FORBES® BOOK OF QUOTATIONS

Forbes

BOOK OF
QUOTATIONS

10,000 Thoughts on the Business of Life

REVISED AND UPDATED

EDITED BY TED GOODMAN

BLACK DOG
& LEVENTHAL
PUBLISHERS

Black Dog & Leventhal Publishers
Hachette Book Group
1290 Avenue of the Americas
New York, NY 10104
www.hachettebookgroup.com
www.blackdogandleventhal.com

First Edition: May 2016

Black Dog & Leventhal Publishers is an imprint of Hachette Books,
a division of Hachette Book Group. The Black Dog & Leventhal Publishers
name and logo are trademarks of Hachette Book Group, Inc.
The publisher is not responsible for websites (or their content) that
are not owned by the publisher.

The Hachette Speakers Bureau provides a wide range of
authors for speaking events. To find out more, go to www.
HachetteSpeakersBureau.com or call (866) 376-6591.

Print book interior design by Elizabeth Driesbach

Library of Congress Cataloging-in-Publication Data available upon request.

ISBNs: 978-0-3163-1004-8 (hardcover), 978-0-3163-1005-5 (ebook)

Printed in China
IM
10 9 8 7 6 5 4 3 2 1

CONTENTS

FOREWORD

Many things about *Forbes* Magazine have changed since its first issue appeared in 1917. One that has not is "Thoughts on the Business of Life." This last page of the magazine, which collects wisdom new and old, consistently has been among the most read in the magazine.

It was almost half a century ago that our grandfather, B.C. Forbes, first collected "Thoughts" between hard covers. With each edition, the selection has expanded and changed, but the animating idea has not. His introduction to the original volume follows. It eloquently explains the underlying purpose of "Thoughts" and, indeed, of *Forbes* Magazine itself.

Undoubtedly, B.C. would be delighted and proud that continued demand led to the current volume. So are we!

Steve Forbes

INTRODUCTION

The moving motive in establishing *Forbes* Magazine, in 1917, was ardent desire to promulgate humaneness in business, then woefully lacking.

Too many individual and corporate employers were merely mercenarily-minded, obsessed only with determination to roll up profits regardless of the suicidal consequences of their shortsighted conduct.

They were without consciousness of their civic, social, patriotic responsibilities.

This writer warned, a third-of-a-century ago, that unless employers altered their tactics, unless they exhibited more consideration for their workers, time would come when "Politicians will step in and do the job in a way that employers will not like."

That had happened with a vengeance!

Every issue of *Forbes*, since its inception, has appeared under the masthead: "With all thy getting, get understanding."

Not only so, but we have devoted, all through the years, a full page to "Thoughts on the Business of Life," reflections by ancient and modern sages calculated to inspire a philosophic mode of life, broad sympathies, charity towards all.

Having assiduously sought all these years to pursue this objective, I would—having already passed the Biblical span of three-score-years-and-ten—pass on contented if I could conscientiously feel that we have rendered at least a little service to our day and generation, that we have done something towards bequeathing a better world for my four sons and an increasing number of grandchildren.

This volume is a humble contribution to furthering human, humane Understanding.

I'm convinced, despite all the woes, wars, strife, bloodshed afflicting mankind at this moment, that Robert Burns was truly prophetic when he wrote:

It's comin' yet for a' that,
That Man to Man, the world o'er.
Shall be brothers for a' that.

I have faith that time will eventually come when employees and employers, as well as humankind, will realize that they serve themselves best when they serve others most.

B.C. Forbes

ABILITY

Because your own strength is unequal to the task, do not assume that it is beyond the powers of man; but if anything is within the powers and province of man, believe that it is within your own compass also.
Marcus Aurelius Antoninus

Ability has nothing to do with opportunity.
Napoleon Bonaparte

It is in destroying and pulling down that skill is displayed? The shallowest understanding, the rudest hand, is more than equal to the task.
Edmund Burke

Men who undertake considerable things, even in a regular way, ought to give us ground to presume ability.
Edmund Burke

Behind an able man there are always other able men.
Chinese proverb

Natural ability without education has more often raised a man to glory and virtue than education without natural ability.
Cicero

Capacity never lacks opportunity. It cannot remain undiscovered because it is sought by too many anxious to use it.
Bourke Cockran

I will not be concerned at other men's not knowing me; I will be concerned at my own want of ability.
Confucius

The superior man is distressed by the limitations of his ability; he is not distressed by the fact that men do not recognize the ability that he has.
Confucius

People are always ready to admit a man's ability after he gets there.
Bob Edwards

What I need is someone who will make me do what I can.
Ralph Waldo Emerson

A smooth sea never made a skilled mariner.
English proverb

Almost any idea is good if a man has ability and is willing to work hard. The best idea is worthless if the creator is a loafer and ineffective.
William Feather

The ultimate high: A man's abilities equaling his opinion of 'em.
Malcolm Forbes

The tools to him who has the ability to handle them.
French proverb

There are few, if any, jobs in which ability alone is sufficient. Needed, also, are loyalty, sincerity, enthusiasm and team play.
William B. Given, Jr.

The man who occupies the first place seldom plays the principal part.
Johann Wolfgang von Goethe

If I accept you as you are, I will make you worse; however, if I treat you as

though you are what you are capable of becoming, I help you become that.
Johann Wolfgang von Goethe

Ability is useless unless it's used.
Robert Half

When ability exceeds ambition, or ambition exceeds ability, the likelihood of success is limited.
Ralph Half

Skill and confidence are an unconquered army.
George Herbert

It is a fine thing to have ability, but the ability to discover ability in others is the true test.
Elbert Hubbard

There is something that is much more scarce, something finer far, something rarer than ability. It is the ability to recognize ability.
Elbert Hubbard

A human being feels able and competent only so long as he is permitted to contribute as much as, or more, than he has contributed to him.
L. Ron Hubbard

There is nothing of permanent value (putting aside a few human affections), nothing that satisfies quiet reflection, except the sense of having worked according to one's capacity and light to make things clear and get rid of cant and shams of all sorts.
Thomas H. Huxley

A man with ability and the desire to accomplish something can do anything.
Donald Kircher

Ability wins us the esteem of the true men; luck that of the people.
François de La Rochefoucauld

The art of using moderate abilities to advantage often brings greater results than actual brilliance.
François de La Rochefoucauld

Abilities wither under faultfinding, blossom under encouragement.
Donald A. Laird

Latent abilities are like clay. It can be mud on shoes, brick in a building or a statue that will inspire all who see it. The clay is the same. The result is dependent on how it is used.
James F. Lincoln

We should be on our guard against the temptation to argue directly from skill to capacity, and to assume when a man displays skill in some feat, his capacity is therefore considerable.
Tom H. Pear

In private matters everyone is equal before the law. In public matters, when it is a question of putting power and responsibility into the hands of one man rather than another, what counts is not rank or money, but the ability to do the job well.
Pericles

Executive ability is deciding quickly and getting somebody else to do the work.
John G. Pollard

Ability and necessity dwell near each other.
Pythagoras

It is always pleasant to be urged to do something on the ground that one can do it well.
George Santayana

A man's ability cannot possibly be of one sort and his soul of another. If his soul be well-ordered, serious and restrained, his ability also is sound and sober.

Conversely, when the one degenerates, the other is contaminated.
Seneca

The young man of native ability, the will to work and good personality will, in the long run, get the equivalent of a college education in the tasks he will set for himself. If he has ability and determination, he will find ways to learn and to get ahead.
Edward G. Seubert

To think we are able is almost to be so; to determine upon attainment is frequently attainment itself; earnest resolution has often seemed to have about it almost a savor of omnipotence.
Samuel Smiles

To be what we are, and to become what we are capable of becoming, is the only end of life.
Baruch Spinoza

The fine points that are uncovered in our work as a result of close study, diligent care, constant application and always trying to improve our methods represent the best and most valuable knowledge we get in business—and the sum total of that attentive attitude is what we call skill.
Roderick Stevens

Anyone can hold the helm when the sea is calm.
Publilius Syrus

Not because of an extraordinary talent did he succeed, but because he had a capacity of a level for business and not above it.
Tacitus

The abilities of man must fall short on one side or the other, like too scanty a blanket when you are abed.
William J. Temple

Forget yourself in your work. If your employer sees that you are more concerned about your own interests than about his, that you are fussy about getting credit of every little or big thing you do, then you are apt to be passed by when a responsible job has to be filled. . . . Don't worry about how big an increase in your salary you can contrive to get. Don't let your mind dwell on money at all, if you can help it. Throw yourself, body, soul, and spirit, into whatever you are doing. . . . The truth is that in every organization, no matter how large or how small, someone is taking notice of any employee who shows special ability.
Harry B. Thayer

They are able because they think they are able.
Virgil

Men are often capable of greater things than they perform. They are sent into the world with bills of credit, and seldom draw to their full extent.
Horace Walpole

Ability is a poor man's wealth.
Matthew Wren

ABSURDITY

What happens to the hole when the cheese is gone?
Bertolt Brecht

To tax and to please, no more than to love and be wise, is not given to men.
Edmund Burke

My turn of mind is so given to taking things in the absurd point of view that it breaks out in spite of me every now and then.
Lord Byron

At any street corner the feeling of absurdity can strike any man in the face.
Albert Camus

The absurd is sin without God.
Albert Camus

I went to a bookstore and asked the saleswoman, "Where's the self-help section?" She said if she told me, it would defeat the purpose.
George Carlin

If it was so, it might be; and if it were so, it would be; but as it isn't, it ain't. That's logic.
Lewis Carroll

In a world where everything is ridiculous, nothing can be ridiculed. You cannot unmask a mask.
G. K. Chesterton

No folly is more costly than the folly of intolerant idealism.
Winston Churchill

There is no opinion so absurd but that some philosopher will express it.
Cicero

He who hath not a dram of folly in his mixture hath pounds of much worse matter.
Charles Caleb Colton

There is no fact that cannot be vulgarized and presented in a ludicrous light.
Fyodor Dostoyevsky

Ridicule may be the evidence of with or bitterness and may gratify a little mind, or an ungenerous temper, but it is no test of reason or truth.
Tryon Edwards

No man is quite sane. Each has a vein of folly in his composition—a slight determination of blood to the head, to make

sure of holding him hard to some one point which he has taken to heart.
Ralph Waldo Emerson

The magnificent and the ridiculous are so close that they touch.
Bertrand de Fontenelle

Life is a jest, and
All things show it;
I thought so once,
But now I know it.
John Gay

America how can I write a holy litany in your silly mood?
Allen Ginsberg

Only exceptionally rational men can afford to be absurd.
Allan Goldfein

Modern man must descend the spiral of his own absurdity to the lowest point; only then can he look beyond it. It is obviously impossible to get around it, jump over it, or simply avoid it.
Vaclav Havel

The deeper the experience of an absence of meaning—in other words, of absurdity—the more energetically meaning is sought.
Vaclav Havel

The privilege of absurdity, to which no other living creature is subject, but man only.
Thomas Hobbes

American freedom consists largely in talking nonsense.
Edgar Watson Howe

It is not in the world of ideas that life is *lived*. Life is lived for better or worse *in* life, and to a man *in* life, his life can be no

more absurd than it can be the opposite of absurd, whatever that opposite may be.
Archibald MacLeish

One morning I shot an elephant in my pajamas. How he got in my pajamas, I don't know.
Groucho Marx (*Animal Crackers*)

What is certain is that I am no Marxist.
Karl Marx

Silly is you in a natural state, and serious is something you have to do until you can get silly again.
Mike Myers

One step above the sublime makes the ridiculous, and one step above the ridiculous makes the sublime again.
Thomas Paine

Oh, life is a glorious cycle of song,
A medley of extemporanea;
And love is a thing than can never go wrong;
And I am Marie of Roumania.
Dorothy Parker

Life is full of infinite absurdities, which, strangely enough, do not even need to appear plausible, because they are true.
Luigi Pirandello

Look for the ridiculous in everything, and you will find it.
Jules Renard

People who cannot recognize a palpable absurdity are very much in the way of civilization.
Agnes Repplier

Much of the wisdom of one age is the folly of the next.
Arthur Schopenhauer

Ridicule: The weapon of all others most feared by enthusiasts of every description, and which from its predominance over such minds, often checks what is absurd, and fully as often smothers that which is noble.
Sir Walter Scott

In the sphere of thought, absurdity and perversity remain the masters of the world, and their dominion is suspended only for brief periods.
Charles Simmons

I'll sail to Ka-Troo And bring back an it-kutch, A preep, and a proo, A nerkle, a NERD, And a seersucker, too!
Dr. Seuss

The ultimate result of shielding men from the effects of folly is to fill the world with fools.
Herbert Spencer

The *reductio ad absurdum* is God's favorite argument.
George Tyrrell

If people never did silly things, nothing intelligent would ever get done.
Ludwig Wittgenstein

I used to work in a fire hydrant factory. You couldn't park anywhere near the place.
Steven Wright

ACCOMPLISHMENTS

We can accomplish almost anything within our ability if we but think that we can! Every great achievement in this world was first carefully thought out.... Think—but to a purpose. Think constructively. Think as you read. Think as you listen. Think as you travel and your eyes reveal new situations. Think as you work daily at your desk, or in the field, or while strolling. Think to rise and improve your place in life. There can

be no advancement or success without serious thought.
George Matthew Adams

Financial rewards follow accomplishment, they don't precede it.
Harry F. Banks

Sweat is the cologne of accomplishment.
Heywood Hale Broun

There is nothing that God has judged good for us that He has not given us the means to accomplish, both in the natural and moral world. If we cry, like children, for the moon, like children we must cry on.
Edmund Burke

"I can't do it" never yet accomplished anything; "I will try" has performed wonders.
George P. Burnham

Life is the art of drawing sufficient conclusions from insufficient premises.
Samuel Butler

Knowledge may give weight, but accomplishments give lustre, and many more people see than weigh.
Lord Chesterfield

Always there will be, along the sidelines of life, inferior souls who throw mud at those whose attainments they do not quite understand. The man who really accomplishes doesn't pay attention to such detractors. If he did, he'd be on their level. He keeps an eye singled on the higher goal—and the mud never touches him.
Jerome P. Fleishman

Too few accomplish twice as much as too many.
Malcolm Forbes

It's more fun to arrive at a conclusion than to justify it.
Malcolm Forbes

In the long run, a short cut seldom is.
Malcolm Forbes

Too many of us, when we accomplish what we set out to do, exclaim, "See what I have done!" instead of saying, "See where I have been led."
Henry Ford

In the United States, to an unprecedented degree, the individual's social role has come to be determined not by who he is but by what he can accomplish.
John W. Gardner

Everyone has his superstitions. One of mine has always been when I started to go anywhere, or to do anything, never to turn back or to stop until the thing intended was accomplished.
Ulysses S. Grant

If well thou hast begun, go on; it is the end that crowns us, not the fight.
Robert Herrick

You can do what you want to do, accomplish what you want to accomplish, attain any reasonable objective you may have in mind. . . . Not all of a sudden, perhaps, not in one swift and sweeping act of achievement. . . . But you can do it gradually—day by day and play by play—if you want to do it, if you will to do it, if you work to do it, over a sufficiently long period of time.
William E. Holler

The most agreeable thing in life is worthy accomplishment. It is not possible that the idle tramp is as contented as the farmers along the road who own their own farms, and whose credit is good at the bank in town. When the tramps get together at night,

they abuse the farmers, but do not get as much satisfaction out of it as do the farmers who abuse the tramps. The sounder your argument, the more satisfaction you get out of it.
Edgar Watson Howe

It's amazing what ordinary people can do if they set out without preconceived notions.
Charles F. Kettering

For truth and duty it is ever the fitting time; who waits until circumstances completely favor his undertaking, will never accomplish anything.
Martin Luther

In our own days we have seen no princes accomplish great results save those who have been accounted miserly.
Niccolò Machiavelli

We would accomplish many more things if we did not think of them as impossible.
C. Malesherbes

No institution which does not continually test its ideals, techniques and measure of accomplishment can claim real vitality.
John Milton

If you have known how to compose your life, you have accomplished a great deal more than the man who knows how to compose a book. Have you been able to make your stride? You have done more than man who has taken cities and empires.
Michel de Montaigne

I wonder if there is anyone in the world who can really direct the affairs of the world, or of his country, with any assurance of the result his actions would have.
Montagu C. Norman

The man who has accomplished all that he thinks worth while, has begun to die.
E.T. Trigg

The great accomplishments of man have resulted from the transmission of ideas and enthusiasm.
Thomas J. Watson

It is by what we ourselves have done, and not by what others have done for us, that we shall be remembered in after ages.
Francis Wayland

The secret of the true love of work is the hope of success in that work; not for the money reward, for the time spent, or for the skill exercised, but for the successful result in the accomplishment of the work itself.
Sidney A. Weltmer

I am an acme of things accomplished, and I am an encloser of things to be.
Walt Whitman

ACHIEVEMENTS

It is a favorite belief of mine that no student ever attains very eminent success by simply doing what is required of him; it is the amount and excellence of what is over and above the required, that determines the greatness of ultimate distinction.
Charles Kendall Adams

The only worthwhile achievements of man are those which are socially useful.
Dr. Alfred Adler

Our prayers are answered not when we are given what we ask, but when we are challenged to be what we can be.
Morris Adler

Who works achieves and who sows reaps.
Arabian proverb

Nothing splendid has ever been achieved except by those who dared believe that something inside them was superior to circumstance.
Bruce Barton

We shall never have more time. We have, and have always had, all the time there is. No object is served in waiting until next week or even until to-morrow. Keep going day in and out. Concentrate on something useful. Having decided to achieve a task, achieve it at all costs.
Arnold Bennett

Achievement is the death of endeavor and the birth of disgust.
Ambrose Bierce

The only conquests which are permanent and leave no regrets are our conquest over ourselves.
Napoleon Bonaparte

The full-grown modern human being who seeks but refuge finds instead boredom and mental dissolution, unless he can be, even in his withdrawal, creative. He can find the quality of happiness in the strain and travail only of achievement and growth. And he is conscious of touching the highest pinnacle of fulfillment which his life-urges demand when his is consumed in the service of an idea, in the conquest of the goal pursued.
R. Briffault

When a great man has some one object in view to be achieved in a given time, it may be absolutely necessary for him to walk out of all the common roads.
Edmund Burke

Every attempt, by whatever authority, to fix a maximum of productive labor by a given worker in a given time is an unjust restriction upon his freedom and a limitation of his right to make the most of himself in order that he may rise in the scale of the social and economic order in which he lives. The notion that all human beings born into this world enter at birth into a definite social and economic classification, in which classi-fication they must remain permanently through life, is wholly false and fatal to a progressive civilization.
Dr. Nicholas Murray Butler

The great Law of culture:
Let each become all that he was created capable of being.
Thomas Carlyle

The thorough man of business knows that only by years of patient, unremit-ting attention to affairs can he earn his reward, which is the result, not of chance, but of well-devised means for the attainment to ends.
Andrew Carnegie

Think of yourself as on the threshold of unparalleled success. A whole clear, glorious life lies before you. Achieve! Achieve!
Andrew Carnegie

Innovation! One cannot be forever inno-vating. I want to create classics.
Coco Chanel

Instead of being concerned that you have no office, be concerned to think how you may fit yourself for office. Instead of being concerned that you are not known, see to the worthy of being known.
Confucius

It is not the ship so much as the skillful sailing that assures the prosperous voyage.
George William Curtis

I have always admired the ability to bite off more than one can chew and then chew it.
William DeMille

A dark horse, which had never been thought of, rushed past the grandstand in sweeping triumph.
Benjamin Disraeli

They can conquer who believe they can.
William Dryden

You can't achieve anything without getting in someone's way. You can't be detached and effective.
Abba Eban

The devotion of thought to an honest achievement makes the achievement possible.
Mary Baker Eddy

The three great essentials to achieve anything worth while are, first, hard work; second, stick-to-itiveness; third, common sense.
Thomas A. Edison

What is the recipe for successful achievement? To my mind there are just four essential ingredients: Choose a career you love. . . . Give it the best there is in you. . . . Seize your opportunities. . . . And be a member of the team. In no country but America, I believe, is it possible to fulfill all four of these requirements.
Benjamin F. Fairless

We all know that the nation can't divide more than the people produce, but as individuals we try to get more than our share and that's how we get ahead.
William Feather

It is well for civilization that human beings constantly strive to gain greater and greater rewards, for it is this urge, this ambition, this aspiration that moves men and women to bestir themselves to rise to higher and higher achievement. Individual success is to be won in most instances by studying and diagnosing the kind of rewards human hearts seek today and are likely to seek tomorrow.
B.C. Forbes

Always fall in with what you're asked to accept. Take what is given, and make it over your way. My aim in life has always been to hold my own with whatever's going. Not against: with.
Robert Frost

The significance of man is not what he attains, but rather in what he longs to attain.
Kahlil Gibran

If you think you're tops, you won't do much climbing.
Arnold Glasow

It is only after an unknown number of unrecorded labors, after a host of noble hearts have succumbed in discouragement, convinced that their cause is lost; it is only then that the cause triumphs.
François Guizot

A fellow doesn't last long on what he has done. He's got to keep on delivering as he goes along.
Carl Hubbell

The rung of a ladder was never meant to rest upon, but only to hold a man's foot long enough to enable him to put the other somewhat higher.
Thomas H. Huxley

Our business in life is not to get ahead of others but to get ahead of ourselves—to break our own records, to outstrip our yesterdays by our today, to do our work with more force than ever before.
Stewart B. Johnson

Spurts don't count. The final score makes no mention of a splendid start if the finish proves that you were an also ran.
Herbert Kaufman

The great scientists, as all great men, have not been concerned with fame. The joy of achievement that comes from finding something new in the universe is by far their greatest joy. A great research scientist is constantly discovering new things in his field. This is his reward. He knows how to spend long years in preparation and long hours in investigation, with no thought of public honor or reward.
William P. King

Keep a definite goal of achievement constantly in view. Realize that work well and worthily done makes life truly worth living.
Grenville Kleiser

Nothing worthwhile ever happens quickly and easily. You achieve only as you are determined to achieve . . . and as you keep at it until you have achieved.
Robert H. Lauer

I have done what I could do in life, and if I could not do better, I did not deserve it. In vain have I tried to step beyond what bound me. Despite my years, I am still trying!
Maurice Maeterlinck

A hero is a man who would argue with the gods, and so awakens devils to contest his vision. The more a man can achieve, the more he may be certain that the devil will inhabit a part of his creation.
Norman Mailer

In time of difficulties, we must not lose sight of our achievements.
Mao Tse-tung

It is more important to know where you are going than to get there quickly. Do not mistake activity for achievement.
Mabel Newcomber

The balance between price in past achievements and consciousness of present shortcomings is difficult to strike.
John O'Ren

Take a look at those two open hands of yours. They are tools with which to serve, make friends, and reach out for the best in life. Open hands open the way to achievement. Put them to work today.
Wilfred A. Peterson

Five minutes, just before going to sleep, given to a bit of directed imagination regarding achievement possibilities of the morrow, will steadily and increasingly bear fruit, particularly if all ideas of difficulty, worry or fear are resolutely ruled out and replaced by those of accomplishment and smiling courage.
Frederick Pierce

The great achievements have always been individualistic. Indeed, any original achievement implies separation from the majority. Though society may honor achievement, it can never produce it.
George Charles Roche

There's a lot more in each of us than any of us suspects. Undoubtedly many former athletes had the power to run the four-minute mile. It was a barrier only until one man achieved it!
Charles K. Rudman

Many things which cannot be overcome when they stand together yield themselves up when taken little by little.
Sertorius

How my achievements mock me!
William Shakespeare

There's no thrill in easy sailing when the skies are clear and blue, there's no joy in merely doing things which any one can do. But there is some satisfaction that is mighty sweet to take, when you reach a destination that you thought you'd never make.
Spirella

Is there anything in life so disenchanting as achievement?
Robert Louis Stevenson

If one advances confidently in the direction of his dreams, and endeavors to live the life which he has imagined, he will meet with a success unexpected in common hours.
Henry David Thoreau

The awareness of the ambiguity of one's highest achievements (as well as one's deepest failures) is a definite symptom of maturity.
Paul Tillich

In every triumph there's a lot of try.
Frank Tyger

There's a man in the world who is never turned down, whatever he chances to stray; he gets the glad hand in the populous town, or out where the farmers make hay; he's greeted with pleasure on deserts of sand, and deep in the aisles of the woods; wherever he goes there's a welcoming hand—he's the man who delivers the goods.
Walt Whitman

He who finds diamonds must grapple in mud and mire because diamonds are not found in polished stones. They are made.
Henry B. Wilson

Capital which overreaches for profits; labor which overreaches for wages, or a public which overreaches for bargains will all destroy such other. There is no salvation for us on that road.
Owen D. Young

ACTING

Generally speaking, success brings out the actors' worst qualities and failure the best.
George Abbott

The trouble with plays these days is that they're too easy to understand.
Robert Allen Arthur

Daddy warned me about men and alcohol. But he never warned me about women and cocaine.
Tallulah Bankhead

It's one of the tragic ironies of the theatre that only one man in it can count on steady work—the night watchman.
Tallulah Bankhead

One of my chief regrets during my years in the theater is that I couldn't sit in the audience and watch me.
John Barrymore

There is an audience for every play; it's just that sometimes it can't wait long enough to find it.
Shirley Booth

An actor's a guy who, if you ain't talking about him, ain't listening.
Marlon Brando

Tallulah Bankhead barged down the Nile last night as Cleopatra—and sank.
John Mason Brown

On Tynan: He never quite loses his posture of amused admiration, presenting himself as a dandy delicately negotiating the rim of a volcano; but

his seriousness is none the less real for lacking any moral dimension.
Simon Callow

Tallulah Bankhead is always skating on thin ice. Everyone wants to be there when it breaks.
Mrs. Patrick Campbell

After my screen test, the director clapped his hands gleefully and yelled: "She can't talk! She can't act! She's wonderful!"
Ava Gardner

When I first went into the movies Lionel Barrymore played my grandfather. Later he played my father and finally my husband. If he had lived, I'm sure I would have played his mother. That's the way it is in Hollywood. The men get younger and the women get older.
Lillian Gish

Too caustic? To hell with the cost. If it's a good picture, we'll make it anyway.
Samuel Goldwyn

The most important thing in acting is honesty. Once you've learned to fake that, you're in.
Samuel Goldwyn

There are all sorts of kisses, lad, from the sticky confection to the kiss of death. Of them all, the kiss of an actress is the most unnerving. How can we tell if she means it or if she's just practicing?
Ruth Gordon

Harold has actually rung me up to say, "I have a rewrite. Page 37. Cut the pause."
Peter Hall

I believe that God felt sorry for actors so he created Hollywood to give them a place in the sun and a swimming pool. The price they had to pay was to surrender their talent.
Sir Cedric Hardwicke

Actors are the only honest hypocrites. Their life is a voluntary dream; and the height of their ambition is to be beside themselves.
William Hazlitt

I can't bear another minute of Noël's inane chatter. Who's interested in a bunch of old English actresses he's picked up from the gutter? Not me. If he wags that silly finger once more I may hit him.
Ernest Hemingway

Acting is the most minor of gifts and not a very high-class way to earn a living. After all, Shirley Temple could do it at age four.
Katharine Hepburn

I think there are probably more closet conservatives in Hollywood than there are closet homosexuals.
Charlton Heston

Is it a stale remark to say that I have constantly found the interest excited at a playhouse to bear an exact inverse proportion to the price paid for admission?
Charles Lamb

The audience is not the least important actor in the play, and if it will not do its allotted share the play falls to pieces.
Somerset Maugham

The structure of a play is always the story of how the birds came home to roost.
Arthur Miller

On Osborne: He had to be plied with extremely expensive champagne. He became more and more like the old Edwardian father he kept attacking in *Look Back in Anger.* That was what he always wanted to be. His fury in the 1950s was that he wasn't a rich squire.
Jonathan Miller

Some of the greatest love affairs
I've known have involved one
actor—unassisted.
Wilson Mizner

I never deliberately set out to shock, but
when people don't walk out of my plays I
think there is something wrong.
John Osborne

Oh, this dread word *Pinteresque*. It makes
people reach for their guns. Or behave
as if they were going to church. But
when the audience is actually there, I am
always gratified when I hear laughter.
Harold Pinter

One half of the pleasure experienced
at a theatre arises from the spectator's
sympathy with the rest of the audience,
and, especially from his belief in their
sympathy with him.
Edgar Allan Poe

It's easy to direct while acting; there's
one less person to argue with.
Roman Polanski

I don't want to read about some of these
actresses who are around today. They
sound like my niece in Scarsdale. I love
my niece in Scarsdale, but I won't buy
tickets to see her act.
Vincent Price

The stage is actor's country. You have to
get your passport stamped every so often
or they take away your citizenship.
Vanessa Redgrave

Acting is standing up naked and turning
around very slowly.
Rosalind Russell

It is with life as with a play—it matters
not how long the action is spun out, but
how good the acting is.
Seneca

I do not want actors and actresses
to understand my plays. That is not
necessary. If they will only pronounce
the correct sounds I can guarantee the
results.
George Bernard Shaw

An actor is never so great as when he
reminds you of an animal, falling like a
cat, lying like a dog, moving like a fox.
François Truffaut

On Coward: Taut, facially, as an appalled
monolith; gracious, socially, as a royal
bastard; tart, vocally, as a hollowed lemon.
Kenneth Tynan

Tennessee Williams recognized that
great theater begins with great talkers,
and that great talkers obey two rules:
they never sound like anyone else and
they never say anything directly.
Edmund White

You can pick out actors by the glazed
look that comes into their eyes when
the conversation wanders away from
themselves.
Michael Wilding

Every now and then, when you're on the
stage, you hear the best sound a player
can hear. It's a sound you can't get in
movies or in television. It is the sound
of a wonderful, deep silence that means
you've hit them where they live.
Shelley Winters

Acting is a child's prerogative. Children
are born to act. Usually, people grow up
and out of it. Actors always seem to me
to be people who never quite did grow
out of it.
Joanne Woodward

ACTION

Trust only movement.
Alfred Adler

Action is only coarsened thought—
thought become concrete, obscure and
unconscious.
Henri Frédéric Amiel

For purposes of action, nothing is more
useful than narrowness of thought
combined with energy of will.
Henri Frédéric Amiel

Effective action is always unjust.
Jean Anouilh

To live well is to work well, to show a
good activity.
Thomas Aquinas

In the arena of human life the honors
and rewards fall to those who show their
good qualities in action.
Aristotle

All our actions take their hue from the
complexion of the heart, as landscapes
their variety from light.
Francis Bacon

We live in deeds, not years; in thoughts,
not figures on a dial. We should count
time by heart throbs. He most lives who
thinks most, feels the noblest, acts the
best.
Philip James Bailey

The secret of success is the consistency
to pursue.
Harry F. Banks

Action without study is fatal. Study
without action is futile.
Mary Beard

Consistency requires you to be as ignorant today as you were a year ago.
Bernard Berenson

Think like a man of action, act like a man
of thought.
Henri Bergson

A thought that does not result in action is
nothing much, and an action that does not
proceed from a thought is nothing at all.
Georges Bernanos

The greatest felony in the news business
today is to be behind, or to miss a big
story. So speed and quantity substitute
for thoroughness and quality, for accuracy and context.
Carl Bernstein

The wise man never initiates any action.
Bhagavad Gita

The individual activity of one man with
backbone will do more than a thousand
men with a mere wishbone.
William J.H. Boetcker

Active natures are rarely melancholy.
Activity and sadness are incompatible.
Christian Bovée

The noblest deeds are well enough set
forth in simple language; emphasis spoils
them.
Jean de la Bruyére

Every person has some splendid traits
and if we confine our contacts so as to
bring those traits into action, there is no
need of ever being bored or irritated or
indignant.
Gelett Burgess

No men can act with effect who do not act
in concert; no men can act in concert who
do not act with confidence; no men can
act with confidence who are not bound

together with common opinions, common affections, and common interests.
Edmund Burke

It is not what a lawyer tells me I may do, but what humanity, reason and justice tell me I ought to do.
Edmund Burke

The most drastic and usually the most effective remedy for fear is direct action.
William Burnham

Every noble work is at first impossible.
Thomas Carlyle

The end of man is action, and not thought, though it be of the noblest.
Thomas Carlyle

He that has done nothing has known nothing.
Thomas Carlyle

There is no Fate that plans men's lives. Whatever comes to us, good or bad, is usually the result of our own action or lack of action.
Herbert N. Casson

Good actions ennoble us, and we are the sons of our own deeds.
Miguel de Cervantes

We inherit nothing truly, but what our actions make us worthy of.
John Chapman

An adventure is only an inconvenience rightly considered. An inconvenience is only an adventure wrongly considered.
G.K. Chesterton

I am myself so exceedingly Nordic, as far as physical constitution is concerned, that I can enjoy almost any weather except what is called glorious weather. At the end of a few days, I am left wondering how the men of the Mediterranean ever managed to do almost all the most active and astonishing things that have been done.
G.K. Chesterton

I never worry about action, but only about inaction.
Winston Churchill

A nation's character is the sum of its splendid deeds; they constitute one common patrimony, the nation's inheritance. They awe foreign powers, they arouse and animate our own people.
Henry Clay

No two things differ more than hurry and dispatch. Hurry is the mark of a weak mind, dispatch of a strong one. A weak man in office, like a squirrel in a cage, is laboring eternally, but to no purpose, and is in constant motion without getting on a job; like a turnstile, he is in everybody's way, but stops nobody; he talks a great deal, but says very little; looks into everything but sees nothing; and has a hundred irons in the fire, but very few of them are hot, and with those few that are, he only burns his fingers.
Charles Caleb Colton

The only things in which we can be said to have any property are our actions. Our thoughts may be bad, yet produce no poison; they may be good, yet produce no fruit. Our riches may be taken away by misfortune, our reputation by malice, our spirits by calamity, our health by disease, our friends by death. But our actions must follow us beyond the grave; with respect to them alone, we cannot say that we shall carry nothing with us when we die, neither that we shall go naked out of the world.
Charles Caleb Colton

The most important part of every business is to know what ought to be done.
Lucius Columella

Each honest calling, each walk of life, has its own elite, its own aristocracy based on excellence of performance.
James Bryant Conant

A true history of human events would show that a far larger proportion of our acts are the results of sudden impulses and accident, than of that reason of which we so much boast.
Myers Y. Cooper

Unless a capacity for thinking be accompanied by a capacity for action, a superior mind exists in torture.
Benedetto Croce

You cannot be buried in obscurity: you are exposed upon a grand theater to the view of the world. If your actions are upright and benevolent, be assured they will augment your power and happiness.
Cyrus

This is a world of action, and nor for moping and droning in.
Charles Dickens

Action may not always bring happiness; but there is no happiness without action.
Benjamin Disraeli

Those who do the most for the world's advancement are the ones who demand the least.
Henry L. Doherty

Through unity of action we can be a veritable colossus in support of peace. No one can defeat us unless we first defeat ourselves. Every one of us must be guided by this truth.
Dwight D. Eisenhower

We must not sit down and wait for miracles. Up and be going!
John Eliot

Act as though everything you do, rightly or wrongly, accurately or carelessly, may tip the scale of the bigger things of tomorrow for all of us, as indeed every act, potentially, can. Remember: Enemies try to break through at the weakest point. Don't let it be on your sector.
L.G. Elliott

A little consideration of what takes place around us every day would show us that a higher law than that of our will regulates events; that only in our easy, simple spontaneous action are we strong, and by contenting ourselves with obedience we become divine.
Ralph Waldo Emerson

Congratulate yourselves if you have done something strange and extravagant and broken the monotony of a decorous age.
Ralph Waldo Emerson

What you do speaks so loudly that I cannot hear what you say.
Ralph Waldo Emerson

There is no strong performance without a little fascination in the performer.
Ralph Waldo Emerson

He who does a good deed is instantly ennobled. He who does a mean deed is by the action itself contracted.
Ralph Waldo Emerson

Unnecessary hustle is one of the American follies. We hustle at both work and play, and consequently enjoy neither to the utmost.
William Feather

The sweaty players in the game of life always have more fun than the supercilious spectators.
William Feather

Contemplation is necessary to generate an object, but action must propagate it.
Owen Feltham

All worthwhile men have good thoughts, good ideas and good intentions—but precious few of them ever translate those into action.
John Hancock Field

Pressure is on us by the nature of the job. Performance releases pressure.
J.T. Fisher

The victors of the battles of tomorrow will be those who can best harness thought to action. From office boy to statesman, the prizes will be for those who most effectively exert their brains, who take deep, earnest and studious counsel of their minds, who stamp themselves as thinkers.
B.C. Forbes

The hardest time to tell: when to stop.
Malcolm Forbes

If you do what you should not, you must bear what you would not.
Benjamin Franklin

Up, sluggard, and waste not life; in the grave will be sleeping enough.
Benjamin Franklin

When confronted with two courses of action I jot down on a piece of paper all the arguments in favor of each one—then on the opposite side I write the arguments against each one. Then by weighing the arguments pro and con and canceling them out, one against the other, I take the course indicated by what remains.
Benjamin Franklin

Words may show a man's wit but actions his meaning.
Benjamin Franklin

It seems to me that man is made to act rather than to know. The principles of things escape our most persevering researches.
Frederick the Great

Haste and rashness are storms and tempests, breaking and wrecking business; but nimbleness is a full, fair wind, blowing it with speed to the haven.
Thomas Fuller

It is good to dream, but it is better to dream and work. Faith is mighty, but action with faith is mightier. Desiring is helpful, but work and desire are invincible.
Thomas Robert Gaines

The fundamental principle of human action . . . is that men seek to gratify their desires with the least exertion.
Henry George

Unless there be correct thought, there cannot be any action, and when there is correct thought, right action will follow.
Henry George

The deed is everything, the glory naught.
Johann Wolfgang von Goethe

Noble blood is an accident of fortune; noble actions are the chief mark of greatness.
Carlo Goldoni

Hurry is the weakness of fools.
Baltasar Gracián

Act quickly, think slowly.
Greek proverb

The greatest ability in business is to get along with others and influence their actions. A chip on the shoulder is too heavy a piece of baggage to carry through life.
John Hancock

Great thoughts reduced to practice become great acts.
William Hazlitt

Indolence is a delightful but distressing state; we must be doing something to be happy. Action is no less necessary than thought to the instinctive tendencies of the human frame.
William Hazlitt

The men of action are, after all, only the unconscious instruments of the men of thought.
Heinrich Heine

Pleasure and pain are the only springs of action in man, and always will be.
Claude Adrien Helvétius

Who hath no haste in his business, mountains to him seem valleys.
George Herbert

A man should share the action and passion of his times at peril of being judged not to have lived.
Oliver Wendell Holmes

An acre of performance is worth a whole world of promise.
William Dean Howells

Action is thought tempered by illusion.
Elbert Hubbard

A fellow doesn't last long on what he has done. He has to keep on delivering.
Carl Hubbell

For man's greatest actions are performed in minor struggles. Life, misfortune, isolation, abandonment and poverty are battlefields which have their heroes— obscure heroes who are at times greater than illustrious heroes.
Victor Hugo

Logical consequences are the scarecrows of fools and the beacons of wise men.
Thomas H. Huxley

The world belongs to those who think and act with it, who keep a finger on its pulse.
William Ralph Inge

Man has been called the representative product of the universe; and we will do well to remember that in this position his actions represent the worst of which nature is capable as well as the best.
L.V. Jacks

Action and feeling go together and by regulating the action which is under the more direct control of the will, we can regulate the feeling, which is not.
William James

We are all ready to be savage in some cause. The difference between a good man and a bad one is the choice of the cause.
William James

None so little enjoy themselves, and are such burdens to themselves, as those who have nothing to do. Only the active have the true relish of life.
William Jay

It is happily and kindly provided that in every life there are certain pauses, and interruptions which force consideration upon the careless, and seriousness upon the light; points of time where one course of action ends and another begins.
Samuel Johnson

Sorrow is the mere rust of the soul.
Activity will cleanse and brighten it.
Samuel Johnson

Many persons wonder why they don't
amount to more than they do, have good
stuff in them, energetic, persevering,
and have ample opportunities. It is all a
case of trimming the useless branches
and throwing the whole force of power
into the development of something that
counts.
W.J. Johnston

Life is the faculty of spontaneous activity,
the awareness that we have powers.
Immanuel Kant

Act in such a way that you always treat
humanity, whether in your own person or
in the person of any other, never simply
as a means but always also as an end.
Immanuel Kant

Act so that the maxim of your act could
be made the principle of a universal law.
Immanuel Kant

You will never stub your toe standing
still. The faster you go, the more chance
there is of stubbing your toe, but the more
chance you have of getting somewhere.
Charles F. Kettering

You cannot antagonize and influence at
the same time.
J.S. Knox

However brilliant an action may be, it
ought not to pass for great when it is not
the result of a great design.
François de La Rochefoucauld

Act well at the moment, and you have
performed a good action to all eternity.
Johann Lavater

He is incapable of a truly good action
who finds not a pleasure in contemplating the good actions of others.
Johann Lavater

A word that has been said may be
unsaid—it is but air. But when a deed is
done, it cannot be undone, nor can our
thoughts reach out to all the mischiefs
that may follow.
Henry Wadsworth Longfellow

All the beautiful sentiments in the world
weigh less than a single lovely action.
James Russell Lowell

The man who saves time by galloping
loses it by missing his way; the shepherd who hurries his flock to get them
home spends the night on the mountain
looking for the lost; economy does not
consist in haste, but in certainty.
Ramsay MacDonald

It is well to think well; it is divine to act
well.
Horace Mann

We live in an age of haste. Some people
look at an egg and expect it to crow.
Orison Swett Marden

It is the direct man who strikes sledge-
hammer blows, who penetrates the very
marrow of a subject at every stroke and
gets the meat out of a proposition, who
does things.
Orison Swett Marden

So much one man can do that does both
act and know.
Andrew Marvell

Give a good deed the credit of a good
motive; and give an evil deed the benefit
of the doubt.
Brander Matthews

There is a sort of man who pays no attention to his good actions, but is tormented by his bad ones. This is the type that most often writes about himself.
Somerset Maugham

We cannot live only for ourselves. A thousand fibers connect us with our fellow-men; and along those fibers, as sympathetic threads, our actions run as causes, and they come back to us as effects.
Herman Melville

Every duty brings its peculiar delight, every denial its appropriate compensation, every thought its recompense, every cross its crown; pay goes with performance as effect with cause.
Charles Mildmay

The ordinary man is involved in action, the hero acts. An immense difference.
Henry Miller

Life is a short day; but it is a working day. Activity may lead to evil, but inactivity cannot lead to good.
Hannah More

A good way to rid one's self of a sense of discomfort is to do something. That uneasy, dissatisfied feeling is actual force vibrating out of order; it may be turned to practical account by giving proper expression to its creative character.
William Morris

And the deeds that ye do upon this earth, it is for fellowship's sake that ye do them.
William Morris

Nothing is unthinkable, nothing impossible to the balanced person, provided it comes out of the needs of life and is dedicated to life's further developments.
Lewis Mumford

One will not go far wrong if one attributes extreme actions to vanity, average ones to habit, and petty ones to fear.
Friedrich Wilhelm Nietzsche

The very essence of all power to influence lies in getting the other person to participate. The mind that can do that has a powerful leverage on his human world.
Harry A. Overstreet

Without consistency there is no moral strength.
Robert Owen

It is our individual performances, no matter how humble our place in life may be, that will in the long run determine how well ordered the world may become.
Paul C. Packer

Never tell people how to do things. Tell them what to do and they will surprise you with their ingenuity.
George S. Patton

What we have done for ourselves alone dies with us. What we have done for others and the world remains and is immortal.
Albert Pine

American businessmen must learn human nature to the point of accepting as necessary the Rabble Rouser of the Right. . . . To get fast action somebody must stir millions to genuine anger over conditions which are adversely affecting their lives.
Walter B. Pitkin

Let deeds match words.
Plautus

Only actions give life strength; only moderation gives it charm.
Jean Paul Richter

In modern times, it is only by the power of association that men of any calling exercise their due influence in the community.
Elihu Root

In my opinion, he only may be truly said to live and enjoy his being who is engaged in some laudable pursuit, and acquires a name by some illustrious action, or useful art.
Sallust

We like to think it is enough if we keep our own lives straight. Quite plainly it is not. If we talk cynically or encourage a lowering of standards, even though we still control our own actions, we become responsible for the failure of those who, weakened by our influence, fail to stand upright.
George P.T. Sargent

We are not forced into unpleasant activities. We either allow them to come about or we encourage them to come about.
William Saroyan

The most important single influence in the life of a person is another person. We may say to our children: Here is art, science, philosophy, mathematics, music, psychology, history, religion—and we may open innumerable doors along the corridors of living so that they will have a broad and even a minute acquaintance with the segments of life; but these introductions are not as important as knowing people whose characters and actions, personalities and words have grown after similar introductions and have become worthy of emulation.
Paul D. Shafer

Suit the action to the word, the word to the action; with this special observation, that you overstep not the modesty of nature.
William Shakespeare

If our impulses were confined to hunger, thirst and desire, we might be nearly free, but now we are moved by every wind that blows, and a chance word or scene that that word may convey to us.
Mary Shelley

Stagnation is something worse than death; it is corruption also.
William Simms

When you cannot make up your mind which of two evenly balanced courses of action you should take—choose the bolder.
W.J. Slim

Rightness expresses of actions, what straightness does of lines; and there can no more be two kinds of right action than there can be two kinds of straight lines.
Herbert Spencer

Heaven never helps the man who will not act.
Sophocles

Allow time and moderate delay; haste manages all things badly.
Publius Papinius Statius

It is the mark of a good action that it
appears inevitable in retrospect.
Robert Louis Stevenson

The end of all knowledge should be in
virtuous action.
Sir Philip Sydney

What is done hastily cannot be done
prudently.
Publilius Syrus

What we do best or most perfectly is
what we have most thoroughly learned
by the longest practice, and at length it
falls from us without our notice, as a leaf
from a tree.
Henry David Thoreau

Why should we live with such hurry and
waste of life? We are determined to be
starved before we are hungry. Men say
that a stitch in time saves nine, and so
they take a thousand stitches today to
save nine tomorrow.
Henry David Thoreau

There hath grown no grass on my heels
since I went hence.
Nicholas Udall

Activity makes more men's fortunes than
cautiousness.
Marquis de Vauvenargues

Iron rusts from disuse, stagnant water
loses its purity, and in cold weather
becomes frozen; even so does inaction
sap the vigors of the mind.
Leonardo da Vinci

A slender acquaintance with the world
must convince every man that actions,
not words, are the true criterion of the
attachment of friends.
George Washington

The chiefest action for a man of spirit is
never to be out of action; the soul was
never put into the body to stand still.
John Webster

Nothing is impossible for the man who
doesn't have to do it himself.
A.H. Weller

Actions lie louder than words.
Carolyn Wells

No man doth think others will be better
to him than he is to them.
Benjamin Whichcote

A race preserves its vigor so long as it
harbors a real contrast between what
has been and what may be; and so long
as it is nerved by the vigor to adventure
beyond the safeties of the past. Without
adventure civilization is in full decay.
Alfred North Whitehead

Any use of a human being in which less is
demanded of him and less is attributed to
him than his full status is a degradation
and a waste.
Norbert Wiener

Action is the last resource of those who
know not how to dream.
Oscar Wilde

Consistency is the last refuge of the
unimaginative.
Oscar Wilde

We should not only master questions, but
also act upon them, and act definitely.
Woodrow Wilson

Thought and theory must precede all
salutary action; yet action is nobler in
itself than either thought or theory.
William Wordsworth

Activity back of a very small idea will produce more than inactivity and the planning of genius.
James A. Worsham

The effects of our actions may be postponed but they are never lost. There is an inevitable reward for good deeds and an inescapable punishment for bad. Meditate upon this truth, and seek always to earn good wages from Destiny.
Wu Ming Fu

Influence is like a savings account. The less you use it, the more you've got.
Andrew Young

In an active life is sown the seed of wisdom; but he who reflects not, never reaps; has no harvest from it, but carries the burden of age without the wages of experience; nor knows himself old, but from his infirmities, the parish register, and the contempt of mankind. And age, if it has not esteem, has nothing.
Edward Young

I really believe that more harm is done by old men who cling to their influence than by young men who anticipate that influence.
Owen D. Young

We protract the career of time by employment, we lengthen the duration of our lives by wise thoughts and useful actions. Life to him who wishes not to have lived in vain is thought and action.
Johann Zimmermann

ADVERSITY

Adversity introduces a man to himself.
Anonymous

You never will be the person you can be if pressure, tension and discipline are taken out of your life.
Dr. James G. Bilkey

In every kind of adversity, the bitterest part of a man's affliction is to remember that he once was happy.
Boethius

'Tis looking downward makes one dizzy.
Robert Browning

Adversity is a severe instructor, set over us by one who knows us better than we do ourselves, as he loves us better too. He that wrestles with us strengthens our nerves and sharpens our skill. Our antagonist is our helper. This conflict with difficulty makes us acquainted with our object, and compels us to consider it in all its relations. It will not suffer us to be superficial.
Edmund Burke

Adversity is sometimes hard upon a man, but for one man who can stand prosperity, there are a hundred that will stand adversity.
Thomas Carlyle

Don't be disquieted in time of adversity. Be firm with dignity and self-reliant with vigor.
Chiang Kai-shek

It is the character of a brave and resolute man not to be ruffled by adversity and not to desert his post.
Cicero

All adverse and depressing influences can be overcome, not by fighting, but by rising above them.
Charles Caleb Colton

Oh the nerves, the nerves; the mysteries of this machine called man! Oh the little

that unhinges it, poor creatures that we are!
Charles Dickens

Rule Number 1 is, don't sweat the small stuff. Rule Number 2 is, it's all small stuff. And if you can't fight and you can't flee, flow.
Robert Eliot

Adversity is the trial of principle. Without it, a man hardly knows whether he is honest or not.
Henry Fielding

He that can heroically endure adversity will bear prosperity with equal greatness of soul; for the mind that cannot be dejected by the former is not likely to be transported with the later.
Henry Fielding

Some people as a result of adversity are sadder, wiser, kinder, more human. Most of us are better, though, when things go better. Knowing when to keep your mouth shut is invariably more important than opening it at the right time. Always listen to a man when he describes the faults of others. Often times, most times, he's describing his own, revealing himself.
Malcolm Forbes

Adversity makes men; good fortune makes monsters.
French proverb

A leaf that is destined to grow large is full of grooves and wrinkles at the start. Now if one has no patience and wants it smooth offhand like a willow leaf, there is trouble ahead.
Johann Wolfgang von Goethe

Stress is an ignorant state. It believes that everything is an emergency. Nothing is that important.
Natalie Goldberg

The greatest object in the universe, says a certain philosopher, is a good man struggling with adversity; yet there is still a greater, which is the good man that comes to relieve it.
Oliver Goldsmith

Adversity has the effect of eliciting talents which in prosperous circumstances would have lain dormant.
Horace

In time of prosperity friends will be plenty; in time of adversity not one in twenty.
James Howell

Adversity has ever been considered the state in which a man most easily becomes acquainted with himself, then, especially, being free from flatterers.
Samuel Johnson

In the adversity of our best friends we often find something that is not wholly displeasing to us.
François de La Rochefoucauld

Sometimes what a man escapes to is worse than what he escapes from.
Stan Lynde

Kites rise against, not with the wind. No man has ever worked his passage anywhere in a dead calm.
John Neal

To reduce stress, avoid excitement. Spend more time with your spouse.
Robert Orben

Often when economic pressure is lifted, a man must pump back into himself a feeling of must.
A.F. Osborn

If thou faint in the day of adversity, thy strength is small.
Proverbs 24:10

Adversity makes a man wise, not rich.
John Ray

In this world without quiet corners, there
can be no easy escapes from history, from
hullabaloo, from terrible unquiet fuss.
Salman Rushdie

Genuine morality is preserved only in the
school of adversity; a state of continuous
prosperity may easily prove a quicksand
to virtue.
Johann Friedrich von Schiller

In prosperous times I have sometimes
felt my fancy and powers of language
flag, but adversity is to me at least a tonic
and bracer.
Sir Walter Scott

Great men rejoice in adversity, just as
brave soldiers triumph in war.
Seneca

The good things of prosperity are to be
wished; but the good things that belong
to adversity are to be admired.
Seneca

It is not every calamity that is a curse,
and early adversity is often a blessing.
Surmounted difficulties not only teach,
but hearten us in our future struggles.
James Sharp

Adversity has made many a man great
who, had he remained prosperous, would
only have been rich.
Maurice Switzer

By trying we can easily learn to endure
adversity. Another man's, I mean.
Mark Twain

You can't hold a man down without
staying down with him.
Booker T. Washington

People seldom want to walk over you
until you lie down.
Elmer Wheeler

ADVERTISING

Time spent in the advertising business
seems to create a permanent deformity
like the Chinese habit of foot-binding.
Dean Acheson

An advertising agency is 85% confusion
and 15% commission.
Fred Allen

In good times people want to advertise;
in bad times they have to.
Bruce Barton

Advertisements in a newspaper are more
full of knowledge in respect to what is
going on in a community than the edito-
rial columns are.
Henry Ward Beecher

The business that considers itself
immune to the necessity for advertising
sooner or later finds itself immune to
business.
Derby Brown

There are different ways of saying It pays
to advertise. It pays, too, to have a quality
product, adequate distribution, good
salesmen. Advertising is just one factor
in the balance mechanism that leads to a
sale: product, quality, distribution, advertising and selling. Advertising is really
salesmanship in print. Although capacity
may be oversold, you can never oversell
the product. You can always continue
to sell the goodwill and the assurance
of quality and service that make buyers
seek out your brand beyond all others.
Paul B. Buckwalter

The advertiser is the over rewarded court jester and court pander at the democratic court.
Joseph Wood Crutch

Advertising is the principle of mass production applied to selling.
John T. Dorrance

You can tell the ideals of a nation by its advertisements.
Norman Douglas

Advertising is a racket, like the movies and the brokerage business. You cannot be honest without admitting that its constructive contribution to humanity is exactly minus zero.
F. Scott Fitzgerald

We grew up founding our dreams on the infinite promise of American advertising. I still believe that one can learn to play the piano by mail and that mud will give you a perfect complexion.
Zelda Fitzgerald

The advertising man is a liaison between the products of business and the mind of the nation. He must know both before he can serve either.
Glenn Frank

There is nothing in the way of amelioration of the conditions of life, of politics, of social and ethical matters, that may not be affected through the skilful application of those principles of advertising that, in business, have proved to be so wonderfully effective.
George French

Advertisements contain the only truths to be relied on in a newspaper.
Thomas Jefferson

Promise, large promise, is the soul of an advertisement.
Samuel Johnson

The critic is the only independent source of information. The rest is advertising.
Pauline Kael

Society drives people crazy with lust and calls it advertising.
John Lahr

The product that will not sell without advertising, will not sell profitably with advertising.
Albert Lasker

Advertising may be described as the science of arresting human intelligence long enough to get money out of it.
Stephen Leacock

Hollywood has its Oscars. Television has its Emmys. Broadway has its Tonys. And advertising has its Clios. And its Andys, Addys and Effies. And 117 other assorted awards. And those are just the big ones.
Joanne Lipman

Advertising is the greatest art form of the 20th century.
Marshall McLuhan

Advertising may be the only business in the world where the clients with the most money can make demands until they get the agency's worst product, while the small client with little to spend must meekly accept the agency's best.
Thomas D. Murray

Advertising is one of the few callings in which it is advisable to pay attention to some one else's business.
Howard W. Newton

Advertising in the final analysis should be news. If it is not news it is worthless.
Adolph S. Ochs

Advertising is the rattling of a stick inside a swill bucket.
George Orwell

Advertising helps everybody: by showing comparative values and new products, thus increasing sales, resulting in greater production and lower prices.
John Henry Patterson

Advertising gives industry an opportunity to keep its clean hands before the public. If industry is clean and has no dirty hands to hide, it should be proud to display its purity.
Robert W. Sparks

When someone stops advertising, someone stops buying. When someone stops buying, someone stops selling. When someone stops selling, someone stops making. When someone stops making, someone stops earning. When someone stops earning, someone stops buying. (Think it over.)
Edwin Stuart

ADVICE

There is nothing which we receive with so much reluctance as advice.
Joseph Addison

It is an easy thing for one whose foot is on the outside of calamity to give advice and to rebuke the sufferer.
Aeschylus

He that gives good advice builds with one hand; he that gives good counsel and example builds with both; but he that gives good admonition and bad example builds with one hand and pulls down with the other.
Francis Bacon

The light that a man receiveth by counsel from another is drier and purer than that which cometh from his own understanding and judgment, which is ever

infused and drenched in his affections and customs.
Francis Bacon

Listen to everything a man has to say about what he knows, but don't let him advise you about what he doesn't know. And usually he doesn't know too much about what's best for you.
Barney Balaban

Advice: The suggestions you give someone else which you hope will work for your benefit.
Ambrose Bierce

Advice is like castor oil, easy enough to give but dreadful uneasy to take.
Josh Billings

What you do not use yourself, do not give to others. For example: advice.
Sri Chinmoy

In those days he was wiser than he is now; he used frequently to take my advice.
Winston Churchill

Advice; it's more fun to give than to receive.
Pat H. Coil

Advice is like snow; the softer it falls, the longer it dwells upon, and the deeper it sinks into the mind.
Samuel Taylor Coleridge

To profit from good advice requires more wisdom than to give it.
John Churton Collins

We ask advice, but we mean approbation.
Charles Caleb Colton

When we feel a strong desire to thrust our advice upon others, it is usually

because we suspect their weakness; but we ought rather to suspect our own.
Charles Caleb Colton

Advice after injury is like medicine after death.
Danish proverb

In every society some men are born to rule, and some to advise.
Ralph Waldo Emerson

It is better to advise than upbraid, for the one corrects the erring; the other only convicts them.
Epictetus

The best advice I can give to any young man or young woman upon graduation from school can be summed up in exactly eight words, and they are—be honest with yourself and tell the truth.
James A. Farley

I've learned that you can't expect your children to listen to your advice and ignore your example.
51-year-old's discovery

Advice: It's more fun to give than to receive.
Malcolm Forbes

How can you avoid people who say, "Let me tell you," and then do?
Malcolm Forbes

Listening to advice often accomplishes far more than heeding it.
Malcolm Forbes

Once you've given advice to someone, you're obligated.
Malcolm Forbes

Families break up when people take hints you don't intend and miss hints you do intend.
Robert Frost

If a man knows where to get good advice, it is as though he could supply it himself.
Johann Wolfgang von Goethe

To accept good advice is but to increase one's own ability.
Johann Wolfgang von Goethe

Do not be inaccessible. None is so perfect that he does not need at times the advice of others. He is an incorrigible ass who will never listen to anyone. Even the most surpassing intellect should find a place for friendly counsel. Sovereignty itself must learn to lean. There are some that are incorrigible simply because they are inaccessible: They fall to ruin because none dares to extricate them. The highest should have the door open for friendship; it may prove the gate of help. A friend must be free to advise, and even to upbraid, without feeling embarrassed.
Baltasar Gracián

When you counsel someone, you should appear to be reminding him of something he had forgotten, not of the light he was unable to see.
Baltasar Gracián

Facts are worthless to a man if he has to keep running to somebody else for advice on how to use them.
Sven Halla

By the time a man asks you for advice, he has generally made up his mind what he wants to do, and is looking for confirmation rather than counseling.
Sydney J. Harris

Harsh counsels have no effect; they are like hammers which are always repulsed by the anvil.
Claude Adrien Helvétius

It is expedient to have an acquaintance with those who have looked into the

world; who know men, understand business, and can give you good intelligence and good advice when they are wanted.
B. Horne

A bad cold wouldn't be so annoying if it weren't for the advice of our friends.
Kin Hubbard

Teeth placed before the tongue give good advice.
Italian proverb

Advice is what we ask for when we already know the answer but wish we didn't.
Erica Jong

No man is so foolish but he may sometimes give another good counsel, and no man so wise that he may not easily err if he takes no other counsel than his own. He that is taught only by himself has a fool for a master.
Ben Jonson

He who can take advice is sometimes superior to him who can give it.
Karl Ludwig von Knebel

The toad beneath the harrow knows
Exactly where each tooth point goes;
The butterfly upon the road
Preaches contentment to that toad.
Rudyard Kipling

You will always find some Eskimos willing to instruct the Congolese on how to cope with heat waves.
Stanislaw Jerzy Lec

We are so happy to advise others that occasionally we even do it in their interest.
Jules Renard

Men give away nothing so liberally as advice.
François de La Rochefoucauld

One can advise comfortably from a safe port.
Johann Friedrich von Schiller

Don't follow any advice, no matter how good, until you feel as deeply in your spirit as you think in your mind that the counsel is wise.
David Seabury

How is it possible to expect that mankind will take advice when they will not so much as take warning?
Jonathan Swift

Many receive advice, only the wise profit by it.
Publilius Syrus

I have found the best way to give advice to your children is to find out what they want and then advise them to do it.
Harry S Truman

I am, at heart, a tiresome nag complacently positive that there is no human problem which could not be solved if people would simply do as I advise.
Gore Vidal

The only thing to do with good advice is to pass it on; it is never of any use to oneself.
Oscar Wilde

AGING

Middle age occurs when you are too young to take up golf and too old to rush up to the net.
Franklin P. Adams

The Indian summer of life should be a little sunny and sad, like the season, and infinite in wealth and depth of tone—but never hustled.
Henry Brooks Adams

He who would pass the declining years of his life with honor and comfort should, when young, consider that he may one day become old, and remember, when he is old, that he has once been young.
Joseph Addison

While one finds company in himself and his pursuits, he cannot feel old, no matter what his years may be.
Amos Bronson Alcott

To keep the heart unwrinkled, to be hopeful, kindly, cheerful, reverent—that is to triumph over old age.
Thomas Bailey Aldrich

To know how to grow old is the master-work of wisdom, and one of the most difficult chapters in the great art of living.
Henri Frédéric Amiel

That judges of important causes should hold office for life is not a good thing, for the mind grows old as well as the body.
Aristotle

Middle age is a time of life
That a man first notices in his wife.
Richard Armour

I refuse to admit that I am more than 52, even if that does make my sons illegitimate.
Nancy Astor

I think your whole life shows in your face and you should be proud of that.
Lauren Bacall

Discern of the coming on of years, and think not to do the same things still, for age will not be defied.
Francis Bacon

Men of age object too much, consult too long, adventure too little, repeat too soon, and seldom drive business home to the full period, but content themselves with a mediocrity of success.
Francis Bacon

The secret of staying young is to live honestly, eat slowly, and lie about your age.
Lucille Ball

Old age comes at a bad time.
Sue Banducci

A man is not old until regrets take the place of dreams.
John Barrymore

With maturity comes the wish to econo-mize—to be more simple. Maturity is the period when one finds the just measure.
Béla Bartók

To me—old age is 15 years older than I am.
Bernard M. Baruch

The essence of any plan for financing old age is saving—to put aside some part of today's earnings for the future. Anything that saps the value of savings—and inflation is the worst single threat—is the enemy of the aged and of those who expect to grow old.
Bernard M. Baruch

I entered my Seventies
A decade ago.
My span here on earth
Has been quite a good show.
I owe a great deal
To my relative peace,
And I'm terribly grateful

For such a long lease.
Cecil Baxter

We grow neither better nor worse as we get old, but more like ourselves.
May Lamberton Becker

The war years count double. Things and people not actively in use age twice as fast.
Arnold Bennett

When I was 40, my doctor advised me that a man in his forties shouldn't play tennis. I heeded his advice carefully and could hardly wait until I reached 50 to start again.
Hugo L. Black

The child's toys and the old man's reasons are the fruits of two seasons.
William Blake

Men in the uniform of Wall Street retirement: black Chesterfield coat, rimless glasses and the *Times* folded to the obituary page.
Jimmy Breslin

Grow old along with me! The best is yet to be, the last of life, for which the first was made.
Robert Browning

I'm finding, as I've thrived and aged,
That much I'd thought was good was bad.
I doubt I'd want to age again
Without the harmful fun I had.
Art Buck

The toll of time brings few delights
In facing age's deadly spike;
Atop the list
Perhaps is this:
Outliving those we didn't like.
Art Buck

If you wish to be positive, which means youthful, never speak of the past any more than you can help.
Gelett Burgess

The old say, "I remember when." The young say, "What's the news?"
Gelett Burgess

I smoke cigars because at my age if I don't have something to hang on to I might fall down.
George Burns

Retirement at 65 is ridiculous. When I was 65 I still had pimples.
George Burns

As the fruit ripens, so does man mature; after many rains, suns and blows.
José de la Luz y Caballero

Given three requisites—means of existence, reasonable health, and an absorbing interest—those years beyond sixty can be the happiest and most satisfying of a lifetime.
Earnest Elmo Calkins

Those who enjoy the large pleasures of advanced age are those who have sacrificed the small pleasures of youth.
Charles E. Carpenter

We are but older children, dear,
Who fret to find our bedtime near.
Lewis Carroll

Sure I'm for helping the elderly. I'm going to be old myself some day.
Lillian Carter (in her 80s)

The dead might as well try to speak to the living as the old to the young.
Willa Cather

The greatest comfort of my old age, and that which gives me the highest satisfaction, is the pleasing remembrance of the many benefits and friendly offices I have done to others.
Marcus Cato

Middle age is when your classmates are so gray and wrinkled and bald they don't recognize you.
Bennett Cerf

I would not say that old men grow wise, for men never grow wise; and many old men retain a very attractive childishness and cheerful innocence. Elderly people are often much more romantic than younger people, and sometimes even more adventurous, having begun to realize how many things they do not know.
G.K. Chesterton

One pleasure attached to growing older is that many things seem to be growing younger; growing fresher and more lively than we once supposed them to be.
G.K. Chesterton

Growing old isn't so bad when you consider the alternative.
Maurice Chevalier

As I approve of a youth that has something of the old man in him, so I am no less pleased with an old man that has something of the youth. He that follows this rule may be old in body, but can never be so in mind.
Cicero

Short as life is, some find it long enough to outlive their characters, their constitutions and their estates.
Charles Caleb Colton

Don't die until you're dead.
Billy Connolly

Old age: I fall asleep during the funerals of my friends.
Mason Cooley

How foolish to think that one can ever slam the door in the face of age. Much wiser to be polite and gracious and ask him to lunch in advance.
Noël Coward

To what do I owe my longevity? Bad luck.
Quentin Crisp

It is better to wear out than to rust out.
Richard Cumberland

Growing old is not for sissies.
Bette Davis

The really frightening thing about middle age is that you know you'll grow out of it.
Doris Day

I know I can't cheat death, but I can cheat old age, and I've lived my life that way.
Darwin Deason

These are the effects of doting age: vain doubts, idle cares and overcaution.
John Dryden

Old men's eyes are like old men's memories, they are strongest for things a long way off.
George Eliot

A man's years should not be counted until he has something else to count.
Ralph Waldo Emerson

It is time to be old, to take in sail.
Ralph Waldo Emerson

Life is eating us up. We shall be fables presently. Keep cool: It will all be one a hundred years hence.
Ralph Waldo Emerson

The years teach much which the days never know.
Ralph Waldo Emerson

To a longer and worse life, a shorter and better is by all means to be preferred.
Epictetus

If youth knew; if age could.
Henri Estienne

If we could be twice young and twice old we could correct all our mistakes.
Euripides

One of the many things nobody ever tells you about middle age is that it's such a nice change from being young.
Dorothy Canfield Fisher

It can be set down as a broad, general principle that we cannot indulge in idleness and abundance during both the first and second half of our life. Study, application, industry, enthusiasm while we are young usually enable us to enjoy life when we grow older. But unless we toil and strive and earn all we can in the first half, the second half of our life is liable to bring disappointment, discomfort, distress. The time to put forth effort is when we are most able to do it, namely, in the years of our greatest strength. The law of compensation hasn't ceased to function.
B.C. Forbes

Age isn't important until you run out of it.
Malcolm Forbes

After 40, one's face begins to tell more than one's tongue.
Malcolm Forbes

As you get older there shouldn't be anything you won't try. The payoff is that you open up whole new avenues that are fun. It's a misinterpretation of life to live it only in preparation for the next one. To subordinate the one you've got to an indefinite next round is foolish. It's a waste of this life not to live this life. What's next is anybody's guess.
Malcolm Forbes

That everyone earning should contribute to Social Security is indisputable; that everyone, regardless of how he's financially fixed at retirement age, should collect Social Security is indisputably wrong. As it was well put in *Washington Monthly*, Social Security's a device for taking money from present workers to support retired ones. Fair enough. But by what standard can we justify a system that taxes a $14,000-a-year secretary with two kids and gives that money to a Malcolm Forbes?

At what to set the cap should be, can be, debated. But there should not be any debate as to whether a cap should be.
Malcolm Forbes (1985)

You have to be old before you can enjoy being young in spirit.
Malcolm Forbes

If you take all the experience and judgment of men over fifty out of the world, there wouldn't be enough left to run it.
Henry Ford

There's only one way to avoid getting old, and that is to die young.
Georgia physician

The better part of maturity is knowing your goals.
Arnold Glasow

So then the year is repeating its old story again. We are come once more to its most charming chapter.
Johann Wolfgang von Goethe

Age that lessens the enjoyment of life, increases our desire of living.
Oliver Goldsmith

No one can avoid aging, but aging productively is something else.
Katharine Graham

Gray hair is a sign of age, not wisdom.
Greek proverb

The old age of an eagle is better than the youth of a sparrow.
Greek proverb

Most people say that as you get old, you have to give up things. I think you get old because you give up things.
Theodore Francis Green

It's hard to believe that some day I'll be an ancestor.
Robert Half

Old age, believe me, is a good and pleasant time. It is true that you are quietly shouldered off the stage, but then you are given such a comfortable front seat as spectator, and if you have really played your part you are more content to sit down and watch.
Jane Ellen Harrison

There's worse ways to get old than rummaging around in your memories.
Jon Hassler

Like it or not, whatever identity we have in this country, especially for men, comes from what we do for a living. It's among the first questions we ask and are asked. "Retired" is not an identity, it's the lack of one. It's Limbo, the waiting room for the Beyond. The best thing about it is the naps.
James Hennigan

A snow year, a rich year.
George Herbert

Old people have fewer diseases than the young, but their diseases never leave them.
Hippocrates

I think "retirement" goes hand in hand with people who make a living by having a "job." I don't think we—the .00001 percent of the population who are so fortunate to love passionately what we do—consider it a "job."
Dustin Hoffman

Age, like distance, lends a double charm.
Oliver Wendell Holmes

I credit my youthfulness at eighty to the fact of a cheerful disposition and contentment in every period of my life with what I was.
Oliver Wendell Holmes

Men, like peaches and pears, grow sweet a little while before they begin to decay.
Oliver Wendell Holmes

To be seventy years young is sometimes far more cheerful and hopeful than to be forty years old.
Oliver Wendell Holmes

Geriatric Logic:
Take one good breath while still in bed,
One cautious stretch from toe to head.
If nothing hurts—I must be dead!
Hospital Rhyme

You'll find as you grow older that you weren't born such a very great while ago after all. The time shortens up.
William Dean Howells

Forty is the old age of youth; fifty is the youth of old age.
Victor Hugo

Young people think they know it all, but a lot of old salts around know they don't.
Richard Jackson

Let us not look at ourselves but onwards, onwards to the ideal life of man, and take strength from the leaf and the signs of the field. Let us labor to make the heart grow larger as we become older, as the spreading oak gives more shelter.
Richard Jeffries

It is the height of absurdity to sow little but weeds in the first half of one's lifetime and expect to harvest a valuable crop in the second half.
Percy H. Johnston

This evening of a well-spent life brings its lamps with it.
Joseph Joubert

If you wish to live long, you must be willing to grow old.
George Lawton

Aging is not simply decay; it is an accumulation of choices and consequences which, if there is any education at all, consists also of alternatives, an experience of strangeness, a sense of other possibilities, an appreciation of might-have-been.
John Leonard

The thing about getting old is the number of things you think that you can't say aloud because it would be too shocking.
Doris Lessing

My grandfather used to make home movies and edit out the joy.
Richard Lewis

How do you know when you're old? When you double your current age and realize you're not going to live that long.
Michael J. Leyden II

Maturity is achieved when a person accepts life as full of tension; when he does not torment himself with childish guilt feelings, but avoids tragic adult sins; when he postpones immediate pleasures for the sake of long-term values. . . . Our generation must be inspired to search for that maturity which will manifest itself in the qualities of tenacity, dependability, co-operativeness and the inner drive to work and sacrifice for a nobler future of mankind.
Joshua L. Liebman

Psychologically I should say that a person becomes an adult at the point when he produces more than he consumes or earns more than he spends. This may be at the age of eighteen, twenty-five, or thirty-five. Some people remain unproductive and dependent children forever and therefore intellectually and emotionally immature.
Henry C. Link

Nobody grows old by merely living a number of years. People grow old only by deserting their ideals. Years wrinkle the face, but to give up enthusiasm wrinkles the soul. Worry, doubt, self-interest, fear, despair—these are the long, long years that bow the head and turn the growing spirit back to dust.
Watterson Lowe

At sixty a man has passed most of the reefs and whirlpools. Excepting only death, he has no enemies left to meet. . . . That man has awakened to a new youth. . . . Ergo, he is young.
George Luks

A man knows when he is growing old because he begins to look like his father.
Gabriel García Márquez

From the earliest time the old have rubbed it into the young that they are wiser, and before the young had discovered what nonsense this was they were

old too, and it profited them to carry on the imposture.
Somerset Maugham

Old age has its pleasures, which, though different, are not less than the pleasures of youth.
Somerset Maugham

Growing old is no more than a bad habit which a busy man has no time to form.
André Maurois

I wish it were O.K. in this country to look one's age, whatever it is. Maturity has a lot going for it, even in terms of esthetics. For example, you no longer get bubblegum stuck in your braces.
Cyra McFadden

Old age is like a plane flying through a storm. Once you are aboard there is nothing you can do.
Golda Meir

Old age is always wakeful; as if, the longer linked with life, the less man has to do with aught that looks like death.
Herman Melville

The best years are the forties; after fifty a man begins to deteriorate, but in his forties he is at the maximum of his villainy.
H.L. Mencken

The older I grow, the more I distrust the familiar doctrine that age brings wisdom.
H.L. Mencken

It is 11 years since I have seen my figure in a glass [mirror]. The last reflection I saw there was so disagreeable I resolved to spare myself such mortification in the future.
Lady Mary Wortley Montagu

Every period of life has its peculiar prejudices; whoever saw old age that did not applaud the past and condemn the present time?
Michel de Montaigne

Gauge a country's prosperity by its treatment of the aged.
Nachman of Bratzlav

If each of us can be helped by science to live a hundred years, what will it profit us if our hates and fears, our loneliness and our remorse will not permit us to enjoy them?
David Neiswanger

You can judge your age by the amount of pain you feel when you come in contact with a new idea.
John Nuveen

When you're fifty you start thinking about things you haven't thought about before. I used to think getting old was about vanity, but actually it's about losing people you love. Getting wrinkles is trivial.
Joyce Carol Oates

A man is sane morally at thirty, rich mentally at forty, wise spiritually at fifty—or never!
Sir William Osler

Even under a harsh God—and I do not believe in a harsh God—one is entitled to serenity in old age.
Albert Outler

How old would you be if you didn't know how old you was?
Satchel Paige

A comfortable old age is the reward of a well-spent youth. Instead of its bringing

sad and melancholy prospects of decay, it should give us hopes of eternal youth in a better world.
R. Palmer

We are all prisoners of cell biology.
H.B. Pearl

We get too soon old, und too late schmart.
Pennsylvania Dutch proverb

Youth is not a time of life; it is a state of mind. People grow old only by deserting their ideals and by outgrowing the consciousness of youth. Years wrinkle the skin, but to give up enthusiasm wrinkles the soul. . . . You are as old as your doubt, your fear, your despair. The way to keep young is to keep your faith young. Keep your self-confidence young. Keep your hope young.
Luella F. Phelan

The belief that youth is the happiest time of life is founded on a fallacy. The happiest person is the person who thinks the most interesting thoughts, and we grow happier as we grow older.
William Lyon Phelps

You know you're old when you notice how young the derelicts are getting.
Jeanne Phillips

Old age: A great sense of calm and freedom. When the passions have relaxed their hold, you have escaped, not from one master but from many.
Plato

Our youth and manhood are due to our country, but our declining years are due to ourselves.
Pliny

The years that a woman subtracts from her age are not lost. They are added to other women's.
Diane de Poitiers

Years following years steal something every day;
At last they steal us from ourselves away.
Alexander Pope

When we are young, we are slavishly employed in procuring something whereby we may live comfortably when we grow old; and when we are old, we perceive it is too late to live as we proposed.
Alexander Pope

Growing old is like being increasingly penalized for a crime you haven't committed.
Anthony Powell

If by the time we are sixty we haven't learned what a knot of paradox and contradiction life is, and how exquisitely the good and bad are mingled in every action we take, and what a compromising hostess Our Lady of Truth is, we haven't grown old to much purpose.
John Cowper Powys

No one grows old by living—only by losing interest in living.
Marie Beynon Ray

You can only hold your stomach in for so many years.
Burt Reynolds

As a man grows older it is harder and harder to frighten him.
Jean Paul Richter

As winter strips the leaves from around us, so that we may see the distant regions they formerly concealed, so old age takes away our enjoyments only to enlarge the prospect of the coming eternity.
Jean Paul Richter

Memory, wit, fancy, acuteness, cannot grow young again in old age, but the heart can.
Jean Paul Richter

What can a man do to move along in some kind of grace through his days and years?
William Saroyan

Nothing is more disgraceful than that an old man should have nothing to show to prove that he has lived long, except his years.
Seneca

My age is as a lusty winter Frosty, but kindly.
William Shakespeare

It's all that the young can do for the old, to shock them and keep them up to date.
George Bernard Shaw

The secret of a long life is knowing when it's time to go.
Michelle Shocked

When you have lived longer in this world and outlived the enthusiastic and pleasing illusions of youth, you will find your love and pity for the race increase tenfold, your admiration and attachment to a particular party or opinion fall away altogether.
Joseph Henry Shorthouse

The greatest danger to an adequate old-age security plan is rising prices. A rise of 2 per cent a year in prices would cut the purchasing power of pensions about 45 per cent in thirty years. The greatest danger of rising prices is from wages rising faster than output per man-hour. . . . Whether the nation succeeds in providing adequate security for retired workers depends in large measure upon the wage policies of trade unions.
Sumner H. Slichter

As A Man Grows Older

He values the voice of experience more and the voice of prophecy less.

He finds more of life's wealth in the common pleasures—home, health, children.

He thinks more about worth of men and less about their wealth.

He begins to appreciate his own father a little more.

He boasts less and boosts more.

He hurries less, and usually makes more progress.

He esteems the friendship of God a little higher.
Roy L. Smith

Being over seventy is like being engaged in a war. All our friends are going or gone and we survive amongst the dead and the dying as on a battlefield.
Muriel Spark

The mark of the immature man is that he wants to die nobly for a cause, while the mark of the mature man is that he wants to live humbly for one.
William Stekel

Emotional maturity is ability to stick to a job and to struggle through until it is finished; to endure unpleasantness, discomfort and frustration; to give more than is asked for or required; to size things up and make independent decisions; to work under authority and to cooperate with others; to defer to time, others persons, and to circumstances.
Edward A. Strecker

Years do not make sages; they only make old men.
Anne Swetchine

Everyone desires long life, not one old age.
Jonathan Swift

There cannot live a more unhappy creature than an ill-natured old man, who is neither capable of receiving pleasures, nor sensible of conferring them on others.
William J. Temple

If one would understand older people, one should first forget age. Oldness is not so much passing a certain birthday as it is the rearrangement of a complicated set of physical, mental, social and economic circumstances. One must not label a man who has lived a lot of years as an old person. For an individual who has early formed good habits of living, picked up the important techniques of adjustment and acquired a good attitude or philosophy, life continues to be an ever-increasing adventure in development. Development can continue at sixty, seventy and eighty as surely as it did in youth.
William B. Terhune

Old age is the most unexpected of all the things that can happen to a man.
Leon Trotsky

We have no simple problems or easy decisions after kindergarten.
John W. Turk

Last spring I stopped frolicking with the mince pie after midnight. Up to then I had always believed it wasn't loaded.
Mark Twain

The first half of life consists of the capacity to enjoy without the chance; the last half consists of the chance without the capacity.
Mark Twain

Whatever a man's age, he can reduce it several years by putting a bright-colored flower in his buttonhole.
Mark Twain

Nobody grows old by merely living a number of years. People grow old by deserting their ideals.
Samuel Ullman

In the beginning, there was no retirement. There were no old people. In the Stone Age, everyone was fully employed until age twenty, by which time nearly everyone was dead, usually of unnatural causes. Any early man who lived long enough to develop crow's-feet was either worshiped or eaten as a sign of respect.
Mary-Lou Weisman

You end up as you deserve. In old age you must put up with the face, the friends, the health, and the children you have earned.
Fay Weldon

Youth is a silly, vapid state;
Old age with fears and ills is rife;
This simple boon I beg of Fate—
A thousand years of Middle Life!
Carolyn Wells

A man's liberal and conservative phases seem to follow each other in a succession of waves from the time he is born. Children are radicals. Youths are conservatives, with a dash of criminal negligence. Men in their prime are liberals (as long as their digestion keeps pace with their intellect).
E.B. White

Old age: The estuary that enlarges and spreads itself grandly as it pours into the Great Sea.
Walt Whitman

More women grow old nowadays through the faithfulness of their admirers than through anything else.
Oscar Wilde

The tragedy of old age is not that one is old, but that one is young.
Oscar Wilde

More women grow old nowadays through the faithfulness of their admirers than through anything else.
Oscar Wilde

Young men want to be faithful and are not; old men want to be faithless and cannot.
Oscar Wilde

It haunts me, the passage of time. I think time is a merciless thing. I think life is a process of burning oneself out and time is the fire that burns you. But I think the spirit of man is a good adversary.
Tennessee Williams

Now, aged fifty, I'm just poised to shoot forth quite free straight and undeflected my bolts whatever they are.
Virginia Woolf

In masks outrageous and austere,
The years go by in single file;
But none has merited my fear,
And none has quite escaped my smile.
Elinor Wylie

An aged man is but a paltry thing, A tattered coat upon a stick.
William Butler Yeats

I really believe that more harm is done by old men who cling to their influence than by young men who anticipate it.
Owen D. Young

ALCOHOL

The cocktail is a pleasant drink;
It's mild and harmless I don't think.
When you've had one, you call for two,
And then you don't care what you do.
George Ader

Bronze is the mirror of the form; wine, of the heart.
Aeschylus

On hangovers: He resolved, having done it once, never to move his eyeballs again.
Kingsley Amis

The vine bears three kinds of grapes: the first of pleasure, the next of intoxication, and the third of disgust.
Anacharsis

The driver is safer when the roads are dry, and vice versa.
Anonymous

When the cock is drunk, he forgets about the hawk.
Ashanti proverb

The weather is hot, and, yes indeed, the wine is pink. If you have even the slightest doubt, let me assure you: Rosé madness continues.
Eric Asimov

Drinking makes such fools of people, and people are such fools to begin with, that it's compounding a felony.
Robert Benchley

My misdeeds are accidental happenings and merely the result of having been in the wrong bar or bed at the wrong

time, say most days between midday and midnight.
Jeffrey Bernard

The whole world is about three drinks behind.
Humphrey Bogart

I write to discover what I think. After all, the bars aren't open that early.
Daniel Boorstin

When you stop drinking, you have to deal with this marvelous personality that started you drinking in the first place.
Jimmy Breslin

The bar was like a funeral parlor with a beverage service.
Bill Bryson

If you were to ask me if I'd ever had the bad luck to miss my daily cocktail, I'd have to say that I doubt it; where certain things are concerned, I plan ahead.
Luis Buñuel

The bar is an exercise in solitude. Above all else, it must be quiet, dark, very comfortable and, contrary to modern mores, no music of any kind, no matter how faint. In sum, there should be no more than a dozen tables, and a clientele that doesn't like to talk.
Luis Buñuel

I have to think hard to name an interesting man who does not drink.
Richard Burton

If the headache would only precede the intoxication, alcoholism would be a virtue.
Samuel Butler

Most Americans are born drunk, and really require a little wine or beer to sober them. They have a sort of permanent intoxication from within, a sort of invisible champagne.
G.K. Chesterton

I have taken more out of alcohol than alcohol has taken out of me.
Winston Churchill

When I was younger I made it a rule never to take a strong drink before lunch. Now it is my rule never to do so before breakfast.
Winston Churchill

Wine, to a gifted bard, is a
Mount that merrily races;
From watered wits,
No good has ever grown.
Cratinus

I drink too much. Last time I gave a urine sample there was an olive in it.
Rodney Dangerfield

Drink never made a man better, but it made many a man think he was better.
Finley Peter Dunne

He talked with more claret than clarity.
Susan Ertz

Can you imagine opening a bottle of champagne with a bottle opener? I can't. It would eliminate half the fun.
Alain de Vogue

O City city, I can sometimes hear
Beside a public bar in Lower Thames Street,
The pleasant whining of a mandoline
And a clatter and a chatter from within
Where fishmen lounge at noon: where the walls
Of Magnus Martyr hold
Inexplicable splendour of Ionian white and gold.
T.S. Eliot

New York is the greatest city in the world for lunch. That's the gregarious time. When that first martini hits the liver like a silver bullet, there is a sigh of contentment that can be heard in Dubuque.
Willliam Emerson, Jr.

A man's got to believe in something. I believe I'll have another drink.
W.C. Fields

I feel sorry for people who don't drink, because when they get up in the morning, it's as good as they'll feel all day.
W.C. Fields

The bar is the male kingdom. For centuries it was the bastion of male privilege, the gathering place for men away from their women, a place where men could go to freely indulge in The Bull Session.
Shulamith Firestone

Would you have suspected drunk or drugged train drivers couldn't be checked by the railroads to see if they were until now? This, despite the fact that in the past ten years there have been dozens of railroad accidents, deaths and injuries, plus tens of millions in property damage directly attributed (after the fact) to alcohol or drug consumption by the trainmen. It was not until a couple of weeks ago that the Department of Transportation gave the railroads the power to test suspected employees. Only in December will it become for the first time illegal for train operators to be drunk on duty.
Malcolm Forbes (1985)

The three-martini lunch is the epitome of American efficiency.
Gerald Ford

Wine is constant proof that God loves us and loves to see us happy.
Benjamin Franklin

Many people believe the more they pay for a wine, the better it is. But it went against my grain.
Ernest Gallo

Some people spend the day in complaining of a headache, and the night in drinking the wine that gives it.
Johann Wolfgang von Goethe

Champagne, if you are seeking the truth, is better than a lie detector. It encourages a man to be expansive, even reckless, while lie detectors are only a challenge to tell lies successfully.
Graham Greene

On the name of her hangover cure: People kind of universally have a negative reaction to it. They think of Hootie & the Blowfish. Or blowing chunks. There's also the poisonous sushi, so people tend to think, "Blowfish, that's a weird name." But people remember it.
Brenna Haysom

I have drunk since I was 15, and few things have given me more pleasure. When you work hard all day with your head and you must work again the next day, what else can change your ideas and make them run on a different plane like whiskey?
Ernest Hemingway

The proximity of a desirable thing tempts one to overindulgence. On that path lies danger.
Frank Herbert

When you consider how many millions of workdays begin with hangovers great and small, it is mildly surprising to find how few real descriptions of the experience our literature can boast.
Christopher Hitchens

Malt does more than Milton can,
To justify God's ways to man.
A.E. Housman

Possible reason for his success: I'm still drinking.
Joseph Jamail, Jr.

I don't need any more goddamn money. The only thing I'm buying these days is better scotch.
Joseph Jamail, Jr.

The sway of alcohol over mankind is unquestionably due to its power to stimulate the mystical faculties of human nature, usually crushed to earth by the cold facts and dry criticisms of the sober hour. Sobriety diminishes, discriminates, and says no; drunkenness expands, unites and says yes.
William James

The habit of intemperance by men in office has occasioned more injury to the public, and more trouble to me, than all other causes; and, were I to commence my administration again, the first question I would ask respecting a candidate for office, would be, Does he use ardent spirits?
Thomas Jefferson

One of the disadvantages of wine is that it makes a man mistake words for thoughts.
Samuel Johnson

Even though a number of people have tried, no one has yet found a way to drink for a living.
Jean Kerr

It was a cliché that champagne did well when times were bad. But this recession has an added element to it in which conspicuous spending—bling—is out of fashion.
Robert Joseph

I often wonder what the vintners buy. One half so precious as the stuff they sell.
Omar Khayyáam

A telephone survey says that 51% of college students drink until they pass out at least once a month. The other 49% didn't answer the phone.
Craig Kilborn

I don't drink liquor. I don't like it. It makes me feel good.
Oscar Levant

By the time a bartender knows what drink a man will have before he orders, there is little else about him worth knowing.
Don Marquis

Wine is like rain: when it falls on the mire it but makes it fouler, but when it strikes the good soil wakes it to beauty and bloom.
John May

Winston Churchill's habit of guzzling a quart or two a day of good cognac is what saved civilization from the Luftwaffe, Hegelian logic, Wagnerian love-deaths and potato pancakes.
Charles McCabe

I drank at every vine.
The last was like the first.
I came upon no wine
So wonderful as thirst.
Edna St. Vincent Millay

Watlington, which combined the distinction of being the smallest town in England with having more pubs per head of the population than I believed possible.
John Mortimer

[Taverns] are universal places, like churches, hallowed meeting places of all mankind.
Iris Murdoch

We cannot move around large quantities of necessary fluids without spilling them occasionally. Those of us who drink have proven this by experimental method.
P.J. O'Rourke

In wine there is truth.
Pliny the Elder

The ideal barroom ambience evokes neither rush-hour subway frenzy nor the torpor of a government office on a summer afternoon.
Eno Putain

The only wise thing about having a third martini is that you're not yet having a fourth.
Eno Putain

The promised land at day's end, where gelid martinis—conical pools of bliss—glow with platinum dew and sit atop their long pelican legs on the mahogany bar, sentries overlooking bowls of salty nuts.
Eno Putain

Yes, God is in the details, but at some point even God says, "Enough, let's go have a cocktail!"
Eno Putain

I drink no more than a sponge.
François Rabelais

If you can't explain your physics to a barmaid, it is probably not very good physics.
Ernest Rutherford

After eating, an epicure gives a thin smile of satisfaction; a gastronome, burping into his napkin, praises the food in a magazine; a gourmet, repressing his burp, criticizes the food in the same magazine; a gourmand belches happily and tells everybody where he ate; a glutton embraces the white porcelain altar, or, more plainly, he barfs.
William Safire

It is all nonsense about not being able to work without ale, and gin, and cider, and fermented liquors. Do lions and cart-horses drink ale?
Sydney Smith

An alcoholic is someone you don't like who drinks as much as you do.
Dylan Thomas

Water taken in moderation cannot hurt anybody.
Mark Twain

How much of our literature, our political life, our friendships and love affairs, depend on being able to talk peacefully in a bar!
John Wain

Contrarians drink to remember.
Dave Weinbaum

I must get out of these wet clothes and into a dry martini.
Alexander Woollcott

When I read about the evils of drinking, I gave up reading.
Henny Youngman

AMBITION

Ambition is the subtlest beast of the intellectual and moral field. It is wonderfully adroit in concealing itself from its owner.
John Adams

The ambitious climbs up high and perilous stairs and never cares how to

come down; the desire of rising hath swallowed up his fear of a fall.
Thomas Adams

God is not dead but alive and working on a much less ambitious project.
Anonymous Graffito

A man's worth is no greater than the worth of his ambitions.
Marcus Aurelius Antoninus

In this country, every man is the architect of his own ambitions.
Horton Bain

Ambition is a poor excuse for not having sense enough to be lazy.
Edgar Bergen

It's stasis that kills you off in the end, not ambition.
Bono

Ambition is the path to success. Persistence is the vehicle you arrive in.
Bill Bradley

Say what we will, we may be sure that ambition is an error. Its wear and tear on the heart are never recompensed.
Edward Bulwer-Lytton

The same sun which gilds all nature, and exhilarates the whole creation, does not shine upon disappointed ambition.
Edmund Burke

He who would rise in the world should veil his ambitions with the forms of humanity.
Chinese proverb

It is by attempting to reach the top at a single leap that so much misery is caused in the world.
William Cobbett

Ambition is to the mind what the cap is to the falcon; it blinds us first, and then compels us to tower by reason of our blindness.
Charles Caleb Colton

All ambitions are lawful except those which climb upward on the miseries or credulities of mankind.
Joseph Conrad

Ambition, having reached the summit, longs to descend.
Pierre Corneille

Ambition is a Dead Sea fruit, and the greatest peril to the soul is that one is likely to get precisely what he is seeking.
Edward Dahlberg

Without ambition one starts nothing. Without work one finishes nothing. The prize will not be sent to you. You have to win it. The man who knows how will always have a job. The man who also knows why will always be his boss. As to methods there may be a million and then some, but principles are few. The man who grasps principles can successfully select his own methods. The man who tries methods, ignoring principles, is sure to have trouble.
Ralph Waldo Emerson

Ambition is the germ from which all growth of nobleness proceeds.
Thomas D. English

First say to yourself what you would be; and then do what you have to do.
Epictetus

For the spear was a desert physician,
That cured not a few of ambition,
And drave not a few to perdition,
With medicine bitter and strong.
James Elroy Flecker

Ambition and the belly are the two worst counselors.
German proverb

Ambition is most aroused by the trumpet-clang of another's fame.
Baltasar Gracián

From its very beginnings ambition was a political word, born of the Latin *ambitus*, the walking around that a Roman politician did when buttering up the voters.
John P. Grier

What is my loftiest ambition? I've always wanted to throw an egg into an electric fan.
Oliver Herford

Ambition is not a weakness unless it be disproportioned to the capacity.

To have more ambition than ability is to be at once weak and unhappy.
George S. Hillard

Man is the only creature that strives to surpass himself, and yearns for the impossible.
Eric Hoffer

God gives every bird its food, but he does not throw it into the nest.
Josiah G. Holland

Men are more often bribed by their loyalties and ambitions than by money.
Robert H. Jackson

To be unhappy at home is the ultimate result of all ambition.
Samuel Johnson

When you go in search of honey you must expect to be stung by bees.
Kenneth Kaunda

I would sooner fail than not be among the greatest.
John Keats

The thrust of ambition is, and always has been, great, but among the bright-eyed it had once a more adventurous and

individualistic air, a much more bracing rivalry.
Louis Kronenberger

Ambition is a poor excuse for not having sense enough to be lazy.
Milan Kundera

The slave has but one master; the man of ambition has as many as there are people useful to his fortune.
Jean de La Bruyère

We often pass from love to ambition, but we hardly ever return from ambition to love.
François de La Rochefoucauld

Ambition does not see the earth she treads on: The rock and the herbage are of one substance to her.
Walter Savage Landor

Ambition and suspicion always go together.
Georg Christoph Lichtenberg

Most people would succeed in small things if they were not troubled by great ambitions.
Henry Wadsworth Longfellow

Ambition is so powerful a passion in the human breast, that however high we reach, we are never satisfied.
Niccolò Machiavelli

It is a psychological law that whatever we desire to accomplish we must impress upon the subjective or subconscious mind; that is, we must register a vow with ourselves, we must make our resolution with vigor, with faith that we can do the thing we want to do; we must register our conviction with such intensity that the great creative forces within us will tend to realize them. Our impressions will become expressions just in proportion to the vigor with which

we register our vows to accomplish our ambitions, to make our visions realities.
Orison Swett Marden

If you have a great ambition, take as big a step as possible in the direction of fulfilling it, but if the step is only a tiny one, don't worry if it is the largest one now possible.
Mildred McAfee

If men cease to believe that they will one day become gods then they will surely become worms.
Henry Miller

Ambition is the spur that makes men struggle with destiny. It is heaven's own incentive to make purpose great and achievement greater.
Donald G. Mitchell

Ambition is a lust that is never quenched, but grows more inflamed and madder by enjoyment.
Thomas Otway

People Who Do Things exceed my endurance. God, for a man that solicits insurance!
Dorothy Parker

The tallest trees are most in the power of the winds, and ambitious men of the blasts of fortune.
William Penn

The same ambition can destroy or save, And makes a patriot as it makes a knave.
Alexander Pope

Though ambition may be a fault in itself, it is often the mother of virtues.
Quintilian

It is the constant fault and inseparable evil quality of ambition, that it never looks behind it.
Seneca

The very substance of the ambitious is merely the shadow of a dream.
William Shakespeare

Ambition is an idol on whose wings great minds are carried to extremes, to be sublimely great, or to be nothing.
Thomas Southern

Many people have the ambition to succeed; they may even have special aptitude for their job. And yet they do not move ahead. Why? Perhaps they think that since they can master the job, there is no need to master themselves.
John Stevenson

In private enterprises men may advance or recede, whereas they who aim at empire have no alternative between the highest success and utter downfall.
Tacitus

I always wanted to be somebody, but I should have been more specific.
Lily Tomlin and Jane Wagner

It is the nature of ambition to make men liars and cheats, to hide truth in their breasts, and show, like jugglers, another thing in their mouths, to cut all friendships and enmities to the measure of their own interest.
Kenneth Tynan

A young man's ambition is to get along in the world and make a place for himself— half your life goes that way, till you're 45 or 50. Then, if you're lucky, you make terms with life, you get released.
Robert Penn Warren

How like a mounting devil in the heart rules the unreined ambition.
Nathanial P. Willis

They build too low who build beneath the skies.
Edward Young

AMERICA

The whole of the American Dream has been based on the chance to get ahead, for one's self or one's children. Would this country have ever reached the point it has if the individual had always been refused the rewards of his labors and dangers?
James Truslow Adams

Yesterday the greatest question was decided which was ever debated in America; and a greater perhaps never was, nor will be, decided upon men. A resolution was passed without one dissenting colony, that those United Colonies are, and of right ought to be, free and independent states.
John Adams (July 3, 1776)

America's future will be determined by the home and the school. The child becomes largely what it is taught, hence we must watch what we teach it, how we live before it.
Jane Addams

Good Americans, when they die, go to Paris.
Thomas Appleton

The American Republic and American business are Siamese twins; they came out of the same womb at the same time; they are born in the same principles and when American business dies, the American Republic will die, and when the American Republic dies, American business will die.
Josiah W. Bailey

In America, it is sport that is the opiate of the masses.
Russell Baker

The making of an American begins at that point where he himself rejects all other ties, any other history, and himself adopts the vesture of his adopted land.
James Baldwin

America is the country where you buy a lifetime supply of aspirin for one dollar, and use it up in two weeks.
John Barrymore

In America there are two classes of travel, first class and with children.
Robert Benchley

Alligator: The crocodile of America, superior in every detail to the crocodile of the effete monarchies of the Old World.
Ambrose Bierce

Despite whatever agreement there may be between some of us, let us never forget that we are all working whole-heartedly and humbly for the same goal—a country of peace, abundance and prosperity—for all of our people of all races, of all groups— whoever they may be, wherever they may live.
Chester Bowles

If you will help run our government in the American way, then there will never be any danger of our government running America in the wrong way.
Omar N. Bradley

It is to the United States that all freemen look for the light and the hope of the world. Unless we dedicate ourselves completely to this struggle, unless we combat hunger with food, fear with trust, suspicion with faith, fraud with justice—and threats with power, nations will surrender to the futility, the hopelessness, the panic on which wars feed.
Omar N. Bradley

America has believed that in differentiation, not in uniformity, lies the path

of progress. It acted on this belief; it has advanced human happiness, and it has prospered.
Louis D. Brandeis

No one in this country has any root anywhere; we don't live in America, we board here, we are like spiders that run over the surface of the water.
Van Wyck Brooks

Americans are a broad-minded people. They'll accept the fact that a person can be an alcoholic, a dope fiend, a wife beater, and even a newspaperman; but if a man doesn't drive there's something wrong with him.
Art Buchwald

The history of the building of the American nation may justly be described as a laboratory experiment in understanding and in solving the problems that will confront the world tomorrow.
Dr. Nicholas Murray Butler

It's a scientific fact that if you stay in California you lose one point of your IQ every year.
Truman Capote

Americans are a backward people, with all the very real virtues of a backward people; the patriarchal simplicity and human dignity of a democracy, and a respect for labor uncorrupted by cynicism.
G.K. Chesterton

I like the Americans for a great many reasons. I like them because even the modern thing called industrialism has not entirely destroyed in them the very ancient thing called democracy. I like them because they have a respect for work which really curbs the human tendency to snobbishness.
G.K. Chesterton

Most Americans are born drunk, and really require a little wine or beer to sober them. They have a sort of permanent intoxication from within, a sort of invisible champagne.
G.K. Chesterton

The historic glory of America lies in the fact that it is the one nation that was founded like a church. That is, it was founded on a faith that was not merely summed up after it had existed; it was defined before it existed.
G.K. Chesterton

There is nothing the matter with Americans except their ideals. The real American is all right: It is the ideal American who is all wrong.
G.K. Chesterton

There are no people in the world who are so slow to develop hostile feelings against a foreign country as the Americans, and no people who, once estranged, are more difficult to win back.
Winston Churchill

America is the only nation in history which miraculously has gone directly from barbarism to degeneration without the usual interval of civilization.
Georges Clemenceau

Race tensions thrive on the restricted educational opportunities for Southern Negroes. When earning power is limited or foreshortened by lack of education, whole populations suffer. A potential great producing force, as well as a large possible market for goods, is thus being ignored.
Dr. Rufus E. Clement

When the Pilgrims landed they fell on their knees and then they fell on the aborigines.
Prescott C. Cleveland

More material progress has been made during the past one hundred and fifty years under the American system of business enterprise than during all the preceding centuries in world history. This record of achievement is a challenge to those who would radically change that system.
Karl T. Compton

It is a great advantage to a President, and a major source of safety to the country, for him to know that he is not a great man.
Calvin Coolidge

The government of the United States is a device for maintaining in perpetuity the rights of the people, with the ultimate extinction of all privileged classes.
Calvin Coolidge

America grew great from the seed of the will to do and dare; the will to get up and go on and not to quit after we had erred and fallen; the will to struggle to our feet and plod along and not to give up and lie down when we wavered and stumbled from fatigue. It grew not from the seed of slumping down and giving in when laden with apparent discouragement and seeming defeat, but from the seed of the will to rise to the occasion, shake it off, stand firm and resolute, and challenge defeat. Yes, it seems what we in America need is to get back to the planting and cultivating of that good old American seed.
Arnold W. Craft

There are certain fundamental requisites for wise and resolute democratic leadership. It must build on hope, not on fear; on honesty, not on falsehood; on justice, not on injustice; on public tranquility, not on violence; on freedom, not on enslavement. It must weave a social fabric in which the most important strands are a devotion to truth and a commitment to righteousness. These are essential ingredients of the American way of life. They are the necessary conditions for the achievement of freedom and human progress the world over.
Dr. Edmund Ezra Day

A vision of the future has been one of the sustaining marks of the American experience. Without that vision and without the men who devote themselves to realizing that vision, there can be no true American way of life. We must beware of the thoughtless men who proclaim that a particular stage of our social development, or any special set of conditions, is the best that progress can offer. These men would immobilize us in the great stream of history. They would let its great challenges and chances pass us by ... forgetting that the American way of life is a way of acting, not a state of inactivity.
Cornelius W. De Kiewit

By patience and determination, rather than by a harsh upsetting of tradition, we move toward our national aspirations. . . . This is the way we get things done in America. One man tells another, does what he can, till the sum of these efforts grows into a national aspiration—a precious goal. Then occurs our miracle of democracy: because the groundwork has been surely laid, the goal is already within our grasp.
Newton B. Drury

America came of God, without question, and we ought to dedicate ourselves to her service so that the goodness of America would make her eternal. . . . And if we live so that the people of the world want to be like us, want to be like what we are instead of what we have, then America will be safe and the world will be safe.
Ulysses G. Dubach

In a world where so much seems to be hidden by the smoke of falsity and moral degeneration, we Americans must grasp firmly the ideals which have made this country great. We must reaffirm the basic human values that have guided our forefathers. A revival of old-fashioned patriotism and a grateful acknowledgment of what our country has done for us would be good for all our souls.
Manton S. Eddy

American working men are principals in the three-member team of capital, management, labor. Never have they regarded themselves as a servile class that could attain freedom only through destruction of the industrial economy.
Dwight D. Eisenhower

Every gathering of Americans—whether a few on the porch of a crossroads store or massed thousands in a great stadium—is the possessor of a potentially immeasurable influence on the future.
Dwight D. Eisenhower

I don't think the United States needs superpatriots. We need patriotism, honestly practiced by all of us, and we don't need these people that are more patriotic than you or anyone else.
Dwight D. Eisenhower

Men of widely divergent views in our own country live in peace together because they share certain common aspirations which are more important than their differences. . . . The common responsibility of all Americans is to become effective, helpful participants in a way of life that blends and harmonizes the fiercely competitive demands of the individual and society.
Dwight D. Eisenhower

Whatever America hopes to bring to pass in the world must first happen in the heart of America. More than escape from death, it is a way of life. More than a haven for the weary, it is a hope for the brave.
Dwight D. Eisenhower

When American life is most American it is apt to be most theatrical.
Ralph Ellison

America is another name for opportunity.
Ralph Waldo Emerson

Every ship that comes to America got its chart from Columbus.
Ralph Waldo Emerson

In America nature is autocratic, saying, "I am not arguing, I am telling you."
Erik H. Erikson

America is so vast that almost everything said about it is likely to be true, and the opposite is probably equally true.
James T. Farrell

The superiority of the American system is eloquently proved by the pressure of people who want to crash our borders.
William Feather

As I steamed into New York this month, exactly 20 years after first landing in America, the thought uppermost in my mind after visiting Europe was this: How mightily the United States has progressed in wealth and power, and how Europe has failed to keep step. America has exhibited qualities of a strong, industrious, generous-hearted, enthusiastic youth. Europe has exhibited signs of age. . . . America, the Youth, has not been eaten up with jealousies and bitterness and strife. Europe, the veteran, has.
B.C. Forbes

Is America becoming decadent? Do we no longer regard our promises and pledges as sacred? . . . We promised

to make peace with Germany only in conjunction with the Allies; but we brought forward a separate peace, demanding for ourselves all the advantages of the Treaty of Versailles but rejecting all the responsibilities embodied in the Treaty. It was America's President who induced Europe to form a League of Nations; and then America was the first country that refused to joint it. . . . If these are not the symptoms of national decadency, what are they?
B.C. Forbes

The British have their own conception of what constitutes the typical American. He must have a flavor of the Wild West about him. He must do spectacular things. He must not be punctilious about dignity, decorum and other refinements characteristic of the real British gentleman. The Yankee pictured by the Briton must be a bustler. If he is occasionally flagrantly indiscreet in speech and action, then he is so much more surely stamped the genuine article. The most typical American the British ever set their eyes on was, in their judgment, Theodore Roosevelt.
B.C. Forbes

What would you call America's most priceless asset? Surely not its limitless natural resources, not its matchless national wealth, not its unequalled store of gold, not its giant factories, not its surpassing railroads, not its unprecedented volume of cheap power. Is not its most priceless asset the character of its people, their indomitable self-confidence, their transcendent vision, their sleepless initiative and, perhaps above all, their inherent, irrepressible optimism?
B.C. Forbes

Blaming the U.S. for most of their problems is usually food for bursts of applause among our allies, and ever more frequently within the Third World. . . . But where do they put what's nearest and dearest to them—their money? Here. In the last year and a half oversea-ers have invested more money in the U.S. than ever before; more, for the first time, than Americans have invested abroad. So, too, their cash stash in U.S. stocks, bonds and Treasuries soars. The French send the Socialists to power and their money to New York.
Malcolm Forbes

For some of us it seems like yesterday when Ike was in the White House, the U.S. Senate censured Joe McCarthy, and the Supreme Court unanimously ruled that racial segregation in public school was unconstitutional.
Malcolm Forbes

It's hard to put your finger on just what it was about Dwight Eisenhower that gave him his unique place in the hearts of his countrymen. War hero? Not really. He never personally led a charge up any San Juan hills [or] Deweyed any enemy fleets at Manila Bay. A spectacular, dramatic, colorful President and Presidency? No one would so describe the Eisenhower years. . . . No, it wasn't any of the obvious Pedestal things. It wasn't his Greatness with a capital G; rather it was his goodness without the capital G; the compelling decency of the man; the unconscious yet visible guidance by his conscience.
Malcolm Forbes

Rightly, we constantly berate ourselves—mostly everybody else but me and thee—about the things wrong in our country. . . . Something has to account, though, for this country's ongoing greatness, innate and actual. And I think the Conference Board's latest survey has put a finger on that something—four out of five Americans are satisfied with their

jobs, one-third of those very satisfied. It's not surprising that job satisfaction climbs with earnings, but more significant is the fact that such satisfaction climbs with age [with] 86% of those 55 and over happy at what they're doing . . .
Malcolm Forbes

The Johnson Administration may have messed up a lot of major programs, according to which party you support . . . but I don't think too many thinking Americans will fault the President and the First Lady for their consistent, determined support of parks, our wilderness areas and some unspoiled, unbelievably attractive American scenery.

[Johnson] has proposed a National Trails system, with four trails to start with . . .

I don't know if you have even taken a walk in the country or . . . joined contemporary neighboring adventurers on hikes. If you did, you know what a wondrous thing it is for mind as well as muscle.
Malcolm Forbes

Our country is still young and its potential is still enormous. We should remember, as we look toward the future, that the more fully we believe in and achieve freedom and equal opportunity—not simply for ourselves but for others—the greater our accomplishments as a nation will be.
Henry Ford

We Americans say that the Constitution made the nation. Well, the Constitution is a great document and we never would have been a nation without it, but it took more than that to make the nation. Rather it was our forefathers and foremothers, who made the Constitution and then made it work. The government they constructed did get great things out of them, but it was not the government primarily that put the great things into

them. What put the great things into them was their home life, their religion, their sense of personal responsibility to Almighty God, their devotion to education, their love of liberty, their personal character.
Harry Emerson Fosdick

We get twitted now and then on how we made this country. Well, we took the whole business, of course. It's not just that corner that we took away from Mexico. When we got it all together, we got a very shapely country—the best continental cut in all the world, between the two oceans and in the right temperature zone.
Robert Frost

Talleyrand once said to the first Napoleon that the United States is a giant without bones. Since that time our gristle has been rapidly hardening.
James A. Garfield

Make no mistake about it. The first man who will walk on the moon has already been born. I hope in America.
General James Gavin (1958)

When the white man came, we had the land and they had the Bibles. Now they have the land and we have the Bibles.
Chief Dan George

In America an hour is 40 minutes.
German saying

The greatness of the United States is due simply to this fact: Under the principle of individual liberty, human incentive has been given its widest scope.
Crawford H. Greenewalt

Every citizen of this country, whether he pounds nails, raises corn, designs rockets or writes poetry, should be taught to

know and love his American heritage; to use the language well; to understand the physical universe, and to enjoy the arts. The dollars he gains in the absence of enlightenment like this will be earned in drudgery and spent in ignorance.
Calvin E. Gross

It is as if all America were but a giant workshop, over the entrance of which is the blazing inscription, "No admission here, except on business."
F.J. Grund (1837)

No citizen of this nation is worthy of the name unless he bears unswerving loyalty to the system under which he lives, the system that gives him more benefits than any other system yet devised by man. Loyalty leaves room to change the system when need be, but only under the ground rules by which we Americans live.
John A. Hannah

Ideals are the incentive payment of practical men. The opportunity to strive for them is the currency that has enriched America through the centuries.
Robert E. Hannegan

The American economic story, despite defects and drawbacks and dreams turned nightmares, is such a good and strong and persuasive story that it needs no attempt to conceal or gloss over blemishes and imperfections. It can stand on its own with its virtues and deficiencies fully displayed. Like Cromwell's face, the U.S. economy is best portrayed warts and all.
Herbert Harris

You can't appreciate home until you've left it, money till it's spent, your wife till she's joined a woman's club, nor Old Glory till you see it hanging on a broomstick on the shanty of a consul in a foreign town.
O. Henry

Every U.S. citizen owes allegiance to our nation. Some Americans consider that anything less than high treason is allegiance.
Cullen Hightower

You cannot gauge the intelligence of an American by talking with him; you must work with him. The American polishes and refines his way of doing things—even the most commonplace—the way the French of the 17th century polished their maxims.
Eric Hoffer

In the homes of America are born the children of America, and from them go out into American life American men and women. They go out with the stamp of these homes upon them and only as these homes are what they should be, will they be what they should be.
Josiah G. Holland

If America is to be run by the people, it is the people who must think. And we do not need to put on sackcloth and ashes to think. Nor should our minds work like a sundial which records only sunshine. Our thinking must square against some lessons of history, some principles of government and morals, if we would preserve the rights and dignity of men to which this nation is dedicated.
Herbert Hoover

It is those moral and spiritual qualities which rise alone in free men, which will fulfill the meaning of the word American. And with them will come centuries of further greatness to our country.
Herbert Hoover

The priceless treasure of boyhood is his endless enthusiasm, his high store of idealism, his affections and his hopes. When we preserve these, we have made men. We have made citizens and we have made Americans.
Herbert Hoover

We [the Government] are here not as masters but as servants, we are not here to glory in power, but to attest our loyalty to the commands and restrictions laid down by our sovereign, the people of the United States, in whose name and by whose will we exercise our brief authority.
Charles Evans Hughes

The thing that impresses me most about this country is its hopefulness. It is this which distinguishes it from Europe, where there is hopeless depression and fear.
Aldous Huxley

I tremble for my country when I reflect that God is just.
Thomas Jefferson

If some period be not fixed, either by the Constitution or by practice, to the services of the First Magistrate, his office, though nominally elective, will, in fact, be for life, and that will soon degenerate into an inheritance.
Thomas Jefferson

It is a very dangerous doctrine to consider the [Supreme Court] judges as the ultimate arbiters of all constitutional questions. It is one which would place us under the despotism of an oligarchy.
Thomas Jefferson

The policy of the American government is to leave their citizens free, neither restraining nor aiding them in their pursuits.
Thomas Jefferson

Science and time and necessity have propelled us, the United States, to be the general store for the world, dealers in everything. Most of all, merchants for a better way of life.
Lady Bird Johnson

Solitude is un-American.
Erica Jong

Rome endured as long as there were Romans. America will endure as long as we remain American in spirit and in thought.
David Starr Jordan

Whither goest thou, America, in thy shiny car in the night?
Jack Kerouac

True nostalgia is an ephemeral composition of dis-jointed memories, but American-style nostalgia is about as ephemeral as copyrighted déjà vu.
Florence King

The earlier days of the republic went into the acquisition of money and the provision for material things is now finding an outlet in the espousal of art. Now America has the leisure and the culture to foster beauty.
Fritz Kreisler

America is a tune. It must be sung together.
Gerald Stanley Lee

Abandon your animosities and make your sons Americans!
Robert E. Lee

I have been up to see the [Confederate] Congress, and they do not seem to be able to do anything except to eat peanuts

and chew tobacco, while my army is starving.
Robert E. Lee (1865)

Intellectually I know that America is no better than any other country; emotionally I know she is better than every other country.
Sinclair Lewis

The abundant life of which we have heard so much recently does not come to those who have all obstacles removed from their paths by others. It develops from within and is rooted in strong mental and moral fiber. To look to government to supply all material safeguards is to sound the doom of the great American tradition. If America is to go forward, we must develop in our colleges ideals of courage, industry, and independence.
Dr. William Mather Lewis

The great social adventure of America is no longer the conquest of the wilderness but the absorption of fifty different peoples.
Walter Lippmann

If a man is going to be an American at all let him be so without any qualifying adjectives; and if he is going to be something else let him drop the word American from his personal description.
Henry Cabot Lodge

In the mighty and almost limitless potential of American industry—the brilliance and rugged determination of its leaders; the skill, energy and patriotism of its workers—there has been welded an almost impregnable defense against the evil designs of any who would threaten the security of the American continent. It is indeed the most forceful and convincing argument yet evolved to restrain the irresponsibility of those who would recklessly bring down upon the good and peace-loving peoples of all the nations of the earth the disaster of total war.
Douglas MacArthur

The map of America is a map of endlessness, of opening out, of forever and ever. No man's face would make you think of it but his hope might, his courage might.
Archibald MacLeish

Americanism is not an accident of birth, but an achievement in terms of worth. Government does not create Americanism, but Americanism creates Government. Americanism is not a race, but a vision, a hope and an ideal.
Dr. Louis I. Mann

Education is the indispensable means by which the ideas of the men who founded the American Republic can be disseminated and perpetuated. Only through education can the people be kept from becoming greedy and ignorant, from degenerating into a populace incapable of self-government. It is only by education, religion, and morality that the people can save themselves from becoming a willing instrument of their own debasement and ruin. The American Republic will endure only as long as the ideas of the men who founded it continue dominant.
Daniel L. Marsh

No political dreamer was ever wild enough to think of breaking down the lines which separate the States and compounding the American people into one common mass.
John Marshall

America must remain, at any cost, the custodian of freedom, human dignity and economic security. The United States

must be strong, so that no nation may dare attack.
Louis B. Mayer

America's love has never been equalled in human history. She turns her cheek seventy times seven. She fights only to defend her family. But when she has defeated her enemies she binds their wounds, feeds their children, pays their bills and hands forth billions of dollars to restore them to an honorable place among the nations of the world.
Emmett McLoughlin

America is the only country ever founded on the printed word.
Marshall McLuhan

American youth attributes much more importance to arriving at driver's-license age than at voting age.
Marshall McLuhan

The most fearful phenomenon of these midcentury years is not the atom bomb; atomic energy does have its constructive possibilities.... The most fearful event of these times is the colossal expansion of the government of the United States and the constant increase of executive power within the government.
Wheeler McMillen

Those tragic comedians, the Chamber of Commerce red hunters, the Women's Christian Temperance Union smellers, the censors of books, the Klan regulators, the Methodist prowlers, the Baptist guardians of sacred vessels—we have the national mentality of a police lieutenant.
H.L. Mencken

Things on the whole are faster in America; people don't *stand for election*, they *run for office*. If a person says he's sick, it doesn't mean regurgitating, it means ill. *Mad* means angry, not insane.

Don't ask for the left-luggage; it's called a *checkroom*.
Jessica Mitford

To be a good American means to understand the simple principles on which our nation was founded, to observe them in our daily life and to fight for them.
Newbold Morris

Wilderness to the people of America is a spiritual necessity, an antidote to the high pressure of modern life, a means of regaining serenity and equilibrium.
Sigurd F. Olson

Never, I say, had a country so many openings to happiness as this.... Her cause was good. Her principles just and liberal. Her temper serene and firm.... The remembrance then of what is past, if it operates rightly must inspire her with the most laudable of an ambition, that of adding to the fair fame she began with. The world has seen her great adversity.... Let then, the world see that she can bear prosperity; and that her honest virtue in time of peace is equal to the bravest virtue in time of war.
Thomas Paine

Double—no, triple—our troubles and we'd still be better off than any other people on earth.
Ronald Reagan

A Primer of American Self-Government

1. Understand, honor and preserve the Constitution of the United States.

2. Keep forever separate and distinct the legislative, executive and judicial functions of government.

3. Remember that government belongs to the people, is inherently inefficient, and that its activities should be limited to those which government alone can perform.

4. Be vigilant for freedom of speech, freedom of worship, and freedom of action.

5. Cherish the system of Free Enterprise which made America great.

6. Respect thrift and economy, and beware of debt.

7. Above all, let us be scrupulous in keeping our word and in respecting the rights of others.
Philip D. Reed

The four cornerstones of character on which the structure of this nation was built are: Initiative, Imagination, Individuality and Independence.
Edward Rickenbacker

The world position which our country holds today is due to the wide vision of the statesmen who founded these United States and to the daring and indomitable persistence of the great industrial leaders, together with the myriads of men who with faith in their leadership have co-operated to rear the marvelous industrial structure of which our country is justly so proud.
John D. Rockefeller, Jr.

It's a great country, but you can't live in it for nothing.
Will Rogers

Everything is un-American that tends either to government by a plutocracy or government by a mob. To divide along the lines of section or caste or creed is un-American. All privileges based on wealth, and all enmity to honest men merely because they are wealthy, are un-American—both of them equally so. The things that will destroy America are prosperity-at-any-price, peace-at-any-price, safety-first instead of duty-first, the love of soft living and the get-rich-quick theory of life.
Theodore Roosevelt

I wish all Americans would realize that American politics is world politics.
Theodore Roosevelt

America remained a land of promise for lovers of freedom. Even Byron, at a moment when he was disgusted with Napoleon for not committing suicide, wrote an eloquent stanza in praise of Washington.
Bertrand Russell

Always the path of American destiny has been into the unknown. Always there arose enough reserves of strength, balances of sanity, portions of wisdom to carry the nation through to a fresh start with ever-renewing vitality.
Carl Sandburg

If I added to their pride of America, I am happy.
Carl Sandburg

Not often in the story of mankind does a man arrive on earth who is both steel and velvet, who is as hard as rock and soft as drifting fog, who holds in his heart and mind the paradox of terrible storm and peace unspeakable and perfect.
Carl Sandburg (on Lincoln)

Americans still believe they are cut out to be successful—in everything: love, love-making, luck, luck-giving, money-making, sense-making, cancer-avoiding, clothes-wearing, car-driving, and so on.
William Saroyan

One of the main differences between our American form of republic and other forms of government is the freedom of the individual to choose and exercise his means to earn his livelihood. Time has proved that our system of private

enterprise, making a team of labor, investment of savings and management, with the minimum of state and Federal Government interference generates the greatest number of opportunities for individuals to earn a decent living.
Fred G. Singer

We have a glorious future within our grasp. The American people have learned a lot in the past twenty-five years about how to make our country the kind of land in which everyone can live in dignity, comfort and personal content-ment, if he so wishes.
Charles R. Sligh, Jr.

The nations of the world look to the people of this country for leadership. They have seen our youth in action. They have seen their courage and their strength. Off the battlefield they have seen and admired the human kind-ness and the tolerance of the men who went overseas for us and for them. May we stand firm in our conviction that America has achieved a way of life that we can all cherish—and cherishing, strive ever to guard and improve.
George A. Sloan

Six things we individual Americans can never afford are: Intolerance, indolence, injustice, indifference, intemperance and ingratitude. Whenever any of these enter, they lead to deterioration, defeat and disaster. Any nation given to them inevitably falls.
J. Richard Sneed

It took thrift and savings, together with tremendous character and vision, to make our nation what it is today. And it will take thrift and savings, together with constant ingenuity and stamina, to conserve our remaining resources to enable us to continue to be a great nation.
John W. Snyder

In the United States there is more room where nobody is than where anybody is. That is what makes America what it is.
Gertrude Stein

Our forefathers gave us a system of government which has produced greater liberties and higher living standards than ever before experienced in the history of the world. As citizens it is our duty and our responsibility to do our utmost to protect that system and to provide moral leadership for the rest of the world.
George E. Stringfellow

The New Dealers, labor politicians and Socialists have tried to take advantage of the natural American instinct for charity to forward their plans to socialize the furnishing of the necessities of life to all. If the Government gives free medical care to everybody, why not free food, clothing and housing?
Robert A. Taft

The reason American cities are pros-perous is that there is no place for people to sit down.
Alfred J. Talley

In America one of the first things done in a new State is to make the post go there; in the forests of Michigan there is no cabin so isolated, no valley so wild, but that letters and newspapers arrive at least once a week.
Alexis de Tocqueville

Of all the countries in the world, America is that in which the spread of ideas and of human industry is the most continual and most rapid.
Alexis de Tocqueville

The worst country to be poor in is America.
Arnold Toynbee

There are many humorous things in the world; among them, the white man's notion that he is less savage than the other savages.
Mark Twain

The United States is the richest, and, both actually and potentially, the most powerful state on the globe. She has much to give to the world; indeed, to her hands is chiefly entrusted the shaping of the future. If democracy in the broadest and truest sense is to survive, it will be mainly because of her guardianship.
Lord Tweedsmuir

Teach our children the wholesome ideals of America today—and the threat of vicious Communism will be dead tomorrow.
Martin Vanbee

I know that all things considered, the United States of America, with all of its abuses of democracy and of liberty itself, is still the garden spot of the world, where peace, co-operation and constructive effort can and should prevail always and the cause of a higher Christian civilization advanced.
George M. Verity

If we mean to support the liberty and independence which have cost us so much blood and treasure to establish, we must drive far away the demon of party spirit and local reproach.
George Washington

God grants liberty only to those who love it and are always ready to guard and defend it. Let our object be our country. And, by the blessing of God, may that country itself become a vast and splendid monument, not of oppression and terror, but of wisdom, of peace, and of liberty, upon which the world may gaze with admiration forever!
Daniel Webster

Let our object be our country, our whole country and nothing but our country.
Daniel Webster

It's becoming increasingly difficult to reach the down-trodden masses in America, a comrade wrote to his superior. In the spring they're forever polishing their cars. In the summer they take vacations. In the fall they go to the world series and football games. And in the winter you can't get them away from their television sets. Please give me suggestions on how to let them know how oppressed they are.
Prof. Dexter Williams

Our way of living together in America is a strong but delicate fabric. It is made up of many threads. It has been woven over many centuries by the patience and sacrifice of countless liberty-loving men and women. It serves as a cloak for the protection of poor and rich, of black and white, of Jew and Gentile, of foreign and native born. Let us not tear it asunder. For no man knows, once it is destroyed, where or when man will find its protective warmth again.
Wendell Willkie

The interesting and inspiring thing about America is that she asks nothing for herself except what she has a right to ask for humanity itself.
Woodrow Wilson

We want the spirit of America to be efficient; we want American character to be efficient; we want American character to display itself in what I may, perhaps, be allowed to call spiritual efficiency—clear

disinterested thinking and fearless action along the right lines of thought.
Woodrow Wilson

ANCESTORS

Genealogy: An account of one's descent from an ancestor who did not particularly care to trace his own.
Ambrose Bierce

A man's ancestry is a positive property to him.
Edward G. Bulwer-Lytton

People will not look forward to posterity, who never look backward to their ancestors.
Edmund Burke

I'd rather have an inch of dog than miles of pedigree.
Dana Burnet

There are many kinds of conceit, but the chief one is to let people know what a very ancient and gifted family one descends from.
Benvenuto Cellini

To forget one's ancestors is to be a brook without a source, a tree without a root.
Chinese proverb

Man is descended from a hairy-tailed quadruped, probably arboreal in his habits.
Charles Darwin

Genealogy: A perverse preoccupation of those who seek to demonstrate that their forebears were better people than they are.
Sydney J. Harris

Every man is his own ancestor, and every man his own heir. He devises his own future, and he inherits his own past.
H.F. Hedge

Many a family tree needs trimming.
Kin Hubbard

If you would civilize a man, begin with his grandmother.
Victor Hugo

The proper time to influence the character of a child is about a hundred years before he is born.
William Ralph Inge

We pay for the mistakes of our ancestors, and it seems only fair that they should leave us the money to pay with.
Don Marquis

It is indeed a desirable thing to be well descended, but the glory belongs to our ancestors.
Plutarch

Our ancestors are very good kind of folks, but they are the last people I should choose to have a visiting acquaintance with.
Richard B. Sheridan

Whoever serves his country well has no need of ancestors.
Voltaire

ANGER

How much more grievous are the consequences of anger than the causes of it.
Marcus Aurelius Antoninus

When thou art above measure angry, bethink thee how momentary a man's life is.
Marcus Aurelius Antoninus

The most complete revenge is not to imitate the aggressor.
Marcus Aurelius Antoninus

Anger represents a certain power, when a great mind, prevented from executing its own generous desires, is moved by it.
Pietro Aretino

Angry men are blind and foolish, for reason at such time takes flight and, in her absence; wrath plunders all the riches of the intellect, while the judgment remains the prisoner of its own pride.
Pietro Aretino

Anybody can become angry—that is easy; but to be angry with the right person, and to the right degree, and at the right time, and for the right purpose, and in the right way—that is not within everybody's power and is not easy.
Aristotle

Meanness is incurable; it cannot be cured by old age, or by anything else.
Aristotle

A man that studieth revenge keeps his own wounds green.
Francis Bacon

Rage can only with difficulty, and never entirely, be brought under the domination of the intelligence, and therefore is not susceptible to any arguments whatsoever.
James Baldwin

A man that does not know how to be angry does not know how to be good.
Henry Ward Beecher

Never forget what a man has said to you when he was angry. If he has charged you with anything, you had better look it up.
Henry Ward Beecher

There is another man within me that's angry with me.
Thomas Browne

When one is in a good sound rage, it is astonishing how calm one can be.
Edward Bulwer-Lytton

He that wrestles with us strengthens our nerves and sharpens our skill. Our antagonist is our helper.
Edmund Burke

Human anger is a higher thing than what is called divine discontent. For you must be angry with something; but you can be discontented with everything.
G.K. Chesterton

If you are patient in one moment of anger, you will escape a hundred days of sorrow.
Chinese proverb

A man is about as big as the things that make him angry.
Winston Churchill

Anger is the most impotent of passions. It effects nothing it goes about, and hurts the one who is possessed by it more than the one against whom it is directed.
Lord Clarendon

I know of no more disagreeable situation than to be left feeling generally angry without anybody in particular to be angry at.
Frank Moore Colby

When anger rises, think of the consequences.
Confucius

It is the growling man who lives a dog's life.
Coleman Cox

Conflict is the gadfly of thought. It stirs us to observation and memory. It

instigates to invention. It shocks us out of sheeplike passivity, and sets us at noting and contriving.
John Dewey

I've learned that if you want to get even with someone at camp, you rub their underwear with poison ivy.
11-year-old's discovery

We boil at different degrees.
Ralph Waldo Emerson

He is a fool who cannot be angry; but he is a wise man who will not.
English proverb

If you do not wish to be prone to anger, do not feed the habit; give it nothing which may tend to its increase. At first, keep quiet and count the days when you were not angry: I used to be angry every day, then every other day: next, every two, then every three days! and if you succeed in passing thirty days, sacrifice to the gods in thanksgiving.
Epictetus

Whenever you are angry, be assured that it is not only a present evil, but that you have increased a habit.
Epictetus

Keeping score of old scores and scars, getting even and one-upping, always make you less than you are.
Malcolm Forbes

It doesn't take much of a rule to measure a mean man.
Malcolm Forbes

Meanness demeans the demeaner far more than the demeaned.
Malcolm Forbes

Anger is never without a reason, but seldom with a good one.
Benjamin Franklin

A string of reproaches against other people leads one to suspect the existence of a string of self-reproaches with the same content.
Sigmund Freud

Act nothing in furious passion. It's putting to sea in a storm.
Thomas Fuller

A man in a passion rides a horse that runs away with him.
Thomas Fuller

The best answer to anger is silence.
German proverb

Anger is never without an argument, but seldom with a good one.
Lord Halifax

He who curbs his wrath merits forgiveness for his sins.
Hebrew proverb

Getting even with somebody is no way to get ahead of anybody.
Cullen Hightower

Anger is a prelude to courage.
Eric Hoffer

Reproach is infinite, and knows no end

So voluble a weapon is the tongue;

Wounded, we wound; and neither side can fail

For every man has equal strength to rail.
Homer

Anger is a short madness.
Horace

Righteous indignation: Your own wrath as opposed to the shocking bad temper of others.
Elbert Hubbard

A grouch escapes so many little annoy-
ances that it almost pays to be one.
Frank McKinney Hubbard

Anger may be foolish and absurd, and
one may be irritated when in the wrong;
but a man never feels outraged unless in
some respect he is at bottom right.
Victor Hugo

When angry, count ten before you speak;
if very angry, 100.
Thomas Jefferson

Life is but short; no time can be afforded
but for the indulgence of real sorry,
or contests upon questions seriously
momentous. Let us not throw away any
of our days upon useless resentment, or
contend who shall hold out longest in
stubborn malignity. It is best not to be
angry; and best, in the next place, to be
quickly reconciled.
Samuel Johnson

Anger is really disappointed hope.
Erica Jong

Revenge is always the weak pleasure of a
little and narrow mind.
Juvenal

Men must either be caressed or else
annihilated; they will revenge themselves for small injuries, but cannot do
so for great ones; the injury therefore
that we do to a man must be such that we
need not fear his vengeance.
Niccolò Machiavelli

Vengeance is gnawing on a leg and
looking down and realizing it's your own.
Gary Michelson

No man can think clearly when his fists
are clenched.
George Jean Nathan

All anger is not sinful, because some
degree of it, and on some occasions, is
inevitable. But it becomes sinful and
contradicts the rule of Scripture when it
is conceived upon slight and inadequate
provocation, and when it continues long.
William Paley

Every stroke our fury strikes is sure to hit
ourselves at last.
William Penn

Reprove not, in their wrath, excited men;
good counsel comes all out of season
then; but when their fury is appeased
and past, they will perceive their faults,
and mend at last. When he is cool and
calm, then utter it.
John Randolph

Mean spirits under disappointment, like
small beer in a thunderstorm, always
turn sour.
John Randolph

Anger, if not restrained, is frequently
more hurtful to us than the injury that
provokes it.
Seneca

The greatest remedy for anger is delay.
Seneca

Wise men ne'er sit and wail their loss, but
cheerily seek how to redress their harms.
William Shakespeare

A good man and a wise man may, at
times, be angry with the world, and at
times grieved for it; but no man was ever
discontented with the world if he did his
duty in it.
Robert Southey

An angry man is again angry with
himself when he returns to reason.
Publilius Syrus

It becomes no man to nurse despair, but, in the teeth of clenched antagonisms, to follow up the worthiest till he die.
Alfred Lord Tennyson

When angry, count four, when very angry, swear.
Mark Twain

Keep cool; anger is not argument.
Daniel Webster

There is something among men more capable of shaking despotic power than lightning, whirlwind, or earthquake; that is the threatened indignation of the whole civilized world.
Daniel Webster

Moral indignation is jealousy with a halo.
H.G. Wells

ANIMALS

Is it not wonderful that the love of the animal parent should be so violent while it lasts and that it should last no longer than is necessary for the preservation of the young?
Joseph Addison

Never try to teach a pig to think. It doesn't work and it annoys the pig.
Anonymous

The reason dogs have so many friends is because they wag their tails and not their tongues.
Anonymous

In seeking honey expect the sting of bees.
Arabian proverb

The dog was created especially for children. He is the god of frolic.
Henry Ward Beecher

Animals are not brethren, they are not underlings; they are other nations, caught with ourselves in the net of life and time.
Henry Beston

A dog is the only thing on earth that loves you more than he loves himself.
Josh Billings

Each outcry of the hunted hare
A fiber from the brain doth tear.
William Blake

Dogs come when they're called; cats take a message and get back to you.
Mary Bly

Before you kick the dog, find out the name of its master.
Ray E. Brown

All animals except man know that the principal business of life is to enjoy it.
Samuel Butler

Never look for birds of this year in the nest of the last.
Miguel de Cervantes

Dogs look up to you, cats look down on you. Give me a pig. He just looks you in the eye and treats you as an equal.
Winston Churchill

Elephants suffer from too much patience. Their exhibitions of it may seem superb—such power and such restraint, combined, are noble—but a quality carried to excess defeats itself.
Clarence Day

Animals are such agreeable friends; they ask no questions, they pass no criticisms.
George Eliot

Consider the mosquito—he sings at his work and he keeps everlastingly at it. The only way to stop him is to kill him.
J.T. Fisher

The Latin proverb *homo homini lupus*—man is a wolf to man—is a libel on the wolf, which is gentle to other wolves.
Geoffrey Gorer

It is not the bee's touching on the flowers that gathers the honey, but her abiding for a time upon them, and drawing out the sweet.
Joseph Hall

On Nim Chimpsky, subject of her 2008 book: Nim was a great survivor, and that's another reason I chose him. He did a lot better than many of the other chimpanzees who were part of his generation, which was the first generation of chimps born in research labs in the U.S. His lifeboat was that he could communicate. He understood people.
Elizabeth Hess

More on the monkey wedding in India: I have come all the way just to watch God's marriage and now the police are telling me to go back and stay away from the temple. They told me the monkeys have been captured. They can't capture God!
Prem Jain

A forest ranger on a recent wedding of two monkeys in Talwas, India: It's illegal to marry a monkey. Anyone found doing that or attending the marriage ceremony will be arrested.
Bhavar Singh Kaviya

There's an old cliche, "Sick as a dog." After you have seen as many sick dogs as I have, you realize it's more truth than cliché. A dog who hurts can't reason that he has felt bad before and recovered to chase cats. He can't comfort himself that this too will pass. He doesn't even care whether the doctor, the nurse or the other patients think he's a coward. He's sick as a dog.
James R. Kinney

The toad beneath the harrow knows
Exactly where each tooth point goes.
Rudyard Kipling

To understand what the outside of an aquarium looks like, it's better not to be a fish.
André Malraux

More on Chimpsky, who was also the subject of the documentary film Project Nim: I liked him, but I wouldn't want to meet him as a fully grown chimpanzee on my own. I would be scared of him, and he'd know that, and he would then monster me, or try to hump me, or something.
Director James Marsh

Bees aren't as busy as we think they are: They just can't buzz any slower.
Abe Martin

When I play with my cat, who knows but that she regards me more as a plaything than I do her?
Michel de Montaigne

The trouble with a kitten is
That
Eventually it becomes a
Cat.
Ogden Nash

One who is too wise an observer of the business of others, like one who is too curious in observing the labor of bees, will often be stung for his curiosity.
Alexander Pope

The use of butterflies is to adorn the world and delight the eyes of men, to brighten the countryside, serving like so many golden spangles to decorate the fields.
John Ray

There is one respect in which brutes show real wisdom when compared with us—I mean their quiet, placid enjoyment of the present moment.
Arthur Schopenhauer

Don't make the mistake of treating your dogs like humans, or they'll treat you like dogs.
Martha Scott

Some people say that cats are sneaky, evil and cruel. True, and they have many other fine qualities as well.
Missy Sizick

A sparrow fluttering about the church is an antagonist which the most profound theologian in Europe is wholly unable to overcome.
Sydney Smith

When a dog runs at you, whistle for him.
Henry David Thoreau

It does not do to leave a live dragon out of your calculations, if you live near him.
J.R.R. Tolkien

My favorite animal is the mule. He has a lot more horse sense than a horse. He knows when to stop eating. And he knows when to stop working.
Harry S Truman

If you pick up a starving dog and make him prosperous, he will not bite you. This is the principal difference between a dog and a man.
Mark Twain

Of all God's creatures there is only one that cannot be made the slave of the lash. That one is the cat. If man could be crossed with the cat, it would improve man, but it would deteriorate the cat.
Mark Twain

We hope that, when the insects take over the world, they will remember with gratitude how we took them along on all our picnics.
Bill Vaughan

In the history of the world the prize has not gone to those species which specialized in methods of violence, or even in defensive armor. In fact, nature began with producing animals encased in hard shells for defense against the ill of life. But smaller animals, without external armor, warm-blooded, sensitive, alert, have cleared those monsters off the face of the earth.
Alfred North Whitehead

APPEARANCE

Half the work that is done in this world is to make things appear what they are not.
E.R. Beadle

A large nose is the mark of a witty, courteous, affable, generous and liberal man.
Cyrano de Bergerac

I don't mind that I'm fat. You still get the same money.
Marlon Brando

Does she or doesn't she? Only her hairdresser knows for sure.
Clairol Advertisement

There is always a period when a man with a beard shaves it off. This period does not last. He returns headlong to his beard.
Jean Cocteau

Keeping your clothes well pressed will keep you from looking hard pressed.
Coleman Cox

Looking the part helps get the chance to fill it. But if you fill the part, it matters not if you look it.
Malcolm Forbes

More often than not, things and people are as they appear.
Malcolm Forbes

Beware, so long as you live, of judging men by their outward appearance.
Jean de La Fontaine

Never trust a man who combs his hair straight from his left armpit.
Alice Roosevelt Longworth

A chaste woman ought not to dye her hair yellow.
Menander

Some of the worst mistakes of my life have been haircuts.
Jim Morrison

Things are not always what they seem; the first appearance deceives many; the intelligence of few perceives what has been carefully hidden in the recesses of the mind.
Phaedrus

The time men spend in trying to impress others they could spend in doing the things by which others would be impressed.
Frank Romer

One man is more concerned with the impression he makes on the rest of mankind, another with the impression the rest of mankind makes on him.
Arthur Schopenhauer

When I went to the Olympics, I had every intention of shaving the mustache off, but I was getting so many comments about it that I decided to keep it.
Mark Spitz

We do not see things as they are, we see things as we are.
Talmudic saying

A narcissist is someone better looking than you are.
Gore Vidal

The world is governed more by appearances than by realities, so that it is fully as necessary to seem to know something as to know it.
Daniel Webster

ARCHITECTURE

Any work of architecture that does not express serenity is a mistake.
Luis Barragan

Solitude is good company and my architecture is not for those who fear or shun it.
Luis Barragan

Architect: One who drafts a plan of your house, and plans a draft of your money.
Ambrose Bierce

The future of architecture does not lie so much in continuing to fill up the landscape as in bringing back life and order to our cities and towns.
Gottfried Boehm

Architecture is inhabited sculpture.
Constantin Brancusi

Architecture is the alphabet of giants; it is the largest set of symbols ever made to meet the eyes of men. A tower stands up like a sort of simplified stature, of much more than heroic size.
G.K. Chesterton

All architecture is great architecture after sunset; perhaps architecture is really a nocturnal art, like the art of fireworks.
G.K. Chesterton

We shape our buildings; thereafter they shape us.
Winston Churchill

The brevity of human life gives a melancholy to the profession of the architect.
Ralph Waldo Emerson

When I have finished, if the solution is not beautiful, I know it is wrong.
R. Buckminster Fuller

I call architecture petrified music. Really there is something in this: The tone of mind produced by architecture approaches the effect of music.
Johann Wolfgang von Goethe

A building, if it's beautiful, is the love of one man, he's made it out of his love for space, materials, things like that.
Martha Graham

Architecture begins where engineering ends.
Walter Gropius

The worst of a modern stylish mansion is that it has no place for ghosts.
Oliver Wendell Holmes

Architecture is to make us know and remember who we are.
Geoffrey Jellicoe

All architecture is shelter, all great architecture is the design of space that contains, cuddles, exalts, or stimulates the persons in that space.
Philip Johnson

Every time a student walks past a really urgent, expressive piece of architecture that belongs to his college, it can help reassure him that he does have that mind, does have that soul.
Louis Kahn

Architecture is the learned game, correct and magnificent, of forms assembled in the light.
Le Corbusier

Of all the forms of visible otherworldliness, the Gothic is at once the most logical and the most beautiful. It reaches up magnificently—and a good half of it is palpably worthless.
H.L. Mencken

A chair is a very difficult object. A skyscraper is almost easier. That is why Chippendale is famous.
Ludwig Mies van der Rohe

Architecture is the will of an epoch translated into space.
Ludwig Mies van der Rohe

In architecture the pride of man, his triumph over gravitation, his will to power, assume visible form. Architecture is a sort of oratory of power by means of form.
Friedrich Wilhelm Nietzsche

You begin with a group of objects and then build a room like a glove to hold them.
Gaillard Ravenel

Any jackass can kick down a barn but it takes a good carpenter to build one.
Sam Rayburn

The surroundings householders crave are glorified autobiographies ghostwritten by willing architects and interior designers who, like their clients, want to show off.
T.H. Robsjohn-Gibbings

No architecture is so haughty as that which is simple.
John Ruskin

When we build, let us think that we build forever. Let it not be for present delight, nor for present use alone; let it be such work as our descendants will thank us for, and let us think, as we lay stone on stone, that a time is to come when those stones will be held sacred because our hands have touched them, and that men will say as they look upon the labor and wrought substance of them, See! this our fathers did for us.
John Ruskin

Small rooms or dwellings discipline the mind; large ones weaken it.
Leonardo da Vinci

The ancient Romans built their greatest master pieces of architecture, their amphitheaters, for wild beasts to fight in.
Voltaire

Heredity is a strong factor, even in architecture. Necessity first mothered invention. Now invention has little ones of her own, and they look just like grandma.
E.B. White

A doctor can bury his mistakes but an architect can only advise his client to plant vines.
Frank Lloyd Wright

ART

The sheer ease with which we can produce a superficial image often leads to creative disaster.
Ansel Adams

He was the world's only armless sculptor. He put the chisel in his mouth and his wife hit him on the back of the head with a mallet.
Fred Allen

Style is not neutral. It gives moral directions.
Martin Amis

If you practice an art, be proud of it and make it proud of you. . . . It may break your heart, but it will fill your heart before it breaks it; it will make you a person in your own right.
Maxwell Anderson

A gentleman is a man who can play the accordion but doesn't.
Anonymous

Art is simply a right method of doing things. The test of the artist does not lie in the will with which he goes to work, but in the excellence of the work he produces.
Thomas Aquinas

A photograph is a secret about a secret. The more it tells you the less you know.
Diane Arbus

I don't want people who want to dance. I want people who have to dance.
George Balanchine

The creative person is both more primitive and more cultivated, more destructive and more constructive, a lot madder and a lot saner, than the average person.
Dr. Frank Barron

Buy Old Masters. They fetch a much better price than old mistresses.
Lord Beaverbrook

All the arts in America are a gigantic racket run by unscrupulous men for unhealthy women.
Thomas Beecham

Artists who have won fame are often embarrassed by it; thus their first works are often their best.
Ludwig van Beethoven

I wonder whether art has a higher function than to make me feel, appreciate, and enjoy natural objects for their art value. So, as I walk in the garden, I look at the flowers and shrubs and trees and discover in them an exquisiteness of contour, a vitality of edge or a vigor of spring as well as an infinite variety of color that no artifact I have seen in the last 60 years can rival.
Bernard Berenson

No art passes our conscience in the way film does, and goes directly to our feelings, deep down into the dark rooms of our souls.
Ingmar Bergman

Art can never exist without naked beauty displayed.
William Blake

The camera can photograph thought. It's better than a paragraph of sweet polemic.
Dirk Bogarde

Each living art object, taken out of its native habitat so we can conveniently gaze at it, is like an animal in a zoo. Something about it has died in the removal.
Daniel J. Boorstin

We treat the lyrics like the woman any man wants to impress the most. We give the lyrics all the attention we can. I'm not sure other formats are remembering that the lyrics are what it's all about.
Garth Brooks

The artist has never been a dictator, since he understands better than anybody else the variations in human personality.
Heywood Broun

As I define it, rock 'n' roll is dead. The attitude isn't dead, but the music is no longer vital. It doesn't have the same meaning. The attitude, though, is still very much alive and it still informs other kinds of music.
David Byrne

Certainly we [the Musée d'Orsay] have bad paintings. We have only the "greatest" bad paintings.
Françoise Cachin

An artist conscientiously moves in a direction which for some good reason he takes, putting one work in front of the other with the hope he'll arrive before death overtakes him.
John Cage

My fan mail is enormous. Everyone is under 6.
Alexander Calder

If lawyers are disbarred and clergymen defrocked, doesn't it follow that electricians can be delighted, musicians denoted?
George Carlin

In every photographer there is something of a stroller.
Henri Cartier-Bresson

My mother told me to keep on singing, and that kept me working through the cotton fields. She said God has his hand on you. You'll be singing for the world someday.
Johnny Cash

Religion and art spring from the same root and are close kin. Economics and art are strangers.
Willa Cather

I like using the thriller genre because when people go see a thriller—unless it's

really worthless—they never say, "We've wasted our time."
Claude Chabrol

Great art picks up where nature ends.
Marc Chagall

Art, like morality, consists of drawing the line somewhere.
G.K. Chesterton

Artistic temperament is a disease that afflicts amateurs.
G.K. Chesterton

The dignity of the artist lies in his duty of keeping awake the sense of wonder in the world. In this long vigil he often has to vary his methods of stimulation; but in this long vigil he is also himself striving against a continual tendency to sleep.
G.K. Chesterton

An artist carries on throughout his life a mysterious, uninterrupted conversation with his public.
Maurice Chevalier

I like to play saxophone because you don't inhale.
Bill Clinton

An artist cannot speak about his art any more than a plant can discuss horticulture.
Jean Cocteau

A film is a petrified fountain of thought.
Jean Cocteau

Art produces ugly things which frequently become beautiful with time. Fashion, on the other hand, produces beautiful things which always become ugly with time.
Jean Cocteau

I have a foolproof device for judging whether a picture is good or bad. If

my fanny squirms, it's bad. If my fanny doesn't squirm, it's good.
Harry Cohn

There has never been a boy painter, nor can there be. The art requires a long apprenticeship, being mechanical as well as intellectual.
John Constable

Creativity is inventing, experimenting, growing, taking risks, breaking rules, making mistakes, and having fun.
Mary Lou Cook

Extraordinary how potent cheap music is.
Noël Coward

On kissing Marilyn Monroe: It's like kissing Hitler.
Tony Curtis

Art imitates nature as well as it can, as a pupil follows his master; thus it is sort of a grandchild of God.
Dante

If I had my life to live over again, I would have made a rule to read some poetry and listen to some music at least once a week; for perhaps the parts of my brain now atrophied would have thus been kept active through use. The loss of these tastes is a loss of happiness, and may possibly be injurious to the intellect, and more probably to the moral character, by enfeebling the emotional part of our nature.
Charles Darwin

Nowadays Robert Mitchum doesn't so much act as point his suit at people.
Russell Davies

What I have crossed out I didn't like. What I haven't crossed out I'm dissatisfied with.
Cecil B. DeMille

Painting is easy when you don't know how, but very difficult when you do.
Edgar Degas

When an artist reasons, it's because he no longer understands anything.
André Derain

Rock music should be gross: that's the fun of it. It gets up and drops its trousers.
Bruce Dickinson

The principle underlying all art is of a purely religious nature.
Vincent d'Indy

Painting is the effort to produce order; order in yourself. There is much chaos in me, much chaos in our time.
Otto Dix

Art is the most frenzied orgy man is capable of.
Jean Dubuffet

Style reflects one's idiosyncrasies. Your personality is apt to show more to the degree that you did not solve the problem than to the degree that you did.
Charles Eames

Commercial rock 'n' roll music is a brutalization of the stream of contemporary Negro church music, an obscene looting of a cultural expression.
Ralph Ellison

If a man have a genius for painting, poetry, music, architecture, or philosophy, he makes a bad husband, and an ill provider.
Ralph Waldo Emerson

Nature is everything a man is born to, and art is the difference he makes in it.
John Erskine

The day after a performance I am limp, useless, worn out, but I don't regret it.

I've given my all, and nothing less than that satisfies me.
Geraldine Farrar

The aim of every artist is to arrest motion, which is life, by artificial means and hold it fixed so that a hundred years later, when a stranger looks at it, it moves again since it is life.
William Faulkner

The stamping out of the artist is one of the blind goals of every civilization. When a civilization becomes so standardized that the individual can no longer make an imprint on it, then that civilization is dying. The mass mind has taken over and another set of national glories is heading for history's scrap heap.
Elie Faure

I was tired of painting. So many collectors bought paintings and locked them in bank vaults. The stained glass windows allowed me to make public art.
Marcelle Ferron

Having once found the intensity of art, nothing else that can happen in life can ever again seem as important as the creative process.
F. Scott Fitzgerald

If the artist sees nothing within him, then he should also refrain from painting what he sees before him.
Caspar David Friedrich

You're always believing ahead of your evidence. What was the evidence I could write a poem? I just believed it. The most creative thing in us is to believe in a thing.
Robert Frost

I'm just trying to change the world one sequin at a time.
Lady Gaga

On Madonna: She's a gay man trapped in a woman's body.
Boy George

When you want to know how things really work, study them when they're coming apart.
William Gibson

An artist cannot get along without a public; and when the public is absent, what does he do? He invents it, and turning his back on his age, he looks toward the future for what the present denies.
André Gide

Art is a collaboration between God and the artist, and the less the artist does the better.
André Gide

Style is just the outside of content, and content the inside of style, like the outside and the inside of the human body both go together, they can't be separated.
Jean-Luc Godard

A man should hear a little music, read a little poetry, and see a fine picture every day of his life, in order that worldly cares may not obliterate the sense of the beautiful which God has implanted in the human soul.
Johann Wolfgang von Goethe

A painting in a museum hears more ridiculous opinions than anything else in the world.
Edmond de Goncourt

All men are creative but few are artists.
Paul Goodman

If I had wanted to be the center of attention I'd have bought a Stratocaster.
Greg Goth

No artist is ahead of his time. He is his time. It's just that the others are behind the time.
Martha Graham

The body is your instrument in dance, but your art is outside that creature, the body. I don't leap and jump any more. I look at young dancers and am envious, more aware of what glories the body contains. But sensitivity is not made dull by age.
Martha Graham

The liberal arts inform and enlighten the independent citizen of a democracy in the use of his own resources. . . . They enlarge his capacity for self-knowledge and expand his opportunities for self-improvement. . . . They are the wellsprings of a free society.
A. Whitney Griswold

Only work which is the product of inner compulsion can have spiritual meaning.
Walter Gropius

If Venice sinks, [my] collection should be preserved somewhere in the vicinity of Venice.
Peggy Guggenheim

The idea of a Christian art is a contradiction in terms.
Ernst Haeckel

We are all, it seems, saving ourselves for the senior prom. But many of us forget that somewhere along the way we must learn to dance.
Alan Harrington

One is never tired of painting, because you have to set down, not what you already knew, but what you have just discovered.
William Hazlitt

If I don't practice one day, I know it; two days, the critics know it; three days, the public knows it.
Jascha Heifetz

I think most of the people involved in any art always secretly wonder whether they are there because they're good or there because they're lucky.
Katharine Hepburn

A highbrow is the kind of person who looks at a sausage and thinks of Picasso.
A.P. Herbert

Comic-strip artists do not make good husbands, and God knows they do not make good comic strips.
Don Herold

On working with actor Klaus Kinski: It was always, How can I domesticate the wild beast, and how do I survive his next tantrum where he destroys the whole set? How do I make his utter madness and irresponsibility productive onscreen?
Werner Herzog

Self-plagiarism is style.
Alfred Hitchcock

The moment you cheat for the sake of beauty, you know you're an artist.
David Hockney

The genuine artist is as much a dissatisfied person as the revolutionary, yet how diametrically opposed are the products each distills from his dissatisfaction.
Eric Hoffer

I think it is owing to the good sense of the English that they have not painted better.
William Hogarth

Great art is an instant arrested in eternity.
James Gibbon Huneker

If it were not for the intellectual snobs who pay—in solid cash—the tribute which philistinism owes to culture, the arts would perish with their starving practitioners. Let us thank heaven for hypocrisy.
Aldous Huxley

We tend to think and feel in terms of the art we like; and if the art we like is bad then our thinking and feeling will be bad. And if the thinking and feeling of most of the individuals composing a society is bad, is not that society in danger?
Aldous Huxley

In art, economy is always beauty.
Henry James

Hank Williams Syndrome: Come to Nashville, write some good songs, cut some hit records, make money, take all the drugs you can and drink all you can, become a wild man and all of a sudden die.
Waylon Jennings

On Keith Richards: He's like a monkey with arthritis.
Elton John

People never talked about my music. They just counted how many knickers were on stage.
Tom Jones

The cinema, like the detective story, makes it possible to experience without danger all the excitement, passion and desirousness that must be repressed in a humanitarian ordering of life.
Carl Jung

I understand your new play is full of single entendre.
George S. Kaufman

On working with director Werner Herzog: I have to shoot without any breaks. I yell at Herzog and hit him. I have to fight for

every sequence. I wish Herzog would catch the plague.
Klaus Kinski

Art does not reproduce the visible; rather, it makes visible.
Paul Klee

One eye sees; the other feels.
Paul Klee

Style is a fraud. I always felt the Greeks were hiding behind their columns.
Willem de Kooning

On his habit of playing his Steinway grand piano every night at midnight: A great piece of music can take you to a place that is pretty powerful and positive.
Bruce Kovner

Johnny Cash was the champion of the voiceless, the underdogs and the down-trodden. He was also something of a holy terror, like Abraham Lincoln with a wild side. He represented the best of America.
Kris Kristofferson

Country music was a part of my life. Now it isn't. We had a good relationship, really, but we wanted each other at arm's length. The people in Nashville didn't want to be responsible for my looks or my actions. But they sure did like the listeners I brought.
k.d. lang

A museum is not a first-hand contact: it is an illustrated lecture. And what one wants is the actual vital touch.
D. H. Lawrence

Having your book turned into a movie is like seeing your oxen turned into bouillon cubes.
John le Carré

I am the most curious of all to see what will be the next thing that I will do.
Jacques Lipchitz

I don't like my music, but what is my opinion against that of millions of others?
Frederick Loewe

All music is based on country music. And that's why so many different kinds of people relate to it. There are more country music fans in New Jersey than there are down South.
Loretta Lynn

I'm anal retentive. I'm a workaholic. I have insomnia. And I'm a control freak. That's why I'm not married. Who could stand me?
Madonna

Rock 'n' roll is a combination of good ideas dried up by fads, terrible junk, hideous failings in taste and judgment, gullibility and manipulation, moments of unbelievable clarity and invention, plea-sure, fun, vulgarity, excess, novelty and utter enervation.
Greil Marcus

I believe entertainment can aspire to be art, and can become art, but if you set out to make art you're an idiot.
Steve Martin

Art for art's sake makes no more sense than gin for gin's sake.
Somerset Maugham

The artist isn't particularly keen on getting a thing done, as you call it. He gets his pleasure out of doing it, playing with it, fooling with it, if you like. The mere completion of it is an incident.
William McFee

Rock 'n' roll doesn't necessarily mean a band. It doesn't mean a singer, and it

doesn't mean a lyric, really. It's that question of trying to be immortal.
Malcolm McLaren

Country music is a form letter. You fill in the blanks. You move from one broken heart to the next one and from this marriage to that divorce, from a beating here to a beating there.
Ben Mink

I try to apply colors like words that shape poems, like notes that shape music.
Joan Miró

Arts and sciences are not cast in a mould, but are found and perfected by degrees, by often handling and polishing.
Michel de Montaigne

Dreams are the true interpreters of our inclinations, but Art is required to sort and understand them.
Michel de Montaigne

The public history of modern art is the story of conventional people not knowing what they are dealing with.
Robert Motherwell

The artist has a special task and duty: the task of reminding men of their humanity and the promise of their creativity.
Lewis Mumford

It is better to create than to be learned; creating is the true essence of life.
Reinhold Niebuhr

I don't very much enjoy looking at paintings in general. I know too much about them. I take them apart.
Georgia O'Keeffe

Nothing is more useful to man than those arts which have no utility.
Ovid

Rock 'n' roll might best be summed up as monotony tinged with hysteria.
Vance Packard

You can't lock up art in a vault and keep it frozen for posterity. Then the artist is betrayed, history is betrayed
Walter Persegati

God is really only another artist. He invented the giraffe, the elephant and the cat. He has no real style, He just goes on trying other things.
Pablo Picasso

I'm a joker who has understood his epoch and has extracted all he possibly could from the stupidity, greed and vanity of his contemporaries.
Pablo Picasso

Painting is a *jeu d'esprit*.
Pablo Picasso

We all know art is not truth. Art is a lie to make us realize the truth.
Pablo Picasso

Every child is an artist. The problem is how to remain an artist once he grows up.
Pablo Picasso

Your skin starts itching once you buy that gimmick about something called love.
Iggy Pop

Thanks to art, instead of seeing a single world, our own, we see it multiply until we have before us as many worlds as there are original artists.
Marcel Proust

Design can be art. Design can be aesthetics. Design is so simple; that's why it's so complicated.
Paul Rand

To me, a painter, if not the most useful, is the least harmful member of our society.
Man Ray

Art is always the index of social vitality, the moving finger that records the destiny of a civilization. A wise statesman should keep an anxious eye on this graph, for it is more significant than a decline in exports or a fall in the value of a nation's currency.
Herbert Read

A room hung with pictures is a room hung with thoughts.
Sir Joshua Reynolds

On rock: Music for the neck downwards.
Keith Richards

You desire a popular art? Begin by having a people whose minds are liberated, a people not crushed by misery and cease-less toil, not brutalized by every super-stition and every fanaticism, a people master of itself, and victor in the fight that is being waged today.
Romain Rolland

Artists—by definition innocent—don't steal. But they do borrow without giving back.
Ned Rorem

For me, painting is a way to forget life. It is a cry in the night, a strangled laugh.
Georges Rouault

My only objective is to paint a Christ so moving that those who see him will be converted.
Georges Rouault

Life without industry is guilt, industry without art is brutality.
John Ruskin

Perfection is achieved not when there is nothing more to add, but when there is nothing left to take away.
Antoine de Saint-Exupéry

An artist is a dreamer consenting to dream of the actual world.
George Santayana

I don't think it's very useful to open wide the door for young artists; the ones who break down the door are more interesting.
Paul Schrader

Styles may change, details may come and go, but the broad demands of aesthetic judgment are permanent.
Roger Scruton

Collectors would purchase work about people whom they would probably never have a relationship with, but are safe for them to admire from a distance.
Andres Serrano

Dance is the only art of which we ourselves are the stuff of which it is made.
Ted Shawn

The plastic arts are gross arts, dealing joyously with gross material facts. They call, in their servants, for a robust stomach and a great power of endur-ance, and while they will flourish in the scullery or on a dunghill, they fade at a breath from the drawing room.
Paul Sickert

On rock music: The most brutal, ugly, desperate, vicious form of expression it has been my misfortune to hear.
Frank Sinatra

Industrial societies turn their citizens into image junkies; it is the most irresist-ible form of mental pollution.
Susan Sontag

Art is like a border of flowers along the course of civilization.
Lincoln Steffens

Everywhere in the world, music enhances a hall, with one exception: Carnegie Hall enhances the music.
Isaac Stern

Style is not something applied. It is something that permeates. It is of the nature of that in which it is found, whether the poem, the manner of a god, the bearing of a man. It is not a dress.
Wallace Stevens

He who has learned to love an art or science has wisely laid up riches against the day of riches.
Robert Louis Stevenson

Harpists spend 90% of their lives tuning their harps and 10% playing out of tune.
Igor Stravinsky

A piano is full of suppressed desires, recalcitrance, inhibition, conflict.
Anita Sullivan

Art is the only way to run away without leaving home.
Twyla Tharp

Art is a human activity consisting in this, that one man consciously, by means of certain external signs, hands on to others feelings he has lived through, and that other people are infected by these feelings, and also experience them.
Leo Tolstoy

It's the most psychedelic experience I ever had, going to see Hendrix play. When he started to play, something changed: colors changed, everything changed.
Pete Townshend

Can it be possible that the painters make John the Baptist a Spaniard in Madrid and an Irishman in Dublin?
Mark Twain

A man's style is intrinsic and private with him like his voice or his gesture, partly a matter of inheritance, partly of cultivation. It is the pattern of the soul.
Maurice Valency

Where the spirit does not work with the hand there is no art.
Leonardo da Vinci

I like Thelonious Monk, he's so gnarled, he's like a piece of machinery that's pulled up the bolts on the floor and gone off on its own.
Tom Waits

If you break open a song, you'll find the eggs of other songs. Misunderstandings are really kind of an epidemic and acceptable. I think it's about one thing, but someone else will say, "That song is kind of a rhino in hot pants on a burnt rocking horse with a lariat shouting 'Repent, repent!'"
Tom Waits

It's hard to play with a bagpipe player. It's like an exotic bird. I love the sound, it's like strangling a goose.
Tom Waits

I'd asked 10 or 15 people for suggestions. Finally one lady friend asked the right question: "What do you love most?" That's how I started painting money.
Andy Warhol

Beautiful forms and compositions are not made by chance, nor can they ever, in any material, be made at small expense. A composition for cheapness and not excellence of workmanship is the most frequent and certain cause of the rapid

decay and entire destruction of arts and manufactures.
Josiah Wedgwood

An artist's career always begins tomorrow.
James McNeill Whistler

There are three kinds of people in the world: those who can't stand Picasso, those who can't stand Raphael, and those who've never heard of either of them.
John White

Lying, a telling of beautiful untrue things, this is the proper aim of art.
Oscar Wilde

No great artist ever sees things as they really are. If he did he would cease to be an artist.
Oscar Wilde

On how he planned to shoot the bizarre scene in Sunset Boulevard *in which Norma's monkey is buried:* You know, the usual monkey-funeral sequence.
Billy Wilder

On Ernst Lubitsch: He could do more with a closed door than other directors could do with an open fly.
Billy Wilder

Art is about making something out of nothing and selling it.
Frank Zappa

ATTITUDE

Without constancy there is neither love, friendship, nor virtue in the world.
Joseph Addison

I happen to think that the degree of a person's intelligence is directly reflected by the number of conflicting attitudes she can bring to bear on the same topic.
Lisa Alther

An optimist is someone who thinks the future is uncertain.
Anonymous

Optimism approves of everything, submits to everything, believes everything; it is the virtue above all of the taxpayer.
Georges Bernanos

The essence of optimism is that it takes no account of the present, but it is a source of inspiration, of vitality and hope where others have resigned; it enables a man to hold his head high, to claim the future for himself and not to abandon it to his enemy.
Dietrich Bonhoeffer

If Christianity is pessimistic as to man, it is optimistic as to human destiny. I can say that, pessimistic as to human destiny, I am optimistic as to man.
Albert Camus

A good man it is not mine to see. Could I see a man possessed of constancy that would satisfy me.
Confucius

Optimism doesn't wait on facts. It deals with prospects.
Norman Cousins

A little learning is a dangerous thing, but a little patronage more so.
Charles Dickens

Coolness and absence of heat and haste indicate fine qualities.
Ralph Waldo Emerson

I am an impatient optimist. The world is getting better, but it's not getting better

fast enough, and it's not getting better for everyone.
Bill Gates

I'm a pessimist because of intelligence, but an optimist because of will.
Antonio Gramsci

The greatest revolution of our generation is the discovery that human beings, by changing the inner attitudes of their minds, can change the outer aspects of their lives.
William James

If once the people become inattentive to the public affairs, you and I and Congress and Assemblies, Judges and Governors, shall all become wolves.
Thomas Jefferson

Science may have found a cure for most evils; but it has found no remedy for the worst of them all—the apathy of human beings.
Helen Keller

Neutrality, as a lasting principle, is an evidence of weakness.
Louis Kossuth

Obstinacy is the strength of the weak. Firmness founded upon principle, upon truth and right, order and law, duty and generosity, is the obstinacy of sages.
Johann Lavater

Your living is determined not so much by what life brings to you as by the attitude you bring to life; not so much by what happens to you as by the way your mind looks at what happens. Circumstances and situations do color life but you have been given the mind to choose what the color shall be.
John Homer Miller

Nothing bad's going to happen to us. If we get fired, it's not failure; it's a midlife vocational reassessment.
P.J. O'Rourke

My optimism wears heavy boots and is loud.
Henry Rollins

A man's greatest enemies are his own apathy and stubbornness.
Frank Tyger

B

BANKING

Business and life are like a bank account—you can't take out more than you put in.
William Feather

A bank is a place where they lend you an umbrella in fair weather and ask for it back again when it begins to rain.
Robert Frost

Banking may well be a career from which no man really recovers.
John Kenneth Galbraith

Global banking sector confidence is gone.
Brian Hunsaker

We still expect huge volatility and more negative surprises. Fasten your seat belt.
Matthias Jasper

When the dust settles, I think Asia will come out ahead of the U.S.
Henry Lee

The federal [bank deposit] insurance scheme has worked up to now simply

and solely because there have been very few bank failures. The next time we have a pestilence of them it will come to grief quickly enough, and if the good banks escape ruin with the bad ones it will be only because the taxpayer foots the bill.
H.L. Mencken (1936)

For a country, everything will be lost when the jobs of an economist and a banker become highly respected professions.
Montesquieu

Stay out of banks. You may never get as rich as you could with other people's money and some luck, but the tradeoff is sleeping at night.
Old southern saying

There was the South Ozone National Bank looking as though it had been waiting for me.
Willie Sutton

This is full-fledged panic.
Wall Street Trader

BEAUTY

You can only perceive real beauty in a person as they get older.
Anouk Aimée

Beauty: The adjustment of all parts proportionately so that one cannot add or subtract or change without impairing the harmony of the whole.
Leon Battista Alberti

Beauty is one of the rare things that do not lead to doubt of God.
Jean Anouilh

Anything in any way beautiful derives its beauty from itself, and asks nothing beyond itself. Praise is not part of it,

for nothing is made worse or better by praise.
Marcus Aurelius Antoninius

Beauty is a greater recommendation than any letter of introduction.
Aristotle

There is no excellent beauty that hath not some strangeness in the proportion.
Francis Bacon

After all, it is not where one washes one's neck that counts but where one moistens one's throat.
Djuna Barnes

If you get simple beauty and nought else, you get about the best God invents.
Robert Browning

It has been said that a pretty face is a passport. But it's not, it's a visa, and it runs out fast.
Julie Burchill

Beauty in distress is much the most affecting beauty.
Edmund Burke

Where does beauty begin and where does it end? It ends where the artist begins.
John Cage

The love of beauty in its multiple forms is the noblest gift of the human cerebrum.
Alexis Carrel

Those who contemplate the beauty of the earth find reserves of strength that will endure as long as life lasts.
Rachel Carson

It is the beautiful bird that gets caged.
Chinese proverb

There is in true beauty, as in courage, somewhat which narrow souls cannot dare to admire.
William Congreve

Zest is the secret of all beauty. There is no beauty that is attractive without it.
Christian Dior

It seems to me we can never give up longing and wishing while we are thoroughly alive. There are certain things we feel to be beautiful and good, and we must hunger after them.
George Eliot

Some thoughts always find us young, and keep us so. Such a thought is the love of the universal and eternal beauty.
Ralph Waldo Emerson

Things are pretty, graceful, rich, elegant, handsome, but until they speak to the imagination, not yet beautiful.
Ralph Waldo Emerson

Though we travel the world over to find the beautiful, we must carry it with us or we will find it not.
Ralph Waldo Emerson

We fly to beauty as an asylum from the terrors of our finite natures.
Ralph Waldo Emerson

Let's face it, there are no plain women on television.
Anna Ford

Without grace, beauty is an unbaited hook.
French proverb

The beautiful is a phenomenon which is never apparent of itself, but is reflected in a thousand different works of the creator.
Johann Wolfgang von Goethe

The soul that sees beauty may sometimes walk alone.
Johann Wolfgang von Goethe

Beauty and folly are generally companions.
Baltasar Gracián

Beauty is a precious trace that eternity causes to appear to us and that it takes away from us. A manifestation of eternity, and a sign of death as well.
Eugène Ionesco

Ugliness creates bitterness. Ugliness is an eroding force on the people of our land. We are all here to try to change that.
Lady Bird Johnson

Beauty is as relative as light and dark. Thus, there exists no beautiful woman, none at all, because you are never certain that a still far more beautiful woman will not appear and completely shame the supposed beauty of the first.
Paul Klee

The autumn of the beautiful is beautiful.
Latin proverb

The task of man is not to discover new worlds, but to discover his own world in terms of human comprehension and beauty.
Archibald MacLeish

Beauty is an ecstasy; it is as simple as hunger. There is really nothing to be said about it.
Somerset Maugham

No one ever called me pretty when I was a little girl.
Marilyn Monroe

No power on earth, however, can abolish the merciless class distinction between those who are physically desirable and the lonely, pallid, spotted, silent, unfancied majority.
John Mortimer

There is always the possibility of beauty where there is an unsealed human eye; of music where there is an unstopped human ear; and of inspiration where there is a receptive human spirit.
Charles Henry Parkhurst

Beauty and wisdom are seldom found together.
Petronius

Beauty is rather a light that plays over the symmetry of things than that symmetry itself.
Plotinus

That pleasure which is at once the most pure, the most elevating and the most intense, is derived, I maintain, from the contemplation of the beautiful.
Edgar Allan Poe

To live with beauty is not only to give oneself a joy, it is to have the power of beauty at one's call. A man's life would be in a deep and manly way purified and sweetened if each day he could gain a little of the inspiration that poets fuse into their verse and have it share his visions for that day. The wise poet was right who advised us, daily to see a beautiful picture, daily to read a beautiful poem. He was right, he was practical.
Martin W. Sampson

The beauty that addresses itself to the eyes is only the spell of the moment; the eye of the body is not always that of the soul.
George Sand

Beauty is but a vain and doubtful good;
A shining gloss that fadeth suddenly;
A flower that dies when first it 'gins to bud,
A brittle glass that's broken presently.
William Shakespeare

Those who skim over the surface in a hit-or-miss fashion not only forfeit the best returns on their efforts, but are ever barred from the keen pleasure of seeing beauty in the results of their labor.
Roderick Stevens

There are women who have an indefinable charm in their faces which makes them beautiful to their intimates, but a cold stranger who tried to reason the matter out and find this beauty would fail.
Mark Twain

Beauty always promises, but never gives anything.
Simone Weil

Industry is the root of all ugliness.
Oscar Wilde

The beauty myth moves for men as a mirage: Its power lies in its ever-receding nature. When the gap is closed, the lover embraces only his own disillusion.
Naomi Wolf

BEGINNING

Affairs are easier of entrance than exit; and it is but common prudence to see our way out before we venture in.
Aesop

Begin: To have commenced is half the deed. Half yet remains;
Begin again on this and thou wilt finish all.
Ausonius

What the carburetor, sparkplug and self-starter are to an automobile, initiative, private enterprise and executive ability are to industry as a whole, including the wage earner, wage payer, wage spender and wage saver, i.e., the investor. If the sparkplug and self-starter get out

of commission, the car will come to a standstill.
William J.H. Boetcker

He who commences many things finishes but few.
H.G. Bohn

The beginnings of all things are small.
Cicero

America, in the eyes of the world, typifies above all else this quality of initiative. The greatest successes are nearly all the fruit of initiative. Why do we hold in such high esteem the achievements of the Wright brothers? Because they were illustrious examples of initiative and tenacity. And ideas are born of initiative, the children of men and women of initiative. Advancement is applied initiative. Don't imitate. Initiate.
B.C. Forbes

Are you in earnest? Seize this very minute. What you can do, or dream you can do, begin it. Begin it and the work will be completed.
Johann Wolfgang von Goethe

Dare to be wise; begin! He who postpones the hour of living rightly is like the rustic who waits for the river to run out before he crosses.
Horace

Initiative consists of doing the right thing without being told.
Irving Mack

The beginnings of all things are weak and tender. We must therefore be clearsighted in the beginnings, for, as in their budding we discern not the danger, so in their full growth we perceive not the remedy.
Michel de Montaigne

The last thing one knows—is what to put first.
Blaise Pascal

The only joy in the world is to begin.
Cesare Pavese

When the ancients said a work well begun was half done, they meant to impress the importance of always endeavoring to make a good beginning.
Polybius

While we ponder when to begin it becomes too late to do.
Quintilian

In our complex world, there cannot be fruitful initiative without government, but unfortunately, there can be government without initiative.
Bertrand Russell

The difference between getting somewhere and nowhere is the courage to make an early start. The fellow who sits still and does just what he is told will never be told to do big things.
Charles M. Schwab

To do anything in this world worth doing, we must not stand back shivering and thinking of the cold and danger, but jump in, and scramble through as well as we can.
Sydney Smith

BELIEFS

It's a wonderful feeling when you discover some evidence to support your beliefs.
Anonymous

Much bending breaks the bow; much unbending the mind.
Francis Bacon

Confronted with the impossibility of remaining faithful to one's beliefs, and the equal impossibility of becoming free of them, one can be driven to the most inhuman excesses.
James Baldwin

When you want to believe in something, you also have to believe in everything that's necessary for believing in it.
Ugo Betti

I'm pro-choice. I'm pro-gay rights. I'm pro-immigration. I'm pro-gun control. I believe in Darwin.
Michael Bloomberg

No man is happy without a delusion of some kind. Delusions are as necessary to our happiness as realities.
Christian Bovée

No more important duty can be urged upon those who are entering the great theater of life than simple loyalty to their best convictions.
Edwin H. Chapin

Dogma does not mean the absence of thought, but the end of thought.
G.K. Chesterton

An unaspiring person believes according to what he achieves. An aspiring person achieves according to what he believes.
Sri Chinmoy

This is the lesson: Never give in . . . never, never, never, never . . . in nothing, great or small, large or petty—never give in except to convictions of honor or good taste.
Winston Churchill

No human beings [are] more dangerous than those who have suffered for a belief: The great persecutors are recruited from the martyrs not quite beheaded.
E.M. Cioran

All the strength and force of man comes from his faith in things unseen. He who believes is strong; he who doubts is weak. Strong convictions precede great actions.
J.F. Clarke

Never believe anything until it has been officially denied.
Claud Cockburn

Unless the man who works in an office is able to sell himself and his ideas, unless he has the power to convince others of the soundness of his convictions, he can never achieve his goal. He may have the best ideas in the world, he may have plans which would revolutionize entire industries. But unless he can persuade others that his ideas are good, he will never get the chance to put them into effect. Stripped of non-essentials, all business activity is a sales battle. And everyone in business must be a salesman.
Robert E.M. Cowie

Believe only half of what you see and nothing that you hear.
Dinah Mulock Craik

A firm belief attracts facts. They come out iv' holes in th' ground an' cracks in th' wall to support belief, but they run away fr'm doubt.
Finley Peter Dunne

All business proceeds on beliefs, or judgments of probabilities, and not on certainties.
Charles W. Eliot

As long as our civilization is essentially one of property, of fences, of exclusiveness, it will be mocked by delusions.
Ralph Waldo Emerson

The believing we do something when we do nothing is the first illusion of tobacco.
Ralph Waldo Emerson

I have found that the greatest help in meeting any problem with decency and self-respect and whatever courage is demanded, is to know where you yourself stand. That is, to have in words what you believe and are acting from.
William Faulkner

At 18 our convictions are hills from which we look; at 45 they are caves in which we hide.
F. Scott Fitzgerald

A big league baseball manager declares that he would have the public feel extremely doubtful early in the season regarding the chances of his team to win the championship. Cocksureness, he implies, could not fail to have a bad effect upon his players, whereas public skepticism acted upon them as a challenge. There is wisdom in this for business concerns. The man who is smugly confident that he has arrived is ripe for the return trip. A measure of self-confidence is an asset when you are battling your way to the top. But cocksureness is not an asset but a liability. It tends to dull the edge of effort. Also, it breeds arrogance that is distasteful.
B.C. Forbes

Believe in yourself, your neighbors, your work, your ultimate attainment of more complete happiness. It is only the farmer who faithfully plants seeds in the Spring, who reaps a harvest in the Autumn.
B.C. Forbes

The man who is cocksure that he has arrived is ready for the return journey.
B.C. Forbes

Whether you believe you can do a thing or not, you are right.
Henry Ford

A supremely religious man or woman is one who believes deeply and consistently in the veracity of his highest experiences. He has his hours in the cellar . . . but he believes in the truth of the hours he spends upstairs.
Harry Emerson Fosdick, D.D.

Devout believers are safeguarded in a high degree against the risk of certain neurotic illnesses; their acceptance of the universal neurosis spares them the task of building a personal one.
Sigmund Freud

We cannot tell some people what it is believe, partly because they are too stupid to understand, partly because we are too proudly vague to explain.
Robert Frost

The men who succeed best in public life are those who take the risk of standing by their own convictions.
James A. Garfield

Everyone has his superstitions. One of mine has always been when I started to go anywhere, or to do anything, never to turn back or to stop until the thing intended was accomplished.
Ulysses S. Grant

The will to believe is perhaps the most powerful but certainly the most dangerous human attribute.
John P. Grier

Those who stand for nothing fall for anything.
Alexander Hamilton

As soon as we cease to pry about at random, we shall come to rely upon accredited bodies of authoritative dogma; and as soon as we come to rely upon accredited bodies of authoritative dogma, not only are the days of our liberty over, but we have lost the

password that has hitherto opened to us the gates of success as well.
Learned Hand

Men are tattooed with their special beliefs like so many South Sea Islanders; but a real human heart with divine love in it beats with the same glow under all the patterns of all earth's thousand tribes.
Oliver Wendell Holmes

Disbelief in futurity loosens in a great measure the ties of morality, and may be for that reason pernicious to the peace of civil society.
David Hume

Too few have the courage of my convictions.
Robert M. Hutchins

Be not afraid of life. Believe that life is worth living, and your belief will help create the fact.
William James

Assertion is not argument; to contradict the statement of an opponent is not proof that you are correct.
Samuel Johnson

Convictions are the mainsprings of action, the driving powers of life. What a man lives are his convictions.
Francis C. Kelley

Credulity is the man's weakness, but the child's strength.
Charles Lamb

Believe that you have it, and you have it.
Latin proverb

Some like to understand what they believe in. Others like to believe in what they understand.
Stanislaw Jerzy Lec

With most people, unbelief in one thing is founded upon blind belief in another.
Georg C. Lichtenberg

That which you vividly imagine, sincerely believe, ardently desire and enthusiastically act upon will inevitably come to pass.
William R. Lucas

I wish I was as sure of anything as he is of everything.
Thomas B. Macaulay

Man is so inconsistent a creature that it is impossible to reason from his beliefs to his conduct, or from one part of his belief to another.
Thomas B. Macaulay

Nothing is so firmly believed as what we least know.
Michel de Montaigne

Convictions are more dangerous enemies of truth than lies.
Friedrich Wilhelm Nietzsche

When you affirm big, believe big, and pray big, big things happen.
Norman Vincent Peale, D.D.

The man who believes he can do it is probably right, and so is the man who believes he can't.
Lawrence J. Peter

Remember that what you believe will depend very much upon what you are.
Noah Porter

It is desire that engenders belief; if we fail as a rule to take this into account, it is because most of the desires that create beliefs end only with out own life.
Marcel Proust

We still had belief. And I think belief goes further than momentum.
Jimmy Rollins

The nobility of a human being is strictly independent of that of his convictions.
Jean Rostand

Emphatic and reiterated assertion, especially during childhood, produces in most people a belief so firm as to have a hold even over the unconscious.
Bertrand Russell

As the essence of courage is to stake one's life on a possibility, so the essence of faith is to believe that the possibility exists.
William Salter

What a man believes may be ascertained, not from his creed, but from the assumptions on which he habitually acts.
George Bernard Shaw

He who is surety is never sure himself. Take advice, and never be security for more than you are quite willing to lose. Remember the word of the wise man: He that is surety for a stranger shall smart for it; and he that hateth suretyship is sure.
Charles H. Spurgeon

Our affections and beliefs are wiser than we; the best that is in us is better than we can understand; for it is grounded beyond experience, and guides us, blindfold but safe, from one age on to another.
Robert Louis Stevenson

To have integrity the individual cannot merely be a weathervane turning briskly with every doctrinal wind that blows. He must possess key loyalties and key convictions which can serve as a basis of judgment and a standard of action.
John Studebaker

In religion and politics, people's beliefs and convictions are in almost every case gotten at second hand, and without examination.
Mark Twain

They can conquer who believe they can.
Virgil

As one may bring himself to believe almost anything he is inclined to believe, it makes all the difference whether we begin or end with the inquiry, "What is truth?"
Richard Whately

Believe things, rather than man.
Benjamin Whichcote

BEST

All I want of the world is very little. I only want the best of everything, and there is so little of that.
Michael Arlen

Do what you know best; if you're a runner, run, if you're a bell, ring.
Ignas Bernstein

Be true to the best you know. This is your high ideal. If you do your best, you cannot do more. Do your best every day and your life will gradually expand into satisfying fullness. Cultivate the habit of doing one thing at a time with quiet deliberateness. Always allow yourself a sufficient margin of time in which to do your work well. Frequently examine your working methods to discover and eliminate unnecessary tension. Aim at poise, repose, and self-control. The relaxed worker accomplishes most.
H.W. Dresser

The man who has done his level best, and who is conscious that he has done

his best, is a success, even though the world may write him down a failure.
B.C. Forbes

The best is good enough.
German proverb

When the best things are not possible, the best may be made of those that are.
Richard Hooker

I do the very best I know how—the very best I can; and mean to keep doing so until the end. If the end brings me out all right, what is said against me won't amount to anything. If the end brings me out wrong, ten angels swearing I was right would make no difference.
Abraham Lincoln

I have simply tried to do what seemed best each day, as each day came.
Abraham Lincoln

When we have done our best, we should wait the result in peace.
J. Lubbock

It is a funny thing about life—if you refuse to accept anything but the best you very often get it.
Somerset Maugham

Life's greatest adventure is in doing one's level best.
Arthur E. Morgan

It is one's duty to make the most of the best that is in him.
Duncan Stuart

All is for the best in the best of possible worlds.
Voltaire

BLAME

When a man points a finger at someone else, he should remember that three of his fingers are pointing at himself.
Anonymous

It is quite gratifying to feel guilty if you haven't done anything wrong: how noble! Whereas it is rather hard and certainly depressing to admit guilt and to repent.
Hannah Arendt

Henry Ward Beecher, so the story goes, was once asked by a young preacher how he could keep his congregation wide awake and attentive during his sermons. Beecher replied that he always had a man watch for sleepers, with instructions, as soon as he saw anyone start nodding or dozing, to hasten to the pulpit and wake up the preacher. Aren't you and I usually less sensible? Would we not be inclined to have the watcher wake up not ourselves but the fellows caught sleeping? In other words, aren't we disposed always to blame others?
B.C. Forbes

How we love to blame others for our misfortunes! Almost every individual who has lost money in stock speculation has on the tip of his tongue an explanation which he trots out to show that it wasn't his own fault at all. . . . Hardly one loser has the manliness to say frankly, I was wrong.
B.C. Forbes

Accepting blame when it's not really due sometimes makes the point better.
Malcolm Forbes

When it's your own fault, things hurt worse than when someone else is to blame.
Malcolm Forbes

If something goes wrong, it is more important to talk about who is going to fix it, than who is to blame.
Francis J. Gable

The search for someone to blame is always successful.
Robert Half

What we call real estate is the broad foundation on which nearly all the guilt of this world rests.
Nathaniel Hawthorne

How extraordinary it is that one feels most guilt about the sins one is unable to commit.
V.S. Pritchett

It is rascally to steal a purse, daring to steal a million, and a proof of greatness to steal a crown. The blame diminishes as the guilt increases.
Johann Friedrich von Schiller

People are always blaming their circumstances for what they are. I don't believe in circumstances. The people who get on in this world are they who get up and look for the circumstances they want, and, if they can't find them, make them.
George Bernard Shaw

BLESSINGS

If one should give me a dish of sand, and tell me there were particles of iron in it, I might look for them with my eyes, and search for them with my clumsy fingers, and be unable to detect them; but let me take a magnet and sweep through it, and how would it draw to itself the almost invisible particles by the mere power of attraction? The unthinkful heart, like my finger in the sand, discovers no mercies; but let the thankful heart sweep through the day, and as the magnet finds the iron, so it will find, in every hour, some heavenly blessings.
Henry Ward Beecher

A patient, humble temper gathers blessings that are marred by the peevish and overlooked by the aspiring.
Edwin H. Chapin

Certain of our blessings can never change. The important things of life will not perish. In whatever brave new world emerges from this chaos, homes will be created, good deeds will be done and sacrifices will be made. God will be reverently worshipped in many a church and chapel. Hospital, libraries and colleges will be organized and endowed. The greatest things will endure—faith, hope and love, and the moral nature in man.
Claude M. Fuess

Take, I pray thee, my blessing that is brought to thee; because God hath dealt graciously with me, and because I have enough.
Genesis 33:11

Reflect that life, like every other blessing, derives its value from its use alone.
Samuel Johnson

The private and personal blessings we enjoy, the blessings of immunity, safeguard, liberty and integrity, deserve the thanksgiving of a whole life.
Jeremy Taylor

Blessings we enjoy daily; and for the most of them, because they be so common, most men forget to pay their praise.
Izaak Walton

BOASTING

Exaggeration is a blood relation to false-hood and nearly as blamable.
Hosea Ballou

We exaggerate misfortune and happiness alike. We are never either so wretched or so happy as we say we are.
Honoré de Balzac

Falsehood often lurks upon the tongue of him, who, by self-praise, seeks to enhance his value in the eyes of others.
James Gordon Bennett

Some persons are exaggerators by temperament. They do not mean untruth, but their feelings are strong, and their imaginations vivid, so that their statements are largely discounted by those of calm judgment and cooler temperament. They do not realize that we always weaken what we exaggerate.
Tryon Edwards

He was like a cock who thought the sun had risen to hear him crow.
George Eliot

Every ass loves to hear himself bray.
Thomas Fuller

An exaggeration is a truth that has lost its temper.
Kahlil Gibran

There is nothing quite so dead as a self-centered man—a man who holds himself up as a self-made success, and measures himself by himself and is pleased with the result.
Wesley G. Huber, D.D.

The man has not anything to boast of but his illustrious ancestors is like a potato—the only belonging to him is underground.
Thomas Overbury

What is the use of acquiring one's heart's desire if one cannot handle and gloat over it, show it to one's friends and gather an anthology of envy and admiration?
Dorothy Sayers

A man has the right to toot his own horn to his heart's content, so long as he stays in his own home, keeps the windows closed and does not make himself obnoxious to his neighbors.
Tiorio

The time is undoubtedly coming when it will be a confession of inferiority to overstate or distort the merits and special uses of any commodity, just as any boaster is self-branded a lightweight rather than a man of parts.
Dr. Harvey W. Wiley

BODY

Man consists of two parts, his mind and his body, only the body has more fun.
Woody Allen

No one hates his body.
St. Augustine

It is a scientific fact that your body will not absorb cholesterol if you take it from another person's plate.
Dave Barry

Our bodies are where we stay; Our souls are what we are.
Cecil Baxter

Nakedness reveals itself. Nudity is placed on display. The nude is condemned to never being naked. Nudity is a form of dress.
John Berger

In the nude, all that is not beautiful is obscene.
Robert Bresson

The human body is an energy system which is never a complete structure; never static; is in perpetual self-construction and self-destruction; we destroy it in order to make it new.
Norman O. Brown

To shake your rump is to be environmentally aware.
David Byrne

I'm the female equivalent of a counterfeit $20 bill. Half of what you see is a pretty good reproduction, the rest is a fraud.
Cher

A woman watches her body uneasily, as though it were an unreliable ally in the battle for love.
Leonard Cohen

Know ye not that ye are the temple of God, and that the Spirit of God dwelleth in you? If any man defile the temple of God, him shall God destroy; for the temple of God is holy, which temple ye are.
I Corinthians 3:16–17

I often think that a slightly exposed shoulder emerging from a long satin nightgown packs more sex than two naked bodies in bed.
Bette Davis

I live in company with a body, a silent companion, exacting and eternal. He it is who notes that individuality which is the seal of the weakness of our race. My soul has wings, but the brutal jailer is strict.
Eugène Delacroix

I wish you could only see Dizzy in his bath, then you would know what a white skin is.
Mary Anne Disraeli

But even the President of the United States sometimes must have to stand naked.
Bob Dylan

The human body is the magazine of inventions, the patent office, where are the models from which every hint is taken. All the tools and engines on earth are only extensions of its limbs and senses.
Ralph Waldo Emerson

Our theological Church, as we know, has scorned and vilified the body till it has seemed almost a reproach and a shame to have one, yet at the same time has credited it with the power to drag the soul to perdition.
Eliza Farnham

Anatomy is destiny.
Sigmund Freud

I am sitting in bed this morning, my head more full of undesirable fluids than the Cambridge public swimming baths.
Stephen Fry

Animals, we have been told, are taught by their organs. Yes, I would add, and so are men, but men have this further advantage that they can also teach their organs in return.
Johann Wolfgang von Goethe

For me, the naked and the nude
(By lexicographers construed
As synonyms that should express
The same deficiency of dress
Or shelter) stand as wide apart
As love from lies, or truth from art.
Robert Graves

Our body is a well-set clock, which keeps good time, but if it be too much or indiscreetly tampered with, the alarm runs out before the hour.
Joseph Hall

Alfred Hitchcock thought of himself as looking like Cary Grant. That's tough, to think of yourself one way and look another.
Tippi Hedren

Erogenous zones are either everywhere or nowhere.
Joseph Heller

The human body was designed to walk, run or stop; it wasn't built for coasting.
Cullen Hightower

The undressed is vulgar—the nude is pure.
Robert Ingersoll

Obesity is really widespread.
Joseph Kern II

Nature gave men two ends—one to sit on and one to think with. Ever since then man's success or failure has been dependent on the one he used most.
George R. Kirkpatrick

The body of man is a machine which winds its own springs.
J.O. de La Mettrie

It is so much more difficult to live with one's body than with one's soul. One's body is so much more exacting: What it won't have it won't have, and nothing can make bitter into sweet.
D.H. Lawrence

The left side controls the right side of your body and right controls the left half. Therefore, left-handers are the only people in their right minds.
Bill (Spaceman) Lee

In the old days, women wore so many girdles, corsets, pantaloons, bloomers, stockings, garters, step-ins and God knows what all that you had to practically be a prospector to get to first base, to even find first base.
Danny McGoorty

After 30, a body has a mind of its own.
Bette Midler

Our own physical body possesses a wisdom which we who inhabit the body lack. We give it orders which make no sense.
Henry Miller

It's not true that I had nothing on. I had the radio on.
Marilyn Monroe

When I get up in the morning, I stay nude for three or four hours. If I really feel like getting formal, I'll put on board shorts.
Iggy Pop

Another good reducing exercise consists in placing both hands against the table edge and pushing back.
Robert Quillen

A feeble body weakens the mind.
Jean-Jacques Rousseau

What is more important in life than our bodies or in the world than what we look like?
George Santayana

I just use my muscles as a conversation piece, like someone walking a cheetah down 42nd Street.
Arnold Schwarzenegger

He will be the slave of many masters who is his body's slave.
Seneca

'Tis not enough to help the feeble up, but to support him after.
William Shakespeare

Stomach: A slave that must accept everything that is given to it, but which avenges wrongs as slyly as does the slave.
Emile Souvester

The authority of any governing institution must stop at its citizen's skin.
Gloria Steinem

I haven't got the figure for jeans.
Margaret Thatcher

Every man is the builder of a temple, called his body, to the god he worships, after a style peculiarly his own, nor can he get off by hammering marble instead. We are all sculptors and painters, and our material is our own flesh and blood and bones.
Henry David Thoreau

It cannot be said that nude sunbathing on a beach is a form of expression likely to be understood by the viewer as an attempt to convey a particular point of view.
Judge Vito J. Titone

Whose property is my body? Probably mine. I so regard it. If I experiment with it, who must be answerable? I, not the State. If I choose injudiciously, does the State die? Oh, no.
Mark Twain

Being naked approaches being revolutionary; going barefoot is mere populism.
John Updike

Body: A cell state in which every cell is a citizen.
Rudolf Virchow

If anything is sacred the human body is sacred.
Walt Whitman

When I die, I'm leaving my body to science fiction.
Steven Wright

BOLDNESS

We make way for the man who boldly pushes past us.
Christian Bovée

Boldness becomes rarer, the higher the rank.
Karl von Clausewitz

Whatever you do, or dream you can do, begin it. Boldness has genius, power and magic in it.
Johann Wolfgang von Goethe

Put a grain of boldness in everything you do.
Baltasar Gracián

It is better by a noble boldness to run the risk of being subject to half of the evils we anticipate, than to remain in cowardly listlessness for fear of what may happen.
Herodotus

There are some things one can only achieve by a deliberate leap in the opposite direction. One has to go abroad in order to find the home one has lost.
Franz Kafka

In great straits and when hope is small, the boldest counsels are the safest.
Livy

By audacity, great fears are concealed.
Lucan

Both fortune and love befriend the bold.
Ovid

Only the bold get to the top.
Publilius Syrus

BOOKS

That is a good book which opened with expectation and closed with profit.
Amos Bronson Alcott

I took a course in speed reading and was able to read *War and Peace* in 20 minutes. It's about Russia.
Woody Allen

Book: A garden carried in a pocket.
Arabian proverb

Some books are undeservedly forgotten; none are undeservedly remembered.
W.H. Auden

To feel most beautifully alive means to be reading something beautiful, ready always to apprehend in the flow of language the sudden flash of poetry.
Gaston Bachelard

For several days after my first book was published I carried it about in my pocket, and took surreptitious peeps at it to make sure the ink had not faded.
J.M. Barrie

Books are the compass and telescopes and sextants and charts which other men have prepared to help us navigate the dangerous seas of human life.
Jesse Lee Bennett

Diary: A daily record of that part of one's life which he can relate to himself without blushing.
Ambrose Bierce

The failure to read good books both enfeebles the vision and strengthens our most fatal tendency—the belief that the here and now is all there is.
Allan Bloom

I had always imagined paradise as a kind of library.
Jorge Luis Borges

In science, ready by preference the newest works; in literature, the oldest. The classics are always modern.
Edward Bulwer-Lytton

The possession of a book becomes a substitute for reading it.
Anthony Burgess

A classic is a book that has never finished saying what it has to say.
Italo Calvino

All that mankind has done, thought, gained or been: it is lying as in magic preservation in the pages of books.
Thomas Carlyle

Biography is the most universally pleasant and profitable of all reading.
Thomas Carlyle

The true university of these days is a collection of books.
Thomas Carlyle

Autobiography is probably the most respectable form of lying.
Humphrey Carpenter

The novel can't compete with cars, the movies, television, liquor. A guy who's had a good feed and tanked up on good wine gives his old lady a kiss after supper and his day is over. Finished.
Louis-Ferdinand Céline

Books are true levelers. They give to all, who will faithfully use them, the society,

the spiritual presence, of the best and greatest of our race.
William Ellery Channing

The most valuable book we can read, about countries we have visited, is that which recalls to us something that we did notice, but did not notice that we noticed.
G.K. Chesterton

Other relaxations are peculiar to certain times, places and stages of life, but the study of letters is the nourishment of our youth, and the joy of our old age. They throw an additional splendor on prosperity, and are the resource and consolation of adversity; they delight at home, and are no embarrassment abroad; in short, they are company to us at night, our fellow travelers on a journey, and attendants in our rural recesses.
Cicero

To add a library to a house is to give that house a soul.
Cicero

An autobiography should give the reader opportunity to point out the author's follies and misconceptions.
Claud Cockburn

Autobiography is an obituary in serial form with the last installment missing.
Quentin Crisp

The world of books is the most remark-able creation of man. Nothing else that he builds ever lasts. Monuments fall, nations perish, civilizations grow old and die out, and after an era of darkness new races build others. But in the world of books are volumes that have seen this happen again and again and yet live on, still young, still as fresh as the day they were written, still telling men's hearts of the hearts of men centuries dead.
Clarence Day

Reading, to most people, means an ashamed way of killing time disguised under a dignified name.
Ernest Dimnet

All autobiography is self-indulgent.
Daphne du Maurier

Don't join the book burners. Don't think you are going to conceal faults by concealing evidence that they ever existed. Don't be afraid to go in your library and read every book.
Dwight D. Eisenhower

I always read the last page of a book first so that if I die before I finish I'll know how it turned out.
Nora Ephron

When I get a little money, I buy books; if any is left, I buy food and clothes.
Desiderius Erasmus

Over the years, I've evolved a somewhat heretical but time- and mind-saving approach to books, articles, editorials that deal with weighty matters. More often than not, by beginning at the end and contemplating the conclusions, one can determine if it's worth going through the whole to get there.
Malcolm Forbes

A dollar put into a book and a book mastered might change the whole course of a boy's life. It might easily be the beginning of the development of lead-ership that would carry the boy far in service to his fellow men.
Henry Ford

I suggest that the only books that influ-ence us are those for which we are ready, and which have gone a little farther

down our particular path than we have yet got ourselves.
E.M. Forster

Thou mayest as well expect to grow stronger by always eating, as wiser by always reading. Too much overcharges Nature, and turns more into disease than nourishment. 'Tis thought and digestion which make books serviceable, and give health and vigor to the mind.
Thomas Fuller

I don't think anyone should write his autobiography until after he's dead.
Samuel Goldwyn

Paperbacks blink in and out of print like fireflies. They also, as older collectors have ruefully discovered, fade and fall apart even more rapidly than their owners.
Paul Gray

Autobiography is an unrivaled vehicle for telling the truth about other people.
Philip Guedalla

Were I to pray for a taste which should stand me in good stead under every variety of circumstances and be a source of happiness and a cheerfulness to me during life and a shield against its ills, however things might go amiss and the world frown upon me, it would be a taste for reading.
Sir John Herschel

Do give books, religious or otherwise, for Christmas. They're never fattening, seldom sinful, and permanently personal.
Lenore Hershey

I do not look with favor on the collecting of first editions and autographs, but it is a vice which is sometimes found in otherwise virtuous persons.
A.E. Housman

It is those books which a man possesses but does not read which constitute the most suspicious evidence against him.
Victor Hugo

To be well informed, one must read quickly a great number of merely instructive books. To be cultivated, one must read slowly and with a lingering appreciation the comparatively few books that have been written by men who lived, thought, and felt with style.
Aldous Huxley

Books are never out of humour; never envious or jealous, they answer all questions with readiness; . . . they teach us how to live and how to die; they dispel melancholy by their mirth, and amuse by their wit; they prepare the soul to suffer everything and desire nothing; they introduce us to ourselves.
Holbrook Jackson

He that reads and grows no wiser seldom suspects his own deficiency, but complains of hard words and obscure sentences, and asks why books are written which cannot be understood.
Samuel Johnson

I am a part of all that I have read.
John Kieran

Where do I find the time for not reading so many books?
Karl Kraus

Book—what they make a movie out of for television.
Leonard Louis Levinson

The things I want to know are in books; my best friend is the man who'll get me a book I ain't read.
Abraham Lincoln

A good book is the precious lifeblood of a master spirit, embalmed and treasured up on purpose to life beyond life.
John Milton

Nowadays the illiterates can read and write.
Alberto Moravia

What is the virtue and service of a book? Only to help me live less gingerly and shabbily.
Christopher Morley

Books worth reading once are worth reading twice; and what is most important of all, the masterpieces of literature are worth reading a thousand times.
John Morley

A dose of poison can do its work but once, but a bad book can go on poisoning minds for generations.
W. John Murray

Just the knowledge that a good book is awaiting one at the end of a long day makes that day happier.
Kathleen Norris

If minds are truly alive they will seek out books, for books are the human race recounting its memorable experiences, confronting its problems, searching for solutions, drawing the blueprints of its futures. To read books is one way of growing along with one's fellows-in-growth.
Harry A. Overstreet

Books come at my call and return when I desire them; they are never out of humor and they answer all my questions with readiness. Some present in review before me the events of past ages; others reveal to me the secrets of Nature. These teach me how to live, and those how to die; these dispel my melancholy by their mirth, and amuse me by their sallies of

wit. Some there are who prepare my soul to suffer everything, to desire nothing, and to become thoroughly acquainted with itself. In a word, they open the door to all the arts and sciences.
Petrarch

I hate books, for they only teach people to talk about what they do not understand.
Jean-Jacques Rousseau

It is a pity, in my opinion, that no prize exists for the writer who best refrains from adding to the world's bad books.
William Saroyan

Any book which is at all important should be reread immediately.
Arthur Schopenhauer

Books are good enough in their own way, but they are a mighty bloodless substitute for living.
Robert Louis Stevenson

A truly good book is something as wildly natural and primitive, mysterious and marvelous, ambrosial and fertile as a fungus or a lichen.
Henry David Thoreau

On editing: I always begin at the left with the opening word of the sentence and read toward the right and I recommend this method.
James Thurber

I don't believe a committee can write a book. It can, oh, govern a country, perhaps, but I don't believe it can write a book.
Arnold Toynbee

The habit of reading is the only one I know in which there is no alloy. It lasts when all other pleasures fade. It will be there to support you when all other resources are gone. It will be present to you when the energies of your body have

fallen away from you. It will make your hours pleasant to you as long as you live.
Anthony Trollope

On reading while dining out: A book does not make bad jokes, drink too much or eat more than you can afford to pay for.
Kenneth Turan

It is with the reading of books the same as with looking at pictures; one must, without doubt, without hesitations, with assurance, admire what is beautiful.
Vincent van Gogh

I keep to old books, for they teach me something; from the new I learn very little.
Voltaire

Only when one has lost all curiosity about the future has one reached the age to write an autobiography.
Evelyn Waugh

BOREDOM

A bore is someone who, when you ask him how he is, tells you.
Anonymous

Perhaps the world's second-worst crime is boredom; the first is being a bore.
Cecil Beaton

A dull ax never loves grindstones.
Henry Ward Beecher

A bore is a person who talks when you wish him to listen.
Ambrose Bierce

Alienation is practiced by whole groups and classes of people. We may all bore one another to death this way, and the young, who are the most self-conscious about their alienation, can be the most boring of all.
John Corry

Nobody has any right to find life uninteresting or unrewarding who sees within the sphere of his own activity a wrong he can help to remedy, or within himself an evil he can hope to overcome.
Charles W. Eliot

Each man reserves to himself alone the right of being tedious.
Ralph Waldo Emerson

A bore: Someone who persists in holding to his own views after we have enlightened him with ours.
Malcolm Forbes

Some of the biggest bores I've ever known are men who have been highly successful in business, particularly self-made heads of big companies. Before the first olive has settled into the first martini, they pour the stories of their lives into the nearest and sometimes the remotest ears capturable....

These men have indeed paid the price of success. To rise to the top of a big company often takes a totality of effort, concentration and dedication. Others, too, have to pay part of the price. Wife and children are out of mind even when in sight....
Malcolm Forbes

Drudgery is as necessary to call out the treasures of the mind as harrowing and planting those of the earth.
Margaret Fuller

Desire is half of life; indifference is half of death.
Kahlil Gibran

When people are bored, it is primarily with their own selves that they are bored.
Eric Hoffer

The most destructive criticism is indifference.
Edgar Watson Howe

Most of my contemporaries at school entered the World of Business, the logical destiny of bores.
Barry Humphries

A bore is a vacuum cleaner of society, sucking up everything and giving nothing. Bores are always eager to be seen talking to you.
Elsa Maxwell

We are raising a generation that has a woefully small stock of ideas and inter-ests and emotions. It must be amused at all costs but it has little skill in amusing itself. It pays some of its members to do what the majority can no longer do for themselves. It is this inner poverty that makes for the worst kind of boredom.
Robert J. McCracken, D.D.

No one really listens to anyone else, and if you try it for a while you'll see why.
Mignon McLaughlin

Indifference is the invincible giant of the world.
Ouida

I am one of those unhappy persons who inspire bores to the greatest flights of art.
Edith Sitwell

Somebody's boring me; I think it's me.
Dylan Thomas

Punctuality is the virtue of the bored.
Evelyn Waugh

Boredom is the legitimate kingdom of the philanthropic.
Virginia Woolf

BRAVERY

I count him braver who overcomes his desires than him who conquers his enemies; for the hardest victory is the victory over self.
Aristotle

The world has a way of giving what is demanded of it. If you are frightened and look for failure and poverty, you will get them, no matter how hard you may try to succeed. Lack of faith in yourself, in what life will do for you, cuts you off from the good things of the world. Expect victory and you make victory. Nowhere is this truer than in business life, where bravery and faith bring both material and spiritual rewards.
Preston Bradley

True valor lies in the middle, between cowardice and rashness.
Miguel de Cervantes

Bravery: A cheap and vulgar quality, of which the brightest instances are frequently found in the lowest savages.
Paul Chatfield

Each man is a hero and an oracle to somebody.
Ralph Waldo Emerson

All brave men love; for he only is brave who has affections to fight for, whether in the daily battle of life, or in physical contests.
Nathaniel Hawthorne

My advice to you, if you should ever be in a hold-up, is to line up with the cowards

and save your bravery for an occasion when it may be of some benefit to you.
O. Henry

What excites and interests the looker-on at life, what the romances and the statues celebrate, and the grim civic monuments remind us of, is the everlasting battle of the powers of light with those of darkness; with heroism reduced to its bare chance, yet ever and anon snatching victory from the jaws of death.
William James

Heroism, the Caucasian mountaineers say, is endurance for one moment more.
George F. Kennan

Physical bravery is an animal instinct; moral bravery is a much higher and truer courage.
Wendell Phillips

Valor is a gift. Those having it never know for sure whether they have it till the test comes. And those having it in one test never know for sure if they have it when the next test comes.
Carl Sandburg

Bravery escapes more dangers than cowardice.
Joseph Segur

Valor grows by daring, fear by holding back.
Publilius Syrus

They are sure to be esteemed bravest who, having the clearest sense of both the pains and pleasures of life, do not on that account shrink from danger.
Thucydides

Except a person be part coward, it is not a compliment to say he is brave.
Mark Twain

I do not like heroes; they make too much noise in the world. The more radiant their glory, the more odious they are.
Voltaire

BRITAIN

The extremes of opulence and of want are more remarkable, and more constantly obvious, in [Great Britain] than in any other place that I ever saw.
John Quincy Adams

I think the British have the distinction above all other nations of being able to put new wine into old bottles without bursting them.
Clement R. Atlee

The English may not like music, but they absolutely love the noise it makes.
Thomas Beecham

It is a curious fact about British Islanders, who hate drill and have not been invaded for nearly a thousand years, that as danger comes nearer and grows they become progressively less nervous; when it is imminent they are fierce, when it is mortal they are fearless.
Winston Churchill

The lowest and vilest alleys of London do not present a more dreadful record of sin than does the smiling and beautiful countryside.
Sir Arthur Conan Doyle

An Anglo-Saxon, Hinnissy, is a German that's forgot who was his parents.
Finley Peter Dunne

The difference between the vanity of a Frenchman and an Englishman is this: The one thinks everything right that is French, while the other thinks everything wrong that is not English.
William Hazlitt

A blaspheming Frenchman is a spectacle more pleasing to the Lord than a praying Englishman.
Heinrich Heine

An Englishman is never so natural as when he's holding his tongue.
Henry James

If an earthquake were to engulf England tomorrow, the English would manage to meet and dine somewhere among the rubble, just to celebrate the event.
Douglas Jerrold

Oats: a grain, which in England is generally given to horses, but in Scotland supports the people.
Samuel Johnson

When a man is tired of London, he is tired of life, for there is in London all that life can afford.
Samuel Johnson

In the dark days and darker nights when England stood alone—and most men save Englishmen despaired of England's life— he [Churchill] mobilized the English language and sent it into battle.
John F. Kennedy

If England was what England seems,
An' not the England of our dreams,
But only putty, brass and paint,
'Ow quick we'd chuck her!
But she ain't!
Rudyard Kipling

We know no spectacle so ridiculous as the British public in one of its periodic fits of morality.
Thomas B. Macaulay

I'm leaving because the weather is too good. I hate London when it's not raining.
Groucho Marx

[England] is the only country in the world where the food is more dangerous than sex.
Jackie Mason

The English are proud; the French are vain.
Jean-Jacques Rousseau

England is the paradise of individuality, eccentricity, heresy, anomalies, hobbies and humors.
George Santayana

There is nothing so bad or so good that you will not find Englishmen doing it; but you will never find an Englishman in the wrong. He does everything on principle.
George Bernard Shaw

What two ideas are more inseparable than beer and Britannia?
Sydney Smith

How hard it is to make an Englishman acknowledge that he is happy.
William Makepeace Thackeray

England has 42 religions and only two sauces.
Voltaire

If one could only teach the English how to talk and the Irish how to listen, society would be quite civilized.
Oscar Wilde

BUDGET

The budget should be balanced, the Treasury should be refilled, public debt should be reduced, the arrogance of officialdom should be tempered and controlled, and the assistance to foreign lands should be curtailed lest Rome become bankrupt.
Cicero (63 B.C.)

A budget tells us what we can't afford, but it doesn't keep us from buying it.
William Feather

It's discouraging how hard it is for a president to slice away large chunks of a $305 billion budget.
Gerald Ford

Budgets are not merely affairs of arithmetic, but in a thousand ways go to the root of prosperity of individuals, the relation of classes and the strength of kingdoms.
William E. Gladstone

The budget is a mythical bean bag. Congress votes mythical beans into it, and then tries to reach in and pull real beans out.
Will Rogers

BUREAUCRACY

A memorandum is written not to inform the reader but to protect the writer.
Dean Acheson

There's nothing which cannot be made a mess of again by officials.
Konrad Adenauer

Bureaucracies are designed to perform public business. But as soon as a bureaucracy is established, it develops an autonomous spiritual life and comes to regard the public as its enemy.
Brooks Atkinson

The perfect bureaucrat everywhere is the man who manages to make no decisions and escape all responsibility.
Brooks Atkinson

Bureaucracy is a giant mechanism operated by pygmies.
Honoré de Balzac

Poor fellow, he suffers from files.
Aneurin Bevan

Remove the document, and you remove the man.
Mikhail Bulgakov

Man is the only animal that laughs and has a state legislature.
Samuel Butler

The atmosphere of officialdom would kill anything that breathes the air of human endeavor.
Joseph Conrad

Bureaucracy gives birth to itself and then expects maternity benefits.
Dale Dauten

I love being a writer. What I can't stand is the paperwork.
Peter De Vries

Bureaucracy is the death of any achievement.
Albert Einstein

To be a corporation, a board of directors is required, though there's mighty little agreement about what directors are supposed to do.
Malcolm Forbes

One of the enduring truths of the nation's capital is that bureaucrats survive.
Gerald Ford

Hell hath no fury like a bureaucrat scorned.
Milton Friedman

The only thing that saves us from bureaucracy is its inefficiency. An efficient bureaucracy is the greatest threat to freedom.
Eugene McCarthy

Bureaucracy, the rule of no one, has become the modern form of despotism.
Mary McCarthy

Bureaucratic time, which is slower than geologic time but more expensive than time spent with Madame Claude's girls in Paris.
P.J. O'Rourke

On Soviet bureaucrats: They don't ask much of you. They only want you to hate the things you love and to love the things you hate.
Boris Pasternak

Bureaucrats write memoranda both because they appear to be busy when they are writing and because the memos, once written, immediately become proof that they were busy.
Charles Peters

If you're going to sin, sin against God, not the bureaucracy. God will forgive you but the bureaucracy won't.
Hyman Rickover

The working of great institutions is mainly the result of a vast mass of routine, petty malice, self-interest, care-lessness and sheer mistake.
George Santayana

Bureaucracy is not an obstacle to democracy but an inevitable complement to it.
Joseph Schumpeter

A committee should consist of three men, two of whom are absent.
Herbert Beerbohm Tree

There is something about a bureaucrat that does not like a poem.
Gore Vidal

We can lick gravity, but sometimes the paperwork is overwhelming.
Wernher von Braun

Bureaucrats: they are dead at 30 and buried at 60.
Frank Lloyd Wright

BUSINESS

I love deadlines. I like the whooshing sound they make as they fly by.
Douglas Adams

We are all manufacturers—making good, making trouble or making excuses.
H.V. Adolt

The person who minds nobody's business but his own is probably a millionaire.
Anonymous

Professionals are people who can do their job when they don't feel like it. Amateurs are people who can't do their job when they do feel like it.
Anonymous

The true worth of a man is to be measured by the objects he pursues.
Marcus Aurelius Antoninus

Business or toil is merely utilitarian. It is necessary, but does not enrich or ennoble a human life.
Aristotle

Business is religion, and religion is business. The man who does not make a business of his religion has a religious life of no force, and the man who does not make a religion of his business has a business life of no character.
Maltbie Babcock

In all negotiations of difficulty, a man may not look to sow and reap at once; but must prepare business, and so ripen it by degrees.
Francis Bacon

Business is really more agreeable than pleasure; it interests the whole mind, the aggregate nature of man more continuously, and more deeply. But it does not look as if it did.
Walter Bagehot

Our problem in money-making or government affairs is how to remain properly venturesome and experimental without making fools of ourselves.
Bernard M. Baruch

There is too much emphasis on the alleged need for more purchasing power. What the country needs is stable purchasing power. Increased wages, higher pensions, more unemployment insurance, all are of no avail if the purchasing power of money falls faster.
Bernard M. Baruch

To prosper soundly in business, you must satisfy not only your customers, but you must lay yourself out to satisfy also the men who make your product and the men who sell it.
Harry Bassett

Corporation: An ingenious device for obtaining individual profit without individual responsibility.
Ambrose Bierce

If your business keeps you so busy that you have no time for anything else, there must be something wrong, either with you or with your business.
William J.H. Boetcker

Life is too short to be unhappy in business. If business were not a part of the joy of living, we might almost say that we have no right to live, because it is a pretty poor man who cannot get into the line for which he is fitted.
George L. Brown

I am a better investor because I am a businessman, and a better businessman because I am no investor.
Warren Buffet

On Bill Gates: He may be the smartest guy I've ever met. But I don't know what those little [computer] things do.
Warren Buffett

When a manager with a reputation for brilliance tackles a business with a reputation for bad economics, the reputation of the business remains intact.
Warren Buffett

The humanities of business in this age have become more important than the techniques of business. Each business and industry has to sweep the public misunderstandings and the false notions off its own front walk. Thus will a pathway be cleared for popular appreciation of the important rôle of business in our freedom and in our way of life.
Harry A. Bullis

I like business because it is competitive, because it rewards deeds rather than words. I like business because it compels earnestness and does not permit me to neglect today's task while thinking about tomorrow. I like business because it undertakes to please, not reform; because it is honestly selfish, thereby avoiding hypocrisy and sentimentality. I like business because it promptly penalizes mistakes, shiftlessness and inefficiency, while rewarding well those who give it the best they have in them. Lastly, I like business because each day is a fresh adventure.
R.H. Cabell

Business is always a struggle. There are always obstacles and competitors. There is never an open road, except the wide road that leads to failure. Every great

success has always been achieved by fight. Every winner has scars. . . . The men who succeed are the efficient few. They are the few who have the ambition and will-power to develop themselves.
Herbert N. Casson

Never arrive on time; this stamps you as a beginner. Don't say anything until the meeting is half over; this stamps you as being wise. Be the first to move for adjournment; this will make you popular; it's what everyone is waiting for.
Harry Chapman

The best mental effort in the game of business is concentrated on the major problem of securing the consumer's dollar before the other fellow gets it.
Stuart Chase

The American businessman cannot consider his work done when he views the income balance in black at the end of an accounting period. It is necessary for him to trace the social incidence of the figures that appear in his statement and prove to the general public that his management has not only been profitable in the accounting sense but salutary in terms of popular benefits.
Colby M. Chester

Few people do business well who do nothing else.
Lord Chesterfield

Some see private enterprise as a predatory target to be shot, others as a cow to be milked, but few are those who see it as a sturdy horse pulling the wagon.
Winston Churchill

My precept to all who build, is, that the owner should be an ornament to the house, and not the house to the owner.
Cicero

Modern business requires that its salesmen be business men in the best sense of the word—men who know the ins and outs of the product or service they are selling . . . men who can make an intelligent and effective presentation . . . and most of all, men who have the modern concept of service to the customer.
Hugh W. Coburn

A committee is a cul-de-sac down which ideas are lured and then quietly strangled.
Sir Barnett Cocks

Business will be better or worse.
Calvin Coolidge

No enterprise can exist for itself alone. It ministers to some great need, it performs some great service, not for itself, but for others; or failing therein, it ceases to be profitable and ceases to exist.
Calvin Coolidge

The business of America is business.
Calvin Coolidge

All of the things now enjoyed by civilization have been created by some man and sold by another man before anybody really enjoyed the benefits of them.
James G. Daly

It may never come, but I fancy that no man who has sympathy for the human race does not wish that sometime those who labor should have the whole product of their toil. Probably it will never come, but I wish that the time might come when men who work in the industries would own the industries.
Clarence Darrow

If it is not in the interest of the public it is not in the interest of business.
Joseph H. Defrees

Things that are bad for business are bad for the people who work for business.
Thomas E. Dewey

There ought to be more scrupulous honesty in big business men than in any other human relation. For big business requires teamwork on a gigantic scale.
Henry L. Doherty

I spend 90% of my time with people who don't report to me, which also allows for serendipity, since I'm walking around the office all the time. You don't have to schedule serendipity. It just happens.
Jack Dorsey

Never shrink from doing anything which your business calls you to do. The man who is above his business may one day find his business above him.
John Drew

Innovation is the specific instrument of entrepreneurship, the act that endows resources with a new capacity to create wealth.
Peter Drucker

The only things that evolve by themselves in an organization are disorder, friction and malperformance.
Peter Drucker

The crossroads of trade are the meeting place of ideas, the attrition ground of rival customs and beliefs; diversities beget conflict, comparison, thought; superstitions cancel one another, and reason begins.
Will Durant

There is far more danger in a public monopoly than there is in a private monopoly, for when government goes into business it can always shift its losses to the taxpayer. The Government never really goes into business, for it never makes ends meet, and that is the first

requisite of business. It just mixes a little business with a lot of politics, and no one ever gets a chance to find out what is actually going on.
Thomas A. Edison

Commerce is a game of skill, which every man cannot play, which few men can play well. The right merchant is one who has the just average of faculties we call commonsense; a man of strong affinity for facts, who makes up his decision on what he has seen. He is thoroughly persuaded of the truths of arithmetic. There is always a reason, in the man, for his good or bad fortune; and so, in making money. Men talk as if there were some magic about this, and believe in magic, in all parts of life. He knows that all goes on the old road, pound for pound, cent for cent—for every effect a perfect cause—and that good luck is another name for tenacity of purpose.
Ralph Waldo Emerson

Big business can't prosper without small business to supply its needs and buy its products. Labor can't prosper so long as capital lies idle. Capital can't prosper while labor is unemployed.
DeWitt M. Emery

Business demands faith, compels earnestness, requires courage, is honestly selfish, is penalized for mistakes, and is the essence of life.
William Feather

The first mark of good business is the ability to deliver. To deliver its product or service on time and in the condition which the client was led to expect. This dedication to provision and quality gives rise to corporate reliability. It makes friends and, in the end, is the reason why solvent companies remain solvent.
Michel J.T. Ferguson

There is nothing so useful to man in general, nor so beneficial to particular societies and individuals, as trade. This is that alma mater, at whose plentiful breast all mankind are nourished.
Henry Fielding

No grand idea was ever born in a conference, but a lot of foolish ideas have died there.
F. Scott Fitzgerald

You cannot afford to make the mistake of thinking you cannot be replaced. And your employer cannot afford to have a man around that he cannot afford to do without.
Frank Irving Fletcher

A big business man was telling Henry Ford about a coach driver of super-expertness with his whip. The driver was telling how he could flick a fly off his horse's ear with his whip—and, a fly alighting just then, he promptly did so. Next he spied a grasshopper beside the road, and he flicked it off with equal dexterity. A little further along the road the passenger noticed an insect on a bush, and nudged the driver to get him.

Not on your life, replied the master of the whip. That there insect is a hornet sitting on his nest with an organization behind him. I leave him alone.
B.C. Forbes

I have known not a few men who, after reaching the summits of business success, found themselves miserable on attaining retirement age. They were so exclusively engrossed in their day-to-day affairs that they had no time for friend-making. . . . They may flatter themselves that their unrelaxing concentration on business constitutes patriotism of the highest order. They may tell themselves that the existing emergency will pass,

and that they can then adopt different, more sociable, more friendly habits. [But] such a day is little likely to come for such individuals.
B.C. Forbes

Lord Northcliffe [British press magnate] once told me that he had discovered in America a tendency to install and worship system to such an extent that so much time was spent on system that little time was left for rounding up business to keep the system going. Is it not so with conferences? Isn't the legitimate purpose of conferences being lost sight of? Just how far should businessmen go in spending hours in conferences with their colleagues and shut out, meanwhile, all communication with those from whom they derive their business? Executives cannot make a business pay by taking in one another's washing.
B.C. Forbes

The world seems to have forgotten that, finally, business must be settled almost wholly by barter. Certainly, American bankers, investment bankers and promoters overlooked this basic fact when they joyfully proceeded to lend hundreds of millions and even billions to almost every foreign country on the face of the earth after the World War and before the collapse of our speculative boom. They never stopped to ask how the overseas borrowers could settle the colossal sums advanced to them. . . . The world had drifted too far away from the A.B.C. truth that trade and commerce must necessarily represent barter.
B.C. Forbes

When you delve deep enough, you find that practically every great fortune and great enterprise in America have sprung from the courageous enterprise of some individual. It was Commodore Vanderbilt's enterprise in switching first from

running a ferryboat to running other ships, and then, when he was well along in years, his enterprise in switching into railroading, that created what was to become one of the most notable fortunes in the history of the world.
B.C. Forbes

Anyone who says businessmen deal only in facts, not fiction, has never read old five-year projections.
Malcolm Forbes

Economists' unanimity that bad business is ahead is the most reassuring news possible. It's very unlikely that this will be the one time they're right.
Malcolm Forbes

In business, there's such a thing as an invaluable person, but no such thing as an indispensable one.
Malcolm Forbes

Speculator: One who bought stocks that went down.
Malcolm Forbes

U.S. Steel. It's probably hard for the younger generation to realize what a giant in every way, shape and form United States Steel once was in our economy. The fabled ogre of corporate folklore is now sick and tired, more likely to be pitied than pilloried. Since Ben Fairless' day, Big Steel has fumbled from one costly wrong decision to another, been heard when silence would have been wiser, been silent when speaking up would have been in order; spent wads for what were often the wrong new facilities and saved when salvation lay in modernizing. Sure it's still big. But it's sad to see the giant in such need of succor.
Malcolm Forbes (1971)

When reading forecasts tied to percent rates of this and that, it's well to keep in mind that extending them too far into the future—no matter that they have been valid for several years past—is to presume a continuity of circumstances that never holds for any great length of time. . . . How about the not-so-long-ago projections for the continuing growth of utilities? Or natural gas, gasoline and oil consumption? Forecasts that run way out are invariably way off.
Malcolm Forbes

Where are most of the millions of new jobs? An overwhelming percentage has been, and is being, created in companies with fewer than 100 employees.
Malcolm Forbes

Business is never so healthy as when, like a chicken, it must do a certain amount of scratching for what it gets.
Henry Ford

Let all your things have their places; let each part of your business have its time.
Benjamin Franklin

No nation was ever ruined by trade.
Benjamin Franklin

The first mistake in public business is the going into it.
Benjamin Franklin

Business is the salt of life.
Thomas Fuller

All our institutions rest upon business. Without it we should not have schools, colleges, churches, parks, playgrounds, pavements, books, libraries, art, music, or anything else that we value.
Cassius E. Gates

The meek shall inherit the earth, but not the mineral rights.
J. Paul Getty

As you cherish the things most worthwhile in your family life, cherish the things most worthwhile in your company.
William B. Given, Jr.

How can you not be fond of a company you built into the largest insurance company in the world? But I don't share a feeling of warmth toward certain people on the board.
Maurice (Hank) Greenberg

It is the customer, and the customer alone, who casts the vote that determines how big any company should be. . . . The regulations laid down by the consuming public are far more potent and far less flexible than any code of law, merely through the exercise of the natural forces of trade.
Crawford H. Greenewalt

A "tired businessman" is one whose business is usually not a successful one.
Joseph R. Grundy

The more people who own little businesses of their own, the safer our country will be, and the better off its cities and towns; for the people who have a stake in their country and their community are its best citizens.
John Hancock

What is a committee? A group of the unwilling, picked from the unfit, to do the unnecessary.
Richard Harkness

I have found [public relations] to be the craft of arranging truths so that people will like you. Public-relations specialists make flower arrangements of the facts, placing them so that the wilted and less attractive petals are hidden by the sturdy blooms.
Alan Harrington

The most sensible people to be met with in society are men of business and of the world, who argue from what they see and know, instead of spinning cobweb distinctions of what things ought to be.
William Hazlitt

It is probably safe to say that the best brains of the nation are to be found in industry. This is partly because industry can afford to pay the highest prices for talent, and also because of the training men receive in that field. That this fact is not more apparent is due in part to the reluctance of business men to reveal their accomplishments to the public, and also because they have directed their energies in the past almost exclusively to production problems.
Ralph Hendershot

A company's business would increase 50% if you cleared the conference room of chairs.
W.F. Heneghan

The are more goods bought by the heart then by the head.
George Henning

Great business turns on a little pin.
George Herbert

All men's gains are the fruit of venturing.
Herodotus

One of the eternal conflicts out of which life is made up is that between the efforts of every man to get the most he can for his services and that of society disguised under the name of capital to get his services for the least possible return.
Oliver Wendell Holmes

No one is born a CEO, but no one tells you that. The magazine stories make it sound like Mark Zuckerberg woke up one day and wanted to redefine how

the world communicates [by creating] a billion-dollar company. He didn't.
Drew Houston

In thousands of years there has been no advance in public morals, in philosophy, in religion or in politics, but the advance in business has been the greatest miracle the world has ever known.
Edgar Watson Howe

Most business problems require common sense rather than legal reference. They require good judgment and honesty of purpose rather than reference to the courts.
Edward N. Hurley

In the takeover business, if you want a friend, you buy a dog.
Carl Icahn

Commerce is the great civilizer. We exchange ideas when we exchange fabrics.
Robert Ingersoll

He who will not apply himself to business, eventually discovers that he means to get his bread by cheating, stealing, or begging, or else is wholly void of reason.
Ischomachus

No one fouls his hands in his own business.
Italian proverb

I do not believe you can do today's job with yesterday's methods and be in business tomorrow.
Nelson Jackson

Agriculture, manufactures, commerce and navigation, the four pillars of our prosperity, are most thriving when left most free to individual enterprise.
Thomas Jefferson

When speculation has done its worst, two and two still make four.
Samuel Johnson

Morale is faith in the man at the top.
Albert S. Johnstone

Whoever said, If it ain't broke, don't fix it, probably never heard of preventative maintenance.
Steven Kasper

Industry prospers when it offers people articles which they want more than they want anything they now have. The fact is that people never buy what they need. They buy what they want.
Charles F. Kettering

To venture causes anxiety, but not to venture is to lose one's self . . . and to venture in the highest sense is precisely to become conscious of one's self.
Søren Kierkegaard

Men who pay whole-hearted attention to business, who train themselves, who develop every power to the full, are favored by the ill-training of the average man. Despite our boasted institutions of learning, most men are only half-educated, have no clear purpose in life or little real ambition, and are not honest in the highest meaning of the word. The only wonder is that well-trained, honest, ambitious, creative men do not forge to the front more rapidly.
Darwin P. Kingsley

A big corporation is more or less blamed for being big; it is only big because it gives service. If it doesn't give service, it gets small faster than it grew big.
William S. Knudsen

The morale of an organization is not built from the bottom up; it filters from the top down.
Peter B. Kyne

I don't play golf or all those things people normally do for business. I do parties. That's where I bring people in, showcase ideas and, in the end, do deals.
Guy Laliberté

A committee is an animal with four back legs.
John le Carré

People will buy anything that's *one to a customer*.
Sinclair Lewis

I've never been in a business where anybody understood what I was doing.
George Lindemann

Calling me a billionaire is shocking. My wife will be surprised.
Leonard Litwin

There is no better ballast for keeping the mind steady on its keel, and saving it from all risk of crankiness, than business.
James Russell Lowell

Your market has a free choice, and only by supplying what the market wants, and not by your efforts to impose your merchandise, will you get your maximum share of the market's potential.
Walter H. Lowy

Business more than any other occupation is a continual dealing with the future; it is a continual calculation, an instinctive exercise in foresight.
Henry R. Luce

The trade-unionist has the same limitation imposed upon him as the capitalist. He cannot advance his interests at the expense of society.
Ramsay MacDonald

No man will ever be a big executive who feels that he must, either openly or under cover, follow up every order he gives

and see that it is done—nor will he ever develop a capable assistant.
John Lee Mahin

I am not going to retire until we're the largest apartment owner in the U.S.
John P. Manning

Be methodical if you would succeed in business, or in anything. Have a work for every moment, and mind the moment's work. Whatever your calling, master all its bearings and details, its principles, instruments and applications. Method is essential if you would get through your work easily and with economy of time.
William Matthews

Business is a combination of war and sport.
André Maurois

All too much of the wage structure has been based on the time workers put in, rather than upon the product put out. The consumer dollar has no interest in how much time it buys—only in the character and quality of the product itself.
Wheeler McMillen

Not even computers will replace committees, because committees buy computers.
Edward Shepherd Mead

If the spirit of business adventure is killed, this country will cease to hold the foremost position in the world.
Andrew W. Mellon

If you buy a few great companies, you can sit on your ass.
Charles Munger

We have three baskets for investing: yes, no, and too tough to understand.
Charles Munger

A ship, to run a straight course, can have but one pilot and one steering wheel.

The same applies to the successful operation of a business. There cannot be a steering wheel at every seat in an organization.
Jules Ormont

Public relations, in this country, is the art of adapting big business to a democracy so that the people have confidence that they are being well served and at the same time the business has the freedom to serve them well.
Arthur W. Page

It is very sad for a man to make himself servant to a single thing; his manhood all taken out of him by the hydraulic pressure of excessive business.
Theodore Parker

A self-contained nation is a backward nation, with large numbers of people either permanently out of work, or very poorly paid in purchasing power. A nation which trades freely with all the world, selling to others those commodities which it can best produce, and buying from others those commodities which others can best produce, is by far the best conditioned nation for all practical purposes.
Walter Parker

We do not say that a man who takes no interest in public affairs is a man who minds his own business. We say he has no business being here at all.
Pericles

Business is like a man rowing a boat upstream. He has no choice; he must go ahead or he will go back.
Lewis E. Pierson

Adoption and continuation of policies that incorporate a maximum of forward thinking should be the most vital single consideration of all executives.
Charles Presbrey

Seest thou a man diligent in his business? He shall stand before kings; he shall not stand before mean men.
Proverbs 22:29

The next generation of businessmen will be articulate, knowing what they believe and entering joyously into the battle of ideas, or there will be no business as we have known it heretofore.
Clarence B. Randall

Running a company on market research is like driving while looking in the rearview mirror.
Anita Roddick

A man who is at the top is a man who has the habit of getting to the bottom.
Joseph E. Rogers

Even if you're on the right track you'll get run over if you just sit there.
Will Rogers

You never get a second chance to make a good first impression.
Will Rogers

Every business should have its biographer—not after its head is dead but to show that he's very much alive.
Frank Romer

We demand that big business give people a square deal; in return we must insist that when anyone engaged in big business honestly endeavors to do right, he shall himself be given a square deal.
Theodore Roosevelt

When we control business in the public interest we are also bound to encourage it in the public interest or it will be a bad thing for everybody and worst of all

for those on whose behalf the control is nominally exercised.
Theodore Roosevelt

The most important difference between business and academia is this: In business everything is dog eat dog. In academia it's just the reverse.
E. John Rosenwald, Jr.

This is a great time to be in real estate. This is the 15 seconds of sun.
Stephen Ross

He should be the owner of the land who rubs it between his hands every spring.
Russian peasant saying

A man who cannot mind his own business is not to be trusted with the king's.
George Savile (Lord Halifax)

He who thinks his place below him, will certainly be below his place.
George Savile (Lord Halifax)

Keeping a little ahead of conditions is one of the secrets of business; the trailer seldom goes far.
Charles M. Schwab

Get the confidence of the public and you will have no difficulty in getting their patronage. Inspire your whole force with the right spirit of service; encourage every sign of the true spirit. So display and advertise wares that customers shall buy with understanding. Treat them as guests when they come and when they go, whether or not they buy. Give them all that can be given fairly, on the principle that to him that giveth shall be given. Remember always that the recollection of quality remains long after the price is forgotten. Then your business will prosper by a natural process.
H. Gordon Selfridge

The length of a meeting rises with the square of the number of people present.
Eileen Shanahan

Consumption is the sole end and purpose of all production, and the interest of the producer ought to be attended to, only so far as it may be necessary for promoting that of the consumer.
Adam Smith

I've made a life out of putting a business aspect to my innovative mind.
James Sorenson

A dinner lubricates business.
Baron Stowell

The chicken business is an old business. I'm bringing new technology to it.
Glen Taylor

A jack-of-all-trades is king of none.
P.K. Thomajan

What recommends commerce to me is its enterprise and bravery. It does not clasp its hands and pray to Jupiter.
Henry David Thoreau

In democracies, nothing is more great or more brilliant than commerce: It attracts the attention of the public and fills the imagination of the multitude; all energetic passions are directed towards it.
Alexis de Tocqueville

I have the same credo with my land as I had with my business: He who profits most serves the best.
Ted Turner

A businessman is a hybrid between a dancer and a calculator.
Paul Valéry

No legitimate business man ever got started on the road to permanent success by any other means than that of hard, intelligent work, coupled with an earned credit, plus character.
F.D. Van Amburgh

The most successful businessman is the man who holds onto the old just as long as it is good and grabs the new just as soon as it is better.
Robert P. Vanderpoel

Being good in business is the most fascinating kind of art. Making money is art and working is art and good business is the best art.
Andy Warhol

I think I have learned, in some degree at least, to disregard the old maxim "Do not get others to do what you can do yourself." My motto on the other hand is: "Do not do that which others can do as well."
Booker T. Washington

There is always room at the top.
Daniel Webster

Call on a business man only at business times, and on business; transact your business, and go about your business, in order to give him time to finish his business.
Duke of Wellington

My own business always bores me to death; I prefer other people's.
Oscar Wilde

The manufacturer who waits in the woods for the world to beat a path to his door is a great optimist. But the manufacturer who shows his mousetraps to the world keeps the smoke coming out of his chimney.
O.B. Winters

When two men in a business always agree, one of them is unnecessary.
William Wrigley, Jr.

In modern business it is not the crook who is to be feared most, it is the honest man who doesn't know what he is doing.
Owen D. Young

I could be on the beach, but I can't wait to get to the office every day. Risk-taking is like a giant jigsaw puzzle.
Samuel Zell

BUSY

Every man is worth just as much as the things he busies himself with.
Marcus Aurelius Antoninus

Whoever admits that he is too busy to improve his methods has acknowledged himself to be at the end of his rope. And that is always the saddest predicament which anyone can get into.
J. Ogden Armour

It is an undoubted truth that the less one has to do the less time one finds to do it in. One yawns, one procrastinates, one can do it when one will, and, therefore, one seldom does it at all; whereas, those who have a great deal of business must buckle to it; and then they always find time enough to do it.
Lord Chesterfield

None are so busy as the fool and the knave.
John Dryden

The busiest men have the most leisure.
English proverb

The happiest people are those who are too busy to notice whether they are or not.
William Feather

The busy man has few idle visitors; to the boiling pot the flies come not.
Benjamin Franklin

The more we do, the more we can do; the more busy we are, the more leisure we have.
William Hazlitt

Occupation is the necessary basis of all enjoyment.
Leigh Hunt

The busier we are, the more acutely we feel that we live.
Immanuel Kant

No thoroughly occupied man was ever yet very miserable.
Letitia Landon

A man who is very busy seldom changes his opinions.
Friedrich Wilhelm Nietzsche

You can't be asleep in business—at the ends of the arms of Morpheus are the hands of the receiver.
Frank Romer

Be busy in trading, receiving, and giving, for life is too good to be wasted in living.
John Sterling

Extreme busyness, whether at school or college, kirk or market, is a symptom of deficient vitality; and a faculty for idleness implies a catholic appetite and a strong sense of personal identity.
Robert Louis Stevenson

Many are idly busy. Domitian was busy, but then it was in catching flies.
Jeremy Taylor

It is not enough to be busy; so are the ants. The question is: What are we busy about?
Henry David Thoreau

CAPITALISM

Capitalism without bankruptcy is like Christianity without hell.
Frank Borman

It is just as illogical to suggest abolishing capitalism because it hasn't abolished poverty as it would be to suggest abolishing the churches because the churches haven't abolished sin.
C. Donald Dallas

Capitalism is the only system in the world founded on credit and character.
Hubert Eaton

There are 100 men seeking security to one able man who is willing to risk his fortune.
J. Paul Getty

And the word is capitalism. We are too mealy-mouthed. We fear the word capitalism is unpopular. So we talk about the free enterprise system and run to cover in the folds of the flag and talk about the American Way of Life.
Eric A. Johnston

There can be no freedom of the individual, no democracy, without the capital system, the profit system, the private enterprise system. These are, in the end, inseparable. Those who would destroy freedom have only first to destroy the

hope of gain, the profit of enterprise and risk-taking, the hope of accumulating capital, the hope to save something for one's old age and for one's children. For a community of men without property, and without the hope of getting it by honest effort, is a community of slaves of a despotic State.
Russell C. Leffingwell

American capitalism has been both over-praised and overindicted. It is neither the Plumed Knight nor the monstrous Robber Baron.
Max Lerner

The capitalistic system is the oldest system in the world, and any system that has weathered the gales and chances of thousands of years must have something in it that is sound and true. We believe in the right of a man to himself, to his own property, to his own destiny, and we believe the government exists as the umpire in the game, not to come down and take the bat, but to see that the other fellows play the game according to the principles of fairness and justice.
Nicholas Longworth

The record of the last century has been impressive. The problem for the future is to keep our capitalism dynamic—continue to raise living standards and yet to reduce, as much as possible, the human costs as reflected in insecurity and instability.
W. Walter Williams

CAREER

Let a man practice the profession which he best knows.
Cicero

Each man has his own vocation. The talent is the call.
Ralph Waldo Emerson

One principal reason why men are so often useless is that they neglect their own profession or calling, and divide and shift their attention among a multitude of objects and pursuits.
Nathaniel Emmons

Think not of yourself as the architect of your career but as the sculptor. Expect to have to do a lot of hard hammering and chiseling and scraping and polishing.
B.C. Forbes

Look before or you'll find yourself behind.
Benjamin Franklin

Everyone has a vocation by which he earns his living, but he also has a vocation in an older sense of the word—the vocation to use his powers and live his life well.
Richard W. Livingstone

If a man has any brains at all, let him hold on to his calling, and, in the grand sweep of things, his turn will come at last.
William McCune

A decent man is not responsible for the vice or absurdity of his profession; and he ought not on that account refuse to pursue it; it is the custom of the country, there is money to be got by it, a man must live in the world and make the best of it, such as it is.
Michel de Montaigne

A career, like a business, must be budgeted. When it is necessary, the budget can be adjusted to meet changing conditions. A life that hasn't a definite plan is likely to become driftwood.
David Sarnoff

The test of a vocation is the love of the drudgery it involves.
Logan Pearsall Smith

To find a career to which you are adapted by nature, and then to work hard at it, is about as near to a formula for success and happiness as the world provides. One of the fortunate aspects of this formula is that, granted the right career has been found, the hard work takes care of itself. Then hard work is not hard work at all.
Mark Sullivan

Every profession does imply a trust for the service of the public.
Benjamin Whichcote

CHANCE

I felt sorry for myself because I had no hands until I met a man who had no chips.
Kent Anderson

Last year people won more than $1 billion playing poker. And casinos made $27 billion just by being around those people.
Samantha Bee

We cannot bear to regard ourselves simply as play-things of blind chance; we cannot admit to feeling ourselves abandoned.
Ugo Betti

The urge to gamble is so universal and its practice so pleasurable that I assume it must be evil.
Heywood Broun

He who distrusts the security of chance takes more pains to effect the safety which results from labor. To find what you seek in the road of life, the best

proverb of all is that which says: "Leave no stone unturned."
Edward Bulwer-Lytton

What I say is, patience, and shuffle the cards.
Miguel de Cervantes

There is no such thing as chance or accident; the words merely signify our ignorance of some real and immediate cause.
Adam Clarke

Those who trust to chance must abide by the results of chance. They have no legitimate complaint against anyone but themselves.
Calvin Coolidge

When we conquer without danger, our triumph is without glory.
Pierre Corneille

Pleased, the fresh packs on cloth of green they see,

And seizing, handle with preluding glee;

They draw, they sit, they shuffle, cut and deal,

Like friends assembled, but like foes to feel.

George Crabbe

The bizarre world of cards is a world of pure power politics where rewards and punishments are meted out immediately.
Ely Culbertson

People who don't take risks generally make about two big mistakes a year. People who do take risks generally make about two big mistakes a year.
Peter Drucker

If you want a guarantee, buy a toaster.
Clint Eastwood

I returned, and saw under the sun, that the race is not to the swift, nor the battle

to the strong, neither yet riches to men of understanding, nor yet favour to men of skill; but time and chance happeneth to them all.
Ecclesiastes 9:11

There is nothing in life so irrational, that good sense and chance may not set it to rights; nothing so rational, that folly and chance may not utterly confound it.
Johann Wolfgang von Goethe

Chance has something to say in everything, even how to write a good letter.
Baltasar Gracián

True luck consists not in holding the best of the cards at the table: Luckiest he who knows just when to rise and go home.
John Hay

Be not too presumptuously sure in any business; for things of this world depend on such a train of unseen chances that if it were in man's hands to set the tables, still he would not be certain to win the game.
Lord Herbert

When in doubt, win the trick.
Edmond Hoyle

Some luck lies in not getting what you thought you wanted but getting what you have, which once you have got it you may be smart enough to see is what you would have wanted had you known.
Garrison Keillor

You will never stub your toe standing still. The faster you go, the more chance there is of stubbing your toe, but the more chance you have of getting somewhere.
Charles F. Kettering

There are no chances so unlucky from which clever people are not able to reap some advantage; and none so lucky that the foolish are not able to turn them to their own disadvantage.
François de La Rochefoucauld

I figure you have the same chance of winning the lottery whether you play or not.
Fran Lebowitz

What chance has made yours is not really yours.
Lucilius

The poker player learns that sometimes both science and common sense are wrong; that the bumblebee can fly; that, perhaps, one should never trust an expert; that there are more things in heaven and earth than are dreamt of by those with an academic bent.
David Mamet

Unless a man has trained himself for his chance, the chance will only make him ridiculous. A great occasion is worth to a man exactly what his antecedents have enabled him to make of it.
William Matthews

The only safe thing is to take a chance.
Elaine May

Remember the Three Princes of Serendip who went out looking for treasure? They didn't find what they were looking for, but they kept finding things just as valuable. That's serendipity, and our business [drugs] is full of it.
George Merck

If you're playing a poker game and you look around the table and can't tell who the sucker is, it's you.
Paul Newman

Chance favors the prepared mind.
Louis Pasteur

The best chess player in Christendom may be little more than the best player of chess; but proficiency in whist implies capacity for success in all these more important undertakings where mind struggles with mind.
Edgar Allan Poe

Why not go out on a limb? That's where the fruit is.
Will Rogers

On the 2008 Forbes 400 charity poker tournament (after winning in 2007): Give me better competition this time. (We won again in 2008.)
Phillip Ruffin

If you're offered a seat on a rocket ship, don't ask what seat—just get on.
Sheryl Sandberg

Because people have no thoughts to deal in, they deal cards, and try to win another's money. Idiots!
Arthur Schopenhauer

The roulette table pays nobody except him that keeps it. Nevertheless, a passion for gambling is common, though a passion for keeping roulette tables is unknown.
George Bernard Shaw

Life is a gamble at terrible odds. If it was a bet, you wouldn't take it.
Tom Stoppard

We are in the world like men playing at tables; the chance is not in our power, but to pay it is; and when it is fallen, we must manage it as we can.
Jeremy Taylor

Chance does nothing that has not been prepared beforehand.
Alexis de Tocqueville

Necessity is the mother of taking chances.
Mark Twain

Chance is a word devoid of sense, nothing can exist without a cause.
Voltaire

Gambling is the child of avarice, the brother of iniquity, and the father of mischief.
George Washington

Last night I stayed up late playing poker with Tarot cards. I got a full house and four people died.
Steven Wright

CHANGE

All great changes are irksome to the human mind, especially those which are attended with great dangers and uncertain effects.
John Quincy Adams

He who reforms himself, has done much toward reforming others; and one reason why the world is not reformed, is, because each would have others make a beginning, and never thinks of himself doing it.
Thomas Adams

Change is no modern invention. It is as old as time and as unlikely to disappear. It has always to be counted on as of the essence of human experience.
James Rowland Angell

All things change, and you yourself are constantly wasting away. So also is the universe.
Marcus Aurelius Antoninus

It is change, continuing change, inevitable change, that is the dominant factor in society today. No sensible decision can be made any longer without taking into account not only the world as it is, but the world as it will be.
Isaac Asimov

Things do change. The only question is that since things are deteriorating so quickly, will society and man's habits change quickly enough?
Isaac Asimov

The main dangers in this life are the people who want to change every thing or nothing.
Nancy Astor

The absurd man is he who never changes.
Auguste Barthéelemy

Every so often we hear people clamor for a change. Let's change the Constitution, change the form of Government, change everything for better or worse except to change the only thing that needs changing first: The human heart and our standard of success and human values.
William J.H. Boetcker

I can think of few important movements for reform in which success was won by any method other than an energetic minority presenting the indifferent majority with a fait accompli, which was then accepted.
Vera Brittain

To know what one can have and to do with it, being prepared for no more, is the basis of equilibrium.
Pearl S. Buck

A state without some means of change is without the means of its conservation.
Edmund Burke

Desperation is the raw material of drastic change. Only those who can leave behind everything they have ever believed in can hope to escape.
William S. Burroughs

Today is not yesterday. We ourselves change. How can our works and thoughts, if they are always to be the fittest, continue always the same? Change, indeed, is painful, yet ever needful; and if memory has its force and worth, so also has hope.
Thomas Carlyle

There is nothing wrong with change, if it is in the right direction.
Winston Churchill

Every reform, however necessary, will by weak minds be carried to an excess, that itself will need reforming.
Samuel Taylor Coleridge

We ought not to be overanxious to encourage innovation, for an old system must ever have two advantages over a new one; it is established and it is understood.
Charles Caleb Colton

Change is inevitable in a progressive country. Change is constant.
Benjamin Disraeli

A man who has reformed himself has contributed his full share towards the reformation of his neighbor.
Norman Douglas

But innovation is more than a new method. It is a new view of the universe, as one of risk rather than of chance or of certainty. It is a new view of man's role in the universe; he creates order by taking risks. And this means that innovation, rather than being an assertion of

human power, is an acceptance of human responsibility.
Peter Drucker

We are reformers in spring and summer. In autumn and winter we stand by the old. Reformers in the morning, conservatives at night. Reform is affirmative; conservatism, negative. Conservatism goes for comfort; reform for truth.
Ralph Waldo Emerson

Change, not habit, is what gets most of us down; habit is the stabilizer of human society, change accounts for its progress.
William Feather

Elders always lament change—and the young cannot wait for it.
Malcolm Forbes

Just as no mode is enduring, so, too, no mood.
Malcolm Forbes

All changes, even the most longed for, have their melancholy; for what we leave behind us is a part of ourselves; we must die to one life before we can enter into another!
Anatole France

Something really big happened in the world's wiring in the last decade, but it was obscured by the financial crisis and post-9/11. We went from a connected world to a hyperconnected world. I'm always struck that Facebook, Twitter, 4G, iPhones, iPads, ubiquitous wireless and Web-enabled cellphones, the cloud, Big Data, cellphone apps and Skype did not exist or were in their infancy a decade ago.
Thomas Friedman

There is danger in reckless change, but greater danger in blind conservatism.
Henry George

Consider how hard it is to change yourself and you'll understand what little chance you have trying to change others.
Arnold Glasow

Let no one be ashamed to say yes today if yesterday he said no.

Or to say no today if yesterday he said yes. For that is life.

Never to have changed—what a pitiable thing of which to boast!
Johann Wolfgang von Goethe

You can't expect that what you've become a master in will keep you valuable throughout the whole of your career, and most people are now going to be working into their 70s. Being a generalist is very unwise. Your major competitor is Wikipedia or Google.
Lynda Gratton

Every man is a reformer until reform tramps on his toes.
Edgar Watson Howe

The path of least resistance is what makes rivers run crooked.
Elbert Hubbard

There is a certain relief in change, even though it be from bad to worse; as I have found in traveling in a stage coach, that it is often a comfort to shift one's position and be bruised in a new place.
Washington Irving

Great innovations should not be forced on slender majorities.
Thomas Jefferson

Long customs are not easily broken: He that attempts to change the course of his own life very often labors in vain; and how shall we do for others, what we are seldom able to do for ourselves?
Samuel Johnson

Such is the state of life that none are happy but by the anticipation of change. The change itself is nothing; when we have made it the next wish is to change again.
Samuel Johnson

To men pressed by their wants all change is ever welcome.
Ben Jonson

All things are changed, and we change with them.
Lothair I

The most effective way to cope with change is to help create it.
L.W. Lynett

Every moment of one's existence one is growing into more or retreating into less. One is always living a little more or dying a little bit.
Norman Mailer

Who does more earnestly long for a change than he who is uneasy in his present circumstances? And who run to create confusions with so desperate a boldness as those who have nothing to lose, hope to gain by them?
Sir Thomas More

The art of living does not consist in preserving and clinging to a particular mood of happiness, but in allowing happiness to change its form without being disappointed by the change, for happiness, like a child, must be allowed to grow up.
Charles L. Morgan

Have no fear of change as such and, on the other hand, no liking for it merely for its own sake.
Robert Moses

Grant me the serenity to accept the things I cannot change, the courage to change the things I can and the wisdom to know the difference.
Reinhold Niebuhr

An intelligent heart acquires knowledge, and the ear of the wise seeks knowledge.
Proverbs 18:15

A little and a little, collected together, become a great deal; the heap in the barn consists of single grains, and drop and drop make the inundation.
Sa'di

Living in a world where everything is changing constantly, you learn to change.
K. Ram Shriram

The less things change, the more they remain the same.
Sicilian proverb

All in all it's a pretty great day for major league sports. At long last they've decided that gay people are fit to be included in their elite club—one that's already allowed in adulterers, wife-swappers, gamblers, cheaters, rapists, racists and slaughterers of man. Those who've abused spouses, drugs, alcohol, family members and animals. Congratulations, gay athletes. Are you sure you want to hang out with these people?
Jon Stewart

There is nothing in this world constant but inconstancy.
Jonathan Swift

It will always do to change for the better.
James Thomson

An individual is more apt to change, perhaps, than all the world around him.
Daniel Webster

If you want to make enemies, try to change something.
Woodrow Wilson

CHARACTER

We often pray for purity, unselfishness, for the highest qualities of character, and forget that these things cannot be given, but must be earned.
Lyman Abbott

Good character is that quality which makes one dependable whether being watched or not, which makes one truthful when it is to one's advantage to be a little less than truthful, which makes one courageous when faced with great obstacles, which endows one with the firmness of wise self-discipline.
Arthur S. Adams

Among the sentiments of most powerful operation upon the human heart, and most highly honorable to the human character, are those of veneration for our forefathers and of love for our posterity.
John Quincy Adams

I never knew an early-rising, hard-working, prudent man, careful of his earnings and strictly honest, who complained of hard luck. A good character, good habits and iron industry are impregnable to the assaults of all ill-luck that fools ever dreamed.
Joseph Addison

Wherever man goes to dwell, his character goes with him.
African proverb

The dearest to me are those of best character.
Arabian proverb

Character is that which reveals moral purpose, exposing the class of things a man chooses or avoids.
Aristotle

Don't mistake personality for character.
Wilma Askinas

A character standard is far more important than even a gold standard. The success of all economic systems is still dependent upon both righteous leaders and righteous people. In the last analysis, our national future depends upon our national character—that is, whether it is spiritually or materially minded.
Roger Babson

Character is a diamond that scratches every other stone.
Cyrus R. Bartol

A man's ledger does not tell what he is, or what he is worth. Count what is in man, not what is on him, if you would know what he is worth—whether rich or poor.
Henry Ward Beecher

Good taste is better than bad taste, but bad taste is better than no taste.
Arnold Bennett

One can acquire everything in solitude except character.
Marie Henri Beyle

Honor your commitments with integrity.
Les Brown

You gotta do it with class and integrity. If not, you're gonna drag yourself through the mud.
Solomon Burke

Character is formed, not by laws, commands, and decrees, but by quiet influence, unconscious suggestion, and personal guidance.
Marion L. Burton

Every man's work, whether it be literature or music or pictures or anything else, is always a portrait of himself, and the more he tries to conceal himself the more clearly will his character appear in spite of him.
Samuel Butler

Integrity has no need of rules.
Albert Camus

Every man is a volume, if you know how to read him.
William Ellery Channing

In men of the highest character and noblest genius there is to be found an insatiable desire for honor, command, power, and glory.
Cicero

Before you are five and twenty you must establish a character that will serve you all your life.
Lord Collingwood

No man knows his true character until he has run out of gas, purchased something on the installment plan and raised an adolescent.
Marcelene Cox

Though intelligence is powerless to modify character, it is a dab hand at finding euphemisms for its weaknesses.
Quentin Crisp

Characters never change. Opinions alter; characters are only developed.
Benjamin Disraeli

Judge of your natural character by what you do in your dreams.
Ralph Waldo Emerson

Some men are born to own; can animate all their possessions. Others cannot: Their owning is not graceful; seems to be a compromise of their character; they seem to steal their own dividends.
Ralph Waldo Emerson

You can easily judge the character of others by how they treat those who can do nothing for them or to them.
Malcolm Forbes

Deep down, I'm pretty superficial.
Ava Gardner

Faced with crisis, the man of character falls back on himself.
Charles de Gaulle

Good taste is the modesty of the mind; that is why it cannot be either imitated or acquired.
Emile de Girardin

It's only by the hard blows of adverse fortune that character is tooled.
Arnold Glasow

A talent can be cultivated in tranquility; a character only in the rushing stream of life.
Johann Wolfgang von Goethe

Nothing tells more about the character of a man than the things he makes fun of.
Johann Wolfgang von Goethe

Talents are best nurtured in solitude; character is best formed in the stormy billows of the world.

You can cultivate taste, as you can the intellect. Full understanding whets the appetite and desire, and, later, sharpens the enjoyment of possession.
Baltasar Gracián

Fame is a vapor, popularity an accident, riches take wings. Only one thing endures, and that is character.
Horace Greeley

Character is the real foundation of all worthwhile success.
John Hays Hammond

To keep your character intact you cannot stoop to filthy acts. It makes it easier to stoop the next time.
Katharine Hepburn

Character is destiny.
Heraclitus

Character is power; it makes friends, draws patronage and support, and opens a sure way to wealth, honor and happiness.
John Howe

Only what we have wrought into our character during life can we take way with us.
Alexander Humboldt

The character that needs law to mend it is hardly worth the tinkering.
Douglas William Jerrold

The fact that a man is a newspaper reporter is evidence of some flaw of character.
Lyndon Baines Johnson

Every man has three characters—that which he exhibits, that which he has, and that which he thinks he has.
Alphonse Karr

Character, like a photograph, develops in darkness.
Yousuf Karsh

It is fortunate to be of high birth, but it is no less to be of such character that people do not care to know whether you are or are not.
Jean de La Bruyère

There is a kind of revolution of so general a character that it changes the tastes as well as the fortunes of the world.
François de La Rochefoucauld

You cannot build character and courage by taking away man's initiative and independence.
Abraham Lincoln

Between ourselves and our real natures we interpose that wax figure of idealizations and selections we call our character.
Walter Lippmann

In this world a man must be either anvil or hammer.
Henry Wadsworth Longfellow

The measure of a man's real character is what he would do if he knew he would never be found out.
Thomas B. Macaulay

The experience of the ages that are past, the hopes of the ages that are yet to come, unite their voices in an appeal to us; they implore us to think more of the character of our people than of its vast numbers; to look upon our vast natural resources, not as tempters to ostentation and pride, but as means to be converted, by the refining alchemy of education, into mental and spiritual treasures—and thus give to the world the example of a nation whose wisdom increases with its prosperity, and whose virtues are equal to its power.
Horace Mann

The goods of Fortune, even such as they really are, still need taste to enjoy them. It is the enjoying, not the possessing, that makes us happy.
Michelangelo

Character consists of what you do on the third and fourth tries.
James Michener

A man's reputation is the opinion people have of him; his character is what he really is.
Jack Miner

Character development is the great, if not the sole, aim of education.
William O'Shea

The force, the mass of character, mind, heart or soul that a man can put into any work is the most important factor in that work.
A.P. Peabody

The real judges of your character aren't your neighbors, your relatives, or even the people you play bridge with. The folks who really know you are the waiters and clerks.
Katherine Piper

The highest of characters is his who is as ready to pardon the moral errors of mankind as if he were every day guilty of them himself; and as cautious of committing a fault as if he never forgave one.
Pliny the Younger

The character we exhibit in the latter half of our life need not necessarily be, though it often is, our original character, developed further, dried up, exaggerated, or diminished. It can be its exact opposite, like a suit worn inside out.
Marcel Proust

The most important thing for a young man is to establish a credit—a reputation, character.
John D. Rockefeller

Only a man's character is the real criterion of worth.
Eleanor Roosevelt

I care not what others think of what I do, but I care very much about what I think of what I do: That is character!
Theodore Roosevelt

Men best show their character in trifles, where they are not on guard. It is in insignificant matters, and in the simplest habits, that we often see the boundless egotism which pays no regard to the feelings of others, and denies nothing to itself.
Arthur Schopenhauer

To wilful men, the injuries that they themselves procure must be their schoolmasters.
William Shakespeare

It seems that the analysis of character is the highest human entertainment. And literature does it, unlike gossip, without mentioning names.
Isaac Bashevis Singer

I'm a fun target to write about—the maverick rich Texan in the Caribbean.
Allen Stanford

Society asks of most men more than sheer intellect ability—it demands also moral hardiness, self-discipline, a competitive spirit and other qualities that in more old-fashioned terms we might simply call character.
Julius Adams Stratton

Fame is what you have taken, character is what you give. When to this truth you awaken, then you begin to live.
Bayard Taylor

Nature has written a letter of credit upon some men's faces that is honored wherever presented. You cannot help trusting such men. Their very presence gives confidence. There is promise to pay in their faces which gives confidence and you prefer it to another man's endorsement. Character is credit.
William Makepeace Thackeray

You can never have a greater or a less dominion than over yourself.
Leonardo da Vinci

The character of a generation is moulded by personal character.
Brooke Foss Westcott

Character is a by-product; it is produced in the great manufacture of daily duty
Woodrow Wilson

If you will think about what you ought to do for other people, your character will take care of itself.
Woodrow Wilson

The noblest contribution which any man can make for the benefit of posterity, is that of character. The richest bequest which any man can leave to the youth of his native land, is that of a shining, spotless example.
Robert C. Winthrop

CHARITY

Charity brings to life again those who are spiritually dead.
Thomas Aquinas

Charity makes no decrease in property.
Arabian proverb

The unfortunate need people who will be kind to them; the prosperous need people to be kind to.
Aristotle

It is heaven upon earth to have a man's mind move in charity, rest in providence and turn upon the poles of truth.
Francis Bacon

The charities of life are scattered everywhere, enameling the vales of human beings as the flowers paint the meadows. They are not the fruit of study, nor the privilege of refinement, but a natural instinct.
George Bancroft

In necessary things, unity; in doubtful things, liberty; in all things, charity.
Richard Baxter

Having leveled my palace, don't erect a hovel and complacently admire your own charity in giving me that for a home.
Emily Brontë

If we can't turn the world around we can at least bolster the victims.
Liz Carpenter

Did universal charity prevail, earth would be a heaven and hell a fable.
Charles Caleb Colton

Though I speak with the tongues of men and of angels, and have not charity, I am as sounding brass, or a tinkling cymbal.
I Corinthians 13:1

And though I have the gift of prophecy, and understand all mysteries, and all knowledge; and though I have all faith, so that I could remove mountains, and have not charity, I am nothing.
I Corinthians 13:2

He who has no charity deserves no mercy.
English proverb

And if thou draw out thy soul to the hungry, and satisfy the afflicted soul; then shall thy light rise in obscurity, and thy darkness be as the noonday.
Isaiah 58:10

Bounty always receives part of its value from the manner in which it is bestowed.
Samuel Johnson

You are much surer that you are doing good when you pay money to those who work, as the recompense of their labors, than when you give money merely in charity.
Samuel Johnson

Be charitable and indulgent to everyone but yourself.
Joseph Joubert

He is truly great who hath a great charity.
Thomas à Kempis

Charity has in it sometimes, perhaps often, a savor of superiority.
James Russell Lowell

Charity . . . is kind, it is not easily provok'd, it thinks no evil, it believes all things, hopes all things.
Cotton Mather

As for charity, it is a matter in which the immediate effect on the persons directly concerned, and the ultimate consequence to the general good, are apt to be at complete war with one another.
John Stuart Mill

When faith and hope fail, as they do sometimes, we must try charity, which is love in action.
Dinah Maria Mulock

The charitable give out at the door, and God puts in at the window.
John Ray

Charity is injurious unless it helps the recipient to become independent of it.
John D. Rockefeller, Jr.

On his charity work for children: Give them the right values. Give them the love they need. And give them the health that they so desperately need.
T. Denny Sanford

All that I abandon, all that I give, I enjoy in a higher manner through the fact that I give it away. To give is to enjoy possessively the object that one gives.
Jean-Paul Sartre

Charity begins at hame, but shouldna end there.
Scottish proverb

Our true acquisitions lie only in our charities, we get only as we give.
William Simms

While actions are always to be judged by the immutable standard of right and wrong, and judgments we pass upon men must be qualified by considerations of age, country, station and other accidental circumstances; and it will then be found that he who is most charitable in his judgment is generally the least unjust.
Robert Southey

Charity is to will and do what is just and right in every transaction.
Emanuel Swedenborg

He who has never denied himself for the sake of giving, has but glanced at the joys of charity.
Anne Swetchine

People that trust wholly to others' charity, and without industry of their own, will always be poor.
William J. Temple

CHILDREN

In every child who is born, under no matter what circumstances, and of no matter what parents, the potentiality of the human race is born again; and in him, too, once more, and of each of us, our terrific responsibility towards human life.
James Agee

Blessed be childhood, which brings down something of heaven into the midst of our rough earthliness.
Henri Frédéric Amiel

Of all the needs (there are none imaginary) a lonely child has, the one that must be satisfied, if there is going to be

hope and a hope of wholeness, is the unshaking need for an unshakable God.
Maya Angelou

The easy way to teach children the value of money is to borrow from them.
Anonymous

We are the buffoons of our children.
Pietro Aretino

The life of children, as much as that of intemperate men, is wholly governed by their desires.
Aristotle

Childhood lasts all through life. It returns to animate broad sections of adult life. Poets will help us to find this living childhood within us, this permanent, durable, immobile world.
Gaston Bachelard

Children have never been very good at listening to their elders, but they have never failed to imitate them.
James Baldwin

If there is a species which is more maltreated than children, then it must be their toys, which they handle in an incredibly off-hand manner. Toys are thus the end point in that long chain in which all the conditions of despotic high-handedness are in play which enchain beings one to another.
Jean Baudrillard

Badgered, snubbed and scolded on the one hand; petted, flattered and indulged on the other—it is astonishing how many children work their way up to an honest manhood in spite of parents and friends. Human nature has an element of great toughness in it.
Henry Ward Beecher

To bring up a child in the way he should go, travel that way yourself once in a while.
Josh Billings

Never lend your car to anyone to whom you have given birth.
Erma Bombeck

If we had paid no more attention to our plants than we have to our children, we would now be living in a jungle of weed.
Luther Burbank

Children feel the whiteness of the lily with a graphic and passionate clearness which we cannot give them at all. The only thing we can give them is information—the information that if you break the lily in two it won't grow again.
G.K. Chesterton

A child's life is like a piece of paper on which every passerby leaves a mark.
Chinese proverb

When I was a child, I spake as a child, I understood as a child, I thought as a child: but when I became a man, I put away childish things.
I Corinthians 13:11

Who takes a child by the hand takes the mother by the heart.
Danish proverb

If you have never been hated by a child, you have never been a parent.
Bette Davis

The intimation never wholly deserts us that there is, in the unformed activities of childhood and youth, the possibilities of a better life for the community as well as for individuals here and there. This dim sense is the ground of our abiding idealization of childhood.
John Dewey

My hair stands on end at the cost and charges of these boys. Why was I ever a father! Why was my father ever a father!
Charles Dickens

Cleaning your house while your kids are still growing is like shoveling the walk before it stops snowing.
Phyllis Diller

If you want to see what children can do, you must stop giving them things.
Norman Douglas

There's no tragedy in life like the death of a child. Things never get back to the way they were.
Dwight D. Eisenhower

There never was a child so lovely but that his mother was glad to get him asleep.
Ralph Waldo Emerson

Children are poor men's riches.
English proverb

Any man who hates children can't be all bad.
W.C. Fields

Upon our children—how they are taught—rests the fate—or fortune—of tomorrow's world.
B.C. Forbes

It's an adult myth that childhood is idyllic.
Malcolm Forbes

On raising kids: Love, without discipline, isn't.
Malcolm Forbes

Speaking of birthdays, our firstborn [recently turned 2]. As parents sometimes fondly do, we reminisced a bit about his early days on earth—the excitement, the wonder, the fears when we brought him home. His every squeak or squawk we were sure heralded some terrible crisis; I tested the warmth of formulas from dusk to dawn, it seemed. We were so germ-conscious my wife even sterilized the skin of the oranges before squeezing them. How firstborns ever survive their parents' attentions is beyond me. However, they do, and he did, and, in spite of our efforts, he turned out to be quite a good guy.
Malcolm Forbes

The other evening around 10 p.m. we were finishing dinner in a fine, famed San Francisco restaurant, when a relatively young parental pair came in with youngsters—two girls is about nine and seven, and a boy of about five or six. The boy had on long pants and a bow tie and the girls were dressed like you'd think middle teenagers might be—in high heels and so forth. It always seems to me such a waste, such a missing of the point . . . There's a time—all too brief as it too soon becomes apparent to parents—to be little; a time to be in between; and a time to be old. Let each have its season . . . Let the little be little.
Malcolm Forbes

She discovered with great delight that one does not love one's children just because they are one's children but because of the friendship formed while raising them.
Gabriel García Márquez

There were giants in the earth in those days; and also after that, when the sons of God came in unto the daughters of men, and they bear children to them, the same became mighty men which were of old, men of renown.
Genesis 6:4

Children, love one another, and if that is not possible—at least try to put up with one another.
Johann Wolfgang von Goethe

There is always one moment in childhood when the door opens and lets the future in.
Graham Greene

Do not handicap your children by making their lives easy.
Robert A. Heinlein

A boy becomes an adult three years before his parents think he does, and about two years after he thinks he does.
Lewis B. Hershey

Adolescence is the period of life when we first become obsessed with trying to prove we are not a child—an obsession that can last a lifetime.
Cullen Hightower

The antidote for crime should be administered in childhood, by the parents. The problem is not fundamentally that of the improper child so much as it is that of the improper home.
John W. Hill

Pretty much all the honest truthtelling there is in the world is done by children.
Oliver Wendell Holmes

The glory of the nation rests in the character of her men. And character comes from boyhood. Thus every boy is a challenge to his elders. It is for them that we must win the war—it is for them that we must make a just and lasting peace. For the world of tomorrow, about which all of us are dreaming and planning, will be carried forward by the boys of today.
Herbert Hoover

All persons who bear the blessed title of parent have the personal responsibility to see that their children are growing up fully appreciative of the rights of God and their fellowmen.
J. Edgar Hoover

We like little children, because they tear out as soon as they get what they want.
Kin Hubbard

Each child is an adventure into a better life, an opportunity to change the old pattern and make it new.
Hubert Humphrey

Being a good psychoanalyst has the same disadvantage as being a good parent: The children desert one as they grow up.
Morton Hunt

Children are remarkable for their intelligence and ardor, for their curiosity, their intolerance of shams, the clarity and ruthlessness of their vision.
Aldous Huxley

Sons have always a rebellious wish to be disillusioned by that which charmed their fathers.
Aldous Huxley

Blessed be the hand that prepares a pleasure for a child, for there is no saying when and where it may bloom forth.
Douglas Jerrold

Allow children to be happy in their own way, for what better way will they ever find?
Samuel Johnson

You teach your daughters the diameters of the planets, and wonder when they have done that they do not delight in your company.
Samuel Johnson

Nothing you do for children is ever wasted. They seem not to notice us, hovering, averting our eyes, and they

seldom offer thanks, but what we do for them is never wasted.
Garrison Keillor

If you bungle raising your children, I don't think whatever else you do well matters very much.
Jacqueline Kennedy

Our greatest obligation to our children is to prepare them to understand and to deal effectively with the world in which they will live and not with the world we have known or the world we would prefer to have.
Grayson Kirk

Children enjoy the present because they have neither a past nor a future.
Jean de La Bruyère

In the final analysis it is not what you do for your children but what you have taught them to do for themselves that will make them successful human beings.
Ann Landers

Only two kids enjoy high school. One is the captain of the football team. The other is his girlfriend.
Letter to Ann Landers

The secret of dealing successfully with a child is not to be its parent.
Mell Lazarus

Ask your child what he wants for dinner only if he's buying.
Fran Lebowitz

Remember that as a teenager you are in the last stage of your life when you will be happy to hear the phone is for you.
Fran Lebowitz

A child is a person who is going to carry on what you have started . . . the fate of humanity is in his hands.
Abraham Lincoln

It must be a hard life to be the child of a psychologist.
Tom Masson

But Jesus said, Suffer little children, and forbid them not, to come unto me: for of such is the kingdom of heaven.
Matthew 19:14

When their children fail to charm others, few parents can stay neutral.
Mignon McLaughlin

Childhood is the kingdom where no one dies.
Edna St. Vincent Millay

The first idea that the child must acquire is that of the difference between good and evil.
Maria Montessori

There's only one thing we can be sure of, and that is the love that we have for our children, for our families, for each other. The warmth of a small child's embrace, that is true. The memories we have of them, the joy that they bring, the wonder we see through their eyes, that fierce and boundless love we feel for them, a love that takes us out of ourselves and binds us to something larger, we know that's what matters. We know we're always doing right when we're taking care of them, when we're teaching them well, when we're showing acts of kindness. We don't go wrong when we do that.
Barack Obama

The best way to keep children at home is to make the home atmosphere pleasant, and let the air out of the tires.
Dorothy Parker

The elements of instruction should be presented to the mind in childhood, but not with any compulsion.
Plato

Children's children are the crown of old men; and the glory of children are their fathers.
Proverbs 17:6

Train up a child in the way he should go: and when he is old, he will not depart from it.
Proverbs 22:6

A child may have too much of his mother's blessing.
John Ray

The conscience of children is formed by the influences that surround them; their notions of good and evil are the result of the moral atmosphere they breathe.
John Paul Richter

The words that a father speaks to his children in the privacy of home are not heard by the world, but, as in whispering galleries, they are clearly heard at the end, and by posterity.
John Paul Richter

For unflagging interest and enjoyment, a household of children, if things go reasonably well, certainly makes all other forms of success and achievement lose their importance by comparison.
Theodore Roosevelt

The first thing a child should learn is how to endure. It is what he will have most need to know.
Jean-Jacques Rousseau

How pleasant it is for a father to sit at his child's board. It is like an aged man reclining under the shadow of an oak which he has planted.
Sir Walter Scott

A child hasn't a grown-up person's appetite for affection. A little of it goes a long way with them; and they like a good imitation of it better than the real thing, as every nurse knows.
George Bernard Shaw

I've learned that if you spread the peas out on your plate, it looks like you ate more.
6-year-old's discovery

I do not love him because he is good, but because he is my little child.
Rabindranath Tagore

If you wish to study men you must not neglect to mix with the society of children.
Jesse Torrey

Living with kids is like living with a bunch of drunks. You know you really have to be on your toes all the time. Things are falling over and breaking and spilling. If you live on the second story, you really have to keep the windows shut all the time.
Tom Waits

Children begin by loving their parents. After a time they judge them. Rarely, if ever, do they forgive them.
Oscar Wilde

I am convinced that, except in a few extraordinary cases, one form or another of an unhappy childhood is essential to the formation of exceptional gifts.
Thornton Wilder

CHOICE

There is no better measure of a person than what he does when he is absolutely free to choose.
Wilma Askinas

More errors arise from inhibited indecision than from impulsive behavior.
Morris Ernst

Very few live by choice. Every man is placed in his present condition by causes which acted without his foresight, and with which he did not always willingly cooperate; and therefore you will rarely meet one who does not think the lot of his neighbor better than his own.
Samuel Johnson

The measure of choosing well, is, whether a man likes and finds good in what he has chosen.
Charles Lamb

Choose always the way that seems the best, however rough it may be; custom will soon render it easy and agreeable.
Pythagoras

You seldom get what you go after unless you know in advance what you want. Indecision has often given an advantage to the other fellow because he did his thinking beforehand.
Maurice Switzer

My own view of history is that human beings do have genuine freedom to make choices. Our destiny is not predetermined for us; we determine it for ourselves.
Arnold Toynbee

Between two evils I always pick the one I never tried before.
Mae West

The more decisions that you are forced to make alone, the more you are aware of your freedom to choose.
Thornton Wilder

CIVILIZATION

Civilization is the lamb's skin in which barbarism masquerades.
Thomas Bailey Aldrich

For 25 centuries Western knowledge has tried to look upon the world. It has failed to understand that the world is not for beholding. It is for hearing. It is not legible, but audible.
Jacques Attali

The origin of civilization is man's determination to do nothing for himself which he can get done for him.
H.C. Bailey

We are no longer in a state of growth; we are in a state of excess. We are living in a society of excrescence.
Jean Baudrillard

In the whole history of law and order the longest step forward was taken by primitive man when, as if by common consent, the tribe sat down in a circle and allowed only one man to speak at a time.
Curtis Bok

We used to build civilizations. Now we build shopping malls.
Bill Bryson

Look back along the endless corridors of time and you will see that four things have built civilization: the spirit of religion, the spirit of creative art, the spirit of research and the spirit of business enterprise.
Neil Carothers

There is nothing more fragile than civilization.
Havelock Ellis

The true test of civilization is, not the census nor the size of cities, nor the crops—no, but the kind of man the country turns out.
Ralph Waldo Emerson

Man was not intended by nature to live in communities and be civilized.
Epicurus

What men call civilization is the condition of present customs; what they call barbarism, the condition of past ones.
Anatole France

A civilized society is one which tolerates eccentricity to the point of doubtful sanity.
Robert Frost

On New York subways in the 1980s:
Riding on the IRT is usually a matter of serving time in one of the city's most squalid environments—noisy, smelly, crowded and overrun with a ceaseless supply of graffiti.
Paul Goldberger

New York is a granite beehive, where people jostle and whir like molecules in an overheated jar.
Nigel Goslin

Every civilization when it loses its inner vision and its cleaner energy, falls into a new sort of sordidness; more vast and more stupendous than the old savage sort. An Augean stable of metallic filth.
D.H. Lawrence

Towns are full of people, houses full of tenants, hotels full of guests, trains full of travelers, cafes full of customers, parks full of promenaders, consulting-rooms of famous doctors full of patients, theaters full of spectators and beaches full of bathers. What previously was, in general, no problem, now begins to be an everyday one, namely, to find room.
José Ortega y Gasset

You can't say that civilization don't advance, for in every war they kill you a new way.
Will Rogers

In antiquity there was only silence. In the 19th century, with the invention of the machine, Noise was born. Today, Noise triumphs and reigns supreme over the sensibility of men.
Luigi Russolo

Unless man has the wit and the grit to build his civilization on something better than material power, it is surely idle to talk of plans for a stable peace.
Francis B. Sayre

If we are to preserve civilization, we must first remain civilized.
Louis St. Laurent

The central question is whether the wonderfully diverse and gifted assemblage of human beings on this earth really knows how to run a civilization.
Adlai Stevenson

In a living civilization there is always an element of unrest, for sensitiveness to ideas means curiosity, adventure, change. Civilized order survives on its merits and is transformed by its power of recognizing its imperfections.
Alfred North Whitehead

There are some circles in America where it seems to be more socially acceptable to carry a handgun than a packet of cigarettes.
Katharine Whitehorn

CLASS

Snobs talk as if they had begotten their own ancestors.
Herbert Agar

No state will be well administered unless the middle class holds sway.
Aristotle

Aristocrats: Fellows that wear downy hats and clean shirts—guilty of education and suspected of bank accounts.
Ambrose Bierce

The true policy of a government is to make use of an aristocracy, but under the forms and in the spirit of democracy.
Napoleon Bonaparte

When the interval between the intellectual classes and the practical classes is too great, the former will possess no influence, the latter will reap no benefit.
Henry Thomas Buckle

Every attempt, by whatever authority, to fix a maximum of productive labor by a given worker in a given time is an unjust restriction upon his freedom and a limitation of his right to make the most of himself in order that he may rise in the scale of the social and economic order in which he lives. The notion that all human beings born into this world enter at birth into a definite social and economic classification, in which classification they must remain permanently through life, is wholly false and fatal to a progressive civilization.
Dr. Nicholas Murray Butler

Just because I have made a point of never losing my accent it doesn't mean I'm an eel-and-pie yob.
Michael Caine

The aristocracy of feudal parchment has passed away with a mighty rushing, and now, by a natural course, we arrive at aristocracy of the money-bag.
Thomas Carlyle

Aristocracy is an atmosphere; it is sometimes a healthy atmosphere; but it is very hard to say when it becomes an unhealthy atmosphere. You can prove that a man is not the son of a king, or that he is not the delegate of a definite number of people. But you cannot prove that a man is not a gentleman.
G.K. Chesterton

Aristocracy: What is left over from rich ancestors after the money is gone.
John Ciardi

M is for Marx
And movement of Masses
And massing of Arses
And clashing of classes.
Cyril Connolly

Aristocracy: A combination of many powerful men, for the purpose of maintaining their own particular interests. It is consequently a concentration of all the most effective parts of a community for a given end, hence its energy, efficiency and success.
James Fenimore Cooper

Errors look so very ugly in persons of small means—one feels they are taking quite a liberty in going astray; whereas people of fortune may naturally indulge in a few delinquencies.
George Eliot

English history is aristocracy with the doors open. Who has courage and faculty, let him come in.
Ralph Waldo Emerson

An intelligent class can scarce ever be, as a class, vicious, and never, as a class, indolent. The excited mental activity operates as a counterpoise to the stimulus of sense and appetite.
Edward Everett

Which class is happiest, the rich, the middle class or the poor? A very successful executive of a large

organization touches upon this vital subject in a long letter to all his salesmen. He uses as his text a passage from *Robinson Crusoe* which included this: "My Father bid me observe it, and I should always find that the calamities of life were shared among the upper and lower part of mankind; but that the middle station had the fewest disasters, and were not exposed to so many vicissitudes as the higher or lower part of mankind."
B.C. Forbes

I distrust great men. . . . I believe in aristocracy, though. Its members are to be found in all nations and classes, and all through the ages, and there is a secret understanding between them when they meet. . . . They are sensitive for others as well as for themselves, they are considerate without being fussy, their pluck is not swankiness but the power to endure and they can take a joke.
E.M. Forster

Americans are the only people in the world known to me whose status anxiety prompts them to advertise their college and university affiliations in the rear window of their automobiles.
Paul Fussell

A sort of moral blackmail is exerted from both poles. The underclass, one gathers, should be dulled with charity and welfare provision lest it turn nasty. The upper class must likewise be conciliated by vast handouts, lest it lose the "incentive" to go on generating wealth.
Christopher Hitchens

There is a natural aristocracy among men. The grounds of this are virtue and talent.
Thomas Jefferson

I believe it to be most true that it seldom happens that men rise from low condition to high rank without employing either force or fraud.
Niccolò Machiavelli

Of all the hokum with which this country [America] is riddled, the most odd is the common notion that it is free of class distinctions.
Somerset Maugham

In America we have an upper crust and a lower crust, but it's what's between—the middle class—that gives the real flavor.
Virginia L. McCleary

There is one thing to be said for country clubs; they drain off a lot of people you wouldn't want to associate with anyway.
Joseph Prescott

There is something to be said for government by a great aristocracy which has furnished leaders for the nation in peace and war for generations; even a democrat like myself must admit this.
Theodore Roosevelt

A status symbol is an instrument you clash when you want someone to know you are there.
William Sansom

Wearing overalls on weekdays, painting somebody else's house to earn money? You're working class. Wearing overalls on weekends, painting your own house to save money? You're middle class.
Lawrence Sutton

The blunting effects of slavery upon the slaveholder's moral perceptions are known and conceded the world over; and a privileged class, an aristocracy, is but a band of slaveholders under another name.
Mark Twain

COMPETITION

There is a tendency among some businesses to criticize and belittle their competitors. This is a bad procedure. Praise them. Learn from them. There are times when you can co-operate with them to their advantage and to yours! Speak well of them and they will speak well of you. You can't destroy good ideas. Take advantage of them.
George Matthew Adams

Does anyone believe for one moment that the progress we have made would have been possible under bureaucratic control of any government. This country was founded upon the principle of the regulation of private effort, of making rules for the game, and under that system alone can we look for the same success in the future which has been ours in the past. Our position today is the direct result of the free play among our people of private competitive effort.
Roger Babson

By competition the total amount of supply is increased, and by increase of the supply a competition in the sale ensues, and this enables the consumer to buy at lower rates. Of all human powers operating on the affairs of mankind, none is greater than that of competition.
Henry Clay

No amount of artificial protection can permanently maintain an obsolete product, an inferior process or a moribund organization against competitors which are based on scientifically improved products or methods.
Karl T. Compton

A man comes to measure his greatness by the regrets, envies and hatreds of his competitors.
Ralph Waldo Emerson

We find the instinct to shut out competition deep-rooted even among banks and corporations, among corner grocers and haberdasheries, among peanut vendors and shoeshine boys—and even among young ladies in search of a husband.
James A. Farley

Competition is the keen cutting edge of business, always shaving away at costs.
Henry Ford

Competition whose motive is merely to compete, to drive some other fellow out, never carries very far. The competitor to be feared is one who never bothers about you at all, but goes on making his own business better all the time. Businesses that grow by development and improvement do not die. But when a business ceases to be creative, when it believes it has reached perfection and needs to do nothing but produce—no improvement, no development—it is done.
Henry Ford

Without the spur of competition we'd loaf out our life.
Arnold Glasow

Don't knock your competitors. By boosting others you will boost yourself. A little competition is a good thing and severe competition is a blessing. Thank God for competition.
Jacob Kindleberger

In business, the competition will bite you if you keep running; if you stand still, they will swallow you.
Semon Knudsen

Today's competitiveness, so much imposed from without, is exhausting, not exhilarating; is unending—a part of one's social life, one's solitude, one's sleep, one's sleeplessness.
Louis Kronenberger

You cannot do away with the competitive system so long as trademarks remain to distinguish one product from another. You cannot cut out large-scale manufacture so long as there are established brands which breed consumer confidence and thus make mass production not only possible and profitable, but also economical.
Philip Salisbury

The idea of imposing restrictions on a free economy to assure freedom of competition is like breaking a man's leg to make him run faster.
Morris R. Sayre

Whenever I may be tempted to slack up and let the business run for awhile on its own impetus, I picture my competitor sitting at a desk in his opposition house, thinking and thinking with the most devilish intensity and clearness, and I ask myself what I can do to be prepared for his next brilliant move.
H. Gordon Selfridge

Competition, as the life of trade, surely is a tremendous spur to progress. Is it not the pursued man or business that advances through persistent effort to keep ahead? The constant striving to maintain leadership ever involves new ways and means of accomplishing more efficiently and thus it is the pursued is the progressive man. Put your pursuers on the pay roll.
W.D. Toland

CONFIDENCE

Confidence is the foundation for all business relations. The degree of confidence a man has in others, and the degree of confidence others have in

him, determines a man's standing in the commercial and industrial world.
William J.H. Boetcker

True prosperity is the result of well placed confidence in ourselves and our fellow man.
Benjamin Burt

Confidence is that feeling by which the mind embarks in great and honorable courses with a sure hope and trust in itself.
Cicero

Life is not easy for any of us. But what of that? We must have perseverance and, above all, confidence in ourselves. We must believe that we are gifted for something, and that this thing, at whatever cost, must be attained.
Marie Curie

It is not so much our friends' help that helps as the confidence of their help.
Epicurus

He can inspire a group only if he himself is filled with confidence and hope of success.
Floyd V. Filson

Skill and confidence are an unconquered army.
George Herbert

We should place confidence in our employee. Confidence is the foundation of friendship. If we give it, we will receive it. Any person in a managerial position, from supervisor to president, who feels that his employee is basically not as good as he is and who suspects his employee is always trying to put something over on him, lacks the necessary qualities for human leadership—to say nothing of human friendship.
Harry E. Humphreys, Jr.

In returning and rest shall ye be saved; in quietness and in confidence shall be your strength.
Isaiah 30:15

I have seen boys on my baseball team go into slumps and never come out of them, and I have seen others snap right out and come back better than ever. I guess more players lick themselves than are ever licked by an opposing team. The first thing any man has to know is how to handle himself. Training counts. You can't win any game unless you are ready to win.
Connie Mack

Confidence is a plant of slow growth in an aged bosom.
William Pitt

Calm self-confidence is as far from conceit as the desire to earn a decent living is remote from greed.
Channing Pollock

To do anything in this world worth doing, we must not stand back shivering and thinking of the cold and danger, but jump in, and scramble through as well as we can.
Sydney Smith

Have confidence that if you have done a little thing well, you can do a bigger thing well, too.
Joseph Storey

Confidence is a thing not to be produced by compulsion. Men cannot be forced into trust.
Daniel Webster

CONSCIENCE

Conscience: A small, still voice that makes minority reports.
Franklin P. Adams

Everyone in daily life carries such a heavy, mixed burden on his own conscience that he is reluctant to penalize those who have been caught.
Brooks Atkinson

It is an accepted law of ethics that punishment in the Court of Conscience, unlike that in Courts of Law, lessens with each repeated and unrebuked offense.
Joseph S. Auerbach

A disciplined conscience is a man's best friend. It may not be his most amiable, but it is his most faithful monitor.
Henry Ward Beecher

Reason often makes mistakes, but conscience never does.
Josh Billings

Wisdom and beauty are the twin arches of that invisible bridge which leads from the individual conscience—ever rebellious against its destiny—to man's collective conscience, ever in search of general progress.
Jaime Torres Bodet

Guilt: the gift that keeps on giving.
Erma Bombeck

The world has achieved brilliance without conscience. Ours is a world of nuclear giants and ethical infants.
Omar N. Bradley

When it was seen that many of the wicked seemed quite untroubled by evil conscience . . . then the idea of future suffering was advanced.
Lewis Browne

A quiet conscience makes one so serene.
Lord Byron

A guilty conscience needs to confess. A work of art is a confession.
Albert Camus

It is far more important to me to preserve an unblemished conscience than to compass any object however great.
William Ellery Channing

He who sacrifices his conscience to ambition burns a picture to obtain the ashes.
Chinese proverb

Whatever is done without ostentation, and without the people being witnesses of it, is, in my opinion, most praiseworthy: not that the public eye should be entirely avoided, for good actions desire to be placed in the light; but notwithstanding this, the greatest theater for virtue is conscience.
Cicero

Our consciences are littered like an old attic with the junk of sheer conviction.
Wilfred Cross

The truth is not so much that man has conscience as that conscience has man.
Isaac Dorner

Solomon's Proverbs, I think, have omitted to say, that as the sore palate findeth grit, so an uneasy consciousness heareth innuendos.
George Eliot

A magazine editor recently asked me to sit down on my 40th birthday and write an article on the most important things I had learned in my first 40 years. I told him that the chief thing I had learned was that the copybook maxims are true, but that too many people forget this once they go out into the heat and hustle and bustle of the battle of life and only realize their truth once one foot is beginning to slip into the grave. The man who has

won millions at the cost of his conscience is a failure.
B.C. Forbes

A quiet conscience sleeps in thunder.
Thomas Fuller

A lot of people mistake a short memory for a clear conscience.
Doug Larson

Conscience admonishes as a friend before punishing us as a judge.
Stanislaus Leszcynski

If your conscience won't stop you, pray for cold feet.
Elmer G. Leterman

The Anglo-Saxon conscience doesn't keep you from doing what you shouldn't, it just keeps you from enjoying it.
Salvador de Madariaga y Rojo

Many people weigh the guilt they will feel against the pleasure of the forbidden action they want to take.
Peter McWilliams

Conscience is the inner voice that warns us that someone may be looking.
H.L. Mencken

Conscience is the voice of values long and deeply infused into one's sinew and blood.
Elliot Richardson

Whence do I get my rules of conduct? I find them in my heart. Whatever I feel to be good is good. Whatever I feel to be evil is evil. Conscience is the best of casuists.
Jean-Jacques Rousseau

It is truly enough said that a corporation has no conscience; but a corporation of

conscientious men is a corporation with a conscience.
Henry David Thoreau

The foundation of the true joy is in the conscience.
Seneca

Fear is the tax that conscience pays to guilt.
George Sewell

Whoever attempts to suppress liberty of conscience finishes some day by wishing for the Inquisition.
Jules Simon

There is no witness so terrible—no accuser so powerful as conscience which dwells within us.
Sophocles

Conscience is God's presence in Man.
Emanuel Swedenborg

There is a difference between him who does no misdeeds because of his own conscience and him who is kept from wrongdoing because of the presence of others.
The Talmud

Labor to keep alive that little spark of celestial fire, called conscience.
George Washington

If a dog will not come to you after he has looked you in the face, you ought to go home and examine your conscience.
Woodrow Wilson

CONTENTMENT

If a man has come to that point where he is so content that he says; I do not want to know any more, or do any more or

be any more, he is in a state in which he ought to be changed into a mummy.
Henry Ward Beecher

Contentment is not happiness. An oyster may be contented.
Christian Bovée

One who is contented with what he has done will never become famous for what he will do. He has laid down to die, and the grass is already growing over him.
Christian Bovée

I am content with what I have, little be it, or much.
John Bunyan

It is not being out at heels that makes a man discontented, it is being out at heart. To be contented is to be good friends with yourself.
Bliss Carman

Intelligent discontent is the mainspring of civilization.
Eugene V. Debs

All our discontents spring from the want of thankfulness for what we have.
Daniel Defoe

A man who is contented with what he has done will never become famous for what he will do.
Fred Estabrook

Contentment gives a crown where fortune hath denied it.
John Ford

Content makes poor men rich; discontent makes rich men poor.
Benjamin Franklin

Let thy discontents be thy secrets; if the world knows them 'twill despise thee and increase them.
Benjamin Franklin

Who is rich? He that is content. Who is that? Nobody.
Benjamin Franklin

Contentment does not consist in heaping up more fuel, but in taking away some fire.
Thomas Fuller

Nine requisites for contented living:
Health enough to make work a pleasure. Wealth enough to support your needs. Strength to battle with difficulties and overcome them. Grace enough to confess your sins and forsake them. Patience enough to toil until some good is accomplished. Charity enough to see some good in your neighbor. Love enough to move you to be useful and helpful to others. Faith enough to make real the things of God. Hope enough to remove all anxious fears concerning the future.
Johann Wolfgang von Goethe

There are two kinds of discontent in this world; the discontent that works, and the discontent that wrings its hands. The first gets what it wants, and the second loses what it has. There's no cure for the first but success; and there's no cure at all for the second.
Gordon Graham

All the discontented people I know are trying to be something they are not, to do something they cannot do.
David Grayson

Moral stimulation is good but moral complacency is the most dangerous habit of mind we can develop, and that danger is serious and ever-present.
Joseph C. Grew

It is much easier in many ways for me— and for other Presidents, I think, who felt the same way—when Congress is not in town.
John F. Kennedy

We shall be made truly wise if we be made content; content, too, not only with what we can understand, but content with what we do not understand—the habit of mind which theologians call, and rightly, faith in God.
Charles Kingsley

When we cannot find contentment in ourselves, it is useless to seek it elsewhere.
François de La Rochefoucauld

It is right to be contented with what we have, never with what we are.
James Mackintosh

Think of what would happen to us in America if there were no humorists; life would be one long Congressional Record.
Tom Masson

Contentment preserves one from catching cold.
Has a woman who knew that she was well dressed ever caught a cold? No, not even when she had scarcely a rag on her back.
Friedrich Wilhelm Nietzsche

In a body [like Congress] where there are more than one hundred talking lawyers, you can make no calculation upon the termination of any debate, and frequently the more trifling the subject the more animated and protracted the discussion.
Franklin Pierce

If you are content, you have enough to live comfortably.
Plautus

The great menace to the life of an industry is industrial self-complacency.
David Sarnoff

If the principles of contentment are not within us, the height of station and worldly grandeur will as soon add a cubit to a man's stature as to his happiness.
Laurence Sterne

When a man is discontented with himself, it has one advantage . . . that it puts him into an excellent frame of mind for making a bargain.
Laurence Sterne

Complacency is the enemy of progress.
Dave Stutman

COURAGE

Courage and perseverance have a magical talisman, before which difficulties disappear and obstacles vanish into air.
John Quincy Adams

Courage that grows from constitution often forsakes a man when he has occasion for it; courage which arises from a sense of duty acts in a uniform manner.
Joseph Addison

It is easy to be brave from a safe distance.
Aesop

Often the test of courage is not to die but to live.
Vittorio Alfieri

Until the day of his death, no man can be sure of his courage.
Jean Anouilh

Courage: The lovely virtue—the rib of Himself that God sent down to His children.
J.M. Barrie

Courage is a special kind of knowledge: the knowledge of how to fear what ought to be feared and how not to fear what ought not to be feared.
David Ben-Gurion

Courage is like love; it must have hope for nourishment.
Napoleon Bonaparte

The paradox of courage is that a man must be a little careless of his life even in order to keep it.
G.K. Chesterton

Courage is rightly esteemed the first of human qualities because it's the quality which guarantees all others.
Winston Churchill

Courage is what it takes to stand up and speak; courage is also what it takes to sit down and listen.
Winston Churchill

Physical courage, which despises all danger, will make a man brave in one way; and moral courage, which despises all opinion, will make a man brave in another.
Charles Caleb Colton

In his last public message: Every man of courage is a man of his word.
Pierre Corneille

Nothing gives a fearful man more courage than another's fear.
Umberto Eco

My message to you is: Be courageous! I have lived a long time. I have seen history repeat itself again and again. I have seen many depressions in business. Always America has come out stronger and more prosperous. Be as brave as your fathers before you. Have faith! Go forward.
Thomas A. Edison

A great part of courage is having done the thing before.
Ralph Waldo Emerson

Courage consists in equality to the problem before us.
Ralph Waldo Emerson

Whatever you do, you need courage. Whatever course you decide upon, there is always someone to tell you you are wrong. There are always difficulties arising which tempt you to believe that your critics are right. To map out a course of action and follow it to an end, requires some of the same courage which a soldier needs. Peace has its victories, but it takes brave men to win them.
Ralph Waldo Emerson

And have you not received faculties which will enable you to bear all that happens to you? Have you not received greatness of spirit? Have you not received courage? Have you not received endurance?
Epictetus

Anger is a prelude to courage.
Eric Hoffer

Nothing is too high for the daring of mortals; we storm heaven itself in our folly.
Horace

The first step in handling anything is gaining the ability to face it.
L. Ron Hubbard

Courage without conscience is a wild beast.
Ralph Ingersoll

It is better to be a coward for a minute than dead for the rest of your life.
Irish proverb

One man with courage makes a majority.
Andrew Jackson

Timid men prefer the calm of despotism to the boisterous sea of liberty.
Thomas Jefferson

Courage is a quality so necessary for maintaining virtue that it is always respected, even when it is associated with vice.
Samuel Johnson

Only be thou strong and very courageous, that thou mayest observe to do according to all the law, which Moses my servant commanded thee: turn not from it to the right hand or to the left, that thou mayest prosper whithersoever thou goest.
Joshua 1:7

Have I not commanded thee? Be strong and of good courage; be not afraid, neither be thou dismayed: for the Lord thy God is with thee whithersoever thou goest.
Joshua 1:9

Hope awakens courage. He who can implant courage in the human soul is the best physician.
Karl Ludwig von Knebel

Hidden valor is as bad as cowardice.
Latin proverb

The only security is courage.
François de La Rochefoucauld

Courage is not simply one of the virtues, but the form of every virtue at the testing point.
C.S. Lewis

Pugnacity is a form of courage, but a very bad form.
Sinclair Lewis

It's easy to be courageous when you have no choice.
Michael Maggio

Courage is the most common and vulgar of the virtues.
Herman Melville

The strongest, most generous and proudest of all virtues is courage.
Michel de Montaigne

Life shrinks or expands in proportion to one's courage.
Anaïs Nin

Courage conquers all things.
Ovid

Courage in danger is half the battle.
Plautus

Courage is a cold Bombay martini.
Eno Putain

Don't foul, don't flinch—hit the line hard.
Theodore Roosevelt

Far better it is to dare mighty things, to win glorious triumphs, even though checkered by failure, than to take rank with those poor spirits who neither enjoy much nor suffer much, because they live in the gray twilight that knows not victory nor defeat.
Theodore Roosevelt

Personal courage is really a very subordinate virtue—a virtue, indeed, in which we are surpassed by the lower animals; or else you would not hear people say, as brave as a lion.
Arthur Schopenhauer

The will to do, the soul to dare.
Sir Walter Scott

There is nothing in the world so much admired as a man who knows how to bear unhappiness with courage.
Seneca

The most sublime courage I have ever witnessed has been among that class too poor to know they possessed it, and too humble for the world to discover it.
George Bernard Shaw

I would define true courage to be a perfect sensibility of the measure of danger, and a mental willingness to endure it.
William Tecumseh Sherman

The test of tolerance comes when we are in a majority; the test of courage comes when we are in a minority.
Ralph W. Sockman, D.D.

Let the man who has to make his fortune in life remember this maxim: Attacking is the only secret. Dare and the world always yields; or if it beats you sometimes, dare it again and it will succumb.
William Makepeace Thackeray

Success is never final and failure never fatal. It's courage that counts.
George F. Tilton

Courage is resistance to fear, mastery of fear—not absence of fear. Except a creature be part coward it is not a compliment to say it is brave; it is merely a loose missapplication of the word.
Mark Twain

It is curious that physical courage should be so common in the world, and moral courage so rare.
Mark Twain

True courage is not the brutal force of vulgar heroes, but the firm resolve of virtue and reason.
Alfred North Whitehead

Only as a grand gesture of defeat will men creep into the arms of the state and seek refuge in its power rather than their own courage.
Henry M. Wriston

Why should we honor those that die upon the field of battle? A man may show as reckless a courage in entering into the abyss of himself.
William Butler Yeats

It takes vision and courage to create—it takes faith and courage to prove.
Owen D. Young

CRIME

On Bernie Madoff: To every con artist, he is the godfather, the don.
Anonymous prison inmate

Behind every great fortune there is a crime.
Honoré de Balzac

I ran the wrong kind of business, but I did it with integrity.
Sydney Biddle Barrows

The world of crime is a last refuge of the authentic, uncorrupted, spontaneous event.
Daniel Boorstin

What is robbing a bank compared with founding a bank?
Bertolt Brecht

Getting caught is the mother of invention.
Robert Byrne

The fear of burglars is not only the fear of being robbed, but also the fear of a sudden and unexpected clutch out of the darkness.
Elias Canetti

My rackets are run on strictly American lines and they're going to stay that way.
Al Capone

If crime fighters fight crime and fire fighters fight fire, what do freedom fighters fight?
George Carlin

Like art and politics, gangsterism is a very important avenue of assimilation into society.
E.L. Doctorow

I wouldn't be in a legitimate business for all the money in the world.
Anguilo Gennaro

Crime is naught but misdirected energy.
Emma Goldman

On eluding conviction after a mistrial: Why me? I am blessed. I can't complain. I am walking out the door. I am going to have a healthy and happy Christmas.
John Gotti, Jr.

After all, crime is only a left-handed form of human endeavor.
John Huston

Obviously crime pays, or there'd be no crime.
G. Gordon Liddy

I believe that people would be alive today if there were a death penalty.
Nancy Reagan

It is a rather pleasant experience to be alone in a bank at night.
Willie Sutton

Society often forgives the criminal; it never forgives the dreamer.
Oscar Wilde

The truth of the matter is that muggers are very interesting people.
Michael Winner

CRITICISM

It is ridiculous for any man to criticize the works of another who has not distinguished himself by his own performance.
Joseph Addison

Before you criticize someone, walk a mile in his shoes. Then when you do criticize that person, you'll be a mile away and have his shoes!
Anonymous

You cannot raise a man up by calling him down.
William J.H. Boetcker

A critic is a man who prefers the indolence of opinion to the trials of action.
John Mason Brown

Any fool can criticize, condemn and complain—and most fools do.
Dale Carnegie

Censure is often useful, praise often deceitful.
Winston Churchill

I criticize by creation, not by finding fault.
Cicero

What the public criticizes in you, cultivate. It is you.
Jean Cocteau

The chronic knocker gets more discomfort from his continual criticism than do all of the people that he is raving against.
Charles J. Dennis

It is much easier to be critical than to be correct.
Benjamin Disraeli

Most of our censure of others is only oblique praise of self, uttered to show the wisdom and superiority of the speaker.
Tryon Edwards

As to people saying a few idle words about us, we must not mind that any more than the old church steeple minds the rooks cawing about it.
George Eliot

Criticism should not be querulous and wasting, all knife and rootpuller, but guiding, instructive, inspiring.
Ralph Waldo Emerson

We are told we should always speak well of the dead. But wouldn't that sometimes be hypocrisy? The writer did not hesitate to criticize [American Woolen Co. head] William M. Wood during his life and now feels that his tragic death, by suicide, contains a lesson for at least a few of America's large employers.

When infirmity overtook him, he [attempted] works of repentance, but it was too late. . . . The writer knows that too many men of vast affairs are blind to the realities, the worthwhile things of life, and do not acquire a correct perspective until they feel themselves slipping toward the grave.
B.C. Forbes

There are no exceptions to the rule that everybody likes to be an exception to the rule.
Malcolm Forbes

I like people to come back and tell me what I did wrong. That's the kindest thing you can do.
Lillian Gish

Many receive a criticism and think it is fine; think they got their money's worth; think well of the teacher for it, and then go on with their work just the same as

before. That is the reason much of the wisdom of Plato is still locked up in the pages of Plato.
Robert Henri

To avoid criticism do nothing, say nothing, be nothing.
Elbert Hubbard

It is harder to avoid censure than to gain applause, for this may be done by one great or wise action in an age; but to escape censure a man must pass his whole life without saying or doing one ill or foolish thing.
David Hume

A tart temper never mellows with age; and a sharp tongue is the only edged tool that grows keener with constant use.
Washington Irving

I find the pain of little censure, even when it is unfounded, is more acute than the pleasure of much praise.
Thomas Jefferson

Criticism is a study by which men grow important and formidable at very small expense.
Samuel Johnson

It behooves the minor critic, who hunts for blemishes, to be a little distrustful of his own sagacity.
Junius

The pleasure of criticism deprives us of that of being deeply moved by beautiful things.
Jean de La Bruyère

Some critics are like chimneysweepers; they put out the fire below, and frighten the swallows from their nests above; they scrape a long time in the chimney, cover themselves with soot, and bring nothing away but a bag of cinders, and then sing from the top of the house as if they had built it.
Henry Wadsworth Longfellow

I have never found, in a long experience of politics, that criticism is ever inhibited by ignorance.
Harold Macmillan

A bad review is even less important than whether it is raining in Patagonia.
Iris Murdoch

When men speak ill of thee, live so as nobody may believe them.
Plato

It is a thing of no great difficulty to raise objections against another man's oration—nay, it is very easy; but to produce a better in its place is a work extremely troublesome.
Plutarch

It is not the critic who counts, nor the man who points out how the strong man stumbles or where the doers of deeds could have done better.
Theodore Roosevelt

Stones and sticks are thrown only at fruit-bearing trees.
Sa'di

Show yourself more human than critical and your pleasure will increase.
Domenico Scarlatti

I have yet to find the man, however exalted his station, who did not do better work and put forth greater effort under a spirit of approval than under a spirit of criticism.
Charles Schwab

Pay no attention to what the critics say; there has never been a statue erected to a critic.
Jean Sibelius

He who would acquire fame must not show himself afraid of censure. The dread of censure is the death of genius.
William Simms

I know of no manner of speaking so offensive as that of giving praise, and closing it with an exception.
Richard Steele

Censure is the tax a man pays to the public for being eminent.
Jonathan Swift

I have ever held that the rod with which popular fancy invests criticism is properly the rod of divination: a hazel switch for the discovery of buried treasure, not a birch twig for the castigation of offenders.
Arthur Symons

You do not get a man's most effective criticism until you provoke him. Severe truth is expressed with some bitterness.
Henry David Thoreau

You do ill if you praise, but worse if you censure, when you do not rightly understand.
Leonardo da Vinci

Has anybody ever seen a dramatic critic in the daytime? Of course not. They come out after dark, up to no good.
P.G. Wodehouse

CULTURE

Every man's ability may be strengthened or increased by culture.
Sir John Joseph Caldwell Abbott

Culture, the acquainting ourselves with the best that has been known and said in the world.
Matthew Arnold

The acquiring of culture is the developing of an avid hunger for knowledge and beauty.
Jesse Lee Bennett

We are in the process of creating what deserves to be called the idiot culture. For the first time, the weird and the stupid and the coarse are becoming our cultural norm, even our cultural ideal.
Carl Bernstein

Without culture, and the relative freedom it implies, society, even when perfect, is but a jungle.
Albert Camus

The boundaries of culture and rainfall never follow survey lines.
J. Frank Dobie

The most distinctive mark of a cultured mind is the ability to take another's point of view; to put one's self in another's place, and see life and its problems from a point of view different from one's own. To be willing to test a new idea; to be able to live on the edge of difference in all matters intellectually; to examine without heat the burning question of the day; to have imaginative sympathy, openness and flexibility of mind, steadiness and poise of feeling, cool calmness of judgment, is to have culture.
Arthur H.R. Fairchild

As a student of American culture, I am willing to argue that the Twist is a valid manifestation of the Age of Anxiety.
Marshall Fishwick

For corporations to be bedfellows with the arts is good business for both. The architecture that houses a company is a more visible statement than the president's in the annual report. Ditto interiors, particularly of offices and sometimes, dramatically, in plants. For solvent

businesses, support of community cultural undertakings in music, drama, dance creates great goodwill. Also, the existence of such activities is often important to the executives and their families that companies want to keep or attract to keep.
Malcolm Forbes

I do not want my house to be walled in on all sides and my windows to be stuffed. I want the cultures of all lands to be blown about my house as freely as possible. But I refuse to be blown off my feet by any.
Mahatma Gandhi

We have ignored cultural literacy in thinking about education. We ignore the air we breathe until it is thin or foul. Cultural literacy is the oxygen of social intercourse.
E.D. Hirsch, Jr.

Culture is simply how one lives and is connected to history by habit.
LeRoi Jones (Amiri Baraka)

Culture is simply the hospitality of the intellect. Your mind is open to new ideas and larger views; when they enter, you know how to receive them, and to entertain, to be entertained, and take what they have to offer without allowing them to dominate you.
Thomas Kettle

Culture's worth huge, huge risks. Without culture we're all totalitarian beasts.
Norman Mailer

Culture is the sum of all the forms of art, of love and of thought, which, in the course of centuries, have enabled man to be less enslaved.
André Malraux

Culture is not just an ornament; it is the expression of a nation's character, and at the same time it is a powerful instrument to mould character. The end of culture is right living.
Somerset Maugham

Culture is half-way to heaven.
George Meredith

Culture is what your butcher would have if he were a surgeon.
Mary Pettibone Poole

The law of Raspberry Jam: The wider any culture is spread, the thinner it gets.
Alvin Toffler

What other culture could have produced someone like Hemingway and not seen the joke?
Gore Vidal

Culture is an instrument wielded by professors to manufacture professors, who when their turn comes will manufacture professors.
Simone Weil

D

DAY

A cloudy day, or a little sunshine, have as great an influence on many constitutions as the most real blessings or misfortunes.
Joseph Addison

In the morning let this thought be present: I am rising to a man's work.
Marcus Aurelius Antoninus

Live not one's life as though one had a thousand years, but live each day as the last.
Marcus Aurelius Antoninus

Goodnight stars
Goodnight air
Goodnight noises everywhere.
Margaret Wise Brown

The sun was like a great visiting presence that stimulated and took its due from all animal energy. When it flung wide its cloak and stepped down over the edge of the fields at evening, it left behind a spent and exhausted world.
Willa Cather

It was a Sunday afternoon, wet and cheerless; and a duller spectacle this earth of ours has not to show than a rainy Sunday in London.
Thomas De Quincey

One of the illusions of life is that the present hour is not the critical, decisive hour. Write it on your heart that every day is the best day of the year.
Ralph Waldo Emerson

To be seeing the world made new every morning, as if it were the morning of the first day, and then to make the most of it for the individual soul, as if it were the last day—is the daily curriculum of the mind's desire.
Dr. John H. Finley

Early rising maketh a man whole in body, wholer in soul and richer in goods.
John Fitzherbert

One ought at least to hear a little melody every day, read a fine poem, see a good picture, and, if possible make a few sensible remarks.
Johann Wolfgang von Goethe

Those that dare lose a day are dangerously prodigal; those that dare misspend it, desperate.
Bishop Joseph Hall

The dullest observer must be sensible of the order and serenity prevalent in those households where the occasional exercise of a beautiful form of worship in the morning gives, as it were, the keynote to every temper for the day, and attunes every spirit to harmony.
Washington Irving

The happiest part of a man's life is that which he passes lying awake in bed in the morning.
Samuel Johnson

Thou shalt ever joy at eventide if thou spend the day fruitfully.
Thomas à Kempis

It was such a lovely day I thought it was a pity to get up.
Somerset Maugham

The clean tongue, the clear head, and the bright eye are birthrights of each day.
Dr. William Osler

The feeling of Sunday is the same everywhere, heavy, melancholy, standing still. Like when they say, "As it was in the beginning, is now, and ever shall be, world without end."
Jean Rhys

The trouble with dawn is that it comes too early in the day.
Susan Richman

Sunday is the day people go quietly mad, one way or another.
William Saroyan

Each day is a little life: every waking and rising a little birth, every fresh morning a

little youth, every going to rest and sleep a little death.
Arthur Schopenhauer

One should count each day a separate life.
Seneca

The day of the sun is like the day of a king. It is a promenade in the morning, a sitting on the throne at noon, a pageant in the evening.
Wallace Stevens

One golden day redeems a weary year.
Celia Thaxter

Only that day dawns to which we are awake.
Henry David Thoreau

When you say good morning to the rabbi, say good morning also to the rabbi's wife.
Yiddish proverb

DEATH

I've done made a deal with the devil. He said he's going to give me an air-conditioned place when I go down there, if I go there, so I won't put all the fires out.
Red Adair

Dying is one of the few things that can be done as easily lying down.
Woody Allen

Death is the sound of distant thunder at a picnic.
W.H. Auden

As for death, one gets used to it, even if it is only other people's death you get used to.
Enid Bagnold

We usually meet all of our relatives only at funerals where somebody always

observes: "Too bad we can't get together more often."
Bernard Berenson

The fence around a cemetery is foolish, for those inside can't come out and those outside don't want to get in.
Arthur Brisbane

One realization does dawn upon the death of the second parent, namely that you've now moved into the green room to the River Styx. You're next.
Christopher Buckley

To live in hearts we leave behind is not to die.
Claude Campbell

I knew a man who gave up smoking, drinking, sex and rich food. He was healthy right up to the time he killed himself.
Johnny Carson

No one could ever meet death for his country without the hope of immortality.
Cicero

I never wanted to see anybody die, but there are a few obituary notices I have read with pleasure.
Clarence Darrow

Worldly faces never look so worldly as at a funeral.
George Eliot

True, you can't take it with you, but then, that's not the place where it comes in handy.
Brendan Francis

One must wait until the evening to see how splendid the day was; one cannot judge life until death.
Charles de Gaulle

The graveyards are full of indispensable men.
Charles de Gaulle

Death is the most convenient time to tax rich people.
David Lloyd George

We have long had death and taxes as the two standards of inevitability. But there are those who believe that death is the preferable of the two.
Erwin N. Griswold

Death is the penalty we all pay for the privilege of life.
Robert Half

Once you're dead, you're made for life.
Jimi Hendrix

But there the glorious Lord will be unto us a place of broad rivers and streams; wherein shall go no galley with oars, neither shall gallant ship pass thereby.
Isaiah 33:21

I hope and trust to meet you in Heaven, both white and black—both white and black.
Andrew Jackson

Only death reveals what a nothing the body of man is.
Juvenal

They say such nice things about people at their funerals that it makes me sad to realize that I'm going to miss mine by just a few days.
Garrison Keillor

I never go to funerals. To me a person is dead when he breathes for the last time. After that, your memories should be personal.
Hedy Lamarr

To judge of the real importance of the individual, we should think of the effect his death would produce.
Françoise Gaston de Lévis

If they do kill me, I shall never die another death.
Abraham Lincoln

Only those are fit to live who are not afraid to die.
Douglas MacArthur

A woman has a much better chance than a man of acquittal on a murder charge. Of course, if she happens to be a blonde, her chances rise about 45%.
Dr. John McGeorge

Public display of mourning is no longer made by people of fashion, although some flashier kinds of widows may insist on sleeping with only black men during the first year after the death.
P.J. O'Rourke

The days of our years are threescore years and ten; and if by reason of strength they be fourscore years, yet is their strength labor and sorrow; for it is soon cut off, and we fly away.
Psalms 90:10

There's no reason to be the richest man in the cemetery. You can't do any business from there.
Colonel Sanders

We can't always have things to please us, Little Johnny has gone to Jesus.
Southern cemetery epitaph

If this is dying, then I don't think much of it.
Lytton Strachey

When it's time to die, let us not discover that we have never lived.
Henry David Thoreau

All say, "How hard it is we have to die"—a strange complaint to come from the mouths of people who have had to live.
Mark Twain

I did not attend his funeral, but I wrote a nice letter saying I approved it.
Mark Twain

Let us endeavor so to live that when we come to die even the undertaker will be sorry.
Mark Twain

Whoever has lived long enough to find out what life is, knows how deep a debt of gratitude we owe to Adam, the first great benefactor of our race. He brought death into the world.
Mark Twain

They are all gone into the world of light, And I alone sit lingering there.
Henry Vaughan

Dying is the most embarrassing thing that can ever happen to you, because someone's got to take care of all your details.
Andy Warhol

If we take eternity to mean not infinite temporal duration but timelessness, then eternal life belongs to those who live in the present.
Ludwig Wittgenstein

Better a noble death than a wretched life.
Yiddish proverb

Death, the terror of the rich, the desire of the poor.
Joseph Zabara

DEBT

An economist on Americans' recent increase in credit card spending: It's unsustainable. At some point when the bills come due, I expect that we will see a very sharp retrenchment in consumer spending, and that could put the recovery in jeopardy.
Bernard Baumohl

It is very iniquitous to make me pay debts, you have no idea, of the pain it gives one.
Lord Byron

There are but two ways of paying debt—increase of industry in raising income, increase of thrift in laying out.
Thomas Carlyle

Owing money has never concerned me so long as I know where it could be repaid.
Col. Henry Crown

Debt is a prolific mother of folly and of crime.
Benjamin Disraeli

Debt is the worst poverty.
Thomas Fuller

Pay all your debts so you can sleep at night.
Guilford Glazer

Let us live is as small a circle as we will, we are either debtors or creditors before we have had time to look around.
Johann Wolfgang von Goethe

The American way is the way most law-abiding, tax-paying Americans live—in debt. Does this make a balanced budget un-American?
Cullen Hightower

Blessed are the young, for they shall inherit the national debt.
Herbert Hoover

A creditor is worse than a slave-owner; for the master owns only your person, but a creditor owns your dignity, and can command it.
Victor Hugo

To preserve their independence, we must not let our rules load us with perpetual debt. We must make our election between economy and liberty, or profusion and servitude.
Thomas Jefferson

Debt is the secret foe of thrift, as vice and idleness are its open foes. The debt-habit is the twin brother of poverty.
Theodore Munger

I feel these days like a very large flamingo. No matter what way I turn, there is always a very large bill.
Joseph O'Connor

Good times are when people make debts to pay in bad times.
Robert Quillen

Debt is the slavery of the free.
Publilius Syrus

If you want the time to pass quickly, just give a banker your note for 90 days.
R.B. Thomas

I had plastic surgery last week. I cut up my credit cards.
Henny Youngman

DECEPTION

The easiest person to deceive is oneself.
Edward Bulwer-Lytton

Beware lest any man spoil you through philosophy and vain deceit, after the tradition of men, after the rudiments of the world, and not after Christ.
Colossians 2:8

Deceivers are the most dangerous members of society. They trifle with the best affections of our nature, and violate the most sacred obligations.
George Crabbe

The easiest thing of all is to deceive one's self; for what a man wishes he generally believes to be true.
Demosthenes

Every man takes care that his neighbor shall not cheat him. But a day comes when he begins to care that he does not cheat his neighbor. Then all goes well.
Ralph Waldo Emerson

Better to be occasionally cheated than perpetually suspicious.
B.C. Forbes

It is in the ability to deceive oneself that the greatest talent is shown.
Anatole France

Cheat me in the price, but not in the goods.
Thomas Fuller

Cynicism is cheap—you can buy it at any Monoprix store—it's built into all poor-quality goods.
Graham Greene

No man was ever so much deceived by another, as by himself.
Lord Greville

A cynic is not merely one who reads bitter lessons from the past; he is one who is prematurely disappointed in the future.
Sydney Harris

The natural man has a difficult time getting along in the world. Half the people think he is a scoundrel because he is not a hypocrite.
Edgar Watson Howe

It is more shameful to distrust your friends than it is to be deceived by them.
François de La Rochefoucauld

We often shed tears that deceive ourselves after deceiving others.
François de La Rochefoucauld

You are never so easily fooled as when trying to fool someone else.
François de La Rochefoucauld

Half the people in America are faking it.
Robert Mitchum

It is very noble hypocrisy not to talk of one's self.
Friedrich Wilhelm Nietzsche

They speak vanity every one with his neighbor: with flattering lips and with a double heart do they speak. The Lord shall cut off all flattering lips, and the tongue that speaketh proud things: Who have said, With our tongue will we prevail; our lips are our own: who is lord over us?
Psalms 12:2–4

When there are two conflicting versions of a story, the wise course is to believe the one in which people appear at their worst.
H. Allen Smith

No matter how cynical you get, it is impossible to keep up.
Lily Tomlin

I hope you have not been leading a double life, pretending to be wicked, and being really good all the time. That would be hypocrisy.
Oscar Wilde

DECISIONS

The rarest gift that God bestows on man is the capacity for decision.
Dean Acheson

When a man takes the road to destruction, the gods help him along.
Aeschylus

He used to be fairly indecisive, but now he's not so certain.
Peter Alliss

The man who insists upon seeing with perfect clearness before he decides, never decides. Accept life, and you cannot accept regret.
Henri Frédéric Amiel

The man who insists upon seeing with perfect clearness before he decides, never decides. Accept life, and you cannot accept regret.
Henri Frédéric Amiel

A wise person decides slowly but abides by these decisions.
Arthur Ashe

A monologue is not a decision.
Clement R. Attlee

He has conferred on the practice of vacillation the aura of statesmanship.
Kenneth Baker

When you come to a fork in the road—take it.
Yogi Berra

It is the characteristic excellence of the strong man that he can bring momentous issues to the fore and make a decision about them. The weak are always forced

to decide between alternatives they have not chosen themselves.
Dietrich Bonhoeffer

When you approach a problem, strip yourself of preconceived opinions and prejudice, assemble and learn the facts of the situation, make the decision which seems to you to be the most honest, and then stick to it.
Chester Bowles

Indecision may or may not be my problem.
Jimmy Buffett

Nothing can be more destructive to vigor of action than protracted, anxious fluctuation, through resolutions adopted, rejected, resumed, and suspended, and nothing causes a greater expense of feeling. A man without decision can never be said to belong to himself; he is as a wave of the sea, or a feather in the air which every breeze blows about as it listeth.
John Foster Dulles

When it is not necessary to make a decision, it is necessary not to make a decision.
Lord Falkland

In many lines of work, it isn't how much you do that counts, but how much you do well and how often you decide right.
William Feather

I have to be wrong a certain number of times in order to be right a certain number of times. However, in order to be either, I must first make a decision.
Frank N. Giampietro

When possible make the decisions now, even if action is in the future. A reviewed decision usually is better than one reached at the last moment.
William B. Given, Jr.

Decision is a sharp knife that cuts clean and straight; indecision, a dull one that hacks and tears and leaves ragged edges behind it.
Gordon Graham

There is nothing more to be esteemed than a manly firmness and decision of character. I like a person who knows his own mind and sticks to it; who sees at once what, in given circumstances, is to be done, and does it.
William Hazlitt

Deliberate with caution, but act with decision; and yield with graciousness or oppose with firmness.
Charles Hole

A weak man has doubts before a decision, a strong man has them afterwards.
Karl Kraus

The truth is that many people set rules to keep from making decisions.
Mike Krzyzewski

Once I make up my mind, I'm full of indecision.
Oscar Levant

When, against one's will, one is high pressured into making a hurried decision, the best answer is always No, because No is more easily changed to Yes, than Yes is changed to No.
Charles E. Nielson

The man who is denied the opportunity of taking decisions of importance begins to regard as important the decisions he is allowed to take.
C. Northcote Parkinson

An executive is a man who decides; sometimes he decides right, but always he decides.
John Henry Patterson

You can't make someone else's choices. You shouldn't let someone else make yours.
Colin Powell

Style is the principle of decision in a work of art.
Susan Sontag

Quick decisions are unsafe decisions.
Sophocles

The first step to getting the things you want out of life is this: Decide what you want.
Ben Stein

I've made up my mind both ways.
Casey Stengel

Decision is a risk rooted in the courage of being free.
Paul Tillich

When people ask for time, it's always for time to say no. Yes has one more letter in it, but it doesn't take half as long to say.
Edith Wharton

DEMOCRACY

I've never known a country to be starved into democracy.
George D. Aiken

Lincoln's reference to government of the people, by the people, for the people is a generally satisfactory definition of democracy. I say generally because when it comes to fair and workable details, democracy fails to completely meet the criteria enunciated by Lincoln by a rather wide margin.
George D. Aiken

If liberty and equality are chiefly to be found in democracy, they will be best attained when all persons alike share in government to the utmost.
Aristotle

An informed people is one of the best guarantees of a continuing democracy.
Harry F. Banks

A man is judged by the company he keeps, and a company is judged by the men it keeps, and the people of Democratic nations are judged by the type and caliber of officers they elect.
William J.H. Boetcker

We cannot possibly reconcile the principle of democracy, which means co-operation, with the principle of governmental omniscience under which everyone waits for an order before doing anything. That way lies loss of freedom, and dictatorship.
Lewis H. Brown

Democracy is something we must always be working at. It is a process never finished, never ending. And each new height gained opens broader vistas for the future. Thus it has been as one looks back over the sweep of history; thus it must continue to be if democracy is to continue as a working tool in the hands of free men.
Edmund De S. Brunner

Democracy is being allowed to vote for the candidate you dislike least.
Robert Byrne

Democracy, as I understand it, requires me to sacrifice myself for the masses, not to them. Who knows not that if you

would save the people, you must often oppose them?
John C. Calhoun

Democratic living is not a station at which people arrive; it is a method of traveling.
Clyde Campbell

All real democracy is an attempt like that of a jolly hostess to bring the shy people out.
G.K. Chesterton

It has been said that democracy is the worst form of government except all those other forms that have been tried from time to time.
Winston Churchill

The chief support of an autocracy is a standing army. The chief support of a democracy is an educated people.
Lotus D. Coffman

No democratic world will work as it should work until we recognize that we can only enjoy any right so long as we are prepared to discharge its equivalent duty. This applies just as much to states in their dealing with one another as to individuals within the states.
Anthony Eden

Democracy is a way of life. Democracy is sincerity, friendliness, courage and tolerance. If your life and mine do not exemplify these characteristics, we do not have the right to call ourselves full-fledged citizens of the world's greatest democracy.
Melvin J. Evans

Wipe out college—the Electoral College, that is. It's not merely that the constitutional provisions for it are anachronistic, but its continued existence is downright dangerous to our democratic system. It's not merely that Presidents can be

and have been elected who have lost the popular vote, but its existence forces Presidential candidates to emphasize issues . . . not necessarily of national importance . . . From all I've read, studied and thought about the matter, I can't find one good reason why the President and Vice President shouldn't be elected by popular vote.
Malcolm Forbes

Two cheers for democracy, one because it admits variety and two because it permits criticism. Two cheers are quite enough: There is no occasion to give three.
E.M. Forster

Democracy is based upon the conviction that there are extraordinary possibilities in ordinary people.
Harry Emerson Fosdick, D.D.

In a democracy dissent is an act of faith. Like medicine, the test of its value is not in its taste, but its effects.
J. William Fulbright

The only thing wrong with democratic process is the failure to use it.
Seymour Graubard

Economic nationalism is a tenacious and potent enemy of world order. To combat this foe, world citizens must become more active. . . . To secure better legislation, the best informed citizens should be the most vocal in their own communities in demanding that measures of dubious sectional short-run benefit give way to policies better calculated to advance the interests of a free, democratic world civilization with material abundance for all of Adam's children.
Robert L. Gulick, Jr.

Democracy is ever eager for rapid progress, and the only progress which can be rapid is progress downhill.
Sir James Jeans

Democracy is threatened by the inertia of good people, by the selfishness of most people, and by the evil designs of a few people.
Stanley King

Democracy and religion stand or fall together. Where democracy has been destroyed, religion has been doomed. Where religion has been trampled down, democracy has ceased to exist. . . . Tyrants have come and have had their day and then have passed while religion has survived them all.
Herbert H. Lehman

In this and like communities public sentiment is everything. With public sentiment nothing can fail; without it nothing can succeed; consequently he who moulds public sentiment goes deeper than he who enacts statutes and decisions. He makes statutes and decisions possible or impossible to be executed.
Abraham Lincoln

In a democracy, the opposition is not only tolerated as constitutional, but must be maintained because it is indispensable.
Walter Lippmann

Democracy is never a thing done. Democracy is always something that a nation must be doing. What is necessary now is one thing and one thing only . . . that democracy become again democracy in action, not democracy accomplished and piled up in goods and gold.
Archibald MacLeish

Democracy is eternal and human. It dignifies the human being; it respects humanity.
Thomas Mann

The experience of a century and a half has demonstrated that our system of free government functions best when the maximum degree of information is made available to our people. In fact, free and candid discussion of vexing problems is the bedrock of democracy and it may be our surest safeguard for peace.
Brien McMahon

Democracy is the art of running the circus from the monkey cage.
H.L. Mencken

Democracy is the theory that the common people know what they want, and deserve to get it good and hard.
H.L. Mencken

We don't need democratization of privilege. What we need is the self-discipline of democracy.
Thomas I. Parkinson

In our democracy we must have a partnership of labor, of business and of government.
Charles H. Percy

Democracy does not contain any force which will check the constant tendency to put more and more on the public payroll. The state is like a hive of bees in which the drones display, multiply and starve the workers so the idlers will consume the food and the workers will perish.
Plato

That businessmen should from time to time direct candid criticism toward our Government is only understandable but salutary in a free democracy.
Clarence B. Randall

The real strength of democracy is that anyone who is not specifically against it must ultimately be for it, while communism suffers from the great tactical liability that anyone who is not specifically for it is eventually forced to oppose it.
Edwin O. Reichauer

The goal of a great democracy should be fulfillment, not ease. It should be adequacy, not serenity.
Abram Sachar

For democracy to survive, every person must realize that mere insistence on his rights alone will be of little avail, that a recognition of one's obligations is imperative—and that one of the most important obligations is that of respecting the rights of others.
I. David Satlow

If you want to raise a crop for one year, plant corn.

If you want to raise a crop for decades, plant trees.

If you want to raise a crop for centuries, raise men.

If you want to plant a crop for eternities, raise democracies.
Carl A. Schenk

Autocracies may survive for intermittent periods with populations of "yes men" but democracies need a perennially renewed supply of "know men."
Dr. Robert Gordon Sproul

Many Americans cannot define democracy; like the schoolboy when asked to define an elephant confessed he was unable to do so, but insisted he would recognize an elephant when he saw one.
Adlai Stevenson

The real danger of democracy is, that the classes which have the power under it will assume all the rights and reject all the duties—that is, that they will use the political power to plunder those-who-have.
William Graham Sumner

Each generation must win democracy for itself. Many young persons wish they might have lived in the historic and courageous time of George Washington, for example, when there were victories to be made and real history written. On the contrary, there are just as big problems today, and every opportunity for development.
Frank Thayer

One of the distinguishing characteristics of a democratic period is the taste that all men have for easy success and present enjoyment. This occurs in the pursuits of the intellect as well as in others.
Alexis de Tocqueville

The progress of democracy seems irresistible, because it is the most uniform, the most ancient and the most permanent tendency which is to be found in history.
Alexis de Tocqueville

When Benjamin Franklin was asked after a session of the Constitutional Convention, "What kind of a government have you given us?" he replied, "A democracy, if you can keep it." Our republic is founded on the principle that it will continue only as long as the people keep democracy alive. From Lexington to Korea, American youth have fought to preserve democracy. With each political campaign, the people who vote keep democracy alive. Each citizen who participates in community affairs is keeping democracy alive. Every act of mercy and helpfulness, every word spoken for freedom, keeps the democratic

spirit alive. Democracy is maintained by passing it on from one generation to another in the school, in place of worship, in the home. At every stage, it must be strengthened. Let us therefore resolve to give to our successors a stronger republic than was passed on to us.
Thomas A. Watson

I cannot too often repeat that Democracy is a word the real gist of which still sleeps, quite unawakened, notwithstanding the resonance and the many angry tempests out of which its syllables have come, from pen or tongue. It is a great word, whose history, I suppose, remains unwritten because that history has yet to be enacted.
Walt Whitman

DESIRES

Though we seem grieved at the shortness of life in general, we are wishing every period of it at an end. The minor longs to be at age, then to be a man of business, then to make up an estate, then to arrive at honors, then to retire.
Joseph Addison

If things do not turn out as we wish, we should wish for them as they turn out.
Aristotle

We should aim rather at leveling down our desires than leveling up our means.
Aristotle

The desire of power in excess caused the angels to fall; the desire of knowledge in excess caused man to fall.
Francis Bacon

The greatest provocations of lust are from our apparel.
Robert Burton

Better return and make a net, than to go down to the stream and merely wish for fish.
Chinese proverb

One great difference between a wise man and a fool is, the former only wishes for what he may possibly obtain; the latter desires impossibilities.
Democritus

When electricity was invented people became discontent with oil lamps. And so our missionaries employ this sound business principle: Show the people something better and they'll want it.
Horace W.B. Donegan, D.D.

You can get what you desire and in just the measure of that desire.
Thomas Dreier

It seems to me we can never give up longing and wishing while we are thoroughly alive. There are certain things we feel to be beautiful and good, and we must hunger after them.
George Eliot

Beware of what you want—for you will get it.
Ralph Waldo Emerson

There are three wants which can never be satisfied: that of the rich, who want something more; that of the sick, who want something different; and that of the traveler, who says, Anywhere but here.
Ralph Waldo Emerson

We'd all like to be taken for what we'd like to be.
Malcolm Forbes

If your desires be endless, your cares and fears will be so too.
Thomas Fuller

Most of us have a pretty clear idea of the world we want. What we lack is an understanding of how to go about getting it.
Hugh Gibson

Beware of wishing for anything in youth, because you will get it in middle age.
Johann Wolfgang von Goethe

Happy the man who early learns the wide chasm that lies between his wishes and his powers!
Johann Wolfgang von Goethe

Sometimes a man devotes all his life to the development of one part of his body . . . his wishbone.
Allen Gray

A successful man is one who can lay a firm foundation with the bricks that others throw at him.
Sidney Greenberg

By annihilating the desires, you annihilate the mind. Every man without passions has within him no principle of action, nor motive to act.
Claude Adrien Helvétius

He begins to die that quits his desires.
George Herbert

Appetite, with an opinion of attaining, is called hope; the same without such opinion, despair.
Thomas Hobbes

Now that fate has brought me what so long I so desired, it is too late, I am too tired.
Laurence Hope

Besides the pleasure derived from acquired knowledge, there lurks in the mind of man, and tinged with a shade of sadness, an unsatisfactory longing for something beyond the present—a striving toward regions yet unknown and unopened.
Wilhelm von Humboldt

Lord, grant that I may always desire more than I can accomplish.
Michelangelo

I have learned to seek my happiness by limiting my desires, rather than attempting to satisfy them.
John Stuart Mill

Any refusal to recognize reality, for any reason whatever, has disastrous consequences. There are no evil thoughts except one: the refusal to think. Don't ignore your own desires. . . . Don't sacrifice them. Examine their cause. There is a limit to how much you should have to bear.
Ayn Rand

We don't know what we want, but we are ready to bite somebody to get it.
Will Rogers

It is not the man who has little, but he who desires more, that is poor.
Seneca

As long as I have a want, I have a reason for living. Satisfaction is death.
George Bernard Shaw

It is foolish to be ambitious for things one does not really want—or for things one cannot have.
Giuseppe Silva

The earnestness of your desire will indicate the distance you are likely to travel.
Clark C. Stockford

The only limitless thing I know of is human want. Civilization itself is nothing more than the creation of wants, followed by methods of satisfying those wants. At the moment we had better give

consideration to the fact that we may not be creating enough stuff to satisfy the wants this education has inspired.
Dr. James Shelby Thomas

We make ourselves rich by making our wants few.
Henry David Thoreau

Wishes cost nothing unless you want them to come true.
Frank Tyger

Human society is based on want. Life is based on want. Wild-eyed visionaries may dream of a world without need. Cloud-cuckoo-land. It can't be done.
H.G. Wells

In this world there are only two tragedies: One is not getting what one wants, and the second is getting it.
Oscar Wilde

The fewer the desires, the more peace.
Woodrow Wilson

The problem of abolishing want is not a problem in division, as the politicians so often aver; it is a problem in multiplication.
Henry M. Wriston

DESTINY

Thy lot or portion of life is seeking after thee; therefore be at rest from seeking after it.
Ali ibn Ali Talib

How true it is that our destinies are decided by nothings and that a small imprudence helped by some insignificant accident, as an acorn is fertilized by a drop of rain, may raise the trees on which perhaps we and others shall be crucified.
Henri Frédéric Amiel

Love nothing but that which comes to you woven in the pattern of your destiny.
Marcus Aurelius Antoninus

Destiny: A tyrant's authority for crime and a fool's excuse for failure.
Ambrose Bierce

The law of harvest is to reap more than you sow. Sow an act, and you reap a habit; sow a habit, and you reap a character; sow a character and you reap a destiny.
G.D. Boardman

A word, a look, an accent, may affect the destiny not only of individuals, but of nations. He is a bold man who calls anything a trifle.
Andrew Carnegie

It is a mistake to look too far ahead. Only one link of the chain of destiny can be handled at a time.
Winston Churchill

Every man carries with him the world in which he must live.
F. Marion Crawford

How easy 'tis, when

Destiny proves kind,

With full-spread sails to run before the wind!
John Dryden

Blaming destiny is a poor out for those who don't reach desired destinations.
Malcolm Forbes

Failure or success seem to have been allotted to men by their stars. But they retain the power of wriggling, of fighting with their star or against it, and in the whole universe the only really interesting movement is this wriggle.
E.M. Forster

He that is born to be hanged shall never be drowned.
French proverb

We are not permitted to choose the frame of our destiny. But what we put into it is ours.
Dag Hammarskjöld

Men heap together the mistakes of their lives, and create a monster they call Destiny.
John Oliver Hobbes

Lots of folks confuse bad management with destiny.
Kin Hubbard

We still have it in our power to rise above the fears, imagined and real, and to shoulder the great burdens which destiny has placed upon us, not for our country alone, but for the benefit of all the world. That is the only destiny worthy of America.
Helen Keller

'Tis all a chequerboard of nights and days

Where Destiny with men for pieces plays:

Hither and thither moves, and mates, and slays,

And one by one back in the closet lays.
Omar Khayyám

It's odd to think we might have been
Sun, moon and stars unto each other;
Only I turned down one little street
As you went up another.
Fanny Heaslip Lea

No wind favors him who has no destined port.
Michel de Montaigne

Most of the critical things in life, which become the starting points of human destiny, are little things.
R. Smith

Let us follow our destiny, ebb and flow. Whatever may happen, we master fortune by accepting it.
Virgil

DIFFICULTIES

Even when he falls on straw, Schlemiel stumbles on a stone.
Sholem Aleichem

No great advance has ever been made in science, politics, or religion, without controversy.
Lyman Beecher

The difficulties and struggles of today are but the price we must pay for the accomplishments and victories of tomorrow.
William J.H. Boetcker

If you would only recognize that life is hard, things would be so much easier for you.
Louis D. Brandeis

They wrong man greatly who say he is to be seduced by ease. Difficulty, abnegation, martyrdom, death are the allurements that act on the heart of man.
Thomas Carlyle

The weak sinews become strong by their conflict with difficulties.
Edwin H. Chapin

Every difficulty slurred over will be a ghost to disturb your repose later on.
Frédéric Chopin

No one is useless in this world who lightens the burdens of it for another.
Charles Dickens

Life has no smooth road for any of us: and in the bracing atmosphere of a high aim the very roughness stimulates the

climber to steadier steps, till the legend, over the steep ways to the stars, fulfills itself.
William C. Doane

Difficulties exist to be surmounted.
Ralph Waldo Emerson

Difficulties are things that show what men are.
Epictetus

What ought one to say then as each hardship comes? I was practising for this, I was training for this.
Epictetus

Unless a man has been kicked around a little, you can't really depend upon him to amount to anything.
William Feather

The greatest difficulties lie where we are not looking for them.
Johann Wolfgang von Goethe

You've got to take the bull between your teeth.
Samuel Goldwyn

When I hear somebody sigh that Life is hard, I am always tempted to ask, Compared to what?
Sydney Harris

Nothing is difficult, it is only we who are indolent.
Benjamin R. Haydon

A man's worst difficulties begin when he is able to do as he likes.
Thomas H. Huxley

Is not this the fast that I have chosen? To break the bands of wickedness, to undo the heavy burdens, and to let the oppressed go free, and that ye break every yoke?
Isaiah 58:6

Life affords no higher pleasure than that of surmounting difficulties, passing from one step of success to another, forming new wishes and seeing them gratified. He that labors in any great or laudable undertaking has his fatigues first supported by hope and afterward rewarded by joy.
Samuel Johnson

If at times our actions seem to have made life difficult for others, it is only because history has made life difficult for us all.
John F. Kennedy

Much of truth is found upon the battlefield of controversy, and it is kept alive by sharp exchanges.
Lawrence A. Kimpton

It is surmounting difficulties that makes heroes.
Louis Kossuth

No man ever sank under the burden of the day. It is when to-morrow's burden is added to the burden of to-day that the weight is more than a man can bear.
George MacDonald

The difficulties, hardships and trials of life, the obstacles one encounters on the road to fortune are positive blessings. They knit the muscles more firmly, and teach self-reliance. Peril is the element in which power is developed.
William Matthews

It cannot be too often repeated that it is not helps, but obstacles, not facilities, but difficulties that make men.
William Matthews

There is no learned man but will confess he hath much profited by reading controversies; his senses awakened, his judgment sharpened, and the truth which he holds more firmly established. In logic they teach that contraries laid together

more evidently appear; and controversy being permitted, falsehood will appear more false, and truth more true.
John Milton

We can easily manage, if we will only take, each day, the burden appointed for it. But the load will be too heavy for us if we carry yesterday's burden over again today, and then add the burden of the morrow to the weight before we are required to bear it.
John Newton

Undertake something that is difficult; it will do you good. Unless you try to do something beyond what you have already mastered, you will never grow.
Ronald E. Osborn

Burdens become light when cheerfully borne.
Ovid

The individual who knows the score about life sees difficulties as opportunities.
Norman Vincent Peale, D.D.

Accustom yourself to master and overcome things of difficulty; for if you observe, the left hand for want of practice is insignificant, and not adapted to general business, yet it holds the bridle better than the right, from constant use.
Pliny

That which renders life burdensome to us, generally arises from the abuse of it.
Jean-Jacques Rousseau

The most savage controversies are those about matters as to which there is no good evidence either way.
Bertrand Russell

It is not the burden but the overburden that kills the beast.
Spanish proverb

If the way which, as I have shown, leads hither seems very difficult, it can nevertheless be found. It must indeed be difficult, since it is so seldom discovered; for if salvation lay ready to hand and could be discovered without great labor, how could it be possible that it should be neglected almost by everybody? But all noble things are as difficult as they are rare.
Baruch Spinoza

Many men owe the grandeur of their lives to their tremendous difficulties.
Charles H. Spurgeon

Nowadays most men lead lives of noisy desperation.
James Thurber

I sit on a man's back, choking him and making him carry me, and yet assure others that I am very sorry for him and wish to ease his lot by all possible means—except by getting off his back.
Leo Tolstoy

Real difficulties can be overcome; it is only the imaginary ones that are unconquerable.
Theodore N. Vail

Take heart again; put your dismal fears away. One day, who knows? Even these hardships will be grand things to look back on.
Virgil

It is a good rule to face difficulties at the time they arise and not allow them to increase unacknowledged.
Edward W. Ziegler

DIGNITY

There is a proper dignity and proportion to be observed in the performance of every act of life.
Marcus Aurelius Antoninus

The sum of behavior is to retain a man's own dignity, without intruding upon the liberty of others.
Francis Bacon

The dignity of man is vindicated as much by the thinker and poet as by the statesman and soldier.
Dr. James Bryant Conant

Nothing is more destructive of human dignity than a rule which imposes a mute and blind obedience.
Anthony Eden

It is more offensive to outshine in dignity than in personal attractions.
Baltasar Gracián

There is a healthful hardiness about real dignity that never dreads contact and communion with others, however humble.
Washington Irving

True dignity is never gained by place, and never lost when honors are withdrawn.
Philip Massinger

Let none presume to wear an undeserved dignity.
William Shakespeare

No race can prosper until it learns that there is as much dignity in tilling a field as in writing a poem.
Booker T. Washington

It is base and unworthy to live below the dignity of our nature.
Benjamin Whichcote

Dignity is often a veil between us and the real truth of things.
Edwin P. Whipple

True dignity abides with him only, who, in the silent hour of inward thought, can still suspect, and still revere himself, in lowliness of heart.
William Wordsworth

DISAGREEMENT

The people to fear are not those who disagree with you, but those who disagree with you and are too cowardly to let you know.
Napoleon Bonaparte

How come nobody wants to argue with me? Is it because I'm always so right?
Jim Bouton

The great mind knows the power of gentleness, only tries force because persuasion fails.
Robert Browning

Somebody has to have the last word. If not, every argument could be opposed by another and we'd never be done with it.
Albert Camus

No man lives without jostling and being jostled; in all ways he has to elbow himself through the world, giving and receiving offense.
Thomas Carlyle

People generally quarrel because they cannot argue.
G.K. Chesterton

The effects of opposition are wonderful. There are men who rise refreshed on hearing of a threat—men to whom a crisis which intimidates and paralyzes

the majority, comes graceful and beloved as a bride!
Ralph Waldo Emerson

The worthless and offensive members of society, whose existence is a social pest, invariably think themselves the most ill-used people alive, and never get over their astonishment at the ingratitude and selfishness of their contemporaries.
Ralph Waldo Emerson

In theory it is easy to convince an ignorant person; in actual life, men not only object to offer themselves to be convinced, but hate the man who has convinced them.
Epictetus

He who has learned to disagree without being disagreeable has discovered the most valuable secret of a diplomat.
Robert Estabrook

The last sound on the worthless earth will be two human beings trying to launch a homemade spaceship and already quarreling about where they are going next.
William Faulkner

In the course of my observation, the disputing, contradicting and confuting people are generally unfortunate in their affairs. They get victory sometimes, but they never get good will, which would be of more use to them.
Benjamin Franklin

Convincing yourself does not win an argument.
Robert Half

No matter what side of an argument you're on, you always find some people on your side that you wish were on the other side.
Jascha Heifetz

We may convince others by our arguments, but we can only persuade them by their own.
Joseph Joubert

What occasions the greater part of the world's quarrels? Simply this: Two minds meet and do not understand each other in time enough to prevent any shock of surprise at the conduct of either party.
John Keats

Business today consists in persuading crowds.
Gerald S. Lee

Persuasion, kind, unassuming persuasion, should be adopted to influence the conduct of men. The opposite course would be a reversal of human nature, which is God's decree and can never be reversed.
Abraham Lincoln

Men are more ready to offend one who desires to be beloved than one who wishes to be feared.
Niccolò Machiavelli

The difficult part in an argument is not to defend one's opinion but rather to know it.
André Maurois

A certain amount of opposition is a great help to a man; it is what he wants and must have to be good for anything. Hardship and opposition are the native soil of manhood and self-reliance.
John Neal

Before you try to convince anyone else be sure you are convinced, and if you cannot convince yourself, drop the subject.
John H. Patterson

Take the course opposite to custom and you will almost always do well.
Jean-Jacques Rousseau

Opposition inflames the enthusiast, never converts him.
Johann Friedrich von Schiller

A long dispute means that both parties are wrong.
Voltaire

I am not arguing with you—I am telling you.
James McNeill Whistler

DISCIPLINE

Hold yourself responsible for a higher standard than anybody else expects of you. Never excuse yourself. Never pity yourself. Be a hard master to yourself—and be lenient to everybody else.
Henry Ward Beecher

The most we can get out of life is its discipline for ourselves, and its usefulness for others.
Tryon Edwards

Only the man who can impose discipline on himself is fit to discipline others or can impose discipline on others.
William Feather

If we don't discipline ourselves the world will do it for us.
William Feather

No horse gets anywhere until he is harnessed. No steam or gas ever drives anything until it is confined. No Niagara is ever turned into light and power until it is tunneled. No life ever grows great until it is focused, dedicated, disciplined.
Harry Emerson Fosdick, D.D.

Life is tons of discipline.
Robert Frost

Discipline without freedom is tyranny. Freedom without discipline is chaos.
Cullen Hightower

Man must be disciplined, for he is by nature raw and wild.
Immanuel Kant

I've never known a man worth his salt who in the long run, deep down in his heart, didn't appreciate the grind, the discipline... I firmly believe that any man's finest hour—this greatest fulfillment to all he holds dear—is that moment when he has worked his heart out in a good cause and lies exhausted on the field of battle victorious.
Vince Lombardi

A stern discipline pervades all nature, which is a little cruel that it may be very kind.
Edmund Spenser

DISCOVERIES

Greater even than the greatest discovery is to keep open the way to future discovery.
John Jacob Abel

A great discovery is a fact whose appearance in science gives rise to shining ideas, whose light dispels many obscurities and shows us new paths.
Claude Bernard

I am more of a sponge than an inventor. I absorb ideas from every source. I take half-matured schemes for mechanical development and make them practical. I am a sort of a middleman between the long-haired and impractical inventor and the hard-headed business man who measures all things in terms of dollars

and cents. My principal business is giving commercial value to the brilliant but misdirected ideas of others.
Thomas A. Edison

The intellect has little to do on the road to discovery. There comes a leap in consciousness, call it intuition or what you will, and the solution comes to you and you don't know how or why. All great discoveries are made in this way.
Albert Einstein

Things don't turn up in this world until somebody turns them up.
James A. Garfield

New discoveries in science . . . will continue to create a thousand new frontiers for those who still would adventure.
Herbert Hoover

I do not much wish well to discoveries, for I am always afraid they will end in conquest and robbery.
Samuel Johnson

No man ever made a great discovery without the exercise of the imagination.
George Henry Lewes

Nearly every great discovery in science has come as the result of providing a new question rather than a new answer.
Paul A. Meglitsch

Invention, strictly speaking, is little more than a new combination of those images which have been previously gathered and deposited in the memory. Nothing can be made of nothing; he who has laid up no materials can produce no combinations.
Sir Joshua Reynolds

The greatest inventions were produced in the times of ignorance, [such] as the

use of the compass, gunpowder and printing.
Jonathan Swift

Name the greatest of all inventors. Accident.
Mark Twain

We are called the nation of inventors. And we are. We could still claim that title and wear its loftiest honors if we had stopped with the first thing we ever invented, which was human liberty.
Mark Twain

Discoveries are often made by not following instructions; by going off the main road; by trying the untried.
Frank Tyger

Scientific discovery consists in the interpretation for our own convenience of a system of existence which has been made with no eye to our convenience at all.
Norbert Wiener

Benjamin Franklin may have discovered electricity, but it was the man who invented the meter who made the money.
Earl Wilson

DISHONESTY

Dishonesty is a forsaking of permanent for temporary advantage.
Christian Bovée

To admire nothing is the motto which men of the world always affect. They think it vulgar to wonder or be enthusiastic. They have so much corruption and charlatanism, that they think the credit of all high policies must be delusive.
Samuel Brydges

Corrupt influence is itself the perennial spring of all prodigality, and of all disorder; it loads us more than millions

of debt; takes away vigor from our arms, wisdom from our councils, and every shadow of authority and credit from the most venerable parts of our constitution.
Edmund Burke

Falsehood is invariably the child of fear in one form or another.
Aleister Crowley

I have known a vast quantity of nonsense talked about bad men not looking you in the face. Don't trust that conventional idea. Dishonesty will stare honesty out of countenance, any day in the week, if there is anything to be got by it.
Charles Dickens

Shower on him every blessing, drown him in a sea of happiness, give him economic prosperity such that he should have nothing else to do but sleep, eat cakes, and busy himself with the continuation of the species, and even then, out of sheer ingratitude, sheer spite, man would play you some nasty trick.
Fyodor Dostoyevsky

Many corporate managements and a lot of security analysts have reacted with much fuming and even more fumbling to the Texas Gulf Sulphur decision and the SEC's actions against trading on inside information.
I don't know why everyone is in such a hot sweat over these two things. The one had been illegal—and damned well properly so—for over 30 years. . . . The initial reaction of some managements that these actions meant they could no longer talk to any publications or analysts was—is—asinine. Such sour silliness is quite the reverse of what was intended.
Malcolm Forbes

Dishonesty, cowardice and duplicity are never impulsive.
George Knight

Men are so simple and yield so readily to the wants of the moment that he who will trick will always find another who will suffer himself to be tricked.
Niccolò Machiavelli

Even a secret agent can't lie to a Jewish mother.
Peter Malkin

Our first duty is to war against dishonesty . . . war against it in public life, and . . . war against it in business life. Corruption in every form is the arch enemy of this Republic, the arch enemy of free institutions and of government by the people, an even more dangerous enemy than the open lawlessness of violence, because it works in hidden and furtive fashion.
Theodore Roosevelt

DOING

Don't just do something, stand there.
Dean Acheson

One must learn by doing the thing, for though you think you know it, you have no certainty until you try.
Aristotle

If you have something to do that is worthwhile doing, don't talk about it, but do it. After you have done it, your friends and enemies will talk about it.
George W. Blount

Everywhere in life the true question is, not what we have gained, but what we do.
Thomas Carlyle

Men do less than they ought, unless they do all that they can.
Thomas Carlyle

What one does easily, one does well.
Andrew Carnegie

The shortest way to do many things is to do only one thing at a time.
Richard Cecil

Do as you would be done by, is the surest method of pleasing.
Lord Chesterfield

Whatever is worth doing at all is worth doing well.
Lord Chesterfield

If a thing is worth doing, it is worth doing badly.
G.K. Chesterton

It's not enough that we do our best; sometimes we have to do what's required.
Winston Churchill

One never notices what has been done; one can only see what remains to be done.
Marie Curie

When I go into my garden with a spade, and dig a bed, I feel such an exhilaration and health that I discover that I have been defrauding myself all this time in letting others do for me what I should have done with my own hands.
Ralph Waldo Emerson

When looking back, usually I'm more sorry for the things I didn't do than for the things I shouldn't have done.
Malcolm Forbes

Well done is better than well said.
Benjamin Franklin

I am only one, but still I am one. I cannot do everything, but still I can do something and because I cannot do everything, I will not refuse to do the something that I can do.
Edward Everett Hale

You have not done enough, you have never done enough, so long as it is still possible that you have something to contribute.
Dag Hammarskjöld

Now is no time to think of what you do not have. Think of what you can do with what there is.
Ernest Hemingway

The shortest answer is doing.
George Herbert

The greatest thing in the world is for a man to be able to do something well, and say nothing about it.
Edgar Watson Howe

For if any be a hearer of the word, and not a doer, he is like a man beholding his natural face in a glass: for he beholdeth himself, and goeth his way, and straightaway forgetteth what manner of man he was.
James 1:23–24

In the dim background of our mind, we know what we ought to be doing, but somehow we cannot start. Every moment, we expect the spell to break, but it continues, pulse after pulse, and we float with it.
William James

One of the greatest failings of today's executive is his inability to do what he's supposed to do.
Malcolm Kent

What you do when you don't have to, determined what you will be when you can no longer help it.
Rudyard Kipling

You cannot help men permanently by doing for them what they could and should do for themselves.
Abraham Lincoln

There is no pleasure in having nothing to do; the fun is having lots to do and not doing it.
Mary Wilson Little

It takes less time to do a thing right than to explain why you did it wrong.
Henry Wadsworth Longfellow

So much one man can do that does both act and know.
Andrew Marvell

To do each day two things one dislikes is a precept I have followed scrupulously: Every day I have got up and I have gone to bed.
Somerset Maugham

What ever fortune brings, don't be afraid of doing things.
A.A. Milne

It is not only what we do, but also what we do not do, for which we are accountable.
Molière

The world is divided into people who do things and people who get the credit. Try, if you can, to belong to the first class. There's far less competition.
Dwight Morrow

Many enjoy the shade . . . but few rake leaves.
Jack Morton

He was a wise man who said: "As I grow older I pay less attention to what men say. I just watch what they do."
Wilfred A. Peterson

Thinking well is wise; planning well;, wiser; doing well wisest and best of all.
Persian proverb

Where you are is of no moment, but only what you are doing there. It is not the place that ennobles you, but you the place, and this only by doing that which is great and noble.
Petrarch

Do to others as you would have others do to you, inspires all men with that other maxim of natural goodness a great deal less perfect, but perhaps more useful: Do good to yourself with as little prejudice as you can to others.
Jean-Jacques Rousseau

Doing is the great thing. For if, resolutely, people do what is right, in time they come to like doing it.
John Ruskin

I feel that the greatest reward for doing is the opportunity to do more.
Jonas Salk

Oh what men dare do! what men may do! what men daily do, not knowing what they do!
William Shakespeare

Some have an idea that the reason we in this country discard things so readily is because we have so much. The facts are exactly opposite—the reason we have so much is simply because we discard things so readily. We replace the old in return for something that will serve us better.
Alfred P. Sloan, Jr.

It is the greatest of all mistakes to do nothing because you can only do a little. Do what you can.
Sydney Smith

Better do a little well, than a great deal badly.
Socrates

Make it a point to do something every day that you don't want to do. This is the golden rule for acquiring the habit of doing your duty without pain.
Mark Twain

Even doing nothing takes doing.
Frank Tyger

If we could only make our hands move as actively as our tongues, what wonders we could accomplish! Almost everyone loves to hear his own voice. It is so easy, too! Yet if we could say less and do more for each other's good, not alone would every home be happier, but communities would be enriched thereby. Instead of criticism by speech, to show someone a better way to do a thing would be of much greater value.
John Wanamaker

I will just create, and if it works, it works, and if it doesn't, I'll create something else. I don't have any limitations on what I think I could do or be.
Oprah Winfrey

Not merely what we do, but what we try to do and why, are the true interpreters of what we are.
C.H. Woodward

DOUBT

If we begin with certainties, we shall end in doubts; but if we begin with doubts, and are patient in them, we shall end in certainties.
Francis Bacon

Weary the path that does not challenge. Doubt is an incentive to truth and patient inquiry leadeth the way.
Hosea Ballou

For if the trumpet give an uncertain sound, who shall prepare himself to the battle?
I Corinthians 14:8

Uncertain ways unsafest are, and doubt a greater mischief than despair.
John Denham

Seeking to know is only too often learning to doubt.
Antoinette Deshoulières

Uncertainty hurts business. It annoys individuals. Why keep the whole country, including business and individuals, in uncertainty over the extent of the tax burdens to be placed upon us? How many of those who voted for Calvin Coolidge imagined for a moment that would do nothing to bring about tax relief before 1926?. . . . But if the Administration persists in opposing a special session then it will inevitably be 1926 before action is taken. . . . Coolidge and Congress should ease our minds and grease our activities by reforming and reducing taxation as soon as feasible after March 4.
B.C. Forbes

When young, you're shocked by the number of people who turn out to have feet of clay. Older, you're surprised by the number of people who don't.
Malcolm Forbes

The believer is happy; the doubter is wise.
Hungarian proverb

Doubts and jealousies often beget the facts they fear.
Thomas Jefferson

Nothing will ever be attempted if all possible objections must be first overcome.
Samuel Johnson

The more uncertain I have felt about myself, the more there has grown up in me a feeling of kinship with all things.
Carl Jung

Men become civilized not in proportion to their willingness to believe, but in proportion to their willingness to doubt.
H.L. Mencken

Doubts are more cruel than the worst of truths.
Molière

Four be the things
I'd been better without:
Love, curiosity,
Freckles and doubt.
Dorothy Parker

He that is overcautious will accomplish little.
Johann Friedrich von Schiller

Our doubts are traitors and cause us to miss the good we oft might win by fearing to attempt.
William Shakespeare

Among the safe courses, the safest of all is to doubt.
Spanish proverb

Open your mouth and purse cautiously, and your stock of wealth and reputation shall, at least in repute, be great.
Johann Zimmermann

DREAMS

Sleep is an 8-hour peep show of infantile erotica.
J.G. Ballard

Dreams have only the pigmentation of fact.
Djuna Barnes

If there were dreams to sell, what would you buy!
Thomas Lovell Beddoes

There couldn't be a society of people who didn't dream. They'd be dead in two weeks.
William S. Burroughs

Sleep hath its own world, and a wide realm of wild reality.
Lord Byron

If I had influence with the good fairy who is supposed to preside over the christening of all children, I should ask that her gift to each child in the world be a sense of wonder so indestructible that it would last throughout life, as an unfailing antidote against boredom and disenchantments of later years, the sterile preoccupation with things that are artificial, the alienation from our sources of strength.
Rachel Carson

To believe in one's dreams is to spend all of one's life asleep.
Chinese proverb

Last night I dreamed I ate a 10-pound marshmallow, and when I woke up the pillow was gone.
Tommy Cooper

Dreaming permits each and every one of us to be quietly and safely insane every night of our lives.
William Dement

Dreams and beasts are two keys by which we find out the keys of our own nature.
Ralph Waldo Emerson

Always dream and shoot higher than you know you can do. Don't bother just to be better than your contemporaries or predecessors. Try to be better than yourself.
William Faulkner

Living and dreaming are two different things—but you can't do one without the other.
Malcolm Forbes

When you cease to dream you cease to live.
Malcolm Forbes

Dreaming is an act of pure imagination, attesting in all men a creative power, which, if it were available in waking, would make every man a Dante or a Shakespeare.
H.F. Hedge

We do not really feel grateful toward those who make our dreams come true; they spoil our dreams.
Eric Hoffer

Hold fast to dreams, for if dreams die, life is a broken-winged bird that cannot fly.
Langston Hughes

No one should negotiate their dreams. Dreams must be free to fly high. No government, no legislature, has a right to limit your dreams. You should never agree to surrender your dreams.
Jesse Jackson

We sometimes from dreams pick up some hint worth improving by . . . reflection.
Thomas Jefferson

No man will be found in whose mind airy notions do not sometimes tyrannize him and thus force him to hope or fear beyond the limits of sober probability.
Samuel Johnson

Dream research is a wonderful field. All you do is sleep for a living.
Stephen Laberge

One half of the world must sweat and groan that the other half may dream.
Henry Wadsworth Longfellow

I make beanstalks; I'm a builder, like yourself.
Edna St. Vincent Millay

True vision is always twofold. It involves emotional comprehensions as well as physical perception.
Ross Parmenter

I have a feeling—as compelling as a religious conviction—that if industry will constantly pass on to the worker and the customer all the savings of labor-saving machinery and invention, rather than siphon them off into the pools of watered securities, it will by that process keep distribution and production in balance and go as far toward Utopia as our poor human natures will go or be driven.
Samuel B. Pettengill

Wonder is the feeling of a philosopher; and philosophy begins in wonder.
Plato

It has never been my object to record my dreams, just the determination to realize them.
Man Ray

The fellow that can only see a week ahead is always the popular fellow, for he is looking with the crowd. But the one that can see years ahead, he has a telescope but he can't make anybody believe he has it.
Will Rogers

Keep your eyes on the stars, and your feet on the ground.
Theodore Roosevelt

A rock pile ceases to be a rock pile the moment a single man contemplates it, bearing within him the image of a cathedral.
Antoine de Saint-Exupéry

Keep true to the dreams of thy youth.
Johann Friederich von Schiller

You see things; and you say Why? But I dream things that never were; and I say Why not?
George Bernard Shaw

Happy are those who dream dreams and are ready to pay the price to make them come true.
Leon J. Suenens

Vision is the art of seeing things invisible.
Jonathan Swift

I have learned this at least by my experiment: that if one advances confidently in the direction of his dreams, and endeavors to live the life which he has imagined, he will meet with a success unexpected in common hours.
Henry David Thoreau

If you have built castles in the air, your work need not be lost; there that is where they should be. Now put foundations under them.
Henry David Thoreau

We grow great by dreams. All big men are dreamers. They see things in the soft haze of a spring day or in the red fire of a long winter's evening. Some of us let these great dreams die, but others nourish and protect them, nurse them through bad days till they bring them to the sunshine and light which come always to those who sincerely hope that their dreams will come true.
Woodrow Wilson

Dreams never hurt anybody if he keeps working right behind the dream to make as much of it come real as he can.
F.W. Woolworth

DUTY

Our duty is to be useful, not according to our desires but according to our powers.
Henri Frédéric Amiel

The reward of doing one duty is the power to do another.
Rabbi Ben Azai

The best security for people's doing their duty is that they should not know anything else to do.
Walter Bagehot

All higher motives, ideals, conceptions, sentiments in a man are of no account if they do not come forward to strengthen him for the better discharge of the duties which devolve upon him in the ordinary affairs of life.
Henry Ward Beecher

There is not a moment without some duty.
Cicero

Is duty a mere sport, or an employ? Life an entrusted talent or a toy?
Samuel Taylor Coleridge

Do your duty and leave the rest to the gods.
Pierre Corneille

Where duty is plain delay is both foolish and hazardous; where it is not, delay may be both wisdom and safety.
Tryon Edwards

The reward of one duty done is the power to fulfill another.
George Eliot

We must find our duties in what comes to us, not in what we imagine might have been.
George Eliot

Duty is that mode of action on the part of the individual which constitutes the best possible application of his capacity to the general benefit.
William Godwin

Knowledge of our duties is the most essential part of the philosophy of life. If you escape duty you avoid action. The world demands results.
George W. Goethals

How can you come to know yourself? Never by thinking; always by doing. Try to do your duty, and you'll know right away what you amount to. And what is your duty? Whatever the day calls for.
Johann Wolfgang von Goethe

I declare my belief that it is not your duty to do anything that is not to your own interest. Whenever it is unquestionably your duty to do a thing, then it will benefit you to perform that duty.
Edgar Watson Howe

It is worthy of special remark that when we are not too anxious about happiness and unhappiness, but devote ourselves to the strict and unsparing performance of duty, then happiness comes of itself.
Wilhelm von Humboldt

Only aim to do your duty, and mankind will give you credit where you fail.
Thomas Jefferson

Duty is the sublimest word in the language; you can never do more than your duty; you shall never wish to do less.
Robert E. Lee

New occasions teach new duties.
James Russell Lowell

There is nothing in the universe that I fear, but that I shall not know all my duty, or shall fail to do it.
Mary Lyon

Where it is a duty to worship the sun it is pretty sure to be a crime to examine the laws of heat.
John Morley

A duty dodged is like a debt unpaid; it is only deferred, and we must come back and settle the account at last.
Joseph Fort Newton

Who escapes a duty, avoids a gain.
Theodore W. Parker

We ought to use the best means we can to be well informed of our duty.
Thomas B. Reed

Next to doing the right thing, the most important thing is to let people know you are doing the right thing.
John D. Rockefeller

A sense of duty is useful in work, but offensive in personal relations.
Bertrand Russell

It is not enough to be ready to go where duty calls. A man should stand around where he can hear the call!
Robert Louis Stevenson

Do not keep away from the measure which has no limit, or from the task which has no end.
Rabbi Tarfon

For many years I was self-appointed inspector of snowstorms and rainstorms, and did my duty faithfully.
Henry David Thoreau

A man who neglects his duty as a citizen is not entitled to his rights as a citizen.
Tiorio

The consideration that human happiness and moral duty are inseparably connected will always continue to prompt me to promote the former by inculcating the practice of the latter.
George Washington

To persevere in one's duty and be silent is the best answer to calumny.
George Washington

Duty is what one expects from others.
Oscar Wilde

It is just as hard to do your duty when men are sneering at you as when they are shooting at you.
Woodrow Wilson

E

ECONOMY

We've seen crisis. We've seen recession. But we've not seen the core of the financial system shaken like this. It's just crazy.
Joseph Balestrino

Colleges don't teach economics properly. Unfortunately we learn little from the experience of the past. An economist must know, besides his subject, ethics, logic, philosophy, the humanities and sociology, in fact everything that is part of how we live and react to one another.
Bernard M. Baruch

A science of economics must be developed before a science of politics can be logically formulated. Essentially, economics is the science of determining whether the interests of human beings are harmonious or antagonistic. This must be known before a science of politics can be formulated to determine the proper functions of government.
Claude Frédéric Bastiat

Inflation is a form of hidden taxation which it is almost impossible to measure.
John Beckley

Thrift and prosperity have gone hand in hand since Abraham's flocks grew and multiplied. Thrift is not, as many suppose, a self repression. It is self expression, the demonstration of a will and ability to raise one's self to a higher plane of living. No depression was ever caused by people having too much money in reserve. No human being ever became a social drifter through the practice of sensible thrift.
Harvey A. Blodgett

Oil is seldom found where it is most needed, and seldom most needed where it is found.
L.E.J. Brouwer

Mere parsimony is not economy. . . . Expense, and great expense, may be an essential part in true economy. . . . Economy is a distributive virtue, and consists, not in saving, but in selection. Parsimony requires no providence, no sagacity, no powers of combination, no comparison, no judgment.
Edmund Burke

Thrift is that habit of character that prompts one to work for what he gets, to earn what is paid him; to invest a part of his earnings; to spend wisely and well; to save, but not hoard.
Arthur Chamberlain

He who will not economize will have to agonize.
Confucius

Inflation is repudiation.
Calvin Coolidge

The oil can is mightier than the sword.
Everett Dirksen

Everyone is always in favor of general economy and particular expenditure.
Anthony Eden

Economy does not consist in saving the coal, but in using the time while it burns.
Ralph Waldo Emerson

Economy has frequently nothing whatever to do with the amount of money being spent, but with the wisdom used in spending it.
Henry Ford

Economists are economical, among other things, of ideas; most make those of their graduate days do for a lifetime.
John Kenneth Galbraith

Economic independence doesn't set anyone free. Or it shouldn't, for the higher up you go, the more responsibilities become yours.
Bernard F. Gimbel

He that spareth in everything is an inexcusable niggard. He that spareth in nothing is an inexcusable madman. The mean is to spare in what is least necessary, and to lay out more liberally in what is most required.
Lord Halifax

Economy is going without something you do want in case you should, some day, want something which you probably won't want.
Anthony H. Hawkins

If one could divine the nature of the economic forces in the world, one could foretell the future.
Robert Heilbroner

Radicalism itself ceases to be radical when absorbed mainly in preserving its control over a society or an economy.
Eric Hoffer

Economic depression cannot be cured by legislative action or executive pronouncement. Economic wounds must be healed by the action of the cells of the economic body, the producers and consumers themselves.
Herbert Hoover

Once upon a time my opponents honored me as possessing the fabulous intellectual and economic power by which I created a worldwide depression all by myself.
Herbert Hoover

I place economy among the first and most important virtues, and public debt as the greatest of dangers to be feared . . . . To preserve our independence, we must not let our rulers load us with perpetual debt. . . . We must make our choice between economy and liberty or profusion and servitude. . . . If we run into such debts, we must be taxed in our meat and drink, in our necessities and our comforts, in our labors and in our amusements. . . . If we can prevent the Government from wasting the labors of the people, under the pretense of caring for them, they will be happy.
Thomas Jefferson

Thrift is care and scruple in the spending of one's means. It is not a virtue and it requires neither skill nor talent.
Immanuel Kant

No gain is so certain as that which proceeds for the economical use of what you already have.
Latin proverb

The consumer today is the victim of the manufacturer who launches on him a regiment of products for which he must make room in his soul.
Mary McCarthy

Large enterprises make the few rich, but the majority prosper only through the carefulness and detail of thrift.
Theodore T. Munger

I would rather have people laugh at my economies than weep for my extravagance.
King Oscar II of Sweden

Natural resources and oil have been good to me, but the big money to be made in those sectors is all over.
Richard Rainwater

Economy is in itself a great source of revenue.
Seneca

Economy is too late at the bottom of the purse.
Seneca

Economy is the art of making the most of life. The love of economy is the root of all virtue.
George Bernard Shaw

The regard one shows economy, is like that we show an old aunt, who is to leave us something at last.
William Shenstone

Parsimony, and not industry, is the immediate cause of the increase of capital. But whatever industry might acquire, if parsimony did not save and store up, the capital would never be the greater.
Adam Smith

Economic growth is not only unncessary, but ruinous.
Aleksandr Solzhenitsyn

Economy is half the battle of life; it is not so hard to earn money as to spend it well.
Charles H. Spurgeon

Oil prices have fallen lately. We include this news for the benefit of gas stations, which otherwise wouldn't learn of it for six months.
Bill Tammeus

We are not to judge thrift solely by the test of saving or spending. If one spends what he should prudently save, that certainly is to be deplored. But if one saves what he should prudently spend, that is not necessarily to be commended. A wise balance between the two is the desired end.
Owen D. Young

EDUCATION

Knowledge accumulates in universities, because the freshmen bring a little in and the seniors take none away.
Academic saying

A teacher affects eternity: he can never tell where his influence stops.
Henry Adams

Education makes a greater difference between man and man than nature has made between man and brute.
John Adams

American critics are like American universities. They both have dull and half-dead faculties.
Edward Albee

A true teacher defends his pupils against his own personal influence.
Amos Bronson Alcott

The avocation of assessing the failures of better men can be turned into a comfortable livelihood, provided you back it up with a Ph.D.
Nelson Algren

The man who knows not and knows that he knows not is a child—teach him.
Arabian proverb

All who have meditated on the art of governing mankind have been convinced that the fate of empires depends on the education of youth.
Aristotle

The roots of education are bitter, but the fruit is sweet.
Aristotle

Those who educate children well are more to be honored than parents, for these only gave life, those the art of living well.
Aristotle

If your civilization is to be enriched, it must be relived by every single child. It is in the schoolroom—or mostly in the schoolroom—while assimilating little tidbits of what has been the experience of men before him, that the child first makes the acquaintance of the human person, of the spiritual being he is.
Max Ascoli

Teachers are the one and only people who save nations.
Mustafa Kemal Atatürk

It takes most men five years to recover from a college education, and to learn that poetry is as vital to thinking as knowledge.
Brooks Atkinson

A professor is one who talks in someone else's sleep.
W.H. Auden

A schoolmaster should have an atmosphere of awe, and walk wonderingly, as if he was amazed at being himself.
Walter Bagehot

The man who graduates today and stops learning tomorrow is uneducated the day after.
Newton D. Baker

The paradox of education is precisely this, that as one begins to become conscious one begins to examine the society in which he is being educated.
James Baldwin

Teaching is not a lost art, but the regard for it is a lost tradition.
Jacques Barzun

The test and the use of man's education is that he finds pleasure in the exercise of his mind.
Jacques Barzun

A republican government is in a hundred points weaker than one that is autocratic; but in this one point it is the strongest that ever existed—it has educated a race of men that are men.
Henry Ward Beecher

Education is not a discipline at all. It's half vocational, half an emptiness dressed up in garments borrowed from philosophy, psychology, literature.
Edward Blishen

Life is amazing; and the teacher had better prepare himself to be a medium for that amazement.
Edward Blishen

The liberally educated person is one who is able to resist the easy and preferred answers, not because he is obstinate but because he knows others worthy of consideration.
Allan Bloom

There is no real teacher who in practice does not believe in the existence of the soul, or in a magic that acts on it through speech.
Allan Bloom

You should have education enough so that you won't have to look up to people; and then more education so that you will be wise enough not to look down on people.
M.L. Boren

Education makes a people easy to lead, but difficult to drive; easy to govern, but impossible to enslave.
Omar N. Bradley

Thoughts on education: American economic security is at risk without better public education.
Eli Broad

Housework is a breeze. Cooking is a pleasant diversion. Putting up a retaining wall is a lark. But teaching is like climbing a mountain.
Fawn Brodie

Prejudices, it is well known, are most difficult to eradicate from the heart whose soil has never been loosened or fertilized by education; they grow there, firm as weeds among stones.
Charlotte Brontë

Education makes a people easy to lead, but difficult to drive; easy to govern, but impossible to enslave.
Henry Brougham

Education is anything that we do for the purpose of taking advantage of the experience of some one else.
Lyman Bryson

Education is the chief defense of nations.
Edmund Burke

The teaching of any science, for purposes of liberal education, without linking it with social progress and teaching its social significance, is a crime against the student mind. It is like teaching a child how to pronounce words but not what they mean.
Vernon Carter

The most effective teacher will always be biased, for the chief force in teaching is confidence and enthusiasm.
Joyce Cary

A true university can never rest upon the will of one man. A true university always rests upon the wills of many divergent-minded old men, who refuse to be disturbed, but who growl in their kennels.
John Jay Chapman

Properly speaking, there is no such thing as education. Education is simply the soul of a society as it passes from one generation to another. Whatever the soul is like, it will have to be passed on somehow, consciously or unconsciously; and that transition may be called education.
G.K. Chesterton

Without education we are in a horrible and deadly danger of taking educated people seriously.
G.K. Chesterton

The authority of those who teach is often an obstacle to those who want to learn.
Cicero

Examinations are formidable even to the best prepared, for the greatest fool may ask more than the wisest man can answer.
Charles Caleb Colton

Better build schoolrooms for "the boy"
Than cells and gibbets for "the man."
Eliza Cook

To read a newspaper is to refrain from
reading something worthwhile. The first
discipline of education must therefore be
to refuse resolutely to feed the mind with
canned chatter.
Aleister Crowley

A good education is usually harmful to a
dancer. A good calf is better than a good
head.
Agnes de Mille

Nature and education are somewhat
similar. The latter transforms man, and
in so doing creates a second nature.
Democritus

The devotion of democracy to education
is a familiar fact. The superficial explanation is that a government resting upon
popular suffrage cannot be successful
unless those who elect and who obey
their governors are educated. Since a
democratic society repudiates the principle of external authority, it must find a
substitute in voluntary disposition and
interest; these can be created only by
education.
John Dewey

There is no more vulnerable human
combination than an undergraduate.
John Sloan Dickey

A school is a place through which you
have to pass before entering life, but
where the teaching proper does not
prepare you for life.
Ernest Dimnet

Children have to be educated, but
they have also to be left to educate
themselves.
Ernest Dimnet

A university should be a place of light, of
liberty and of learning.
Benjamin Disraeli

The most important aspect of freedom of
speech is freedom to learn. All education
is a continuous dialogue—questions and
answer that pursue every problem to the
horizon. That is the essence of academic
freedom.
William O. Douglas

Sixty years ago I knew everything; now I
know nothing; education is a progressive
discovery of our own ignorance.
Will Durant

The great end of education is, to discipline rather than to furnish the mind;
to train it to the use of its own powers,
rather than fill it with the accumulations
of others.
Tyron Edwards

Education is that which remains when
one has forgotten everything he learned
in school.
Albert Einstein

Never regard study as a duty, but as the
enviable opportunity to learn to know
the liberating influence of beauty in the
realm of the spirit for your own personal
joy and to the profit of the community to
which your later work belongs.
Albert Einstein

Schools need not preach political
doctrine to defend democracy. If they
shape men capable of critical thought
and trained in social attitudes, that is all
that is necessary.
Albert Einstein

Liberal education develops a sense
of right, duty and honor; and more
and more in the modern world, large

business rests on rectitude and honor as well as on good judgment.
Charles W. Eliot

That which we do not call education is more precious than that which we call so.
Ralph Waldo Emerson

The things taught in schools and colleges are not an education, but the means of education.
Ralph Waldo Emerson

There is no teaching until the public is brought into the same state or principle in which you are; a transfusion takes place; he is you and you are he; then is a teaching, and by no unfriendly chance or bad company can he ever quite lose the benefit.
Ralph Waldo Emerson

Education is the process by which the individual relates himself to the universe, gives himself citizenship in the changing world, shares the race's mind and enfranchises his own soul.
Dr. John H. Finley

Nations have recently been led to borrow billions for war; no nation has ever borrowed largely for education.
Abraham Flexner

Vitally important for a young man or woman is, first, to realize the value of education, and then to cultivate earnestly, aggressively, ceaselessly, the habit of self-education. Without fresh supplies of knowledge, the brain will not develop healthily and vigorously any more than the body can be sustained without fresh supplies of food.
B.C. Forbes

It's the less-bright students who make teachers teach better.
Malcolm Forbes

We can't take a slipshod and easygoing attitude toward education in this country. And by "we" I don't mean "somebody else," but I mean me and I mean you. It is the future of our country—yours and mine—which is at stake.
Henry Ford II

On digging ditches: The single biggest motivation to get an education.
Paul Foster

The whole art of teaching is only the art of awakening the natural curiosity of young minds for the purpose of satisfying it afterwards.
Anatole France

A Bible and a newspaper in every house, a good school in every district—all studied and appreciated as they merit—are the principal support of virtue, morality, and civil liberty.
Benjamin Franklin

Education is the ability to listen to almost anything without losing your temper or your self-confidence.
Robert Frost

Next in importance to freedom and justice is popular education, without which neither freedom nor justice can be permanently maintained.
James A. Garfield

Every man who rises above the common level has received two educations: the first from his teachers; the second, more personal and important, from himself.
Edward Gibbon

One of the chief objects of education should be to widen the windows through which we view the world.
Arnold Glasow

Good teaching is one-fourth preparation and three-fourths theatre.
Gail Godwin

Alas! how much there is in education, and in our social institutions, to prepare us and our children for insanity.
Johann Wolfgang von Goethe

If you feel that you have both feet planted on solid ground, then the university has failed you.
Robert Goheen

Higher education must lead the march back to the fundamentals of human relationships, to the old discovery that is ever new, that man does not live by bread alone.
John A. Hannah

It may be that we should stop putting so much emphasis in our own minds on the monetary value of a college education and put more emphasis on the intangible social and cultural values to be derived from learning. The time may be coming when we will have to start accepting the idea that education is life, not merely a preparation for it.
Seymour E. Harris

The two basic processes of education are knowing and valuing.
Robert J. Havighurst

An important personal quality for a teacher is that he care about humanity. If he doesn't, he is taking his pay illegally.
Edward C. Helwick

A good education prepares a child to be a good employee and a good citizen—in that order, with the importance of the former never exceeding the importance of the latter.
Cullen Hightower

A teacher must believe in the value and interest of his subject as a doctor believes in health.
Gilbert Higuet

Our world is a college, events are teachers, happiness is the graduating point, character is the diploma God gives man.
Newell Dwight Hillis

A child's education should begin at least 100 years before he is born.
Oliver Wendell Holmes

We need education in the obvious more than investigation of the obscure.
Oliver Wendell Holmes

My idea of education is to unsettle the minds of the young and inflame their intellects.
Robert M. Hutchins

When we listen to the radio, look at television and read the newspapers we wonder whether universal education has been the great boon that its supporters have always claimed it would be.
Robert M. Hutchins

I care not what subject is taught if only it be taught well.
Thomas H. Huxley

Perhaps the most valuable result of all education is the ability to make yourself do the thing you have to do, whether you like it or not.
Thomas H. Huxley

University degrees are a bit like adultery:
You may not want to get involved with
that sort of thing, but you don't want to
be thought incapable.
Peter Imbert

Colleges are places where pebbles are
polished and diamonds are dimmed.
Robert Ingersoll

Experts are men who educate themselves by reading each other's books.
Irish jurist

Let no youth have any anxiety about the
upshot of his education, whatever the
line of it may be. If he keep faithfully
busy each hour of the working-day, he
may safely leave the result to itself. He
can with perfect certainty count on
waking up some fine morning to find
himself one of the competent ones of his
generation.
William James

I know of no safe repository for the ultimate powers of society but the people
themselves; and if we think them not
enlightened enough to exercise their
control with a wholesome discretion, the
remedy is not to take it from them, but to
increase their discretion by education.
Thomas Jefferson

He that teaches us anything which we
knew not before is undoubtedly to be
reverenced as a master.
Samuel Johnson

To find out what we presently are and
where we are going, we must know what
we have been and what others have
done; and this, because the humanities
are at once the creation and the interpreters of the past, is the great purpose
of humanistic scholarship.
Howard Mumford Jones

I am now past the craggy paths of study,
and come to the flowery plains of honor
and reputation.
Ben Jonson

One looks back with appreciation to the
brilliant teachers, but with gratitude to
those who touch our human feelings.
The curriculum is so much necessary
raw material, but warmth is the vital
element for the growing plant and for the
soul of a child.
Carl Jung

I find the three major problems on a
campus are sex for the students, athletics
for the alumni, and parking for the
faculty.
Clark Kerr

The quality of a university is measured
more by the kind of student it turns out
than the kind it takes in.
Robert Kibbee

It is on the sound education of the people
that the security and destiny of every
nation chiefly rests.
Louis Kossuth

When I hear somebody's got an M.B.A., I
have a feeling of dread, because normally
they come to me with an overpompous
sense of their own importance. And no
way are you going to prick that bubble,
with the result that one day there will be
a cave-in in their department.
Robert Kuok

America's future walks through the
doors of our schools every day.
Mary Jean LeTendre

Men, in teaching others, learn
themselves.
Thomas Lodge

Jails and prisons are the complement of
schools; so many less as you have of the

latter, so many more you must have of the former.
Horace Mann

No man is worthy the honored name of a statesman who does not include the highest practicable education of the people in all his plans of administration. He may have eloquence, he may have a knowledge of all history, diplomacy, jurisprudence; and by these he might claim, in other countries, the elevated rank of a statesman; but, unless he speaks, plans, labors, at all times and in all places, for the culture and edification of the whole people, he is not, he cannot be, an American statesman.
Horace Mann

What office is there which involves more responsibility, which requires more qualifications, and which ought, therefore, to be more honorable, than that of teaching?
Harriet Martineau

The aim of education should be to convert the mind into a living fountain, and not a reservoir. That which is filled by merely pumping in, will be emptied by pumping out.
John M. Mason

I touch the future. I teach.
Christa McAuliffe

A man who knows a subject thoroughly, a man so soaked in it that he eats it, sleeps it and dreams it—this man can always teach it with success, no matter how little he knows of technical pedagogy.
H.L. Mencken

Education is no longer thought of as a preparation for adult life, but as a continuing process of growth and development from birth until death.
Stephen Mitchell

We teachers can only help the work going on, as servants wait upon a master.
Maria Montessori

Industry must fight just as passionately for educational freedom as it does for economic freedom because that which threatens educational freedom threatens all freedoms.
Charles F. Moore, Jr.

Just as education without humanity is the most dangerous thing in the world, so education in love, human understanding and cooperation is the greatest hope of the world.
Joy Elmer Morgan

Intelligence plus experience creates ideas, and experimentation with that form of chemistry—the contact of ideas with events—is the field of adult education.
Felix Morley

I was greatly influenced by one of my teachers. She had a zeal not so much for perfection as for steady betterment—she demanded not excellence so much as integrity.
Edward R. Murrow

The possession of knowledge does not kill the sense of wonder and mystery. There is always more mystery.
Anaïs Nin

I've learned that my teacher always calls on me the one time I don't know the answer.
9-year-old's discovery

No bubble is so iridescent or floats longer than that blown by the successful teacher.
William Osler

Education is a debt due from the present to the future generations.
George Peabody

Education is a method whereby one acquires a higher grade of prejudices.
Laurence J. Peter

Being educated means to prefer the best not only to the worst but to the second best.
William Lyon Phelps

The direction in which education starts a man will determine his future life.
Plato

The mind is not a vessel to be filled but a fire to be kindled.
Plutarch

Thank goodness I was never sent to school; it would have rubbed off some of the originality.
Beatrix Potter

Give instruction to a wise man, and he will be still wiser; teach a just man, and he will increase in learning.
Proverbs 9:9

The noblest exercise of the mind within doors . . . is study.
William Ramsey

There is nothing so stupid as an educated man, if you get him off the thing he was educated in.
Will Rogers

Education is either from nature, from man or from things. The developing of our faculties and organs is the education of nature; that of man is the application we learn to make of this very developing; and that of things is the experience we acquire in regard to the different objects by which we are affected. All that we have not at our birth, and that we stand in need of at the years of maturity, is the gift of education.
Jean-Jacques Rousseau

Education is leading human souls to what is best, and making what is best out of them; and these two objects are always attainable together, and by the same means; the training which makes men happiest in themselves also makes them most serviceable to others.
John Ruskin

Men are born ignorant, not stupid; they are made stupid by education.
Bertrand Russell

In a society safe and worthy to be free, teaching which produces a willingness to lead, as well as a willingness to follow, must be given to all.
William F. Russell

The well-meaning people who talk of education as if it were a substance distributable by coupon in large or small quantities never exhibit any understanding of the truth that you cannot teach anybody anything that he does not want to learn.
George Sampson

The great difficulty in education is to get experience out of ideas.
George Santayana

A well-educated population, trained by mental discipline and culture, and deeply imbued with the religious principle, is the strongest bulwark of a nation.
David Scott

A man cannot leave a better legacy to the world than a well-educated family.
Thomas Scott

My joy in learning is partly that it enables me to teach.
Seneca

Teachers should be held in the highest honor. They are the allies of legislators; they have agency in the prevention of crime; they aid in regulating the atmosphere, whose incessant action and pressure cause the life-blood to circulate, and to return pure and healthful to the heart of the nation.
Lydia Sigourney

Education is the biggest business in America. It has the largest number of owners, the most extensive and costly plant, and utilizes the most valuable raw material. It has the greatest number of operators. It employs our greatest investment in money and time, with the exception of national defense. Its product has the greatest influence on both America and the world.
Charles R. Sligh Jr.

The future of civilization is, to a great extent, being written in the classrooms of the world.
Milton L. Smith

An educated man is one on whom nothing is lost.
Wendell Smith

The great aim of education is not knowledge but action.
Herbert Spencer

Education is not any more the pale flower, to be nurtured in cloistered seclusion, away from the crass world's bruising conflict for material gain. Today education is part of that conflict. It is the prerequisite for material gain. Nor

can even the scholar withdraw into the academic life. The academic life is right out there now, trying to make a living in competition with all the other forms of life.
Francis W. Springer

The worst education which teaches self-denial is better than the best which teaches everything else and not that.
John Sterling

Study to shew thyself approved unto God, a workman that needeth not to be ashamed, rightly dividing the word of truth. But shun profane and vain babblings: for they will increase unto more ungodliness.
II Timothy 2:15–16

I like to instruct people. It is noble to teach oneself. It is still nobler to teach others, and less trouble.
Mark Twain

I never let my schooling interfere with my education.
Mark Twain

It used to take me all vacation to grow a new hide in place of the one they flogged off me during the school term.
Mark Twain

Training is everything. The peach was once a bitter almond; the cauliflower is nothing but cabbage with a college education.
Mark Twain

Four years was enough of Harvard. I still had a lot to learn, but had been given the liberating notion that now I could teach myself.
John Updike

Poor is the pupil who does not surpass his master.
Leonardo da Vinci

Education is an admirable thing, but it is well to remember from time to time that nothing that's worth knowing can be taught.
Oscar Wilde

Education is the mother of leadership.
Wendell Willkie

Education today, more than ever before, must see clearly the dual objectives: Educating for living and educating for making a living.
James Mason Wood

One good teacher in a lifetime may sometimes change a delinquent into a solid citizen.
Philip Wylie

EFFORT

How much easier our work would be if we put forth as much effort trying to improve the quality of it as most of us do trying to find excuses for not properly attending to it.
George W. Ballenger

Know what thou canst work at, and work at it like a Hercules.
Thomas Carlyle

A man is relieved and gay when he has put his heart into his work and done his best.
Ralph Waldo Emerson

So with slight efforts, how should one obtain great results? It is foolish even to desire it.
Euripides

Virtue proceeds through effort.
Euripides

Keep the faculty of effort alive in you by a little gratuitous exercise every day.

That is, be systematically ascetic or heroic in little unnecessary points, do every day or two something for no other reason than that you would rather not do it, so that when the hour of dire need draws nigh, it may find you not unnerved and untrained to stand the test.
William James

Life is either a daring adventure or nothing at all.
Helen Keller

Whether our efforts are, or not, favored by life, let us be able to say, when we come near to the great goal, I have done what I could.
Louis Pasteur

Man's capacities have never been measured. Nor are we to judge of what he can do by precedents, so little has been tried.
Henry David Thoreau

Whatever your work is, dignify it with your best thought and effort.
Esther Baldwin York

EGO

Egotist: A man of low taste, more interested in himself than in me.
Ambrose Bierce

The bigger a man's head gets, the easier it is to fill his shoes.
Henry A. Courtney

I like the moment when I break a man's ego.
Bobby Fischer

Ego trip: a journey to nowhere.
Robert Half

The nice thing about egotists is that they don't talk about other people.
Lucille Harper

Egotism: The art of seeing in yourself what others cannot see.
George Higgins

Our ego is our silent partner—too often with a controlling interest.
Cullen Hightower

They that observe lying vanities forsake their own mercy.
Jonah 2:8

Egotism is the anesthetic that dulls the pain of stupidity.
Frank Leahy

Left-wingers are incapable of conspiring because they're all egomaniacs.
Norman Mailer

Knowledge that puffs up the possessor's mind is ever more of a pernicious kind.
William Mather

I have never seen a greater monster or miracle than myself.
Michel de Montaigne

When any man is more stupidly vain and outrageously egotistic than his fellows, he will hide his hideousness in humanitarianism.
George Moore

Egotism is usually subversive of sagacity.
Marianne Moore

An egotist is not a man who thinks too much of himself; he is a man who thinks too little of other people.
Joseph Fort Newton

To men and women who want to do things, there is nothing quite so driving as the force of an imprisoned ego. . . . All genius comes from this class.
Mary Roberts Rinehart

The egoist does not tolerate egoism.
Joseph Roux

Egotism is the anesthetic which nature gives us to deaden the pain of being a fool.
Dr. Herbert Shofield

If the egotist is weak, his egotism is worthless. If the egotist is strong, acute, full of distinctive character, his egotism is precious, and remains a possession of the race.
Alexander Smith

No one has learned the meaning of life until he has surrendered his ego to the service of his fellow men.
Beran Wolfe

EMOTIONS

It may be true of all relationships, not only between fathers and sons, but between men and women. Nothing seems fixed. Everything is always changing. We seem to have very little control over our emotional life.
Sherwood Anderson

Sensitiveness is closely allied to egotism. Indeed, excessive sensitiveness is only another name for morbid self-consciousness. The cure for it is to make more of our objects, and less of ourselves.
Christian Bovée

There is no fire like passion, there is no shark like hatred, there is no snare like folly, there is no torrent like greed.
Buddha

The guilty think all talk is of themselves.
Geoffrey Chaucer

People hate those who make them feel
their own inferiority.
Lord Chesterfield

The tragedy of life is in what dies inside
a man while he lives—the death of
genuine feeling, the death of inspired
response, the death of the awareness that
makes it possible to feel the pain or the
glory of other men in yourself.
Norman Cousins

Your intellect may be confused, but your
emotions will never lie to you.
Roger Ebert

Are you not justified in feeling inferior,
when you seek to cover it up with arrogance and insolence?
Malcolm Forbes

The heart errs like the head; its errors
are not any the less fatal, and we have
more trouble getting free of them
because of their sweetness.
Anatole France

The appearance of things change
according to the emotions and thus we
see magic and beauty in them, while the
magic and beauty are really in ourselves.
Kahlil Gibran

Systems die—instincts remain.
Oliver Wendell Holmes

Our ideas are here today and gone
tomorrow, whereas our feelings are
always with us, and we recognize those
who feel like us, and at once, by a sort of
instinct.
George Moore

The active part of man consists of
powerful instincts, some of which are
gentle and continuous; others violent
and short; some baser, some nobler, and
all necessary.
F.W. Newman

When I cry, do you want the tears to run
all the way or shall I stop halfway down?
Margaret O'Brien (age 6)

The acceptance of the truth that joy
and sorrow, laughter and tears are not
confined to any particular time, place or
people, but are universally distributed,
should make us more tolerant of and
more interested in the lives of others.
William M. Peck

Our emotions are the driving powers of
our lives. When we are aroused emotionally, unless we do something great and
good, we are in danger of letting our
emotions become perverted. William
James used to tell the story of a Russian
woman who sat weeping at the tragic
fate of the hero in the opera while her
coachman froze to death outside.
Earl Riney

No one can make you feel inferior
without your consent.
Eleanor Roosevelt

The degree of one's emotion varies
inversely with one's knowledge of the
facts—the less you know the hotter
you get.
Bertrand Russell

The advantage of the emotions is that
they lead us astray.
Oscar Wilde

Swift instinct leaps; slow reason feebly
climbs.
Edward Young

EMPLOYEES

For employee success, loyalty and integrity are equally as important as ability.
Harry F. Banks

There is no way of making a business successful that can vie with the policy of promoting those who render exceptional service.
Andrew Carnegie

Plenty of men can do good work for a spurt and with immediate promotion in mind, but for promotion you want a man in whom good work has become a habit.
Henry L. Doherty

Frank W. Woolworth once told me that the turning-point in his career did not come until he was thrown flat on his back by illness. He was sure that his business would go to pieces during his long, enforced absence. Instead, he discovered that he had in his employ men who could overcome difficulties when given power to exercise initiative. After that Woolworth left many problems and difficulties to be solved by subordinates and turned his attention to big things.
B.C. Forbes

H.P. Davison, who became the number one Morgan partner and was widely recognized as among the ablest bankers America ever produced, modestly explained to me how he went about qualifying for promotion. Briefly, he always taught whoever was immediately below him to do his (Davison's) work; next he learned all he could about the job immediately ahead. In this way, whenever changes became necessary, his supervisors found it easy to promote him. After he rose to the top he followed the same principle of teaching others how to pinch-hit for him, thus avoiding delay or dislocation should he be absent at any time.
B.C. Forbes

New Year, the season for changes in positions and advances in salaries, approaches. If you have in your employ some who deserve more salary, do not compel them to go through the unpleasant ordeal of asking for a raise, but, rather, voluntarily increase their remuneration. A raise that comes from the boss without asking is worth a lot more than one that has to be gouged out of him. Is it not true that a great many employers who would not dream of overcharging their customers have no qualms whatever about underpaying their employees if the latter will submit without protest?
B.C. Forbes

All too often we say of a man doing a good job that he is indispensable. A flattering canard, as so many disillusioned and retired and fired have discovered when the world seems to keep on turning without them. In business, a man can come nearest to indispensability by being dispensable in his current job. How can a man move up to new responsibilities if he is the only one able to handle his present tasks? It matters not how small or large the job you now have, if you have trained no one to do it as well, you're not available; you've made your promotion difficult if not impossible.
Malcolm Forbes

Never hire someone who knows less than you do about what he's (or she's) hired to do.
Malcolm Forbes

I tell you, sir, the only safeguard of order and discipline in the modern world is a standardized worker with interchangeable parts. That would solve the entire problem of management.
Jean Giraudoux

When you hire people who are smarter than you are, you prove you are smarter than they are.
Richard Grant

People work for people, not for companies. A worker's regard for his supervisor will affect his opinion of his employer. Production is related to attitude, so much so that an organization which disregards this human equation will not achieve as much as it could achieve.
Gerard R. Griffin

We should place confidence in our employee. Confidence is the foundation of friendship. If we give it, we will receive it. Any person in a managerial position, from supervisor to president, who feels that his employee is basically not as good as he is and who suspects his employee is always trying to put something over on him, lacks the necessary qualities for human leadership—to say nothing of human friendship.
Harry E. Humphreys, Jr.

When people are against profits they're against business; when they're against business, they're against employment; when they're against employment, it's not surprising that a large number of them are unemployed.
Richard J. Needham

I have never met a business man in my life who is not delighted to take on additional employees whenever the demand for his goods and services makes it possible for him to do so.
H.W. Prentis, Jr.

You can employ men and hire hands to work *for* you, but you must win their hearts to have them work *with* you.
Tiorio

EMPLOYERS

The employer generally gets the employees he deserves.
Sir Walter Bilbey

A man who tries to make the workmen believe that their employers are their natural enemies is indeed the worst enemy of workmen. For the employees of yesterday are the employers of today, and the employees of today can and will partly be the employers of tomorrow.
William J.H. Boetcker

With a full century of contrary proof in our possession and despite our demonstrated capacity for cooperative teamwork, some among us seem to accept the shibboleth of an unbridgeable gap between those who hire and those who are employed. We miserably fail to challenge the lie that what is good for management is necessarily bad for labor; that for one side to profit, the other must be depressed. Such distorted doctrine is false and foreign to the American scene where common ideals and purpose permit us a common approach toward the common good.
Dwight D. Eisenhower

Many men who do creditable things refuse to let it be known. This is a mistake. While we all admire modesty, nevertheless there is a great national need to do everything possible to bring home to the rank and file of the people that all employers and all wealthy men are not grinding, mercenary, selfish skinflints, but that many of them take delight in doing helpful things for others. . . . Shortcomings of employers are constantly paraded. Why not let the public become acquainted with the better side which most present-day employers possess?
B.C. Forbes

To be soft-hearted may be handicapping, in a sense. But on the whole, a soft heart is to be preferred to a hard heart. Hard-hearted, severe, dominating giants sometimes manage to get further and to amass

more money. But they get less genuine joy out of life. . . . It is the hard-boiled employer, not the softhearted species, that incites most of our strikes and does most to endanger the harmonious progress of democracy.
B.C. Forbes

The man who gives me employment, which I must have or suffer, that man is my master, let me call him what I will.
Henry George

If, traditionally, employers and employees have blasted at each other, often without dignity and courtesy, could it not be that they were talking two separate dialects? Because capital and labor both have such important contributions to make to the public welfare, it is particularly important that they exhibit, through men of good will, their evolution from a historic precedent of "trading blasts" to a new enlightenment which comes only from "trading places."
J. Richard Sneed

ENEMIES

We often give our enemies the means for our own destruction.
Aesop

Pay attention to your enemies, for they are the first to discover your mistakes.
Antisthenes

In all differences consider that both you and your opponent or enemy are mortal, and that ere long your very memories will be extinguished.
Aurel

The man who never makes a mistake always takes orders from one who does. No man or woman who tries to pursue

an ideal in his or her own way is without enemies.
Daisy Bates

When my enemies stop hissing, I shall know I'm slipping.
Maria Callas

When you go to dig a grave for your enemy—dig two.
Chinese proverb

Choose a friend. He will help you. Alas, he deserts you. Choose an enemy. He will fight against you. Lo, he corrects and perfects you.
Sri Chinmoy

I bring out the worst in my enemies and that's how I get them to defeat themselves.
Roy M. Cohn

Abatement in the hostility of one's enemies must never be thought to signify they have been won over. It only means that one has ceased to constitute a threat.
Quentin Crisp

A strong foe is better than a weak friend.
Edward Dahlberg

Let my enemies devour each other.
Salvador Dalí

Love your enemies in case your friends turn out to be a bunch of bastards.
R.A. Dickson

Take heed of enemies reconciled, and of meat twice boiled.
English proverb

You can calculate the worth of a man by the number of his enemies, and the importance of a work of art by the harm that is spoken of it.
Gustave Flaubert

We have friends but they have not been made by silence or pussyfooting. If we have enemies we do not placate them.
William H. Grimes

If appeasing our enemies is not the answer, neither is hating them. . . . Somewhere between the extremes of appeasement and hate there is a place for courage and strength to express themselves in magnanimity and charity, and this is the place we must find.
A. Whitney Griswold

You can discover what your enemy fears most by observing the means he uses to frighten you.
Eric Hoffer

Treating your adversary with respect is giving him an advantage to which he is not entitled.
Samuel Johnson

Forgive your enemies, but never forget their names.
John F. Kennedy

Every virtuous man would rather meet an open foe than a pretended friend who is a traitor at heart.
H.F. Kletzing

I don't have a warm personal enemy left. They've all died off. I miss them terribly because they helped define me.
Clare Boothe Luce

I am gratified when a friend slaps me on the back and tells me I'm a fine fellow, but I do a little resent it when with his other hand he picks my pocket.
Somerset Maugham

The enemy who forces you to retreat is himself afraid of you at that very moment.
André Maurois

Learning from one's enemies is the best way to love them, for it puts one into a grateful mood toward them.
Friedrich Wilhelm Nietzsche

To have a good enemy, choose a friend: He knows where to strike.
Diane de Poitiers

Rejoice not when thine enemy falleth, and let not thy heart be glad when he stumbleth; Lest the Lord see it, and it displease him, and he turn away his wrath from him.
Proverbs 24:17–18

It's easier to fight one's enemies than to get on with one's friends.
Cardinal de Retz

Whenever thy hand can reach it, tear out thy foe's brain, for such an opportunity washes anger from the mind.
Sa'di

One very important ingredient of success is a good, wide-awake, persistent, tireless enemy. An enemy to an ambitious man is like the rhinoceros bird to the rhinoceros. When the enemy comes the rhinoceros bird tells about it. When a successful man is making mistakes the enemy immediately calls attention and warns the man. Get for yourself a first class enemy, cultivate him as an enemy, and when you achieve success, thank him.
Col. Frank B. Shutts

Your worst enemy is always a man of your own trade.
Spanish proverb

In order to have an enemy, one must be somebody. One must be a force before he can be resisted by another force. A malicious enemy is better than a clumsy friend.
Anne Swetchine

It takes your enemy and your friend, working together, to hurt you: the one to slander you, and the other to bring the news to you.
Mark Twain

ENERGY

Our culture runs on coffee and gasoline, the first often tasting like the second.
Edward Abbey

The difference between one man and another is not mere ability—it is energy.
Thomas Arnold

Energy, like the Biblical grain of mustard seed, will move mountains.
Hosea Ballou

Energy is the only life, and is from the body; and reason is the bound or outward circumference of energy. Energy is eternal delight.
William Blake

Energy is liberated matter; matter is energy waiting to happen.
Bill Bryson

The longer I live, the more deeply I am convinced that that which makes the difference between one man and another—between the weak and the powerful, the great and the insignificant, is energy—invisible determination—a purpose once formed and then death or victory. This quality will do anything that has to be done in the world, and no talents, no circumstances, no opportunities, will make one a man without it.
Thomas Buxton

The average person puts only 25% of his energy and ability into his work. The world takes off its hat to those who put in more than 50% of their capacity, and

stands on its head for those few and far between souls who devote 100%.
Andrew Carnegie

When I first started paying $4 a gallon for gas, I didn't mind; I thought I was just getting better gas.
Stephen Colbert

I guess I am not naturally energetic. I like to sit around and talk.
Calvin Coolidge

Intelligence and the spirit of adventure can be combined to create new energies, and out of these energies may come exciting and rewarding new prospects.
Norman Cousins

Instead of begging OPEC to drop its oil prices, let's use American leadership and ingenuity to solve our own energy problems.
Pete Domenici

I'd put my money on the sun and solar energy. What a source of power! I hope we don't have to wait until oil and coal run out before we tackle that.
Thomas A. Edison

The world belongs to the energetic.
Ralph Waldo Emerson

The real difference between men is energy. A strong will, a settled purpose, an invincible determination, can accomplish almost anything; and in this lies the distinction between great men and little men.
Thomas Fuller

Energy will do anything that can be done in the world; and no talents, no circumstances, no opportunities will make a two-legged animal a man without it.
Johann Wolfgang von Goethe

A man doesn't need brilliance or genius, all he needs is energy.
Albert M. Greenfield

Our energy is in proportion to the resistance it meets. We attempt nothing great but from a sense of the difficulties we have to encounter; we persevere in nothing great but from a pride in overcoming them.
William Hazlitt

It takes wit and interest and energy to be happy. The pursuit of happiness is a great activity. One must be open and alive. It is the greatest feat man has to accomplish, and spirits must flow. There must be courage. There are no easy ruts to get into which lead to happiness. A man must become interesting to himself and must become actually expressive before he can be happy.
Robert Henri

He also has energy who cannot be deprived of it.
Johann Lavater

There is no genius in life like the genius of energy and industry.
D.G. Mitchell

In addition to contributing to erosion, pollution, food poisoning and the dead zone, corn requires huge amounts of fossil fuel—it takes a half gallon of fossil fuel to produce a bushel of corn.
Michael Pollan

I have a great deal of difficulty with those who live in a hugely prosperous country telling people in the developing world that they should be deprived of a critical source of energy.
Lee Raymond

It is sad that my emotional dependence on the man I love should have killed so much of my energy and ability; there was certainly once a great deal of energy in me.
Sonya Tolstoy

I found that the men and women who got to the top were those who did the jobs they had in hand, with everything they had of energy and enthusiasm and hard work.
Harry S Truman

We are all addicts of fossil fuels in a state of denial, about to face cold turkey.
Kurt Vonnegut

The Stone Age did not end for lack of stone and the Oil Age will end long before the world runs out of oil.
Sheikh Ahmed Zaki Yamani

ENJOYMENT

That one who does not get fun and enjoyment out of every day in which he lives, needs to reorganize his life. And the sooner the better, for pure enjoyment throughout life has more to do with one's happiness and efficiency than almost any other single element.
George Matthew Adams

All of the animals except man know that the principal business of life is to enjoy it.
Samuel Butler

To enjoy and give enjoyment, without injury to yourself or others; this is true morality.
Nicolas Chamfort

Let us not be too prodigal when we are young, nor too parsimonious when we are old. Otherwise we shall fall into the common error of those, who, when they had the power to enjoy, had not the

prudence to acquire; and when they had the prudence to acquire, had no longer the power to enjoy.
Charles Caleb Colton

And also that every man should eat and drink, and enjoy the good of all his labor, it is the gift of God.
Ecclesiastes 3:13

I like large parties. They're so intimate. At small parties there isn't any privacy.
F. Scott Fitzgerald

Enjoyment is not a goal, it is a feeling that accompanies important ongoing activity.
Paul Goodman

There is nothing like fun, is there? I haven't any myself, but I do like it in others.
Thomas Haliburton

Taking fun as simply fun and earnestness in earnest shows how thoroughly thou none of the two discernest.
Piet Hein

Fun is like life insurance: the older you get, the more it costs.
Kin Hubbard

True enjoyment comes from activity of the mind and exercise of the body; the two are ever united.
Wilhelm von Humboldt

Restraint is the golden rule of enjoyment.
Letitia Landon

Man only plays when in the full meaning of the word he is a man, and he is only completely a man when he plays.
Johann Friedrich von Schiller

The test of an enjoyment is the remembrance which it leaves behind.
Logan Pearsall Smith

No enjoyment, however inconsiderable, is confined to the present moment. A man is the happier for life from having made once an agreeable tour, or lived for any length of time with pleasant people, or enjoyed any considerable interval of innocent pleasure.
Sydney Smith

Never run after your own hat—others will be delighted to do it; why spoil their fun?
Mark Twain

Work consists of whatever a body is obliged to do, and play consists of whatever a body is not obliged to do.
Mark Twain

One of the principal features of my entertainment is that it contains so many things that don't have anything to do with it.
Artemus Ward

ENTHUSIASM

The worst bankrupt in the world is the man who has lost his enthusiasm. Let a man lose everything else in the world but his enthusiasm and he will come through again to success.
H.W. Arnold

From the glow of enthusiasm I let the melody escape. I pursue it. Breathless I catch up with it. It flies again, it disappears, it plunges into a chaos of diverse emotions. I catch it again, I seize it, I embrace it with delight. . . . I multiply it by modulations, and at last I triumph in the first theme. There is the whole symphony.
Ludwig van Beethoven

Nothing is so contagious as enthusiasm.
Edward George Bulwer-Lytton

Enthusiasm is a virtue rarely to be met with in seasons of calm and unruffled prosperity.
Thomas Chalmers

Enthusiasm is the greatest asset in the world. It beats money and power and influence. It is no more or less than faith in action.
Henry Chester

Every production of genius must be the production of enthusiasm.
Benjamin Disraeli

There is a sort of human paste that when it comes near the fire of enthusiasm is only baked into harder shape.
George Eliot

Experience and enthusiasm are two fine business attributes seldom found in one individual.
William Feather

It's so much easier to be enthusiastic—especially when there are grounds for it.
Malcolm Forbes

Enthusiasm is at the bottom of all progress. With it there is accomplishment. Without it there are only alibis.
Henry Ford

A mother should give her children a superabundance of enthusiasm, that after they have lost all they are sure to lose on mixing with the world, enough may still remain to prompt and support them through great actions.
Julius C. Hare

Weakness, fear, melancholy, together with ignorance, are the true sources of superstition. Hope, pride, presumption, a warm indignation, together with ignorance, are the true sources of enthusiasm.
David Hume

Enthusiasts soon understand each other.
Washington Irving

Study the unusually successful people you know, and you will find them imbued with enthusiasm for their work which is contagious. Not only are they themselves excited about what they are doing, but they also get you excited.
Paul W. Ivey

Men are nothing until they are excited.
Michel de Montaigne

If you can't get enthusiastic about your work, it's time to get alarmed—something is wrong. Compete with yourself; set your teeth and dive into the job of breaking your own record. No one keeps up his enthusiasm automatically. Enthusiasm must be nourished with new actions, new aspirations, new efforts, new vision. It is one's own fault if his enthusiasm is gone; he has failed to feed it. If you want to turn hours into minutes, renew your enthusiasm.
Papyrus

The essential in this time of moral poverty is to create enthusiasm.
Pablo Picasso

It is energy—the central element of which is will—that produces the miracles of enthusiasm in all ages. Everywhere it is the mainspring of what is called force of character and the sustaining power of all great action.
Samuel Smiles

The language of excitement is at best picturesque merely. You must be calm before you can utter oracles.
Henry David Thoreau

Apathy can only be overcome by enthusiasm, and enthusiasm can only be aroused by two things: first, an ideal which takes the imagination by storm,

and second, a definite intelligible plan for carrying that ideal into practice.
Arnold Toynbee

National enthusiasm is the great nursery of genius.
Henry Tuckerman

Enthusiasm is that temper of the mind in which the imagination has got the better of the judgment.
William Warburton

ENVY

One reason why so many people are unhappy, not knowing why, is that they have burdened their minds with resentments. These evil thoughts pile right on top of happier and generous ones and smother them so that they never get expression. Resentments are a form of hate. . . . What a dearth of good will and co-operation there are among human beings and nations! What a world this would be if we all worked together, and as a popular diplomat recently expressed it—played together!
George Matthew Adams

Few men have the natural strength to honor a friend's success without envy.
Aeschylus

Envy ought to have no place allowed it in the heart of man; for the goods of this present world are so vile and low that they are beneath it, and those of the future world are so vast and exalted that they are above it.
Charles Caleb Colton

A man shall never be enriched by envy.
Thomas Draxe

Again, I considered all travail, and every right work, that for this a man is envied of his neighbor. This is also vanity and vexation of spirit.
Ecclesiastes 4:4

Men are so constituted that every one undertakes what he sees another successful in, whether he has aptitude for it or not.
Johann Wolfgang von Goethe

Let your conversation be without covetousness; and be content with such things as ye have.
Hebrews 13:5

It is better to be envied than to be pitied.
Herodotus

The envious man grows lean at the success of his neighbor.
Horace

There is more self-love than love in jealousy.
François de La Rochefoucauld

The truest mark of being born with great qualities, is being born without envy.
François de La Rochefoucauld

Envy always implies conscious inferiority wherever it resides.
Pliny

We love in others what we lack ourselves, and would be everything but what we are.
Richard H. Stoddard

Grudges get heavier, the longer they are carried.
P.K. Thomajan

No man is greatly jealous who is not in some measure guilty.
Benjamin Whichcote

EQUALITY

The defect of equality is that we only desire it with our superiors.
Henry Becque

Whatever difference there may appear to be in men's fortunes, there is still a certain compensation of good and ill in all, that makes them equal.
Pierre Charron

The doctrine of human equality reposes on this: that there is no man really clever who has not found that he is stupid. There is no big man who has not felt small. Some men never feel small; but these are the few men who are.
G.K. Chesterton

The English are no nearer than they were a hundred years ago to knowing what Jefferson really meant when he said that God had created all men equal.
G.K. Chesterton

We hold these truths to be self-evident, that all men are created equal, that they are endowed by their Creator with certain unalienable Rights, that among these are Life, Liberty and the pursuit of Happiness. That to secure these rights, Governments are instituted among Men, deriving their just powers from the consent of the governed. That whenever any Form of Government becomes destructive of these ends, it is the Right of the People to alter or to abolish it, and to institute new Government, laying its foundation on such principles and organizing its powers in such form, as to them shall seem most likely to effect their Safety and Happiness.
The Declaration of Independence

If by saying that all men are born free and equal, you mean that they are all equally born, it is true, but true in no other sense; birth, talent, labor, virtue, and providence, are forever making differences.
Eugene Edwards

Some persons are always ready to level those above them down to themselves, while they are never willing to level those below them up to their own position. But he that is under the influence of true humility will avoid both these extremes. On the one hand, he will be willing that all should rise just so far as their diligence and worth of character entitle them to; and on the other hand, he will be willing that his superiors should be known and acknowledged in their place, and have rendered to them all the honors that are their due.
Jonathan Edwards

Some will always be above others. Destroy the inequality today, and it will appear again tomorrow.
Ralph Waldo Emerson

Men are by nature equal. It is vain, therefore, to treat them as if they were equal.
James A. Froude

Let him who expects one class of society to prosper in the highest degree, while the other is in distress, try whether one side of his face can smile while the other is pinched.
Thomas Fuller

Every Frenchman wants to enjoy one or more privileges; that's the way he shows his passion for equality.
Charles de Gaulle

We are all born equal—equally helpless and equally indebted to others for whatever our survival turns out to be worth.
Cullen Hightower

All men are equal before fish.
Herbert Hoover

The hole and the patch should be commensurate.
Thomas Jefferson

For the reason that we are equal before God, we are made equal before the law of this land. And when you have said that, you have summed up and tied with a bowknot the complete American doctrine of equality.
Clarence E. Manion

The good Lord sees your heart, not the braid on your jacket; before him we are all in our birthday suits, generals and common men alike.
Thomas Mann

ERRORS

An error is always the more dangerous in proportion to the degree of truth which it contains.
Henri Frédéric Amiel

There is no such source of error as the pursuit of absolute truth.
Samuel Butler

An error is simply a failure to adjust immediately from a preconception to an actuality.
John Cage

The greatest mistake is to imagine that we never err.
Thomas Carlyle

Honest error is to be pitied, not ridiculed.
Lord Chesterfield

It is human to err; and the only final and deadly error, among all our errors, is denying that we have ever erred.
G.K. Chesterton

Ignorance is a blank sheet on which we may write; but error is a scribbled one from which we must first erase.
Charles Caleb Colton

It is almost as difficult to make a man unlearn his errors as his knowledge.
Charles Caleb Colton

I beseech you, in the bowels of Christ, think it possible you may be mistaken.
Oliver Cromwell

The chief cause of human errors is to be found in prejudices picked up in childhood.
René Descartes

Man is made for error; it enters his mind naturally, and he discovers a few truths only with the greatest effort.
Frederick the Great

An old error is always more popular than a new truth.
German proverb

I hate all bungling like sin, but most of all bungling in state affairs, which produces nothing but mischief to thousands and millions.
Johann Wolfgang von Goethe

While man's desires and aspirations stir he cannot choose but err.
Johann Wolfgang von Goethe

To err is human, but when the eraser wears out ahead of the pencil, you're overdoing it.
J. Jenkins

Error is not a fault of our knowledge, but a mistake of our judgment giving assent to that which is not true.
John Locke

Sometimes we may learn more from a man's errors than from his virtues.
Henry Wadsworth Longfellow

We come to learn that it does not pay to grieve too much over our errors. Ordinarily we try to do the best we can.
Robert L. Masson

The world always makes the assumption that the exposure of an error is identical with the discovery of the truth—that error and truth are simply opposite. They are nothing of the sort. What the world turns to, when it is cured of one error, is usually simply another error, and maybe one worse than the first one.
H.L. Mencken

The credit belongs to the man who is actually in the arena; whose face is marred with dust and sweat; who strives valiantly; who errs and may fall again and again, because there is no effort without error or shortcoming.
Theodore Roosevelt

To err is human—but it feels divine.
Mae West

If a man is in too big a hurry to give up an error he is liable to give up some truth with it, and in accepting the argument of the other man he is sure to get some error with it. After I get hold of a truth I hate to lose it again, and I like to sift all the truth out before I give up an error.
Wilbur Wright

The pain that others give passes away in their later kindness, but that of our own blunders, especially when they hurt our vanity, never passes away.
William Butler Yeats

ESPIONAGE

Every man is surrounded by a neighborhood of voluntary spies.
Jane Austen

When I was at Cambridge it was, naturally enough, I felt, my ambition to be approached in some way by an elderly homosexual don and asked to spy for or against my country.
Stephen Fry

The life of spies is to know, not to be known.
George Herbert

A prince should have a spy to observe what is necessary, and what is unnecessary, in his own as well as in his enemy's country
Hitopadesha

He that spies is the one that kills.
Irish proverb

What do you think spies are: priests, saints and martyrs? They're a squalid procession of vain fools, traitors too, yes; pansies, sadists and drunkards, people who play cowboys and Indians to brighten their rotten lives.
John le Carré

There are some who become spies for money, or out of vanity and megalomania, or out of ambition, or out of a desire for thrills. But the malady of our time is of those who become spies out of idealism.
Max Lerner

On the Profumo affair: When I was in Venice I thought that perhaps masked naked men, orgies and unlimited spying are an accompaniment of maritime powers in decline.
Nancy Mitford

It is only the enlightened ruler and the wise general who will use the highest intelligence of the army for the purposes of spying, and thereby they achieve great results.
Sun Tzu

From infancy on we are all spies; the shame is not this but that the secrets to be discovered are so paltry and few.
John Updike

I cannot think that espionage can be recommended as a technique for building an impressive civilization. It's a lout's game.
Rebecca West

EVIL

Eighty percent of our criminals come from unsympathetic homes.
Hans Christian Andersen

Hell is more bearable than nothingness.
Philip James Bailey

The contagion of crime is like that of the plague. Criminals collected together corrupt each other. They are worse than ever when, at the termination of their punishment, they return to society.
Napoleon Bonaparte

When bad men combine, the good must associate, else they will fall one by one, an unpitied sacrifice in a contemptible struggle.
Edmund Burke

Only one thing is worse than a devil and that is an educated devil.
George A. Butterick

Men's hearts ought not be set against one another, but set with one another, and all against evil only.
Thomas Carlyle

The old assumption of the approximate impossibility of war really rested on a similar assumption about the impossibility of evil—and especially of evil in high places.
G.K. Chesterton

Evils in the journey of life are like the hills which alarm travelers on the road. Both appear great at a distance, but when we approach them we find they are far less insurmountable than we had conceived.
Charles Caleb Colton

Evil, which is our companion all our days, is not to be treated as a foe. It is wrong to cocker vice, but we grow narrow and pithless if we are furtive about it, for this is at best a pretense, and the sage knows good and evil are kindred. The worst of men harm others, and the best injure themselves.
Edward Dahlberg

Because sentence against an evil work is not executed speedily, therefore the heart of the sons of men is fully set in them to do evil.
Ecclesiastes 8:11

Preventives of evil are far better than remedies; cheaper and easier of application, and surer in result.
Tryon Edwards

One soweth and another reapeth is a verity that applies to evil as well as good.
George Eliot

There is no sort of wrong deed of which a man can bear the punishment alone; you can't isolate yourself and say that the evil that is in you shall not spread. Men's lives are as thoroughly blended with each other as the air they breathe; evil spreads as necessarily as disease.
George Eliot

The first lesson of history is that evil is good.
Ralph Waldo Emerson

For we wrestle not against flesh and blood, but against principalities, against powers, against the rulers of the darkness of this world, against a spiritual wickedness in high places.
Ephesians 6:12

The gift of a bad man can bring no good.
Euripides

Crime in the city streets is more than a political issue. It's a too rampant fact. . . . In Indianapolis they have come up with a most sensible, affordable approach to the problem. Policemen are assigned their police patrol cars for personal use after hours. They are encouraged to use the police car while taking the family shopping, to the movies, and everywhere one takes one's family. As a result, says the Police Chief's assistant, we may have as many as 400 cars on the street instead of 100 or so per shift. [And] the presence of the police car obviously indicates the proximity of policemen.
Malcolm Forbes

How in heck are they handling their surplus population in Hell these days? Maybe by the time you and I are in the queue there won't be room for us.
Malcolm Forbes

The usual choice is not between the good and the bad but between the bad and the worse.
French proverb

Don't let us make imaginary evils, when you know we have so many real ones to encounter.
Oliver Goldsmith

One uncooperative employee can sabotage an entire organization because bad spirit is more contagious than good spirit.
Robert Half

Wherever they burn books they will also, in the end, burn human beings.
Heinrich Heine

It is only when men associate with the wicked with the desire and purpose of doing them good, that they can rely upon the protection of God to preserve them from contamination.
Charles Hodge

Knowest thou not this of old, since man was placed upon earth, That the triumphing of the wicked is short, and the joy of the hypocrite but for a moment?
Job 20:4–5

Woe unto them that call evil good, and good evil; that put darkness for light, and light for darkness; that put bitter for sweet, and sweet for bitter.
Isaiah 5:20

Evil acts of the past are never rectified by evil acts of the present.
Lyndon Baines Johnson

Combinations of wickedness would overwhelm the world, by the advantage which licentious principles afford, did not those who have long practised perfidy grow faithless to each other.
Samuel Johnson

Where secrecy or mystery begins, vice or roguery is not far off.
Samuel Johnson

No man ever became very wicked all at once.
Juvenal

Whoever takes it upon himself to establish a commonwealth and prescribe laws must presuppose all men naturally bad, and that they will yield to their innate evil passions as often as they can do so with safety.
Niccolò Machiavelli

Hell begins on the day when God grants us a clear vision of all that we might have achieved, of all the gifts which we have wasted, of all that we might have done which we did not do.
Gian Carlo Menotti

Real evils can be either cured or endured; it is only imaginary evils that make people anxiety-ridden for a lifetime.
Earl Nightingale

We sometimes learn more from the sight of evil than from an example of good; and it is well to accustom ourselves to profit by the evil which is so common, while that which is good is so rare.
Blaise Pascal

A good end cannot sanctify evil means, nor must we ever do evil that good may come of it.
William Penn

It is not noble to return evil for evil, at no time ought we to do an injury to our neighbors.
Plato

Fret not thyself because of evildoers, neither be thou envious against the workers of iniquity. For they shall soon be cut down like the grass, and wither as the green herb.
Psalms 37:1–2

It is the law of our humanity that man must know good through evil. No great principle ever triumphed but through much evil. No man ever progressed to greatness and goodness but through great mistakes.
Frederick W. Robertson

There is evil in the world, but it can be overcome through repentance and aspiration, and therein lies the true meaning and adventure of life.
Abba Hillel Silver

Never let a man imagine that he can pursue a good end by evil means, without sinning against his own soul. The evil effect on himself is certain.
Robert Southey

The wise man avoids evil by anticipating it.
Publilius Syrus

There can be no such thing as a necessary evil. For, if a thing is really necessary, it cannot be an evil and if it is an evil, it is not necessary.
Tiorio

There is only one way to put an end to evil, and that is to do good for evil.
Leo Tolstoy

EXAMPLE

Example is the school of mankind, and they will learn at no other.
Edmund Burke

When you try to step into someone else's shoes, you'll find they are either too big or too small.
Simha Dinitz

It is a trite but true definition that examples work more forcibly on the mind than precepts.
Henry Fielding

You can preach a better sermon with your life than with your lips.
Oliver Goldsmith

If birds of a feather flock together, they don't learn enough.
Robert Half

The first great gift we can bestow on others is a good example.
Thomas Morell

Example is contagious behavior.
Charles Reade

Men trust their eyes rather than their ears; the road by precept is long and tedious, by example short and effectual.
Seneca

Example teaches better than precept. It is the best modeler of the character of men and women. To set a lofty example is the richest bequest a man can leave behind him.
Samuel Smiles

Few things are harder to put up with than the annoyance of a good example.
Mark Twain

EXCELLENCE

In every business there is always someone who knows exactly what is going on. And that person should be fired.
Anonymous

Excellence is an art won by training and habituation. We do not act rightly because we have virtue or excellence, but we rather have those because we have acted rightly. We are what we repeatedly do. Excellence, then, is not an act but a habit.
Aristotle

Striving for excellence motivates you; striving for perfection is demoralizing.
Harriet Braiker

The secret of joy in work is contained in one word, excellence. To know how to do something well is to enjoy it.
Pearl S. Buck

Men have various subjects in which they may excel, or at least would be thought to excel, and though they love to hear justice done to them where they know they excel, yet they are most and best flattered upon those points where they wish to excel and yet are doubtful whether they do or not.
Lord Chesterfield

He who stops being better stops being good.
Oliver Cromwell

One that desires to excel should endeavor it in those things that are in themselves most excellent.
Epictetus

One fact stands out in bold relief in the history of man's attempts for betterment. That is that when compulsion is used, only resentment is aroused, and the end is not gained. Only through moral suasion and appeal to man's reason can a movement succeed.
Samuel Gompers

The less justified a man is in claiming excellence for his own self, the more ready he is to claim all excellence for his nation, his religion, his race or his holy cause.
Eric Hoffer

Strive for excellence in your calling, but as a subsidiary to this: Do not fail to enrich your whole capital as man. To be a giant, and not a dwarf in your profession, you must always be growing. The man

that has ceased to go up intellectually
has begun to go down.
William Matthews

There is no excellency without difficulty.
Ovid

Excellence is never granted to man
but as the reward of labor. It argues
no small strength of mind to persevere in habits of industry without the
pleasure of perceiving those advances,
which, like the hand of a clock, whilst
they make hourly approaches to their
point, yet proceed so slowly as to escape
observation.
Joshua Reynolds

I tell you that as long as I can conceive
something better than myself I cannot be
easy unless I am striving to bring it into
existence or clearing the way for it.
George Bernard Shaw

Our priceless heritage is the American
way of life, and nothing is more typical of
the average American than his constant
search for something better. The everlasting demand for better homes, better
automobiles, better schools . . . better
everything . . . has gone hand in hand
with our devotion to freedom.
James H. Shields

Each excellent thing, once learned,
serves for a measure of all other
knowledge.
Sir Philip Sidney

In seasons of tumult and discord bad
men have most power; mental and moral
excellence require peace and quietness.
Tacitus

Next to excellence is the appreciation
of it.
William Makepeace Thackeray

We succeed in enterprises which
demand the positive qualities we possess,
but we excel in those which can also
make use of our defects.
Alexis de Tocqueville

EXECUTIVES

Good executives never put off until
tomorrow what they can get someone
else to do today.
Anonymous

A committee is a group that keeps the
minutes and loses hours.
Milton Berle

Very few big executives want to be
surrounded by "yes" men. Their greatest
weakness often is the fact that "yes" men
build up around the executive a wall of
fiction, when what the executive wants
most of all is plain facts.
Burton Bigelow

A valuable executive must possess
a willingness and ability to assume
responsibility, a fair knowledge of his
particular branch of business, and a nice
understanding of business principles
in general, also to be able to read and
understand human nature. There is no
phase of knowledge which anyone can
safely dismiss as valueless.
Charles Cheney

If you don't take it for granted that the
other man will do his job, you're not an
executive.
William Feather

After visiting several of America's most
fashionable playgrounds, I have reached
the conclusion that men who work hard
enjoy life most. The men at such places
can be divided into two classes, first,
busy men of affairs . . . and, second, rich
loafers. I was impressed by the obvious

enjoyment corporation heads and other important executives were deriving from their vacation activities. . . . The idle rich fellows, on the other hand, although indulging in exactly the same activities, palpably were bored.
B.C. Forbes

Do too many executives still indulge in the short-sighted habit of issuing orders without taking the slightest pains to explain to those responsible for carrying them out the whyfor and wherefor of the orders? Where employees come in daily and hourly contact with the public, surely it is important that care be taken to fit them to reply intelligently to courteous questions. "Because them are orders" isn't a satisfying reply—even less satisfactory to the management than to the public.
B.C. Forbes

It is a great mistake for presidents and other leading executives of organizations having branches throughout the country to chain themselves to their desks at headquarters and send out rigid instructions to those in charge of distant branches and offices. Because a man sits in a palatial office in New York or Chicago or Philadelphia or Detroit and draws a big salary, it does not necessarily follow that he knows better than the man on the spot what ought to be done. . . . Paul, Caesar, Napoleon did not merely sit at home and issue long-range instructions.
B.C. Forbes

The more I move among workers and factories and other plants, the stronger I become convinced that it is advisable to have as [a company] president a practical man, preferably one who has risen from the very bottom of the ladder. Workmen, I find, have far more respect for such men than for collar-and-cuff executives

knowing little or nothing about the different kinds of work which have to be done by the workers. Wherever circumstances call for placing a financier or lawyer or a papa's son at the head of a large organization, he should be made chairman or some other title, but not president.
B.C. Forbes

Whenever possible, I like to have the supreme head of a company show me over the works. It is extremely illuminating to note the attitude of workers towards their boss, and equally interesting to note the attitude towards the workers. It is tragic to notice how many chief executives of large concerns are absolutely unknown, even by sight, to the rank and file of their workers.
B.C. Forbes

An inadequate chief executive officer's time at the top is always too long no matter how short.
Malcolm Forbes

Executives who get there and stay suggest solutions when they present the problems.
Malcolm Forbes

Hopeless cases: Executives who assert themselves by saying No when they should say Yes.
Malcolm Forbes

People are talking about the new "civilized" way to fire executives. You kick 'em upstairs. They're given a little, a liberal tithe, nothing to do, and a secretary to do it with. What a way to go!
Malcolm Forbes

The top people of the biggest companies are, surprisingly, often the nicest ones in their company. I'm not sure, though, if they got there because they were good

guys or that they're now good guys
because they can afford to be.
Malcolm Forbes

Twelve experts gathered in one room
equal one big idiot.
Carl Jung

Committees are to get everybody
together and homogenize their thinking.
Art Linkletter

When you know men and you know how
to handle men, you've licked the problem
of running a business. The executive's job
is to provide leadership, the kind of leadership that develops the best efforts of
the men under him. He can't do that if he
shuts himself up in his office. He has to
get out and get acquainted with his men.
Roy W. Moore

The best executive is the one who has
sense enough to pick good men to do
what he wants done, and self-restraint
enough to keep from meddling with
them while they do it.
Theodore Roosevelt

Even for the neurotic executive—as for
everyone else—work has great ther-
apeutic value; it is generally his last
refuge, and deterioration there marks the
final collapse of the man; his marriage,
his social life, and the outside interests—
all have suffered beforehand.
Richard A. Smith

EXPECTATIONS

What a pleasure life would be to live if
everybody would try to do only half of
what he expects others to do.
William J.H. Boetcker

The element of the unexpected and the
unforeseeable is what gives some of its
relish to life and saves us from falling
into the mechanical thralldom of the
logicians.
Winston Churchill

As long as there are postmen, life will
have zest.
William James

We love to expect, and when expectation
is either disappointed or gratified, we
want to be again expecting.
Samuel Johnson

We are living in a period which all too
readily scraps the old for the new.....
As a nation, we are in danger of forgetting that the new is not true because
it is novel, and that the old is not false
because it is ancient.
Joseph P. Kennedy

It must be remembered that there is
nothing more difficult to plan, more
doubtful of success, nor more dangerous
to manage, that the creation of a new
system. For the initiator has the enmity
of all who would profit by the preservation of the old institutions and merely
lukewarm defenders in those who would
gain by the new ones.
Niccolò Machiavelli

Presumption is our natural and original
malady. When I play with my cat, who
knows if I am not a pastime to her more
than she is to me.
Michel de Montaigne

One does not expect in this world; one
hopes and pays carfares.
Josephine Preston Peabody

There is nothing more miserable and
foolish than anticipation.
Seneca

Oft expectation fails, and most oft there
where most it promises.
William Shakespeare

We must expect everything and fear everything from time to time.
Marquis de Vauvenargue

EXPERIENCE

The man who views the world at 50 the same as he did at 20 has wasted 30 years of his life.
Muhammad Ali

Experience is a good teacher, but she sends in terrific bills.
Minna Antrim

By experience we find out a short way by a long wandering.
Roger Ascham

Experience is a private, very largely speechless affair.
James Baldwin

Experience is the comb that Nature gives us after we are bald.
Belgian proverb

Experience isn't interesting until it begins to repeat itself, in fact, till it does that, it hardly is experience.
Elizabeth Bowen

Experience takes dreadfully high school-wages, but he teaches like no other.
Thomas Carlyle

Experience is the universal mother of sciences.
Miguel de Cervantes

You cannot speak of ocean to a well-frog, the creature of a narrower sphere. You cannot speak of ice to a summer insect, the creature of a season.
Chuang Tzu

If men could learn from history, what lessons it might teach us! But passion and party blind our eyes, and the light which experience gives us is a lantern on the stern which shines only on the waves behind us.
Samuel Taylor Coleridge

The trouble with experience is that by the time you have it you are too old to take advantage of it.
Jimmy Connors

Experience is the child of thought, and thought is the child of action. We cannot learn men from books.
Benjamin Disraeli

It takes a lot of time to get experience, and once you have it you ought to go on using it.
Benjamin M. Duggar

For everything you have missed you have gained something else.
Ralph Waldo Emerson

Experience seems to be the only thing of any value that's widely distributed.
William Feather

Life is a series of experience, each one of which makes us bigger, even though sometimes it is hard to realize this. For the world was built to develop character, and we must learn that the setbacks and griefs which we endure help us in our marching onward.
Henry Ford

You take all the experience and judgment of men over 50 out of the world and there wouldn't be enough left to run it.
Henry Ford

In the business world, everyone is paid in two coins: cash and experience. Take the experience first; the cash will come later.
Harold Geneen

An M.B.A's first shock could be the realization that companies require

experience before they hire a chief executive officer.
Robert Half

I have but one lamp by which my feet are guided, and that is the lamp of experience. I know of no way of judging of the future by the past.
Patrick Henry

Experience is something I always think I have until I get more of it.
Burton Hillis

Experience is not what happens to a man. It is what a man does with what happens to him.
Aldous Huxley

The one who thinks over his experiences most, and weaves them into systematic relations with each other, will be the one with the best memory.
William James

The ordinary affairs of a nation offer little difficulty to a person of any experience.
Thomas Jefferson

Experience is the worst teacher; it gives the test before presenting the lesson.
Vernon Law

Growing up is, after all, only the understanding that one's unique and incredible experience is what everyone shares.
Doris Lessing

The story of any one man's real experience finds its startling parallel in that of every one of us.
James Russell Lowell

Age should not have its faith lifted but rather teach the world to admire wrinkles as the etchings of experience and the firm lines of character.
Ralph Barton Perry

There are many arts among men, the knowledge of which is acquired bit by bit by experience. For it is experience that causeth our life to move forward by the skill we acquire, while want of experience subjects us to the effects of chance.
Plato

Experience is a jewel, and it had need be so, for it is often purchased at an infinite rate.
William Shakespeare

Men are wise in proportion, not to their experience, but to their capacity for experience.
George Bernard Shaw

The rules which experience suggests are better than those which theorists elaborate in their libraries.
Richard Storrs

All experience is an arch wherethro' gleams that untraveled world whose margins fade forever and forever as we move.
Alfred, Lord Tennyson

Experience does not err; only your judgements err by expecting from her what is not in her power.
Leonardo da Vinci

FACTS

It is not the facts which guide the conduct of men, but their opinions about facts; which may be entirely wrong. We can only make them right by discussion.
Sir Norman Angell

Every man has a right to his opinion, but no man has a right to be wrong in his facts.
Bernard M. Baruch

Facts that are not frankly faced have a habit of stabbing us in the back.
Sir Harold Bowden

Facts are to the mind what food is to the body. On the due digestion of the former depend the strength and wisdom of the one, just as vigor and health depend on the other. The wisest in council, the ablest in debate, and the most agreeable companion in the commerce of human life, is that man who has assimilated to his understanding the greatest number of facts.
Edmund Burke

Let us keep our mouths shut and our pens dry until we know the facts.
Dr. A.J. Carlson

The moment you step into the world of facts, you step into the world of limits. You can free things from alien or accidental laws, but not from the laws of their own nature.
G.K. Chesterton

Only feeble minds are paralyzed by facts.
Arthur C. Clarke

Creative thinking will improve as we relate the new fact to the old and all facts to each other.
John Dewey

Facts are the most important thing in business. Study facts and do more than is expected of you.
Frederick H. Ecker

Facts are God's arguments; we should be careful never to misunderstand or pervert them.
Tryon Edwards

In some small field each child should attain, within the limited range of its experience and observation, the power to draw a justly limited inference from observed facts.
Charles W. Eliot

No facts are to me sacred; none are profane; I simply experiment, an endless seeker, with no past at my back.
Ralph Waldo Emerson

Any fact is better established by two or three good testimonies than by a thousand arguments.
Nathanial Emmons

That's the kind of ad I like: facts, facts, facts.
Samuel Goldwyn

Facts do not cease to exist because they are ignored.
Aldous Huxley

Facts mean nothing unless they are rightly understood, rightly related and rightly interpreted.
R.L. Long

No fact is so simple that it is not harder to believe than to doubt at the first presentation. Equally, there is nothing so mighty or so marvelous that the wonder it evokes does not tend to diminish in time.
Lucretius

We should keep so close to facts that we never have to remember the second time what we said the first time.
F. Marion Smith

Never face facts; if you do, you'll never get up in the morning.
Marlo Thomas

The brightest flashes in the world of thought are incomplete until they have

been proved to have their counterparts in the world of fact.
John Tyndall

It is the individual citizen's understanding of facts that counts in a democracy. In totalitarian states, only a few people have to know the significance of facts. Here in America everyone has to know what facts mean.
Paul A. Wagner

He that has a spirit of detail will do better in life than many who figured beyond him in the university.
Daniel Webster

FAILURE

Nothing resembles pride so much as discouragement.
Henri Frédéric Amiel

Whoever admits that he is too busy to improve his methods, has acknowledged himself to be at the end of his rope. And that is always the saddest predicament which any one can get into.
J. Ogden Armour

Failures either do not know what they want, or jib at the price.
W.H. Auden

One of the things that drives me is the excitement that I could fail. What better buzz can you get?
Calvin Ayre

One of the things I learned the hard way was it does not pay to get discouraged. Keeping busy and making optimism a way of life can restore your faith in yourself.
Lucille Ball

Discouragement is of all ages: In youth it is a presentiment, in old age a remembrance.
Honoré de Balzac

Try as we may, none of us can be free of conflict and woe. Even the greatest men have had to accept disappointments as their daily bread. . . . The art of living lies less in eliminating our troubles than in growing with them. Man and society must grow together. Each individual's efforts to discipline himself must be matched by society's struggle to enforce the rules of law and of justice under the law.
Bernard M. Baruch

Ever tried. Ever failed. No matter. Try again. Fail again. Fail better.
Samuel Beckett

It is defeat that turns bone to flint, and gristle to muscle, and makes a man invincible, and forms those heroic natures that are now in ascendancy in the world. Do not, then, be afraid of defeat. You are never so near to victory as when defeated in a good cause.
Henry Ward Beecher

There is much to be said for failure. It is more interesting than success.
Max Beerbohm

Seven national crimes: 1. I don't think. 2. I don't know. 3. I don't care. 4. I am too busy. 5. I leave well enough alone. 6. I have no time to read and find out. 7. I am not interested.
William J.H. Boetcker

Time after time . . . today's crisis shrinks to next week's footnote to a newly headline disaster.
Hal Borland

Those whom the gods would destroy
they first call promising.
Jan Carew

Don't take no for an answer, never submit
to failure. Do not be fobbed off with mere
personal success or acceptance. You will
make all kinds of mistakes, but as long
as you are generous and true, and also
fierce, you cannot hurt the world or even
seriously distress her. She was made to be
wooed and won by youth.
Winston Churchill

Our greatest glory is not in never falling,
but in rising every time we fall.
Confucius

Try to do to others as you would have
them do to you, and do not be discouraged if they fail sometimes. It is much
better that they should fail than that you
should.
Charles Dickens

The disappointment of manhood
succeeds the delusion of youth.
Benjamin Disraeli

Giving up is the ultimate tragedy.
Robert J. Donovan

Sometimes a noble failure serves the
world as faithfully as a distinguished
success.
Edward Dowden

Many of life's failures are people who
did not realize how close they were to
success when they gave up.
Thomas A. Edison

I'm proof against that word failure. I've
seen behind it. The only failure a man
ought to fear is failure in cleaving to the
purpose he sees to be best.
George Eliot

When a man is pushed, tormented,
defeated, he has a chance to learn something; he has been put on his wits; on his
manhood; he has gained the facts; learns
his ignorance; is cured of the insanity
of conceit; has got moderation and real
skill.
Ralph Waldo Emerson

Don't let life discourage you; everyone
who got where he is had to begin where
he was.
Richard L. Evans

No man is a failure who enjoys life.
William Feather

Never let us be discouraged with
ourselves. It is not when we are conscious
of our faults that we are the most wicked;
on the contrary, we are less so.
François Fénelon

Failure is success if we learn from it.
Malcolm Forbes

How to fail: Try too hard.
Malcolm Forbes

One who fears failure limits his activities. Failure is only the opportunity more
intelligently to begin again.
Henry Ford

He that is good for making excuses, is
seldom good for anything else.
Benjamin Franklin

He's no failure. He's not dead yet.
W.L. George

An excuse's only virtue is to salve its
maker's guilt.
Stanley Goldstein

There is no such thing as a good excuse.
John P. Grier

It is only after an unknown number of
unrecorded labors, after a host of noble

hearts have succumbed in discouragement, convinced that their cause is lost; it is only then that the cause triumphs.
François Guizot

The longer is the excuse, the less likely it's the truth.
Robert Half

Why should anybody be interested in some old man who was a failure?
Ernest Hemingway

Don't make excuses—make good.
Elbert Hubbard

There is the greatest practical benefit in making a few failures early in life.
Thomas H. Huxley

The greatest test of courage on earth is to bear defeat without losing heart.
Robert Green Ingersoll

Don't be discouraged by a failure. It can be a positive experience. Failure is, in a sense, the highway to success, inasmuch as every discovery of what is false leads us to seek earnestly after what is true, and every fresh experience points out some form of error which we shall afterwards carefully avoid.
John Keats

There is not a fiercer hell than the failure in a great object.
John Keats

The only time you don't want to fail is the last time you try.
Charles F. Kettering

We have forty million reasons for failure, but not a single excuse.
Rudyard Kipling

Let no feeling of discouragement prey upon you, and in the end you're sure to succeed.
Abraham Lincoln

In great attempts, it is glorious even to fail.
Cassius Longinus

Because a fellow has failed once or twice, or a dozen times, you don't want to set him down as a failure till he's dead or loses his courage—and that's the same thing.
George Horace Lorimer

The only failure which lacks dignity is the failure to try.
Malcolm F. MacNeil

Lack of will power and drive cause more failure than lack of imagination and ability.
Dennis Mahoney

When we begin to take our failures nonseriously, it means we are ceasing to be afraid of them. It is of immense importance to learn to laugh at ourselves.
Katherine Mansfield

There is no sweeter sound than the crumbling of one's fellow man.
Groucho Marx

The same disappointments in life will chasten and refine one man's spirit, embitter another's.
William Matthews

How far high failure overleaps the bounds of low success.
Lewis Morris

Show me a good loser and I will show you a loser.
Paul Newman

What is defeat? Nothing but education; nothing but the first step to something better.
Wendell Phillips

The world is divided into two categories: failures and unknowns.
Francis Picabia

Rejoice not when thine enemy falleth, and let not thine heart be glad when he stumbleth.
Proverbs 24:17

It is a healthy symptom when a man is dissatisfied without being discouraged.
Roy L. Smith

Formula for failure: Try to please everybody.
Herbert Bayard Swope

What is called resignation is confirmed desperation.
Henry David Thoreau

Whatever we succeed in doing is a transformation of something we have failed to do. Thus, when we fail, it is only because we have given up.
Paul Valéry

The girl who can't dance says the band can't play.
Yiddish proverb

FAITH

Faith is kept alive in us, and gathers strength, more from practice than from speculations.
Joseph Addison

Without faith a man can do nothing. But faith can stifle all science.
Henri Frédéric Amiel

Inflexible in faith, invincible in arms.
James Beattie

Every tomorrow has two handles. We can take hold of it with the handle of anxiety or the handle of faith. We should live for the future, and yet should find our life in the fidelities of the present; the last is only the method of the first.
Henry Ward Beecher

A man of courage is also full of faith.
Cicero

As ye have therefore received Christ Jesus the Lord, so walk ye in him: rooted and built up in him, and established in the faith, as ye have been taught, abounding therein with thanksgiving.
Colossians 2:6–7

Faith is the great motive power, and no man realizes his full possibilities unless he has the deep conviction that life is eternally important and that his work well done is a part of an unending plan.
Calvin Coolidge

We need not be afraid of the future, for the future will be in our own hands. We shall need courage, energy and determination, but above all, we shall need faith—faith in ourselves, in our communities and in our country.
Thomas E. Dewey

Send the harmony of a Great Desire vibrating through every fiber of your being. Pray for a task that will call forth your faith, your courage, your perseverance, and your spirit of sacrifice. Keep your hands and your soul clean, and the conquering current will flow freely.
Thomas Dreier

Faith is not trying to believe something regardless of the evidence; faith is daring to do something regardless of the consequences.
Sherwood Eddy

Faith and love are apt to be spasmodic in the best minds. Men live on the brink of mysteries and harmonies into which they never enter, and with their hand on the door-latch they die outside.
Ralph Waldo Emerson

The business man who has faith is not very likely to go wrong. He is going to steer his ship of commerce through the troubled waters of misfortune, perhaps even adversity, with a serenity born of the consciousness that nothing can harm him permanently so long as he sees clearly and acts wisely. There will be many hands eager to retard his progress. Slander will raise its ugly head from many little by-ways along his path. Ill health may come; the loss of loved ones; the crippling of his finances; the striking down of his most cherished hopes; and yet—the man who has Faith—who believes that right is right will triumph.
Jerome P. Fleishman

Faith springs from inward conviction of worthiness.
B.C. Forbes

Please, I would like to ask all those who have positions of responsibility in economic, political and social life, and all men and women of good will: Let us be "protectors" of creation, protectors of God's plan inscribed in nature, protectors of one another and of the environment. Let us not allow omens of destruction and death to accompany the advance of this world.
Pope Francis

In the affairs of this world, men are saved, not by faith, but by the want of it.
Benjamin Franklin

Only a person who has faith in himself can be faithful to others.
Erich Fromm

Faith is positive, enriching life in the here and now. Doubt is negative, robbing life of glow and meaning. So though I do not understand immortality, I choose to believe.
Webb B. Garrison

But without faith it is impossible to please him: for he that cometh to God must believe that he is, and that he is a rewarder of them that diligently seek him.
Hebrews 11:6

Absolute faith corrupts as absolutely as absolute power.
Eric Hoffer

It's faith in something and enthusiasm for something that makes life worth looking at.
Oliver Wendell Holmes

You can change your faith without changing gods, and vice versa.
Stanislaw Jerzy Lec

He who keeps his faith only, cannot be discrowned.
James Russell Lowell

If we have no faith in ourselves and in the kind of future we can create together, we are fit only to follow, not to lead. Let us remember that the Bible contains two proverbs we cannot afford to forget. The first is "Man does not live by bread alone" and the second is "Where there is no vision, the people perish."
Charles Luckman

Faith, like light, should always be simple and unbending; while love, like warmth, should beam forth on every side, and bend to every necessity of our brethren.
Martin Luther

If ye have faith as a grain of mustard seed, ye shall say unto the mountain,

Remove hence to yonder place; and it shall remove; and nothing shall be impossible unto you.
Matthew 17:20

There is many a thing which the world calls disappointment, but there is no such word in the dictionary of faith.
John Newton

Nothing in life is more wonderful than faith—the one great moving force which we can neither weigh in the balance nor test in the crucible.
William Osler

The errors of faith are better than the best thoughts of unbelief.
Thomas Russell

Faith is indispensable, and the world at times does not seem to have quite enough of it. It can and has accomplished what seems to be the impossible. Wars have been started and men and nations lost for the lack of it. Faith starts from the individual and builds men and nations. America was built by and on the faith of our ancestors.
Carl Sandburg

Columbus found a world, and had no chart save one that Faith deciphered in the skies.
George Santayana

In actual life, every great enterprise begins with and takes its first forward step in faith.
August Wilhelm von Schlegel

No ray of sunlight is ever lost, but the green which it awakes into existence needs time to sprout, and it is not always granted to the sower to see the harvest. All work that is worth anything is done in faith.
Albert Schweitzer

There are glimpses of heaven to us in every act, or thought, or word, that raises us above ourselves.
A.P. Stanley

In the harsh face of life faith can read a bracing gospel.
Robert Louis Stevenson

Kind hearts are more than coronets,
And simple faith than Norman blood.
Alfred, Lord Tennyson

'Tis not the dying for a faith that's so hard; 'tis the living up to it that is difficult.
William Makepeace Thackeray

The mason asks but a narrow shelf to spring his brick from; man requires only an infinitely narrower one to spring his arch of faith from.
Henry David Thoreau

Doubt is the disease of this inquisitive, restless age. It is the price we pay for our advanced intelligence and civilization—the dim night of our resplendent day. But as the most beautiful light is born of darkness, so the faith that springs from conflict is often the strongest and best.
R. Turnbull

It was the schoolboy who said, "Faith is believing what you know ain't so."
Mark Twain

Faith is raising the sail of our little boat until it is caught up in the soft winds above and picks up speed, not from anything within itself, but from the vast resources of the universe around us.
W. Ralph Ward, Jr.

Faith is the root of all good works; a root that produces nothing is dead.
Daniel Wilson

It takes vision and courage to create—it takes faith and courage to prove.
Owen D. Young

FALSE

Thou shalt not get found out is not one of God's commandments; and no man can be saved by trying to keep it.
Leonard Bacon

If you can't imitate him, don't copy him.
Yogi Berra

If I take refuge in ambiguity, I assure you that it's quite conscious.
Kingman Brewster Jr.

Falsehood is never so successful as when she baits her hook with truth, and no opinions so fatally mislead us as those that are not wholly wrong, as no watches so effectively deceive the wearer as those that are sometimes right.
Charles Caleb Colton

There are more fakers in business than in jail.
Malcolm Forbes

It is astonishing what force, purity and wisdom it requires for a human being to keep clear of falsehoods.
Margaret Fuller

The united voice of millions cannot lend the smallest foundation to falsehood.
Oliver Goldsmith

False gods must be repudiated, but that is not all: The reasons for their existence must be sought beneath their masks.
Alexander Herzen

Very much of what we call the progress of today consists in getting rid of false ideas, false conceptions of things, and in taking a point of view that enables us to see the principles, ideas and things in right relation to each other.
William D. Hoard

An imitator is a man who succeeds in being an imitation.
Elbert Hubbard

No man ever yet became great by imitation.
Samuel Johnson

There is a false modesty, which is vanity; a false glory, which is levity; a false grandeur, which is meanness; a false virtue, which is hypocrisy; and a false wisdom, which is prudery.
Jean de La Bruyère

It is a poor wit who lives by borrowing the words, decisions, mien, inventions and actions of others.
Johann Lavater

Men walk almost always in the paths trodden by others, proceeding in their actions by imitation.
Niccoló Macchiavelli

False conclusions which have been reasoned out are infinitely worse than blind impulse.
Horace Mann

A great part of art consists in imitation. For the whole conduct of life is based on this: that what we admire in others we want to do ourselves.
Quintilian

Man is an imitative creature.
Johann Friedrich von Schiller

Deep breaths are very helpful at shallow parties.
Barbara Walters

Only the shallow know themselves.
Oscar Wilde

FAME

I don't want to achieve immortality through my work. I want to achieve it through not dying.
Woody Allen

Penélope Cruz belongs to the Mediterranean school of acting, a style that is characterized by its carnality, gutsiness, shamelessness, messy hair, generous cleavage, and shouting as a natural form of communication.
Pedro Almodóvar

Fame often makes a writer vain, but seldom makes him proud.
W.H. Auden

Fame is like a river that beareth up things light and swollen, and drowns things weighty and solid.
Francis Bacon

The easiest kind of relationship for me is with ten thousand people. The hardest is with one.
Joan Baez

The surest way to make a monkey of a man is to quote him.
Robert Benchley

Celebrity-worship and hero worship should not be confused. Yet we confuse them every day, and by doing so we come dangerously close to depriving ourselves of all real models. We lose sight of the men and women who do not simply seem great because they are famous, but famous because they are great.
Daniel Boorstin

The fact that people do not understand and respect the very best things, such as Mozart's concertos, is what permits men like us to become famous.
Johannes Brahms

Happy is the man who hath never known what it is to taste of fame—to have it is a purgatory, to want it is a hell.
Edward George Bulwer-Lyton

Fame you get accustomed to, but if it ever takes possession of you, then quite clearly you're in dead trouble.
Richard Burton

On his marriages to Elizabeth Taylor: I might run from her for a thousand years, and she is still my baby child. Our love is so furious that we burn each other out.
Richard Burton

All hunt for fame, but most mistake the way.
Charles Churchill

The life given us by nature is short, but the memory of a well-spent life is eternal.
Cicero

What the owner of a gay bar Elizabeth Taylor often visited said when she called one night: I told her not to come. It was too busy. And there were already a half-dozen Elizabeth Taylors here anyway.
David Cooley

Worldly fame is but a breath of wind that blows now this way, and now that, and changes name as it changes in direction.
Dante

Fame is the beauty parlor of the dead.
Benjamin De Casseres

"What's fame, after all, me la-ad?" 'Tis apt to be what some wan writes on ye'er tombstone.
Finley Peter Dunne

I ought to be jealous of the tower. She is more famous than I am.
Gustave Eiffel

The wise man thinks of fame just enough to avoid being despised.
Epicurus

Millions long for immortality who do not know what to do with themselves on a rainy Sunday afternoon.
Susan Ertz

It quite often happens. A man bounds into sudden success, becomes obsessed by vanity, builds or buys a palace—and then has to close up the palace. The latest example is Clarence Saunders, who founded the Piggly Wiggly stores, launched a company, gathered in a lot of money, started building a million dollar home, tried to fight Wall Street at its own game of speculating in stocks, gloried in having cornered his stock, lost out, and now makes this announcement concerning his palace now under construction at Memphis: "I am going to nail up the place and lock the gates until I can make the money to complete it."
B.C. Forbes

She was notorious for being late, and my father learned to allow for the inevitable three to four hours of delay. Thus, in Japan, when he was told that his plane had to leave by 4 p.m., he told Elizabeth [Taylor] she must be at the plane for a prompt noontime takeoff. She got there at five minutes past 4.
Steve Forbes

Sam Jackson is a director's dream. Some actors hope to find their character during shooting. He knows his character before shooting. Sam's old-school. I just got out of his way. I never did more than two takes with Sam.
William Friedkin

I'm an actor. I do a job and I go home. Why are you interested in me? You don't ask a truck driver about his job.
James Gandolfini

I was born at the age of 12 on a Metro-Goldwyn-Mayer lot.
Judy Garland

Wood burns because it has the proper stuff in it; and a man becomes famous because he has the proper stuff in him.
Johann Wolfgang von Goethe

The cult of individuality and personality, which promotes painters and poets only to promote itself, is really a business. The greater the "genius" of the personage, the greater the profit.
George Grosz

Glory is largely a theatrical concept. There is no striving for glory without a vivid awareness of an audience.
Eric Hoffer

The nice thing about being a celebrity is that, if you bore people, they think it's their fault.
Henry Kissinger

The fame of men ought always to be estimated by the means used to acquire it.
François de La Rochefoucauld

The best fame is a writer's fame: It's enough to get a table at a good restaurant, but not enough that you get interrupted when you eat.
Fran Lebowitz

On celeb Twitter feuds: It's a combination of self-importance gone awry, the headiness of having followers, the lack of self-censorship. It's not really to communicate some bone of contention, it's to humiliate the person in front of the whole world. Social media in general,

and Twitter in particular, is the coward's way of expressing yourself.
Carole Lieberman, A-list psychiatrist

She was the most incredible vision of loveliness I have ever seen in my life. And she was sheer innocence.
Joseph L. Mankiewicz

Immortality is not a gift, immortality is an achievement; and only those that strive mightily shall possess it.
Edgar Lee Masters

In Hollywood now when people die they don't say, "Did he leave a will?" but "Did he leave a diary?"
Liza Minnelli

Renown is a source of toil and sorrow; obscurity is a source of happiness.
Johann L. Von Mosheim

Fame has only the span of a day they say. But to live in the hearts of the people— that is worth something.
Ouida

The celebrity monuments of our age have grown so huge that they dwarf the aspirations of ordinary people, who are asked to yield their dreams to the gods: to flash their favorite singer's corporate logo at concerts, to pour open their lives (and data) on Facebook, to adopt Apple as a lifestyle. We know our stars aren't inviting us to think we can be just like them. Their success is based on leaving the rest of us behind.
George Packer

I don't care what people say about my relationship; I don't care what they say about my boobs. People are buying my songs; I have a sold-out tour. I'm getting incredible feedback from my music.
Katy Perry

Mankind differ in their notions of happiness; but in my opinion he truly possesses it who lives in the anticipation of honest fame, and the glorious figure he shall make in the eyes of posterity.
Pliny the Younger

Those who desire fame are fond of praise and flattery, though it comes from their inferiors.
Pliny the Younger

True glory consists in doing what deserves to be written; in writing what deserves to be read; and in so living as to make the world happier and better for our living in it.
Pliny the Younger

Fame due to the achievements of the mind never perishes.
Propertius

Never throughout history has a man who lived a life of ease left a name worth remembering.
Theodore Roosevelt

How men long for celebrity! Some would willingly sacrifice their lives for fame, and not a few would rather be known by their crimes than not known at all.
John Sinclair

Nothing is easier to avoid than publicity. If one genuinely doesn't want it, one doesn't get it.
C.P. Snow

Fame and rest are utter opposites.
Richard Steele

The desire for fame is the last weakness wise men put off.
Tacitus

The desire for glory clings even to the best men longer than any other passion.
Tacitus

Fame is what you have taken, character is what you give. When to this truth you awaken, then you begin to live.
Bayard Taylor

Any star can be devoured by human adoration, sparkle by sparkle.
Shirley Temple Black

Celebrity is a mask that eats into the face. As soon as one is aware of being somebody, to be watched and listened to with extra interest, input ceases, and the performer goes blind and deaf in his overanimation.
John Updike

There is only one way to get ready for immortality, and that is to love this life and live it as bravely and faithfully and cheerfully as we can.
Henry van Dyke

Heroes must see to their own fame. No one else will.
Gore Vidal

It would be glamorous to be reincarnated as a great big ring on Liz Taylor's finger.
Andy Warhol

Better was it to go unknown and leave behind you an arch . . . than to burn like a meteor and leave no dust.
Virginia Woolf

In fame's temple there is always to be found a niche for rich dunces, importunate scoundrels, or successful butchers of the human race.
Johann Zimmerman

FAMILY

My father never raised his hand to any one of his children, except in self-defense.
Fred Allen

It is a truth universally acknowledged, that a single man in possession of a good fortune must be in want of a wife.
Jane Austen

Could you possibly whistle to your father and put him back on his lead, please?
Alan Ayckbourn

Wife and children are a kind of discipline of humanity.
Francis Bacon

If the relationship of father to son could really be reduced to biology, the whole earth would blaze with the glory of fathers and sons.
James Baldwin

God forgive us but most of us grew up to be the sort of men our mothers warned us against.
Brendan Behan

Advice for mothers: Moms are becoming much more real in terms of admitting that the job is a difficult one and that a nice glass of wine at the end of the day sure helps.
Marile Borden

Other things may change us, but we start and end with the family.
Anthony Brandt

Happiness is having a large, loving, caring, close-knit family in another city.
George Burns

A man first quarrels with his father about three-quarters of a year before he is born.
Samuel Butler

Some people seem compelled by unkind fate to parental servitude for life. There is no form of penal service worse than this.
Samuel Butler

Cautiously avoid speaking of the domestic affairs either of yourself, or of other people. Yours are nothing to them but tedious gossip; and theirs are nothing to you.
Lord Chesterfield

Few fathers care much for their sons, or at least, most of them care more for their money. Of those who really love their sons, few know how to do it.
Lord Chesterfield

Twenty thousand years ago the family was the social unit. Now the social unit has become the world, in which it may truthfully be said that each person's welfare affects that of every other.
Arthur H. Compton

The father who does not teach his son his duties is equally guilty with the son who neglects them.
Confucius

Secrets with girls, like loaded guns with boys,
Are never valued till they make a noise.
George Crabbe

The graveyards are full of women whose houses were so spotless you could eat off the floor. Remember, the second wife always has a maid.
Heloise Cruise

my father moved through dooms of love through sames of am through haves of give,
singing each morning out of each night
my father moved through depths of height
e.e. cummings

I was nothing special as a father. But I loved [my kids] and they knew it.
Sammy Davis, Jr.

On privacy and the birth of Prince William: I felt the whole country was in labor with me.
Princess Diana

In order to get as much fame as one's father one has to be much more able than he.
Denis Diderot

As thou knowest not what is the way of the spirit, nor how the bones do grow in the womb of her that is with child: even so thou knowest not the works of God who maketh all.
Ecclesiastes 11:5

Some people are your relatives but others are your ancestors, and you choose the ones you want to have as ancestors. You create yourself out of those values.
Ralph Ellison

Our family is not yet so good as to be degenerating.
Kurt Ewald

It isn't success if it costs you the companionship and chumminess and love of your children. Very often busy, wealthy men of momentous affairs discover too late that they have sacrificed the finest thing in life, the affection of their family. Let me relate an incident [containing] a priceless suggestion for many ultra-busy businessmen. Frank L. Baker, prominent public utility executive, told a friend that he was going to give his young son an unusual Christmas present. I am going to write my boy a letter telling him I am going to give him an hour of my time every day. Alas, Mr. Baker died two weeks later.
B.C. Forbes

Occasionally we all inherit, or are given, or get something or some things that are too good to use for a variety of seemingly sound but really quite silly reasons—they're heirlooms or too rare or too expensive or too fragile or too pretty. The result is heirloom linen handed down from generation to generation that falls apart when some benighted heiress decides to air it.

While I'm glad that past generations saved some things we now enjoy, we are enjoying them by using them instead of carefully storing them for our kids—in turn to store. Unused beautiful things are a waste.
Malcolm Forbes

A father is a banker provided by nature.
French proverb

I could not point to any need in childhood as strong as that for a father's protection.
Sigmund Freud

Husbands are like fires:
They go out when unattended.
Zsa Zsa Gabor

A father loves best his worst son.
Moses Gentili

My father was frightened of his father, I was frightened of my father, and I am damned well going to see to it that my children are frightened of me.
King George V

A good father lives so he is a credit to his children.
Arnold Glasow

I chose my wife, as she did her wedding gown, for qualities that would wear well.
Oliver Goldsmith

Only mothers can think of the future, because they give birth to it in their children.
Maxim Gorky

Families are about love overcoming emotional torture.
Matt Groening

Family is the most effective form of government.
Robert Half

Features alone do not run in the blood; vices and virtues, genius and folly, are transmitted through the same sure but unseen channel.
William Hazlitt

There is probably no more terrible instant of enlightenment than the one in which you discover your father is a man with human flesh.
Frank Herbert

One father is more than a hundred schoolmasters.
George Herbert

The antidote for crime should be administered in childhood, by the parents. The problem is not fundamentally that of the improper child so much as it is that of the improper home.
Justice John W. Hill

Heredity: An omnibus in which all our ancestors ride, and every now and then one of them puts his head out and embarrasses us.
Oliver Wendell Holmes

The great virtue of parents is a great dowry.
Horace

Call it a clan, call it a network, call it a tribe, call it a family. Whatever you call it, whoever you are, you need one.
Jane Howard

When you consider what a chance women have to poison their husbands, it's a wonder there isn't more of it done.
Kin Hubbard

I had rather be shut up in a very modest cottage, with my books, my family and a few old friends, dining on simple bacon, and letting the world roll on as it liked, than to occupy the most splendid post which any human power can give.
Thomas Jefferson

The mother is a matchless beast.
James Kelly

Whenever I heard thunder in the mountains it was like the iron of my mother's love.
Jack Kerouac

Fathers don't curse, they disinherit. Mothers curse.
Irma Kurtz

I am determined that my children shall be brought up in their father's religion, if they can find out what it is.
Charles Lamb

When I was a boy I used to do what my father wanted. Now I have to do what my boy wants. My problem is: When am I going to do what I want?
Sam Levenson

I regard no man as poor who has a godly mother.
Abraham Lincoln

Parents wonder why the streams are bitter, when they themselves have poisoned the fountain.
John Locke

Woman knows what Man has too long forgotten, that the ultimate economic and spiritual unit of any civilization is still the family.
Clare Boothe Luce

Why his parents gave him his quirky nickname: My dad wanted a dog.
Sparky Lyle

His father watched him across the gulf of years and pathos which always must divide a father from his son.
J.P. Marquand

How easily a father's tenderness is recalled, and how quickly a son's offenses vanish at the slightest word of repentance!
Molière

It is only reasonable to allow the administration of affairs to mothers before their children reach the age prescribed by law at which they themselves can be responsible. But that father would have reared them ill who could not hope that in their maturity they would have more wisdom and competence than his wife.
Michel de Montaigne

There is not much less vexation in the government of a private family than in the managing of an entire state.
Michel de Montaigne

Children aren't happy with nothing to ignore, And that's what parents were created for.
Ogden Nash

Family: A unit composed not only of children, but of men, women, an occasional animal, and the common cold.
Ogden Nash

Some mothers need happy children; others need unhappy ones—otherwise they cannot prove their maternal virtues.
Friedrich Wilhelm Nietzsche

The worst misfortune that can happen to an ordinary man is to have an extraordinary father.
Austin O'Malley

On the joys of making dinner for her family: I have to go throw food to the animals.
Mary Jane O'Neill

Families are nothing other than the idolatry of duty.
Ann Oakley

I phoned my dad to tell him that I had stopped smoking. He called me a quitter.
Steven Pearl

To be as good as our fathers we must be better, imitation is not discipleship.
Wendell Phillips

The just man walketh in his integrity: his children are blessed after him.
Proverbs 20:7

What a father says to his children is not heard by the world, but it will be heard by posterity.
Jean Paul Richter

It was dangerous to hit the wrong kid in my neighborhood, because a lot of the guys I played with had fathers in the Mafia.
Tim Robbins

The place of the father in the modern suburban family is a very small one, particularly if he plays golf.
Bertrand Russell

There is no such thing as fun for the whole family.
Jerry Seinfeld

If you would reform the world from its errors and vices, begin enlisting the mothers.
Charles Simmons

A family's photograph album is generally about the extended family, and, often, is all that remains of it.
Susan Sontag

To a hoarding father succeeds an extravagant son.
Spanish proverb

It is not only paying wages, and giving commands, that constitute a master of a family; but prudence, equal behavior, with a readiness to protect and cherish them, is what entitles man to that character in their very hearts and sentiments.
Richard Steele

To be a parent without an assistant is hard work.
William J. Temple

When I was a boy of fourteen, my father was so ignorant I could hardly stand to have the old man around. But when I got to be twenty-one, I was astonished at how much the old man had learned in seven years.
Mark Twain

In Biblical times, a man could have as many wives as he could afford. Just like today.
Abigail Van Buren

It no longer bothers me that I may be constantly searching for father figures; by this time, I have found several and dearly enjoyed knowing them all.
Alice Walker

All women become like their mothers.
That is their tragedy. No man does.
That's his.
Oscar Wilde

Fathers should be neither seen nor
heard. That is the only proper basis for
family life.
Oscar Wilde

FATE

It is a singular fact that many men of
action incline to the theory of fatalism,
while the greater part of men of thought
believe in a divine providence.
Honoré de Balzac

Fate is not the ruler, but the servant of
Providence.
Edward Bulwer-Lytton

If you believe in fate, believe in it, at
least, for your good.
Ralph Waldo Emerson

Whatever limits us we call Fate.
Ralph Waldo Emerson

Fate with impartial hand turns out the
doom of high and low; her capacious urn
is constantly shaking out the names of all
mankind.
Horace

Granting our wish is one of Fate's
saddest jokes.
James Russell Lowell

It is the fate of the coconut husk to float,
of the stone to sink.
Malay proverb

Fate often puts all the material for happiness and prosperity into a man's hands
just to see how miserable he can make
himself with them.
Don Marquis

If fate means you to lose, give him a good
fight anyhow.
William McFee

Fate is something you believe in when
things are not going well. When they are,
you forget it.
Aubrey Menen

Our wills and fates do so contrary run,
that our devices still are overthrown; our
thoughts are ours, their ends none of our
own.
William Shakespeare

Dreadful is the mysterious power of
fate; there is no deliverance from it by
wealth or by war, by walled city or dark,
seabeaten ships.
Sophocles

I do not believe in that word Fate. It is
the refuge of every self-confessed failure.
Andrew Soutar

FAULTS

Vices are their own punishment.
Aesop

We make a ladder of our vices, if we
trample those same vices underfoot.
St. Augustine

Every man should have a fair-sized
cemetery in which to bury the faults of
his friends.
Henry Ward Beecher

When dealing with people, remember
you are not dealing with creatures of
logic, but with creatures of emotion,
creatures bristling with prejudice and
motivated by pride and vanity.
Dale Carnegie

Think of your own faults the first part
of the night when you are awake, and of

the faults of others the latter part of the night when you are asleep.
Chinese proverb

To copy faults is want of sense.
Charles Churchill

Everybody loves to find fault, it gives a feeling of superiority.
William Feather

We can often do more for other men by correcting our own faults than by trying to correct theirs.
François Fénelon

Whether the stone bumps the jug or the jug bumps the stone it is bad for the jug.
Folk saying

If a friend tell thee a fault, imagine always that he telleth thee not the whole.
Thomas Fuller

There is no reward for finding fault.
Arnold Glasow

It is easier to discover a deficiency in individuals, in states, and in Providence, than to see their real import and value.
Georg Wilhelm Hegel

I may have my faults, but being wrong ain't one of them.
Jimmy Hoffa

When we try to avoid one fault, we are led to the opposite, unless we be very careful.
Horace

I have long been disposed to judge men by their average. If it is reasonably high, I am charitable with faults that look pretty black.
Edgar W. Howe

In the intercourse of life, we please more by our faults than by our good qualities.
François de La Rochefoucauld

To many people virtue consists chiefly in repenting faults, not in avoiding them.
Georg Lichtenberg

I have not hated the man, but his faults.
Martial

It is not so much the being exempt from faults, as having overcome them, that is an advantage to us.
Alexander Pope

I never yet heard man or woman much abused that I was not inclined to think the better of them, and to transfer the suspicion or dislike to the one who found pleasure in pointing out the defects of another.
Jane Porter

However good you may be you have faults; however dull you may be you can find out what some of them are, and however slight they may be you had better make some—not too painful, but patient efforts to get rid of them.
John Ruskin

Faultfinding without suggestions for improvement is a waste of time.
Ralph C. Smedley

Don't tell your friends their social faults; they will cure the fault and never forgive you.
Logan Pearsall Smith

Always acknowledge a fault quite frankly. This will throw those in authority off their guard and give you an opportunity to commit more.
Mark Twain

It is easy to find fault, if one has that disposition. There was once a man who, not being able to find any other fault with his coal, complained that there were too many prehistoric toads in it.
Mark Twain

Whosoever does not know how to recognize the faults of great men is incapable of estimating their perfections.
Voltaire

FEAR

Fear gives intelligence even to fools.
Anonymous

An ugly sight, a man who is afraid.
Jean Anouilh

No man loves the man he fears.
Aristotle

A fool without fear is sometimes wiser than an angel with fear.
Nancy Astor

Fear is an insidious virus. Given a breeding place in our minds, it will permeate the whole body of our work; it will eat away our spirit and block the forward path of our endeavors. Fear is the greatest enemy of progress. Progress moves ever on, and does not linger to consider microscopically the implications of each particular action. Only small and overcautious minds see the shadows of lurking enemies and dangers everywhere, and shrink away from the increased efforts needed to overcome them. Fear is met and destroyed with courage. Again and again, when the struggle seems hopeless and all opportunity lost—some man or woman with a little more courage, a little more effort, brings victory.
James F. Bell

The worst sorrows in life are not in its losses and misfortunes, but its fears.
Arthur Christopher Benson

Behind everything we feel, there is always a sense of fear.
Ugo Betti

The people to fear are not those who disagree with you, but those who disagree with you and are too cowardly to let you know.
Napoleon Bonaparte

A panic is a sudden desertion of us, and a going over to the enemy of our imagination.
Christian Bovée

He doesn't know the meaning of the word fear, but then again he doesn't know the meaning of most words.
Bobbie Bowden

The man who has ceased to fear has ceased to care.
F.H. Bradley

The concessions of the weak are the concessions of fear.
Edmund Burke

Fear has many eyes and can see things underground.
Miguel de Cervantes

No power is strong enough to be lasting if it labors under the weight of fear.
Cicero

A superior man is the one who is free from fear and anxieties.
Confucius

The way of a superior man is threefold. Virtuous, he is free from anxieties; wise, he is free from perplexities; bold, he is free from fear.
Confucius

You always have two choices: your commitment versus your fear.
Sammy Davis, Jr.

It is our attitude toward events, not events themselves, which we can control. Nothing is by its own nature

calamitous—even death is terrible only if we fear it.
Epictetus

A man who causes fear cannot be free from fear.
Epicurus

Who bathes in worldly joys, swims in a world of fears.
Phineas Fletcher

All of the great leaders have had one characteristic in common: it was the willingness to confront unequivocally the major anxiety of their people in their time.
John Kenneth Galbraith

The truth is that there is no terror untempered by some great moral idea.
Jean-Luc Godard

To tremble before anticipated evils, is to bemoan what thou hast never lost.
Johann Wolfgang von Goethe

The original of all great and lasting societies consisted not in the mutual good will men had toward each other, but in the mutual fear they had of each other.
Thomas Hobbes

A good scare is worth more to a man than advice.
Edgar W. Howe

The great Big Black Things that have loomed against the horizon of my life, threatening to devour me, simply loomed and nothing more. The things that have really made me miss my train have always been sweet, soft, pretty, pleasant things of which I was not in the least afraid.
Elbert Hubbard

He knew no fear except the fear of doing wrong.
Robert Green Ingersoll

Never take counsel of your fears.
Andrew Jackson

Feel the fear and do it anyway.
Susan Jeffers

Evil is uncertain in the same degree as good, and for the reason that we ought not to hope too securely, we ought not to fear with too much dejection.
Samuel Johnson

If fear is cultivated it will become stronger. If faith is cultivated it will achieve the mastery. We have a right to believe that faith is the stronger emotion because it is positive whereas fear is negative.
John Paul Jones

The only thing we have to fear on this planet is man.
Carl Jung

My "fear" is my substance, and probably the best part of me.
Franz Kafka

I find no foeman in the road but fear; to doubt is failure and to dare success.
Frederic Knowles

It is better to have a right destroyed than to abandon it because of fear.
Philip Mann

What the world has to eradicate is fear and ignorance.
Jan Masaryk

There is nothing strange about fear: no matter in what guise it presents itself it is something with which we are all so familiar that when a man appears who

is without it we are at once enslaved by him.
Henry Miller

The thing in the world I am most afraid of is fear.
Michel de Montaigne

He who is afraid of a thing gives it power over him.
Moorish proverb

Traffic is like a bad dog. It isn't important to look both ways when crossing the street. It's important to not show fear.
P.J. O'Rourke

Fear has the largest eyes of all.
Boris Pasternak

Fortunately for themselves and the world, nearly all men are cowards and dare not act on what they believe. Nearly all our disasters come of a few fools having the courage of their convictions.
Coventry Patmore

The fear of the Lord tendeth to life: and he that hath it shall abide satisfied; he shall not be visited with evil.
Proverbs 19:23

God is our refuge and strength, a very present help in trouble. Therefore will not we fear, though the earth be removed, and though the mountains be carried into the midst of the sea.
Psalms 46:1–2

Of all the passions, fear weakens judgment most.
Cardinal de Retz

I believe that anyone can conquer fear by doing the things he fears to do, provided he keeps doing them until he gets a record of successful experiences behind him.
Eleanor Roosevelt

Fear is the main source of superstition, and one of the main sources of cruelty. To conquer fear is the beginning of wisdom.
Bertrand Russell

Present fears are less than horrible imaginings.
William Shakespeare

Things done well and with a care, exempt themselves from fear.
William Shakespeare

There is no fear without some hope, and no hope without some fear.
Baruch Spinoza

Fear could never make virtue.
Voltaire

The basis of optimism is sheer terror.
Oscar Wilde

Love is what we were born with. Fear is what we learned here.
Marianne Williamson

On starting her new cable network, OWN:
I woke up one morning clutching my chest in fear. I realized fear ain't good.
Oprah Winfrey

FIGHT

When the fight begins within himself, a man's worth something.
Robert Browning

Every act of rebelling expresses a nostalgia for innocence.
Albert Camus

A child's instinct is almost perfect in the matter of fighting. The child's hero is always the man or boy who defends himself suddenly and splendidly against aggression.
G.K. Chesterton

We should not forget that our tradition is one of protest and revolt, and it is stultifying to celebrate the rebels of the past . . . while we silence the rebels of the present.
Henry Steele Commager

I propose to fight it out on this line if it takes all summer.
Ulysses S. Grant

It isn't the size of the dog in the fight, but the size of the fight in the dog that counts.
Woody Hayes

Fight! Be somebody! If you have lost confidence in yourself, make believe you are somebody else, somebody that's got brains, and act like him.
Sol Hess

A little rebellion is a medicine necessary for the sound health of government.
Thomas Jefferson

FOOD

A fat paunch never bred a subtle mind.
Anonymous

You are where you eat.
Anonymous

There are all kinds of myths going on in the Italian culture, and the way they celebrate is through their food. It's the tradition of the table where the Italians celebrate most of their triumphs and successes.
Mario Batali

Sadder than destitution, sadder than a beggar is the man who eats alone in public.
Jean Baudrillard

Food: Part of the spiritual expression of the French, and I do not believe that they have ever heard of calories.
Beverly Baxter

I believe that if ever I had to practice cannibalism, I might manage if there were enough tarragon around.
James Beard

A gourmet who thinks of calories is like a tart who looks at her watch.
James Beard

A gourmet can tell from the flavor whether a woodcock's leg is the one on which the bird is accustomed to roost.
Lucius Beebe

Be content to remember that those who can make omelettes properly can do nothing else.
Hilaire Belloc

Edible: Good to eat, and wholesome to digest, as a worm to a toad, a toad to a snake, a snake to a pig, a pig to a man, and a man to a worm.
Ambrose Bierce

I've been on a constant diet for the last two decades. I've lost a total of 789 pounds. By all accounts, I should be hanging from a charm bracelet.
Erma Bombeck

Never order food in excess of your body weight.
Erma Bombeck

Thanksgiving dinners take 18 hours to prepare. They are consumed in 12 minutes. Half-times take 12 minutes. This is not coincidence.
Erma Bombeck

How long would we remain free in a daily, desperate, overpopulated scramble for bread?
David Brinkley

If what we already know were simply applied to all the agricultural land of the world and the problem of proper distribution were given consideration, the world could feed itself well.
Louis Bromfield

You can tell how long a couple has been married by whether they are on their first, second or third bottle of Tabasco.
Bruce Bye

I am bound to add that the excess in too little has ever proved in me more dangerous than the excess in too much; the last may cause indigestion, but the first causes death.
Giacomo Casanova

As long as there's pasta and Chinese food in the world, I'm okay.
Michael Chang

We are always giving foreign names to very native things. If there is a thing that reeks of the glorious tradition of the old English tavern, it is toasted cheese. But for some wild reason we call it Welsh rarebit. I believe that what we call Irish stew might more properly be called English stew, and that it is not particularly familiar in Ireland.
G.K. Chesterton

In France, cooking is a serious art form and a national sport.
Julia Child

The more you eat, the less flavor; the less you eat, the more flavor.
Chinese proverb

The one way to get thin is to reestablish a purpose in life.
Cyril Connolly

To eat is human; to digest, divine.
Charles Townsend Copeland

Gluttony is an emotional escape, a sign that something is eating us.
Peter De Vries

Let the stoics say what they please, we do not eat for the good of living, but because the meat is savory and the appetite is keen.
Ralph Waldo Emerson

Last night we went to a Chinese dinner at six and a French dinner at nine, and I can feel the sharks' fins navigating unhappily in the Burgundy.
Peter Fleming

If you don't watch your figure, you'll have more figure to watch.
Malcolm Forbes

Wanna waste money? Buy diet books. Wanna make money? Write one. Wanna waist away? Eat less.
Malcolm Forbes

Slender people bury the dead.
Eileen Ford

Gourmet: Usually little more than a glutton festooned with charge cards.
Sidney J. Harris

Think of weight gain as merely a rounding error.
Richard Hyfler

If cooking becomes an art form rather than a means of providing a reasonable diet, then something is clearly wrong.
Tom Jaine

We never repent having eaten too little.
Thomas Jefferson

Ye shall eat in plenty, and be satisfied, and praise the name of the Lord your God, that hath dealt wondrously with you; and my people shall never be ashamed.
Joel 2:26

Diets are mainly food for thought.
N. Wylie Jones

The American does not drink at meals as a sensible man should. Indeed, he has no meals. He stuffs for ten minutes thrice a day.
Rudyard Kipling

The best way to lose weight is to close your mouth—something very difficult for a politician. Or watch your food—just watch it, don't eat it.
Ed Koch

An optimist is a person who starts a new diet on Thanksgiving Day.
Irv Kupcinet

A restaurant is a fantasy—a kind of living fantasy in which diners are the most important members of the cast.
Warner Leroy

Everything you see I owe to spaghetti.
Sophia Loren

People often feed the hungry so that nothing may disturb their own enjoyment of a good meal.
Somerset Maugham

Kissing don't last: cookery do!
George Meredith

The qualities of an exceptional cook are akin to those of a successful tightrope walker: an abiding passion for the task, courage to go out on a limb and an impeccable sense of balance.
Bryan Miller

The toughest part of being on a diet is shutting up about it.
Gerald Nachman

A fruit is a vegetable with looks and money. Plus, if you let fruit rot, it turns into wine, something Brussels sprouts never do.
P.J. O'Rourke

Avoid fried meats which angry up the blood. If your stomach disputes you, lie down and pacify it with cool thoughts.
Satchel Paige

I highly recommend worrying. It is much more effective than dieting.
William Powell

Creole is New Orleans city food. Communities were created by the people who wanted to stay and not go back to Spain or France.
Paul Prudhomme

In Ethiopia, where I was born, all the cooks are women. When I grew up in Sweden, my mom and my grandmother did predominantly all the cooking. Then I changed to restaurant kitchens, where all of a sudden there were just more men than women, and I always thought that was weird.
Marcus Samuelsson

Eating well gives a spectacular joy to life and contributes to goodwill and happy companionship. It is of great importance to the morale.
Elsa Schiaparelli

Before long it will be the animals who do the dieting so that the ultimate consumer does not have to.
Mimi Sheraton

If you think Independence Day is America's defining holiday, think

again. Thanksgiving deserves that title, hands-down.
Tony Snow

I always say this to the young chefs and mean it: The customer is excited, he says you are an artist, but we are not just craftspeople with a little talent. If the chef is an artist, he doesn't succeed. Why? Because he is inspired today but not tomorrow. We cannot do that.
André Soltner

A hungry man is not a free man.
Adlai Stevenson

I celebrated Thanksgiving in an old-fashioned way. I invited everyone in my neighborhood to my house, we had an enormous feast, and then I killed them and took their land.
Jon Stewart

In eating, a third of the stomach should be filled with food, a third with drink and the rest left empty.
The Talmud

Seeing is deceiving. It's eating that's believing.
James Thurber

Health food makes me sick.
Calvin Trillin

Keeping off a large weight loss is a phenomenon about as common in American medicine as an impoverished dermatologist.
Calvin Trillin

When it comes to Chinese food I have always operated under the policy that the less known about the preparation the better. A wise diner who is invited to visit the kitchen replies by saying, as politely as possible, that he has a pressing engagement elsewhere.
Calvin Trillin

Don't let love interfere with your appetite. It never does with mine.
Anthony Trollope

The true Southern watermelon is a boon apart, and not to be mentioned with common things. It is chief of this world's luxuries, king by the grace of God over all the fruits of the earth. When one has tasted it, he knows what the angels eat. It was not a Southern watermelon that Eve took; we know it because she repented.
Mark Twain

For my 16th birthday, my parents took me to Auberge de l'Ill, a three-star Michelin restaurant in Alsace. I loved the ballet of the waiters and the food. When the chef came to the table, my father said, "My son is good for nothing. Do you need anybody to wash dishes?" The chef said, "Come in next week." That was the first restaurant I worked in.
Jean-Georges Vongerichten

Ask not what you can do for your country, ask what's for lunch.
Orson Welles

To ask women to become unnaturally thin is to ask them to relinquish their sexuality.
Naomi Wolf

When a poor man eats a chicken, one of them is sick.
Yiddish proverb

FOOLS

If a fool and his money are soon parted, why are there so many rich fools?
Anonymous

There is a foolish corner in the brain of the wisest man.
Aristotle

Only intuition can protect you from the most dangerous individual of all, the articulate incompetent.
Robert Bernstein

Never play down the importance of incompetence in the organization. It has always been the seed of discontent, independence and successful entrepreneurship.
William Bliss

Make it idiot-proof and someone will make a better idiot.
Bumper sticker

The greatest pleasure of a dog is that you may make a fool of yourself with him, and not only will he not scold you, but he will make a fool of himself, too.
Samuel Butler

Fool me once, shame on you; fool me twice, shame on me.
Chinese proverb

It is the peculiar quality of a fool to perceive the faults of others and to forget his own.
Cicero

To follow foolish precedents, and wink with both our eyes, is easier than to think.
William Cowper

How to get taken: Spend most of your time making sure you're not.
Malcolm Forbes

If 50 million people say a foolish thing, it is still a foolish thing.
Anatole France

Young people tell what they are doing, old people what they have done and fools what they wish to do.
French proverb

He who laughs at everything is as big a fool as he who weeps at everything.
Baltasar Gracián

The fool has set in his heart that he can get more money through the tiring of his muscle and the starvation of his brain—but he can't.
William D. Hoard

He dares to be a fool, and that is the first step in the direction of wisdom.
James Gibbons Huneker

There are two kinds of fools. One says, "This is old, therefore it is good." The other says, "This is new, therefore it is better."
William Ralph Inge

Sometimes a fool has talent, but never judgment.
François de La Rochefoucauld

An erudite fool is a greater fool than an ignorant fool.
Molière

If you wish to avoid seeing a fool you must first break your mirror.
François Rabelais

Professing themselves to be wise, they became fools.
Romans 1:22

When we are born we cry that we are come to this great stage of fools.
William Shakespeare

Arguing with a fool proves there are two.
Doris M. Smith

When a fool has made up his mind the market has gone by.
Spanish proverb

No man really becomes a fool until he stops asking questions.
Charles P. Steinmetz

Let us be thankful for the fools; but for them the rest of us could not succeed.
Mark Twain

On July 4th: Statistics show that we lose more fools on this day than on all the other days of the year put together. This proves, by the number left in stock, that one Fourth of July per year is now inadequate, the country has grown so.
Mark Twain

A fool is his own informer.
Yiddish proverb

Send a fool to close the shutters and he'll close them all over town.
Yiddish proverb

FORCEFULNESS

Epithets are not arguments. Abuse does not persuade.
Robert Green Ingersoll

Some degree of abuse is inseparable from the proper use of everything.
James Madison

Who overcomes by force, hath overcome but half his foe.
John Milton

Forces rule the world, and not opinion; but opinion is that which makes use of force.
Blaise Pascal

Forcefulness in the character of a chief executive is an invaluable quality.
Robert K. Patterson

FORGIVENESS

Forgive many things in others; nothing in yourself.
Ausonius

They who forgive most, shall be most forgiven.
Josiah W. Bailey

One can't relive one's life. Forgiveness is not what's difficult; one's always too ready to forgive. And it does no good, that's obvious.
Louis-Ferdinand Céline

If men wound you with injuries, meet them with patience; hasty words rankle the wound, soft language dresses it, forgiveness cures it, and oblivion takes away the scar. It is more noble by silence to avoid an injury than by argument to overcome it.
Francis Beaumont

If the people around you are spiteful and callous and will not hear you, fall down before them and beg their forgiveness; for in truth you are to blame for their not wanting to hear you.
Fyodor Dostoyevsky

Let all bitterness, and wrath, and anger, and clamour, and evil speaking, be put away from you, with all malice; and be ye kind to one another, tender-hearted, forgiving one another, even as God for Christ's sake hath forgiven you.
Ephesians 4:31–32

The only unforgivable sin: Being unforgiving.
Malcolm Forbes

The sweetest revenge is to forgive.
Isaac Friedmann

God will pardon: That's His business.
Heinrich Heine

He that cannot forgive others, breaks the bridge over which he must pass himself; for every man has need to be forgiven.
Lord Herbert

One thing you will probably remember well is any time you forgive and forget.
Franklin P. Jones

Two persons cannot long be friends if they cannot forgive each other's little failings.
Jean de La Bruyère

When a deep injury is done to us, we never recover until we forgive.
Alan Paton

It's far easier to forgive an enemy after you've gotten even with him.
Olin Miller

As freely as the firmament embraces the world, or the sun pours forth impartially his beams, so mercy must encircle both friend and foe.
Johann Friedrich von Schiller

Mercy is the twin sister of truth.
George Seaver

It is very easy to forgive others their mistakes; it takes more grit and gumption to forgive them for having witnessed our own.
Jessamyn West

Always forgive your enemies, nothing annoys them so much.
Oscar Wilde

Execute true judgment, and shew mercy and compassions every man to his brother: And oppress not the widow, nor the fatherless, the stranger nor the poor; and let none of you imagine evil against his brother in your heart.
Zechariah 7:9–10

FORTUNE

Fortune is for all; judgment is theirs who have won it for themselves.
Aeschylus

If a man look sharply and attentively, he shall see Fortune; for though she is blind, she is not invisible.
Francis Bacon

It cannot be denied that outward accidents conduce much fortune, but chiefly, the mold of a man's fortune is in his hands.
Francis Bacon

The use we make of our fortune determines as to its sufficiency. A little is enough if used wisely, and too much if expended foolishly.
Christian Bovée

Fortune always leaves some door open in disasters whereby to come at a remedy.
Miguel de Cervantes

The brave man carves out his fortune, and every man is the son of his own works.
Miguel de Cervantes

Man's life is ruled by fortune, not by wisdom.
Cicero

The wheel of fortune turns around incessantly, and who can say to himself, I shall today be uppermost.
Confucius

It is not Justice the servant of men, but accident, hazard, Fortune—the ally of patient Time—that holds an even and scrupulous balance.
Joseph Conrad

No one is ever satisfied with his fortune or dissatisfied with his understanding.
Antoinette Deshoulières

Fortune is an evil chain to the body, and vice to the soul.
Epictetus

Fortune favors the audacious.
Erasmus

When fortune smiles, what need of friends?
Euripides

He is a good man whom fortune makes better.
Thomas Fuller

Fortune pays sometimes for the intensity of her favors by the shortness of their duration.
Baltasar Gracián

There sometimes wants only a stroke of fortune to discover numberless latent good or bad qualities, which would otherwise have been eternally concealed.
Lord Greville

The greatest reverses of fortune are the most easily borne from a sort of dignity belonging to them.
William Hazlitt

You never find people laboring to convince you that you may live very happily upon a plentiful fortune.
Samuel Johnson

There is nothing keeps longer than a middling fortune, and nothing melts away sooner than a great one. Poverty treads on the heels of great and unexpected riches.
Jean de La Bruyère

High fortune makes both our virtues and vices stand out as objects that are brought clearly to view by the light.
François de La Rochefoucauld

I certainly think that it is better to be impetuous than cautious, for fortune is a woman, and it is necessary if you wish to master her, to conquer her by force.
Niccolò Machiavelli

Men may second fortune, but they cannot thwart her—They may weave her web, but they cannot break it.
Niccolò Machiavelli

Fortune gives many too much, but none enough.
Martial

The tallest trees are most in the power of the winds, and ambitious men of the blasts of fortune.
William Penn

Good fortune will elevate even petty minds, and give them the appearance of a certain greatness and stateliness, as from their high place they look down upon the world; but the truly noble and resolved spirit raises itself, and becomes more conspicuous in times of disaster and ill fortune.
Plutarch

I made my fortune by being able to spot a certain kind of man.
Ayn Rand

Industry is fortune's right hand and frugality her left.
John Ray

It requires a great deal of boldness and a great deal of caution to make a great fortune; and when you have got it, it requires ten times as much wit to keep it.
Meyer Rothschild

A great fortune is a great servitude.
Seneca

Happy is the man who can endure the highest and lowest fortune. He who has

endured such vicissitudes with equanimity has deprived misfortune of its power.
Seneca

We are sure to get the better of fortune if we do but grapple with her.
Seneca

There is a tide in the affairs of men, which, taken at the flood, leads on to fortune; omitted, all the voyage of their life is bound in shallows and in miseries.
William Shakespeare

When fortune smiles,
I smile to think,
How quickly she will frown.
Robert Southwell

There is no fortune so good that you can find nothing in it to complain of.
Publilius Syrus

This is the posture of fortune's slaves: one foot in the gravy, one foot in the grave.
James Thurber

Whatever may happen, every kind of fortune is to be overcome by bearing it.
Virgil

Fortune's a right whore. If she give aught, she deals it in small parcels, That she may take away all at one swoop.
John Webster

If Fortune calls, offer him a seat.
Yiddish proverb

FREE ENTERPRISE

To the infantryman, his country's military might is only those buddies he can see, and the equipment they have at hand; likewise, to the wage-earner, free enterprise is primarily the way his boss treats him and those around him.
Malcolm Forbes

I think things that contribute to the destruction of our free-incentive system are wrong. A trend against that free-incentive system is wrong, and should only be temporarily engaged in, in the event that war or something of that kind requires it. Otherwise, it should be reduced.
George Humphrey

Free enterprise is a rough and competitive game. It is a hell of a lot better than a government monopoly.
Ronald Reagan

We must lift the level of understanding both at home and abroad of what the free enterprise system is, what it is not, and how it benefits the people who live under it. We must somehow get these elementary truths across, not only to the people of other lands but to millions here at home who do not understand it, if we are to generate a powerful demand and desire for its retention.
Philip D. Reed

FREEDOM

Posterity! You will never know how much it cost the present generation to preserve your freedom. I hope you will make good use of it.
John Quincy Adams

If ye love wealth greater than liberty, the tranquility of servitude greater than the animating contest for freedom, go home from us in peace. Crouch down and lick the hand that feeds you, and may posterity forget that ye were once our countrymen.
Samuel Adams

There is no better measure of a person than what he does when he is absolutely free to choose.
Wilma Askinas

The free man is not he who defies the rules . . . but he who, recognizing the compulsions inherent in his being, seeks rather to read, mark, learn, and inwardly digest each day's experience.
Bernard I. Bell

Freedom of press and freedom of speech: What a blessing for a country while in the hands of honest, patriotic men; what a curse if in the hands of designing demagogues.
William J.H. Boetcker

Without free speech no search for truth is possible; without free speech progress is checked and the nations no longer march forward toward the nobler life which the future holds for man. Better a thousandfold abuse of free speech than denial of free speech. The abuse dies in a day, but the denial stays the life of the people, and entombs the hope of the race.
Charles Bradlaugh

Depend upon it that the lovers of freedom will be free.
Edmund Burke

Human freedom is . . . an achievement by man, and, as it was gained by vigilance and struggle, it can be lost by indifference and supineness.
Harry F. Byrd

Freedom is no heritage. Preservation of freedom is a fresh challenge and a fresh conquest for each generation. It is based on the religious concept of the dignity of man. The discovery that man is free is the greatest discovery of the ages.
C. Donald Dallas

The objectives of education and industry are identical. Both are interested in good citizenship, in serving society, in a better life—and both firmly believe in freedom.
Herman L. Donovan

One of our greatest assets is that all men aspire to be equal and free. This fact haunts the rulers of the Kremlin today for even they cannot change this law of nature and they know it. It is up to us, not only by example but by positive acts, to make the most of this driving force within mankind.
Allen Dulles

The supreme belief of our society is the dignity and freedom of the individual. To the respect of that dignity, to the defense of that freedom, all effort is pledged.
Dwight D. Eisenhower

Freedom may come quickly in robes of peace or after ages of conflict and war, but come it will, and abide it will, so long as the principles by which it was acquired are held sacred.
Edward Everett

What's the very first step taken by every dictatorship since history has been recorded? The prohibition of free speech, the curbing and elimination of a free press. A perhaps unintended but insidious assault on the freedom of the press to probe, to inform, is the effort by the Department of Justice to subpoena journalists and force them to reveal sources of information. . . . The decision by a federal court upholding a journalist's right to protect his sources is immensely valuable to all. . . . To let rage and pique at the press, for good or bad reasons, lead to a curbing of enterprising reporting would be a disaster. . . .
Malcolm Forbes

Without freedom of thought, there can be no such thing as wisdom; and no such thing as public liberty without freedom of speech; which is the right of every man as far as by it he does not hurt or control the right of another; and this is the only check it ought to suffer and the only bounds it ought to know. . . . Whoever would overthrow the liberty of a nation must begin by subduing the freedom of speech, a thing terrible to traitors.
Benjamin Franklin

Freedom is not worth having if it does not connote freedom to err.
Mahatma Gandhi

None are more hopelessly enslaved than those who falsely believe they are free.
Johann Wolfgang von Goethe

Freedom for workers is in turn conditioned by freedom for enterprise.
William Green

Freedom costs you a great deal.
Lillian Hellman

Perfect freedom is as necessary to the health and vigor of commerce as it is to the health and vigor of citizenship.
Patrick Henry

The basic test of freedom is perhaps less in what we are free to do than in what we are free not to do.
Eric Hoffer

Freedom of speech does not give a person the right to shout Fire in a crowded theater.
Oliver Wendell Holmes

A splendid storehouse of integrity and freedom has been bequeathed to us by our forefathers. In this day of confusion, of peril to liberty, our high duty is to see that this storehouse is not robbed of its contents.
Herbert Hoover

A man who is willing to accept restriction and barriers and is not afraid of them is free. A man who does nothing but fight restrictions and barriers will usually be trapped.
L. Ron Hubbard

Freedom is hammered out on the anvil of discussion, dissent and debate.
Hubert Humphrey

If business is going to continue to sell through the decades, it must also promote an understanding of what made those products possible, what is necessary to a free market, and what our free market means to the individual liberty of each of us, to be certain that the freedoms under which this nation was born and brought to this point shall endure in the future . . . for America is the product of our freedoms.
E.F. Hutton

It is better for a man to go wrong in freedom than to go right in chains.
Thomas H. Huxley

One should never put on one's best trousers to go out to fight for freedom.
Henrik Ibsen

Freedom of religion, freedom of the press, freedom of person under protection of habeas corpus; and trial by juries impartially selected, these principles form the bright constellation which has gone before us, and guided our steps through an age of revolution and reformation.
Thomas Jefferson

If a nation expects to be ignorant and free, in a state of civilization, it expects what never was and never will be.
Thomas Jefferson

In every country where man is free to think and to speak, difference of opinion will arise from difference of perception, and the imperfection of reason; but these differences, when permitted, as in this happy country, to purify themselves by free discussion, are but as passing clouds overspreading our land transiently, and leaving our horizon more bright and serene.
Thomas Jefferson

Our greatest happiness does not depend on the condition of life in which chance has placed us, but is always the result of a good conscience, good health, occupation, and freedom in all just pursuits.
Thomas Jefferson

The path we have chosen for the present is full of hazards, as all paths are. The cost of freedom is always high, but Americans have always paid it. And one path we shall never choose, and that is the path of surrender, or submission.
John F. Kennedy

People hardly ever make use of the freedom they have, for example, freedom of thought; instead they demand freedom of speech as a compensation.
Søren Kierkegaard

Freedom is not what a man does, nor what he is permitted to do. Freedom is part of what a man is.
Robert Lessing

Freedom is the last, best hope of earth.
Abraham Lincoln

If destruction be our lot we must ourselves be its author and finisher. As a nation of free men we must live through all time, or die by suicide.
Abraham Lincoln

Real freedom comes from the mastery, through knowledge, of historic conditions and race character, which makes possible a free and intelligent use of experience for the purpose of progress.
Hamilton Wright Mabie

Only those cities and countries that are free can achieve greatness. . . . In free countries we also see wealth increase more rapidly, both that which results from the culture of the soil and that which is produced by industry and art; for everybody gladly multiplies those things, and seeks to acquire those goods the possession of which he can tranquilly enjoy.
Niccolò Machiavelli

There are more instances of the abridgment of the freedom of the people by gradual and silent encroachments of those in power than by violent and sudden usurpation.
James Madison

If a nation values anything more than freedom, it will lose its freedom; and the irony of it is that if it is comfort or money that it values more, it will lose that too.
Somerset Maugham

No nation deserves freedom or can long retain it which does not win it for itself. Revolutions must be made by the people and for the people.
Giuseppe Mazzini

A people may prefer a free government, but if from indolence, or carelessness, or cowardice, or want of public spirit, they are unequal to the exertions necessary for preserving it; if they will not fight for it when it is directly attacked; . . . if by

momentary discouragement, or temporary panic, or a fit of enthusiasm for an
individual, they can be induced to lay
their liberties at the feet even of a great
man, or trust him with powers which
enable him to subvert their institutions—
in all these cases they are more or less
unfit for liberty; and even though it may
be for their good to have had it even for
a short time, they are unlikely long to
enjoy it.
John Stuart Mill

The only freedom which deserves the
name is that of pursuing our own good,
in our own way, so long as we do not
attempt to deprive others of theirs, or
impede their efforts to obtain it.
John Stuart Mill

Countries are well cultivated, not as they
are fertile, but as they are free.
Montesquieu

Those who expect to reap the blessing of
freedom must undertake to support it.
Thomas Paine

Freedom is like a bag of sand. If there is
a hole anywhere in the bag, all the sand
will run out. If any group of our people
are denied their rights, sooner or later all
groups stand to lose their rights. All the
freedom will run out.
Robert K. Patterson

In order to improve the condition
of mankind all men must be given
the certainty of security through the
exchange of safeguards, the assurance
of prosperity through an exchange of
resources, the reality of freedom through
the free movement of information,
persons and ideas.
Antoine Pinay

Eventually women will learn there's no
such thing as freedom. Their husbands
are just as fastened to the deck as they
are. Men get onto a treadmill and never
get off.
Katherine Anne Porter

We have come to world leadership
because our people have had the opportunity to develop this nation under a
government and a Constitution that
gave them political freedom and encouraged initiative, enterprise, responsibility, industry and thrift. Freedom and
achievement are not unrelated. This
nation has become one of history's
finest illustrations of how a people can
enrich life and raise their whole level
of economic well-being when they are
given justice, liberty and incentive.
Herbert V. Prochnow

To have freedom is only to have that
which is absolutely necessary to enable
us to be what we ought to be, and to
possess what we ought to possess.
Ibn Rahel

Freedom without obligation is anarchy;
freedom with obligation is democracy.
Earl Riney

They say that freedom is a constant
struggle, goes the old song. It is. It is also
more than that. Freedom is the struggle.
It is never achieved except in the effort
to reach it.
Wallace Roberts

The war for freedom will never really
be won because the price of freedom is
constant vigilance over ourselves and
over our Government.
Eleanor Roosevelt

Freedom is not now, any more than
at any other time, something to be
preserved; it is something to be created.

Freedom cannot be protected; it can only be extended.
David Smith

Whoever will be free must make himself free. Freedom is no fairy gift to fall into a man's lap. What is freedom? To have the will to be responsible for one's self.
Max Stirner

In our country we have those three unspeakably precious things: freedom of speech, freedom of conscience, and the prudence never to practice either.
Mark Twain

Progress in America has resulted from the freedom of the individual to venture for himself and to assure the gains and take all the losses as they come.
Robert R. Wason

Freedom is an indivisible word. If we want to enjoy it, and fight for it, we must be prepared to extend it to everyone, whether they are rich or poor, whether they agree with us or not, no matter what their race or the color of their skin.
Wendell Willkie

Only free people can hold their purpose and their honor steady to a common end, and prefer the interests of mankind to any narrow interest of their own.
Woodrow Wilson

FRIENDSHIP

The influence of each human being on others in this life is a kind of immortality.
John Quincy Adams

I keep my friends as misers do their treasure, because, of all things granted us by wisdom, none is greater or better than friendship.
Pietro Aretino

A friend is one who sees through you and still enjoys the view.
Wilma Askinas

Between friends, differences in taste or opinion are irritating in direct proportion to their triviality.
W.H. Auden

Love thy neighbor as thyself, but choose your neighborhood.
Louise Beal

My father and he had one of those English friendships which begin by avoiding intimacies and eventually eliminate speech altogether.
Jorge Luis Borges

People have no idea what a hard job it is for two writers to be friends. Sooner or later you have to talk about each other's work.
Anatole Broyard

Friendship is like money, easier made than kept.
Samuel Butler

Friendship is a pretty full-time occupation if you really are friendly with somebody. You can't have too many friends because then you're just not really friends.
Truman Capote

A man must eat a peck of salt with his friend before he knows him.
Miguel de Cervantes

Most people enjoy the inferiority of their best friends.
Lord Chesterfield

Real friendship is a slow grower and never thrives unless engrafted upon a stock of known and reciprocal merit.
Lord Chesterfield

He who cannot in his own house entertain a guest, when abroad will find few to entertain him.
Chinese proverb

There is only one thing worse than fighting with allies and that is fighting without them.
Winston Churchill

A friend is, as it were, a second self.
Cicero

Friendship is the only thing in the world concerning the usefulness of which all mankind are agreed.
Cicero

Friendship that flows from the heart cannot be frozen by adversity, as the water that flows from the spring cannot congeal in winter.
James Fenimore Cooper

Nothing is more limiting than a closed circle of acquaintanceship where every avenue of conversation has been explored and social exchanges are fixed in a known routine.
Archibald J. Cronin

Fate chooses our relatives, we choose our friends.
Jacques DeLille

The stranger in the land who looks into ten thousand faces for some answering look and never finds it, is in cheering society as compared with him who passes ten averted faces daily, that were once the countenances of friends.
Charles Dickens

It pays to know who your friends are but it also pays to know you ain't got any friends.
Bob Dylan

Forsake not an old friend, for a new one does not compare with him.
Ecclesiastes 9:10

I have friends in overalls whose friendship I would not swap for the favor of the kings of the world.
Thomas A. Edison

What do we live for, if it is not to make life less difficult for each other?
George Eliot

A friend is a person before whom I may think aloud.
Ralph Waldo Emerson

Friends should be like books, easy to find when you need them, but seldom used.
Ralph Waldo Emerson

It is one of the blessings of old friends that you can afford to be stupid with them.
Ralph Waldo Emerson

The only way to have a friend is to be one.
Ralph Waldo Emerson

In prosperity it is very easy to find a friend; in adversity, nothing is so difficult.
Epictetus

It is a good thing to be rich, it is a good thing to be strong, but it is a better thing to be beloved of many friends.
Euripides

Who enters my house as a friend will never be too early, always too late.
Flemish proverb

A certain ultra-dignified gentleman of unusual prominence carried himself so stiffly that nobody felt free to call him by his first name. He quarreled with a friend of earlier days and from then on the two never spoke. The day the friend died an associate found the ultra-dignified

gentleman staring through the window. When he came out of his reverie, he soliloquized with a sigh, "He was the last to call me John." Is any man really entitled to regard himself a success who has failed to inspire at least a goodly number of fellow mortals to greet him by his first name?
B.C. Forbes

The way to make a true friend is to be one. Friendship implies loyalty, esteem, cordiality, sympathy, affection, readiness to aid, to help, to stick, to fight for, if need be. The real friend is he or she who can share all our sorrows and double our joys. Radiate friendship and it will return sevenfold.
B.C. Forbes

Nothing hurts more than the friendly letter that one never got around to writing.
Brendan Francis

I sincerely believe that the word relationships is the key to the prospect of a decent world. It seems abundantly clear that every problem you will have—in your family, in your work, in our nation, or in this world—is essentially a matter of relationships, of interdependence.
Clarence Francis

A brother may not be a friend, but a friend will always be a brother.
Benjamin Franklin

He is my friend, that succoreth me, not he that pitieth me.
Thomas Fuller

So live that your friends can defend you, but never have to.
Arnold Glasow

Tell me with whom thou art found, and I will tell thee who thou art.
Johann Wolfgang von Goethe

A man is judged by his friends, for the wise and the foolish have never agreed.
Baltasar Gracián

The friend of my adversity I shall always cherish most. I can better trust those who helped to relieve the gloom of my dark hours than those who are so ready to enjoy with me the sunshine of my prosperity.
Ulysses S. Grant

The best things in life are never rationed. Friendship, loyalty, love do not require coupons.
George T. Hewitt

Strangers are what friends are made of.
Cullen Hightower

Don't flatter yourself that friendship authorizes you to say disagreeable things to your intimates. The nearer you come into relation with a person, the more necessary does tact and courtesy become. Except in cases of necessity, which are rare, leave your friend to learn unpleasant things from his enemies; they are ready enough to tell him.
Oliver Wendell Holmes

Instead of loving your enemies, treat your friends a little better.
Edgar W. Howe

A friend is a person who knows all about you—and still likes you.
Elbert Hubbard

The free conversation of a friend is what I would prefer to any environment.
David Hume

There is an emanation from the heart in genuine hospitality which cannot be described, but is immediately felt and puts the stranger at once at his ease.
Washington Irving

Make no man your friend before inquiring how he has used his former friends; for you must expect him to treat you as he has treated them. Be slow to give your friendship, but when you have given it, strive to make it lasting; for it is as reprehensible to make many changes in one's associates as to have no friends at all. Neither test your friends to your own injury nor be willing to forego a test of your companions.
Isocrates

I have never considered a difference of opinion in politics, in religion, in philosophy, as a cause for withdrawing from a friend.
Thomas Jefferson

Some friends are like a sundial: useless when the sun sets.
Judah Jeiteles

Friendship, like love, is destroyed by long absence, though it may be increased by short intermissions.
Samuel Johnson

If a man does not make new acquaintance as he advances through life, he will soon find himself left alone. A man, sir, should keep his friendship in constant repair.
Samuel Johnson

To those who have lived long together, everything heard and everything seen recalls some pleasure communicated, some benefit conferred, some petty quarrel or some slight endearment. Esteem of great powers, or amiable qualities newly discovered may embroider a day or a week, but a friendship of twenty years is interwoven with the texture of life.
Samuel Johnson

In a bad marriage, friends are the invisible glue. If we have enough friends, we may go on for years, intending to leave, talking about leaving instead of actually getting up and leaving.
Erica Jong

Greater love than this, he said, no man hath that a man lay down his wife for his friend.
James Joyce

A true friend is the greatest of all blessings, and that which we take the least care of all to acquire.
François de La Rochefoucauld

Friends are thieves of time.
Latin proverb

By your friends I gauge your wealth; by your enemies, your greatness.
Judah Lazerov

There is only one thing better than making a new friend, and that is keeping an old one.
Elmer G. Leterman

He is a fine friend. He stabs you in the front.
Leonard Louis Levinson

Ye shall do no unrighteousness in judgment: thou shalt not respect the person of the poor, nor honor the person of the mighty: but in righteousness shalt thou judge thy neighbor.
Leviticus 19:15

If you would win a man to your cause, first convince him that you are his true friend. Therein is a drop of honey that catches his heart, which, say what he will, is the greatest highroad to his reason, and which when once gained, you will find but little trouble in convincing his judgment of the justice of your cause, if, indeed, that cause be really a just one. On the contrary,

assume to dictate to his judgment, or to command his action, or to make him as one to be shunned or despised, and he will retreat within himself, close all the avenues to his head and heart; and though your cause be naked truth itself, transformed to the heaviest lance, harder than steel and sharper than steel can be made, and though you throw it with more than Herculean force and precision, you shall be no more able to pierce him than to penetrate the hard shell of a tortoise with a rye straw.
Abraham Lincoln

Elvis was one of my best friends. We both were young at the same time and we got old at the same time. I wish he was here.
Little Richard

No small part of the cruelty, oppression, miscalculation, and general mismanagement of human relations is due to the fact that in our dealings with others we do not see them as persons at all, but only as specimens or representatives of some type or other. . . . We react to the sample instead of to the real person.
Robert J. MacIver

I will destroy my enemies by converting them to friends.
Maimonides

There is a way of speaking of people which has the mystical power of calling forth friendship and love for them—originating in friendship and love itself.
Hans Margolius

It is part of the business of life to be affable and pleasing to those whom either nature, chance or circumstance has made our companions.
Sir Thomas More

There is nothing like sexual frustration to give warmth to friendship, which

flourishes in prisons, armies, on Arctic expeditions and did well in wartime Oxford.
John Mortimer

What are friends for if you don't use them?
Freddie Myers

I love a hand that meets my own with a grasp that causes some sensation.
F.S. Osgood

Could we see when and where we are to meet again, we would be more tender when we bid our friends goodbye.
Ouida

My hates have always occupied my mind much more actively and have given greater spiritual satisfactions than my real friendships.
Westbrook Pegler

A true friend unbosoms freely, advises justly, assists readily, adventures boldly, takes all patiently, defends courageously, and continues a friend unchangeably.
William Penn

There can be no friendship where there is no freedom. Friendship loves a free air, and will not be fenced up in straight and narrow enclosures.
William Penn

Let us never adopt the maxim, Rather lose our friend than our jest.
Quintilian

In a letter to a friend the thought is often unimportant, and the feeling, if it be only a desire to entertain him, everything.
Sir Walter Raleigh

We learn our virtues from the friends who love us; our faults from the enemy who hates us. We cannot easily discover our real character from a friend. He is

a mirror, on which the warmth of our breath impedes the clearness of the reflection.
Jean Paul Richter

A friendship founded on business is a good deal better than a business founded on friendship.
John D. Rockefeller

Be kindly affectioned one to another with brotherly love; in honor preferring one another; not slothful in business; fervent in spirit; serving the Lord; rejoicing in hope; patient in tribulation; continuing instant in prayer.
Romans 12:10–12

In a letter to Winston Churchill: There should be no inferiors and no superiors for true world friendship.
Carlos P. Romulo

It is fun being in the same decade with you.
Franklin D. Roosevelt

The only true solution of our political and social problems lies in cultivating everywhere the spirit of brotherhood, of fellow feeling and understanding between man and man, and the willingness to treat a man as a man.
Theodore Roosevelt

It takes a great deal of bravery to stand up to our enemies, but just as much to stand up to our friends.
J.K. Rowling

Friendship is almost always the union of a part of one mind with a part of another; people are friends in spots.
George Santayana

Be friends with everybody. When you have friends you will know there is somebody who will stand by you. You know the old saying, that if you have a single enemy you will find him everywhere. It doesn't pay to make enemies. Lead the life that will make you kindly and friendly to every one about you, and you will be surprised what a happy life you will live.
Charles M. Schwab

If you have no friends to share or rejoice in your success in life—if you cannot look back to those to whom you owe gratitude, or forward to those to whom you ought to afford protection, still it is no less incumbent on you to move steadily in the path of duty; for your active exertions are due not only to society; but in humble gratitude to the Being who made you a member of it, with powers to serve yourself and others.
Sir Walter Scott

Counsel your friend on all things, especially on those which respect yourself. His counsel may then be useful where your own self-love might impair your judgment.
Seneca

The only service a friend can really render is to keep up your courage by holding up to you a mirror in which you can see a noble image of yourself.
George Bernard Shaw

The worst cliques are those which consist of one man.
George Bernard Shaw

Life is the continuous adjustment of internal relations to external relations.
Herbert Spencer

A friend is a present you give yourself.
Robert Louis Stevenson

We are all travelers in the desert of life and the best we can find in our journey is an honest friend.
Robert Louis Stevenson

The essence of true friendship is to make allowances for one another's little lapses.
David Storey

When we are old, our friends find it difficult to please us, and are less concerned whether we be pleased or not.
Jonathan Swift

We would all rather be in the company of somebody we like than in the company of the most superior being of our acquaintance.
Frank Swinnerton

Unless you make allowances for your friend's foibles, you betray your own.
Publilius Syrus

We die as often as we lose a friend.
Publilius Syrus

Friendship is the allay of our sorrows, the ease of our passions, the discharge of our oppressions, the sanctuary to our calamities, the counselor of our doubts, the clarity of our minds, the emission of our thoughts, the exercise and improvement of what we dedicate.
Jeremy Taylor

Friendship is never established as an understood relation. It is a miracle which requires constant proofs. It is an exercise of the purest imagination and of the rarest faith!
Henry David Thoreau

The most I can do for my friend is simply to be his friend.
Henry David Thoreau

John Adams and Thomas Jefferson were political enemies, but they became fast friends. And when they passed away on the same day, the last words of one of them was, "The country is safe. Jefferson still lives." And the last words of the other was, "John Adams will see that things go forward."
Harry S. Truman

The holy passion of Friendship is of so sweet and enduring a nature that it will last through a whole lifetime, if not asked to lend money.
Mark Twain

Good friends are like shock absorbers. They help you take the lumps and bumps on the road of life.
Frank Tyger

I do not believe that friends are necessarily the people you like best; they are merely the people who got there first.
Peter Ustinov

You must not break friendship on account of different religious opinions, for it is universally agreed that all religions are matters of imagination.
Solomon ibn Verga

Be not forward, but friendly and courteous; the first to salute, hear and answer; and be not pensive when it is time to converse.
George Washington

We cherish our friends not for their ability to amuse us but for ours to amuse them.
Evelyn Waugh

He's the kind of man who picks his friends—to pieces.
Mae West

Every organism requires an environment of friends, partly to shield it from violent changes, and partly to supply it with its wants.
Alfred North Whitehead

An acquaintance that begins with a compliment is sure to develop into a real friendship.
Oscar Wilde

Friendship is the only cement that will hold the world together.
Woodrow Wilson

FUTURE

The future you shall know when it has come; before then, forget it.
Aeschylus

Work for your future as if you are going to live forever, for your afterlife as if you are going to die tomorrow.
Arabian proverb

The future is like heaven—everyone exalts it but no one wants to go there now.
James Baldwin

We steal if we touch tomorrow. It is God's.
Henry Ward Beecher

We have embraced the 21st century by entering such cutting-edge industries as brick, carpet, insulation and paint. Try to control your excitement.
Warren Buffett

You can never plan the future by the past.
Edmund Burke

Real generosity toward the future consists in giving all to what is present.
Albert Camus

If we open a quarrel between the past and the present, we shall find that we have lost the future.
Winston Churchill

The empires of the future are the empires of the mind.
Winston Churchill

There is no future in any job. The future lies in the man who holds the job.
George Crane

The world is full of people whose notion of a satisfactory future is, in fact, a return to the idealized past.
Robertson Davies

The future belongs to those who are virile, to whom it is a pleasure to live, to create, to what their intelligence on that of the others.
Sir Henri Deterding

Neither a wise man nor a brave man lies down on the tracks of history to wait for the train of the future to run over him.
Dwight D. Eisenhower

If a man carefully examine his thoughts he will be surprised to find how much he lives in the future. His well-being is always ahead. Such a creature is probably immortal.
Ralph Waldo Emerson

The man least dependent upon the morrow goes to meet the morrow most cheerfully.
Epicurus

Nobody can really guarantee the future. The best we can do is size up the chances, calculate the risks involved, estimate our ability to deal with them and then make our plans with confidence.
Henry Ford II

That man is prudent who neither hopes nor fears anything from the uncertain events of the future.
Anatole France

The danger of the past was that men became slaves. The danger of the future is that men may become robots.
Erich Fromm

Some new machinery with adequate powers must be created now if our fine phrases and noble sentiments are to have substance and meaning for our children.
James William Fulbright

People often overestimate what will happen in the next two years and underestimate what will happen in ten.
Bill Gates

There are admirable potentialities in every human being. Believe in your strength and your youth. Learn to repeat endlessly to yourself: It all depends on me.
André Gide

We are always looking to the future; the present does not satisfy us. Our ideal, whatever it may be, lies further on.
Ezra Gillett

Never before has the future so rapidly become the past.
Arnold Glasow

The hours we pass with happy prospects in view are more pleasing than those crowded with fruition.
Oliver Goldsmith

Never make forecasts, especially about the future.
Samuel Goldwyn

It is a great deed to leave nothing for tomorrow.
Baltasar Gracián

What the future holds for us, depends on what we hold for the future. Hard working todays make high-winning tomorrows.
William E. Holler

I have always sought to guide the future—but it is very lonely sometimes trying to play God.
Oliver Wendell Holmes

Ye that say, today or tomorrow we will go into such a city, and continue there a year, and buy and sell, and make gain: Whereas ye know not what shall be on the morrow. For what is your life? It is even a vapour, that appeareth for a little time, and then vanisheth away.
James 4:13–14

He who can see three days ahead will be rich for three thousand years.
Japanese proverb

Cheer up! The worst is yet to come.
Philander Johnson

The future is purchased by the present.
Samuel Johnson

The testimony of every scientist is that the frontiers that are opening out ahead of us now are far wider and more spectacular than any frontier of America in the past. Our horizons are not closed. We are going to write a greater development in America than has ever been conceived.
Eric Johnston

The future is not in the hands of fate but in ours.
Jules Jusserand

The great French Marshal Lyautey once asked his gardener to plant a tree. The gardener objected that the tree was slow-growing and would not reach maturity for 100 years. The marshal replied: In that case, there is no time to lose, plant it this afternoon.
John F. Kennedy

We work day after day, not to finish things; but to make the future better ... because we will spend the rest of our lives there.
Charles F. Kettering

You can't have a better tomorrow if you are thinking about yesterday all the time.
Charles F. Kettering

Everything that looks to the future elevates human nature; for never is life so low or so little as when occupied with the present.
Walter Savage Landor

I don't know who my grandfather was, I am much more concerned to know what his grandson will be.
Abraham Lincoln

You can't escape the responsibility of tomorrow by evading it today.
Abraham Lincoln

Look not sorrowfully into the past; it comes not back again. Wisely improve the present; it is thine. Go forth to meet the shadowy future without fear, and with a manly heart.
Henry Wadsworth Longfellow

Even if I knew that tomorrow the world would go to pieces, I would still plant my apple tree.
Martin Luther

Take therefore no thought for the morrow: for the morrow shall take thought for the things of itself. Sufficient unto the day is the evil thereof.
Matthew 6:34

In a life well lived, each succeeding day becomes better than the last. Each day, each year, each experience does not stand alone; it cannot be separated from what has happened before or what may happen after. Yesterday determines today, and today helps determine tomorrow.
John Homer Miller

I neither complain of the past, nor do I fear the future.
Michel de Montaigne

Humanity does not know where to go because no one is waiting for it: not even God.
Antonio Porchia

How narrow our souls become when absorbed in any present good or ill! It is only the thought of the future that makes them great.
Jean Paul Richter

As people used to be wrong about the motion of the sun, so they are still wrong about the motion of the future. The future stands still, it is we who move in infinite space.
Rainer Maria Rilke

The only limit to our realization of tomorrow will be our doubts of today.
Franklin D. Roosevelt

That which we know is but little; that which we have a presentiment of is immense; it is in this direction that the poet outruns the learned man.
Joseph Roux

When we build ... let it not be for present delights nor for present use alone. Let it be such work as our descendants will thank us for, and let us think ... that a time is to come when these stones will be held sacred because our hands have touched them, and that men will say as they look upon the labor, and the wrought substance of them, See! This our fathers did for us!
John Ruskin

We must welcome the future, remembering that soon it will be the past, and we must respect the past, knowing that once it was all that was humanly possible.
George Santayana

Live only for today, and you ruin tomorrow.
Charles Simmons

If one listens to the faintest but constant suggestions of his genius, which are certainly true, he sees not to what extremes, or even insanity, it may lead him; and yet that way, as he grows more resolute and faithful, his road lies.
Henry David Thoreau

The trouble with our times is that the future is not what it used to be.
Paul Valéry

The past cannot be changed, the future is still in your power.
Hugh White

On his 70th birthday: I am not afraid of tomorrow, for I have seen yesterday and I love today.
William Allen White

I like men who have a future and women who have a past.
Oscar Wilde

G

GENERATIONS

I have to study politics and war so that my sons can study mathematics, commerce and agriculture, so their sons can study poetry, painting and music.
John Quincy Adams

I hope the World War II generation doesn't lose that quality that made them so appealing: their modesty, and the way they are always looking forward and seldom back.
Tom Brokaw

Tradition means handing on all that is of value to the next generation.
Henry Lewis Bullen

Generations are as the days of toilsome mankind. . . . What the father has made, the son can make and enjoy but has also work of his own appointed him. Thus all things wax and roll onwards; arts, establishments, opinions; nothing is ever completed, but ever completing.
Thomas Carlyle

Only take heed to thyself, and keep thy souls diligently, lest thou forget the things which thine eyes have seen, and lest they depart from thy heart all the days of thy life: but teach them thy sons, and thy sons' sons.
Deuteronomy 4:9

One generation passeth away, and another generation cometh; but the earth abideth forever.
Ecclesiastes 1:4

Most oldsters are fascinated by the Future, while the young love to look back to earlier days, especially their own.
Malcolm Forbes

Recently I labeled the argument—that 18-year-olds were old enough to vote if they were old enough to fight—a perfect example of a non sequitur. This precipitated a spirited discussion by two of my sons at the dinner table; (said) our 15-year-old, Tim: "Pop, fellows at 18

today are a lot smarter than your generation was at 18, and for sure smarter than
teenagers were when voting-age requirements were first set in law." His older
brother Bob elucidated: "Maybe not
smarter, but certainly better informed,
more knowledgeable. . . . More guys
in school and college have helped, but
primarily the boob tube has done it."
Malcolm Forbes

To young people everything looks
permanent, established—and in their
eyes everything should be, needs to be
changed. To older people everything
seems to change, and in their view
almost nothing should.
Malcolm Forbes

Older generations are living proof that
younger generations can survive their
lunacy.
Cullen Hightower

We may consider each generation as a
separate nation, with a right, by the will
of the majority, to bind themselves, but
none to bind the succeeding generation,
more than the inhabitants of another
country.
Thomas Jefferson

We have to hate our immediate predecessors to get free of their authority.
D.H. Lawrence

Few can be induced to labor exclusively
for posterity. Posterity has done nothing
for us.
Abraham Lincoln

Every generation revolts against its
fathers and makes friends with its
grandfathers.
Lewis Mumford

Every age and generation must be as free
to act for itself in all cases as the ages
and generations which preceded it. The

vanity of governing beyond the grave
is the most ridiculous and insolent of
all tyrannies.
Thomas Paine

Every generation, no matter how paltry
its character, thinks itself much wiser
than the one immediately preceding it,
let alone those that are more remote.
Arthur Schopenhauer

The man who sees two or three generations is like one who sits in the conju-
reor's booth at a fair, and sees the same
tricks two or three times. They are meant
to be seen only once.
Arthur Schopenhauer

Tradition is not a fetish to be prayed to—
but a useful record of experiences. Time
should bring improvement—but not all
old things are worthless. We are served
by both the moderns and the ancients.
The balanced man is he who clings to
the best in the old—and appropriates the
desirable in the new.
Richard Steele

Amongst democratic nations, each
generation is a new people.
Alexis de Tocqueville

I have had enough experience in all my
years, and have read enough of the past,
to know that advice to grandchildren is
usually wasted. If the second and third
generations could profit by the experience of the first generation, we would
not be having some of the troubles we
have today.
Harry S Truman

Every one expects to go further than
his father went; every one expects to be
better than he was born and every generation has one big impulse in its heart—to
exceed all the other generations of the

past in all the things that make life worth living.
William Allen White

GENEROSITY

Watch lest prosperity destroy generosity.
Henry Ward Beecher

If a man is prodigal, he cannot be truly generous.
James Boswell

We need to be just before we are generous, as we need shirts before ruffles.
Sébastien Chamfort

He who confers a favor should at once forget it, if he is not to show a sordid, ungenerous spirit. To remind a man of a kindness conferred on him, and talk of it, is little different from reproach.
Demosthenes

The secret pleasure of a generous act is the great mind's bribe.
John Dryden

Generous gestures yield the most when that isn't their purpose.
Malcolm Forbes

Generosity is giving more than you can; pride is taking less than you need.
Kahlil Gibran

True generosity is a duty as indispensably necessary as those imposed on us by law.
Oliver Goldsmith

People who think they're generous to a fault usually think that's their only fault.
Sydney J. Harris

Of all virtues magnanimity is the rarest; there are a hundred persons of merit for one who willingly acknowledges it in another.
William Hazlitt

I would rather be a beggar and spend my money like a king, than be a king and spend money like a beggar.
Robert G. Ingersoll

What seems to be generosity is often no more than disguised ambition, which overlooks a small interest in order to secure a great one.
François de La Rochefoucauld

Generosity during life is a very different thing from generosity in the hour of death; one proceeds from genuine liberality, and benevolence; the other from pride or fear, or from the fact that you cannot take your money with you to the other world.
Martial

I would have a man generous to his country, his neighbors, his kindred, his friends, and most of all his poor friends. Not like some who are most lavish with those who are able to give most of them.
Pliny

Many men have been capable of doing a wise thing, more a cunning thing, but very few a generous thing.
Alexander Pope

Mighty of heart, mighty of mind, magnanimous—to be this is indeed to be great in life.
John Ruskin

He who allows his day to pass by without practicing generosity and enjoying life's pleasure is like a blacksmith's bellows— he breathes but does not live.
Sanskrit proverb

Humanity is the virtue of a woman, generosity of a man. The fair sex, who

have commonly much more tenderness than ours, have seldom so much generosity.
Adam Smith

Almost always the most indigent are most generous.
King Stanislaus of Poland

Favors cease to be favors when there are conditions attached to them.
Thornton Wilder

GENIUS

Doing easily what others find difficult is talent; doing what is impossible for talent is genius.
Henri Frédéric Amiel

Genius is childhood recalled at will.
Charles Baudelaire

Improvement makes straight roads; but the crooked roads without improvement are the roads of genius.
William Blake

Since when was genius found respectable?
Elizabeth Barrett Browning

Genius might be the ability to say a profound thing in a simple way.
Charles Bukowski

Every man who observes vigilantly and resolves steadfastly grows unconsciously into genius.
Edward Bulwer-Lytton

Genius is fostered by industry.
Cicero

Genius must have talent as its complement and implement, just as in like manner imagination must have fancy. In short, the higher intellectual powers can only act through a corresponding energy of the lower.
Samuel Taylor Coleridge

When the creations of a genius collide with the mind of a layman, and produce an empty sound, there is little doubt as to which is at fault.
Salvador Dalí

Genius is the quality of the special spirit, whether in poetry or politics or science, which raises a man above a single locality or nation to influence the people of the world.
Cornelis W. De Kiewiet

Genius is one per cent inspiration and ninety-nine per cent perspiration.
Thomas A. Edison

There are geniuses in trade as well as in war, or the state, or letters; and the reason why this or that man is fortunate is not to be told. It lies in the man: that is all anybody can tell you about it.
Ralph Waldo Emerson

When Nature has work to be done, she creates a genius to do it.
Ralph Waldo Emerson

Genius is entitled to respect only when it promotes the peace and improves the happiness of mankind.
Lord Essex

One of the strongest characteristics of genius is the power of lighting its own fire.
John Foster

The greatest genius will never be worth much if he pretends to draw exclusively from his own resources. What is genius but the faculty of seizing and turning to account everything that strikes us?
Johann Wolfgang von Goethe

Genius may have its limitations, but stupidity is not thus handicapped.
Elbert Hubbard

Genius is initiative on fire.
Holbrook Jackson

It's more fun to be a pirate than to join the navy.
Steve Jobs

No estimate is more in danger of erroneous calculations than those by which a man computes the force of his own genius.
Samuel Johnson

A man of genius makes no mistakes. His errors are volitional and are the portals of discovery.
James Joyce

I do not despise genius—indeed, I wish I had a basketful of it. But yet, after a great deal of experience and observation, I have become convinced that industry is a better horse to ride than genius. It may never carry any man as far as genius has carried individuals, but industry— patient, steady, intelligent industry—will carry thousands into comfort, and even celebrity; and this it does with absolute certainty.
Walter Lippmann

To make the common marvelous is the test of genius.
James Russell Lowell

The highest genius is willingness and ability to do hard work. Any other conception of genius makes it a doubtful, if not a dangerous possession.
Robert S. MacArthur

Genius is eternal patience.
Michelangelo

Genius is an African who dreams up snow.
Vladimir Nabokov

One of the satisfactions of a genius is his willpower and obstinacy.
Man Ray

If there be anything that can be called genius, it consists chiefly in ability to give that attention to a subject which keeps it steadily in the mind, till we have surveyed it accurately on all sides.
Thomas Reid

Genius is only a superior power of seeing.
John Ruskin

In talking about a genius, you would not say that he lies; he sees realities with different eyes from ours.
Constantin Stanislavski

Genius does not need a special language; it uses newly whatever tongue it finds.
Edmund Stedman

When a true genius appears in the world, you may know him by this sign, that the dunces are all in confederacy against him.
Jonathan Swift

No man ever followed his genius until it misled him.
Henry David Thoreau

GIVING

It is more blessed to give than to receive.
Acts 20:35

Thank the Lord that you can give, instead of depending on others to give to you.
Anonymous

Of all the varieties of virtue, liberality is the most beloved.
Aristotle

Blessed are those who can give without remembering and take without forgetting.
Elizabeth Bibesco

You need more tact in the dangerous art of giving presents than in any other social action.
William Bolitho

Examples are few of men ruined by giving. Men are heroes in spending, cravens in what they give.
Christian Bovée

A man there was, and they called him mad; the more he gave, the more he had.
John Bunyan

We make a living by what we get, we make a life by what we give.
Winston Churchill

The Lord shall open unto you his good treasure, the heaven to give the rain unto thy land in his season, and to bless all the work of thine hand: and thou shall lend unto many nations, and thou shalt not borrow.
Deuteronomy 28:12

How painful to give a gift to any person of sensibility, or of equality! It is next worse to receiving one.
Ralph Waldo Emerson

We do not quite forgive a giver. The hand that feeds us is in some danger of being bitten.
Ralph Waldo Emerson

"D'ye think I'm in business for my health?" How often have you heard that? Every time I hear it I conclude that the man doesn't know what he is in business for. What are we in business for? We are in business to benefit others. If we are not, then our business won't prosper permanently. All business is a matter of reciprocity, of giving something in exchange for something else. Unless we give, we cannot receive. And the man or concern that gives us most naturally gets most in return. He reaps most who serves most. The most notably successful businesses are those that have rendered signally valuable services to the people.
B.C. Forbes

Give naught, get same. Give much get same.
Malcolm Forbes

O Divine Master, grant that I may not so much seek to be consoled as to console; to be understood, as to understand, to be loved, as to love; for it is in giving that we receive, it is in pardoning that we are pardoned, and it is in dying that we are born to eternal life.
St. Francis of Assisi

He gives twice that gives soon, i.e., he will soon be called to give again.
Benjamin Franklin

When thou makes presents, let them be of such things as will last long; to the end they may be in some sort immortal, and may frequently refresh the memory of the receiver.
Thomas Fuller

It is better to give than to lend, and it costs about the same.
Sir Philip Gibbs

Two can give as cheap as one.
Arnold Glasow

An idea would never be liberal: It must be vigorous, positive, and without loose ends so that it may fulfill its divine mission and be productive. The proper place for liberality is in the realm of the emotions.
Johann Wolfgang von Goethe

If every American donated five hours a week, it would equal the labor of 20 million full-time volunteers.
Whoopi Goldberg

Share weight and woe, for misfortune falls with double force on him that stands alone.
Baltasar Gracián

Why you are born and why you are living depend entirely on what you are getting out of this world and what you are giving to it. I cannot prove that this is a balance of mathematical perfection, but my own observation of life leads me to the conclusion that there is a very real relationship, both quantitatively and qualitatively, between what you contribute and what you get out of this world.
Oscar Hammerstein II

A gift much expected is paid, not given.
George Herbert

They who give have all things; they who withhold have nothing.
Hindu proverb

There is sublime thieving in all giving. Someone gives us all he has and we are his.
Eric Hoffer

Life cannot subsist in society but by reciprocal concessions.
Samuel Johnson

Money doesn't give you any license to relax. It gives an opportunity to use all your advantages, free of financial worries, to go forward, and to use your superior advantages and talents to help others.
Rose Fitzgerald Kennedy

The giving is the hardest part; what does it cost to add a smile?
Jean de La Bruyère

Let him who exhorts others to give, give himself.
Latin proverb

Give what you have. To someone it may be better than you dare to think.
Henry Wadsworth Longfellow

The greatest grace of a gift, perhaps, is that it anticipates and admits of no return.
Henry Wadsworth Longfellow

The gift without the giver is rare.
James Russell Lowell

Give, and it shall be given unto you; good measure, pressed down, and shaken together, and running over, shall men give into your bosom. For with the same measure that ye mete withal it shall be measured to you again.
Luke 6:38

The heart of the giver makes the gift dear and precious.
Martin Luther

Be ashamed to die until you have won some victory for humanity.
Horace Mann

Whoever makes great presents expects great presents in return.
Martial

For too many giving is occasional, spasmodic, ill-proportioned. It depends on what is left over when other things have had their full share. Sometimes what it

means is that only the small change lying in their pockets goes to the support of good and worthy causes.
Robert J. McCracken, D.D.

Presents which our love for the donor has rendered precious are ever the most acceptable.
Ovid

The gift derives its value from the rank of the giver.
Ovid

He who is not liberal with what he has, does but deceive himself when he thinks he would be liberal if he had more.
William S. Plumer

The weakest among us has a gift, however seemingly trivial, which is peculiar to him and which worthily used will be a gift also to his race.
John Ruskin

Giving, whether it be of time, labor, affection, advice, gifts, or whatever, is one of life's greatest pleasures.
Rebecca Russell

You must give some time to your fellow man. Even if it's a little thing, do something for those who have of help, something for which you get no pay but the privilege of doing it. For remember, you don't live in a world all your own. Your brothers are here, too.
Albert Schweitzer

A benefit consists not in that which is done or given, but in the intention of the giver or doer.
Seneca

It is another's fault if he be ungrateful; but it is mine if I do not give. To find one thankful man, I will oblige a great many that are not so. I had rather never receive a kindness than never bestow one. Not to

return a benefit is a great sin; but not to confer one is a greater.
Seneca

If there be any truer measure of a man than by what he does, it must be by what he gives.
Robert Southey

We are rich only through what we give: and poor only through what we refuse and keep.
Anne Sophie Swetchine

He giveth twice that giveth quickly.
Richard Taverner

Trust not the horse, O Trojans. Be it what it may, I fear the Greeks when they offer gifts.
Virgil

No man who continues to add something to the material, intellectual and moral well-being of the place in which he lives is left long without proper reward.
Booker T. Washington

GOALS

In this life we get only those things for which we hunt, for which we strive, and for which we are willing to sacrifice. It is better to aim for something that you want—even though you miss it—than to get something that you didn't aim to get, and which you don't want! If we look long enough for what we want in life we are almost sure to find it, no matter what that objective may be.
George Matthew Adams

Whether zeal or moderation be the point we aim at, let us keep fire out of the one, and frost out of the other.
Joseph Addison

Far away there in the sunshine are my highest aspirations. I may not reach them, but I can look up and see their beauty, believe in them and try to follow where they lead.
Louisa May Alcott

There is no shame in having fallen. Nor any shame in being born into a lowly estate. There is only shame in not struggling to rise. And also shame for not wishing to attain the better. Or not dreaming about it and praying for it.
Samuel Amalu

Every art and every inquiry, as well as every practical pursuit, seems to aim at some good, whereby it has been well said that the good is that at which all things aim.
Aristotle

Today's put-off objectives reduce tomorrow's achievements.
Harry F. Banks

The life of every man is a diary in which he means to write one story, and writes another, and his humblest hour is when he compares the volume as it is with what he vowed to make it.
J.M. Barrie

By every part of our nature we clasp things above us, one after another, not for the sake of remaining where we take hold, but that we may go higher.
Henry Ward Beecher

If you don't know where you're going, you'll end up somewhere else.
Yogi Berra

My ancestors wandered in the wilderness for 40 years because even in biblical times, men would not stop to ask directions.
Elayne Boosler

A man's reach should exceed his grasp, or what's heaven for?
Robert Browning

The fact is, nothing comes; at least, nothing good. All has to be fetched.
Charles Buxton

Write down on paper your goal in life. With that down in black and white, we really can get somewhere. Few can define their goal, much less write it. You cannot find happiness until your goal is clear and in view.
Ross Byron

If you cry "Forward" you must without fail make plain in what direction to go.
Anton Chekhov

If you aspire to the highest place it is no disgrace to stop at the second, or even the third.
Cicero

If you wish to travel far and fast, travel light. Take off all your envies, jealousies, unforgiveness, selfishness and fears.
Glenn Clark

No one rises so high as he who knows not whither he is going.
Oliver Cromwell

Life has no smooth road for any of us; and in the bracing atmosphere of a high aim the very roughness stimulates the climber to steadier steps, till the legend, over steep ways to the stars, fulfills itself.
W.C. Doane

Perfection of means and confusion of goals seem, in my opinion, to characterize our age.
Albert Einstein

There is no sorrow I have thought more about than that—to love what is great, and try to reach it, and yet to fail.
George Eliot

Hitch your wagon to a star. Let us not fag in paltry works which serve our pot and bag alone.
Ralph Waldo Emerson

In business, as in baseball, the prizes go most often to the organizations that pursue their objective hard and relentlessly every day of the year.
William Feather

How foolish you would be to start on a journey without knowing where you wanted to go. Have you ever sat down and seriously drawn up a plan for your life? Have you ever deliberately mapped out where you want to go during your life's journey? Now, isn't your life infinitely more important to you than any journey you may take? Why, therefore, not devote the most earnest effort to plan your life, to set for yourself a goal? We are now at the New Year season. Isn't this a peculiarly appropriate time to look ahead, to indulge in solemn thinking, to formulate life plans, to lay down a definite course to follow?
B.C. Forbes

If you don't know what you want to do, it's harder to do it.
Malcolm Forbes

When you catch what you're after, it's gone.
Malcolm Forbes

He who moves not forward goes backward.
Johann Wolfgang von Goethe

Not failure, but low aim, is a crime.
Ernest Holmes

The rung of a ladder was never meant to rest upon, but only to hold a man's foot long enough to enable him to put the other somewhat higher.
Thomas H. Huxley

What we truly and earnestly aspire to be, that in some sense we are.
Anna Jameson

If you don't know where you are going, every road will get you nowhere.
Henry Kissinger

Make the most of today. Translate your good intentions into actual deeds. Know that you can do what ought to be done. Improve your plans. Keep a definite goal of achievement constantly in view. Realize that work well and worthily done makes life truly worth living.
Grenville Kleiser

I'm forever raising the high bar and breaking my neck to clear it.
John Kluge

The journey of a thousand miles begins with one step.
Lao-tzu

Unless you know where you are going, and road will take you there.
Theodore Levitt

You can't just go on being a good egg. You must either hatch or go bad!
Clive Staples Lewis

Determine that the thing can and shall be done, and then we shall find the way.
Abraham Lincoln

We must ask where we are and whither we are tending.
Abraham Lincoln

Truly there is a tide in the affairs of men; but there is no gulf-stream setting forever in one direction.
James Russell Lowell

To get anywhere, strike out for somewhere, or you'll get nowhere.
Martha Lupton

When you determine what you want, you have made the most important decision of your life. You have to know what you want in order to attain it.
Douglas Lurton

Ambition is but the evil shadow of aspiration.
George Macdonald

Discover what you want most of all in this world, and set yourself to work on it.
John Homer Miller

Many are stubborn in pursuit of the path they have chosen, few in pursuit of the goal.
Friedrich Wilhelm Nietzsche

You must have long-range goals to keep you from being frustrated by short-range failures.
Charles C. Noble

And in navigation, the more sights we take, the more likely we are to hit port.
Henry Osborn

Thy destiny is only that of man, but thy aspirations may be those of a god.
Ovid

You must make a habit of thinking in terms of a defined objective.
John Henry Patterson

Some men give up their designs when they have almost reached the goal; while others, on the contrary, obtain a victory by exerting, at the last moment, more vigorous efforts than before.
Polybius

The successful man lengthens his stride when he discovers that the signpost has deceived him; the failure looks for a place to sit down.
J.R. Rogers

Take the course opposite to custom and you will almost always do well.
Jean-Jacques Rousseau

What signifies the ladder, provided one rise and attain the end?
Charles Sainte-Beuve

Three men were laying brick.

The first was asked: "What are you doing?"

He answered: "Laying some brick."

The second man was asked: "What are you working for?"

He answered: "Five dollars a day."

The third man was asked: "What are you doing?"

He answered: "I am helping to build a great cathedral."

Which man are you?
Charles M. Schwab

To drift is to be in hell, to be in heaven is to steer.
George Bernard Shaw

Who shoots at the midday sun, though sure he shall never hit the mark, yet sure he is that he shall shoot higher than he who aims at a bush.
Sir Philip Sidney

There are two things to aim at in life: first, to get what you want; and, after that, to enjoy it. Only the wisest of mankind achieve the second.
Logan Pearsall Smith

Every individual should have a purpose in life which is worthy of intense effort—and constantly work toward the definite goal ahead.
Roderick Stevens

The peculiar fascination which the speeding train has for us comes from the evident progress it is making toward its definite goal ahead.
Roderick Stevens

An aim in life is the only fortune worth the finding.
Robert Louis Stevenson

The man with the average mentality, but with control, with a definite goal, and a clear conception of how it can be gained, and above all, with the power of application and labor, wins in the end.
William Howard Taft

Did you ever hear of a man who had striven all his life faithfully and singly toward an object, and in no measure obtained it? If a man constantly aspires, is he not elevated? Did ever a man try heroism, magnanimity, truth, sincerity, and find that there was no advantage in them—that it was a vain endeavor?
Henry David Thoreau

In the long run you hit only what you aim at. Therefore, though you should fail immediately, you had better aim at something high.
Henry David Thoreau

Being easy-going when you have a goal to reach seldom makes the going easy.
Frank Tyger

The first step, my son, which we make in this world, is the one on which depends the rest of our days.
Voltaire

We are all in the gutter, but some of us are looking at the stars.
Oscar Wilde

Not doing more than the average is what keeps the average down.
William Winans

GOD

He that formeth the mountains, and createth the wind, and declareth unto man what is his thought, that maketh the morning darkness, and treadeth upon the high places of the earth, The Lord, The God of hosts, is his name.
Amos 4:13

God will provide the victuals, but He will not cook the dinner.
Anonymous

Differences of opinion give me but little concern; but it is a real pleasure to be brought into communication with any one who is in earnest, and who really look to God's will as his standard of right and wrong, and judges of actions according to their greater or less conformity.
Thomas Arnold

They that deny a God destroy man's nobility; for certainly man is of kin to the beasts by his body; and, if he be not kin to God by his spirit, he is a base and ignoble creature.
Francis Bacon

What you hide from God, don't show your neighbors.
Ignas Bernstein

What America needs is businessman—indeed all men and women—not so much on their knees but on their toes, reaching up ever higher and higher to bring the laws of God down into, and as a part of, the laws of man.
Louis Binstock

Think in the name of Almighty God. We must first have a worldwide awakening of the public conscience, a spiritual revival, a moral regeneration, before there can be permanent peace and real economic recovery. To this end we do not need new laws, but a new spirit; we do not need a change of government, but a change of the human heart. There can be no peace, there will be no recovery without it. Therefore, with a change of heart, let's all make a new start.
William J.H. Boetcker

When I stand before God at the end of my life, I would hope that I would not have a single bit of talent left but could say I've used everything you gave me.
Erma Bombeck

Hardship, unbelief, suffering and poverty have not stopped our soldiery from rendering their service to God and man. The Salvation Army is a great empire, an empire without a frontier made up of a tangle of races, tongues and colors such as never before in all history gathered together under one flag.
Gen. Evangeline Booth

Get the pattern of your life from God, then go about your work and be yourself.
Phillips Brooks

No man has come to true greatness who has not felt in some degree that his life belongs to his race, and that what God gives him He gives him for mankind.
Phillips Brooks

If there was not God, there would be no atheists.
G.K. Chesterton

Those thinkers who cannot believe in any gods often assert that the love of humanity would be in itself sufficient for them; and so, perhaps, it would, if they had it.
G.K. Chesterton

I go walking, and the hills loom above me, range upon range, one against the other. I cannot tell where one begins and another leaves off. But when I talk with God He lifts me up where I can see clearly, where everything has a distinct contour.
Mme. Chiang Kai-shek

With him is an arm of flesh; but with us is the Lord our God to help us, and to fight our battles.
II Chronicles 32:8

I am ready to meet my Maker. Whether my Maker is prepared for the ordeal of meeting me is another matter.
Winston Churchill

If you believe in the Lord, He will do half the work—but the last half. He helps those who help themselves.
Cyrus H.K. Curtis

It is the easiest thing in the world to obey God when He commands us to do what we like, and to trust Him when the path is all sunshine. The real victory of faith is to trust God in the dark, and through the dark.
Theodore L. Cuyler

God is subtle but not malicious.
Albert Einstein

If a man's eye is on the Eternal, his intellect will grow.
Ralph Waldo Emerson

Try first thyself,
And after call in God;
For the worker
God himself lends aid.
Euripides

God does not want us to do extraordinary things: He wants us to do ordinary things extraordinarily well.
Bishop Gore

The word of God is the Christian soul's best weapon, and it is essential to have it with him always. In doubt it decides, in consultation it directs; in anxiety it reassures; in sorrow it comforts; in failure it encourages; in defense it protects; in offense it is mightier than the mighty.
Wilfred T. Grenfell

And the Lord answered me, and said, Write the vision, and make it plain upon tables, that he may run that readeth it.
Habakkuk 2:2

The word of God is quick, and powerful, and sharper than any two edged sword, piercing even to the dividing asunder of soul and spirit, and of the joints and marrow, and is a discerner of the thoughts and intents of the heart.
Hebrews 4:12

For God is not unrighteous to forget your work and labour of love, which ye have shewed toward his name, in that ye have ministered to the saints, and do minister.
Hebrews 6:10

The people that walked in darkness have seen a great light; they that dwell in the shadow of death, upon them hath the light shined.
Isaiah 9:2

How beautiful upon the mountains are the feet of him that bringeth good tidings, that publisheth peace; that bringeth good tidings of good, that publisheth salvation; that sayeth unto Zion, Thy God reigneth!
Isaiah 52:7

But now, O Lord, thou art our father; we are the clay, and thou potter; and we all are the work of thy hand.
Isaiah 64:8

And other sheep I have, which are not of this fold: them also I must bring, and they shall hear my voice; and there shall be one fold, and one shepherd.
John 10:16

Verily, verily, I say unto you, He that believeth on me, the works that I do shall he do also; and greater works than these shall he do; because I go unto my Father.
John 14:12

And this is life eternal, that they might know thee the only true God, and Jesus Christ, whom thou hast sent.
John 17:3

God is action, complete with mistakes, fumblings, persistence, agony. God is not the power that has found eternal equilibrium, but the power that is forever breaking every equilibrium, forever searching for a higher one.
Nikos Kazantzakis

The finger of God never leaves identical fingerprints.
Stanislaus Lec

Men are not flattered by being shown that there has been a difference of purpose between the Almighty and them.
Abraham Lincoln

Take heed that ye do not your alms before men, to be seen of them: otherwise ye have no reward of your Father which is in heaven.
Matthew 6:1

Take my yoke upon you, and learn of me; for I am meek and lowly in heart; and ye shall find rest unto your souls. For my yoke is easy, and my burden is light.
Matthew 11:29–30

It isn't more light we need, it isn't more truth, and it isn't more scientific data. It is more Christ, more courage, more spiritual insight to act on the light we have.
Benjamin E. Mays

God is in the details.
Ludwig Mies van der Rohe

God, I can push the grass apart
And lay my finger on Thy heart!
Edna St. Vincent Millay

God gave man an upright countenance to survey the heavens, and to look upward to the stars.
Ovid

Trust in the Lord with all thine heart; and lean not unto thine own understanding. In all thy ways acknowledge Him, and He shall direct thy paths.
Proverbs 3:5–6

As for God, his way is perfect: the word of the Lord is tried. He is a buckler to all those that trust in him.
Psalms 18:30

The Lord is my shepherd; I shall not want. He maketh me to lie down in green pastures: he leadeth me beside the still waters. He restoreth my soul: he leadeth me in the paths of righteousness for his name's sake.
Psalms 23:1–3

The Lord is my light and my salvation; whom shall I fear? The Lord is the strength of my life; of whom shall I be afraid?
Psalms 27:1

Because he hath set his love upon me, therefore will I deliver him: I will set him on high, because he hath known my name.
Psalms 91:14

I will lift up mine eyes unto the hills, from whence cometh my help. My help cometh from the Lord, which made heaven and earth.
Psalms 121:1–2

He delighteth not in the strength of a horse: he taketh not pleasure in the legs of a man. The Lord taketh pleasure in them that fear him, in those that hope in his mercy.
Psalms 147:11–12

Let them praise his name in the dance: let them sing praises unto him with the timbrel and harp.
Psalms 149:3

The world is a kind of spiritual kindergarten where millions of bewildered infants are trying to spell God with the wrong blocks.
Edwin Arlington Robinson

We are tempted to use God when we ought to be used by God.
Sherman S. Robinson

Let never day nor night unhallow'd pass, but still remember what the Lord hath done.
William Shakespeare

Balance the bad news of life with the good news of Christ.
Ralph W. Sockman

Take what you want, said God, take it—and pay for it.
Spanish proverb

It is by the goodness of God that in our country we have those three unspeakably

precious things: freedom of speech, freedom of conscience, and the prudence never to practice either.
Mark Twain

Only a life built into God's place can succeed. Half of our discouragements are due to the fact that we are not in tune with the infinite harmony of the Great Power. We should be helpers in building the city of God—a city that will endure when all earthly cities crumble to dust.
Bishop Herbert E. Welch

Fear of God builds churches but love of God builds men.
Louis O. Williams

We need to understand that the world's evil is only the accumulation of evils in us. It is the search for God that is urgent and practical in human life.
Paul Austin Wolfe

If God lived on earth, people would break his windows.
Yiddish proverb

GOODNESS

Good nature is more agreeable in conversation than wit, and gives a certain air to the countenance which is more amiable than beauty.
Joseph Addison

No longer talk at all about the kind of man a good man ought to be, but be such.
Marcus Aurelius Antoninus

You exist but as a part inherent in a greater whole. Do not live as though you had a thousand years before you. The common due impends; while you live, and while you may, be good.
Marcus Aurelius Antoninus

Good has two meanings: it means that which is good absolutely and that which is good for somebody.
Aristotle

Goodness is easier to recognize than to define.
W.H. Auden

Amid life's quests, there seems but worthy one: to do men good.
Gamaliel Bailey

Good nature is often a mere matter of health.
Henry Ward Beecher

It is the greatest good to the greatest number which is the measure of right and wrong.
Jeremy Bentham

Good is good, but better carrieth it.
H.G. Bohn

To become a thoroughly good man is the best prescription for keeping a sound mind in a sound body.
Frances Bowen

Reason teaches us that what is good is good for something, and that what is good for nothing is not good at all.
Francis Herbert Bradley

There is no limit to the good a man can do if he doesn't care who gets the credit.
Judson B. Branch

Good order is the foundation of all good things.
Edmund Burke

Whatever mitigates the woes or increases the happiness of others—this is my criterion of goodness. And whatever injures society at large, or any individual in it—this is my measure of iniquity.
Robert Burns

Men should not try to overstrain their goodness more than any other faculty.
Samuel Butler

He cannot long be good that knows not why he is good.
Richard Carew

Goodness is always an asset. A man who is straight, friendly and useful may never be famous, but he is respected and liked by all who know him. He has laid a sound foundation for success and he will have a worthwhile life.
Herbert N. Casson

The best way to keep good acts in memory is to refresh them with new.
Cato

It is impossible for good or evil to last forever; and hence it follows that the evil having lasted so long, the good must be now nigh at hand.
Miguel de Cervantes

While I can crawl upon this planet I think myself obliged to do what good I can, in my narrow domestic spheres, to my fellow creatures, and to wish them all the good I cannot do.
Lord Chesterfield

If you pursue good with labor, the labor passes away but the good remains; if you pursue evil with pleasure, the pleasure passes away and the evil remains.
Cicero

In nothing do men approach so nearly to the gods as doing good to men.
Cicero

Inability to tell good from evil is the greatest worry of man's life.
Cicero

Goodness and greatness go not always together.
John Clarke

He who wishes to secure the good of others has already secured his own.
Confucius

When you see a good man, think of emulating him; when you see a bad man, examine your own heart.
Confucius

Little progress can be made by merely attempting to repress what is evil; our great hope lies in developing what is good.
Calvin Coolidge

He who stops being better stops being good.
Oliver Cromwell

Between two evils, choose neither; between two goods, choose both.
Tryon Edwards

To be good, we must do good; and by doing good, we take a sure means of being good, as the use and exercise of the muscles increase their power.
Tryon Edwards

Nothing is so good as it seems beforehand.
George Eliot

He is good that failed never.
David Fergusson

A good man therefore is a standing lesson to us all.
Henry Fielding

Let no man be sorry he has done good, because others have done evil! If a man has acted right, he has done well, though

alone; if wrong, the sanction of all mankind will not justify him.
Henry Fielding

It's so much easier to do good than to be good.
B.C. Forbes

Make no expense but to do good to others or yourself.
Benjamin Franklin

Learn the luxury of doing good.
Oliver Goldsmith

The power of a man is his present means to obtain some future apparent good.
Thomas Hobbes

Whatsoever is the object of any man's appetite or desire, that is it which he for his part calleth good.
Thomas Hobbes

Nature will not forgive those who fail to fulfill the law of their being. The law of human beings is wisdom and goodness, not unlimited acquisition.
Robert M. Hutchins

An inexhaustible good nature is one of the most precious gifts of heaven, spreading itself like oil over the troubled sea of thought, and keeping the mind smooth and equable in the roughest weather.
Washington Irving

As I know more of mankind I expect less of them, and am ready to call a man a good man upon easier terms than I was formerly.
Samuel Johnson

An action is essentially good if the motive of the agent be good, regardless of the consequences.
Immanuel Kant

Walking on water wasn't built in a day.
Jack Kerouac

How happy the station which every moment furnishes opportunities of doing good to thousands! How dangerous that which every moment exposes to the injuring of millions!
Jean de La Bruyère

The greatest pleasure I know, is to do a good action by stealth, and have it found out by accident.
Charles Lamb

Nothing is rarer than true good nature; they who are reputed to have it are generally only pliant or weak.
François de La Rochefoucauld

When I do good, I feel good. When I do bad, I feel bad. And that's my religion.
Abraham Lincoln

The smallest actual good is better than the most magnificent promise of impossibilities.
Thomas Macaulay

A man who wishes to make a profession of goodness in everything must necessarily come to grief among so many who are not good.
Niccolò Machiavelli

An act of goodness is of itself an act of happiness. No reward coming after the event can compare with the sweet reward that went with it.
Maurice Maeterlinck

A good man doubles the length of his existence; to have lived so as to look back with pleasure on our past life is to live twice.
Martial

Good, the more communicated, more abundant grows.
John Milton

Report followeth not all goodness, except difficulty and rarity be joined thereto.
Michel de Montaigne

It is not enough to do good; one must do it in the right way.
John Morley

The world is my country, all mankind are my brethren, and to do good is my religion.
Thomas Paine

Be rather bountiful than expensive; do good with what thou hast, or it will do thee no good.
William Penn

For so it is the will of God, that with doing good ye may put to silence the ignorance of foolish men.
I Peter 2:15

That state is best ordered when the wicked have no command, and the good have.
Pittacus

Withhold not good from them to whom it is due, when it is in the power of thine hand to do it.
Proverbs 3:27

The backslider in heart shall be filled with his own ways: and a good man shall be satisfied from himself.
Proverbs 14:14

Do not wait for extraordinary circumstances to do good; try to use ordinary situations.
Jean Paul Richter

The sorrow of knowing that there is evil in the best is far out-balanced by the joy of discovering that there is good in the worst.
Dr. Austen Fox Riggs

Nobody does good to men with impunity.
François Auguste Rodin

And we know that all things work together for good to them that love God, to them who are called according to His purpose.
Romans 8:28

I desire to see in this country the decent men strong and the strong men decent, and until we get that combination in pretty good shape, we are not going to be by any means as successful as we should be.
Theodore Roosevelt

My intellect as well as my instincts lead me to the conclusion that men have a positive yearning to be good.
Albert Rosenfeld

He that does good to another does also good to himself.
Seneca

It is not goodness to be better than the worst.
Seneca

The largest part of goodness is the will to become good.
Seneca

We are members of one great body planted by nature in a mutual love, and fitted for a social life. We must consider that we were born for the good of the whole.
Seneca

If to do were as easy as to know what were good to do, chapels had been churches, and poor men's cottages princes' palaces. It is a good divine that

follows his own instructions; I can easier teach twenty what were good to be done, than be one of the twenty to follow mine own teaching.
William Shakespeare

In this earthly world . . . to do harm is often laudable, to do good sometime accounted dangerous folly.
William Shakespeare

Doing good is the only certainly happy action of a man's life.
Sir Philip Sidney

There are two things that men should never weary of—goodness and humility.
Robert Louis Stevenson

There is so much good in the worst of us, and so much bad in the best of us, that it behooves all of us not to talk about the rest of us.
Robert Louis Stevenson

What is the real relation between happiness and goodness? It is only within a few generations that men have found courage to say that there is none.
William Graham Sumner

The world is good-natured to people who are good-natured.
William Makepeace Thackeray

No one would remember the Good Samaritan if he'd only had good intentions; he had money, too.
Margaret Thatcher

You can't keep a good man down or a bad one up.
P.K. Thomajan

Goodness is the only investment which never fails.
Henry David Thoreau

If I repent of anything, it is very likely to be my good behavior.
Henry David Thoreau

There is little pleasure in the world that is true and sincere beside the pleasure of doing our duty and doing good.
John Tillotson

To be good is noble. To tell people how to be good is even nobler and much less trouble.
Mark Twain

The only way to compel men to speak good of us is to do it.
Voltaire

Do all the good you can, in all the ways you can, to all the souls you can, in every place you can, at all the times you can, with all the zeal you can, as long as ever you can.
John Wesley

A good man's life is all of a piece.
Benjamin Whichcote

If you pretend to be good, the world takes you very seriously. If you pretend to be bad, it doesn't. Such is the outstanding stupidity of optimism.
Oscar Wilde

Have as much good nature as good sense since they generally are companions.
William Wycherly

GOODWILL

But if you should take the bond of goodwill out of the universe no house or city could stand, nor would even the tillage of the fields abide. If that statement is not clear, then you may understand how great is the power of friendship and of concord from a consideration of the results of enmity and disagreement. For

what house is so strong, or what state so enduring that it cannot be utterly overthrown by animosities and division?
Cicero

None of us can buy goodwill; we must earn it.
William Feather

Goodwill is the one and only asset that competition cannot undersell or destroy.
Marshall Field

Employers, have you ever stopped to reckon what the goodwill of your workers is worth? . . . In most large concerns it would be worth more in dollars and cents to have the goodwill of the working force than of those on the outside. It has been repeatedly demonstrated that the average working force is capable of increasing its production 25% or more whenever the workers feel so inclined. Workers animated by ill will cannot possibly give results equal to those of workers animated by goodwill. The tragic fact appears to be that a tremendous number of working forces are not so animated. . . .
B.C. Forbes

I have found it helpful to keep constantly in mind that there are really two entries to be made for every transaction—one in terms of immediate dollars and cents, the other in terms of goodwill.
Ralph Hitz

A great asset of any business is goodwill. This is a trite statement but, like so many self-evident truths, it seldom gets the careful consideration it deserves. Goodwill does not come through clarion advertising appeals, exhortations, protestations. Character, from which stems goodwill, is a quality of slow growth through performance.
W. Alton Jones

Goodwill to others is constructive thought. It helps build us up. It is good for your body. It makes your blood purer, your muscles stronger, and your whole form more symmetrical in shape. It is the real elixir of life. The more such thought you attract to you, the more life you will have.
Prentice Mulford

Goodwill is no easy symbol of good wishes. It is an immeasurable and tremendous energy, the atomic energy of the spirit.
Eleanor B. Stock

Goodwill is the mightiest practical force in the universe.
Talmudic saying

Goodwill cannot be insured. The only way to retain it is to keep earning it.
Frank Tyger

By helping one another in times of disaster, nations are strengthening the bonds of goodwill that will yet bring the peoples of earth together.
Walter Van Kirk

Goodwill for a business is built by good goods, service and truthful advertising.
E.R. Waite

GOSSIP

If we knew what will be said about us when we are gone, we would have been gone a long time ago.
Don-Aminado

If we all said to people's faces what we say behind one another's backs, society would be impossible.
Honoré de Balzac

There are many who dare not kill themselves for fear of what the neighbors will say.
Cyril Connolly

If you are told that such an one speaks ill of you, make no defense against what was said, but answer, "He surely knew not my other faults, else he would not have mentioned these only!"
Epictetus

Talking things over has its place in an organization [but] so-called conferences are being grossly over-done. One executive stops at the desk of another to tell him, perhaps, about the wonderful score he made at golf on Saturday afternoon. This chin-chin immediately becomes a conference, and neither the office boy nor the telephone operator must disturb either gentleman. More idle gossip is indulged in at many business conferences these days than an old wives' sewing circle would be guilty of.
B.C. Forbes

If one surveys this culture of Monica Lewinsky and O.J. Simpson and constant gossip and salaciousness, and one tries to trace the roots, you find yourself at Walter Winchell. He was not only present at the creation of this modern journalism but in many respects he was the creation.
Neal Gabler

I don't care what is written about me so long as it isn't true.
Katharine Hepburn

Shun the inquisitive, for you will be sure to find him leaky. Open ears do not keep conscientiously what has been intrusted to them, and a word once spoken flies, never to be recalled.
Horace

If you haven't got anything nice to say about anybody, come sit next to me.
Alice Roosevelt Longworth

Gossip isn't scandal and it's not merely malicious. It's chatter about the human race by lovers of the same.
Phyllis McGinley

The glory of gossip these days is that there are so many celebrities and such quick-access media that the scandal stories blow up huge and all-encompassing, then are replaced by the next one three days later.
Michael Musto

So live that you wouldn't be ashamed to sell the family parrot to the town gossip.
Will Rogers

Gossip is news running ahead of itself in a red satin dress.
Liz Smith

One's own vanities and humiliations I find a delicious subject for conversation. Things said of me behind my back I don't enjoy, and don't listen to them.
Logan Pearsall Smith

There is only one thing in the world worse than being talked about, and that is not being talked about.
Oscar Wilde

Gossip is the art of saying nothing in a way that leaves practically nothing unsaid.
Walter Winchell

GOVERNMENT

While all other sciences have advanced, that of government is at a standstill—little better understood, little better

practiced now than three or four thousand years ago.
John Adams

Whatsoever moveth is stronger than that which is moved, and whatsoever governeth is stronger than that which is governed.
St. Aristides

When any of the four pillars of government—religion, justice, counsel, and treasure—are mainly shaken or weakened, men had need to pray for fair weather.
Francis Bacon

All government is a trust. Every branch of government is a trust, and immemorially acknowledged to be so.
Jeremy Bentham

Most of the time, the war against leaks is much more about a presidential quest for control over information, over his own White House, over the government—than it is about real damage the leak has caused.
Jonathan Bernstein

A reform is a correction of abuses, a revolution is a transfer of power.
Edward Bulwer-Lytton

If you are to stand up for your government you must be able to stand up to your government.
Harold Caccia

Of representative assemblies may not this good be said: that contending parties fight there, since fight they must, by petition [and] parliamentary eloquence, not by sword, bayonet and bursts of military cannon.
Thomas Carlyle

The administration of government, like a guardianship, ought to be directed to the good of those who confer, not of those who receive the trust.
Cicero

Government is a trust, and the officers of the government are trustees; and both the trust and the trustees are created for the benefit of the people.
Henry Clay

A government for the people must depend for its success on the intelligence, the morality, the justice, and the interest of the people themselves.
Grover Cleveland

Phil Gramm and I disagreed on a lot of things, but he can't possibly be wrong about everything. On the Glass-Steagall thing, if you could demonstrate to me that it was a mistake, I'd be glad to look at the evidence. But I can't blame [the Republicans]. This wasn't something they forced me into.
Bill Clinton

The only choice which Providence has graciously left to a vicious government is either to fall by the people if they become enlightened, or with them, if they are kept enslaved and ignorant.
Samuel Taylor Coleridge

There is good government when those who are near are happy, and when those who are far away desire to come.
Confucius

Governments are necessarily continuing concerns. They have to keep going in good times and in bad. They therefore need a wide margin of safety. If taxes and debt are made all the people can bear when times are good, there will be certain disaster when times are bad.
Calvin Coolidge

This is not a great time to be in Congress.
Rep. Jim Cooper

You can only govern men by serving them. The rule is without exception.
Victor Cousin

The state has but one face for me: that of the police. To my eyes, all of the state's ministries have this single face, and I cannot imagine the ministry of culture other than as the police of culture, with its prefect and commissioners.
Jean Dubuffet

There is far more danger in public than in private monopoly, for when Government goes into business it can always shift its losses to the taxpayers. Government never makes ends meet—and that is the first requisite of business.
Thomas A. Edison

I firmly believe that the army of persons who urge greater and greater centralization of authority and greater and greater dependence upon the Federal Treasury are really more dangerous to our form of government than any external threat that can possibly be arrayed against us.
Dwight D. Eisenhower

The less government we have the better—the fewer laws and the less confided power. The antidote to this abuse of formal government is the influence of private character, the growth of the individual.
Ralph Waldo Emerson

Local government is the foundation of democracy, if it fails, democracy will fail.
Robert W. Flack

If the World War [I] demonstrated anything it was that government ownership is fraught with the gravest dangers and usually leads to disaster. Take Britain. The two problems which have caused the greatest trouble since the war ended have been transportation and coal. The government seized both industries when the war broke out. It got them into such a hopeless mess that it does not know how to turn [in] coal; the government now realizes, it took hold of the tail of a wild animal and is afraid to let go.
B.C. Forbes

Civil Service has itself become such a spoils system that a fed-to-the-teeth-with-bureaucracy public threatens to support a return to the old one.

Once in a civil service job, one needs only to live to rise. It's near impossible to be fired for incompetence, indifference, woeful attendance, insubordination, or even being caught red-handed in the cookie jar. . . .

When Congress passed the civil service act slightly more than 100 years ago after a disappointed job-seeker assassinated President Garfield, it surely didn't have in mind that its baby would turn into such an uncivil monster.
Malcolm Forbes

Pundits often poke fun at President Johnson's tendency to grab the phone and personally issue an order or a request to someone 25 layers below the top. I guess though that in these instances Mr. Johnson's long years of experience in government taught him where the inaction begins to set in.

If Presidents have such trouble moving the federal bureaucracy, what chance is there for us mere citizens? It's a point to keep in mind next time we start to say, Let's have the Government do it. That's often a way, it would seem, of making sure that whatever it is that should be done isn't.

Malcolm Forbes

Government is itself an art, one of the subtlest of the arts. It is neither business, nor technology, nor applied science. It is the art of making men live together in peace and with reasonable happiness.
Felix Frankfurter

It is wonderful how preposterously the affairs of the world are managed. We assemble parliaments and councils to have the benefit of collected wisdom, but we necessarily have, at the same time, the inconvenience of their collected passions, prejudices and private interests: for regulating commerce an assembly of great men is the greatest fool on earth.
Benjamin Franklin

If private business should be supervised in the public interest, government, when it assumes a business role, is in equal need of supervision.
James A. Fulton

All free governments are managed by the combined wisdom and folly of the people.
James A. Garfield

It is the duty of government to make it difficult for people to do wrong, easy to do right.
William E. Gladstone

Why has government been instituted at all? Because the passions of men will not conform to the dictates of reason and justice, without constraint.
Alexander Hamilton

All good government must begin in the home. It is useless to make good laws for bad people. Public sentiment is more than law.
H.R. Hawes

No free government, or the blessings of liberty can be preserved to any people but by a firm adherence to justice, moderation, temperance, frugality, and virtue, and by a frequent recurrence to fundamental principles.
Patrick Henry

One shudders to imagine the mischief that some budding J. Edgar Hoover, now playing Call of Duty on his iPad after school, might one day make with the assets of the [NSA's] Utah Data Center.
Hendrik Hertzberg

If we fixed a hangnail the way our government fixes the economy, we'd slam a car door on it.
Cullen Hightower

There is one thing better than good government, and that is government in which all the people have a part.
Walter Hines

There are very few so foolish that they had not rather govern themselves than be governed by others.
Thomas Hobbes

Along this road of spending, the government either takes over, which is Socialism, or dictates institutional and economic life, which is Fascism.
Herbert Hoover

The first lesson in civics is that efficient government should begin at home.
Charles Evans Hughes

There are no necessary evils in government. Its evils exist only in its abuses. If it would confine itself to equal protection, and, as Heaven does its rain, shower its favors alike on the high and on the low, the rich and the poor, it would be an unqualified blessing.
Andrew Jackson

I think we have more machinery of government than is necessary, too many

parasites living on the labor of the industrious.
Thomas Jefferson

My reading of history convinces me that most bad government results from too much government.
Thomas Jefferson

The persons and property of our citizens are entitled to the protection of our government in all places where they may lawfully go.
Thomas Jefferson

The qualifications of self-government in society are not innate. They are the result of habit and long training, and for these they will require time and probably much suffering.
Thomas Jefferson

Those who bear equally the burdens of government should equally participate of its benefits.
Thomas Jefferson

The future holds little hope for any government where the present holds no hope for the people.
Lyndon Baines Johnson

One of the things we have to be thankful for is that we don't get as much government as we pay for.
Charles F. Kettering

As restrictions and prohibitions are multiplied the people grow poorer and poorer. When they are subjected to overmuch government, the land is thrown into confusion.
Lao-tzu

It's easy to forget what intelligence consists of: luck and speculation. Here and there a windfall, here and there a scoop.
John le Carré

It has long been a grave question whether any government, not too strong for the liberties of its people, can be strong enough to maintain its existence in great emergencies.
Abraham Lincoln

Let the people know the truth and the country is safe.
Abraham Lincoln

No man is good enough to govern another man without that other man's consent.
Abraham Lincoln

Dictatorship is always merely an aria, never an opera.
Emil Ludwig

A popular government without popular information, or the means of acquiring it, is but a prologue to a farce or a tragedy, or perhaps both.
James Madison

If it was wise, manly, and patriotic for us to establish a free government, it is equally wise to attend to the necessary means of its preservation.
James Monroe

What the press never does say is who the leaker is and why he wants the story leaked. Yet, more often than not, this is the more important story: What policy wins if the one being disclosed loses?
Daniel Patrick Moynihan

Governments, like clocks, go from the motion men give them, and as governments are made and moved by men, so by them they are ruined also. Therefore governments depend upon men rather then men upon governments.
William Penn

The men of the FBI, with hardly an exception, were proud of their insularity,

of having sprung from the grass roots. They were therefore whisky-drinkers, with beer for light refreshment. By contrast, CIA men flaunted cosmopolitan postures. They would discuss absinthe and serve Burgundy at room temperature.
Kim Philby

The punishment suffered by the wise who refuse to take part in the government, is to live under the government of bad men.
Plato

Men well governed should seek after no other liberty, for there can be no greater liberty than a good government.
Sir Walter Raleigh

Millions of individuals making their own decisions in the marketplace will always allocate resources better than any centralized government planning process.
Ronald Reagan

Industrial combination is not wrong in itself. The danger lies in taking government into partnership.
Franklin D. Roosevelt

Under government ownership corruption can flourish just as rankly as under private ownership.
Theodore Roosevelt

The major problem confronting the world today is: Shall the people govern or be governed?
Dr. John A. Ross, Jr.

Government originated in the attempt to find a form of association that defends and protects the person and property of each with the common force of all.
Jean-Jacques Rousseau

The institution of representative government to us seems an essential part of democracy, but the ancients never thought of it. Its immense merit was that it enabled a large constituency to exert indirect power, and thus made possible the distribution of political responsibility throughout the great states of modern times.
Bertrand Russell

There are times when free markets stop and rational thinking goes out the window. It then isn't enough to be a laissez-faire conservative and let Rome burn. This bill is not perfect, but doing nothing is far worse than passing this bill.
Rep. Paul Ryan

An administration, like a machine, does not create. It carries on.
Antoine de Saint-Exupéry

They that govern the most make the least noise.
John Selden

A hated government does not long survive.
Seneca

As soon as government management begins it upsets the natural equilibrium of industrial relations, and each interference only requires further bureaucratic control until the end is the tyranny of the totalitarian state.
Adam Smith (1776)

I know now why confusion in government is not only tolerated but encouraged. I have learned. A confused people can make no clear demands.
John Steinbeck

It is not the function of the State to make men happy. They must make themselves happy in their own way, and at their own risk. The functions of the State lie

entirely in the conditions or chances under which the pursuit of happiness is carried on.
William Graham Sumner

O divine art of subtlety and secrecy! Through you we learn to be invisible, through you inaudible and hence we can hold the enemy's fate in our hands.
Sun Tzu

To commit violent and unjust acts, it is not enough for a government to have the will or even the power; the habits, ideas and passions of the time must lend themselves to their committal.
Alexis de Tocqueville

It is beyond the vision or ability of any human being to foretell what will follow partial socialization of industry and a governmental supervision over practically all business. . . . I feel, however, that we can assume that we will never go back to the old order of things; that we will find that this is simply the first chapter of a new book and that no one can as yet foretell the trend of the chapters or acts that are to follow.
George M. Verity

In general, the art of government consists of making as much money as possible from one class of citizens to give to the other.
Voltaire

Government is not reason, it is not eloquence—it is force! Like fire it is a dangerous servant and a fearful master; never for a moment should it be left to irresponsible action.
George Washington

The habits of thinking in a free country should inspire caution in those intrusted with its administration to confine themselves within their respective constitutional spheres, avoiding in the exercise of the powers of one department, to encroach upon another.
George Washington

If war should sweep our commerce from the seas, another generation will restore it. If war exhausts our treasury, future industry will replenish it. If war desiccate and lay waste our fields, under new cultivation they will grow green again and ripen to future harvest. If the walls of yonder Capitol should fall and its decorations be covered by the dust of battle, all these can be rebuilt. But who shall reconstruct the fabric of a demolished government; who shall dwell in the well-proportioned columns of constitutional liberty; who shall frame together the skillful architecture which unites sovereignty with state's rights, individual security with prosperity?
Daniel Webster

The history of liberty is the history of the limitations on the power of the government.
Woodrow Wilson

Asking journalists to denounce leaks because of their deleterious effects on the functioning of government is as hopeless as asking an airline to denounce jet fuel because of its impact on the environment.
Benjamin Wittes

The essential problem is how to govern a large-scale world with small-scale local minds.
Alfred Zimmern

GRAMMAR

Sentence structure is innate but whining is acquired.
Woody Allen

Bad spellers of the world, untie!
Anonymous

Boyhood is distracted for years with precepts of grammar that are infinitely prolix, perplexed and obscure.
Johann Comenius

Grammar is a piano I play by ear. All I know about grammar is its power.
Joan Didion

To be loose with grammar is to be loose with the worst woman in the world.
Otis C. Edwards

The adjective is the banana peel of the parts of speech.
Clifton Fadiman

Cut out all these exclamation points. An exclamation point is like laughing at your own joke.
F. Scott Fitzgerald

You can be a little ungrammatical if you come from the right part of the country.
Robert Frost

Grammarians dispute, and the question is still undecided.
Horace

I am the King of Rome, and above grammar.
Emperor Sigismund

Save the gerund and screw the whale.
Tom Stoppard

Caesar is not above the grammarians.
Tiberius

Commas in *The New Yorker* fall with the precision of knives in a circus act, outlining the victim.
E.B. White

Like everything metaphysical the harmony between thought and reality is to be found in the grammar of language.
Ludwig Wittgenstein

GRATITUDE

When people are made to feel secure and important and appreciated, it will no longer be necessary for them to whittle down others in order to seem bigger by comparison.
Virginia Arcastle

Next to ingratitude, the most painful thing to bear is gratitude.
Henry Ward Beecher

Sometimes we need to remind ourselves that thankfulness is indeed a virtue.
William John Bennett

Do you know what is more hard to bear than the reverses of fortune? It is the baseness, the hideous ingratitude of man.
Napoleon Bonaparte

A blessing:
Some hae meat and cannae eat,
And some hae meat but want it;
But we hae meat and we can eat
And sae the Lord be thankit.
Robert Burns

I awoke this morning with devout thanksgiving for my friends, the old and new.
Will Carleton

Gratitude is not only the greatest of virtues, but the parent of all others.
Cicero

He is a man of sense who does not grieve for what he has not, but rejoices in what he has.
Epictetus

When I'm not thank'd at all, I'm thank'd enough. I've done my duty, and I've done no more.
Henry Fielding

Gratitude: A lively sense of future benefit.
French definition

Best of all is it to preserve everything in a pure, still heart, and let there be for every pulse a thanksgiving, and for every breath a song.
Konrad von Gesner

There is one day that is ours. There is one day when all we Americans who are not self-made go back to the old home to eat saleratus biscuits and marvel how much nearer to the porch the old pump looks than it used to . . . Thanksgiving Day . . . is the one day that is purely American.
O. Henry

The deepest principle in human nature is the craving to be appreciated.
William James

Gratitude is the fruit of great cultivation; you do not find it among gross people.
Samuel Johnson

Particular pains particular thanks do ask.
Ben Jonson

Gratitude, in most men, is only a strong and secret hope of greater favors.
François de La Rochefoucauld

One can never pay in gratitude; one can only pay in kind somewhere else in life.
Anne Morrow Lindbergh

Gratitude is the most exquisite form of courtesy.
Jacques Maritain

A man may be ungrateful, but the human race is not so.
John Milton

The worship most acceptable to God comes from a thankful and cheerful heart.
Plutarch

He who receives a benefit with gratitude repays the first installment on his debt.
Seneca

Let the man, who would be grateful, think of repaying a kindness, even while receiving it.
Seneca

The private and personal blessings we enjoy, the blessings of immunity, safeguard, liberty, and integrity, deserve the thanksgiving of a whole life.
Jeremy Taylor

As bread is the staff of life, the simple sustenance of the body, so appreciation is the food of the soul.
Priscilla Wayne

GREATNESS

Great men are the real men, in them nature has succeeded.
Henri Frédéric Amiel

A man's true greatness lies in the consciousness of an honest purpose in life, founded on a just estimate of himself and everything else, on frequent self-examinations, and a steady obedience to the rule which he knows to be right, without troubling himself about what others may think or say, or whether they do or do not that which he thinks and says and does.
Marcus Aurelius Antoninus

All rising to a great place is by a winding stair.
Francis Bacon

Great thoughts, like great deeds, need no trumpet.
James M. Bailey

Man must realize his own unimportance before he can appreciate his importance.
R.M. Baumgardy

Whatever action is performed by a great man, common men follow in his footsteps, and whatever standards he sets by exemplary acts, all the world pursues.
Bhagavad-Gita

A really great man is known by three signs—generosity in the design, humanity in the execution, moderation in success.
Otto von Bismarck

All men who are really great can afford to be really human and to be shown so.
Gamaliel Bradford

A great man leaves clean work behind him, and requires no sweeper up of the chips.
Elizabeth Barrett Browning

Difficulty is the nurse of greatness.
William Cullen Bryant

Seem not greater than thou art.
Samuel Burton

To do great work a man must be very idle as well as very industrious.
Samuel Butler

Great minds discuss ideas, average minds discuss events, small minds discuss people.
Hugh C. Cameron

All greatness is unconscious, or it is little and naught.
Thomas Carlyle

Great men never feel great; small men never feel small.
Chinese proverb

There is a great man who makes every man feel small. But the really great man is the man who makes every man feel great.
Chinese proverb

The price of greatness is responsibility.
Winston Churchill

Great minds had rather deserve contemporaneous applause without obtaining it, than obtain without deserving it. If it follow them it is well, but they will not deviate to follow it.
Charles Caleb Colton

There are three marks of a superior man: being virtuous, he is free from anxiety; being wise, he is free from perplexity; being brave, he is free from fear.
Confucius

From the little spark may burst a mighty flame.
Dante

Anybody can be nobody, but it takes a man to be somebody.
Eugene V. Debs

A great man is one who can have power and not abuse it.
Henry L. Doherty

Man is not merely a combination of appetites, instincts, passions and curiosity. Something more is needed to explain great human deeds, virtues, sacrifices, martyrdom. There is an element in the great mystics, the saints, the prophets, whose influence has been

felt for centuries, which escapes mere intelligence.
Lecomte Du Noüy

Great spirits have always found violent opposition from mediocrities.
Albert Einstein

Half of the harm that is done in this world is due to people who want to feel important . . . they do not mean to do harm . . . they are absorbed in the endless struggle to think well of themselves.
T.S. Eliot

Great men are more distinguished by range and extent than by originality.
Ralph Waldo Emerson

The great man is not convulsible or tormentable; events pass over him without much impression.
Ralph Waldo Emerson

To be great is to be misunderstood.
Ralph Waldo Emerson

I note the derogatory rumors concerning the use of alcoholic stimulants and lavish living. It is the penalty of greatness.
W.C. Fields

The best teachers of humanity are the lives of great men.
Charles H. Fowler

To accomplish great things, we must not only act, but also dream, not only plan, but also believe.
Anatole France

It is a great mistake to think of being great without goodness; and I pronounce it as certain that there was never yet a truly great man that was not at the same time truly virtuous.
Benjamin Franklin

The truly great man is he who would master no one, and who would be mastered by none.
Kahlil Gibran

It doesn't take great men to do things, but it is doing things that make men great.
Arnold Glasow

One is never done with knowing the greatest men or the greatest works of art—they carry you on and on, and at the last you feel that you are only beginning.
T.R. Glover

Every individual has a place to fill in the world, and is important in some respect, whether he chooses to be so or not.
Nathaniel Hawthorne

True greatness, first of all, is a thing of the heart. It is alive with robust and generous sympathies. It is neither behind its age nor too far before it. It is up with its age, and ahead of it only just so far as to be able to lead its march. It cannot slumber, for activity is a necessity of its existence. It is no reservoir, but a fountain.
Roswell D. Hitchcock

The world's idea of greatness has been that he is greatest who succeeds in using his fellow men for the furtherance of his own ends.
A.H. Hoge

As a madman is apt to think himself grown suddenly great, so he that grows suddenly great is apt to borrow a little from the madman.
Samuel Johnson

Those who give too much attention to trifling things become generally incapable of great ones.
François de La Rochefoucauld

There is no right without a parallel duty, no liberty without the supremacy of the law, no high destiny without earnest perseverance, no greatness without self-denial.
Francis Lieber

Lives of great men all remind us we can make our lives sublime!
Henry Wadsworth Longfellow

If any man seeks for greatness, let him forget greatness and ask for truth, and he will find both.
Horace Mann

Lack of something to feel important about is almost the greatest tragedy a man may have.
Dr. Arthur E. Morgan

Great men have been characterized by the greatness of their mistakes as well as by the greatness of their achievements.
Abraham Myerson

Those who cannot feel the littleness of great things in themselves are apt to overlook the greatness of little things in others.
Kakuzo Okakura

Do little things now; so shall big things come to thee by and by asking to be done.
Persian proverb

I go to seek a great perhaps.
François Rabelais

It's great to be great, but it's greater to be human.
Will Rogers

Great men never make bad use of their superiority; they see it, and feel it, and are not less modest. The more they have, the more they know their own deficiencies.
Jean Jacques Rousseau

I fear uniformity. You cannot manufacture great men any more than you can manufacture gold.
John Ruskin

Let a man in a garret but burn with enough intensity, and he will set fire to the world.
Antoine de Saint-Exupéry

The greatest man is he who chooses right with the most invincible resolution; who resists to sorest temptation from within and without; who bears the heaviest burdens cheerfully; who is calmest in storms, and most fearless under menaces and frowns; whose reliance on truth, on virtue, and on God is most unfaltering.
Seneca

There's hope a great man's memory may outlive his life half a year.
William Shakespeare

Life is made up of little things. It is very rarely that an occasion is offered for doing a great deal at once. True greatness consists in being great in little things.
Charles Simmons

The career of a great man remains an enduring monument of human energy. The man dies and disappears, but his thoughts and acts survive and leave an indelible stamp upon his race.
Samuel Smiles

The great man is the man who does a thing for the first time.
Alexander Smith

If thou art rich, then show the greatness of thy fortune; or what is better, the greatness of thy soul, in the meekness of thy conversation; condescend to men of low estate, support the distressed, and patronize the neglected. Be great.
Laurence Sterne

To have read the greatest works of any great poet, to have beheld or heard the greatest works of any great painter or musician, is a possession added to the best things of life.
Algernon Swinburne

Might I give counsel to any man, I would say to him, try to frequent the company of your betters. In books and in life, that is the most wholesome society; learn to admire rightly; the great pleasure of life is that. Note what great men admire.
William Makepeace Thackeray

Great men undertake great things because they are great; fools, because they think them easy.
Marquis de Vauvenargues

When a man realizes his littleness, his greatness can appear.
H.G. Wells

Every great man nowadays has his disciples, and it is always Judas who writes the biography.
Oscar Wilde

None think the great unhappy but the great.
Edward Young

GREED

Avarice, in old age, is foolish; for what can be more absurd than to increase our provisions for the road the nearer we approach to our journey's end?
Cicero

From top to bottom of the ladder, greed is aroused without knowing where to find ultimate foothold. Nothing can calm it, since its goal is far beyond all it can attain. Reality seems valueless by comparison with the dreams of fevered imaginations; reality is therefore abandoned.
Emile Durkheim

Greed is a bottomless pit which exhausts the person in an endless effort to satisfy the need without ever reaching satisfaction.
Erich Fromm

Avarice hoards itself poor; charity gives itself rich.
German proverb

Is not dread of thirst when your well is full, the thirst that is unquenchable?
Kahlil Gibran

Callous greed grows pious very fast.
Lillian Hellman

Avarice, or the desire of gain, is a universal passion which operates at all times, at all places, and upon all persons.
David Hume

There is no calamity greater than lavish desires

There is no greater guilt than discontentment

And there is no greater disaster than greed.
Lao-tzu

Anyone with more than 365 pairs of shoes is a pig.
Barbara Melser Lieberman

Take heed, and beware of covetousness; for a man's life consisteth not in the abundance of the things which he possesseth.
Luke 12:15

We're all born brave, trusting and greedy, and most of us remain greedy.
Mignon McLaughlin

Those who are greedy of praise prove that they are poor in merit.
Plutarch

Covetousness, by a greediness of getting more, deprives itself of the true end of getting; it loses the enjoyment of what it had got.
Thomas Sprat

The point is that you can't be too greedy.
Donald Trump

Happy the man who has learned the cause of things and has put under his feet all fear, inexorable fate, and the noisy strife of the hell of greed.
Virgil

The avaricious man is like the barren sandy ground of the desert which sucks in all the rain and dew with greediness, but yields no fruitful herbs or plants for the benefit of others.
Zeno

GROWTH

The most fatal illusion is the settled point of view. Life is growth and motion; a fixed point of view kills anybody who has one.
Brooks Atkinson

To grow and know what one is growing towards—that is the source of all strength and confidence in life.
James Baillie

Life is growth—a challenge of environment. If we cannot meet our everyday surroundings with equanimity and pleasure and grow each day in some useful direction, then this splendid balance of cosmic forces which we call life is on the road toward misfortune, misery and

destruction. Therefore, health is the most precious of all things.
Luther Burbank

Time ripens all things. No man's born wise.
Miguel de Cervantes

When he who ponders these things cries that all flesh is grass, science joins with faith, replying: Make green, then, in thy season, the place wherein thou growest.
George W. Corner

A man's growth is seen in the successive choirs of his friends.
Ralph Waldo Emerson

No great thing is created suddenly, any more than a bunch of grapes or a fig. If you tell me that you desire a fig, I answer you that there must be time. Let it first blossom, then bear fruit, then ripen.
Epictetus

Everybody wants to be somebody, but nobody wants to grow.
Johann Wolfgang von Goethe

In the business of life, Man is the only product. And there is only one direction in which man can possibly develop if he is to make a better living or yield a bigger dividend to himself, to his race, to nature or to God. He must grow in knowledge, wisdom, kindliness and understanding.
V.C. Kitchen

Just as we outgrow a pair of trousers, we outgrow acquaintances, libraries, principles, etc., at times before they're worn out and at times—and this is the worst of all—before we have new ones.
Georg C. Lichtenberg

We want our children to grow up to be such persons that ill-fortune, if they meet with it, will bring out strength in them,

and that good fortune will not trip them up, but make them winners.
Edward Sandford Martin

Undertake something that is difficult; it will do you good. Unless you try to do something beyond what you have already mastered, you will never grow.
Ronald E. Osborn

Our growth depends not on how many experiences we devour, but on how many we digest.
Ralph W. Sockman

Great occasions do not make heroes or cowards; they simply unveil them to the eyes of men. Silently and imperceptibly, as we wake or sleep, we grow strong or we grow weak, and at last some crisis shows us what we have become.
Bishop Westcott

H

HABITS

Since custom is the principal magistrate of man is life, let men by all means endeavor to obtain good customs.
Francis Bacon

We think according to nature; we speak according to rules; but we act according to custom.
Francis Bacon

You don't get anything clean without getting something else dirty.
Cecil Baxter

Woe unto them that are tired of everything, for everything will certainly be tired of them.
G.K. Chesterton

The nature of man is always the same; it is their habits that separate them.
Confucius

Any man who leads the regular and temperate life, not swerving from it in the least degree where his nourishment is concerned, can be but little affected by other disorders or incidental mishaps. Whereas, on the other hand, I truly conclude that disorderly habits of living are those which are fatal.
Luigi Cornaro

The customs and fashions of men change like leaves on the bough, some of which go and others come.
Dante

Habit is either the best of servants or the worst of masters.
Nathaniel Emmons

A nail is driven out by another nail; habit is overcome by habit.
Erasmus

Custom may lead a man into many errors, but it justifies none.
Henry Fielding

It is not from nature, but from education and habits, that our wants are chiefly derived.
Henry Fielding

Fatigue is no more praiseworthy than drunkenness; both are evidence of bad habits.
L.G. Freeman

If everyone sweeps before his own front door, then the street is clean.
Johann Wolfgang von Goethe

The diligent fostering of a candid habit of mind, even in trifles, is a matter of high moment both to character and opinions.
John S. Howson

Custom, then, is the great guide to human life.
David Hume

No habit has any real hold on you other than the hold you have on it.
Gardner Hunting

We must make automatic and habitual, as early as possible, as many useful actions as we can. The more of the details of our daily life we can hand over to the effortless custody of automatism, the more our higher powers of mind will be set free for their own proper work.
William James

The chains of habit are too weak to be felt until they are too strong to be broken.
Samuel Johnson

Habit is a cable; we weave a thread of it each day, and at last we cannot break it.
Horace Mann

The unfortunate thing about this world is that good habits are so much easier to give up than bad ones.
Somerset Maugham

The despotism of custom is on the wane. We are not content to know that things are; we ask whether they ought to be.
John Stuart Mill

Small habits well pursued betimes may reach the dignity of crimes.
Hannah More

Habits change into character.
Ovid

The best way to stop a bad habit is never to begin it.
J.C. Penney

The fixity of a habit is generally in direct proportion to its absurdity.
Marcel Proust

A deep meaning often lies in old customs.
Johann Friedrich von Schiller

Better keep yourself clean and bright; you are the window through which you must see the world.
George Bernard Shaw

Good habits, which bring our lower passions and appetites under automatic control, leave our natures free to explore the larger experiences of life. Too many of us divide and dissipate our energies in debating actions which should be taken for granted.
Ralph W. Sockman, D.D.

Habit is habit, and not to be flung out of the window by any man, but coaxed downstairs a step at a time.
Mark Twain

Nothing so needs reforming as other people's habits.
Mark Twain

The formation of right habits is essential to your permanent security. They diminish your chance of falling when assailed, and they augment your chance of recovery when overthrown.
John Tyndall

The secret of being tiresome is to tell everything.
Voltaire

HAPPINESS

If you have nothing else to do, look about you and see if there isn't something close at hand that you can improve! It may make you wealthy, though it is more likely that it will make you happy.
George Matthew Adams

A man should always consider how much he has more than he wants and how much more unhappy he might be than he really is.
Joseph Addison

We must dare to be happy, and dare to confess it, regarding ourselves always as the depositories, not as the authors of our own joy.
Henri Frédéric Amiel

The happiness of your life depends upon the quality of your thoughts: therefore, guard accordingly, and take care that you entertain no notion unsuitable to virtue and reasonable nature.
Marcus Aurelius Antoninus

Real happiness is cheap enough, yet how dearly we pay for its counterfeit.
H. Ballou

It is not in doing what you like, but in liking what you do that is the secret of happiness.
James M. Barrie

Pleasure only starts once the worm has got into the fruit; to become delightful, happiness must be tainted with poison.
Georges Bataille

A man without mirth is like wagon without springs, in which one is caused disagreeably to jolt by every pebble over which it turns.
Henry Ward Beecher

Each morning the day lies like a fresh shirt on our bed; this incomparably fine, incomparably tightly woven tissue of pure prediction fits us perfectly. The happiness of the next 24 hours depends on our ability, on waking, to pick it up.
Walter Benjamin

The idea that happiness could have a share in beauty would be too much of a good thing.
Walter Benjamin

Don't mistake pleasure for happiness. They are a different breed of dogs.
Josh Billings

It is the paradox of life that the way to miss pleasure is to seek it first. The very first condition of lasting happiness is that a life should be full of purpose, aiming at something outside self. As a matter of experience, we find that true happiness comes in seeking other things, in the manifold activities of life, in the healthful outgoing of all human powers.
Hugh Black

I had always imagined paradise as a kind of library.
Jorge Luis Borges

Unhappiness indicates wrong thinking; just as ill health indicates a bad regimen.
Paul Bourget

Happiness, whether in business or private life, leaves very little trace in history.
Fernand Braudel

Happiness quite unshared can scarcely be called happiness; it has no taste.
Emily Brontë

Money doesn't always bring happiness. People with ten million dollars are no

happier than people with nine million
dollars.
Hobart Brown

No man, with a man's heart in him gets
far on his way without some bitter,
soul-searching disappointment. Happy
is he who is brave enough to push on to
another stage of the journey.
John Mason Brown

To be happy, you must learn to forget
yourself.
Edward Bulwer-Lytton

There is work that is work and there is
play that is play; there is play that is work
and work that is play. And in only one of
these lies happiness.
Gelett Burgess

Happiness and misery depend not upon
how high up or low down you are—they
depend not upon these, but on the direction in which you are tending.
Samuel Butler

We have all sinned and come short of the
glory of making ourselves as comfortable
as we easily might have done.
Samuel Butler

All who would win joy, must share it;
happiness was born a twin.
Lord Byron

There comes forever something between
us and what we deem our happiness.
Lord Byron

The secret of happiness is renunciation.
Andrew Carnegie

It is with happiness as with watches:
the less complicated, the less easily
deranged.
Sebastien Chamfort

Happy is he who still loves something
he loved in the nursery: He has not been
broken in two by time; he is not two men,
but one, and he has saved not only his
soul but his life.
G.K. Chesterton

True contentment is a thing as active as
agriculture. It is the power of getting out
of any situation all that there is in it.
G.K. Chesterton

Happiness is someone to love, something
to do, and something to hope for.
Chinese proverb

One does not leave a convivial party
before closing time.
Winston Churchill

I do not understand what the man who is
happy wants in order to be happier.
Cicero

A perverse temper and fretful disposition
will make any state of life whatsoever
unhappy.
Cicero

We communicate happiness to others
not often by great acts of devotion and
self-sacrifice, but by the absence of faultfinding and censure, by being ready to
sympathize with their notions and feelings, instead of forcing them to sympathize with ours.
Adam Clarke

It is misery enough to have once been
happy.
John Clarke

Happiness is a hard thing because it is
achieved only by making others happy.
Stuart Cloete

The happiness of life is made up of minute fractions—the little, soon forgotten charities of a kiss or smile, a kind look, a heart-felt compliment, and the countless infinitesimals of pleasurable and genial feeling.
Samuel Taylor Coleridge

We never enjoy perfect happiness; our most fortunate successes are mingled with sadness; some anxieties always perplex the reality of our satisfaction.
Pierre Corneille

A life of ease is a difficult pursuit.
William Cowper

Each time dawn appears, the mystery is there in its entirety.
René Daumal

Search for a single, inclusive good is doomed to failure. Such happiness as life is capable of comes from the full participation of all our powers in the endeavor to wrest from each changing situation of experience its own full and unique meaning.
John Dewey

Action may not always bring happiness; but there is no happiness without action.
Benjamin Disraeli

If we are ever to enjoy life, now is the time—not tomorrow, nor next year, nor in some future life after we have died. The best preparation for a better life next year is a full, complete, harmonious, joyous life this year. Our beliefs in a rich future life are of little importance unless we coin them into a rich present life. Today should always be our most wonderful day.
Thomas Dreier

Happy the man, and happy he alone, he, who can call today his own.
John Dryden

Well-being and happiness never appeared to me as an absolute aim. I am even inclined to compare such moral aims to the ambitions of a pig.
Albert Einstein

Whether happiness may come or not, one should try and prepare one's self to do without it.
George Eliot

Don't be a cynic, and bewail and bemoan. Omit the negative propositions. Don't waste yourself in rejection, nor bark against the bad, but chant the beauty of the good. Set down nothing that will help somebody.
Ralph Waldo Emerson

Happiness is a perfume you cannot pour on others without getting a few drops on yourself.
Ralph Waldo Emerson

The high prize of life, the crowning glory of a man is to be born with a bias to some pursuit which finds him in employment and happiness—whether it be to make baskets, or broadswords, or canals, or statues, or songs.
Ralph Waldo Emerson

There is only one way to happiness, and that is cease worrying about things which are beyond the power of our will.
Epictetus

To be happy is not the purpose of our being, but to deserve happiness.
Immanuel Fichte

To be happy, one must have a good stomach and a bad heart.
Bernard de Fontenelle

A hug's a happy thing while a shrug's so often destructive.
Malcolm Forbes

Profit is a by-product of work; happiness is its chief product.
Henry Ford

Human felicity is produced not so much by great pieces of good fortune that seldom happen, as by little advantages that occur every day.
Benjamin Franklin

A single sunbeam is enough to drive away many shadows.
St. Francis of Assisi

Success is getting what you want, happiness is wanting what you get.
Dave Gardner

To attain happiness in another world we need only to believe something, while to secure it in this world we must do something.
C.P. Gilman

I have the happiness of the passing moment, and what more can a mortal ask?
George Gissing

We take greater pains to persuade others that we are happy, than in endeavoring to be so ourselves.
Oliver Goldsmith

If I could drop dead right now, I'd be the happiest man alive.
Samuel Goldwyn

All happiness depends on a leisurely breakfast.
John Gunther

Planning for happiness is rarely successful. Happiness just happens.
Robert Half

Happiness in this world, when it comes, comes incidentally. Make it the object of pursuit, and it leads us a wild-goose chase, and is never attained. Follow some other object, and very possibly we may find that we have caught happiness without dreaming of it.
Nathaniel Hawthorne

I do not know of any sure way of making others happy as being so one's self.
Arthur Helps

The happiness of this life depends less on what befalls you than the way in which you take it.
Elbert Hubbard

Happiness is the overcoming of not unknown obstacles toward a known goal.
L. Ron Hubbard

The supreme happiness of life is the conviction of being loved for yourself, or more correctly, being loved in spite of yourself.
Victor Hugo

Human happiness seems to consist in three ingredients; action, pleasure and indolence. And though these ingredients ought to be mixed in different proportions, according to the disposition of the person, yet no one ingredient can be entirely wanting without destroying in some measure the relish of the whole composition.
David Hume

I can sympathize with people's pains, but not with their pleasures. There is something curiously boring about somebody else's happiness.
Aldous Huxley

Labor and trouble one can always get through alone, but it takes two to be glad.
Henrik Ibsen

The happiest people seem to be those who have no particular reason for being so except that they are so.
William Ralph Inge

Happiness is not a reward—it is a consequence. Suffering is not a punishment—it is a result.
Robert G. Ingersoll

Happiness is the only good. The time to be happy is now. The place to be happy is here. The way to be happy is to make others so.
Robert G. Ingersoll

The first thing to learn in intercourse with others is non-interference with their own particular ways of being happy, provided those ways do not assume to interfere by violence with ours.
William James

It is neither wealth nor splendor, but tranquillity and occupation, which give happiness.
Thomas Jefferson

Our greatest happiness does not depend on the condition of life in which chance has placed us, but is always the result of a good conscience, good health, occupation, and freedom in all just pursuits.
Thomas Jefferson

Perfect happiness, I believe, was never intended by the Deity to be the lot of one of his creatures in this world; but that he has very much put in our power the nearness of our approaches to it is what I have steadfastly believed.
Thomas Jefferson

Every period of life is obliged to borrow its happiness from time to come.
Samuel Johnson

Philosophers there are who try to make themselves believe that this life is happy; but they believe it only while they are saying it, and never yet produced conviction in a single mind.
Samuel Johnson

Those who are not looking for happiness are the most likely to find it, because those who are searching forget that the surest way to be happy is to seek happiness for others.
Martin Luther King, Jr.

In this sad world of ours, sorry comes to all, and it often comes with bitter agony. Perfect relief is not possible, except with time. You cannot now believe that you will ever feel better. But this is not true. You are sure to be happy again. Knowing this, truly believing it, will make you less miserable now.
Abraham Lincoln

Most people are about as happy as they make up their minds to be.
Abraham Lincoln

Life finds its purpose and fulfillment in the expansion of happiness.
Maharishi Mahesh Yogi

Space plus whatever you feel equals more whatever you feel, marvelous for happiness, God save you otherwise.
Bernard Malamud

There is a wonderful mythical law of nature that the three things we crave most in life—happiness, freedom and peace of mind—are always attained by giving them to someone else.
Peyton Conway March

The first recipe for happiness is: Avoid too-lengthy meditations on the past.
André Maurois

Every job has drudgery, whether it is in the home, in the professional school or in

the office. The first secret of happiness is the recognition of this fundamental fact.
M.C. McIntosh

There is only one honest impulse at the bottom of Puritanism, and that is the impulse to punish the man with a superior capacity for happiness.
H.L. Mencken

Ask yourself whether you are happy, and you cease to be so.
John Stuart Mill

Unquestionably, it is possible to do without happiness; it is done involuntarily by nineteen-twentieths of mankind.
John Stuart Mill

I have no money, no resources, no hopes. I am the happiest man alive.
Henry Miller

Unbroken happiness is a bore: It should have ups and downs.
Molière

False happiness renders men stern and proud, and that happiness is never communicated. True happiness renders them kind and sensible, and that happiness is always shared.
Montesquieu

If one only wished to be happy, this could be easily accomplished; but we wish to be happier than other people, and this is always difficult, for we believe others to be happier than they are.
Montesquieu

Every method is used to prove to men that in given political, economic and social situations they are bound to be happy, and those who are unhappy are mad or criminals or monsters.
Alberto Moravia

The merchant enjoys the felicity both of this world and the next.
Muhammad

There is only one way to achieve happiness on this terrestrial ball, and that is to have either a clear conscience, or none at all.
Ogden Nash

The most intelligent men, like the strongest, find their happiness where others would find only disaster: in the labyrinth, in being hard with themselves and with others, in effort; their delight is self-mastery; in them asceticism becomes second nature, a necessity, as instinct.
Friedrich Wilhelm Nietzsche

What is happiness?—The feeling that power increases—that resistance is overcome.
Friedrich Wilhelm Nietzsche

We are here not to get all we can out of life for ourselves, but to try to make the lives of others happier.
William Osler

If you count the sunny and the cloudy days of the whole year, you will find that the sunshine predominates.
Ovid

Let a man choose what condition he will, and let him accumulate around him all the goods and gratifications seemingly calculated to make him happy in it; if that man is left at any time without occupation or amusement, and reflects on what he is, the meagre, languid felicity of his present lot will not bear him up. He will turn necessarily to gloomy anticipations of the future; and unless his occupation calls him out of himself, he is inevitably wretched.
Blaise Pascal

He who is of a calm and happy nature will hardly feel the pressure of age, but to him who is of an opposite disposition youth and age are equally a burden.
Plato

The man who makes everything that leads to happiness depend upon himself, and not upon other men, has adopted the very best plan for living happily. This is the man of moderation, the man of manly character and of wisdom.
Plato

Do not speak of your happiness to one less fortunate than yourself.
Plutarch

The state of life is most happy where superfluities are not required and necessities are not wanting.
Plutarch

Man's real life is happy, chiefly because he is ever expecting that it soon will be so.
Edgar Allan Poe

False happiness is like false money; it passes for a time as well as the true, and serves some ordinary occasions; but when it is brought to the touch, we find the lightness and alloy, and feel the loss.
Alexander Pope

No one's happiness but my own is in my power to achieve or to destroy.
Ayn Rand

The influences that really make and mar human happiness are beyond the reach of the law. The law can keep neighbors from trespassing, but it cannot put neighborly courtesy and goodwill into their relations.
Walter Rauschenbusch

The road to happiness lies in two simple principles: find what it is that interests

you and that you can do well, and when you find it put your whole soul into it—every bit of energy and ambition and natural ability you have.
John D. Rockefeller III

The genius of American culture and its integrity comes from fidelity to the light. Plain as day, we say. Happy as the day is long. Early to bed, early to rise. American virtues are daylight virtues.
Richard Rodriguez

I must accept life unconditionally. Most people ask for happiness on condition. Happiness can only be felt if you don't set any condition.
Artur Rubinstein

God intends no man to live in this world without working, but it seems to me no less evident that He intends every man to be happy in his work.
John Ruskin

Contempt for happiness is usually contempt for other people's happiness, and is an elegant disguise for hatred of the human race.
Bertrand Russell

To be without some of the things you want is an indispensable part of happiness.
Bertrand Russell

Of all created comforts, God is the lender; you are the borrower, not the owner.
Walter R. Rutherford

I believe in the possibility of happiness, if one cultivates intuition and outlives the grosser passions, including optimism.
George Santayana

The profoundest affinities are the most readily felt; they remain a background

and standard for all happiness and if we trace them out we succeed.
George Santayana

Wealth without virtue is no harmless neighbor. Blend them and walk the peak of happiness.
Sappho

The great happiness of life, I find, after all, to consist in the regular discharge of some mechanical duty.
Johann Friedrich von Schiller

Happiness? That's nothing more than good health and a poor memory.
Albert Schweitzer

Humanity is fortunate, because no man is unhappy except by his own fault.
Seneca

The true felicity of life is to be free from anxieties and pertubations; to understand and do our duties to God and man, and to enjoy the present without any serious dependence on the future.
Seneca

No man is happy but by comparison.
Thomas Shadwell

I had rather have a fool to make me merry than experience to make me sad.
William Shakespeare

We have no more right to consume happiness without producing it than to consume wealth without producing it.
George Bernard Shaw

What can be added to the happiness of a man who is in health, out of debt, and has a clear conscience?
Adam Smith

The pursuit of happiness is a most ridiculous phrase: If you pursue happiness you'll never find it.
C.P. Snow

Objects we ardently pursue bring little happiness when gained; most of our pleasures come from unexpected sources.
Herbert Spencer

To describe happiness is to diminish it.
Stendhal

Positiveness is a most absurd foible. If you are in the right, it lessens your triumph; if in the wrong, it adds shame to your defeat.
Laurence Sterne

A happy man or woman is a better thing to find than a five-pound note. He or she is a radiating focus of goodwill; and their entrance into a room is as though another candle had been lighted.
Robert Louis Stevenson

There is no duty we so much underrate as the duty of being happy. By being happy, we sow anonymous benefits upon the world, which remain unknown even to ourselves, or when they are disclosed, surprise nobody so much as the benefactor.
Robert Louis Stevenson

The best advice on the art of being happy is about as easy to follow as advice to be well when one is sick.
Anne Swetchine

If we take an examination of what is understood by happiness . . . we shall find all its properties . . . under this short definition, that it is a perpetual possession of being well deceived.
Jonathan Swift

Life is long to the miserable, but short to the happy.
Publilius Syrus

No man is happy unless he believes he is.
Publilius Syrus

A man of meditation is happy, not for an hour or a day, but quite round the circle of all his years.
Isaac Taylor

Happiness is in action, and every power is intended for action; human happiness, therefore, can only be complete as all the powers have their full and legitimate play.
David Thomas

What wisdom, what warning can prevail against gladness? There is no law so strong that a little gladness may not transgress.
Henry David Thoreau

Are you so unobservant as not to have found out that sanity and happiness are an impossible combination?
Mark Twain

Doing what you like is freedom. Liking what you do is happiness.
Frank Tyger

You never see the stock called Happiness quoted on the exchange.
Henry van Dyke

I firmly believe, notwithstanding all our complaints, that almost every person upon earth tastes upon the totality more happiness than misery.
Horace Walpole

If only we'd stop trying to be happy we'd have a pretty good time.
Edith Wharton

Felicity, not fluency of language, is a merit.
E.P. Whipple

Rich bachelors should be heavily taxed. It is not fair that some men should be happier than others.
Oscar Wilde

The Constitution of America only guarantees pursuit of happiness—you have to catch up with it yourself. Fortunately, happiness is something that depends not on position but on disposition, and life is what you make it.
Gill Robb Wilson

No life can be barren which hears the whisper of the wind in the branches, or the voice of the sea as it breaks upon the shore; and no soul can lack happiness looking up to the midnight stars.
William Winter

True happiness must arise from well-regulated affections, and an affection includes a duty.
Mary Wollstonecraft

HATE

Politics, as a practice, whatever its professions, has always been the systematic organization of hatreds.
Henry Adams

To be loved is to be fortunate, but to be hated is to achieve distinction.
Minna Antrim

Never marry a man who hates his mother because he'll end up hating you.
Jill Bennett

He who surpasses or subdues mankind must look down on the hate of those below.
Lord Byron

I tell you there is such a thing as creative hate!
Willa Cather

Most men know what they hate, few what they love.
Charles Caleb Colton

There are many that despise half the world; but if there be any that despise the whole of it, it is because the other half despises them.
Charles Caleb Colton

We hate some persons because we do not know them; and we will not know them because we hate them.
Charles Caleb Colton

It is better to give love. Hatred is a low and degrading emotion and is so poisonous that no man is strong enough to use it safely. The hatred we think we are directing against some person or thing or system has a devilish way of turning back upon us. When we seek revenge we administer slow poison to ourselves. When we administer affection it is astonishing what magical results we obtain.
Thomas Dreier

Hating people is like burning down your own house to get rid of a rat.
Harry Emerson Fosdick

I never hated a man enough to give him diamonds back.
Zsa Zsa Gabor

"Hate the sin and not the sinner" is a precept which, though easy enough to understand, is rarely practiced, and that is why the poison of hatred spreads in the world.
Mohandas Gandhi

Impotent hatred is the most horrible of all emotions; one should hate nobody whom one cannot destroy.
Johann Wolfgang von Goethe

Like gluttony or drunkenness, hatred seems an agreeable vice when you practice it yourself, but disgusting when observed in others.
William H. Irwin

If a man say, I love God, and hateth his brother, he is a liar; for he that loveth not his brother whom he has seen, how can he love God whom he hath not seen?
I John 4:20

People hate me because I am a multifaceted, talented, wealthy, internationally famous genius.
Jerry Lewis

I went around the world last year and you want to know something? It hates each other.
Edward Mannix

I don't hate anyone. I dislike. But my dislike is the equivalent of anyone else's hate.
Elsa Maxwell

Any kiddie in school can love like a fool,
But hating, my boy, is an art.
Ogden Nash

He who despises himself nevertheless esteems himself as a self-despiser.
Friedrich Wilhelm Nietzsche

Hatreds are the cinders of affection.
Sir Walter Raleigh

Hatred, for the man who is not engaged in it, is a little like the odor of garlic for one who hasn't eaten any.
Jean Rostand

Hatred is an affair of the heart; contempt that of the head.
Arthur Schopenhauer

It is human nature to hate him whom you have injured.
Tacitus

Despise not small things, either for evil or good, for a look may work thy ruin, or a word create thy wealth. A spark is a little thing, yet it may kindle the world.
M.T. Tupper

HEALTH

The best cure for hypochondria is to forget about your body and get interested in somebody else's.
Goodman Ace

My health is good; it's my age that's bad.
Roy Acuff

There is a limit to the best of health, disease is always a near neighbor.
Aeschylus

Hypochondria is the only disease I haven't got.
Anonymous

Pain is inevitable; suffering is optional.
Anonymous

When pain is unbearable it destroys us; when it does not it is bearable.
Marcus Aurelius Antoninus

I used to jog, but it's bad for the knees. Too much beta carotene makes you orange; too much calcium gives you kidney stones. Health kills.
Margaret Atwood

The greatest evil is physical pain.
St. Augustine

Everybody's heart is open, you know, when they have recently escaped from severe pain, or are recovering the blessing of health.
Jane Austen

A healthy body is a guest-chamber for the soul; a sick body is a prison.
Francis Bacon

People who say you're just as old as you feel are all wrong, fortunately.
Russell Baker

A cough so robust that I tapped into two new seams of phlegm.
Bill Bryson

Gluttony is the source of all our infirmities and the fountain of all our diseases. As a lamp is choked by a superabundance of oil, and a fire extinguished by excess of fuel, so is the natural health of the body destroyed by intemperate diet.
Marion L. Burton

I reckon being ill as one of the great pleasures of life, provided one is not too ill and is not obliged to work till one is better.
Samuel Butler

Fitness: If it came in a bottle, everybody would have a good body.
Cher

The most poetical thing in the world is not being sick.
G.K. Chesterton

The trouble about always trying to preserve the health of the body is that it is so difficult to do so without destroying the health of the mind.
G.K. Chesterton

Never hurry; take plenty of exercise; always be cheerful, and take all the sleep you need, and you may expect to be well.
J.F. Clarke

Faddists are continually proclaiming the value of exercise. Four people out of five are more in need of rest than exercise.
Logan Clendening

You don't get ulcers from what you eat, but from what's eating you.
Albert Cliffe

Real pain can alone cure us of imaginary ills. We feel a thousand miseries till we are lucky enough to feel misery.
Samuel Taylor Coleridge

Minor surgery is surgery someone else is having.
J. Carl Cook

Sleep in the golden chain that ties health and our bodies together.
Thomas Dekker

Those who do not find time for exercise will have to find time for illness.
Earl of Derby

This cough I've got is hacking, The pain in my head is wracking,

I hardly need to mention the flu. The Board of Health has seen me

They want to quarantine me, I might as well be miserable with you.
Howard Dietz

The health of nations is more important than the wealth of nations.
Will Durant

Sickness comes on horseback and departs on foot.
Dutch proverb

Health and appetite impart the sweetness to sugar, bread and meat.
Ralph Waldo Emerson

We forget ourselves and our destinies in health; and the chief use of temporary sickness is to remind us of these concerns.
Ralph Waldo Emerson

Health is better than wealth.
English proverb

My illness is due to my doctor's insistence that I drink milk, a whitish fluid they force down helpless babies.
W.C. Fields

Suggested remedy for the common cold: A good gulp of whiskey at bedtime—it's not very scientific, but it helps.
Dr. Alexander Fleming

There is a certain state of health that does not allow us to understand everything; and perhaps illness shuts us off from certain truths; but health shuts us off just as effectively from others.
André Gide

Don't worry about losing weight; you'll find it exactly where you lost it.
Robert Half

To lose one's health renders science null, are inglorious, strength unavailing, wealth useless, and eloquence powerless.
Herophilus

Keep a watch also upon the faults of the patients, which also makes them lie about the taking of things prescribed.
Hippocrates

There are things about quitting the smoking habit for which nobody prepares you. Did I have any idea that I would indulge in long, droolingnay, dribblinglascivious dreams in which I was

still wreathed in fragrant blue fumes? I would wake with the complete and guilty conviction that I had sinned in word and deed while I was asleep.
Christopher Hitchens

True enjoyment comes from activity of the mind and exercise of the body; the two are united.
Alexander von Humboldt

Health is worth more than learning.
Thomas Jefferson

Beloved, I pray that you may prosper in all things and be in health, just as your soul prospers.
3 John 1:2

Health is so necessary to all the duties, as well as pleasures of life, that the crime of squandering it is equal to the folly.
Samuel Johnson

To preserve health is a moral and religious duty, for health is the basis of all social virtues. We can no longer be useful when not well.
Samuel Johnson

Man needs difficulties; they are necessary for health.
Carl Jung

One of the most difficult things to contend with in a hospital is the assumption on the part of the staff that because you have lost your gall bladder you have also lost your mind.
Jean Kerr

If you look like your passport photo, you're too ill to travel.
Will Kommen

How sickness enlarges the dimensions of a man's self to himself! Supreme

selfishness is inculcated upon him as his only duty.
Charles Lamb

What have I gained by health? Intolerable dullness. What by moderate meals? A total blank.
Charles Lamb

One out of four people in this country is mentally unbalanced. Think of your three closest friends; if they seem OK, then you're the one.
Ann Landers

Disease makes men more physical; it leaves them with nothing but body.
Thomas Mann

It's no longer a question of staying healthy. It's a question of finding a sickness you like.
Jackie Mason

It is easier to change a man's religion than to change his diet.
Margaret Mead

A man in good health is always full of advice to the sick.
Menander

Mental health problems do not affect three or four out of every five persons, but one out of one.
Dr. Karl Menninger

A bear, however hard he tries, grows tubby without exercise.
A.A. Milne

Health is a precious thing, and the only one, in truth, meriting that a man should lay out not only his time, sweat, labor and goods, but also life itself to obtain it.
Michel de Montaigne

Show him death, and he'll be content
with fever.
Persian proverb

Without health, life is not life; it is only a
state of langour and suffering—an image
of death.
François Rabelais

Orthodox medicine has not found an
answer to your complaint. However,
luckily for you, I happen to be a quack.
Mischa Richter cartoon

The diseases which destroy a man are
no less natural than the instincts which
preserve him.
George Santayana

You may tend to get cancer from the
thing that makes you want to smoke so
much, not from the smoking itself.
William Saroyan

Hold fast then to this sound and wholesome rule of life; indulge the body only
as far as is needful for health.
Seneca

It is part of the cure to wish to be cured.
Seneca

I enjoy convalescence. It is the part that
makes the illness worthwhile.
George Bernard Shaw

The sound body is the product of the
sound mind.
George Bernard Shaw

Use your health, even to the point of
wearing it out. That is what it is for.
Spend all you have before you die; and do
not outlive yourself.
George Bernard Shaw

Surgeons can cut out everything except
cause.
Herbert M. Shelton

Illness is the night-side of life, a more
onerous citizenship. Everyone who
is born holds dual citizenship, in the
kingdom of the well and in the kingdom
of the sick.
Susan Sontag

A man too busy to take care of his health
is like a mechanic too busy to take care of
his tools.
Spanish proverb

If you would live in health, be old early.
Spanish proverb

The only way for a rich man to be
healthy is by exercise and abstinence, to
live as if he were poor.
Sir W. Temple

When we are well, we all have good
advice for those who are ill.
Terence

Measure your health by your sympathy
with morning and Spring.
Henry David Thoreau

Men who are occupied in the restoration
of health to other men, by the joint exertion of skill and humanity, are above all
the great of the earth. They even partake
of divinity, since to preserve and renew is
almost as noble as to create.
Voltaire

We are such docile creatures, normally,
that it takes a virus to jolt us out of life's
routine. A couple of days in a fever bed
are, in a sense, health-giving; the change
in body temperature, the change in pulse
rate, and the change of scene have a
restorative effect on the system equal to
the hell they raise.
E.B. White ("The Cold")

HEART

No man can tell whether he is rich or poor by turning to his ledger. It is the heart that makes a man rich. He is rich according to what he is, not according to what he has.
Henry Ward Beecher

There is a dew in one flower and not in another, because one opens in cup and takes it in, while the other closes itself, and the drops run off. God rains His goodness and mercy as widespread as the dew, and if we lack them, it is because we will not open our hearts to receive them.
Henry Ward Beecher

If a good face is a letter of recommendation, a good heart is a letter of credit.
Edward Bulwer-Lytton

To judge human character rightly, a man may sometimes have very small experience, provided he has a very large heart.
Edward Bulwer-Lytton

A loving heart is the beginning of all knowledge.
Thomas Carlyle

Contact with the world either breaks or hardens the heart.
Sébastien Chamfort

If I keep a green bough in my heart, the singing bird will come.
Chinese proverb

But as it is written, eye hath not seen, nor ear heard, neither have entered into the heart of man, the things which God hath prepared for them that love him.
I Corinthians 2:9

What a sober man has in his heart, a drunken man has on his lips.
Danish proverb

Beware what you set your heart upon. For it surely shall be yours.
Ralph Waldo Emerson

No man can deliver the goods if his heart is heavier than the load.
Frank Irving Fletcher

At the heart of any good business is a chief executive officer with one.
Malcolm Forbes

A man not perfect, but of heart so high, and such heroic rage, that even his hopes became a part of earth's eternal heritage.
Richard Gilder

Whatever comes from the heart carries the heat and color of its birthplace.
Oliver Wendell Holmes

It is better to go down on the great seas which human hearts were made to sail than to rot at the wharves in ignoble anchorage.
Hamilton Wright Mabie

The great man is he who does not lose his child's heart.
Mencius

And the heart that is soonest awake to the flowers is always the first to be touched by the thorns.
Sir Thomas More

There are good hearts to serve men in palaces as in cottages.
Robert Owen

No true manhood can be trained by a merely intellectual process. You cannot train men by the intellect alone; you must train them by the heart.
Joseph Parker

No matter how widely you have travelled, you haven't seen the world if you

have failed to look into the human hearts that inhabit it.
Donald C. Peattie

Who shall ascend into the hill of the Lord? or who shall stand in his holy place? He that hath clean hands, and a pure heart.
Psalms 24:3–4

A light heart lives long.
William Shakespeare

The heart has always the pardoning power.
Anne Sophie Swetchine

The most unproductive, empty, fruitless fellow in the world is the man with a barren heart. Happiness can never reach him, for nothing good and lasting can lodge in his heart. It is solid as a billiard ball. Contrast this man with his barren heart with the human that plays the game of life fairly and honestly and is willing to make others happy by his own sacrifices.
F.D. Van Amburgh

What I am concerned about in this fast-moving world in a time of crises, both in foreign and domestic affairs, is not so much a program as a spirit of approach, not so much a mind as a heart. A program lives today and dies tomorrow. A mind, if it be open, may change with each new day, but the spirit and the heart are as unchanging as the tides.
Owen D. Young

HELP

One rooster can't help another scratch the same piece of ground.
African proverb

A helping word to one in trouble is often like a switch on a railroad track—an

inch between wreck and smooth-rolling prosperity.
Henry Ward Beecher

When a person is down in the world, an ounce of help is better than a pound of preaching.
Edward Bulwer-Lytton

Drop the hammer and pick up the shovel.
J.A. Dever

It is one of the most beautiful compensations of this life that no man can sincerely try to help another without helping himself.
Ralph Waldo Emerson

One right and honest definition of business is mutual helpfulness.
William Feather

He who says he never needs help, most does.
Malcolm Forbes

Time and money spent in helping men to do more for themselves is far better than mere giving.
Henry Ford

Three helping one another bear the burden of six.
George Herbert

Help thy brother's boat across, and lo! thine own has reached the shore.
Hindu proverb

All the other pleasures of life seem to wear out, but the pleasure of helping others in distress never does.
Julius Rosenwald

Every great man is always being helped by everybody; for his gift is to get good out of all things and all persons.
John Ruskin

The race of mankind would perish did they cease to aid each other. We cannot exist without mutual help. All therefore that need aid have a right to ask it from their fellow-men; and no one who has the power of granting can refuse it without guilt.
Sir Walter Scott

It is one of the beautiful compensations of this life that no one can sincerely try to help another without helping himself.
Charles Dudley Warner

HISTORY

The historian must not try to know what is truth, if he values his honesty; for if he cares for his truths, he is certain to falsify his facts.
Henry Adams

History is a relay of revolutions.
Saul Alinsky

More than any time in history mankind faces a crossroads. One path leads to despair and utter hopelessness, the other to total extinction. Let us pray that we have the wisdom to choose correctly.
Woody Allen

There is nothing that solidifies and strengthens a nation like reading of the nation's own history, whether that history is recorded in books or embodied in customs, institutions and monuments.
Joseph Anderson

Two things we ought to learn from history: one, that we are not in ourselves superior to our fathers; another, that we are shamefully and monstrously inferior to them, if we do not advance beyond them.
Thomas Arnold

In every age "the good old days" were a myth. No one ever thought they were good at the time. For every age has consisted of crises that seemed intolerable to the people who lived through them.
Brooks Atkinson

Man is a history-making creature who can neither repeat his past nor leave it behind.
W.H. Auden

History, real solemn history, I cannot be interested in. I read it a little as a duty; but it tells me nothing that does not either vex or weary me. The quarrels of popes and kings, with wars and pestilence in every page; the men so good for nothing, and hardly any women at all.
Jane Austen

The best history is but like the art of Rembrandt; it casts a vivid light on certain selected causes, on those which were best and greatest; it leaves all the rest in shadow and unseen.
Walter Bagehot

American history is longer, larger, more various, more beautiful, and more terrible than anything anyone has ever said about it.
James Baldwin

A good writer of history is a guy who is suspicious.
Jim Bishop

There are always some areas world history does not reach, zones of silence and undisturbed ignorance.
Fernand Braudel

When ancient opinions and rules of life are taken away, the loss cannot possibly be estimated. From that moment we have

no compass to govern us, nor can we know distinctly to what port to steer.
Edmund Burke

The true past departs not; no truth or goodness realized by man ever dies, or can die; but all is still here, and, recognized or not, lives and works through endless change.
Thomas Carlyle

Everyone can recognize history when it happens. Everyone can recognize history after is has happened; but only the wise man knows at the moment what is vital and permanent, what is lasting and memorable.
Winston Churchill

If men could learn from history, what lessons it might teach us! But passion and party blind our eyes, and the light which experience gives us is a lantern on the stern which shines only on the waves behind us.
Samuel Taylor Coleridge

We shall not understand the history of men and other times unless we ourselves are alive to the requirements which that history satisfied.
Benedetto Croce

The people who have really made history are the martyrs.
Aleister Crowley

It was the best of times, it was the worst of times, it was the age of wisdom, it was the age of foolishness, it was the epoch of belief, it was the epoch of incredulity, it was the season of Light, it was the season of Darkness, it was the spring of hope, it was the winter of despair.
Charles Dickens

The history of the past interests us only in so far as it illuminates the history of the present.
Ernest Dimnet

We Americans are the best-informed people on earth as to the events of the last 24 hours; we are not the best informed as to the events of the last 60 centuries.
Will and Ariel Durant

History teaches us that men and nations behave wisely once they have exhausted all other alternatives.
Abba Eban

History has many cunning passages, contrived corridors and issues.
T.S. Eliot

I am ashamed to see what a shallow village tale our so-called history is.
Ralph Waldo Emerson

The golden age was never the present age.
English proverb

History is more or less bunk.
Henry Ford

It is a fair summary of history to say that the safeguards of liberty have been forged in controversies involving not very nice people.
Felix Frankfurter

History never looks like history when you are living through it. It always looks confusing and messy, and it always looks uncomfortable.
John W. Gardner

The world's history is a divine poem of which the history of every nation is a canto and every man a word. Its strains have been pealing along down the centuries, and though there have been mingled

the discords of warring cannon and dying men, yet . . . there has been a divine melody running through the song which speaks of hope and halcyon days to come.
James A. Garfield

In the tumult of men and events, solitude was my temptation; now it is my friend. What other satisfaction can be sought once you have confronted History?
Charles de Gaulle

The reason history is by turns gripping, boring and threatening is that it is a play in which the characters make up their lines as they go along.
John P. Grier

History repeats itself. Historians repeat each other.
Philip Guedalla

The use of history is to tell us what we are, for at our birth we are nearly empty vessels and we become what our tradition pours into us.
Learned Hand

A generation which ignores history has no past—and no future.
Robert A. Heinlein

When I want to understand what is happening today, I try to decide what will happen tomorrow; I look back, a page of history is worth a volume of logic.
Oliver Wendell Holmes

The future of nations cannot be frozen . . . cannot be foreseen. If we are going to accomplish anything in our time we must approach our problems in the knowledge that there is nothing rigid or immutable in human affairs. History is a story of growth, decay and change. If no provision, no allowance is made for change by peaceful means, it will come anyway—and with violence.
Herbert Hoover

That men do not learn very much from the lessons of history is the most important of all the lessons history has to teach.
Aldous Huxley

Old myths, old gods, old heroes have never died. They are only sleeping at the bottom of our mind, waiting for our call. They represent the wisdom of our race.
Stanley Kunitz

History is the short trudge from Adam to atom.
Leonard Louis Levinson

At each epoch of history the world was in a hopeless state, and at each epoch of history the world muddled through; at each epoch the world was lost, and at each epoch it was saved.
Jacques Maritain

The historian's first duties are sacrilege and the mocking of false gods. They are his indispensable instruments for establishing the truth.
Jules Michelet

History shows that great economic and social forces flow like a tide over communities only half conscious of that which is befalling them. Wise statesmen foresee what time is thus bringing, and try to shape institutions and mold men's thoughts and purposes in accordance with the change that is silently coming on. The unwise are those who bring nothing constructive to the process, and who greatly imperil the future of mankind by leaving great questions to be fought out between ignorant change on one hand and ignorant opposition to change on the other.
John Stuart Mill

One age cannot be completely understood if all the others are not understood.

The song of history can only be sung as a whole.
José Ortega y Gasset

To be ignorant of the lives of the most celebrated men of antiquity is to continue in a state of childhood all our days.
Plutarch

If anyone wants to understand the course of man on earth, he must consider the fact of the long pause, three million years on the level of savagery, ten thousand years on the level of dependence on the fruits of hand labor, and a hundred or a hundred and fifty years of sudden sharp rise. One hundred or 150 years is the time included in what we call progress in man's history.
E. Parmalee Prentice

The weeks slide by like a funeral procession, but generations pass like a snowstorm.
Ned Rorem

Throughout human history, the apostles of purity, those who have claimed to possess a total explanation, have wrought havoc among mere mixed-up human beings.
Salman Rushdie

Every epoch, under names more or less specious, has deified its peculiar errors.
Percy Bysshe Shelley

Study men, not historians.
Harry S Truman

The man who ventures to write contemporary history must expect to be attacked both for everything he has said and everything he has not said.
Voltaire

History is a race between education and catastrophe.
H.G. Wells

All centuries are dangerous; it is the business of the future to be dangerous. It must be admitted that there is a degree of instability which is inconsistent with civilization. But, on the whole, the great ages have been the unstable ages.
Alfred North Whitehead

HOLIDAYS

May all your troubles last as long as your New Year's resolutions.
Joey Adams

To many people holidays are not voyages of discovery, but a ritual of reassurance.
Phillip Adams

I never had a good year.
Jason Alexander

The human race has not devised any way of dissolving barriers, getting to know the other chap fast, breaking the ice, that is one-tenth as handy and efficient as letting you and the other chap, or chaps, cease to be totally sober at about the same rate in agreeable surroundings.
Kingsley Amis

That's what the holidays are for—for one person to tell the stories and another to dispute them. Isn't that the Irish way?
Lara Flynn Boyle

Dear Lord, I've been asked to thank Thee for the Christmas turkey before us, a turkey which was no doubt a lively, intelligent bird, a social being capable of actual affection. Anyway, it's dead and we're gonna eat it.
Berke Breathed

I won't be going to any New Year's Eve parties because I think they're naff. No one over the age of 15 should bother going to parties.
Julie Burchill

Christmas is a holiday that persecutes the lonely, the frayed and the rejected.
Jimmy Cannon

Christmas is a season not only of rejoicing but of reflection.
Winston Churchill

All holidays can be good times.
John Clayton

If Christmas is for families, what do you do when there are families scattered all over the country? I am pretty sure God wants to make sure I touch all the bases, even if I spend his actual birthday with Delta Airlines.
Gail Collins

It has been an unchallengeable American doctrine that cranberry sauce, a pink goo with overtones of sugared tomatoes, is a delectable necessity of the Thanksgiving board and that turkey is uneatable without it.
Alistair Cooke

The gist of New Year's Day is: Try again.
Frank Crane

What I don't like about office Christmas parties is looking for a job the next day.
Phyllis Diller

Let your holidays be associated with great public events, and they may be the life of patriotism as well as a source of relaxation and personal employment.
Tryon Edwards

Except for excess decoration, excess commercialism, excess editorializing, excess caroling, excess bibbling, and excess cheer, I heartily approve of the Christmas spirit.
William Feather

Christmas is a tonic for our souls. It moves us to think of others rather than of ourselves. It directs our thoughts to giving.
B.C. Forbes

Let us enter the New Year cheerfully. Let us resolve to look on the bright side, to make the best of whatever may befall, to maintain faith that doing the right thing will ultimately bring victory. Let us cultivate sunniness, resist sourness. We can better wrestle with difficulties, obstacles, problems in a spirit of buoyancy than in an abject, morose mood. How much more the radiant mortal gets out of life and puts into life than the downcast, long-faced, self-pitying being!
B.C. Forbes (1937)

The Christmas spirit brings home to us—or should bring home to us—the profound Biblical truth that it is more blessed to give than to receive. Anything which inspires unselfishness makes for our ennoblement. Christmas does that. I am all for Christmas.
B.C. Forbes

There's one post-Christmas chore I love—writing thank-you letters. . . . Lots of companies for many reasonable reasons, I guess, have a policy against sending even Christmas cards, never mind things, at Christmastime. But our clan gets a big kick out of opening the Warner-Lambert box containing an assortment of their wares; we argue over which of the boys is to get the Union Oil Co. necktie [and] all the holiday long we play the marvelous Christmas music sent by Goodyear. . . . None of these things

means that Forbes or Forbeses have been had. But all of us like being thought of.
Malcolm Forbes

On office parties and YouTube: These days, you have to assume that anything you do at your party is going to be broadcast.
Elizabeth Freedman

People are happier at Yuletime because they take the milk of human kindness out of the deep freeze.
Arnold Glasow

I never believed in Santa Claus because I knew no white dude would come into my neighborhood after dark.
Dick Gregory

I get myself a gig somewhere, whether it's in a club or in a bar, it doesn't matter, and I just work on New Year's Eve because I feel it's very symbolic for me for the next year, for the new year.
Debbie Harry

Resolutions are popular because everyone feels they could use a little improvement.
Marilu Henner

Christmas is the season for kindling the fire of hospitality in the hall, the genial flame of charity in the heart.
Washington Irving

Therefore the Lord himself shall give you a sign; Behold, a virgin shall conceive, and bear a son, and shall call his name Immanuel.
Isaiah 7:14

Thanksgiving: Not a good day to be my pants.
Kevin James

Every man who possibly can should force himself to a holiday of a full month in a year, whether he feels like taking it or not.
William James

The joy of brightening other lives, bearing each other's burdens, easing others' loads and supplanting empty hearts and lives with generous gifts becomes for us the magic of Christmas.
W.C. Jones

Now the New Year reviving old Desires, The thoughtful Soul to Solitude retires.
Omar Khayyám

Thanksgiving comes after Christmas for people over 30.
Peter Kreeft

New Year's Day is every man's birthday.
Charles Lamb

No one ever regarded the first of January with indifference. It is the nativity of our common Adam.
Charles Lamb

If all the cars in the United States were placed end to end, it would probably be Labor Day weekend.
Doug Larson

This is the conundrum of holiday parties: You need a drink because it softens the awkwardness of mixing work relationships with holiday merriment, but drink too much and you'll end up in a situation that's far more awkward in the sobering fluorescent light of Monday morning.
Matthew Latkiewicz

As my brother used to say, "A matzo ball without shmaltz is an assimilated matzo ball."
Jack Lebewohl

New Year's Eve is like every other night; and yet no man has quite the same thoughts this evening that come with the coming of darkness on other nights.
Hamilton Wright Mabie

Christmas means a spirit of love, a time when the love of our fellow men should prevail over all hatred and bitterness.
George McDougall

Hangover: The moaning after.
Vernon McLellan

Thanksgiving comes to us out of the prehistoric dimness, universal to all ages and all faiths. At whatever straws we must grasp, there is always a time for gratitude and new beginnings.
J. Robert Moskin

Merry Christmas, Nearly Everybody!
Ogden Nash

Cold, bleak January rolls in, a wake of skull-scraping hangovers, bloated credit card bills, long, tired nights and barren, office-bound days.
Eno Putain

On New Year's Day the best resolution is to take a long walk, mix a stiff drink and eat a hearty meal with old friends.
Eno Putain

After a Christmas comes a Lent.
John Ray

Passover is the most widely recognized Jewish holiday, if you don't count the year-end sale at Neiman Marcus.
Joan Rivers

Christmas, that time of year when people descend into the bunker of the family.
Byron Rogers

For most of us it can be a Happy Christmas if by happiness we mean that we have done with doubts, that we have set our hearts against fear, that we still believe in the Golden Rule for all mankind.
Franklin D. Roosevelt

My mother is such a lousy cook that Thanksgiving at her house is a time of sorrow.
Rita Rudner

Did you know that Christmas Day is absolutely the best day to fly? It is. No crowded airports and crowded planes. I always flew to Australia. That's what Christmas was for me—a plane journey to the next tournament.
Monica Seles

If all the year were playing holidays, to sport would be as tedious as to work; but when they seldom come, wished for come.
William Shakespeare

Nobody shoots at Santa Claus.
Alfred E. Smith

Unfortunately there is nothing more inane than an Easter carol. It is a religious perversion of the activity of Spring in our blood.
Wallace Stevens

In the past people were drinking because they were socially phobic or they needed to blow off steam at the end of the year. Now they're overdoing it because their bonuses were decreased, their hours have gone up or their job security isn't as safe as it used to be.
Harris Stratyner

I stopped believing in Santa Claus when I was six. Mother took me to see him in a department store and he asked for my autograph.
Shirley Temple

Ring out the old, ring in the new, Ring, happy bells, across the snow;

The year is going, let him go; Ring out the false, ring in the true.
Alfred, Lord Tennyson

We don't want any child to go without seeing Santa, but it's not worth bringing your child to the mall, infecting the Santa and infecting the other children.
Nicholas Trolli, president of the amalgamated order of real bearded santas

As you get older, you get tired of doing the same things over and over again, so you think Christmas has changed. It hasn't. It's you who has changed.
Harry S Truman

They have Easter egg hunts in Philadelphia, and if the kids don't find the eggs, they get booed.
Bob Uecker

For what's reputed to be an essential subgenre of cinema, the Christmas film may in fact suffer from the wildest inconsistency of quality of any movie category known to Hollywood.
S.T. VanAirsdale

An optimist stays up until midnight to see the new year in. A pessimist stays up to make sure the old year leaves.
Bill Vaughn

On being Santa: I wear gloves, and that's part of the costume, but it also creates a barrier between the kids and me. I have a very big supply of gloves in my dressing room. The beard gets washed every day.
Jerry Weeks

Of course I don't want to go to a cocktail party. If I wanted to stand around with a load of people I don't know eating bits of cold toast I can get caught shoplifting and go to Holloway.
Victoria Wood

Advice to department store Santas: Santa is even-tempered. Santa does not hit children over the head who kick him. Santa does not have a three-martini lunch. Santa does not borrow money from store employees. Santa wears a good deodorant.
Jenny Zink

Those who refuse to make New Year's resolutions because they always break them anyway miss the point. Making resolutions is a cleansing ritual of self-assessment and repentance that demands personal honesty and reinforces humility. Breaking them is part of the cycle.
Eric Zorn

HOME

The starting points of character and destiny in the young begin with home environment and outside associations.
Harry F. Banks

Many a man who pays rent all his life owns his own home; and many a family has successfully saved for a home only to find itself at last with nothing but a house.
Bruce Barton

Cooking: An art, a noble science; cooks are gentlemen.
Richard Burton

Only the home can found a state.
Joseph Cook

Look well to the hearthstone; therein all hope for America lies.
Calvin Coolidge

When I can no longer bear to think of the victims of broken homes, I begin to think of the victims of intact ones.
Peter De Vries

Many a man who thinks to have found a home discovers that he has merely opened a tavern for his friends.
Norman Douglas

Home is the place where, when you have to go there, they have to take you in.
Robert Frost

A home is no home unless it contains food and fire for the mind as well as for the body. For human beings are not so constituted that they can live without expansion. If they do not get it in one way, they must in another, or perish.
Margaret Fuller

The happiness of the domestic fireside is the first boon to Heaven; and it is well it is so, since it is that which is the lot of the mass of mankind.
Thomas Jefferson

No worldly success can compensate for failure in the home.
David O. McKay

The home is the basis of a righteous life and no other instrumentality can take its place nor fulfill its essential functions.
David O. McKay

If this world affords true happiness, it is to be found in a home where love and confidence increase with the years, where the necessities of life come without severe strain, where luxuries enter only after their cost has been carefully considered.
A. Edward Newton

I hate housework! You make the bed, you do the dishes—and six months later you have to start all over again.
Joan Rivers

Only that traveling is good which reveals to me the value of home and enables me to enjoy it better.
Henry David Thoreau

What a fool he must be who thinks that his El Dorado is anywhere but where he lives.
Henry David Thoreau

The home . . . is the lens through which we get our first look at marriage and all civic duties; it is the clinic where, by conversation and attitude, impressions are created with respect to sobriety and reverence; it is the school where lessons of truth or falsehood, honesty or deceit are learned; it is the mold which ultimately determines the structure of society.
Perry F. Webb

HONESTY

To believe all men honest would be folly. To believe none so, is something worse.
John Quincy Adams

Man's first care should be to avoid the reproaches of his own heart, and next to escape the censures of the world. If the last interfere with the first it should be entirely neglected. But otherwise there cannot be a greater satisfaction to an honest mind than to see its own approbation seconded by the applauses of the public.
Joseph Addison

No man is really honest; none of us is above the influence of gain.
Aristophanes

Aside from the strictly moral standpoint, honesty is—not only the best policy, but the only possible policy from the standpoint of business relations. The fulfillment of the pledged word is of equal necessity to the conduct of all business. If we expect and demand virtue and honor in others, the flame of both must burn brightly within ourselves and shed their light to illuminate the erstwhile dark corners of distrust and dishonesty. . . . The truthful answer rests for the most part within ourselves, for like begets like. Honesty begets honesty; trust, trust; and so on through the whole category of desirable practices that must govern and control the world's affairs.
James F. Bell

How desperately difficult it is to be honest with oneself. It is much easier to be honest with other people.
Edward F. Benson

Men must be honest with themselves before they can be honest with others. A man who is not honest with himself presents a hopeless case.
William J.H. Boetcker

An inch in a man's nose is much.
H.G. Bohn

Put a rogue in the lime-light and he will act like an honest man.
Napoleon Bonaparte

Hard workers are usually honest; industry lifts them above temptation.
Christian Bovée

Make yourself an honest man, and then you may be sure there is one rascal less in the world.
Thomas Carlyle

Honesty: The ability to resist small temptations.
John Ciardi

Ninety-eight out of 100 of the rich men in America are honest. That is why they are rich.
Russell Herman Conwell

There is no twilight zone of honesty in business—a thing is right or it's wrong—it's black or it's white.
John F. Dodge

Honesty is the cornerstone of character. The honest man or woman seeks not merely to avoid criminal or illegal acts, but to be scrupulously fair, upright, fearless in both action and expression. Honesty pays dividends both in dollars and in peace of mind.
B.C. Forbes

Trickery and treachery are the practices of fools that have not wits enough to be honest.
Benjamin Franklin

Nothing is quite honest that is not commercial, but not everything commercial is honest.
Robert Frost

If thou employest plain men, and canst find such as are commonly honest, they will work faithfully, and report fairly. Cunning men will, for their own credit, adventure without command; and from thy business derive credit to themselves.
Thomas Fuller

Honesty of thought and speech and written word is a jewel, and they who curb prejudice and seek honorably to know and speak the truth are the only builders of a better life.
John Galsworthy

The darkest hour in the history of any young man is when he sits down to study how to get money without honestly earning it.
Horace Greeley

Our great error is that we suppose mankind more honest than they are.
Alexander Hamilton

Every man should make up his mind that if he expects to succeed, he must give an honest return for the other man's dollar.
E.H. Harriman

Honesty is one part of eloquence. We persuade others by being in earnest ourselves.
William Hazlitt

There is no well-defined boundary between honesty and dishonesty. The frontiers of one blend with the outside limits of the other, and he who attempts to tread this dangerous ground may be sometimes in one domain and sometimes in the other.
O. Henry

The world wants to be cheated, so cheat.
Xaviera Hollander

No public man can be a little crooked. There is no such thing as a no-man's-land between honesty and dishonesty.
Herbert Hoover

Honesty is largely a matter of information, of knowing that dishonesty is a mistake.
Ed Howe

Honesty pays, but it don't seem to pay enough to suit a lot of people.
Kin Hubbard

Every man who expresses an honest thought is a soldier in the army of intellectual liberty.
Robert G. Ingersoll

I have not observed men's honesty to increase with their riches.
Thomas Jefferson

The more honesty a man has, the less he affects the air of a saint.
Johann Lavater

Honesty isn't any policy at all; it's a state of mind or it isn't honesty.
Eugene L'Hote

Honesty is often in the wrong.
Lucan

An honest man is not accountable for the vice and folly of his trade, and therefore ought not to refuse the exercise of it. It is the custom of his country, and there is profit in it. We must live by the world, and such as we find it, so make use of it.
Michel de Montaigne

Honest men are the soft easy cushions on which knaves repose and fatten.
Thomas Otway

The honest man must be a perpetual renegade, the life of an honest man a perpetual infidelity. For the man who wishes to remain faithful to truth must make himself perpetually unfaithful to all the continual, successive, indefatigable, renascent errors.
Charles Pierre Péguy

If you don't lie to people and you are honest and clear about how you made your money, you can look people in the eye and explain it to them.
Mikhail Prokhorov

No one can ask honestly or hopefully to be delivered from temptation unless he has himself honestly and firmly determined to do the best he can to keep out of it.
John Ruskin

Ay, sir; to be honest, as this world goes, is to be one man picked out of ten thousand.
William Shakespeare

I am afraid we must make the world honest before we can honestly say to our children that honesty is the best policy.
George Bernard Shaw

It's better to be quotable than to be honest.
Tom Stoppard

I hope I shall always possess firmness and virtue enough to maintain what I consider the most enviable of all titles, the character of an honest man.
George Washington

Honesty is the best policy, but he who is governed by that maxim is not an honest man.
Richard Whately

HONOR

Honor's a fine imaginary notion, that draws in raw and unexperienced men to real mischiefs.
Joseph Addison

The place should not honor the man, but the man the place.
Agesilaus

My father always had doubts about the Booker Prize, although they evaporated on the announcement that he had won it.
Martin Amis

At certain times each year, we journalists do almost nothing except apply for the Pulitzers and several dozen other major prizes. During these times you could walk right into most newsrooms and commit a multiple axe murder naked, and it wouldn't get reported in the paper because the reporters and editors would all be too busy filling out prize applications.
Dave Barry

There never was a person who did anything worth doing who did not receive more than he gave.
Henry Ward Beecher

Honor is like the eye, which cannot suffer the least injury without damage; it is a precious stone, the price of which is lessened by the least flaw.
Jacques Bossuet

My career must be slipping. This is the first time I've been available to pick up an award.
Michael Caine

No amount of ability is of the slightest avail without honor.
Andrew Carnegie

Our inheritance of well-founded, slowly conceived codes of honor, morals and manners, the passionate convictions which so many hundreds of millions share together of the principles of freedom and justice, are far more precious to us than anything which scientific discoveries could bestow.
Winston Churchill

No person was ever honored for what he received. Honor has been the reward for what he gave.
Calvin Coolidge

Honor is not a matter of any man's calling merely, but rather of his own actions in it.
John S. Dwight

The Nobel is a ticket to one's funeral. No one has ever done anything after he got it.
T.S. Eliot

The louder he talked of his honor, the faster we counted our spoons.
Ralph Waldo Emerson

I have a lantern. You steal my lantern. What, then, is your honor worth no more to you than the price of my lantern!
Epictetus

On reviewers: It wasn't until the Nobel Prize that they really thawed out. They couldn't understand my books, but they could understand $30,000.
William Faulkner

He that hath a trade hath an estate and he that hath a calling hath an office of profit and honor.
Benjamin Franklin

The award of a pure gold medal for poetry would flatter the recipient unduly: no poem ever attains such carat purity.
Robert Graves

It is extraordinary, an act of illiterates, to give prizes for literature.
Geoffrey Grigson

Awards are like piles. Sooner or later, every bum gets one.
Maureen Lipman

An honor prudently declined often returns with increased luster.
Livy

With all those prizes the most interesting thing is getting on to the shortlist, because that tells you who people see as your peers.
David Malouf

The Oscars demonstrate the will of the people to control and judge those they have elected to stand above them (much, perhaps, as in bygone days, an election celebrated the same).
David Mamet

The honor of a country depends much more on removing its faults than on boasting of its qualities.
Giuseppe Mazzini

The difference between a moral man and a man of honor is that the latter regrets a discreditable act; even when it has worked and he has not been caught.
H.L. Mencken

To honor with hymns and panegyrics those who are still alive is not safe; a man should run his course and make a fair ending, and then we will praise him; and let praise be given equally to women as well as men who have been distinguished in virtue.
Plato

Men show no mercy and expect no mercy, when honor calls, or when they fight for their idols or their gods.
Johann Friedrich von Schiller

Mine honor is my life; both grow in one; take honor from me and my life is done.
William Shakespeare

The shortest and surest way to live with honor in the world, is to be in reality what we would appear to be; all human virtues increase and strengthen themselves by the practice and experience of them.
Socrates

To refuse awards is another way of accepting them with more noise than is normal.
Peter Ustinov

The biggest reward for a thing well done is to have done it.
Voltaire

Our country's honor calls upon us for a vigorous and manly exertion; and if we

now shamefully fail, we shall become infamous to the whole world.
George Washington

People fail you, children disappoint you, thieves break in, moths corrupt, but an Order of the British Empire goes on forever.
Fay Weldon

On receiving a special Academy Award:
Now I'm an old Christmas tree, the roots of which have died. They just come along and while the little needles fall off me replace them with medallions.
Orson Welles

Be honorable yourself if you wish to associate with honorable people.
Welsh proverb

There are only two stimulants to one's best efforts—the fear of punishment, and the hope of reward. When neither is present, one can hardly hope that sales-people will want to be trained or want to do a good job. When disappointment is not expressed that one hasn't done a better job, or when credit is withheld when one has done a good job, there is absolutely no incentive to put forth the best effort.
John M. Wilson

HOPE

How tight can life be without the space of hope?
Arabian proverb

Hope is a waking dream.
Aristotle

Hope is a good breakfast, but it is a bad supper.
Francis Bacon

The illusions of hope are apt to close one's eyes to the painful truth.
Harry F. Banks

The sunrise never failed us yet.
Celia Baxter

Hope! Thou nurse of young desire.
Isaac Bickerstaff

Hope springs exulting on triumphant wing.
Robert Burns

Man is, properly speaking, based upon hope; he has no other possession but hope; this world of his is emphatically the place of hope.
Thomas Carlyle

Hope is a vigorous principle; it is furnished with light and heat to advise and execute; it sets the head and heart to work, and animates a man to do his utmost. And thus, by perpetually pushing and assurance, it puts a difficulty out of countenance, and makes a seeming impossibility give way.
Jeremy Collier

Times of general calamity and confusion have never been productive of the greatest minds. The purest ore is produced from the hottest furnace, and the brightest thunderbolt is elicited from the darkest storms.
Charles Caleb Colton

Hope! Of all ills that men endure, The only cheap and universal cure.
Abraham Cowley

Hope of ill gain is the beginning of loss.
Democritus

Hope is the thing with feathers that perches in the soul.
Emily Dickinson

To help the young soul, to add energy, inspire hope, and blow the coals into a useful flame; to redeem defeat by new thought and firm action, this, though not easy, is the work of divine men.
Ralph Waldo Emerson

A ship ought not to be held by one anchor, nor life by a single hope.
Epictetus

One should . . . be able to see things as hopeless and yet be determined to make them otherwise.
F. Scott Fitzgerald

He that lives upon hope will die fasting.
Benjamin Franklin

It drives me into a frothing frenzy when politicians return from inner cities saying, "What the people of this town need is Hope." What these bleeding hearts mean is Money, but they're too greasy to say so.
Stephen Fry

Great hopes make great men.
Thomas Fuller

He that wants hope is the poorest man alive.
Thomas Fuller

Hope is worth any money.
Thomas Fuller

In old age the consolation of hope is reserved for the tenderness of parents, who commence a new life in their children, the faith of enthusiasts, who sing hallelujahs above the clouds; and the vanity of authors, who presume the immortality of their name and writings.
Edward Gibbon

Correction does much, but encouragement does more. Encouragement after censure is as the sun after a shower.
Johann Wolfgang von Goethe

Hope is a pleasant acquaintance, but an unsafe friend, not the man for your banker, though he may do for a traveling companion.
Thomas Haliburton

Hope is a feeling that life and work have a meaning. You either have it or you don't, regardless of the state of the world that surrounds you.
Vaclav Havel

As a general rule, Providence seldom vouchsafes to mortals any more than just that degree of encouragement which suffices to keep them at a reasonably full exertion of their powers.
Nathaniel Hawthorne

Hope is the best possession. None are completely wretched but those who are without hope, and few are reduced so low as that.
William Hazlitt

It is natural to man to indulge in the illusion of hope. We are apt to shut our eyes against a painful truth, till she transforms us into beasts.
Patrick Henry

It is the around-the-corner brand of hope that prompts people to action, while the distant hope acts as an opiate.
Eric Hoffer

The natural flights of the human mind are not from pleasure to pleasure, but from hope to hope.
Samuel Johnson

Whatever enlarges hope will also exalt courage.
Samuel Johnson

The setting of a great hope is like the setting of the sun. The brightness of our life is gone.
Henry Wadsworth Longfellow

Everything that is done in the world is done by hope. No merchant or tradesman would set himself to work if he did not hope to reap benefit thereby.
Martin Luther

Hope is the worst of evils, for it prolongs the torment of man.
Friedrich Wilhelm Nietzsche

A student never forgets an encouraging private word, when it is given with sincere respect and admiration.
William Lyon Phelps

Hope is brightest when it dawns from fears.
Sir Walter Scott

True hope is swift, and flies with swallow's wings.

Kings it makes gods, and meaner creatures kings.
William Shakespeare

Every heart that has beat strong and cheerfully has left a hopeful impulse behind it in the world, and bettered the tradition of mankind.
Robert Louis Stevenson

To travel hopefully is a better thing than to arrive.
Robert Louis Stevenson

Hope knows not if fear speaks truth, nor fear whether hope be blind as she.
Algernon Swinburne

The mighty hopes that make us men.
Alfred, Lord Tennyson

Hope ever tells us tomorrow will be better.
Tibullus

Hope deceives more men than cunning does.
Marquis de Vauvenargues

When we have lost everything, including hope, life becomes a disgrace and death a duty.
Voltaire

I believe that any man's life will be filled with constant and unexpected encouragement, if he makes up his mind to do his level best each day, and as nearly as possible reaching the high-water mark of pure and useful living.
Booker T. Washington

Hope never abandons you; you abandon it.
George Weinberg

Hope, like faith, is nothing if it is not courageous; it is nothing if it is not ridiculous.
Thornton Wilder

HUMAN NATURE

Inconsistency with ourselves is the great weakness of human nature.
Joseph Addison

Human relations is the most important science in the broad curriculum of living.
Stanley C. Allyn

There is no problem of human nature which is insoluble.
Ralph J. Bunche

It will generally be found that those who sneer habitually at human nature, and

affect to despise it, are among its worst and least pleasant samples.
Charles Dickens

However exquisitely human nature may have been described by writers, the true practical system can be learned only in the world.
Henry Fielding

San Francisco's latest earthquake is a tragically dramatic reminder of how fragile our complicated, contemporary civilization really is. Hurricane Hugo's devastating swath a couple of weeks earlier made the same painful point. Our ever-higher high-tech way of life increases our vulnerability. Remember a decade or so ago how New York City's blackout, uncasualtied though it was, brought to a screeching halt the way of life and livelihood of that huge city's hived millions? But isn't it strangely wondrous how quickly we recover from catastrophic interruptions? Bouncing back dramatizes something vastly more significant than our fragility: the unquenchable, unkillable human spirit.
Malcolm S. Forbes (1989)

The people I respect most behave as if they were immortal and as if society was eternal. Both assumptions are false: both of them must be accepted as true if we are to go on eating and working and loving, and are to keep open a few breathing holes for the human spirit.
E.M. Forster

The people of this country have shown by the highest proofs human nature can give that wherever the path of duty and honor may lead, however steep and rugged it may be, they are ready to walk in it.
James A. Garfield

Perhaps catastrophe is the natural human environment, and even though we spend a good deal of energy trying to get away from it, we are programmed for survival amid catastrophe.
Germaine Greer

The sacred rights of mankind are not to be rummaged for among old parchments or musty records. They are written, as with a sunbeam, in the whole volume of human nature, by the hand of the Divinity itself, and can never be erased or obscured by mortal power.
Alexander Hamilton

Human nature is the same on every side of the Atlantic, and will be alike influenced by the same causes. The time to guard against corruption and tyranny is before they shall have gotten hold of us. It is better to keep the wolf out of the fold than to trust to drawing his teeth and claws after he shall have entered.
Thomas Jefferson

I believe in human dignity as the source of national purpose, human liberty as the source of national action, the human heart as the source of national compassion, and in the human mind as the source of our invention and our ideas.
John F. Kennedy

No small part of the cruelty, oppression, miscalculation, and general mismanagement of human relations is due to the fact that in our dealings with others we do not see them as persons at all, but only as specimens or representatives of some type or other. . . . We react to the sample instead of to the real' person.
Robert J. MacIver

The world and the human condition are not essentially benign.
Ivan Morris

The human spirit is stronger than anything that can happen to it.
C.C. Scott

To feel much for others and little for ourselves; to restrain our selfishness and exercise our benevolent affections, constitute the perfection of human nature.
Adam Smith

HUMANITY

Relations between the sexes are so complicated that the only way you can tell if members of the set are going together is if they are married. Then, almost certainly, they are not.
Cleveland Amory

Most of the trouble in this world has been caused by folks who can't mind their own business, because they have no business of their own to mind, any more than a smallpox virus has.
William S. Burroughs

Wherever humanity has made that hardest of all starts and lifted itself out of mere brutality is a sacred spot.
Willa Cather

Men and women are two locked caskets, of which each contains the key to the other.
Isak Dinesen

All humanity is one undivided and indivisible family, and each one of us is responsible for the misdeeds of all the others.
Mahatma Gandhi

You must not lose faith in humanity. Humanity is an ocean; if a few drops of the ocean are dirty, the ocean does not become dirty.
Mahatma Gandhi

Man is not on the earth solely for his own happiness. He is there to realize great things for humanity.
Vincent van Gogh

While I do not suggest that humanity will ever be able to dispense with its martyrs, I cannot avoid the suspicion that with a little more thought and a little less belief their number may be substantially reduced.
John Haldane

Men and women should live next door and visit each other once in a while.
Katharine Hepburn

The traveler's-eye view of men and women is not satisfying. A man might spend his life in trains and restaurants and know nothing of humanity at the end. To know, one must be an actor as well as a spectator.
Aldous Huxley

My favorite thing about the Internet is that you get to go into the private world of real creeps without having to smell them.
Penn Jillette

Humanity should question itself, once more, about the absurd and always unfair phenomenon of war, on whose stage of death and pain only remains standing the negotiating table that could and should have prevented it.
Pope John Paul II

We are a nation of 20 million bathrooms, with a humanist in every tub.
Mary McCarthy

Every day sees humanity more victorious in the struggle with space and time.
Guglielmo Marconi

There is a destiny that makes us brothers: None goes his way alone: All

that we send into the lives of others comes back into our own.
Edwin Markham

The chief obstacle to the progress of the human race is the human race.
Don Marquis

Each of us brings with him an element, more or less important, of the life of humanity to come.
Giuseppe Mazzini

The only way in which one can make endurable man's inhumanity to man, and man's destruction of his own environment, is to exemplify in your own lives man's humanity to man and man's reverence for the place in which he lives.
Alan Paton

Buy ye are a chosen generation, a royal priesthood, an holy nation, a peculiar people; that you should shew forth the praises of him who hath called you out of darkness into his marvellous light.
I Peter 2:9

Human beings are the only animals of which I am thoroughly and cravenly afraid.
George Bernard Shaw

The desire for the well-being of one's own nation can be—and must be—made compatible with the welfare of all humanity.
Louis L. Snyder

Provision for others is a fundamental responsibility of human life.
Woodrow Wilson

HUMBLE

A just and reasonable modesty does not only recommend eloquence, but sets off every great talent which a man can be

possessed of; it heightens all the virtues which it accompanies; like the shades in paintings, it raises and rounds every figure and makes the colors more beautiful, though not so glaring as they would be without.
Joseph Addison

At home I'm a nice guy: but I don't want the world to know. Humble people, I've found, don't get very far.
Muhammad Ali

Modesty is hardly to be described as a virtue. It is a feeling rather than a disposition. It is a kind of fear of falling into disrepute.
Aristotle

I've never had a humble opinion in my life. If you're going to have one, why bother to be humble about it?
Joan Baez

It is no great thing to be humble when you are brought low; but to be humble when you are praised is a great and rare attainment.
St. Bernard

The more humble a man is before God, the more he will be exalted, the more humble he is before man, the more he will get rode roughshod.
Josh Billings

The true way to be humble is not to stoop till you are smaller than yourself, but to stand at your real height against some higher nature that shall show you what the real smallness of your greatest greatness is.
Phillips Brooks

One must become as humble as the dust before he can discover truth.
Mahatma Gandhi

The society which scorns excellence in plumbing because plumbing is a humble activity and tolerates shoddiness in philosophy because it is an exalted activity will have neither good plumbing nor good philosophy. Neither its pipes nor its theories will hold water.
John W. Gardner

Modesty is of no use to a beggar.
Homer

Modesty in human beings is praised because it is not a matter of nature, but of will.
Lactantius

A fellow once came to me to ask for an appointment as a minister abroad. Finding he could not get that, he came down to some more modest position. Finally, he asked to be made a tide-waiter. When he saw he could not get that, he asked me for an old pair of trousers. It is sometimes well to be humble.
Abraham Lincoln

A humble man can do great things with an uncommon perfection because he is no longer concerned about accidentals, like his own interests and his own reputation, and therefore he no longer needs to waste his efforts in defending them.
Thomas Merton

To be humble to superiors is a duty, to equals courtesy, to inferiors nobleness.
Sir Thomas More

Modest? My word, no. He was an all-the-lights-on man.
Henry Reed

Those who are believed to be most abject and humble are usually most ambitious and envious.
Baruch Spinoza

Few people are modest enough to be estimated at their true worth.
Marquis de Vauvenargues

Strive not with your superiors in argument, but always submit your judgment to others with modesty.
George Washington

Too humble is half proud.
Yiddish proverb

HUMILITY

There is something in humility which strangely exalts the heart.
St. Augustine

Nothing is more deceitful than the appearance of humility. It is often only carelessness of opinion, and sometimes an indirect boast.
Jane Austen

Life is a long lesson in humility.
J.M. Barrie

One of the first businesses of a sensible man is to know when he is beaten, and to leave off fighting at once.
Samuel Butler

Humility is not a weak and timid quality; it must be carefully distinguished from a groveling spirit.
Edwin H. Chapin

The wise person possesses humility. He knows that his small island of knowledge is surrounded by a vast sea of the unknown.
Harold C. Chase

Humility has its origin in an awareness of unworthiness, and sometimes too in a dazzled awareness of saintliness.
Colette

By humility I mean not the abjectness
of a base mind, but a prudent care not to
overvalue ourselves.
Nathaniel Crew

Some persons are always ready to level
those above them down to themselves,
while they are never willing to level
those below them up to their own position. But he that is under the influence
of true humility will avoid both these
extremes. On the one hand, he will be
willing that all should rise just so far as
their diligence and worth of character
entitle them to; and on the other hand,
he will be willing that his superiors
should be known and acknowledged in
their place, and have rendered to them
all the honors that are their due.
Jonathan Edwards

Humility is the most difficult of all
virtues to achieve; nothing dies harder
than the desire to think well of self.
T.S. Eliot

I am no lover of pompous title, but only
desire that my name be recorded in a line
or two, which shall briefly express my
name, my virginity, the years of my reign,
the reformation of religion under it, and
my preservation of peace.
Queen Elizabeth I

It is useless to gather virtues without
humility, for the spirit of the Lord
delighteth to dwell in the hearts of the
humble.
Erasmus

There is no true holiness without
humility.
Thomas Fuller

Humility is not my forte, and whenever
I dwell for any length of time on my own
shortcomings, they gradually begin to
seem mild, harmless, rather engaging

little things, not at all like the staring
defects in other people's characters.
Margaret Halsey

Humility is just as much the opposite of
self-abasement as it is of self-exaltation.
Dag Hammarskjöld

The fruits of humility are love and peace.
Hebrew proverb

Humility is often only a feigned submission, of which we make use to render
others submissive. It is an artifice of
pride which abases in order to exalt
itself.
François de La Rochefoucauld

Of all kinds of shame, the worst, surely, is
being ashamed of frugality or poverty.
Livy

In 1969 I published a small book on
humility. It was a pioneering work,
which has not, to my knowledge, been
superseded.
Long Longford

Humility leads to strength and not
to weakness. It is the highest form of
self-respect to admit mistakes and to
make amends for them.
John J. McCloy

The trodden worm curls up. Thus it
reduces its chance of being stepped
on again. In the language of morality:
Humility.
Friedrich Wilhelm Nietzsche

Sense shines with a double luster when it
is set in humility. An able and yet humble
man is a jewel worth a kingdom.
William Penn

Humility is a virtue all preach, none practice, and yet everybody is content to hear.
John Selden

The more things a man is ashamed of, the more respectable he is.
George Bernard Shaw

Humility is to make a right estimate of oneself.
Charles H. Spurgeon

We come nearest to the great when we are great in humility.
Rabindranath Tagore

If I only had a little humility, I'd be perfect.
Ted Turner

HUMOR

Comedy just pokes at problems, rarely confronts them squarely. Drama is like a plate of meat and potatoes; comedy is rather the dessert, a bit like meringue.
Woody Allen

Men ought to find the difference between saltness and bitterness. Certainly, he that hath a satirical vein, as he maketh others afraid of his wit, so he had need be afraid of others' memory.
Francis Bacon

Humor is falling downstairs if you do it in the act of telling your wife not to.
Kenneth Bird

The righteous one has no sense of humor.
Bertolt Brecht

Being a funny person does an awful lot of things to you. You feel that you mustn't get serious with people. They don't expect it from you and they don't want to see it. You're not entitled to be serious.
Fanny Brice

All my humor is based upon destruction and despair. If the whole world were tranquil, without disease and violence, I'd be standing on the breadline right in back of J. Edgar Hoover.
Lenny Bruce

Humor purges the blood, making the body young, lively, and fit for any manner of employment.
Robert Burton

I remain just one thing, and one thing only, and that is a clown. It places me on a far higher plane than any politician.
Charlie Chaplin

For health and the constant enjoyment of life, give me a keen and ever present sense of humor; it is the next best thing to an abiding faith in providence.
George B. Cheever

A joke's a very serious thing.
Charles Churchill

Men will confess to treason, murder, arson, false teeth, or a wig. How many of them will own up to a lack of humor?
Frank Moore Colby

Humor is by far the most significant activity of the human brain.
Edward de Bono

The last man that makes a joke owns it.
Finley Peter Dunne

A different of taste in jokes is a great strain upon the affections.
George Eliot

An uncontrolled sense of humor is often costly in business.
William Feather

Humor is an affirmation of dignity, a declaration of man's superiority to all that befalls him.
Romain Gary

Advice is sometimes transmitted more successfully through a joke than grave teaching.
Baltasar Gracián

There is certainly no defense against adverse fortune which is, on the whole, so effectual as an habitual sense of humor.
Thomas W. Higginson

A jest often decides matters of importance more effectively and happily than seriousness.
Horace

Be fond of the man who jests at his scars, if you like; but never believe he is being on the level with you.
Pamela Hansford Johnson

Humor, a good sense of it, is to Americans what manhood is to Spaniards, and we will go to great lengths to prove it. Experiments with laboratory rats have shown that, if one psychologist in the room laughs at something a rat does, all of the other psychologists will laugh equally. Nobody wants to be left holding the joke.
Garrison Keillor

Good humor is a tonic for mind and body. It is the best antidote for anxiety and depression. It is a business asset. It attracts and keeps friends. It lightens human burdens. It is the direct route to serenity and contentment.
Grenville Kleiser

Life's more amusing than we thought.
Andrew Lang

I think a sense of humor is the emotional equivalent of a sense of realism. One should not take everything seriously, and everybody takes some things seriously.
Michael Maccoby

Sense of humor: A thread of illuminated intelligence that links two opposite ideas.
Tom Masson

The sense of humor is the oil of life's engine. Without it, the machinery creaks and groans. No lot is so hard, no aspect of things is so grim, but it relaxes before a hearty laugh.
G.S. Merriam

Life does not cease to be funny when people die any more than it ceases to be serious when people laugh.
George Bernard Shaw

Good humor is the best shield against the darts of satirical raillery.
Charles Simmons

Good humor is one of the best articles of dress one can wear in society.
William Makepeace Thackeray

Comedy has ceased to be a challenge to the mental processes. It has become a therapy of relaxation, a kind of tranquilizing drug.
James Thurber

Humor is emotional chaos remembered in tranquility.
James Thurber

Never say a humorous thing to a man who does not possess humor. He will always use it in evidence against you.
Herbert Beerbohm Tree

The humorous story is American, the comic story is English, the witty story is French. The humorous story depends for its effect upon the manner of the telling; the comic and the witty story upon the matter.
Mark Twain

Humor implies a sure conception of the beautiful, the majestic and the true, by

whose light it surveys and shapes their opposites. It is a humane influence, softening with mirth the ragged inequities of existence, prompting tolerant views of life, bridging over the space which separates the lofty from the lowly, the great from the humble.
Edwin P. Whipple

I

IDEALS

The best and noblest lives are those which are set toward high ideals.
René Alemeras

The ideal man bears the accidents of life with dignity and grace, making the best of the circumstances.
Aristotle

To live in the presence of great truths and eternal laws, to be led by permanent ideals—that is what keeps a man patient when the world ignores him, and calm and unspoiled when the world praises him.
Honoré de Balzac

All higher motives, ideals, conceptions, sentiments in a man are of no account if they do not come forward to strengthen him for the better discharge of the duties which devolve upon him in the ordinary affairs of life.
Henry Ward Beecher

It is no good making a fortune if you do not know how to enjoy it. Higher material standards are no good if you do not know how to use them for a better life. Economic ideals must include the ideal

of beauty as well as the ideal of plenty. We want new capital, far more capital than is being created today, but we want it not only to advance material well-being but because we want a better and more beautiful life for the citizens.
Sir Basil Blackett

Idealism is fine; but as it approaches reality, the cost becomes prohibitive.
William F. Buckley, Jr.

Heads are wisest when they are cool, and hearts are strongest when they beat in response to noble ideals.
Ralph J. Bunche

All human things do require to have an ideal in them; to have some soul in them.
Thomas Carlyle

We see facts with our eyes; we see ideas with our minds; we see ideals with our souls. Whatever we see with our souls is real and permanent and cannot be destroyed.
Glenn Clark

The danger to America is not in the direction of the failure to maintain its economic position, but in the direction of the failure to maintain its ideals.
Calvin Coolidge

There is no force so democratic as the force of an ideal.
Calvin Coolidge

We have a system which, though far from perfect, is strong with idealism. It gives elbow room for men of all races and all beliefs. It is vital and dynamic. And it works. We have the means of shaping the world in our pattern. If we do, freedom will be assured for all men. The decision is in the hands of this generation. It is a challenge to our political competence.

For western civilization it is the greatest challenge of all time.
William O. Douglas

We never reach our ideals, whether of mental or moral improvement, but the thought of them shows us our deficiencies, and spurs us on to higher and better things.
Tryon Edwards

An ideal is the only thing that has any real force. We have lost sight of our own ideal and its tremendous force and vigor. Somehow that must be recaptured. It must be passed on to generations to come, to make them believe in it; so that the energy in man which has its source in the ideal will not be lost.
Homer Ferguson

No nation can rise above the level of the ideals of its citizens.
Brooks Fletcher

To die for an idea sets a high price on conjecture.
Anatole France

Man can never come up to his ideal standard. It is the nature of the immortal spirit to raise that standard higher and higher as it goes from strength to strength, still upward and onward.
Margaret Fuller

When ideas fail, words come in very handy.
Johann Wolfgang von Goethe

An ideal is the most practical thing in the world, for it is a force behind action that must be reckoned with by the frankest materialist.
Edward H. Griggs

Words without actions are the assassins of idealism.
Herbert Hoover

Misguided idealism is as unproductive as unconcern.
A. Dodds Kinard

He who, having lost one ideal, refuses to give his heart and soul to another and nobler, is like a man who declines to build a house on the rock because the wind and rain have ruined his house on the sand.
Constance Naden

I looked for great men, but all I found were the apes of their ideals.
Friedrich Wilhelm Nietzsche

All men need something to poetize and idealize their life a little—something which they value for more than its use and which is a symbol of their emancipation from the mere materialism and drudgery of daily life.
Theodore E. Parker

Blessed is he who carries within himself a God, an ideal, and who obeys it.
Louis Pasteur

To live in the presence of great truths and eternal laws, to be led by permanent ideals—that is what keeps a man patient when the world ignores him, and calm and unspoiled when the world praises him.
Dr. A. Peabody

Let us show, not merely in great crises, but in every day affairs of life, qualities of practical intelligence, of hardihood and endurance, and above all, the power of devotion to a lofty ideal.
Theodore Roosevelt

Nobody grows old by merely living a number of years; people grow old only by deserting their ideals.
Samuel Ullman

There are many forms of triumph, but there is no other success that in any shape or way approaches that which is open to the men and women who have the right ideals. These are the men and women who see that it is the intimate and homely things that count most. They are the men and women who have the courage to strive for the happiness which comes only with labor, effort and self-sacrifice, and only to those whose joy in life springs in part from power of work and sense of duty.
Charles R. Wiers

Every great man of business has got somewhere a touch of the idealist in him.
Woodrow Wilson

No art can conquer the people alone—the people are conquered by an ideal of life upheld by authority.
William Butler Yeats

IDEAS

I ran into Isosceles. He has a great idea for a new triangle!
Woody Allen

Theory without experience is sterile, practice without theory is blind.
George Jay Anyon

Life is the application of noble and profound ideas to life.
Matthew Arnold

It seems to me that the thing that makes the theater worthwhile is the fact that it attracts so many people with ideas who are constantly trying to share them with the public. Real art is illumination. It gives a man an idea he never had before or lights up ideas that were formless or only lurking in the shadows of his mind. It adds stature to life.
Brooks Atkinson

He that will not apply new remedies must expect new evils.
Francis Bacon

One of the greatest pains to human nature is the pain of a new idea.
Walter Bagehot

The rewards in business go to the man who does something with an idea.
William Benton

The more an idea is developed, the more concise becomes its expression; the more a tree is pruned, the better is the fruit.
Alfred Bougeart

An idea must not be condemned for being a little shy and incoherent; all new ideas are shy when introduced first among our old ones. We should have patience and see whether the incoherency is likely to wear off or to wear on, in which latter case the sooner we get rid of them the better.
Samuel Butler

Money never starts an idea; it is the idea that starts the money.
W.J. Cameron

The idea is in thyself. The impediment, too, is in thyself.
Thomas Carlyle

The wise only possess ideas; the great part of mankind are possessed by them.
Samuel Taylor Coleridge

The philosopher contemplates ideas; the teacher energizes ideas; the student generates ideas.
Lionel Crocker

Ideas make their way in silence like the waters that, altering behind the rocks of the Alps, loosen then from the mountains upon which they rest.
Jean d'Aubigné

Many blunder in business through inability or an unwillingness to adopt new ideas. I have seen many a success turn to failure also, because the thought which should be trained on big things is cluttered up with the burdensome detail of little things.
Philip S. Delaney

Neither man nor nation can exist without a sublime idea.
Fyodor Dostoyevsky

Although words exist for the most part for the transmission of ideas, there are some which produce such violent disturbance in our feelings that the role they play in the transmission of ideas is lost in the background.
Albert Einstein

Wise men put their trust in ideas and not in circumstances.
Ralph Waldo Emerson

We don't need men with new ideas as much as we need men who will put energy behind the old ideas.
William Feather

The test of a first-rate intelligence is the ability to hold two opposed ideas in mind at the same time and still retain the ability to function. One should, for example, be able to see things as hopeless and yet be determined to make them otherwise.
F. Scott Fitzgerald

Now, ideas are the raw material of progress. Everything first takes shape in the form of an idea. But an idea by itself is worth nothing. An idea, like a machine, must have power applied to it before it can accomplish anything. The men who have won fame and fortune through having an idea are those who devoted every ounce of their strength and every dollar they could muster to putting it into operation. Ford had a big idea, but he had to sweat and suffer and sacrifice in order to make it work.
B.C. Forbes

Most of us have a pretty clear idea of the world we want. What we lack is an understanding of how to go about getting it.
Hugh Gibson

Daring ideas are like chessmen moved forward; they may be beaten, but they may start a winning game.
Johann Wolfgang von Goethe

Behind every advance of the human race is a germ of creation growing in the mind of some lone individual. An individual whose dreams waken him in the night while others lie contentedly asleep.
Crawford H. Greenewalt

Nothing is so corrupting as a great idea whose time is past.
John P. Grier

In the long run of history, the censor and the inquisitor have always lost. The only sure weapon against bad ideas is better ideas.
Whitney Griswold

So many new ideas are at first strange and horrible though ultimately valuable that a very heavy responsibility rests upon those who would prevent their dissemination.
John B.S. Haldane

All the lost mines of Mexico, all the argosies that ever sailed from the Indies, all the gold- and silver-laden ships of the treasure fleets of storied Spain, count no more value than a beggar's dole compared with the wealth that is today

created every eight hours by modern business ideas.
Worthington C. Holman

Many ideas grow better when transplanted into another mind than in the one where they sprang up.
Oliver Wendell Holmes

An idea that is not dangerous is unworthy of being called an idea at all.
Elbert Hubbard

There is one thing stronger than all the armies in the world, and that is an Idea whose time has come.
Victor Hugo

A healthful hunger for a great idea is the beauty and blessedness of life.
Jean Ingelow

An idea, to be suggestive, must come to the individual with the force of a revelation.
William James

Ideas lose themselves as quickly as quail, and one must wing them the minute they rise out of the grass—or they are gone.
Thomas F. Kennedy

So long as new ideas are created, sales will continue to reach new highs.
Charles F. Kettering

To ask at what time a man has first any ideas is to ask when he begins to perceive; having ideas and perception being the same thing.
John Locke

The requisite of a natural resource is an idea. There are no known limits, therefore, to the multiplication of natural resources of the earth, and exhaustion of them is impossible.
James C. Malin

Men's ideas are the direct emanations of their material state. This is true in politics, law, morality, religion, etc.
Karl Marx

There are two things that have to happen before an idea catches on. One is that the idea should be good. The other is that it should fit in with the temper of the age. If it does not, even a good idea may well be passed by.
Jawaharlal Nehru

Most ideas are step-by-step children of other ideas.
Alex Osborn

To get your ideas across, use small words, big ideas and short sentences.
John Henry Patterson

Mere words are cheap and plenty enough, but ideas that rouse and set multitudes thinking come as gold from the mines.
A. Owen Penny

A great idea is usually original to more than one discoverer. Great ideas come when the world needs them. They surround the world's ignorance and press for admission.
Austin Phelps

As there are misanthropists or haters of men, so also are there misologists, or haters of ideas.
Plato

It is a thing of no great difficulty to raise objections against another man's oration—nay, it is a very easy matter; but to produce a better in its place is a work extremely troublesome.
Plutarch

Ideas are a capital that bears interest only in the hands of talent.
Antoine de Rivarol

There are no hard times for good ideas.
H. Gordon Selfridge

Getting an idea should be like sitting down on a pin; it should make you jump up and do something.
E.L. Simpson

It must be remembered that the object of the world of ideas as a whole is not the portrayal of reality—that would be an utterly impossible task—but rather to provide us with an instrument for finding our way about in this world more easily.
Hans Vaihinger

We are healthy only to the extent that our ideas are humane.
Kurt Vonnegut Jr.

Every breeze wafts intelligence from country to country, every wave rolls it and gives it forth, and all in turn receive it. There is a vast commerce of ideas, there are marts and exchanges for intellectual discoveries, and a wonderful fellowship of those individual intelligences which make up the minds and opinions of the age.
Daniel Webster

Human history is, in essence, a history of ideas.
H.G. Wells

The value of an idea has nothing whatever to do with the sincerity of the man who expresses it.
Oscar Wilde

All the really good ideas I ever had came to me while I was milking a cow.
Grant Wood

The power of an idea can be measured by the degree of resistance it attracts.
David Yoho

IDLENESS

It has been said that idleness is the parent of mischief which is very true; but mischief itself is merely an attempt to escape from the dreary vacuum of idleness.
George Barrow

If you are idle you are on the way to ruin, and there are few stopping places upon it. It is rather a precipice than a road.
Henry Ward Beecher

You see men of the most delicate frames engaged in active and professional pursuits who really have no time for idleness. Let them become idle—let them take care of themselves, let them think of their health—and they die! The rust rots the steel which use preserves.
Edward Bulwer-Lytton

Too much idleness, I have observed, fills up a man's time much more completely, and leaves him less his own master, than any sort of employment whatsoever.
Edmund Burke

Idleness is an appendix to nobility.
Robert Burton

There is no greater cause of melancholy than idleness.
Robert Burton

Blessed is the man that has found his work. One monster there is in the world, the idle man.
Thomas Carlyle

He doth all things with sadness and with peevishness, slackness and excusation, with idleness and without good will.
Geoffrey Chaucer

From its very inaction, idleness ultimately becomes the most active cause of evil; as a palsy is more to be dreaded than

a fever. The Turks have a proverb which says that the devil tempts all other men, but that idle men tempt the devil.
Charles Caleb Colton

Idleness is not doing nothing. Idleness is being free to do anything.
Floyd Dell

I never remember feeling tired by work, though idleness exhausts me completely.
Sir Arthur Conan Doyle

An idle brain is the devil's workshop.
English proverb

Sometimes I think that idlers seem to be a special class for whom nothing can be planned, plead as one will with them, their only contribution to the human family is to warm a seat at the common table.
F. Scott Fitzgerald

Nobody can think straight who does not work. Idleness warps the mind. Thinking without constructive action becomes a disease.
Henry Ford

He that is busy is tempted by one devil; he that is idle, by a legion.
Thomas Fuller

Determine never to be idle. No person will have occasion to complain of the want of time who never loses any. It is wonderful how much may be done if we are always doing.
Thomas Jefferson

It is impossible to enjoy idling thoroughly unless one has plenty of work to do.
Jerome K. Jerome

There is no kind of idleness by which we are so easily seduced as that which dignifies itself by the appearance of business.
Samuel Johnson

Far from idleness being the root of all evil, it is rather the only true good.
Søren Kierkegaard

Time is the one thing that can never be retrieved. One may lose and regain a friend; one may lose and regain money; opportunity once spurned may come again; but the hours that are lost in idleness can never be brought back to be used in gainful pursuits. Most careers are made or marred in the hours after supper.
C.R. Lawton

Certainly work is not always required of a man. There is such a thing as a sacred idleness—the cultivation of which is now fearfully neglected.
George MacDonald

There is also an honest and necessary idleness whereby good men are made more apt and ready to do their labors and vocations whereunto they are called.
John Northbrooke

Better sit idle than work for nought.
Scottish proverb

There is one piece of advice, in a life of study, which I think no one will object to: and that is, every now and then to be completely idle, to do nothing at all.
Sydney Smith

He is not only idle who does nothing, but he is idle who might be better employed.
Socrates

Idleness is the burial of a living man.
Jeremy Taylor

Shun idleness. It is a rust that attaches itself to the most brilliant metals.
Voltaire

It is in our idleness, in our dreams, that the submerged truth sometimes comes to the top.
Virginia Woolf

IGNORANCE

Prejudice and self-sufficiency naturally proceed from inexperience of the world, and ignorance of mankind.
Joseph Addison

Beware of ignorance when in motion; look out for inexperience when in action, and beware of the majority when mentally poisoned with misinformation, for collective ignorance does not become wisdom.
William J.H. Boetcker

Behind every argument is someone's ignorance.
Louis D. Brandeis

Ignorance is not innocence but sin.
Robert Browning

If you think education is expensive, try ignorance.
Bumper sticker

The truest characters of ignorance are vanity, and pride and arrogance.
Samuel Butler

Ignorance is an enemy, even to its owner. Knowledge is a friend, even to its hater. Ignorance hates knowledge because it is too pure. Knowledge fears ignorance because it is too sure.
Sri Chinmoy

To be conscious that you are ignorant is a great step to knowledge.
Benjamin Disraeli

It is the ignorant and childish part of mankind that is the fighting part.
Ralph Waldo Emerson

There is nothing more frightening than a bustling ignorance.
Johann Wolfgang von Goethe

The recipe for perpetual ignorance is: Be satisfied with your opinions and content with your knowledge.
Elbert Hubbard

We're trying to eradicate ignorance. It's a losing fight.
Joseph Jamail, Jr.

Ignorance, when voluntary, is criminal, and a man may be properly charged with that evil which he neglected or refused to learn how to prevent.
Samuel Johnson

Nothing in all the world is more dangerous than sincere ignorance and conscientious stupidity.
Martin Luther King, Jr.

Ignorance is voluntary misfortune.
Nicholas Lang

To know one's ignorance is the best part of knowledge.
Lao-tzu

What we know here is very little, but what we are ignorant of is immense.
Pierre Simon Laplace

Half knowledge is worse than ignorance.
Thomas B. Macaulay

It is impossible to defeat an ignorant man by argument.
William McAdoo

To admit ignorance is to exhibit wisdom.
Ashley Montagu

Better be unborn than untaught, for ignorance is the root of misfortune.
Plato

There is a determinable difference between the apparent casualness of mastery and the carelessness of ignorance.
Charles B. Rogers

There is no darkness—but ignorance.
William Shakespeare

It is poverty in a rich man to despise the poor and ignorance in a wise man to despise the ignorant.
Constance C. Vigil

Ignorance is not bliss—it is oblivion.
Philip Wylie

ILLUSIONS

Beware lest you lose the substance by grasping at the shadow.
Aesop

We must select the illusion which appeals to our temperament, and embrace it with passion, if we want to be happy.
Cyril Connolly

Every age is fed on illusions, lest men should renounce life early and the human race come to an end.
Joseph Conrad

What difference is there, do you think, between those in Plato's cave who can only marvel at the shadows and images of various objects, provided they are content and don't know what they miss, and the philosopher who has emerged from the cave and sees the real things?
Erasmus

The illusion that times that were are better than those that are, has probably pervaded all ages.
Horace Greeley

Illusion is always based on reality, for its strength depends upon its fit with the desires, fears and experiences of countless humans.
John P. Grier

Rob the average man of his illusion and you rob him of his happiness at one stroke.
Henrik Ibsen

No man will be found in whose mind airy notions do not sometimes tyrannize, and force him to hope or fear beyond the limits of sober probability.
Samuel Johnson

It appears to me that almost any man may, like the spider, spin from his own inwards his own airy citadel.
John Keats

The most important part of our lives— our sensations, emotions, desire, aspirations—takes place in a universe of illusions which science can attenuate or destroy, but which it is powerless to enrich.
Joseph Wood Krutch

The notion that as a man grows older his illusions leave him is not quite true. What is true is that his early illusions are supplanted by new, and to him, equally convincing illusions.
George Jean Nathan

A man loses his illusions first, his teeth second, and his follies last.
Helen Rowland

A hallucination is a fact, not an error; what is erroneous is a judgment based upon it.
Bertrand Russell

The eyes are not responsible when the mind does the seeing.
Publilius Syrus

It isn't safe to sit in judgment upon another person's illusion when you are not on the inside. While you are thinking it is a dream, he may be knowing it is a planet.
Mark Twain

Illusion is the first of all pleasures.
Voltaire

IMAGINATION

Far away in the sunshine are my highest inspirations. I may not reach them, but I can look up and see the beauty, believe in them and try to follow where they lead.
Louisa May Alcott

No human being is innocent, but there is a class of innocent human actions called games.
W.H. Auden

Man is an imagining being.
Gaston Bachelard

I get the facts, I study them patiently, I apply imagination.
Bernard M. Baruch

Imagination: a warehouse of facts with poet and liar in joint ownership.
Ambrose Bierce

The human race is governed by its imagination.
Napoleon Bonaparte

Fortunately, somewhere between chance and mystery lies imagination, the only thing that protects our freedom, despite the fact that people keep trying to reduce or kill it off altogether.
Luis Buñuel

Imagination is like a lofty building reared to meet the sky—fancy is a balloon that soars at the wind's will.
Gelett Burgess

Your imagination has much to do with your life. It pictures beauty, success, desired results. On the other hand, it brings into focus ugliness, distress, and failure. It is for you to decide how you want your imagination to serve you.
Philip Conley

Every great advance in science has issued from a new audacity of imagination.
John Dewey

The first step is an intuition—and comes with a burst, then difficulties arise. This thing gives out and then that—"Bugs"—as such little faults are called, show themselves.
Thomas A. Edison

Imagination is more important than knowledge.
Albert Einstein

Imagination is not a talent of some men, but is the health of every man.
Ralph Waldo Emerson

The man who will use his skill and constructive imagination to see how much he can give for a dollar, instead of how little he can give for a dollar, is bound to succeed.
Henry Ford

It is the starved imagination, not the well-nourished, that is afraid.
E.M. Forster

The very core of peace and love is imagination. All altruism springs from putting yourself in the other person's place.
Harry Emerson Fosdick, D.D.

Imagination is the secret reservoir of the riches of the human race.
Maude L. Frandsen

Inspiration is and can only be the product of free men.
Howard E. Fritz

Originality is simply a pair of fresh eyes.
Thomas W. Higginson

The principal mark of genius is not perfection but originality, the opening of new frontiers.
Arthur Koestler

My imagination makes me human and makes me a fool; it gives me all the world and exiles me from it.
Ursula Le Guin

Imagination is a very precise thing—it is not fantasy; the man who invented the wheel while he was observing another man walking, that is imagination!
Jacques Lipchitz

Imagination, where it is truly creative, is a faculty, not a quality; its seat is in the higher reason, and it is efficient only as the servant of the will. Imagination, as too often understood, is mere fantasy—the image-making power, common to all who have the gift of dreams.
James Russell Lowell

All good things which exist are the fruits of originality.
John Stuart Mill

Originality is the one thing which unoriginal minds cannot feel the use of.
John Stuart Mill

A strong imagination begetteth opportunity.
Michel de Montaigne

The power of imagination makes us infinite.
John Muir

Imagination, the supreme delight of the immortal and the immature, should be limited. In order to enjoy life, we should not enjoy it too much.
Vladimir Nabokov

The great composer does not set to work because he is inspired, but becomes inspired because he is working. Beethoven, Wagner, Bach and Mozart settled down day after day to the job in hand with as much regularity as an accountant settles down each day to his figures. They didn't waste time waiting for inspiration.
Ernest Newman

Imagination disposes of everything; it creates beauty, justice, happiness, which is everything in this world.
Blaise Pascal

It may well be doubted whether human ingenuity can construct an enigma of the kind which human ingenuity may not, by proper application, resolve.
Edgar Allan Poe

It will be found, in fact, that the ingenious are always fanciful, and the truly imaginative never less than analytic.
Edgar Allan Poe

The world of reality has its limits; the world of imagination is boundless. Not being able to enlarge the one, let us contract the other; for it is from their difference that all the evils arise which render us unhappy.
Jean-Jacques Rousseau

The virtue of the imagination is its reaching, by intuition and intensity, a more essential truth than is seen at the surface of things.
John Ruskin

A man to carry on a successful business must have imagination. He must see things as in a vision, a dream of the whole thing.
Charles M. Schwab

The greatest instrument of moral good is the imagination.
Percy Bysshe Shelley

Originality does not consist is saying what no one has ever said before, but in saying exactly what you think yourself.
James Stephens

The imagination is man's power over nature.
Wallace Stevens

Skill without imagination is craftsmanship and gives us many useful objects such as wickerwork picnic baskets. Imagination without skill gives us modern art.
Tom Stoppard

Men of great parts are often unfortunate in the management of public business because they are apt to go out of the common road by the quickness of their imagination.
Jonathan Swift

Imagination lit every lamp in this country, produced every article we use, built every church, made every discovery, performed every act of kindness and progress, created more and better things for more people. It is the priceless ingredient for a better day.
Henry J. Taylor

So you see, imagination needs moodling-long, inefficient, happy idling, dawdling and puttering.
Brenda Ueland

It is the spirit of the age to believe that any fact, no matter how suspect, is superior to any imaginative exercise, no matter how true.
Gore Vidal

The imagination imitates. It is the critical spirit that creates.
Oscar Wilde

IMPOSSIBLE

The word impossible is not in my dictionary.
Napoleon Bonaparte

I have learned to use the world impossible with the greatest caution.
Wernher von Braun

To wonder at nothing when it happens, to consider nothing impossible before it has come to pass.
Cicero

When a distinguished but elderly scientist states that something is possible, he is almost certainly right. When he states that something is impossible, he is probably wrong.
Arthur C. Clarke

To believe a business impossible is the way to make it so. How many feasible projects have miscarried through despondency, and been strangled in their birth by a cowardly imagination.
Jeremy Collier

Only he who can see the invisible can do the impossible.
Frank L. Gaines

Never tell a young person that something cannot be done. God may have been waiting for centuries for somebody ignorant enough of the impossible to do that thing.
Dr. John Andrew Holmes

Few things are impossible in themselves: application to make them succeed fails us more often than the means.
François de La Rochefoucauld

Nothing is impossible; there are ways that lead to everything, and if we had sufficient will we should always have sufficient means. It is often merely for an excuse that we say things are impossible.
François de La Rochefoucauld

Man can believe the impossible, but man can never believe the improbable.
Oscar Wilde

IMPROVEMENT

A man who truly wants to make the world better should start by improving himself and his attitudes.
Fred de Armond

There isn't a plant or a business on earth that couldn't stand a few improvements—and be better for them. Someone is going to think of them. Why not beat the other fellow to it?
Roger W. Babson

To face tomorrow with the thought of using the methods of yesterday is to envision life at a standstill. To keep ahead, each one of us, no matter what our task, must search for new and better methods—for even that which we now do well must be done better tomorrow.
James F. Bell

It is not the rich man's son that the young struggler for advancement has to fear in the race for life, nor his nephew, nor his cousin. Let him look out for the dark horse in the boy who begins by sweeping out the office.
Andrew Carnegie

Do not hold the delusion that your advancement is accomplished by crushing others.
Cicero

Where we cannot invent, we may at least improve; we may give somewhat of novelty to that which was old, condensation to that which was diffuse, perspicuity to that which was obscure, and currency to that which was recondite.
Charles Caleb Colton

Why are we so blind? That which we improve, we have that which we hoard is not for ourselves.
Dorothée DeLuzy

Every man, however obscure, however far removed from the general recognition, is one of a group of men impressible for good, and impressible for evil, and it is in the nature of things that he cannot really improve himself without in some degree improving other men.
Charles Dickens

People never improve unless they look to some standard or example higher and better than themselves.
Tryon Edwards

Improvement of one's economic position is helped more by cool persistence than by hot enthusiasm.
William Feather

The most essential feature of man is his improvableness.
John Fiske

The opportunity for the average workman to rise to the management

positions in industry was never better than it is today. These opportunities will continue to grow in the next decade. If the average intelligent and honest workman supplements his practical work experience with study of the general problems of business he will find privileged opportunities and promotion awaiting him.
Henry H. Heimann

Men, said the Devil, are good to their brothers; they don't want to mend their own ways, but each other's.
Piet Hein

You will probably get a larger position than you expect when you begin to do larger things than your firm expects you to do.
George C. Hobbs

There is no advancement to him who stands trembling because he cannot see the end from the beginning.
E.J. Klemme

Slumber not in the tents of your fathers. The world is advancing. Advance with it.
Giuseppe Mazzini

The hope, and not the fact, of advancement is the spur to industry.
Henry J. Taylor

INDEPENDENCE

There is often as much independence in not being led, as in not being driven.
Tryon Edwards

The greatest of all human benefits, that, at least, without which no other benefit can be truly enjoyed, is independence.
Parke Godwin

It's easy to be independent when you've got money. But to be independent when you haven't got a thing—that's the Lord's test.
Mahalia Jackson

Let all your views in life be directed to a solid, however moderate, independence; without it no man can be happy, nor even honest.
Junius

Self-government, self-discipline, self-responsibility are the triple safeguards of the independence of man.
Bernice Moore

To be independent is the business of a few only; it is the privilege of the strong.
Friedrich Wilhelm Nietzsche

Independence is of more value than any gifts; and to receive gifts is to lose it.
Sa'di

A great step towards independence is a good-humored stomach.
Seneca

Independency may be found in comparative as well as in absolute abundance; I mean where a person contracts his desires within the limits of his fortune.
William Shenstone

INDIVIDUAL

We are afraid to put men to live and trade each on his own private stock of reason; because we suspect that this stock in each man is small, and that the individuals would do better to avail themselves of the general bank and capital of nations and of age.
Edmund Burke

Individuality is either the mark of genius or the reverse. Mediocrity finds safety in standardization.
Frederick E. Crane

What counts in any system is the intelligence, self-control, conscience and energy of the individual.
Cyrus Eaton

Regardless of circumstances, each man lives in a world of his own making.
Josepha Murray Emms

No task is so humble that it does not offer an outlet for individuality.
William Feather

One man can completely change the character of a country, and the industry of its people, by dropping a single seed in fertile soil.
John C. Gifford

Every individual has a place to fill in the world, and is important in some respect, whether he chooses to be so or not.
Nathaniel Hawthorne

Be thankful not only that you are an individual but also that others are different. The world needs all kinds, but it also needs to respect and use that individuality.
Donald A. Laird

In proportion to the development of his individuality, each person becomes more valuable to others. There is a greater fullness of life about his own existence, and when there is more life in the units there is more in the mass which is composed of them.
John Stuart Mill

Whatever crushes individuality is despotism, by whatever name it may be called.
John Stuart Mill

It is an absolute perfection to know how to get the very most out of one's individuality.
Michel de Montaigne

Individuality is everywhere to be spaced and respected as the root of everything good.
Jean Paul Richter

How beautifully is it ordered, that as many thousands work for one, so must every individual bring his labor to make the whole. The highest is not to despise the lowest, nor the lowest to envy the highest; each must live in all and by all.
G.A. Sala

We seem to want mass production, but we must remember that men are individuals not to be satisfactorily dealt with in masses, and the making of men is more important than the production of things.
Ralph W. Sockman, D.D.

There will never be a really free and enlightened state until the state comes to recognize the individual as a higher and independent power, from which all its own power and authority are derived, and treats him accordingly.
Henry David Thoreau

All great questions of politics and economics come down in the last analysis to the decisions and actions of individual men and women. They are questions of human relations, and we ought always to think about them in terms of men and women—the individual human beings who are involved in them. If we can get human relations on a proper basis, the statistics, finance and all other complicated technical aspects of these questions will be easier to solve.
Thomas J. Watson

Most men are individuals no longer so far as their business, its activities, or its moralities are concerned. They are not units but fractions.
Woodrow Wilson

INDUSTRY

In the ordinary business of life, industry can do anything which genius can do, and very many things which it cannot.
Henry Ward Beecher

There is one rule for industrialists and that is: Make the best quality of goods possible at the lowest cost possible, paying the highest wages possible.
Henry Ford

Sloth makes all things difficult, but industry all things easy.
Benjamin Franklin

The way to wealth is as plain as the way to market. It depends chiefly on two words, industry and frugality; that is, waste neither time nor money, but make the best use of both. Without industry and frugality nothing will do; with them, everything.
Benjamin Franklin

In every rank, both great and small, it is industry that supports us all.
John Gay

To industry, nothing is impossible.
Latin proverb

I do not despise genius—indeed, I wish I had a basketful of it. But yet, after a great deal of experience and observation, I have become convinced that industry is a better horse to ride than genius. It may never carry any man as far as genius has carried individuals, but industry— patient, steady, intelligent industry—will carry thousands into comfort, and even

celebrity; and this it does with absolute certainty.
Walter Lippmann

If you have genius, industry will improve it; if you have none, industry will supply its place.
Sir Joshua Reynolds

I am convinced that when confidence has been established amongst all nations of the world, the present capacity of industrial countries will not be sufficient to satisfy the demand.
Oskar Sempell

National progress is the sum of individual industry, energy, and uprightness, as national decay is of individual idleness, selfishness, and vice.
Samuel Smiles

A man who gives his children habits of industry provides for them better than by giving them a fortune.
Richard Whately

INSULTS

A thick skin is a gift from God.
Konrad Adenauer

He who does not shield himself from vilification receives it.
Arabian proverb

Slander cannot destroy the man ... when the flood recedes, the rock is there.
Chinese proverb

An insult is either sustained or destroyed, not by the disposition of those who insult, but by the disposition of those who bear it.
St. John Chrysostom

Some people would not hesitate to drive up to the gate of heaven and honk.
John Andrew Holmes

A sneer is often the sign of heartless malignity.
Johann Lavater

The habit of sneering marks the egotist, the fool, or the knave, or all three.
Johann Lavater

There are two insults no human will endure: the assertion that he has no sense of humor and the doubly impertinent assertion that he has never known trouble.
Sinclair Lewis

I hold it to be a proof of great prudence for men to abstain from threats and insulting words toward anyone, for neither diminishes the strength of the enemy.
Niccolò Machiavelli

No one is safe from slander. The best way is to pay no attention to it, but live in innocence and let the world talk.
Molière

Man is much more sensitive to the contempt of others than to self-contempt.
Friedrich Wilhelm Nietzsche

The poorest way to face life is to face it with a sneer.
Theodore Roosevelt

Obscenity is whatever happens to shock some elderly and ignorant magistrate.
Bertrand Russell

Rudeness is better than any argument; it totally eclipses intellect.
Arthur Schopenhauer

There is a principle which is a bar against all information, which is proof against all argument and which cannot fail to keep a man in everlasting ignorance. This principle is contempt prior to examination.
Herbert Spencer

Speak not injurious words, neither in jest nor earnest; scoff at none although they give occasion.
George Washington

INTELLIGENCE

Cleverness is serviceable for everything, sufficient for nothing.
Henri Frédéric Amiel

What is an intelligent man? A man who enters with ease and completeness into the spirit of things and the intention of persons, and who arrives at an end by the shortest route.
Henri Frédéric Amiel

It is the mark of an educated mind to be able to entertain a thought without accepting it.
Aristotle

The brave, impetuous heart yields everywhere to the subtle, contriving head.
Matthew Arnold

All human knowledge takes the form of interpretation.
Walter Benjamin

Unintelligent people always look for a scapegoat.
Ernest Bevin

The brain is not an organ to be relied upon.
Alexander Block

Business and action strengthen the brain, but too much study weakens it.
H.G. Bohn

Man's brain is, after all, the greatest natural resource.
Karl Brandt

Intelligence is not to make no mistakes, but to see quickly how to make them good.
Bertolt Brecht

The commerce of intellect loves distant shores. The small retail dealer trades only with his neighbor; when the great merchant trades he links the four quarters of the globe.
Edward Bulwer-Lytton

In the U.S. you have to be a deviant or exist in extreme boredom. Make no mistake, all intellectuals are deviants in the U.S.
William S. Burroughs

An intellectual is someone whose mind watches itself.
Albert Camus

The education of the intellect is a great business; but an unconsecrated intellect is the saddest sight on which the sun looks down.
Edwin Chadwick

Good sense is at the bottom of everything: virtue, genius, wit, talent and taste.
J.J. de Chenier

It required Infinite Intelligence to create it and it requires Infinite Intelligence to keep it on its course. Everything that surrounds us—everything that exists—proves that there are Infinite Laws behind it. There can be no denying this fact. It is mathematical in its precision.
Thomas A. Edison

Intellect annuls fate. So far as a man thinks he is free.
Ralph Waldo Emerson

Cleverness is not wisdom.
Euripides

Brains aren't everything, but they're important.
William Feather

The man who puts $110,000 additional capital into an established business is pretty certain of increased returns; and in the same way, the man who puts additional capital into his brains—information, well directed thought and study of possibilities—will as surely—yes, more surely—get increased returns. There is no capital and no increase in capital safer than that.
Marshall Field

I was street smart. Unfortunately, the street was Rodeo Drive.
Carrie Fisher

Nothing is useless to the man of sense; he turns everything to account.
Charles Fontaine

The best buy by way of management is brains—at any price.
Malcolm Forbes

A clever man commits no minor blunders.
Johann Wolfgang von Goethe

When you hire people who are smarter than you are, you prove you are smarter than they are.
R.H. Grant

The brain is a mass of cranial nerve tissue, most of it in mint condition.
Robert Half

You could imagine you could be smart like Wittgenstein by just thinking hard enough, but Elvis just had it. It was almost spiritual. A kind of grace.
Richard Hell

To meet the great tasks that are before us, we require all our intelligence, and we must be sound and wholesome in mind. We must proceed in order. The price of anger is failure.
Elwood Hendricks

The most fertile soil does not necessarily produce the most abundant harvest. It is the use we make of our faculties which renders them valuable.
Thomas W. Higginson

A moment's insight is sometimes worth a life's experience.
Oliver Wendell Holmes

A rather important contemporary problem: too many unintelligent intellectuals.
Walter Hoving

It takes a clever man to turn cynic and a wise man to be clever enough not to.
Fannie Hurst

No one is mediocre who has good sense and good sentiments.
Joseph Joubert

The difference between intelligence and an education is this—that intelligence will make you a good living.
Charles F. Kettering

College was for people who didn't know they were smart.
Stephen King

"I think, therefore I am" is the statement of an intellectual who underrates toothaches.
Milan Kundera

Not many men have both good fortune and good sense.

Not many men have both good fortune and good sense.
Livy

Talent, taste, wit, good sense are very different things but by no means incompatible. Between good sense and good taste there exists the same difference as between cause and effect, and between wit and talent there is the same proportion as between a whole and its parts.
Jean de La Bruyère

I am clever; and make no scruple of declaring it; why should I?
François de La Rochefoucauld

Intellectual blemishes, like facial ones, grow more prominent with age.
François de La Rochefoucauld

It is great cleverness to know how to conceal one's cleverness.
François de La Rochefoucauld

The earth flourishes, or is overrun with noxious weeds and brambles, as we apply or withhold the cultivating hand. So fares it with the intellectual system of man.
Horace Mann

There's no underestimating the intelligence of the American public.
H.L. Mencken

People of quality know everything without ever having learned anything.
Molière

Go to bed smarter than when you woke up.
Charles Munger

In order to acquire intellect one must need it. One loses it when it is no longer necessary.
Friedrich Wilhelm Nietzsche

Intelligence is the effort to do the best you can at your particular job; the quality that gives dignity to that job, whether it happens to be scrubbing a floor or running a corporation.
J.C. Penney

It's a terrible shame if you're born the brightest guy in your class. If you're not, then you have to hustle—and that's good.
Hal Prince

Scholarship is polite argument.
Philip Rieff

Work alone does not suffice—the effort must be intelligent.
Charles B. Rogers

So far as I can remember, there is not one word in the Gospels in praise of intelligence.
Bertrand Russell

The fundamental cause of the trouble is that in the modern world the stupid are cocksure while the intelligent are full of doubt.
Bertrand Russell

On his career: Only in show business could a guy with a C-minus average be considered an intellectual.
Mort Sahl

It is the mark of a truly intelligent person to be moved by statistics.
George Bernard Shaw

It is only the constant exertion and working of our sensitive, intellectual, moral, and physical machinery that keeps us from rusting, and so becoming useless.
Charles Simmons

The march of intellect is proceeding at quick time; and if its progress be not accompanied by a corresponding improvement in morals and religion, the faster it proceeds, with the more violence will you be hurried down the road to ruin.
Robert Southey

Intellect does not attain its full force until it attacks power.
Madame de Staël

If you would take, you must first give, this is the beginning of intelligence.
Tao Te Ching

In the world a man will often be reputed to be a man of sense, only because he is not a man of talent.
Henry J. Taylor

I doubt not that in due time, when the arts are brought to perfection, some means will be found to give a sound head to a man who has none at all.
Voltaire

A superior and commanding intellect, a truly great man—when Heaven vouchsafes so rare a gift—is not a temporary flame, burning for a while, and then expiring, giving place to eternal darkness. It is rather a spark of fervent heat, as well as radiant light, with power to enkindle the common mass of human mind; so that, when it glimmers in its own decay, and finally goes out in death, no night follows; but it leaves the world all light, all on fire, from the potent contact of its own spirit.
Daniel Webster

Intelligence is quickness to apprehend—as distinct from ability, which is capacity to act wisely on the thing apprehended.
A.N. Whitehead

J

JOBS

I received a letter from a lad asking me for an easy berth. To this I replied: You cannot be an editor; do not try the law; do not think of the ministry; let alone all ships and merchandise; abhor politics; don't practice medicine; be not a farmer or a soldier or a sailor; don't study, don't think. None of these are easy. O, my son, you have come into a hard world. I know of only one easy place in it, and that is the grave!
Henry Ward Beecher

Had I not gone through the ordeal, in more than one country, of landing a job, I would he be tempted to lose patience over the number of letters pouring in from fellows who want me or someone else to hand them a job on a silver platter with a guarantee that they will receive the wonderful promotion their talents warrant. . . . But a tragic number of young men and even older men have a notion that it is not up to them to prosecute the bettering process. They look to someone else to perform the trick for them.
B.C. Forbes

Usually there are responsible jobs going begging because not enough men are willing to sweat enough to master the problems involved.
W. Alton Jones

Unless the job means more than the pay it will never pay more.
H. Bertram Lewis

It is easier to do a job right than to explain why you didn't.
Martin Van Buren

JOY

Joys are bubble-like; what makes them bursts them too.
Philip James Bailey

There are joys which long to be ours. God sends ten thousand truths, which come about us like birds seeking inlet; but we are shut up to them, and so they bring us nothing, but sit and sing awhile upon the roof, and then fly away.
Henry Ward Beecher

The wise man seeks little joys, knowing that life is long and that his quota of great joys is distinctly limited.
William Feather

The greatest joy of a thinking man is to have searched the explored and to quietly revere the unexplored.
Johann Wolfgang von Goethe

When you jump for joy, beware that no one moves the ground from beneath your feet.
Stanislaw Jerzy Lec

They that sow in tears shall reap in joy. He that goeth forth and weepeth, bearing precious seed, shall doubtless come again with rejoicing, bringing his sheaves with him.
Psalms 126:5–6

A joy that's shared is a joy made double.
John Ray

I wish you all the joy that you can wish.
William Shakespeare

Sometimes hath the brightest day a cloud; and after summer evermore succeeds barren winter, with his wrathful nipping cold: So care and joys abound, as seasons fleet.
William Shakespeare

There is the true joy of life; to be used by a purpose recognized by yourself as a mighty one; to be thoroughly worn out before being thrown on the scrap heap; to be a force of nature instead of a feverish, selfish little clod of ailments and grievances complaining that life will not devote itself to making you happy.
George Bernard Shaw

When the power of imparting joy is equal to the will, the human soul requires no other heaven.
Percy Bysshe Shelley

The very society of joy redoubles it; so that, while it lights upon my friend, it rebounds upon myself, and the brighter his candle burns, the more easily will it light mine.
Robert Southey

Shared joy is double joy, and shared sorrow is half-sorrow.
Swedish proverb

Things in which we do not take joy are either a burden upon our minds to be got rid of at any cost; or they are useful, and therefore in temporary and partial relation to us, becoming burdensome when their utility is lost; or they are like wandering vagabonds, loitering for a moment on the outskirts of our recognition, and then passing on. A thing is only completely our own when it is a thing of joy to us.
Rabindranath Tagore

On with the dance, let joy be unconfined is my motto, whether there's a dance to dance or any joy to unconfine.
Mark Twain

Joy is the life of man's life.
Benjamin Whichcote

JUDGMENT

What we do not understand we have no right to judge.
Henri Frédéric Amiel

A good way to judge people is by observing how they treat those who can do them absolutely no good.
Anonymous

Property may be destroyed and money may lose its purchasing power; but, character, health, knowledge and good judgment will always be in demand under all conditions.
Roger Babson

Discretion of speech is more than eloquence.
Francis Bacon

Three things you can be judged by, your voice, your face and your disposition.
Ignas Bernstein

I shall tell you a great secret, my friend. Do not wait for the last judgment, it takes place every day.
Albert Camus

He who has the judge for his father goes into court with an easy mind.
Miguel de Cervantes

In order to judge of the inside of others, study your own; for men in general are very much alike, and though one has one prevailing passion, and another has another, yet their operations are much the same; and whatever engages or disgusts, pleases, or offends you in others will engage, disgust, please or offend others in you.
Lord Chesterfield

Statistics are no substitute for judgment.
Henry Clay

He that opposes his own judgment against the consent of the times ought to be backed with unanswerable truths; and he that has truth on his side is a fool as well as a coward if he is afraid to own it because of other men's opinions.
Daniel Defoe

As in walking it is your great care not to run your foot upon a nail, or to tread awry, and strain your leg; so let it be in all the affairs of human life, not to hurt your mind or offend your judgment. And this rule, if observed carefully in all your deportment, will be a mighty security to you in your undertakings.
Epictetus

Sound judgment, with discernment, is the best of seers.
Euripides

Associate with men of judgment, for judgment is found in conversation, and we make another man's judgment ours by frequenting his company.
Thomas Fuller

Discretion is the perfection of reason, and a guide to us in all the duties of life. It is only found in men of sound sense and understanding.
Jean de La Bruyère

We judge ourselves by what we feel capable of doing, while others judge us by what we have already done.
Henry Wadsworth Longfellow

True scholarship consists in knowing not what things exist, but what they mean; it is not memory but judgment.
James Russell Lowell

Judge not, that ye be not judged. For with what judgment ye judge, ye shall be judged: and with what measure ye mete, it shall be measured to you again.
Matthew 7:1–2

Knowledge is the treasure, but judgment is the treasurer of a wise man.
William Penn

Middle age is when the best exercise is one of discretion.
Laurence J. Peter

Let us not therefore judge one another any more: but judge this rather, that no man put a stumbling-block or an occasion to fall in his brother's way.
Romans 14:13

A right judgment draws us a profit from all things we see.
William Shakespeare

How little do they see what really is, who frame their hasty judgment upon that which seems.
Robert Southey

We do not judge men by what they are in themselves, but by what they are relatively to us.
Anne Sophie Swetchine

No man was ever endowed with a judgment so correct and judicious in regulating his life but that circumstances, time and experience would teach him something new, and apprise him that of those things with which he thought himself the best acquainted he knew nothing; and that those ideas which in theory appeared the most advantageous, were found, when brought into practice, to be altogether inapplicable.
Terence

Your best hope for success is that your associates aren't as good at judging you as you are at judging them.
Frank Tyger

Judge a man by his questions rather than his answers.
Voltaire

One cool judgment is worth a thousand hasty councils. The thing to do is to supply light and not heat.
Woodrow Wilson

JUSTICE

In the same degree that we overrate ourselves, we shall underrate others; for injustice allowed at home is not likely to be correct abroad.
Washington Allston

Justice is a certain rectitude of mind whereby a man does what he ought to do in the circumstances confronting him.
Thomas Aquinas

The greatest injustices proceed from those who pursue excess, not by those who are driven by necessity.
Aristotle

If we do not maintain justice, justice will not maintain us.
Francis Bacon

Above all do not ask that justice be just: It is just, because it is justice. The idea of a just justice could have originated only in the brain of an anarchist.
Honoré de Balzac

Opinions are a private matter. The public has an interest only in judgments.
Walter Benjamin

Justice! Custodian of the world! But since the world errs, justice must be custodian of the world's errors.
Ugo Betti

Justice: a commodity which in a more or less adultered condition the State sells to the citizen as a reward for his allegiance, taxes and personal service.
Ambrose Bierce

The aim of justice is to give everyone his due.
Cicero

It is a besetting vice of democracies to substitute public opinion for law. This is the usual form in which masses of men exhibit their tyranny.
James Fenimore Cooper

All are not just because they do no wrong; but he who will not wrong me when he may, he is truly just.
Richard Cumberland

There is no such thing as justice—in or out of court.
Clarence Darrow

Justice is always violent to the party offending, for each man is innocent in his own eyes.
Daniel Defoe

It is not possible to found a lasting power upon injustice, perjury, and treachery.
Demosthenes

A man is a little thing while he works by and for himself; but when he gives voice to the rules of love and justice, he is godlike.
Ralph Waldo Emerson

There is no such thing as justice in the abstract; it is merely a compact between men.
Epicurus

It is impossible to find twelve fair men in all the world.
W.C. Fields

Most everyone wants to do what's fair, right, and good, but knowing what is often the tough part.
Malcolm Forbes

Justice is as strictly due between neighbor nations as between neighbor citizens.
Benjamin Franklin

Justice delayed, is justice denied.
William E. Gladstone

If we are to keep our democracy, there must be one commandment: Thou shalt not ration justice.
Learned Hand

We ought always to deal justly, not only with those who are just to us, but likewise to those who endeavor to injure us; and this, for fear lest by rendering them evil for evil, we should fall into the same vice.
Hierocles

If you study the history and records of the world, you must admit that the source of justice was the fear of injustice.
Horace

Mankind are always found prodigal both of blood and treasure in the maintenance of public justice.
David Hume

Justice should remove the bandage from her eyes long enough to distinguish between the vicious and the unfortunate.
Robert Ingersoll

Thus saith the Lord: Execute ye justice and righteousness, and deliver the spoiled out of the hand of the oppressor: and do no wrong, do no violence to the stranger, the fatherless, nor the widow, neither shed innocent blood in this place.
Jeremiah 22:3

Nobody is poor unless he stands in need of justice.
Lactantius

Injustice is relatively easy to bear; what stings is justice.
H.L. Mencken

If mankind does not relinquish at once, and forever, its vain, mad and fatal dream of justice, the world will lapse into barbarism.
George Moore

Justice is the insurance we have on our lives, and obedience is the premium we pay for it.
William Penn

To heal the breach between the rich and the poor, it is necessary to distinguish between justice and charity.
Pope Pius X

Charity cannot take the place of justice unfairly withheld.
Pope Pius XI

Justice is a faculty that may be developed. This development is what constitutes the education of the human race.
P.J. Proudhon

No cause is hopeless if it is just. Errors, no matter how popular, carry the seeds of their own destruction.
John W. Scoville

Justice is conscience, not a personal conscience but a conscience of the whole of humanity. Those who clearly recognize the voice of their own conscience usually recognize also the voice of justice.
Alexander Solzhenitsyn

There is a point at which even justice does injury.
Sophocles

The rain falls upon the just and the unjust alike; a thing which would not happen if I were superintending the

rain's affairs. No, I would rain softly and sweetly on the just, but if I caught a sample of the unjust outdoors I would drown him.
Mark Twain

To withdraw ourselves from the law of the strong, we have found ourselves obliged to submit to justice. Justice or might, we must choose between these two masters.
Marquis de Vauvenargues

It is better to risk saving a guilty man than to condemn an innocent one.
Voltaire

Justice is the great interest of man on earth. It is a ligament which holds civilized beings and civilized nations together.
Daniel Webster

Judging from the main portions of the history of the world, so far, justice is always in jeopardy.
Walt Whitman

One should always play fairly when one has the winning cards.
Oscar Wilde

Has justice ever grown in the soil of absolute power? Has not justice always come from the ... heart and spirit of men who resist power?
Woodrow Wilson

The nature of men and of organized society dictates the maintenance in every field of action of the highest and purest standards of justice and of right dealing. .... By justice the lawyer generally means the prompt, fair, and open application of impartial rules; but we call ours a Christian civilization, and a Christian conception of justice must be much higher. It must include sympathy and helpfulness and a willingness to forego

self-interest in order to promote the welfare, happiness, and contentment of others and of the community as a whole.
Woodrow Wilson

K

KINDNESS

Courtesy is the shortest distance between two people.
Anonymous

God is not kind to those who are not kind to others.
Arabian proverb

He who is devoid of kindness is devoid of grace.
Arabian proverb

If a man be gracious to strangers, it shows that he is a citizen of the world, and his heart is no island, cut off from other islands, but a continent that joins them.
Francis Bacon

We may scatter the seeds of courtesy and kindness about us at little expense. Some of them will fall on good ground, and grow up into benevolence in the minds of others, and all of them will bear fruit of happiness in the bosom whence they spring.
Jeremy Bentham

Kindness is a language the dumb can speak and the deaf can hear and understand.
Christian Bovée

Of all the virtues necessary to the completion of the perfect man, there is none to be more delicately implied and less ostentatiously vaunted than that of exquisite feeling or universal benevolence.
Edward Bulwer-Lytton

He who acknowledges a kindness has it still, and he who has a grateful sense of it has requited it.
Cicero

I believe in courtesy, the ritual by which we avoid hurting other people's feelings by satisfying our own egos.
Kenneth Clark

In all the affairs of life, social as well as political, courtesies of a small and trivial character are the ones which strike deepest in the grateful and appreciating heart.
Henry Clay

Amiable people, though often subject to imposition in their contact with the world, yet radiate so much of sunshine that they are reflected in all appreciative hearts.
Dorothée Deluzy

What do we live for if it is not to make life less difficult for each other?
George Eliot

To adorn our characters by the charm of an amiable nature shows at once a lover of beauty and a lover of man.
Epictetus

The prudence of the best heads is often defeated by the tenderness of the best of hearts.
Henry Fielding

Courtesy gives its owner a passport round the world. It transmutes aliens into trusting friends.
James Thomas Fields

Courtesy is doing that which nothing under the sun makes you do but human kindness. Courtesy springs from the heart; if the mind prompts the action, there is a reason; if there be a reason, it is not courtesy, for courtesy has no reason. Courtesy is good will, and good will is prompted by the heart full of love to be kind. Only the generous man is truly courteous. He gives freely without a thought of receiving anything in return.
B.C. Forbes

What one thing does the world need most today—apart, that is, from the all-inclusive thing we call righteousness? Aren't you inclined to agree that what this old world needs is just the art of being kind? Every time I visit a factory or any other large business concern, I find myself trying to diagnose whether the atmosphere is one of kindliness or the reverse. And somehow, if there is palpably lacking that spirit of kind-ness, the owners . . . have fallen short of achieving 24-carat success no matter how imposing the financial balance sheet may be.
B.C. Forbes

Contrary to the cliché, genuinely nice guys most often finish first or very near it.
Malcolm Forbes

All doors are open to courtesy.
Thomas Fuller

Kindness is the golden chain by which society is bound together.
Johann Wolfgang von Goethe

In human relationships, kindness and lies are worth a thousand truths.
Graham Greene

A man may fight fiercely to hold his own in business; but he does not need to fight to get ahead of someone in the elevator, or up the car steps, or at the post office window. And no matter how strong competition is, business and personal courtesy make it easier and pleasanter for everybody.
William H. Hamby

Kindness is the beginning and the end of the law.
Hebrew proverb

Be kind and considerate to others, depending somewhat upon who they are.
Don Herold

One difference between savagery and civilization is a little courtesy.

There's no telling what a lot of courtesy would do.
Cullen Hightower

One kind word can warm three winter months.
Japanese proverb

To act from pure benevolence is not possible for finite beings. Human benevolence is mingled with vanity, interest or some other motive.
Samuel Johnson

A part of kindness consists in loving people more than they deserve.
Joseph Joubert

Beneficence is a duty; and he who frequently practices it, and sees his benevolent intentions realized comes, at length, really to love him to whom he has done good.
Immanuel Kant

The habit of being uniformly considerate toward others will bring increased happiness to you. As you put into practice the qualities of patience, punctuality, sincerity and solicitude, you will have a better opinion of the world about you.
Grenville Kleiser

Grace is to the body what clear thinking is to the mind.
François de La Rochefoucauld

We should only affect compassion, and carefully avoid having any.
François de La Rochefoucauld

Kindness in ourselves is the honey that blunts the sting of unkindness in another.
Walter Savage Landor

I have three precious things which I hold fast and prize. The first is gentleness; the second is frugality; the third is humility, which keeps me from putting myself before others. Be gentle and you can be bold; be frugal and you can be liberal; avoid putting yourself before others and you can become a leader among men.
Lao-tzu

After years of living with the coldest realities I still believe that one reaps what one sows and that to sow kindness is the best of all investments.
Joseph W. Martin, Jr.

Benevolence is one of the distinguishing characters of man.
Mencius

Grace is indeed required to turn a man into a saint; and he who doubts this does not know what either a man or a saint is.
Blaise Pascal

I expect to pass through life but once. If, therefore, there be any kindness I can show, or any good thing I can do to any fellow-being, let me do it now, and not

defer or neglect it, as I shall not pass this way again.
William Penn

Let me hear thy loving-kindness in the morning; for in thee do I trust: cause me to know the way wherein I should walk; for I lift up my soul unto thee.
Psalms 143:8

The principle of liberty and equality, if coupled with mere selfishness, will make men only devils, each trying to be independent that he may fight only for his own interest. And here is the need of religion and its power, to bring in the principle of benevolence and love to men.
John Randolph

The last, best fruit which comes to late perfection, even in the kindliest soul, is tenderness toward the hard, forbearance toward the unforbearing, warmth of heart toward the cold, philanthropy toward the misanthropic.
Jean Paul Richter

Gentle to others, to himself severe.
Samuel Rogers

Human kindness has never weakened the stamina or softened the fiber of a free people. A nation does not have to be cruel to be tough.
Franklin D. Roosevelt

Guard within yourself that treasure kindness. Know how to give without hesitation, how to lose without regret, how to acquire without meanness.
George Sand

Among the qualities of mind and heart which conduce to worldly success, there is one, the importance of which is more real, and which is generally underrated in our day. . . . It is courtesy.
Herbert Schiffer

Kindness works simply and perseveringly; it produces no strained relations which prejudice its working; strained relations which already exist it relaxes. Mistrust and misunderstanding it puts to flight, and it strengthens itself by calling forth answering kindness. Hence it is the furthest reaching and the most effective of all forces.
Albert Schweitzer

I had rather never receive a kindness than never bestow one.
Seneca

Wherever there is a human being there is a chance for kindness.
Seneca

Dissembling courtesy! How fine this tyrant can trickle when she wounds!
William Shakespeare

In nature there's no blemish but the mind; none can be call'd deform'd but the unkind.
William Shakespeare

What would you have? Your gentleness shall force more than your force move us to gentleness.
William Shakespeare

Compassion is the fellow-feeling of the unsound.
George Bernard Shaw

A churlish courtesy rarely comes but either for gain or falsehood.
Sir Philip Sidney

There never was any heart truly great and generous, that was not also tender and compassionate.
Robert Southey

That should be considered long which can be decided but once.
Publilius Syrus

Kindness is very indigestible. It disagrees with very proud stomachs.
William Makepeace Thackeray

Never lose a chance of saying a kind word. As Collingwood never saw a vacant place in his estate but he took an acorn out of his pocket and planted it, so deal with your compliments through life. An acorn costs nothing, but it may spread into a prodigious timber.
William Makepeace Thackeray

Kindness is the one commodity of which you should spend more than you earn.
T.N. Tiemeyer

Kindness is a language which the deaf can hear and the blind can see.
Mark Twain

High station in life is earned by the gallantry with which appalling experiences are survived with grace.
Tennessee Williams

The best portion of a good man's life is his little, nameless, unremembered acts of kindness and of love.
William Wordsworth

All values in this world are more or less questionable, but the most important thing in life is human kindness.
Yevgeny Yevtushenko

KNOWLEDGE

I find that a great part of the information I have was acquired by looking up something and finding something else on the way.
Franklin P. Adams

You are your greatest investment. The more you store in that mind of yours, the more you enrich your experience, the more people you meet, the more books you read, and the more places you visit, the greater is that investment in all that you are. Everything that you add to your peace of mind, and to your outlook upon life, is added capital that no one but yourself can dissipate.
George Matthew Adams

People who think they know it all are especially annoying to those of us who do.
Anonymous

Real knowledge, like everything else of the highest value, is not to be obtained easily. It must be worked for, studied for, thought for, and, more than all, it must be prayed for.
Thomas Arnold

What is all our knowledge worth? We do not even know what the weather will be tomorrow.
Berthold Auerbach

To wisdom belongs the intellectual apprehension of eternal things; to knowledge, the rational knowledge of temporal things.
St. Augustine

Knowledge and human power are synonymous, since the ignorance of the cause frustrates the effect.
Francis Bacon

Of true knowledge at any time, a good part is merely convenient, necessary indeed to the worker, but not to an understanding of his subject: One can judge a building without knowing where to buy the bricks; one can understand a violin sonata without knowing how to score for the instrument. The work may in fact be better understood without a knowledge of the details of its

manufacture, of attention to these tends
to distract from meaning and effect.
Jacques Barzun

It is right it should be so;
Man was made for joy and woe;
And when this we rightly know
Through the world we safely go.
William Blake

The quest for knowledge and the application of that knowledge for man's
benefit will not be denied.
Roger M. Blough

Most men believe that it would benefit
them if they could get a little from those
who have more. How much more would
it benefit them if they would learn a little
from those who know more.
William J.H. Boetcker

What a man knows should find expression in what he does. The chief value of
superior knowledge is that it leads to a
performing manhood.
Christian Bovée

Every branch of knowledge which a good
man possesses, he may apply to some
good purpose.
Claudius Buchanan

A little knowledge is a dangerous thing,
but a little want of knowledge is also a
dangerous thing.
Samuel Butler

One of the principal challenges of our
world to the individual is that he must
not only achieve a fairly high degree
of specialization to make him a useful
member of society, but at the same time
achieve enough general knowledge to
enable him to look with sympathy and
understanding on what is going on about
him.
Oliver J. Caldwell

If you don't realize there is always somebody who knows how to do something
better than you, then you don't give
proper respects for others' talents.
Hortense Canady

I've learned one thing—people who
know the least anyways seem to know it
the loudest.
Andy Capp

In every object there is inexhaustible
meaning; the eye sees in it what the eye
brings means of seeing.
Thomas Carlyle

Do not try to entrap others with your
haughty knowledge. To your wide
surprise, they will entrap you with their
lengthy ignorance.
Sri Chinmoy

Knowledge is the only instrument of
production that is not subject to diminishing returns.
J.M. Clark

Pleasure is a shadow, wealth is vanity,
and power a pageant; but knowledge
is ecstatic in enjoyment, perennial in
frame, unlimited in space and indefinite
in duration.
DeWitt Clinton

The worth and value of knowledge is in
proportion to the worth and value of its
object.
Samuel Taylor Coleridge

To know what we know what we know,
and that we do not know what we do not
know, that is true knowledge.
Confucius

Each new development starts from
something else. It does not come out of a
blue sky. You make use of that which has

already entered the mind. . . . That is the real reason for accumulating knowledge.
Robert P. Crawford

A greater poverty than that caused by lack of money is the poverty of unawareness. Men and women go about the world unaware of the beauty, the goodness, the glories in it. Their souls are poor. It is better to have a poor pocketbook than to suffer from a poor soul.
Thomas Dreier

Herein lies the tragedy of the age: not that men are poor—all men know something of poverty; not that men are wicked—who is good? Not that men are ignorant—what is truth? Nay, but that men know so little of men.
W.E.B. DuBois

Knowledge is the eye of desire and can become the pilot of the soul.
Will Durant

Knowledge—full, unfettered knowledge of its own heritage, of freedom's enemies, of the whole world of men and ideas— this knowledge is a free people's surest strength.
Dwight D. Eisenhower

To each individual the world will take on a different connotation of meaning—the important lies in the desire to search for an answer.
T.S. Eliot

Knowledge is the antidote to fear.
Ralph Waldo Emerson

Men of vision caught glimpses of truth and beauty shining aloft like stars: and in these glimpses was a new hope for the unification of mankind through enlightenment.
Sir Robert Falconer

Experts kill me. Economic experts, that is. Corporations, foundations, publications and governments pay them by the bucketful, and they fill buckets with forecasts that change more frequently than white-collar workers do shirts. What Lies Ahead is the usual title. What Lies would often be more appropriate. If women's hemlines changed as rapidly as an economist's forecasts, the fashion people and the textile industry would be more profitable than any other. In fact, if all the country's economists were laid end to end, they still wouldn't reach a conclusion.
Malcolm Forbes

If you don't know, it's not always necessary to admit it.
Malcolm Forbes

Those who act as if they know more than their boss seldom do.
Malcolm Forbes

If money is your only hope for independence, you will never have it. The only real security that a man can have in this world is a reserve of knowledge, experience and ability.
Henry Ford

It is well for the heart to be naïve and for the mind not to be.
Anatole France

If a man empties his purse into his head, no one can take it away from him. An investment in knowledge always pays the best interest.
Benjamin Franklin

The saying that knowledge is power is not quite true. Used knowledge is power, and more than power. It is money, and service, and better living for our fellow-men, and a hundred other good

things. But mere knowledge, left unused, has not power in it.
Dr. Edward E. Free

If you have knowledge, let others light their candles at it.
Margaret Fuller

Knowledge is a treasure but practice is the key to it.
Thomas Fuller

Knowledge and courage take turns at greatness.
Baltasar Gracián

Infinite toil would not enable you to sweep away a mist; but by ascending a little you may often look over it altogether.
Arthur Helps

Who is so deaf or so blind as is he that willfully will neither hear nor see?
John Heywood

The best part of our knowledge is that which teaches us where knowledge leaves off and ignorance begins.
Oliver Wendell Holmes

An expert is a man who knows just that much more about his subject than his associates. Most of us are nearer the top than we think. We fail to realize how easy it is, how necessary it is to learn that fraction more.
William N. Hutchins

If a little knowledge is dangerous, where is the man who has so much as to be out of danger?
Thomas H. Huxley

If you love knowledge, you will be a master of knowledge. What you have come to know, pursue by exercise; what you have not learned, seek to add to your knowledge, for it is as reprehensible to

hear a profitable saying and not grasp it as to be offered a good gift by one's friends and not accept it. Believe that many precepts are better than much wealth, for wealth quickly fails us, but precepts abide through all time.
Isocrates

There is no substitute for accurate knowledge. Know yourself, know your business, know your men.
Randall Jacobs

Man is fed with fables through life, and leaves it in the belief he knows something of what has been passing, when in truth he knows nothing but what has passed under his own eyes.
Thomas Jefferson

See everything. Overlook a great deal, improve a little.
Pope John XXIII

Having harvested all the knowledge and wisdom we can from our mistakes and failures, we should put them behind us and go ahead, for vain regretting interferes with the flow of power into our own personalities.
Edith Johnson

Knowledge always desires increase, it is like fire, which must first be kindled by some external agent, but which will afterwards propagate itself.
Samuel Johnson

A desire of knowledge is the natural feeling of mankind; and every human being whose mind is not debauched will be willing to give all that he has to get knowledge.
Samuel Johnson

All wish to possess knowledge, but few, comparatively speaking, are willing to pay the price.
Juvenal

A business man's judgment is no better than his information.
R.P. Lamont

Those who know do not tell; those who tell do not know.
Lao-tzu

The only people who achieve much are those who want knowledge so badly that they seek it while the conditions are still unfavorable. Favorable conditions never come.
C.S. Lewis

Within the next few years—a decade perhaps—we should be in a position to unlock new knowledge about life and matter so great that wholly new concepts of human life will follow in the wake of this new knowledge.
David E. Lilienthal

The improvement of the understanding is for two ends; first, our own increase of knowledge; secondly, to enable us to deliver that knowledge to others.
John Locke

It is not lawful or proper for you to know everything.
Lucian

Man can never plumb the depths of his own being; his image is not to be discovered in the extent of the knowledge he acquires but in the questions he asks.
André Malraux

It is well when the wise and the learned discover new truths; but how much better to diffuse the truths already discovered amongst the multitudes. Every addition to true knowledge is an addition to human power; and while a philosopher is discovering one new truth, millions of truths may be propagated amongst the people. . . . The whole land must be watered with the streams of knowledge.
Horace Mann

Solitary reading will enable a man to stuff himself with information, but without conversation his mind will become like a pond without an outlet—a mass of unhealthy stag-nature. It is not enough to harvest knowledge by study; the wind of talk must winnow it and blow away the chaff. Then will the clear, bright grains of wisdom be garnered, for our own use or that of others.
William Matthews

As the age of information demands the simultaneous use of all our faculties, we discover that we are most at leisure when we are most intensely involved.
Marshall McLuhan

"Know thyself" is a good saying, but not in all situations. In many it is better to say "Know others."
Menander

Sin, guilt, neurosis—they are one and the same, the fruit of the tree of knowledge.
Henry Miller

We can be knowledgeable with other men's knowledge, but we cannot be wise with other men's wisdom.
Michel de Montaigne

It is not so important to know everything as to know the exact value of everything, to appreciate what we learn and to arrange what we know.
Hannah More

If I have seen farther than others, it is because I have stood on the shoulders of giants.
Sir Isaac Newton

We don't see things as they are, we see things as we are.
Anaïs Nin

The highest purpose of intellectual cultivation is to give a man a perfect knowledge and mastery of his own inner self.
Novalis

Is anyone educated in whom the powers of conscious reasoning are untrained or undeveloped, however great may be the store of accumulated knowledge?
Joseph H. Odell

It is much better to know something about everything than to know everything about one thing.
Blaise Pascal

You can't see clearly if you insist on smoking up your glasses.
Amos Parrish

The cloak of naiveté was the uniform of our success: we didn't know it couldn't be done.
Mark Peters

All knowledge that is divorced from justice must be called cunning.
Plato

Yea, if thou criest after knowledge, and liftest up thy voice for understanding; if thou seekest her as silver, and searchest for her as for hid treasures: Then shalt thou understand the fear of the Lord, and find the knowledge of God.
Proverbs 2:3–5

What harm is there in getting knowledge and learning, were it from a sot, a pot, a fool, a winter mitten or an old slipper?
François Rabelais

Whether you know the shape of a pebble or the structure of a solar system, the axioms remain the same: that it exists and that you know it.
Ayn Rand

Try to put well in practice what you already know; and in so doing, you will in good time, discover the hidden things you now inquire about. Practice what you know, and it will help to make clear what now you do not know.
Rembrandt

Useful knowledge is a great support for intuition.
Charles B. Rogers

There is much pleasure to be gained from useless knowledge.
Bertrand Russell

Whoever acquires knowledge but does not practice it is as one who ploughs but does not sow.
Sa'di

A grain of real knowledge, of genuine controllable conviction, will outweigh a bushel of adroitness; and to produce persuasion there is one golden principle of rhetoric not put down in the books—to understand what you are talking about.
John Seeley

It is better to have useless knowledge than to know nothing.
Seneca

Consultant: an ordinary guy more than 50 miles from home.
Eric Sevareid

The things most people want to know about are usually none of their business.
George Bernard Shaw

We don't live in a world of reality, we live in a world of perceptions.
Gerald J. Simmons

In all living there is a certain narrowness of application which leads to breadth and power. We have to concentrate on a thing in order to master it. Then we must be broad enough not to be narrowed by our specialties.
Ralph W. Sockman

When a man's knowledge is not in order, the more of it he has the greater will be his confusion.
Herbert Spencer

We cannot hold a torch to light another's path without brightening our own.
Ben Sweetland

Knowledge comes by eyes always open and working hands, and there is no knowledge that is not power.
Jeremy Taylor

I said that an expert was a fella who was afraid to learn anything new because then he wouldn't be an expert anymore.
Harry S Truman

Information appears to stew out of me naturally, like the precious ottar of roses out of the otter.
Mark Twain

Though completely armed with knowledge and endowed with power, we are blind and impotent in a world we have equipped and organized—a world of which we now fear the inextricable complexity.
Paul Valéry

Any piece of knowledge I acquire today has a value at this moment exactly proportional to my skill to deal with it. Tomorrow, when I know more, I recall that piece of knowledge and use it better.
Mark Van Doren

The color of the object illuminated partakes of the color of that which illuminates it.
Leonardo da Vinci

Everything is explained now. We live in an age when you say casually to somebody, "What's the story on that?" and they can run to the computer and tell you within five seconds. That's fine, but sometimes I'd just as soon continue wondering. We have a deficit of wonder right now.
Tom Waits

It is the glorious prerogative of the empire of knowledge that what it gains it never loses. On the contrary, it increases by the multiple of its own power: all its ends become means; all its attainments help to new conquests.
Daniel Webster

Evil being the root of mystery, pain is the root of knowledge.
Simone Weil

In the scientific world I find just that disinterested devotion to great ends that I hope will spread at last through the entire range of human activity.
H.G. Wells

There are two ways of spreading light: to be the candle or the mirror that reflects it.
Edith Wharton

There is a thing called knowledge of the world which people do not have until they are middle aged. It is something which cannot be taught to younger people because it is not logical and does not obey laws which are constant. It has no rules.
Theodore H. White

In the advance of civilization, it is new knowledge which paves the way, and the pavement is eternal.
W.R. Whitney

Someone who knows too much finds it hard not to lie.
Ludwig Wittgenstein

L

LABOR

Not only is there no God, but try getting a plumber on weekends.
Woody Allen

Don't condescend to unskilled labor. Try it for half a day first.
Brooks Atkinson

Labor is one of the processes by which A acquires property for B.
Ambrose Bierce

Such hath it been—shall be—beneath the sun: The many still must labor for the one.
Lord Byron

There is no more dreadful punishment than futile and hopeless labor.
Albert Camus

The true epic of our times is not arms and the man, but tools and the man, an infinitely wider kind of epic.
Thomas Carlyle

Labor is discovered to be the grand conqueror, enriching and building up nations more surely than the proudest battles.
William Ellery Channing

When you put on your clothes, remember the weaver's labor; when you take your daily food, remember the husbandman's work.
Chinese proverb

Therefore, my beloved brethren, be ye steadfast, immovable, always abounding in the work of the Lord, forasmuch as ye know that your labor is not in vain in the Lord.
I Corinthians 15:58

If you're in the contracting business in this country, you're suspect. If you're in the contracting business in New Jersey, you're indictable. If you're in the contracting business in New Jersey and are Italian, you're convicted.
Ray Donovan

If I would be a young man again and had to decide how to make my living, I would not try to become a scientist or scholar or teacher. I would rather choose to be a plumber or a peddler in hope to find that modest degree of independence still available under present circumstances.
Albert Einstein

The best investment is in the tools of one's own trade.
Benjamin Franklin

Labor disgraces no man; unfortunately, you occasionally find men who disgrace labor.
Ulysses S. Grant

The dignity of labor depends not on what you do, but how you do it.
Edwin Osgood Grover

The strike is the weapon of the industrial jungle.
Sidney Hillman

Take not from the mouth of labor the bread it has earned.
Thomas Jefferson

Excellence, in any department, can now be attained only by the labor of a lifetime. It is not purchased at a lesser price.
Samuel Johnson

He that never labors may know the pains of idleness, but not the pleasures.
Samuel Johnson

Labor's face is wrinkled with the wind, and swarthy with the sun.
Samuel Johnson

Genius begins great works; labor alone finishes them.
Joseph Joubert

Without labor there is no rest, nor without fighting can the victory be won.
Thomas à Kempis

If work was a good thing the rich would have it all and not let you do it.
Elmore Leonard

As labor is the common burden of our race, so the effort of some to shift their share of the burden onto the shoulders of others is the great durable curse of the race.
Abraham Lincoln

Cheap labor is never cheap for the person who performs it.
Audre Lorde

Blessed is the land that has a labor question.
David Lubin

Take the tools in hand and carve your own best life.
Douglas Lurton

A coin earned by manual labor is worth more than all the revenue the Prince of Captivity derives from gifts.
Maimonides

Labor is a pleasure in itself.
Marcus Manilius

Labor is the divine law of our existence; repose is desertion and suicide.
Giuseppe Mazzini

Toil is man's allotment; toil of brain, or toil of hands, or a grief that's more than either, the grief and sin of idleness.
Herman Melville

I suspect that American workers have come to lack a work ethic. They do not live by the sweat of their brow.
Kiichi Miyazawa

Labor is rest from the sorrows that greet us; from all the petty vexations that meet us; from the sin-promptings that assail us; from the world-sirens that lure us to ill.
Francis S. Osgood

The lottery of honest labor, drawn by time, is the only one whose prizes are worth taking up and carrying home.
Theodore W. Parker

Nothing is denied to well-directed labor, and nothing is to be attained without it.
Joshua Reynolds

I have long been profoundly convinced that in the very nature of things, employers and employees are partners, not enemies; that their interests are common, not opposed; that in the long run the success of each is dependent upon the success of the other. If the labor movement will do its share in outlawing industrial warfare; substituting part-nership therefore; if more men of broad vision and high purpose respond to the opportunity for constructive leadership which labor unionism offers, well may it be that the trade union movement will

enjoy the glory and honor of ushering in industrial peace.
John D. Rockefeller, Jr.

We are coming to see that there should be no stifling of labor by capital, or of capital by labor; and also that there should be no stifling of labor by labor, or of capital by capital.
John D. Rockefeller, Jr.

Don't be misled into believing that somehow the world owes you a living. The boy who believes that his parents, or the government, or anyone else owes him his livelihood and that he can collect it without labor will wake up one day and find himself working for another boy who did not have that belief and, therefore, earned the right to have others work for him.
David Sarnoff

Seven months ago I could give a single command and 541,000 people would immediately obey it. Today I can't get a plumber to come to my house.
Norman Schwarzkopf III

'Tis no sin for a man to labor in his vocation.
William Shakespeare

There is no real wealth but the labor of man. Were the mountains of gold and the valleys of silver, the world would not be one grain of corn richer; not one comfort would be added to the human race.
Percy Bysshe Shelley

To travel hopefully is a better thing than to arrive, and the true success is to labor.
Robert Louis Stevenson

Ah, why should life all labor be?
Alfred, Lord Tennyson

The fruits of labor are the sweetest of all pleasures.
Luc de Vauvenargues

If you do things by the job, you are perpetually driven: the hours are scourges. If you work by the hour, you gently sail on the stream of Time, which is always bearing you on to the haven of Pay, whether you make any effort, or not.
Charles Dudley Warner

America has proved that it is practicable to elevate the mass of mankind—the laboring or lower class—to raise them to self-respect, to make them competent to act a part in the great right and the great duty of self-government; and she has proved that this may be done by education and the diffusion of knowledge. She holds out an example a thousand times more encouraging than ever was presented before to those nine-tenths of the human race who are born without hereditary fortune or hereditary rank.
Daniel Webster

Labor is the great producer of wealth; it moves all other causes.
Daniel Webster

I will not build nothing in Alaska, even my tomb.
Peter Zamarello

LANGUAGE

To break through language in order to touch life is to create or re-create the theater.
Antonin Artaud

Language is the armory of the human mind, and at once contains the trophies of its past and the weapons of its future conquests.
Samuel Taylor Coleridge

Mastery of language affords remarkable power.
Frantz Fanon

Command of English, spoken or written, ranks at the top in business. Our main product is words, so a knowledge of their meaning and spelling and pronunciation is imperative. If a man knows the language well, he can find out about all else.
William Feather

Language is the picture and counterpart of thought.
Mark Hopkins

Language is by its very nature a communal thing; that is, it expresses never the exact thing but a compromise—that which is common to you, me and everybody.
Thomas Ernest Hulme

I am always sorry when any language is lost, because languages are the pedigree of nations.
Samuel Johnson

In human relations a little language goes farther than a little of almost anything else. Whereas one language now often makes a wall, two can make a gate.
Walter V. Kaulfers

Slang is a poor man's poetry.
John Moore

The art of translation lies less in knowing the other language than in knowing your own.
Ned Rorem

England and America are two countries separated by the same language.
George Bernard Shaw

Ours is a precarious language, as every writer knows, in which the merest shadow line often separates affirmation from negation, sense from nonsense, and one sex from the other.
James Thurber

LAUGHTER

Laughter, while it lasts, slackens and unbraces the mind, weakens the faculties, and causes a kind of remissness and dissolution in all the powers of the soul.
Joseph Addison

It's wrong to suppress laughter. It goes back down and spreads to your hips.
Fred Allen

Laughter is a tranquilizer with no side effects.
Anonymous

Among those whom I like or admire, I can find no common denominator, but among those whom I love, I can: All of them make me laugh.
W.H. Auden

You grow up the day you have your first real laugh—at yourself.
Ethel Barrymore

Laughter is day, and sobriety is night; a smile is the twilight that hovers gently between both, more bewitching than either.
Henry Ward Beecher

All laughter is a muscular rigidity spasmodically relieved by involuntary twitching.
Robert Benchley

He who laughs last thinks slowest.
Bumper sticker

The man who cannot laugh is not only fit for treasons, stratagems and spoils, but

his whole life is already a treason and a stratagem.
Thomas Carlyle

If you want to make people weep, you must weep yourself. If you want to make people laugh, your face must remain serious.
Giacomo Casanova

The person who can laugh with life has developed deep roots with confidence and faith—faith in one-self, in people and in the world, as contrasted to negative ideas with distrust and discouragement.
Democritus

No man ever distinguished himself who could not bear to be laughed at.
Marie Edgeworth

He is not laughed at that laughs at himself first.
Thomas Fuller

Laugh to forget, but don't forget to laugh.
Arnold Glasow

He who laughs at everything is as big a fool as he who weeps at everything.
Baltasar Gracián

With mirth and laughter, let old wrinkles come.
Thomas Hardy

Anyone who takes himself too seriously always runs the risk of looking ridiculous; anyone who can consistently laugh at himself does not.
Vaclav Havel

I've always thought that a big laugh is a really loud noise from the soul saying, "Ain't that the truth."
Quincy Jones

There are three things which are real: God, human folly and laughter. The first two are beyond our comprehension, so we must do what we can with the third.
John F. Kennedy

A laugh is worth a hundred groans in any market.
Charles Lamb

With the fearful strain that is on me night and day, if I did not laugh I should die.
Abraham Lincoln

The freedom of any society varies proportionately with the volume of its laughter.
Zero Mostel

Man alone suffers so excruciatingly in the world that he was compelled to invent laughter.
Friedrich Wilhelm Nietzsche

Sayings designed to raise a laugh are generally untrue and never complimentary. Laughter is never far removed from derision.
Quintilian

I am forced to try to make myself laugh that I may not cry: For one or other I must do.
Samuel Richardson

The young man who has not wept is a savage, and the old man who will not laugh is a fool.
George Santayana

The cause of laughter is simply the sudden perception of the incongruity between a concept and the real project.
Arthur Schopenhauer

I am convinced that there can be no regeneration of mankind until laughter is put down.
Percy Bysshe Shelley

I am persuaded that every time a man smiles—but much more so when he laughs—it adds something to this fragment of life.
Laurence Sterne

A good laugh is sunshine in a house.
William Makepeace Thackeray

Power, money, persuasion, supplication, persecution—these can lift a colossal humbug, push it a little, weaken it a little; but only laughter can blow it to rags and atoms at a blast. Against the assault of laughter nothing can stand.
Mark Twain

In laughter there is always a kind of joyousness that is incompatible with contempt or indignation.
Voltaire

Laughter is not a bad beginning for a friendship, and it is the best ending for one.
Oscar Wilde

LAWS

Nobody has a more sacred obligation to obey the law than those who make the law.
Jean Anouilh

Laws are not invented; they grow out of circumstances.
Azarias

That law may be set down as good which is certain in meaning, just in precept, convenient in execution, agreeable to the form of government, and productive of virtue in those that live under it.
Francis Bacon

It usually takes a hundred years to make a law, and then, after it has done its work, it usually takes another hundred years to get rid of it.
Henry Ward Beecher

Laws and institutions are constantly tending to gravitate. Like clocks, they must be occasionally cleansed, and wound up, and set to true time.
Henry Ward Beecher

It is a very easy thing to devise good laws; the difficulty is to make them effective. The great mistake is that of looking upon men as virtuous, or thinking that they can be made so by laws; and consequently the greatest art of a politician is to render vices serviceable to the cause of virtue.
Lord Bolingbroke

Bad laws are the worst sort of tyranny.
Edmund Burke

There is but one law for all; namely the law which governs all law—the law of our Creator, the law of humanity, justice, equity; the law of nature and of nations.
Edmund Burke

The violation of some laws is a normal part of the behavior of every citizen.
Stuart Chase

If you have ten thousand regulations you destroy all respect for the law.
Winston Churchill

The liberty of a people consists in being governed by laws which they have made themselves, under whatsoever form it be of government; the liberty of a private man, in being master of his own time and actions, as far as may consist with the laws of God and of his country.
Abraham Cowley

Laws should be like clothes. They should be made to fit the people they are meant to serve.
Clarence Darrow

Behold, I have taught you statutes and judgments, even as the Lord my God commanded me that ye should do so in the land whither ye go to possess it.
Deuteronomy 4:5

As civilization progresses, we should improve our laws basically, not super-ficially. Many things that are lawful are highly immoral and some things which are moral are unlawful.
Henry L. Doherty

The law, in its majestic equality, forbids all men to sleep under bridges, to beg in the streets and to steal bread—the rich as well as the poor.
Anatole France

An unjust law is itself a species of violence. Arrest for its breach is more so.
Mahatma Gandhi

The more laws, the less justice.
German proverb

The Englishman walks before the law like a trained horse in a circus. He has the sense of legality in his bones, in his muscles.
Maxim Gorky

Four out of five potential litigants will settle their disputes the first day they come together, if you will put the idea of arbitration into their heads.
Moses H. Grossman

Our laws can be friendly to those who obey them, and too often useful to those who don't.
Cullen Hightower

There are not enough jails, not enough policemen, not enough law courts, to enforce a law not supported by the people.
Hubert Humphrey

Hearken unto me, my people; and give ear unto me, O my nation: for a law shall proceed from me, and I will make my judgment to rest for a light of the people.
Isaiah 51:4

The execution of the laws is more important than the making of them.
Thomas Jefferson

This book of the law shall not depart out of thy mouth; but thou shall mediate therein day and night, that thou mayest observe to do according to all that is written therein: for then thou shalt make thy way prosperous, and then thou shalt have good success.
Joshua 1:8

Morality cannot be legislated, but behavior can be regulated. Judicial decrees may not change the heart, but they can restrain the heartless.
Martin Luther King, Jr.

Of all injustice, that is the greatest which goes under the name of law, and of all sorts of tyranny the forcing of the letter of the law against the equity, is the most insupportable.
Roger L'Estrange

Let every man remember that to violate the law is to trample on the blood of his father, and to tear the charter of his own and his children's liberty. Let rever-ence for the laws be breathed by every American mother to the lisping babe that prattles on her lap; let it be written in primers, spelling books, and alma-nacs; let it be preached from the pulpit; proclaimed in the legislative halls, and

enforced in courts of justice. In short, let it become the political religion of the nation.
Abraham Lincoln

No man can be a competent legislator who does not add to an upright intention and a sound judgment a certain degree of knowledge of the subjects on which he is to legislate.
James Madison

The purpose of law is to prevent the strong always having their way.
Ovid

We are here, not because we are law-breakers; we are here in our efforts to become law-makers.
Emmeline Pankhurst

Statutes are mere milestone, telling how far yesterday's thought had traveled; and the talk of the sidewalk today is the law of the land. With us, law in nothing unless close behind it stands a warm, living public opinion.
Wendell Phillips

The law does not generate justice, the law is nothing but a declaration and application of what is already just.
Pierre J. Proudhon

No man is above the law, and no man is below it; nor do we ask any man's permission when we require him to obey it.
Theodore Roosevelt

The cornerstone of this Republic, as of all free government, is respect for and obedience to the law. Where we permit the law to be defied or evaded, whether by rich man or poor man, by black man or white, we are by just so much weakening the bonds of our civilization and increasing the chances of its overthrow, and of the substitution therefore of a

system in which there shall be violent alternations of anarchy and tyranny.
Theodore Roosevelt

It is to law alone that men owe justice and liberty. It is this salutary organ of the will of all which establishes in civil rights the natural equality between men. It is this celestial voice which dictates to each citizen the precepts of public reason, and teaches him to act according to the rules of his own judgment and not to behave inconsistently with himself. It is with this voice alone that political leaders should speak when they command.
Jean-Jacques Rousseau

Government can easily exist without law, but law cannot exist without government.
Bertrand Russell

Revolt and terror pay a price. Order and law have a cost.
Carl Sandburg

When the state is most corrupt, then laws are most multiplied.
Tacitus

Laws are always unstable unless they are founded on the manners of a nation; and manners are the only durable and resisting power in a people.
Alexis de Tocqueville

Laws are sand, customs are rock. Laws can be evaded and punishment escaped, but an openly transgressed custom brings sure punishment.
Mark Twain

A multitude of laws in a country is like a great number of physicians, a sign of weakness and malady.
Voltaire

LAWYERS

Lawsuit: A machine which you go into as a pig and come out of as a sausage.
Ambrose Bierce

If there were no bad people, there would be no good lawyers.
Charles Dickens

God works wonders now and then: Behold! A lawyer and an honest man!
Benjamin Franklin

Lawyer: The only man in whom ignorance of the law is not punished.
Elbert Hubbard

Discourage litigation. Persuade your neighbor to compromise whenever you can. As a peacemaker the lawyer has a superior opportunity of being a good man. There will still be business enough.
Abraham Lincoln

Woe unto you also, ye lawyers! for ye lade men with burdens grievous to be borne, and ye yourselves touch not the burdens with one of your fingers.
Luke 11:46

Lawyers are men who hire out their words and anger.
Martial

The minute you read something you can't understand, you can almost be sure it was drawn up by a lawyer.
Will Rogers

The lawyers' truth is not Truth, but consistency or a consistent expediency.
Henry David Thoreau

LAZINESS

By nature, man is lazy, working only under compulsion; and when he is strong we will always live, as far as he can, upon the labor or the property of the weak.
Henry Brooks Adams

Laziness grows on people; it begins in cobwebs and ends in iron chains. The more one has to do the more he is able to accomplish.
Sir Thomas Buxton

Sloth never arrived at the attainment of a good wish.
Miguel de Cervantes

The love of indolence is universal, or next to it.
Samuel Taylor Coleridge

Sloth, if it has prevented many crimes, has also smothered many virtues.
Charles Caleb Colton

Indolence is the dry rot of even a good mind and a good character; the practical uselessness of both. It is the waste of what might be a happy and useful life.
Tryon Edwards

Laziness is the one common deficiency in mankind that blocks the establishment of a perfect world in which everyone leads a happy life.
William Feather

Sloth, like rush, consumes faster than labor wears, while the key often used is always right.
Benjamin Franklin

Laziness is a secret ingredient that goes into failure. But it's only kept a secret from the person who fails.
Robert Half

The slothful man is the beggar's brother.
James Kelly

If ever this free people, if this Government itself is ever utterly demoralized,

it will come from this incessant human wriggle and struggle for office, which is but a way to live without work.
Abraham Lincoln

We make a pretext of difficulty to excuse our sloth.
Quintilian

Though you may have known clever men who were indolent, you never knew a great man who was so; and when I hear a young man spoken of as giving promise of great genius, the first question I ask about him always is, Does he work?
John Ruskin

LEADERSHIP

Leadership is the initiation and direction of endeavor in the pursuit of consequence. Anything else is criticism from janitors.
Royal Alcott

When a fellow thinks he is putting it over on the boss, the boss is not thinking of putting him over others to boss.
C.K. Anderson

Conductors of great symphony orchestras do not play every musical instrument; yet through leadership the ultimate production is an expressive and unified combination of tones.
Thomas D. Bailey

A leader is a dealer in hope.
Napoleon Bonaparte

It is hard to look up to a leader who keeps his ear to the ground.
James H. Boren

Leadership of a world-economy is an experience of power which may blind the victor to the march of history.
Fernand Braudel

There are no warlike peoples—just warlike leaders.
Ralph J. Bunche

When we think we lead we most are led.
Lord Byron

A symphony may be played by a hundred musicians responsive under the baton of a master conductor or by fifty thousand mechanics playing a blueprint score.
William J. Cameron

We are not altogether here to tolerate. We are here to resist, to control and vanquish withal.
Thomas Carlyle

While once it was the rank and file that cheered with all the partisan passions at their heights, today it is the party leaders who are cheering themselves; and all by themselves. The mob that is their audience is in one vast universal trance, thinking about something else.
G.K. Chesterton

A man who wants to lead the orchestra must turn his back on the crowd.
James Crook

I must follow the people. Am I not their leader?
Benjamin Disraeli

A leader of men must make decisions quickly; be independent; act and stand firm; be a fighter; speak openly, plainly, frankly; make defeats his lessons; co-operate; co-ordinate; use the best of any alliances or allies; walk with active faith courageously toward danger or the unknown; create a staff; know, love and represent the best interests of his followers; be loyal, true, frank and faithful; reward loyalty; have a high, intelligent and worthy purpose and ideal.

Do justice; love mercy; fear no man but fear only God.
John W. Dodge

You do not lead by hitting people over the head—that's assault, not leadership.
Dwight D. Eisenhower

A good man likes a hard boss. I don't mean a nagging boss or a grouchy boss. I mean a boss who insists on things being done right and on time; a boss who is watching things closely enough so that he knows a good job from a poor one. Nothing is more discouraging to a good man than a boss who is not on the job, and who does not know whether things are going well or badly.
William Feather

No one's a leader if there are no followers.
Malcolm Forbes

The question "Who ought to be boss?" is like asking "Who ought to be the tenor in the quartet?" Obviously, the man who can sing tenor.
Henry Ford

If you command wisely, you'll be obeyed cheerfully.
Thomas Fuller

If the modern leader doesn't know the facts, he is in grave trouble, but rarely do the facts provide unqualified guidance.
John W. Gardner

Leaders of men are later remembered less for the usefulness of what they have achieved than for the sweep of their endeavors.
Charles de Gaulle

The great leaders have always stage-managed their effects.
Charles de Gaulle

Real leaders are ordinary people with extraordinary determinations.
John Seaman Garns

The business world reaches out for and rewards leaders who can relegate and delegate.
Arnold Glasow

Faith in the ability of a leader is of slight service unless it be united with faith in his justice.
George W. Goethals

Those who can command themselves command others.
William Hazlitt

Just as the real basics of human nature do not change from one generation to another, so the real basics of human leadership do not change from one leader to another—from one field to the next—but remain always and everywhere the same.
William E. Holler

The weaknesses of the many make the leader possible.
Elbert Hubbard

He that entereth not by the door into the sheep-fold, but climbeth up some other way, the same is a thief and a robber. But he that entereth in by the door is the shepherd of the sheep.
John 10:1–2

The final test of a leader is that he leaves behind him in other men the conviction and the will to carry on.
Walter Lippmann

A person under the firm persuasion that he can command resources virtually has them.
Livy

There is nothing more difficult to take in hand, more perilous to conduct, or more

uncertain in its success than to take the lead in the introduction of a new order of things.
Niccolò Machiavelli

In the birth of societies it is the chiefs of states who give it its special character; and afterward it is this special character that forms the chiefs of state.
Montesquieu

Big shots are little shots who kept shooting.
Christopher Morley

The character and qualifications of the leader are reflected in the men he selects, develops and gathers around him. Show me the leader and I will know his men. Show me the men and I will know their leader. Therefore, to have loyal, efficient employees—be a loyal and efficient employer.
Arthur W. Newcomb

Thou seekest disciples? Then thou seekest ciphers.
Friedrich Wilhelm Nietzsche

I wonder if there is anyone in the world who can really direct the affairs of the world, or of his country, with any assurance of the result his actions would have.
Montagu C. Norman

A great leader never sets himself above his followers except in carrying responsibilities.
Jules Ormont

Leadership appears to be the art of getting others to want to do something you are convinced should be done.
Vance Packard

In any series of elements to be controlled, a selected small fraction, in terms of numbers of elements, always accounts for a large fraction in terms of effect.
Vilfredo Pareto

The best leaders are those most interested in surrounding themselves with assistants and associates smarter than they are—being frank in admitting this—and willing to pay for such talents.
Amos Parrish

A leader has two important characteristics; first, he is going somewhere; second, he is able to persuade other people to go with him.
Maximilien François Robespierre

It's a terrible thing to look over your shoulder when you are trying to lead—and find no one there.
Franklin D. Roosevelt

People ask the difference between a leader and a boss. . . . The leader works in the open and the boss in covert. The leader leads and the boss drives.
Theodore Roosevelt

In a society safe and worthy to be free, teaching which produces a willingness to led, as well as a willingness to follow, must be given to all.
William F. Russell

True leadership stems from individuality that is honestly and sometimes imperfectly expressed. Leaders should strive for authenticity over perfection.
Sheryl Sandberg

We cannot all be masters.
William Shakespeare

What you cannot enforce, do not command.
Sophocles

Reason and judgment are the qualities of a leader.
Tacitus

A man is rich in proportion to the number of things which he can afford to let alone.
Henry David Thoreau

Leadership is the ability to get men to do what they don't want to do and like it.
Harry S Truman

The right of commanding is no longer an advantage transmitted by nature; like an inheritance, it is the fruit of labors, the price of courage.
Voltaire

I say no body of men are fit to make Presidents, judges and generals, unless they themselves supply the best specimens of the same; and that supplying one or two such specimens illuminates the whole body for a thousand years.
Walt Whitman

Produce great men, the rest follows.
Walt Whitman

LEARNING

I find that a great part of the information I have was acquired by looking up something and finding something else on the way.
Franklin P. Adams

They know enough who know how to learn.
Henry Adams

The truth of it is, learning, like traveling and all other methods of improvement, as if finishes good sense, so it makes a silly man ten thousand times more insufferable by supplying variety of matter to his impertinence, and giving him an opportunity of abounding in absurdities.
Joseph Addison

Learning is a treasury whose keys are queries.
Arabian proverb

To think of learning as a preparation for something beyond learning is a defeat of the process. The most important attitude that can be formed is that of desire to go on learning.
Daniel Bell

Some will never learn anything because they understand everything too soon.
Thomas Blount

If you want to earn more—learn more. If you want to get more out of the world you must put more into the world. For, after all, men will get no more out of life than they put into it.
William J.H. Boetcker

It is some compensation for great evils that they enforce great lessons.
Christian Bovée

Never seem wiser or more learned than the company you are with. Treat your learning like a watch and keep it hidden. Do not pull it out to count the hours, but give the time when you are asked.
Lord Chesterfield

Wear your learning, like your watch, in a private pocket. Do not pull it out merely to show that you have one. If asked what o'clock it is, tell it; but do not proclaim it hourly and unasked, like the watchman.
Lord Chesterfield

The man who has ceased to learn ought not to be allowed to wander around loose in these dangerous days.
M.M. Coady

Learning consists of ideas, and not of the noise that is made by the mouth.
William Cobbett

He who learns but does not think is lost, he who thinks but does not learn is in danger.
Confucius

Seeing much, suffering much and studying much, are the three pillars of learning.
Benjamin Disraeli

It is the studying that you do after your school days that really counts. Otherwise, you know only that which everyone else knows.
Henry L. Doherty

In every man there is something wherein I may learn of him, and in that I am his pupil.
Ralph Waldo Emerson

Whoso neglects learning in his youth loses the past and is dead for the future.
Euripides

As long as learning is connected with earning, as long as certain jobs can only be reached through exams, so long must we take the examination system seriously. If another ladder to employment was contrived, much so-called education would disappear, and no one would be a penny the stupider.
E.M. Forster

We have an infinite amount to learn both from nature and from each other.
John Glenn

Go to the place where the thing you wish to know is native; your best teacher is there. Where the thing you wish to know is so dominant that you must breathe its very atmosphere, there teaching is most thorough and learning is most easy. You acquire a language most readily in the country where it is spoken; you study mineralogy best among miners; and so with everything else.
Johann Wolfgang von Goethe

We are all, it seems, saving ourselves for the Senior Prom. But many of us forget that somewhere along the way we must learn to dance.
Alan Harrington

To stay young requires unceasing cultivation of the ability to unlearn of falsehoods.
Robert A. Heinlein

The love of learning and the love of money rarely meet.
George Herbert

The sweetest and most inoffensive path of life leads through the avenues of science and learning; and whoever can either remove any obstruction in this way, or open up any new prospect, ought, so far, to be esteemed a benefactor to mankind.
David Hume

He who devotes 16 hours a day to hard study may become as wise at 60 as he thought himself at 20.
Mary Little

None of the things children are to learn should ever be made a burden to them, or imposed on them as a task. Whatever is so imposed presently becomes irksome; the mind takes an aversion to it, though before it were a thing of delight.
John Locke

There is no easy method of learning difficult things. The method is to close the door, give out that you are not at home, and work.
Joseph de Maistre

In this age, which believes that there is a shortcut to everything, the greatest lesson to be learned is that the most difficult way is, in the long run, the easiest.
Henry Miller

One pound of learning requires ten pounds of commonsense to apply it.
Persian proverb

A wise man will hear, and will increase learning; and a man of understanding shall attain unto wise counsels.
Proverbs 1:5

Learning makes the wise wiser and the fool more foolish.
John Ray

No man is the wiser for his learning: It may administer matter to work in or objects to work upon; but wit and wisdom are born with a man.
John Selden

The more we study, the more we discover our ignorance.
Percy Bysshe Shelley

Learning, like money, may be of so base a coin as to be utterly void of use; or, if sterling, may require good management to make it serve the purposes of sense or happiness.
William Shenstone

If it is sensible for the child to make an effort to learn how to be an adult, then it is essential for the adult to learn how to be aged.
Edward Stieglitz

Learning is either a continuing thing or it is nothing.
Frank Tyger

The purpose of learning to employ every minute properly is to unclutter our hours, deliver us of feverish activity and earn us true leisure.
Robert R. Updegraff

Have you learned lessons only of those who admired you, and were tender with you, and stood aside for you? Have you not learned great lessons from those who rejected you, and braced themselves against you, or disputed the passage with you?
Walt Whitman

Our task as we grow older in a rapidly advancing science, is to retain the capacity of joy in discoveries which correct older ideas, and to learn from our pupils as we teach them.
Hans Zinsser

LEISURE

You can go to doctors until the last cow has been placed in its shed. You can journey the earth in search of peace of mind. You can experiment with a dozen theories, hoping for a relief from worries, or the problems which beset you, but unless you learn to relax you will end up disappointed. Tension is a killer! Just relax and note the immediate effect. One of peace and ease of mind. One in which every organ of the body joins. In relaxation there is unity of mind, body and spirit.
George Matthew Adams

I am never less at leisure than when at leisure, nor less alone than when I am alone.
Scipio Africanus

How many inner resources one needs to tolerate a life of leisure without fatigue.
Natalie Clifford Barney

If I am doing nothing, I like to be doing nothing to some purpose. That is what leisure means.
Alan Bennett

Leisure may prove to be a curse rather than a blessing, unless education teaches a flippant world that leisure is not a synonym for entertainment.
William J. Bogan

Let the world have whatever sports and recreations please them best, provided they be followed with discretion.
Richard Burton

Men cannot labor on always. They must have recreation.
Orville Dewey

Increased means and increased leisure are the two civilizers of man.
Benjamin Disraeli

Don't expect to be paid a dollar an hour for your working hours when you then use your leisure hours as though they were not worth five cents a dozen.
Henry L. Doherty

Many concerns now make part or the whole of their dividends from by-products that formerly went to waste. How do we, as individuals, utilize our principal by-product? Our principal by-product is, of course, our leisure time. Many years of observation forces the conclusion that a man's success or failure in life is determined as much by how he acts during his leisure as by how he acts during his work hours. Tell me how a young man spends his evenings and I will tell you how he is likely to spend the latter part of his life.
B.C. Forbes

Employ thy time well if thou meanest to gain leisure.
Benjamin Franklin

The time to relax is when you don't have time for it.
Sydney J. Harris

There is room enough in human life to crowd almost every art and science in it. If we pass "no day without a line"—visit no place without the company of a book—we may with ease fill libraries or empty them of their contents. The more we do, the more busy we are, the more leisure we have.
William Hazlitt

He who cannot dance puts the blame on the floor.
Hindu proverb

Leisure is the mother of philosophy.
Thomas Hobbes

The right use of leisure is no doubt a harder problem than the right use of our working hours. The soul is dyed the color of its leisure thoughts. As a man thinketh in his heart so is he.
Dean Inge

All intellectual improvement arises from leisure.
Samuel Johnson

It is that unoccupied space which makes a room habitable, as it is our leisure hours which make life endurable.
Lin Yutang

He that will make good use of any part of his life must allow a large part of it to recreation.
John Locke

If the world were not so full of people, and most of them did not have to work so hard, there would be more time for them to get out and lie on the grass, and there would be more grass for them to lie on.
Don Marquis

I would not exchange my leisure hours for all the wealth in the world.
Honoré de Mirabeau

They know but little of society who think we can bear to be always employed, either in duties or meditation, without relaxation.
Hannah More

I would live all my life in nonchalance and insouciance, were it not for making a living, which is rather a nouciance.
Ogden Nash

Make thy recreation servant to thy business, lest thou become a slave to thy recreation.
Francis Quarles

To be able to fill leisure intelligently is the last product of civilization.
Bertrand Russell

Who has more leisure than a worm?
Seneca

It is doing some service to humanity to amuse innocently; and they know very little of society who think we can bear to be always employed, either in duties or meditations, without any relaxation.
Sir Philip Sidney

Sit loosely in the saddle.
Robert Louis Stevenson

Recreation is nothing but a change of work—an occupation for the hands by those who live by their brains, or for the brains by those who live by their hands.
Dorothy Thompson

What the banker sighs for, the meanest clown may have—leisure and a quiet mind.
Henry David Thoreau

Every now and then go away, have a little relaxation, for when you come back to your work your judgment will be surer, since to remain constantly at work will cause you to lose power of judgment. Go some distance away, because then the work appears smaller, and more of it can be taken in at a glance, and lack of harmony and proportion is more readily seen.
Leonardo da Vinci

People who cannot find time for recreation are obliged sooner or later to find time for illness.
John Wanamaker

Be temperate in your work, but don't carry the patience over into your leisure hours.
Monty Woolley

Leisure is pain; take off our chariot wheels; how heavily we drag the load of life!
Edward Young

LIBERTY

If ye love wealth greater than liberty, the tranquility of servitude greater than the animating contest for freedom, go home from us in peace. Crouch down and lick the hand that feeds you, and may posterity forget that ye were once our countrymen.
Samuel Adams (to Tories)

A day, an hour, of virtuous liberty is worth a whole eternity in bondage.
Joseph Addison

If liberty and equality, as is thought by some, are chiefly to be found in democracy, they will be best attained when all persons alike share in the government to the utmost.
Aristotle

Liberty of speech inviteth and provoketh liberty to be used again, and so bringeth much to a man's knowledge.
Francis Bacon

The most essential mental quality for a free people, whose liberty is to be progressive, permanent, and on a large scale, is much stupidity.
Walter Bagehot

The real democratic American idea is not that every man shall be on a level with every other, but that every one shall have liberty, without hindrance, to be what God made him.
Henry Ward Beecher

Liberty is to the collective body, what health is to every individual body. Without health no pleasure can be tasted by man; without liberty, no happiness can be enjoyed by society.
Lord Bolingbroke

The people never give up their liberties but under some delusion.
Edmund Burke

The human race cannot go forward without liberty. If this be correct, then all people everywhere should strive for liberty. If they achieve liberty, they will get a chance to pursue happiness and perhaps will be able to develop toward the ultimate goal of creation.
Richard E. Byrd

Liberty is dangerous.
Albert Camus

Liberty—is one of the choicest gifts that heaven hath bestowed upon man, and exceeds in volume all the treasures which the earth contains within its bosom or the sea covers. Liberty, as well as honor, man ought to preserve at the hazard of his life, for without it, life is insupportable.
Miguel de Cervantes

No matter what the form of the government, the liberty of a people consists in being governed by laws which they have themselves made.
Abraham Cowley

The condition upon which God hath given liberty to man is eternal vigilance.
John Philpot Curran

Liberty is the most jealous and exacting mistress that can beguile the brain and soul of man. From him who will not give her all, she will have nothing. She knows that his pretended love serves but to betray. But when once the fierce heat of her quenchless, lustrous eyes has burned into the victim's heart, he will know no other smile but hers.
Clarence Darrow

Liberty is a product of order.
Will Durant

If the choice is given to us of liberty or security, we must scorn the latter with the proper contempt of free man and the sound judgment of wise men who know that liberty and security are not incompatible in the lives of honest men.
James A. Farley

Liberty will not descend to a people, a people must raise themselves to liberty; it is a blessing that must be earned before it can be enjoyed.
Benjamin Franklin

They that give up essential liberty to obtain a little temporary safety deserve neither liberty nor safety.
Benjamin Franklin

Liberty is not merely a privilege to be conferred; it is a habit to be acquired.
David Lloyd George

Some folks believe liberty is doing as they please, but with controls on others.
Arnold Glasow

If you take a worm's eye view of the ills in American life and our foreign relations; you may worry that we are entering the decline and fall of the greatest nation in history.

If you take a bird's eye view you will see the increasing skills, growing productivity, and the expansion of education and understanding, with improving health and growing strength all over our nation. And from whence came this strength? It lies in freedom of men's initiative and the rewards of their efforts. It comes from our devotion to liberty and religious faith. We will have no decline and fall of this nation, provided we stand guard against the evils which would weaken these forces.
Herbert Hoover

Liberty is a thing of the spirit—to be free to worship, to think, to hold opinions, and to speak without fear—free to challenge wrong and oppression with surety of justice.
Herbert Hoover

To those who think that liberty is a good thing, and that it may someday be possible for people to live in a society fit for free, fully human individuals, a thorough education in the nature of language, its uses and abuses, seems indispensable.
Aldous Huxley

What light is to the eyes—what air is to the lungs—what love is to the heart, liberty is to the soul of man. Without liberty, the brain is a dungeon, where the chained thoughts die with their pinions pressed against the hingeless doors.
Robert G. Ingersoll

I would rather be exposed to the inconveniences attending too much liberty than those attending too small a degree of it.
Thomas Jefferson

If ever there was a holy war, it was that which saved our liberties and gave us independence.
Thomas Jefferson

The people are the only sure reliance for the preservation of our liberty.
Thomas Jefferson

Let it be impressed upon your minds, let it be instilled into your children, that the liberty of the press is the palladium of all the civil, political, and religious rights.
Junius

Liberty without learning is always in peril, and learning without liberty is always in vain.
John F. Kennedy

In the American colonies, the main problem of liberty has been solved, demonstrated and practiced in such a manner as not to leave much to be said by European institutions.
Marquis de Lafayette

The chief end of man, as I see it, is to find security, have liberty to express his abilities, enjoy the love of family and friends, and to secure recognition of his talents, to worship God in his own way, and to participate in a government that will protect him in his exercise of these liberties, and by education and training in the development of the arts and sciences, and the techniques of their application, help him to find his proper place in the scheme of things.
C.S. Lewis

In Europe, charters of liberty have been granted by power. America has set the example, and France has followed it, of charters of power granted by liberty.
James Madison

A nation may lose its liberties in a day and not miss them in a century.
Montesquieu

To do what we will, is natural liberty; to do what we may consistently with the interests of the community to which we belong, is civil liberty, the only liberty to be desired in a state of civil society.
William Paley

There is no doubt that the real destroyer of the liberties of any people is he who spreads among them bounties, donations and largesse.
Plutarch

Liberty is not in any form of government. It is in the heart of the free man, he carries it with him everywhere.
Jean-Jacques Rousseau

A well-governed appetite is a great part of liberty.
Seneca

Liberty means responsibility. That is why most men dread it.
George Bernard Shaw

Liberty is no heirloom. It requires the daily bread of self-denial, the salt of law and, above all, the backbone of acknowledging responsibility for our deeds.
Bishop Fulton J. Sheen

If men use their liberty in such a way as to surrender their liberty, are they thereafter any the less slaves? If people by a plebiscite elect a man despot over them, do they remain free because the despotism was of their own making? Are the coercive edicts issued by him to be regarded as legitimate because they are the ultimate outcome of their own votes?
Herbert Spencer

This is the first nation that organized government on the basis of universal liberty with a free Church and a free State. This meant much at the time; it means much now and will continue to be the beacon of light and guidance for ourselves and of other nations. All that is good and practical and wise in the new developments can best be worked out under our form of government without destroying any of the basic principles upon which it rests.
Oscar S. Straus

Despotism may govern without faith, but Liberty cannot.
Alexis de Tocqueville

Liberty, in my opinion, is the only orthodoxy within the limits of which art may express itself and flourish freely—liberty that is the best of all things in the life of man, if it is all one with wisdom and virtue.
Arturo Toscanini

The contest for ages has been to rescue liberty from the grasp of executive power.
Daniel Webster

Liberty has never come from government. Liberty has always come from the subjects of it. The history of liberty is a history of resistance. The history of liberty is a history of limitations of governmental power, not the increase of it.
Woodrow Wilson

There can be no liberty that isn't earned.
Robert R. Young

LIES

A liar will not be believed, even when he speaks the truth.
Aesop

It is sometimes necessary to lie damnably in the interests of the nation.
Hilaire Belloc

Liars share with those they deceive the desire not to be deceived.
Sissela Bok

Delusions, errors and lies are like huge, gaudy vessels, the rafters of which are rotten and worm-eaten, and those who embark in them are fated to be shipwrecked.
Buddha

The best liar is he who makes the smallest amount of lying go the longest way.
Samuel Butler

Someone who always has to lie discovers that every one of his lies is true.
Elias Canetti

Some of the most frantic lies on the face of life are told with modesty and restraint; for the simple reason that only modesty and restraint will save them.
G.K. Chesterton

A lie leads a man from a grove into a jungle.
Marcelene Cox

Lying to ourselves is more deeply ingrained than lying to others.
Fyodor Dostoyevsky

Lie detectors may have some limited uses, but for sure one of them isn't in the corporate hiring process. For the CIA, the FBI, the military's superse-cret areas, lie detectors may have some psychological value. As proof positive, for sure they are not. According to a recent *New York Times* article, leading academic critics contend that lie detectors are lucky to be right 70% of the time and are often no better than chance. Pentagon officials stress that "no machine can detect a lie"; lie detectors can only detect stress, may well reflect fear, surprise or anger at the interrogation rather than guilt. . . .
Malcolm Forbes

Without lies humanity would perish of despair and boredom.
Anatole France

As hypocrisy is said to be the highest compliment to virtue, the art of lying is the strongest acknowledgment of the force of truth.
William Hazlitt

Sin has many tools, but a lie is the handle which fits them all.
Oliver Wendell Holmes

I detest the man who hides one thing in the depths of his heart and speaks forth another.
Homer

Life is a system of half-truths and lies. Opportunistic, convenient evasion.
Langston Hughes

It is more from carelessness about the truth than from intentional lying that there is so much falsehood in the world.
Samuel Johnson

Society can exist only on the basis that there is some amount of polished lying and that no one says exactly as he thinks.
Lin Yutang

No man has a good enough memory to be a successful liar.
Abraham Lincoln

He was the consummate politician; he didn't lie, neither did he tell the truth.
John Lundberg

One can be absolutely truthful and sincere even though admittedly the most outrageous liar. Fiction and invention are of the very fabric of life.
Henry Miller

Lying is a hateful and accursed vice. We have no other tie upon one another, but our word. If we did but discover the horror and consequences of it, we should pursue it with fire and sword, and more justly than other crimes.
Michel de Montaigne

The most common sort of lie is that by which a man deceives himself: the deception of others is a relatively rare offense.
Friedrich Wilhelm Nietzsche

Museums are just a lot of lies. We have infected the pictures in museums with all our stupidities, all our mistakes, all our poverty of spirit. We have turned them into petty and ridiculous things.
Pablo Picasso

A lie has always a certain amount of weight with those who wish to believe it.
E.W. Rice

Lie: A fault in a boy, an art in a lover, an accomplishment in a bachelor, and second nature in a married woman.
Helen Rowland

People lie because they don't remember clear what they saw. People lie because they can't help making a good story better than it was the way it happened.
Carl Sandburg

Sanity is a cozy lie.
Susan Sontag

A lie is an abomination unto the Lord, and a very present help in time of trouble.
Adlai Stevenson

One man lies in his work, and gets a bad reputation; another in his manners, and enjoys a good one.
Henry David Thoreau

One of the most striking differences between a cat and a lie is that a cat has only nine lives.
Mark Twain

Falsehoods not only disagree with truths, but usually quarrel among themselves.
Daniel Webster

The only form of lying that is absolutely beyond reproach is lying for its own sake.
Oscar Wilde

A half truth is a whole lie.
Yiddish proverb

LIFE

In life as in the dance, grace glides on blistered feet.
Alice Abrams

It's what each of us sows, and how, that gives us character and prestige. Seeds of kindness, goodwill, and human under-standing, planted in fertile soil, spring up into deathless friendshps, big deeds of worth, and a memory that will not soon fade out. We are all sowers of seeds—and let us never forget it!
George Matthew Adams

The goal is the same: life itself; and the price is the same; life itself.
James Agee

Our bravest and best lessons are not learned through success, but through misadventure.
Amos Bronson Alcott

It is not what he has, or even what he does which expresses the worth of a man, but what he is.
Henri Frédéric Amiel

Life is an apprenticeship to constant renunciations, to the steady failure of our claims, our hopes, our powers, our liberty.
Henri Frédéric Amiel

If you can't run with the big dogs, stay up on the porch.
Anonymous

Life is like a grindstone: Whether it grinds you down or polishes you up depends on what you're made of.
Anonymous

Life is a wonderful thing to talk about, or to read about in history books—but it is terrible when one has to live it.
Jean Anouilh

What comes with ease goes with ease.
Arabian proverb

Life is seldom as unendurable as, to judge by the facts, it ought to be.
Brooks Atkinson

In a game, just losing is almost as satisfying as just winning. In life, the loser's score is always zero.
W.H. Auden

What you are must always displease you, if you would attain to that which you are not.
St. Augustine

Man ought to know that in the theater of human life, it is only for Gods and angels to be spectators.
Francis Bacon

One of the most detestable habits of Lilliputian minds is to find their own littleness in others.
Honoré de Balzac

The only questions worth asking are whether humans are going to have any emotions tomorrow, and what the quality of life is going to be if the answer is no.
Lester Bangs

We will often find compensation if we think more of what life has given us and less about what life has taken away.
William Barclay

The life of every man is a diary in which he means to write one story, and writes another, and his humblest hour is when he compares the volume as it is with what he vowed to make it.
J.M. Barrie

We didn't all come over on the same ship, but were all in the same boat.
Bernard M. Baruch

The deeper men go into life, the deeper is their conviction that this life is not all. It is an unfinished symphony. A day may round out an insect's life, and a bird or a beast needs no tomorrow. Not so with him who knows that he is related to God and has felt the power of an endless life.
Henry Ward Beecher

The most important preliminary to the task of arranging one's life so that one may live fully and comfortably within one's daily budget of 24 hours is the calm realization of the extreme difficulty of the task, of the sacrifices and the endless effort which it demands.
Arnold Bennett

Life begets life. Energy creates energy.
It is only by spending oneself that one
becomes rich.
Sarah Bernhardt

You can observe a lot by just watching.
Yogi Berra

Before you can write a check, you must
first make out a deposit slip; before you
can draw money out of a bank, you must
put money into a bank; before you are
entitled to a living, you must give the
world a life; if you want to make a first-
class living, learn to give the world a
first-class life.
William J.H. Boetcker

It is our relation to circumstances that
determines their influence over us. The
same wind that carries one vessel into
port may blow another off shore.
Christian Bovée

The ladder of life is full of splinters,
but they always prick the hardest when
we're sliding down.
William L. Brownell

In life, as in whist, hope nothing from the
way cards may be dealt to you. Play the
cards, whatever they be, to the best of
your skill.
Edward Bulwer-Lytton

To find new things, take the path you
took yesterday.
John Burroughs

Life is the art of drawing sufficient
conclusions from insufficient premises.
Samuel Butler

There is no life of a man, faithfully
recorded, but it is a heroic poem of its
sort, rhymed or unrhymed.
Thomas Carlyle

The first man gets the oyster, the second
man gets the shell.
Andrew Carnegie

There are only two or three human
stories, and they go on repeating themselves as fiercely as if they had never
happened before.
Willa Cather

When one door is shut, another opens.
Miguel de Cervantes

Events are only the shells of ideas; and
often it is the fluent thought of ages that
is crystallized in a moment by the stroke
of a pen or the point of a bayonet.
Edwin H. Chapin

Man must sit in chair with mouth open
for very long time before roast duck fly in.
Chinese proverb

If you're a sailor, best not know how
to swim. Swimming only prolongs the
inevitable—if the sea wants you and your
time has come.
James Clavell

Despite some of the horrors and barba-
risms of modern life which appall and
grieve us, life in the twentieth century
undeniably has—or has the potentiality
of—such richness, joy and adventure as
were unknown to our ancestors except in
their dreams.
Arthur H. Compton

Life is really simple, but men insist on
making it complicated.
Confucius

Those who break down the dikes
will themselves be drowned in the
inundation.
Confucius

To take a gloomy view of life is not part
of my philosophy; to laugh at the idiocies

of my fellow creatures is. However, at this particular moment I cannot find so much to laugh at as I would like.
Noël Coward

Variety is the very spice of life, that gives it all its flavor.
William Cowper

When small men cast long shadows the sun is going down.
Vinita Cravens

A man who dares to waste one hour of life has not discovered the value of life.
Charles Darwin

Life is made up, not of great sacrifices or duties, but of little things, in which smiles and kindnesses, and small obligations, given habitually, are what win and preserve the heart and secure comfort.
Sir Humphry Davy

The real world is not easy to live in. It is rough; it is slippery. Without the most clear-eyed adjustments we fall and get crushed. A man must stay sober; not always, but most of the time.
Clarence Day

Life unexamined, is not worth living.
Democritus

Remember that life is neither pain nor pleasure; it is serious business, to be entered upon with courage and in a spirit of self-sacrifice.
Alexis de Tocqueville

To live is so startling it leaves time for little else.
Emily Dickinson

I'm not finished, because I'm still curious.
Barry Diller

The cure for anything is saltwater: sweat, tears or the sea.
Isak Dinesen

Life is too short to be little.
Benjamin Disraeli

Man is not the creature of circumstances, circumstances are the creatures of man. We are free agents, and man is more powerful than matter.
Benjamin Disraeli

Resolved, to live with all my might while I do live. Resolved, never to lose one moment of time, to improve it in the most profitable way I possibly can. Resolved, never to do anything which I should despise or think meanly of in another. Resolved, never to do anything out of revenge. Resolved, never to do anything which I should be afraid to do if it were the last hour of my life.
Jonathan Edwards

Strange is our situation here upon earth. Each of us comes for a short visit, not knowing why, yet sometimes seeming to divine a purpose.

From the standpoint of daily life, however, there is one thing we do know: that man is here for the sake of other men—above all for those upon whose smile and well-being our own happiness depends, and also for the countless unknown souls with whose fate we are connected by a bond of sympathy. Many times a day I realize how much my own outer and inner life is built upon the labors of my fellow men, both living and dead, and how earnestly I must exert myself in order to give in return as much as I have received. My peace of mind is often troubled by the depressing sense that I have borrowed too heavily from the work of other men.
Albert Einstein

The man who regards his own life and that of his fellow-creatures as meaningless is not merely unfortunate, but almost disqualified for life.
Albert Einstein

The most beautiful thing we can experience is the mysterious. It is the source of all art and science. He to whom this emotion is a stranger, who can no longer pause to wonder and stand rapt in awe, is as good as dead; his eyes are closed.
Albert Einstein

It is not half as important to burn the midnight oil as it is to be awake in the daytime.
E.W. Elmore

Try to enjoy the great festival of life with other men!
Epictetus

We do not choose our own parts in life, and have nothing to do with those parts. Our duty is confined to playing them well.
Epictetus

I envy that man who passes through life safely, to the world and fame unknown.
Euripides

For most men life is a search for a proper manila envelope in which to get themselves filed.
Clifton Fadiman

One way to get the most out of life is to look upon it as an adventure.
William Feather

The secret of prolonging life consists in not shortening it.
Ernst von Feuchtersleben

If the existence of human beings leads to nothing, what is all this comedy about?
Camille Flammarion

That which is useless dies. Animals that fail to serve some useful purpose in the scheme of things slowly but surely become extinct. Let any part of the human body cease to perform its ordained function, and it withers—as when an arm is long kept in a sling. This same decree, that nothing useless is permitted to survive, runs through the industrial world. . . . Let any concern cease to render useful service, and in time it shrivels. True, certain individuals, firms . . . may for a time appear immune. But sooner or later they pay the penalty.
B.C. Forbes

I heard one wheel describe another: "He's absolutely copeless."
Malcolm Forbes

It's great to arrive, but the trip's most always most of the fun.
Malcolm Forbes

People who can't see without glasses should wear them.
Malcolm Forbes

Since we had nothing to do with our arrival and usually are not consulted about our departure, what makes so many of us think we're entitled to so much while we're here?
Malcolm Forbes

Things there are no solution to: Inflation, bureaucracy & dandruff.
Malcolm Forbes

To live your life in the fear of losing it is to lose the point of life.
Malcolm Forbes

Every human life involves an unfathomable mystery, for man is the riddle of the universe, and the riddle of man in his endowment with personal capacities. The stars are not so strange as the mind

that studies them, analyzes their light, and measures their distance.
Harry Emerson Fosdick, D.D.

We do not know what to do with this short life, but we want another that will be eternal.
Anatole France

The eyes of other people are the eyes that ruin us. If all but myself were blind, I should want neither fine clothes, fine houses, nor fine furniture.
Benjamin Franklin

Life is half spent before one knows what it is.
French proverb

Life as we find it is too hard for us; it entails too much pain, too many disappointments, impossible tasks. We cannot do without palliative remedies.
Sigmund Freud

There is more to life than increasing its speed.
Mohandas Gandhi

We must not hope to be mowers
And to gather the ripe gold ears,
Unless we have first been sowers,
And watered the furrows with tears.
It is not just as we take it,
This mystical world of ours:
Life's field will yield as we make it,
A harvest of thorns or of flowers.
Johann Wolfgang Von Goethe

Little things are great to little men.
Oliver Goldsmith

You can preach a better sermon with your life than with your lips.
Oliver Goldsmith

Every day is a little life, and our whole life is but a day repeated. Therefore live every day as if it would be the last. Those that dare lose a day, are dangerously prodigal; those that dare misspend it are desperate.
Joseph Hall

The human question is not how many can possibly survive within the system, but what kind of existence is possible for those who do survive.
Frank Herbert

A handful of good life is better than a bushel of learning.
George Herbert

You cannot make a windmill go with a pair of bellows.
George Herbert

That man lives twice who lives the first life well.
Robert Herrick

With most men life is like backgammon— half skill and half luck.
Oliver Wendell Holmes

He is always a slave who cannot live on little.
Horace

What a folly it is to dread the thought of throwing away life at once, and yet have no regard to throwing it away by parcels and piecemeal?
John Howe

The secret of the man who is universally interesting is that he is universally interested.
William Dean Howells

Every knock is a boost.
Elbert Hubbard

I play it cool, and dig all jive, and that's the reason I stay alive.
Langston Hughes

Life, in all ranks and situations, is an outward occupation, an actual and active work.
Wilhelm von Humboldt

He is happy whose circumstances suit his temper; but he is more excellent who can suit his temper to any circumstances.
David Hume

When thou passeth through the waters, I will be with thee; and through the rivers, they shall not overflow thee: when thou walkest through the fire, thou shall not be burned; neither shall the flames kindle upon thee.
Isaiah 43:2

It's all right letting yourself go, as long as you can get yourself back.
Mick Jagger

Live all you can; it's a mistake not to. It doesn't so much matter what you do in particular, so long as you have your life. If you haven't had that, what have you had?
Henry James

The great use of life is to spend it for something that will outlast it.
William James

If this life be not a real fight, in which something is eternally gained for the universe by success, it is no better than a game of private theatricals from which one may withdraw at will.
William James

The trouble with life in the fast lane is that you get to the other end in an awful hurry.
John Jensen

Human life is everywhere a state in which much is to be endured, and little to be enjoyed.
Samuel Johnson

Life is not long, and too much of it must not pass in idle deliberation how it shall be spent.
Samuel Johnson

Novelty is indeed necessary to preserve eagerness and alacrity; but art and nature have stores inexhaustible by human intellects, and every moment produces something new to him who has quickened his faculties by diligent observation.
Samuel Johnson

The main of life is composed of small incidents and petty occurrences; of wishes for objects not remote, and grief for disappointments of no fatal consequence. . . .
Samuel Johnson

Be a life long or short, its completeness depends on what it was lived for.
David Starr Jordan

There is always some levity even in excellent minds; they have wings to rise, and also to stay.
Joseph Joubert

Welcome, O life! I go to encounter for the millionth time the reality of experience and to forge in the smithy of my soul the uncreated conscience of my race.
James Joyce

Life is truly known only to those who suffer, lose, endure adversity and stumble from defeat to defeat.
Ryszard Kapuscinski

Life is either a daring adventure or nothing.
Helen Keller

We should not lose ourselves in vainglorious schemes for changing human nature all over the planet. Rather, we should learn to view ourselves with a sense of proportion and

Christian humility before the enormous complexity of the world in which it has been given us to live.
George F. Kennan

There will always be a Frontier where there is an open mind and a willing hand.
Charles F. Kettering

Life must be lived forwards, but can only be understood backwards.
Søren Kierkegaard

Repetition is the reality and the seriousness of life.
Søren Kierkegaard

When 'Omer smote 'is bloomin' lyre,
He'd 'eard men sing by land an' sea;
An' what he thought 'e might require,
'E went and took—the same as me!
Rudyard Kipling

If you keep the turkeys out of your life, then good things can happen.
Robert Kraft

He who sleeps half a day has won half a life.
Karl Kraus

For man there are only three important events: birth, life and death; but he is unaware of being born, he suffers when he dies, and he forgets to live.
Jean de La Bruyère

Life is what happens to us while we are making other plans.
Thomas La Mance

You never know where bottom is until you plumb for it.
Frederick Laing

Not many sounds in life, and I include all urban and rural sounds, exceed in interest a knock at the door.
Charles Lamb

Life is like an echo. We get from it what we put in it and, just like an echo, it often gives us much more.
Boris Lauer-Leonardi

We never think of the main business of life till a vain repentance minds us of it at the wrong end.
Roger L'Estrange

Set your goals high; make friends with different kinds of people; enjoy simple pleasures. Stand on high ground; sit on level ground; walk on expansive ground.
Li Ka-shing

A man watches his pear tree day after day, impatient for the ripening of the fruit. Let him attempt to force the process, and he may spoil both fruit and tree. But let him patiently wait, and the ripe fruit at length falls into his lap.
Abraham Lincoln

The lowest ebb is the turn of the tide.
Henry Wadsworth Longfellow

Circumstances are the rulers of the weak; they are but the instruments of the wise.
Samuel Lover

The falling drops at last will wear the stone.
Lucretius

Life never becomes a habit to me. It's always a marvel.
Katherine Mansfield

We win half the battle when we make up our minds to take the world as we find it, including the thorns.
Orison Swett Marden

I have always had a dread of becoming a passenger in life.
Queen Margrethe II of Denmark

A good man doubles the length of his existence; to have lived so as to look back with pleasure on our past life is to live twice.
Martial

The mere lapse of years is not life. To eat, to drink, and sleep; to be exposed to darkness and the light; to pace around in the mill of habit; and turn thought into an instrument of trade—this is not life. Knowledge, truth, love, beauty, goodness, faith, alone can give vitality to the mechanism of existence.
James Martineau

The life force is vigorous. The delight that accompanies it counter-balances all the pains and hardships that confront men.
Somerset Maugham

Life, as it is called, is for most of us one long postponement.
Henry Miller

To know that which lies before us in daily life is the prime wisdom.
John Milton

There are three ingredients in the good life: learning, earning and yearning.
Christopher Morley

There is only one success: To be able to spend your life in your own way.
Christopher Morley

The great business of life is to be, to do, to do without and to depart.
John Morley

Not on one string are all life's jewels strung.
William Morris

Hark, now hear the sailors cry, smell the sea and feel the sky, let your soul and spirit fly into the mystic.
Van Morrison

The best of life is always ahead, always further on.
William Mulock

Life is the only art that we are required to practice without preparation, and without being allowed the preliminary trials, the failures and botches, that are essential for training.
Lewis Mumford

The irrationality of a thing is no argument against its existence, rather a condition of it.
Friedrich Wilhelm Nietzsche

One must be thrust out of a finished cycle in life, and that leap is the most difficult to make—to part with one's faith, one's love, when one would prefer to renew the faith and recreate the passion.
Anaïs Nin

Life is easier to take than you'd think; all that is necessary is to accept the impossible, do without the indispensable, and bear the intolerable.
Kathleen Norris

If you aren't living on the edge, you're taking up too much space.
Nursing home resident

Tell me what ticks you off, and I will tell you what makes you tick.
Lloyd John Ogilvie

Keep your mouth shut and your eyes open.
Samuel Palmer

The sensibility of man to trifles, and his insensibility to great things, indicates a strange inversion.
Blaise Pascal

Life is pain and the enjoyment of love is an anesthetic.
Cesare Pavese

No pain, no palm; no thorns, no throne; no gall, no glory; no cross, no crown.
William Penn

Sooner or later, a man, if he is wise, discovers that life is a mixture of good days and bad, victory and defeat, give and take.
Wilfred A. Peterson

A well-ordered life is like climbing a tower; the view halfway up is better than the view from the base, and it steadily becomes finer as the horizon expands.
William Lyon Phelps

Life is little more than a loan shark: It exacts a high rate of interest for the few pleasures it concedes.
Luigi Pirandello

We feel in one world, we think and name in another. Between the two we can set up a system of references, but we cannot fill the gap.
Marcel Proust

Yea, the darkness hideth not from thee; but the night shinest as the day: the darkness and the light are both alike to thee.
Psalms 139:12

The desire not to be anything is the desire not to be.
Ayn Rand

You can either be squirrel food or the seed of a mighty tree.
Paul Richey

Inspect the neighborhood of thy life; every shelf, every nook of thine abode.
Jean Paul Richter

Who is speaking of victory? To survive is everything.
Rainer Maria Rilke

I believe in the supreme worth of the individual and in his right to life, liberty and the pursuit of happiness.

I believe that every right implies a responsibility; every opportunity, an obligation; every possession, a duty.

I believe that the law was made for man and not man for the law; that government is the servant of the people and not their master.

I believe in the dignity of labor, whether with head or hand; that the world owes no man a living but that it owes every man an opportunity to make a living.

I believe that thrift is essential to well-ordered living and that economy is a prime requisite of a sound financial structure, whether in government, business or personal affairs.

I believe that truth and justice are fundamental to an enduring social order.

I believe in the sacredness of a promise, that a man's word should be as good as his bond; that character—not wealth or power or position—is of supreme worth.

I believe that the rendering of useful service is the common duty of mankind and that only in the purifying fire of sacrifice is the dross of selfishness consumed and the greatness of the human soul set free.

I believe in an all-wise and all-loving God, named by whatever name, and that the individual's highest fulfillment, greatest happiness and widest usefulness are to be found in living in harmony with His will.

I believe that love is the greatest thing in the world; that it alone can overcome hate; that right can and will triumph over might.
John D. Rockefeller, Jr.

You have to accept whatever comes, and the only important thing is that you meet it with the best you have to give.
Eleanor Roosevelt

Whenever I date a guy, I think, is this the man I want my children to spend their weekends with?
Rita Rudner

Life is a magic vase filled to the brim; so made that you cannot dip into it nor draw from it; but it overflows into the hand that drops treasures into it—drop in malice and it overflows hate; drop in charity and it overflows love.
John Ruskin

The good life, as I conceive it, is a happy life. I do not mean that if you are good you will be happy; I mean that if you are happy you will be good.
Bertrand Russell

There is no cure for birth and death save to enjoy the interval.
George Santayana

We cannot withdraw our cards from the game. Were we as silent and mute as stones, our very passivity would be an act.
Jean-Paul Sartre

Consciousness is the mere surface of our minds, of which, as of the earth, we do not know the inside, but only the crust.
Arthur Schopenhauer

Life is a language in which certain truths are conveyed to us; if we could learn them in some other way, we should not live.
Arthur Schopenhauer

Not one of us knows what effect his life produces, and what he gives to others; that is hidden from us and must remain so, though we are often allowed to see some little fraction of it, so that we may not lose courage. The way in which power works is a mystery.
Albert Schweitzer

It is within the power of every man to live his life nobly, but of no man to live forever. Yet so many of us hope that life will go on forever, and so few aspire to live nobly.
Seneca

Levity of behavior is the bane of all that is good and virtuous.
Seneca

Life is neither a good nor an evil, but simply the scene of good and evil.
Seneca

Nothing is so false as human life, nothing so treacherous. God knows no one would have accepted it as a gift, if it had not been given without our knowledge.
Seneca

We should every night call ourselves to an account: What infirmity have I mastered today? What passions opposed? What temptation resisted? What virtue acquired? Our vices will abate of themselves if they be brought every day to the shrift.
Seneca

Man ought always to have something that he prefers to life; otherwise life itself will seem to him tiresome and void.
Johann Seume

That which goeth up must needs come down; and that which is down must needs go up. But Brahma has ordained

that the that that goeth up is seldom the same as the that that hath gone down.
Gautama Shakyamuni

What is life, but a series of inspired follies?
George Bernard Shaw

I have been a wanderer among distant fields. I have sailed down mighty rivers.
Percy Bysshe Shelley

History makes some amends for the shortness of life.
Robert Skelton

Trifles make up the happiness or the misery of mortal life.
Alexander Smith

All the conditions of modern life, its material plenitude, its sheer crowd-edness, conjoin to dull our sensory faculties.
Susan Sontag

A trifle is often pregnant with high importance; the prudent man neglects no circumstance.
Sophocles

Let a salad-maker be a spendthrift for oil, a miser for vinegar, a statesman for salt, and a madman for mixing.
Spanish proverb

Life is the continuous adjustment of external relations.
Herbert Spencer

Life often seems like a long shipwreck of which the debris are friendship, glory and love.
Madame de Staël

To be what we are, and to become what we are capable of becoming, is the only end of life.
Robert Louis Stevenson

It matters not how long you live, but how well.
Publilius Syrus

It matters not what you are thought to be, but what you are.
Publilius Syrus

Life is given to use, we earn it by giving it.
Rabindranath Tagore

Life improves slowly and goes wrong fast, and only catastrophe is clearly visible.
Edward Teller

The shell must break before the bird can fly.
Alfred, Lord Tennyson

The worst is yet to come.
Alfred, Lord Tennyson

Measure your health by your sympathy with morning and Spring. If there is no response in you to the awakening of nature, if the prospect of an early morning walk does not banish sleep, if the warble of the first bluebird does not thrill you, know that the morning and spring of your life are past. Thus you may feel your pulse.
Henry David Thoreau

The cost of a thing is that amount of life which must be exchanged for it.
Henry David Thoreau

The idea shared by many that life is a vale of tears is just as false as the

idea shared by the great majority, the idea to which youth and health and riches incline you, that life is a place of entertainment.
Leo Tolstoy

Every man is born to one possession which outvalues all his others—his last breath.
Mark Twain

Why is it that we rejoice at a birth and grieve at a funeral? It is because we are not the person involved.
Mark Twain

There is a life that is worth living now as it was worth living in the former days, and that is the honest life, the useful life, the unselfish life, cleansed by devotion to an ideal. There is a battle worth fighting now as it was worth fighting then, and that is the battle for justice and equality: to make our city and our state free in fact as well as in name; to break the rings that strangle real liberty, and to keep them broken; to cleanse, so far as in our power lies, the fountains of our national life from political, commercial, and social corruption; to teach our sons and daughters, by precept and example, the honor of serving such a country as America. That is work worthy of the finest manhood and womanhood.
Henry van Dyke

The great man presides over all his states of consciousness with obstinate rigor.
Leonardo da Vinci

Life resembles the banquet of Damocles; the sword is ever suspended.
Voltaire

There is no power on earth that can neutralize the influence of a high, pure, simple and useful life.
Booker T. Washington

The theory that can absorb the greatest number of facts, and persist in doing so, generation after generation through all changes of opinion and detail, is the one that must rule all observation.
John Weiss

Get all you can without hunting your soul, your body, or your neighbor. Save all you can, cutting off every needless expense. Give all you can. Be glad to give, and ready to distribute; laying up in store for yourselves a good foundation against the time to come, that you may attain eternal life.
John Wesley

Life has a way of overgrowing its achievements as well as its ruins.
Edith Wharton

Life is far too important a thing ever to talk seriously about.
Oscar Wilde

One should absorb the color of life, but one should never remember its details.
Oscar Wilde

There are few things easier than to live badly and die well.
Oscar Wilde

When a man says he has exhausted life one always knows life has exhausted him.
Oscar Wilde

Life is an unanswered question, but let's still believe in the dignity and importance of the question.
Tennessee Williams

All things come to him who waits— provided he knows what he is waiting for.
Woodrow Wilson

One likes people much better when they're battered down by a prodigious

siege of misfortune than when they triumph.
Virginia Woolf

Life is divided into three terms—that which was, which is, and which will be. Let us learn from the past to profit by the present, and from the present to live better for the future.
William Wordsworth

Think naught a trifle, though it small appear;

Small stands the mountain, moments make the year, and trifles life.
Edward Young

LISTENING

What a different world this would be if people would listen to those who know more and not merely try to get something from those who have more.
William J.H. Boetcker

The secret of a good memory is attention, and attention to a subject depends upon our interest in it. We rarely forget that which has made a deep impression on our minds.
Tryon Edwards

One often reads about the art of conversation—how it's dying or what's needed to make it flourish, or how rare good ones are. But wouldn't you agree that the infinitely more valuable rara avis is a good listener?
Malcolm Forbes

The art of conversation lies in listening.
Malcolm Forbes

Hearing is one of the body's five senses. But listening is an art.
Frank Tyger

The reason why we have two ears and only one mouth is that we may listen the more and talk the less.
Zeno

LIVING

The art of living is more like wrestling than dancing.
Marcus Aurelius Antoninus

It is so small a thing to have enjoyed the sun, to have lived light in the spring, to have loved, to have thought, to have done?
Matthew Arnold

It matters not how long we live but how.
Philip James Bailey

To live is like to love—all reason is against it, and all healthy instinct is for it.
Samuel Butler

We all live in the past, because there is nothing else to live in. To live in the present is like proposing to sit on a pin. It is too minute, it is too slight a support, it is too uncomfortable a posture, and it is of necessity followed immediately by totally different experiences, analogous to those of jumping up with a yell.
G.K. Chesterton

To live long it is necessary to live slowly.
Cicero

I know I'm not dead, but am I alive?
Frank Conroy

You will find men who want to be carried on the shoulders of others, who think that the world owes them a living. They don't seem to see that we must all lift together and pull together.
Henry Ford

The art of living rightly is like all arts; it must be learned and practiced with incessant care.
Johann Wolfgang von Goethe

The trials of living and the pangs of disease make even the short span of life too long.
Herodotus

To live is to function. That is all there is in living.
Oliver Wendell Holmes

He possesses dominion over himself, and is happy, who can every day say, I have lived. Tomorrow the heavenly Father may either involve the world in dark clouds, or cheer it with clear sunshine; he will not, however, render ineffectual the things which have already taken place.
Horace

I have ever judged of the religion of others by their lives. For it is in our lives, and not from our works, that our religion must be read.
Thomas Jefferson

To improve the golden moments of opportunity and catch the good that is within our reach, is the great art of living.
Samuel Johnson

Having outlived so many of my contemporaries, I ought not to forget that I may be thought to have outlived myself.
James Madison

A man lives not only his personal life as an individual but also, consciously or unconsciously, the life of his epoch and his contemporaries.
Thomas Mann

Live and let live is not enough; live and help live is not too much.
Orison Swett Marden

When a man begins to understand himself he begins to live. When he begins to live he begins to understand his fellow men.
Norvin G. McGranahan

My candle burns at both ends; It will not last the night; But, ah, my foes, and, oh, my friends It gives a lovely light!
Edna St. Vincent Millay

The great and glorious masterpiece of men is to live to the point. All other things—to reign, to hoard, to build—are, at most, but inconsiderable props and appendages.
Michel de Montaigne

No one grows old by living—only by losing interest in living.
Marie Beynon Ray

Half the agony of living is waiting.
Alexander Rose

I think the one lesson I have learned is that there is no substitute for paying attention.
Diane Sawyer

It is silliness to live when to live is torment.
William Shakespeare

The mass of men lead lives of quiet desperation.
Henry David Thoreau

They lived long that have lived well.
Woodrow Wilson

There appears to exist a greater desire to live long than to live well! Measure by man's desires, he cannot live long enough; measure by his good deeds, and he has not lived long enough; measure by his evil deeds, and he has lived too long.
Johann Zimmermann

LONELINESS

It would do the world good if every man in it would compel himself occasionally to be absolutely alone. Most of the world's progress has come out of such loneliness.
Bruce Barton

No one ever discovers the depth of his own loneliness.
George Bernanos

The whole business of your life overwhelms you when you live alone. One's stupefied by it. To get rid of it you try to daub some of it off onto people who come to see you, and they hate that. To be alone trains one for death.
Louis-Ferdinand Céline

A lonely man is a lonesome thing, a stone, a bone, a stick, a receptacle for Gilbey's gin, a stooped figure sitting at the edge of a hotel bed, heaving copious sighs like the autumn wind.
John Cheever

Columbus discovered no isle or key so lonely as himself.
Ralph Waldo Emerson

Loneliness is something you can't walk away from.
William Feather

If I'm such a legend, why am I so lonely?
Judy Garland

The thing that makes you exceptional, if you are at all, is inevitably that which must also make you lonely.
Lorraine Hansberry

There is no loneliness greater than the loneliness of a failure. The failure is a stranger in his own house.
Eric Hoffer

Strife is better than loneliness.
Irish saying

To most people loneliness is a doom. Yet loneliness is the very thing which God has chosen to be one of the schools of training for His very own. It is the fire that sheds the dross and reveals the gold.
Bernard M. Martin

We seek pitifully to convey to others the treasures of our heart, but they have not the power to accept them, and so we go lonely, side by side but not together, unable to know our fellows and unknown by them.
Somerset Maugham

All men are lonely. But sometimes it seems to me that we Americans are the loneliest of all. Our hunger for foreign places and new ways has been with us almost like a national disease. Our literature is stamped with a quality of longing and unrest.
Carson McCullers

People are lonely because they build walls instead of bridges.
Joseph Fort Newton

When so many are lonely as seem to be lonely, it would be inexcusably selfish to be lonely alone.
Tennessee Williams

LOVE

We [Americans] cheerfully assume that in some mystic way love conquers all, that good outweighs evil in the just balances of the universe and that at the eleventh hour something gloriously triumphant will prevent the worst before it happens.
Brooks Atkinson

A false enchantment can all too easily last a lifetime.
W.H. Auden

Almost all of our relationships begin and most of them continue as forms of mutual exploitation, a mental or physical barter, to be terminated when one or both parties run out of goods.
W.H. Auden

A crowd is not company, and faces are but a gallery of pictures, and talk is but a tinkling cymbal, where there is no love.
Francis Bacon

It is as absurd to say that a man can't love one woman all the time as it is to say that a violinist needs several violins to play the same piece of music.
Honoré de Balzac

Love: Two minds without a single thought.
Philip Barry

Love is the delightful interval between meeting a beautiful girl and discovering that she looks like a haddock.
John Barrymore

Paper napkins never return from a laundry, nor love from a trip to the law courts.
John Barrymore

Of all earthly music, that which reaches farthest into heaven is the beating of a truly loving heart.
Henry Ward Beecher

Adam invented love at first sight, one of the greatest labor-saving machines the world ever saw.
Josh Billings

Embraces are comminglings from the head even to the feet,
And not a pompous high priest entering by a secret place.
William Blake

True affection is a body of enigmas, mysteries and riddles, wherein two so become one that they both become two.
Thomas Browne

To live is like to love—all reason is against it, and all healthy instinct is for it.
Samuel Butler

Like the measles, love is most dangerous when it comes late in life.
Lord Byron

Man's love is of man's life a thing apart. 'Tis women's whole existence.
Lord Byron

Anything will give up its secrets if you love it enough.
George Washington Carver

Love means to love that which is unlovable, or it is no virtue at all.
G.K. Chesterton

Many a man has fallen in love with a girl in a light so dim he would not have chosen a suit by it.
Maurice Chevalier

We should measure affection, not like youngsters by the ardor of its passion, but by its strength and constancy.
Cicero

All men, even the most surly, are influenced by affection.
Samuel Taylor Coleridge

And though I bestow all my goods to feed the poor, and though I give my body to

be burned, but have not love, it profiteth
me nothing.
I Corinthians 13:3

The formula for achieving a successful
relationship: You should treat all disasters as if they were trivialities but never
treat a triviality as if it were a disaster.
Quentin Crisp

Most women set out to change a man,
and when they have changed him they
do not like him.
Marlene Dietrich

Burt Reynolds once asked me out. I was
in his room.
Phyllis Diller

The effect of the indulgence of human
affection is a certain cordial exhilaration.
Ralph Waldo Emerson

Take spring when it comes, and rejoice.
Take happiness when it comes, and
rejoice. Take love when it comes, and
rejoice.
Carl Ewald

Love and scandal are the best sweeteners
of tea.
Henry Fielding

The kiss originated when the first male
reptile licked the first female reptile,
implying in a subtle, complimentary way
that she was as succulent as the small
reptile he had for dinner the night before.
F. Scott Fitzgerald

Every time we hold our tongues instead
of returning the sharp retort, show
patience with another's faults, show a
little more love and kindness, we are
helping to stock-pile more of these
peace-bringing qualities in the world
instead of armaments for war.
Constance Foster

Religion has done love a great service by
making it a sin.
Anatole France

In love there is always one who kisses
and one who offers the cheek.
French proverb

And think not you can guide the course
of love. For love, if it finds you worthy,
shall guide your course.
Kahlil Gibran

Work is love made visible.
Kahlil Gibran

Everywhere, we learn only from those
whom we love.
Johann Wolfgang von Goethe

The porcupine, whom one must handle
gloved, may be respected, but never
loved.
Arthur Guiterman

Kindness and intelligence don't always
deliver us from the pitfalls and traps:
There are always failures of love, of will,
of imagination. There is no way to take
the danger out of human relationships.
Barbara Grizzuti Harrison

Love is what's left of a relationship after
all the selfishness has been removed.
Cullen Hightower

We probably have a greater love for those
we support than for those who support
us. Our vanity carries more weight than
our self-interest.
Eric Hoffer

The sound of a kiss is not so loud as that
of a cannon, but its echo lasts a great deal
longer.
Oliver Wendell Holmes

Nothing is more dreadful than a cold,
unimpassioned indulgence. And love

infallibly becomes cold and unimpassioned when it is too lightly made.
Aldous Huxley

Good nature is the cheapest commodity in the world, and love is the only thing that will pay ten percent to both borrower and lender.
Robert Ingersoll

Beloved, let us love one another: for love is of God; and everyone that loveth is born of God, and knoweth God. He that loveth not knoweth not God; for God is love.
I John 4:7–8

A new commandment I give unto you, that ye love one another: as I have loved you, that ye also love one another.
John 13:34

The feeling of friendship is like that of being comfortably filled with roast beef; love, like being enlivened with champagne.
Samuel Johnson

Romance, like the rabbit at the dog track, is the elusive, fake and never attained reward which, for the benefit and amusement of our masters, keeps us running and thinking in safe circles.
Beverly Jones

No time of life is so beautiful as the early days of love, when with every meeting, every glance, one fetches something new home to rejoice over.
Søren Kierkegaard

Love and friendship exclude each other.
Jean de La Bruyère

No disguise can long conceal love where it exists, or long feign it where it is lacking.
François de La Rochefoucauld

There are two sorts of constancy in love; the one comes from the constant discovery in our beloved of new grounds for love, and the other from making it a point of honor to be constant.
François de La Rochefoucauld

There is only one kind of love, but there are one thousand imitations.
François de La Rochefoucauld

We are nearer loving those who hate us than those who love us more than we wish.
François de La Rochefoucauld

We forgive so long as we love.
François de La Rochefoucauld

Graham Greene once referred to a chip of ice that has to be in the writer's heart. And that is the strain: that you must abstain from relationships and yet at the same time engage in them. There you have, I think, the real metaphysical relationship between the writer and the spy.
John le Carré

Talk not of wasted affection; affection never was wasted.
Henry Wadsworth Longfellow

Love is what happens to a man and a woman who don't know each other.
Somerset Maugham

There is no way under the sun of making a man worthy of love, except by loving him.
Thomas Merton

To live without loving is not really to live.
Molière

There is no substitute for the comfort supplied by the utterly taken-for-granted relationship.
Iris Murdoch

Happy is he who dares courageously to defend what he loves.
Ovid

By the time you swear you're his,
Shivering and sighing,
And he vows his passion is
Infinite, undying—
One of you is lying.
Dorothy Parker

His voice was as intimate as the rustle of sheets.
Dorothy Parker

Those who love deeply never grow old; they may die of old age, but they die young.
Arthur Wing Pinero

He whom love touches not walks in darkness.
Plato

I believe that love is the greatest thing in the world; that it alone can overcome hate; that right can and will triumph over might.
John D. Rockefeller, Jr.

Love cannot exists as a duty; to tell a child that it ought to love its parents and its brother and sisters is utterly useless, if not worse.
Bertrand Russell

Perhaps love is the process of my leading you gently back to yourself.
Antoine de Saint-Exupéry

Love doesn't have to be perfect. Even perfect, it is still the best thing there is, for the simple reason that it is the most common and constant truth of all, of all life, all law and order, the very thing which holds everything together, which permits everything to move along in time and be its wonderful or ordinary self.
William Saroyan

Loving can cost a lot, but not loving always costs more, and those who fear to love often find that want of love is an emptiness that robs the joy from life.
Merle Shain

Loving someone means helping them to be more themselves, which can be different from being what you'd like them to be, although often they turn out the same.
Merle Shain

All my life, affection has been showered upon me, and every forward step I have made has been taken in spite of it.
George Bernard Shaw

The fickleness of the women I love is only equalled by the infernal constancy of the women who love me.
George Bernard Shaw

Love rarely overtakes, it mostly comes to meet us.
Wilhelm Stekel

'Tis sweet to feel by what fine-spun threads our affections are drawn together.
Laurence Sterne

It is only when we no longer compulsively need someone that we can have a real relationship with them.
Anthony Storr

Fear less, hope more; eat less, chew more; whine less, breathe more; talk less, say more; hate less, love more; and all good things are yours.
Swedish proverb

One of the most common disrupters of marital bliss is the choice of where to spend a vacation. What this country needs is an ocean in the mountains.
Paul Sweeney

We live in this world when we love it.
Rabindranath Tagore

No one worth possessing
Can be quite possessed.
Sara Teasdale

There is no remedy for love but to love
more.
Henry David Thoreau

Praise is well, compliment is well, but
affection—that is the last and most
precious reward that any man can win,
whether by character or achievement.
Mark Twain

The chains of love are never so binding
as when their links are made of gold.
Royal Tyler

Love conquers all things except poverty
and toothache.
Mae West

What we can do for another is the test of
powers; what we can suffer for is the test
of love.
Bishop Westcott

When one is in love, one always begins
by deceiving one's self; and one always
ends by deceiving others. That is what
the world calls a romance.
Oscar Wilde

Love is an energy which exists of itself. It
is its own value.
Thornton Wilder

There is a land of the living and a land of
the dead and the bridge is love.
Thornton Wilder

We live by admiration, hope and love.
William Wordsworth

LOYALTY

Total loyalty is possible only when
fidelity is emptied of all concrete
content, from which changes of mind
might naturally arise.
Hannah Arendt

There is one element that is worth its
weight in gold and that is loyalty. It will
cover a multitude of weaknesses.
Philip Armour

Loyalty must arise spontaneously from
the hearts of people who love their
country and respect their government.
Hugo L. Black

You stand up for your teammates. Your
loyalty is to them. You protect them
through good and bad, because they'd do
the same for you.
Yogi Berra

An intelligent and conscientious opposition is a part of loyalty to country.
Bainbridge Colby

Loyalty cannot be blueprinted. It cannot
be produced on an assembly line. In fact,
it cannot be manufactured at all, for its
origin is the human heart—the center of
self-respect and human dignity. It is a
force which leaps into being only when
conditions are exactly right for it—and it
is a force very sensitive to betrayal.
Maurice R. Franks

Loyalty is a major force making for unity
in any life—even in the existence of a
civilization. . . . It gives point and flavor,
most of all meaning, to a life or a culture.
Harmon M. Gehr

Whose bread I eat, his song I sing.
German Saying

The strength of a country or creed lies in the true sense of loyalty it can arouse in the hearts of its people.
Louis C. Gerstein

I'll take 50% efficiency to get 100% loyalty.
Samuel Goldwyn

No citizen of this nation is worthy of the name unless he bears unswerving loyalty to the system under which he lives, the system that gives him more benefits than any other system yet devised by man. Loyalty leaves room to change the system when need be, but only under the ground rules by which we Americans live.
John A. Hannah

My honor is my loyalty.
Heinrich Himmler

An ounce of loyalty is worth a pound of cleverness.
Elbert Hubbard

I don't want loyalty. I want *loyalty*! I want him to kiss my ass in Macy's window at high noon and tell me it smells like roses.
Lyndon Baines Johnson

Loyalty is a fine quality, but in excess it fills political graveyards.
Neil Kinnock

A healthy loyalty is not passive and complacent, but active and critical.
Harold Laski

Cheats, liars and criminals may resist every blandishment while respectable gentlemen have been moved to appalling treasons by watery cabbage in a departmental canteen.
John le Carré

It is best not to swap horses while crossing the river.
Abraham Lincoln

How many things in the world deserve our loyalty? Very few indeed. I think one should be loyal to immortality, which is another word for life, a stronger word for it.
Boris Pasternak

If vitality gives a man's perspectives color, if community bonds give them breadth, if awareness of the land makes them realistic, a deep sense of loyalty gives them personal meaning and integrity.
Harry Huntt Ransom

It goes far toward making a man faithful to let him understand that you think him so; and he that does but suspect I will deceive him, gives me a sort of right to do so.
Seneca

I meant what I said
And said what I meant
An elephant's faithful
One hundred percent.
Dr. Seuss

When you betray somebody else, you also betray yourself.
Isaac Bashevis Singer

Think not those faithful who praise all thy words and actions, but those who kindly reprove thy faults.
Socrates

My kind of loyalty was loyalty to one's country, not to its institutions or its office-holders.
Mark Twain

Faithfulness is to the emotional life what consistency is to the life of the intellect— simply a confession of failure.
Oscar Wilde

LUCK

I never knew an early-rising, hard-working, prudent man, careful of his earnings, and strictly honest, who complained of bad luck. A good character, good habits, and iron industry are impregnable to the assaults of all the ill-luck that fools ever dreamed of.
Joseph Addison

If you wait for luck to help you, you'll have often an empty stomach.
Ignas Bernstein

Good luck reaches farther than long arms.
H.G. Bohn

The public man needs but one patron, namely, the lucky moment.
Edward Bulwer-Lytton

I have a notion that gamblers are as happy as most people, being always excited; women, wine, fame, the table, even ambition sate now and then, but every turn of the card and cast of the dice keeps the gambler alive, besides, one can game ten times longer than one can do anything else.
Lord Byron

A stout man's heart breaks bad luck.
Miguel de Cervantes

Good and bad luck is a synonym in the great majority of instances, for good and bad judgment.
John Chatfield

What we call luck is the inner man externalized. We make things happen to us.
Robertson Davies

Backboneless employees are too ready to attribute the success of others to luck. Luck is usually the fruit of intelligent application. The man who is intent on making the most of his opportunities is too busy to bother about luck.
B.C. Forbes

There is an old saying, "The harder you try, the luckier you get." I kind of like that definition of luck.
Gerald Ford

It never occurs to fools that merit and good fortune are closely united.
Johann Wolfgang von Goethe

Luck is an accident that happens to the competent.
Albert M. Greenfield

Make a bet every day, otherwise you might walk around lucky and never know it.
Jimmy Jones

Throw a lucky man into the sea, and he will come up with a fish in his mouth.
Judah Leib Lazerov

I am a great believer in luck, and I find the harder I work the more I have of it.
Stephen Leacock

Your luck is how you treat people.
Bridget O'Donnell

Luck means the hardships and privations which you have not hesitated to endure, the long nights you have devoted to work. Luck means the appointments you have never failed to keep; the trains you have never failed to catch.
Max O'Rell

To say that a schlemiel is a luckless person is to touch only the negative side. It is the schlemiel's avocation and profession to miss out on things, to muff opportunities, to be persistently, organically, preposterously and ingeniously out

of place. A hungry schlemiel dreams of a plate of hot soup, and hasn't a spoon.
Maurice Samuel

Luck never gives; it only lends.
Swedish proverb

M

MAN

One man's poison ivy is another man's spinach.
George Ade

It is not the oath that makes us believe the man, but the man the oath.
Aeschylus

Our dependence outweighs our independence, for we are independent only in our desire, while we are dependent on our health, on nature, on society, on everything in us and outside us.
Henri Frédéric Amiel

A rational nature admits of nothing which is not serviceable to the rest of mankind.
Marcus Aurelius Antoninus

I made man in three stages: when he was young, I overlooked his stumbling; when he was a man, I considered his purpose; and when he grows old, I watch him till he repent.
Apocalypse of Sedrach

All mankind is divided into three classes: Those that are immovable, those that are movable, and those that move.
Arabian proverb

There is a cropping-time in the races of men, as in the fruits of the field; and sometimes, if the shock be good, there springs up for a time a succession of splendid men; and then comes a period of barrenness.
Aristotle

A crowd is not company, and faces are but a gallery of pictures.
Francis Bacon

What is an individual? Just a bit of life shot off from the one Life in the universe—just a bit of love and truth dropped on this globe, just as the globe itself was once a bit of light and heat dropped from the sun.
C.W. Barron

The significance of man is that he is insignificant and aware of it.
Carl Becker

Many men build as cathedrals are built— the part nearest the ground finished, but that part which soars toward heaven, the turrets and the spires, forever incomplete.
Henry Ward Beecher

Despise not any man, and do not spurn anything; for there is no man that has not his hour, nor is there anything that has not its place.
Rabbi ben Azzai

I consider that we are all self-seeking, cruel and destructive beings, except perhaps briefly to those we wish to impress. I am no longer hurt or astonished.
Charity Blackstock

Nought can deform the human race
Like to the armour's iron brace.
William Blake

If a man watches three football games in a row, he should be declared legally dead.
Erma Bombeck

You first parents of the human race . . . who ruined yourselves for an apple, what might you not have done for a truffled turkey?
Anthelme Brillat-Savarin

What a man is is the basis of what he dreams and thinks, accepts and rejects, feels and perceives.
John Mason Brown

Man seeks his own good at the whole world's cost.
Robert Browning

People are much more alike inside than they are on the surface.
Verne Burnett

The world will only, in the end, follow those who have despised as well as served it.
Samuel Butler

In men whom men condemn as ill
I find so much of goodness still,
In men whom men pronounce divine
I found so much of sin and blot,
I do not dare to draw a line
Between the two, where God has not.
Lord Byron

Show me the man you honor, and I will know what kind of a man you are, for it shows me what your ideal of manhood is, and what kind of a man you long to be.
Thomas Carlyle

The true epic of our times is not arms and the man, but tools and the man, an infinitely wider kind of epic.
Thomas Carlyle

There are only two or three human stories, and they go on repeating themselves as fiercely as if they had never happened before.
Willa Cather

Three things too much, and three too little are pernicious to man; to speak much, and know little; to spend much, and have little; to presume much, and be worth little.
Miguel de Cervantes

A true man never frets about his place in the world, but just slides into it by the gravitation of his nature, and swings there as easily as a star.
Edwin H. Chapin

Chins are exclusively a human feature, not to be found among the beasts. If they had chins, most animals would look like each other.
Malcolm de Chazal

In nature a repulsive caterpillar turns into a lovely butterfly. But with human beings a lovely butterfly turns into a repulsive caterpillar.
Anton Chekhov

Man is what he believes.
Anton Chekhov

You must look into people, as well as at them.
Lord Chesterfield

Man is an exception, whatever else he is. If it is not true that a divine being fell, then we can only say that one of the animals went entirely off its head.
G.K. Chesterton

We must be united, we must be undaunted, we must be inflexible. Our qualities and deeds must burn and glow through the gloom of Europe until they become the veritable beacon of its salvation.
Winston Churchill

It is not the place that maketh the person, but the person that maketh the place honorable.
Cicero

It is not until we have passed through the furnace that we are made to know how much dross there is in our composition.
Charles Caleb Colton

The Master was entirely free from four things: prejudice, foregone conclusions, obstinacy, and egoism.
Confucius

The superior man will watch over himself when he is alone. He examines his heart that there may be nothing wrong there, and that he may have no cause of dissatisfaction with himself.
Confucius

The Lord your God hath multiplied you, and, behold, ye are this day as the stars of heaven for multitude.
Deuteronomy 1:10

The man who follows the crowd will never be followed by a crowd.
Richard S. Donnell

Let us teach our children to study man as well as mathematics and to build cathedrals as well as power stations.
David Eccles

It is not a struggle merely of economic theories, or forms of government or of military power. At issue is the true nature of man. Either man is the creature whom the psalmist described as a little lower than the angels . . . or man is a soulless, animated machine to be enslaved, used and consumed by the state for its own glorification. It is, therefore, a struggle which goes to the roots of the human spirit, and its shadow falls across the long sweep of man's destiny.
Dwight D. Eisenhower

A man is known by the books he reads, by the company he keeps, by the praise he gives, by his dress, by his tastes, by his distastes, by the stories he tells, by his gait, by the motion of his eye, by the look of his house, of his chamber; for nothing on earth is solitary, but everything hath affinities infinite.
Ralph Waldo Emerson

A mob is a society of bodies, voluntarily bereaving themselves of reason, and traversing its work. The mob is man, voluntarily descending to the nature of the beast. Its fit hour of activity is night; its actions are insane, like its whole constitution.
Ralph Waldo Emerson

I know and see too well, when not voluntarily blind, the speedy limits of persons called high and worthy.
Ralph Waldo Emerson

We own to man higher succors than food and fire. We owe to man man.
Ralph Waldo Emerson

Nobody can make anybody be someone he or she doesn't want to be.
Malcolm Forbes

The difference between men and boys is the price of their toys.
Malcolm Forbes

Men are not against you; they're merely for themselves.
Gene Fowler

Of all the ways of defining man, the worst is the one which makes him out to be a rational animal.
Anatole France

Mankind are very odd creatures: One half censure what they practice, the

other half practice what they censure; the rest always say and do as they ought.
Benjamin Franklin

For if a man think himself to be something, when he is nothing, he deceiveth himself. But let every man prove his own work, and then shall he have rejoicing in himself alone.
Galatians 6:3–4

Essential characteristics of a gentleman: The will to put himself in the place of others; the horror of forcing others into positions from which he would himself recoil; the power to do what seems to him to be right, without considering what others may say or think.
John Galsworthy

I mean to make myself a man, and if I succeed in that, I shall succeed in everything else.
James A. Garfield

Territory is but the body of a nation. The people who inhabit its hills and valleys are its soul, its spirit, its life.
James A. Garfield

When everyone is somebody then no one's anybody.
William S. Gilbert

Man is to be trained chiefly by studying and by knowing man.
William E. Gladstone

Man is not born to solve the problem of the universe, but to find out what he has to do; and to restrain himself within the limits of his comprehension.
Johann Wolfgang von Goethe

The master proves himself in recognizing his limitations.
Johann Wolfgang von Goethe

Treat people as if they were what they ought to be and you help them become what they are capable of becoming.
Johann Wolfgang von Goethe

In the world men must be dealt with according to what they are, and not to what they ought to be; and the great art of life is to find out what they are, and act with them accordingly.
Charles C.F. Greville

The real gentleman is one who is gentle in everything, at least in everything that depends on himself—in carriage, temper, constructions, aims, desires. He is mild, calm, quiet, even temperate—not hasty in judgment, not exorbitant in ambition, not overbearing, not proud, not rapacious, not oppressive.
Julius C. Hare

None of us know all the potentialities that slumber in the spirit of the population, or all the ways in which that population can surprise us when there is the right interplay of events.
Vaclav Havel

The most insignificant people are the most apt to sneer at others. They are safe from reprisals, and have no hope of rising in their own esteem but by lowering their neighbors.
William Hazlitt

A gentleman is one who never hurts anyone's feelings unintentionally.
Oliver Herford

A dissenting minority feels free only when it can impose its will on the majority; what it abominates most is the dissent of the majority.
Eric Hoffer

A gentleman is one who is too brave to lie, too generous to cheat, and who takes

his share of the world and lets other people have theirs.
Paul G. Hoffman

The gentleman is solid mahogany; the fashionable man is only veneer.
Josiah G. Holland

Of all the creatures that creep and breathe on earth, there is none more wretched than man.
Homer

Government, religion, property, books, are nothing but the scaffolding to build men. Earth holds up to her master no fruit like the finished man.
Wilhelm von Humboldt

Thoughtfulness for others, generosity, modesty and self-respect are the qualities which make a real gentleman or lady.
Thomas Henry Huxley

The real nature of man is originally good, but it becomes clouded by contact with earthly things and therefore needs purification before it can shine forth in its native clarity.
I Ching

A gentleman is man who never insults anyone unintentionally.
P.G. Ivens

Man, biologically considered, and whatever else he may be into the bargain, is the most formidable of all beasts of prey, and indeed, the only one who preys systematically on his own species.
William James

Masses are always breeding grounds of psychic epidemics.
Carl Jung

I refuse to accept the idea that the "isness" of man's present nature makes him morally incapable of reaching up for the eternal "oughtness" that forever confronts him.
Martin Luther King, Jr.

Let us not complain against men because of their rudeness, their ingratitude, their injustice, their arrogance, their love of self, their forgetfulness of others. They are so made. Such is their nature.
Jean de La Bruyère

When you cut open my veins you get cement, not blood.
Samuel Lefrak

Real misanthropes are not found in solitude, but in the real world; since it is experience of life, and not philosophy, which produces real hatred of mankind.
Giacomo Leopardi

Every mob, in its ignorance and blindness and bewilderment, is a League of Frightened Men that seeks reassurance in collective action.
Max Lerner

The history of mankind seems like kite flying; sometimes, when the wind is favorable, we let go the string a little and the kite soars a little higher; sometimes the wind is too rough and we have to lower it a little, and sometimes it gets caught among the tree branches; but to reach the upper strata of pure bliss—ah, perhaps never.
Lin Yutang

In the crowd, herd, or gang, it is a mass-mind that operates—which is to say, a mind without subtlety, a mind without compassion, a mind, finally, uncivilized.
Robert Lindner

Some must follow and some command, through all are made of clay.
Henry Wadsworth Longfellow

Whatever you may be sure of, be sure of this, that you are dreadfully like other people.
James Russell Lowell

There is no kind of bondage which life lays upon us that may not yield both sweetness and strength; and nothing reveals a man's character more fully than the spirit in which he bears his limitations.
Hamilton W. Mabie

In respect to foresight and firmness, the people are more prudent, more stable, and have better judgement than princes.
Niccolò Machiavelli

Speaking generally, men are ungrateful, fickle, hypocritical, fearful of danger and covetous of gain.
Niccolò Machiavelli

I have witnessed the tremendous energy of the masses. On this foundation it is possible to accomplish any task whatsoever.
Mao Tse-tung

Nothing can lift the heart of man like manhood in a fellow man.
Herman Melville

To live is not to live for one's self; let us help one another.
Menander

If there is a look of human eyes that tells of perpetual loneliness, so there is also the familiar look that is the sign of perpetual crowds.
Alice Meynell

Human beings are not like sheep; and even sheep are not undistinguishably alike. A man cannot get a coat or a pair of boots to fit him, unless they are either made to his measure, or he has a whole warehouseful to choose from: and is it easier to fit him with a life than with a coat, or are human beings more like one another in their whole physical and spiritual conformation than in the shape of their feet? If it were only that people have diversities of taste, that is reason enough for not attempting to shape them all after one model.
John Stuart Mill

Mankind are greater gainers by suffering each other to live as seems good themselves, than by compelling each other to live as seems good to the rest.
John Stuart Mill

There are 193 living species of monkeys and apes. One hundred and ninety-two of them are covered with hair. The exception is a naked ape self-named *Homo sapiens*.
Desmond Morris

What we know of man today is limited precisely by the extent to which we have regarded him as a machine.
Friedrich Wilhelm Nietzsche

I require only three things of a man. He must be handsome, ruthless, and stupid.
Dorothy Parker

No man is so great as mankind.
Theodore E. Parker

The multitude which is not brought to act as unity, is confusion. That unity which has not its origin in the multitude is tyranny.
Blaise Pascal

The noblest of all studies is the study of what man is and of what life he should live.
Plato

The nose of a mob is its imagination. By this, at any time, it can be quietly led.
Edgar Allan Poe

The proper study of mankind is man.
Alexander Pope

If you are black, if you are Puerto Rican or Hispanic, be proud of that. But don't let it become a problem. Let it become somebody else's problem.
Colin Powell

Put not your trust in princes, nor in the son of man, in whom there is no help. His breath goeth forth, he returneth to his earth; in that very day his thoughts perish.
Psalms 146:3–4

A man who tries to surpass another may perhaps succeed in equaling if not actually surpassing him, but one who merely follows can never quite come up with him: a follower, necessarily, is always behind.
Quintilian

Man is a paradoxical being—the constant glory and scandal of this world.
Sarvepalli Radhakrishnan

This is the age of the common man, they tell us—a title which any man may claim to the extent of such distinction as he has managed not to achieve.
Ayn Rand

The reason why the race of man moves slowly is because it must move all together.
Thomas B. Reed

I believe that the ultimate object of all activities in a republic should be the development of the manhood of its citizens.
John D. Rockefeller, Jr.

I never met a man I didn't like.
Will Rogers

When a man has put a limit on what he will do, he has put a limit on what he can do.
Charles M. Schwab

Man has become a superman . . . because he not only disposes of innate, physical forces, but because he is in command . . . of latent forces in nature and because he can put them to his service. . . . But the essential fact we must surely all feel in our hearts . . . is that we are becoming inhuman in proportion as we become supermen.
Albert Schweitzer

Those who follow the banners of reason are like the well-disciplined battalions which, wearing a more sober uniform and making a less dazzling show than the light troops commanded by imagination, enjoy more safety, and even more honor, in the conflicts of human life.
Sir Walter Scott

How beauteous mankind is! O brave new world that has such people in it.
William Shakespeare

We must love men ere they will seem to us worthy of our love.
William Shakespeare

Man can climb to the highest summits, but he cannot dwell there long.
George Bernard Shaw

You see, among men who are honored with the common appellation of gentleman, many contradictions to that character.
Richard Steele

Man, unlike any other thing organic or inorganic in the universe grows beyond his work, walks up the stairs of his concepts, emerges ahead of his accomplishments.
John Steinbeck

The trouble with the rat race is that even if you win, you're still a rat.
Lily Tomlin

Everyone is a moon and has a dark side which he never shows to anybody.
Mark Twain

Man seems to be a rickety poor sort of thing, any way you take him; a kind of British Museum of infirmities and inferiorities. He is always undergoing repairs. A machine that was as unreliable as he is would have no market.
Mark Twain

Man is only man at the surface. Remove his skin, dissect, and immediately you come to machinery.
Paul Valéry

There is a loftier ambition that merely to stand high in the world. It is to stoop down and lift mankind a little higher.
Henry van Dyke

Nine-tenths of the people were created so you would want to be with the other tenth.
Horace Walpole

Sleep not when others speak, sit not when others stand, speak not when you should hold your peace, walk not when others stop.
George Washington

The greatest want of the world is the want of men—men who will not be bought or sold; men who in their inmost souls are true and honest; men who do not fear to call sin by its right name; men

whose conscience is as true to duty as the needle to the pole; men who will stand for the right though the heavens fall.
Elwyn Brooks White

The true perfection of man lies, not in what man has, but in what man is. . . . Nothing should be able to harm a man but himself. Nothing should be able to rob a man at all. What a man really has is what is in him. What is outside of him should be a matter of no importance.
Oscar Wilde

So great has been the endurance, so incredible the achievement, that, as long as the sun keeps a set course in heaven, it would be foolish to despair of the human race.
Ernest L. Woodward

Great bodies of people are never responsible for what they do.
Virginia Woolf

I weigh the man, not his title, 'tis not the king's stamp can make the metal better.
William Wycherley

Bachelor: A man who never makes the same mistake once.
Ed Wynn (and others)

Nature revolves, but man advances.
Edward Young

MANAGEMENT

Management, in the sense of employer, is merely the agent for the public, the stockholders and the employees. It is management's job to preserve the balance fairly between all these interests, that each may have his fair share without imperilling the continuity of the effort upon which the whole depends.
James F. Bell

Every person engaged in a given enterprise is called upon to perform a managerial function, or at least to perform a function that is directly serving the purpose of management.
Donaldson Brown

Managers thinking about accounting issues should never forget one of Abraham Lincoln's favorite riddles: How many legs does a dog have, if you call a tail a leg? The answer: Four, because calling a tail a leg doesn't make it a leg.
Warren Buffett

One cannot manage too many affairs: Like pumpkins in the water, one pops up while you try to hold down the other.
Chinese proverb

So much of what we call management consists in making it difficult for people to work.
Peter Drucker

The men who can manage men, manage the men who manage only things, and the men who can manage money manage all.
Will and Ariel Durant

Management is the art of getting three men to do three men's work.
William Feather

Managing the other fellow's business is a fascinating game. Trade unionists all over the country have pronounced ideas for the reform of Wall Street banks; and Wall Street bankers are not far behind in giving plans for the tremendous improvement of trade union policies. Wholesalers have schemes for improving the retailer; the retailer knows just what is wrong in the conduct of wholesale business—and we might go through a long list. . . . Yet for some reason the classes that ought to be helped keep on stubbornly clinging to their own method of running their affairs. . . .
B.C. Forbes

Basically, the problem of management is to produce more goods and services for satisfying people's wants at prices more people can afford to pay.
Paul Garrett

I've been promoted to middle management. I never thought I'd sink so low.
Tim Gould

Quality of management is all-important. After all, what is a company but people? If the people have character, imagination, drive, that's good enough for me.
Donald A. Herman

Lots of folks confuse bad management with destiny.
Elbert Hubbard

Man is the principal syllable in Management.
C.T. McKenzie

I am convinced that much better results can be obtained from operating organizations which are responsible to a competent private management and boards of direction which must show economical operation, adequate upkeep, good public relations, and a profit than can possibly be secured from a national bureaucratic or a local political organization which is responsible to a constantly changing, short-lived political administration without any financial responsibility as to the result.
Henry Earle Riggs

Good management consists in showing average people how to do the work of superior people.
John D. Rockefeller

Take my assets—but leave me my organization and in five years I'll have it all back.
Alfred M. Sloan

Where there is unity there is always victory.
Publilius Syrus

To keep an organization young and fit, don't hire anyone until everybody's so overworked they'll be glad to see the new-comer no matter where he sits.
Robert Townsend

MANNERS

Clothes and manners do not make the man; but when he is made, they greatly improve his appearance.
Arthur Ashe

It pays to be obvious, especially if you have a reputation for subtlety.
Isaac Asimov

Polish doesn't change quartz into a diamond.
Wilma Askinas

Manners are the hypocrisy of a nation.
Honoré de Balzac

When away from home always be like the kind of man you would care to take into your own home.
William J. H. Boetcker

There ought to be a system of manners in every nation which a well-formed mind would be disposed to relish. To make us love our country, our country ought to be lovely.
Edmund Burke

Good breeding differs, if at all, from high breeding only as it gracefully remembers the rights of others, rather than gracefully insists on its own rights.
Thomas Carlyle

Good breeding is the art of showing men, by external signs, the internal reward we have for them. It arises from good sense, improved by conversing with good company.
Marcus Cato

Gravity must be natural and simple; there must be urbanity and tenderness in it. A man must not formalize on everything. He who does so is a fool; and a grave fool is, perhaps, more injurious than a light fool.
William Cecil

A man can buy nothing in the market with gentility.
William Cecil

Some are able and humane men and some are low-grade individuals with the morals of a goat, the artistic integrity of a slot machine and the manners of a floor-walker with delusions of grandeur.
Raymond Chandler

Gentility is what is left over from rich ancestors after the money is gone.
John Ciardi

To be audacious with tact, you have to know to what point you can go too far.
Jean Cocteau

Manners are love in a cool climate.
Quentin Crisp

How majestic is naturalness. I have never met a man whom I really considered a great man who was not always natural and simple. Affectation is inevitably the mark of one not sure of himself.
Charles G. Dawes

The trouble with treating people as equals is that the first thing you know they may be doing the same thing to you.
Peter De Vries

It is the privilege of any human work which is well done to invest the doer with a certain haughtiness.
Ralph Waldo Emerson

Manners are the happy ways of doing things; each one a stroke of genius or of love, now repeated and hardened into usage.
Ralph Waldo Emerson

People who stare deserve the looks they get.
Malcolm Forbes

Good breeding sums up in its instinctive attitude all the efforts a man has made towards perfection, aye, and all that his ancestors have made before him. It is unconscious, the simple acting out of a sound, wholesome nature.
C. Hanford Henderson

Politeness is artificial good humor, it covers the natural want of it, and ends by rendering habitual a substitute nearly equivalent to the real virtue.
Thomas Jefferson

Tact is after all a kind of mind reading.
Sarah Orne Jewett

You never want to give a man a present when he's feeling good. You want to do it when he's down.
Lyndon Baines Johnson

Affected simplicity is refined imposture.
François de La Rochefoucauld

Of all the things you wear, your expression is the most important.
Janet Lane

The telephone is a good way to talk to people without having to offer them a drink.
Fran Lebowitz

Affectation is an awkward and forced imitation of what should be genuine and easy, wanting the beauty that accompanies what is natural.
John Locke

As laws are necessary that good manners may be preserved, so good manners are necessary that laws may be maintained.
Niccolò Machiavelli

A highbrow is a person educated beyond his intelligence.
Brander Matthews

Manner is everything with some people, and something with everybody.
Conyers Middleton

Whom one wants to change manners and customs, one should not do so by changing the laws.
Montesquieu

Good manners are a combination of intelligence, education, taste and style mixed together so that you don't need any of those things.
P.J. O'Rourke

Manners are a sensitive awareness of the feelings of others. If you have that awareness, you have good manners, no matter what fork you use.
Emily Post

Nothing is less important than which fork you use. Etiquette is the science of living. It embraces everything. It is ethics. It is honor.
Emily Post

Manners make often fortunes.
John Ray

In this world we must either institute conventional forms of expression or else pretend that we have nothing to express; the choice lies between a mask and a figleaf.
George Santayana

The great secret is not having bad manners or good manners or any other particular sort of manners, but having the same manner for all human souls; in short, behaving as if you were in heaven, where there are no third-class carriages, and one soul is as good as another.
George Bernard Shaw

The test of a man's or woman's breeding is how they behave in a quarrel.
George Bernard Shaw

Laws are always unstable unless they are founded on the manners of a nation; and manners are the only durable and resisting power in a people.
Alexis de Tocqueville

To succeed in the world it is not enough to be stupid, you must also be well-mannered.
Voltaire

Let your countenance be pleasant, but in serious matters let it be somewhat grave.
George Washington

The test of good manners is to be able to put up pleasantly with bad ones.
Wendell Willkie

It is a good rule in life never to apologize. The right sort of people do not want apologies, and the wrong sort take a mean advantage of them.
P.G. Wodehouse

MARRIAGE

Nowadays 80% of women are against marriage. Why? Because women realize it's not worth buying an entire pig just to get a little sausage.
Anonymous

A divorce is like an amputation; you survive, but there is less of you.
Margaret Atwood

Happiness in marriage is entirely a matter of chance.
Jane Austen

The best way to get most husbands to do something is to suggest that perhaps they're too old to do it.
Anne Bancroft

My wife was too beautiful for words, but not for arguments.
John Barrymore

The curse which lies upon marriage is that too often the individuals are joined in their weakness rather than in their strength—each asking from the other instead of finding pleasure in giving.
Simone de Beauvoir

My wife and I have a perfect understanding. I don't try to run her life, and I don't try to run mine.
Milton Berle

My husband and I have never considered divorce. Murder, sometimes, but never divorce.
Dr. Joyce Brothers

One was never married, and that's his hell; another is, and that's his plague.
Robert Burton

On wife Rosalynn: I've never won an argument with her; and the only times I

thought I had I found out the argument wasn't over yet.
Jimmy Carter

It would be very hard for a man to live with me, unless he's terribly strong.
Coco Chanel

Even hooligans marry, though they know that marriage is but for a little while. It is alimony that is forever.
Quentin Crisp

My wife and I were happy for 20 years. Then we met.
Rodney Dangerfield

The value of marriage is not that adults produce children but that children produce adults.
Peter De Vries

Marriage is the greatest earthly happiness when founded on complete sympathy.
Benjamin Disraeli

His designs were strictly honorable, as the phrase is: that is, to rob a lady of her fortune by way of marriage.
Henry Fielding

Any marriage that survives a big wedding can probably survive.
Malcolm Forbes

One thing that previous practice doesn't always make perfect: Marriage.
Malcolm Forbes

To switch lads and lassies from quickie ceremonies back to the catered works in to-be-worn-only-once white dresses, the [wedding] garment producers have turned to sociology. Through statistics as carefully laid out as a bridal train, they are establishing a correlation showing a higher divorce rate for the informally gowned. . . . They may just have something there. . . . If a bride has sunk a bunk of savings into a dress she can't use again in a second wedding, she might think twice about having a second.
Malcolm Forbes

Where there's marriage without love, there will be love without marriage.
Benjamin Franklin

I have never had an impulse to go to the altar. I am a difficult person to lead.
Greta Garbo

A wedding is just like a funeral except that you get to smell your own flowers.
Grace Hansen

Marriage is honorable among all, and the bed undefiled, but the fornicators and adulterers God will judge.
Hebrews 13:4

If I get married, I want to be very married.
Audrey Hepburn

The concept of two people living together for 25 years without having a cross word suggests a lack of spirit only to be admired in sheep.
A.P. Herbert

There is radicalism in all getting and conservatism in all keeping. Lovemaking is radical, while marriage is conservative.
Eric Hoffer

It takes in reality only one to make a quarrel. It is useless for the sheep to pass resolutions in favor of vegetarianism, while the wolf remains of a different opinion.
William Ralph Inge

A good husband is healthy and absent.
Japanese proverb

Make sure you never, never argue at night. You just lose a good night's sleep, and you can't settle anything until morning anyway.
Rose Kennedy

My parents had only one argument in 45 years. It lasted 43 years.
Cathy Ladman

The poor wish to be rich, the rich wish to be happy, the single wish to be married, and the married wish to be dead.
Ann Landers

My whole working philosophy is that the only stable happiness for mankind is that it shall live married in blessed union to woman kind—intimacy, physical and psychical, between a man and his wife. I wish to add that my state of bliss is by no means perfect.
D.H. Lawrence

There is no good in arguing with the inevitable. The only argument available with an east wind is to put on your overcoat.
James Russell Lowell

There is one thing I would break up over, and that is if she caught me with another woman. I won't stand for that.
Steve Martin

I was married by a judge. I should have asked for a jury.
Groucho Marx

A successful marriage is an edifice that must be rebuilt every day.
Andre Maurois

Christmas carols always brought tears to my eyes. I also cry at weddings. I should have cried at a couple of my own.
Ethel Merman

The trouble with wedlock is that there's not enough wed and too much lock.
Christopher Morley

Think of your ancestors and your posterity, and you will never marry.
Ethel Mumford

Marriage is the alliance of two people, one who never remembers birthdays and the other who never forgets them.
Ogden Nash

Marriage is a book of which the first chapter is written in poetry and the remaining chapters in prose.
Beverley Nichols

The best friend is likely to acquire the best wife, because a good marriage is based on the talent for friendship.
Friedrich Wilhelm Nietzsche

Other people's marriages are a perpetual source of amazement.
Patrick O'Brian

No woman marries for money; they are all clever enough, before marrying a millionaire, to fall in love with him.
Cesare Pavese

Divorce isn't a cure—it's a surgical operation, even if there are no children to consider.
Rosamunde Pilcher

A good marriage is that in which each appoints the other the guardian of his solitude, and shows him this confidence, the greatest in his power to bestow.
Rainer Maria Rilke

I've had so many wives and so many children I don't know whose house to go to first on Christmas.
Mickey Rooney

Quarrels in France strengthen a love affair, in America they end it.
Ned Rorem

Before marriage, a man declares that he would lay down his life to serve you; after marriage, he won't even lay down his newspaper to talk to you.
Helen Rowland

Marriage is popular because it combines the maximum of temptation with the maximum of opportunity.
George Bernard Shaw

No time to marry, no time to settle down—I'm a young woman, and I ain't done runnin' around.
Bessie Smith

By all means marry. If you get a good wife, you'll be happy. If you get a bad one, you'll become a philosopher.
Socrates

What they do in heaven we are ignorant of; but what they do not do we are told expressly; they neither marry nor are given in marriage.
Jonathan Swift

Take it from me, marriage isn't a word—it's a sentence.
King Vidor

Divorce is probably of nearly the same date as marriage. I believe, however, that marriage is some weeks more ancient.
Voltaire

He is dreadfully married. He's the most married man I ever saw in my life.
Artemus Ward

Don't marry a man to reform him—that's what reform schools are for.
Mae West

Marriage is a great institution, but I'm not ready for an institution yet.
Mae West

Bigamy is having one wife too many. Monogamy is the same.
Oscar Wilde

The very essence of romance is uncertainty. If I ever marry, I'll try to forget the fact.
Oscar Wilde

MEDIA

What the mass media offer is not popular art, but entertainment which is intended to be consumed like food, forgotten, and replaced by a new dish.
W.H. Auden

Television knows no night. It is perpetual day. TV embodies our fear of the dark, of night, of the other side of things.
Jean Baudrillard

The greatest felony in the news business today is to be behind, or to miss a big story. So speed and quantity substitute for thoroughness and quality, for accuracy and context.
Carl Bernstein

Nothing is real unless it happens on television.
Daniel Boorstin

The one function that TV news performs very well is that when there is no news we give it to you with the same emphasis as if it were.
David Brinkley

The most important service rendered by the press is that of educating people to approach printed matter with distrust.
Samuel Butler

Other administrations have had a love-hate relationship with the press. The Nixon administration has a hate-hate relationship.
John Chancellor

Television is democracy at its ugliest.
Paddy Chayefsky

Journalism is popular, but it is popular mainly as fiction. Life is one world, and life seen in the newspapers another.
G.K. Chesterton

Television is for appearing on, not looking at.
Noël Coward

And that's the way it is.
Walter Cronkite

Television thrives on unreason, and unreason thrives on television. It strikes at the emotions rather than the intellect.
Robin Day

We call them Twinkies. You've seen them on television acting the news, modeling and fracturing the news while you wonder whether they've read the news or if they've blow-dried their brains, too.
Linda Ellerbee

There was no sex in Ireland before television.
Oliver J. Flanagan

TV cassette players will take ever-bigger bites out of the regular TV-viewing audience, moviegoers, sports and other event-attending spectators. Cassette players are now the hottest thing on the entertainment scene since popcorn . . . Movie cassettes are improving the margin of profit for more and more Hollywood hits that don't at the box office. And of course, there is the home video camera . . . The only limitation is the viewer's time. And there, my friends, is the rub of the matter. With only one pair of eyes and a 24-hour day, tape-popping addicts have less and less time for going out to pay to see things.
Malcolm Forbes

There are no plain women on television.
Anna Ford

Because television can make so much money doing its worst, it often cannot afford to do its best.
Fred Friendly

All you need for a movie is a gun and a girl.
Jean-Luc Godard

On inky rebellion and the publication of the Occupied Wall Street Journal: We thought it was important that there be a media outlet that reflected what was under way. A newspaper is tactile, engages all of the senses, and leads to more immersive reading than what people might do online.
Arun Gupta

From his earliest days, he was one of the hungriest reporters around, wildly competitive, no one was going to beat Walter Cronkite on a story, and as he grew older and more successful, the marvel of it was that he never changed, the wild fires still burned.
David Halberstam

On the power of TV versus the Internet: If you want to reach a mass audience, there's no other way to do it.
Stanley Hubbard

The hand that rules the press, the radio, the screen and the far-spread magazine, rules the country.
Learned Hand

On Cronkite's 1968 visit to Vietnam and his criticism of the war: If I've lost Cronkite, I've lost middle America.
Lyndon Baines Johnson

He stood for a world, a century that no longer exists. His death is like losing the last veteran of a world-changing war, one of those men who saw too much but was never embittered by it. Walter Cronkite's gift was to talk to us about what he saw, and we are very lucky to have been able to listen.
Verlyn Klinkenborg

The most guileful reporters are those who appear friendly and smile and seem to be supportive. They are the ones who will seek to gut you on every occasion.
Ed Koch

In the days of Caesar, kings had fools and jesters. Now network presidents have anchormen.
Ted Koppel

I find television very educating. Every time somebody turns on the set I go into the other room and read a book.
Groucho Marx

Journalism is more addictive than crack cocaine. Your life can get out of balance.
Dan Rather

On Walter Cronkite: We were proud to work with him, for him—we loved him.
Mike Wallace

I hate television. I hate it as much as peanuts. But I can't stop eating peanuts.
Orson Welles

The media is not doing well, and it's not going to get any better. Advertising is falling off dramatically, and we are taking all kinds of what we hope are intelligent methods to respond to that.
Mortimer Zuckerman

MEDICINE

I am dying with the help of too many physicians.
Alexander the Great

You medical people will have more lives to answer for in the other world than even we generals.
Napoleon Bonaparte

The whole imposing edifice of modern medicine is like the celebrated Tower of Pisa—slightly off balance.
Charles, Prince of Wales

The most Mighty hath created medicines out of the earth, and a wise man will not abhor them.
Ecclesiastes 38:4

At today's prices for medicines, doctors and hospitals—if the latter are available at any price—only millionaires can afford to be hurt or sick and pay for it. Very few people want socialized medicine in the U.S. But pressure for it is going to appear with the same hurricane force as the demand for pollution control if the medicine men and hospital operators don't take soon some Draconian measures. . . . At the present rate of doctor fees and hospital costs under Medicare and Medicaid plans [taxpayers] are shovelling in billions with nothing but escalation in sight.
Malcolm Forbes (1970)

A disease known is half cured.
Thomas Fuller

The dignity of a physician requires that he should look healthy, and as plump as nature intended him to be; for the common crowd consider those who are not of this excellent bodily condition to be unable to take care of themselves.
Hippocrates

A good laugh and a long sleep are the best cures in the doctor's book.
Irish proverb

As long as men are liable to die and are desirous to live, a physician will be made fun of, but he will be well paid.
Jean de La Bruyère

To live by medicine is to live horribly.
Linnaeus

All interest in disease and death is only another expression of interest in life.
Thomas Mann

The desire to take medicine is perhaps the greatest feature that distinguishes men from animals.
Sir William Osler

Medicine being a compendium of the successive and contradictory mistakes of medical practitioners, when we summon the wisest of them to our aid, the chances are that we may be relying on a scientific truth the error of which will be recognized in a few years' time.
Marcel Proust

By medicine life may be prolonged, yet death will seize the doctor too.
William Shakespeare

There is no better surgeon than one with many scars.
Spanish proverb

Men who are occupied in the restoration of health to other men, by the joint exertion of skill and humanity, are above all the great of the earth. They even partake of divinity, since to preserve and renew is almost as noble as to create.
Voltaire

MEMORY

Not the power to remember, but its very opposite, the power to forget, is a necessary condition for our existence.
Sholem Asch

God gave us our memories so that we might have roses in December.
J.M. Barrie

You never remember who came to the funeral, but you never forget who didn't.
Monie Begley

The camera relieves us of the burden of memory. It surveys us like God, and it surveys for us. Yet no other god has been so cynical, for the camera records in order to forget.
John Berger

Happiness is good health and a bad memory.
Ingrid Bergman

How strange are the tricks of memory, which, often hazy as a dream about the most important events of a man's life, religiously preserve the merest trifles.
Richard Burton

A friend who cannot at a pinch remember a thing or two that never happened is as bad as one who does not know how to forget.
Samuel Butler

Memory is often the attribute of stupidity; it generally belongs to heavy spirits whom it makes even heavier by the baggage it loads on them.
François de Châteaubriand

There are many books which we think we have read when we have not. There are, at least, many that we think we remember when we do not. An original picture was, perhaps, imprinted upon the

brain, but it has changed with our own changing minds. We only remember our remembrance.
G.K. Chesterton

The palest ink is better than the best memory.
Chinese proverb

Memory is the treasury and guardian of all things.
Cicero

A good storyteller is a person who has a good memory and hopes other people haven't.
Irvin S. Cobb

The difference between false memories and true ones is the same as for jewels: It is always the false ones that look the most real, the most brilliant.
Salvador Dalí

She is an excellent creature, but she can never remember which came first, the Greeks or the Romans.
Benjamin Disraeli

It is sadder to find the past again and find it inadequate to the present than it is to have it elude you and remain forever a harmonious conception of memory.
F. Scott Fitzgerald

Isn't it fortunate how selective our recollections usually are.
Malcolm Forbes

The heart's memory eliminates the bad and magnifies the good; and thanks to this artifice we manage to endure the burdens of the past.
Gabriel García Márquez

We are so constituted that we believe the most incredible things, and once they are engraved upon the memory, woe to him that endeavor to erase them.
Johann Wolfgang von Goethe

The things we remember best are those best forgotten.
Baltasar Gracián

No one remembers who came in second.
Walter Hagen

Memory is a net: One finds it full of fish when he takes it from the brook, but a dozen miles of water have run through it without sticking.
Oliver Wendell Holmes, Sr.

The one who thinks over his experiences most, and weaves them into systematic relations with each other, will be the one with the best memory.
William James

Of all the faculties of the human mind, that of memory is the first that suffers decay from age.
Thomas Jefferson

It would add much to human happiness, if an art could be taught of forgetting all of which the remembrance is at once useless and afflictive, that the mind might perform its functions without encumbrance, and the past might no longer encroach upon the present.
Samuel Johnson

No man has a good enough memory to make a successful liar.
Abraham Lincoln

To be able to enjoy one's past life is to live twice.
Martial

Memory presents to us not what we choose but what it pleases.
Michel de Montaigne

Nothing fixes a thing so intensely in the memory as the wish to forget it.
Michel de Montaigne

Memories may escape the action of the will, may sleep a long time, but when stirred by the right influence, though that influence be light as a shadow, they flash into full stature and life with everything in place.
John Muir

Many a man fails to become a thinker for the sole reason that his memory is too good.
Friedrich Wilhelm Nietzsche

A habit of debt is very injurious to the memory.
Austin O'Malley

What beastly incidents our memories insist on cherishing, the ugly, and the disgusting; the beautiful things we have to keep diaries to remember.
Eugene O'Neill

If you wish to forget something on the spot, make a note that this thing is to be remembered.
Edgar Allan Poe

What was hard to bear is sweet to remember.
Portuguese proverb

The repressed memory is like a noisy intruder being thrown out of the concert hall. You can throw him out, but he will hang on the door and continue to disturb the concert.
Dr. Theodor Reik

A man's memory may almost become the art of continually varying and misrepresenting his past, according to his interest in the present.
George Santayana

Our memories are independent of our wills. It is not easy to forget.
Richard B. Sheridan

A man's real possession is his memory. In nothing else is he rich, in nothing else is he poor.
Alexander Smith

Everything remembered is dear, endearing, touching, precious. At least the past is safe—though we didn't know it at the time. We know it now.
Susan Sontag

That is my major preoccupation, memory, the kingdom of memory. I want to protect and enrich that kingdom, glorify that kingdom and serve it.
Elie Wiesel

Memory is the diary that we all carry about with us.
Oscar Wilde

Life is all memory, except for the present moment that goes by you so quick you hardly catch it going.
Tennessee Williams

In memory everything seems to happen to music.
Tennessee Williams

MERIT

A work of real merit finds favor at last.
Amos Bronson Alcott

Merit is never so conspicuous as when coupled with an obscure origin, just as the moon never appears so lustrous as when it emerges from a cloud.
Christian Bovée

Assuredly men of merit are never lacking at any time, for those are the men who

manage affairs, and it is the affairs that produce the men.
Catherine the Great

We ought not to judge of men's merits by their qualifications, but by the use they make of them.
Pierre Charron

Real merit of any kind cannot long be concealed; it will be discovered, and nothing can depreciate it but a man exhibiting it himself. It may not always be rewarded as it ought; but it will always be known.
Lord Chesterfield

Towers are measured by their shadows, and men of merit by those who are envious of them.
Chinese proverb

Contemporaries appreciate the man rather than the merit; but posterity will regard the merit rather than the man.
Charles Caleb Colton

We can perceive the difference between ourselves and our inferiors, but when it comes to a question of the difference between us and our superiors we fail to appreciate merits of which we have no preconceptions.
James Fenimore Cooper

Never to reward any one equal to his merits; but always to insinuate that the reward was above it.
Henry Fielding

It is of no consequence of what parents a man is born, so he be a man of merit.
Horace

I am told so many ill things of a man, and I see so few in him, that I began to suspect he has a real but troublesome

merit, as being likely too eclipse that of others.
Jean de La Bruyère

Merit, God knows, is very little rewarded.
Charles Lamb

Our merit gains us the esteem of the virtuous—our star that of the public.
François de La Rochefoucauld

We must not judge of a man's merits by his great qualities, but by the use he makes of them.
François de La Rochefoucauld

Arrogance in persons of merit affronts us more than arrogance in those without merit. Merit itself is an affront.
Friedrich Wilhelm Nietzsche

By merit, not favoritism, shall we attain our ends.
Plout

Charm strikes the sight, but merit wins the soul.
Alexander Pope

The sufficiency of merit is to know that my merit is not sufficient.
Francis Quarles

There is a certain noble pride, through which merit shines brighter than through modesty.
Jean Paul Richter

True merit, like a river, the deeper it is, the less noise it makes.
George Savile

MIND

One reason why men and women lose their heads so often is that they use them so little! It is the same with everything. If we have anything that is valuable, it must be put to some sort of use. If a man's

muscles are neglected, he soon has none, or rather none worth mentioning. The more the mind is used the more flexible it becomes, and the more it takes upon itself new interests.
George Matthew Adams

One of the most important but one of the most difficult things for a powerful mind is to be its own master.
Joseph Addison

A man's felicity consists not in the outward and visible blessing of fortune, but in the inward and unseen perfections and riches of the mind.
Anarcharsis

The whole object of education is, or should be, to develop mind. The mind should be a thing that works. It should be able to pass judgment on events as they arise, make decisions.
Sherwood Anderson

Mind is a light which the Gods mock us with to lead false those who trust it.
Matthew Arnold

He who cannot contract the sight of his mind, as well as dilate it, wants a great talent in life.
Francis Bacon

Much bending breaks the bow; much unbending the mind.
Francis Bacon

What impresses men is not mind, but the result of mind.
Walter Bagehot

The Unconscious by definition is what you are not conscious of. But the Analysts already know what's in it; they should, because they put it all in beforehand.
Saul Bellow

There are but two powers in the world, the sword and the mind. In the long run the sword is always beaten by the mind.
Napoleon Bonaparte

Few minds wear out; more rust out.
Christian Bovée

Measure your mind's height by the shade it casts.
Robert Browning

I don't wait for moods. You accomplish nothing if you do that. Your mind must know it has got to get down to earth.
Pearl S. Buck

A mind once cultivated will not lie fallow for half an hour.
Edward Bulwer-Lytton

I don't suffer from insanity: I enjoy every minute of it.
Bumper sticker

It is well for people who think to change their minds occasionally in order to keep them clean. For those who do not think, it is best at least to rearrange their prejudices once in a while.
Luther Burbank

The march of the human mind is slow.
Edmund Burke

An open mind is all very well in its way, but it ought not to be so open that there is no keeping anything in or out of it. It should be capable of shutting its doors sometimes, or it may be found a little draughty.
Samuel Butler

A small mind is obstinate. A great mind can lead and be led.
Alexander Cannon

It is the mind which does the work of the world, so that the more there is of mind, the more work will be accomplished.
William Ellery Channing

Merely having an open mind is nothing. The object of opening the mind, as of opening the mouth, is to shut it again on something solid.
G.K. Chesterton

There is but an inch of difference between the cushioned chamber and the padded cell.
G.K. Chesterton

The empires of the future are the empires of the mind.
Winston Churchill

The proof of a well-trained mind is that it rejoices in which is good and grieves at the opposite.
Cicero

We cannot employ the mind to advantage when we are filled with excessive food and drink.
Cicero

The extreme limit of wisdom—that's what the public calls madness.
Jean Cocteau

If you would stand well with a great mind, leave him with a favorable impression of yourself; if with a little mind, leave him with a favorable opinion of himself.
Samuel Taylor Coleridge

Times of general calamity and confusion have ever been productive of the greatest minds. The purest ore is produced from the hottest furnace, and the brightest thunderbolt is elicited from the darkest storm.
Charles Caleb Colton

The best cure for a sluggish mind is to disturb its routine.
William H. Danforth

Minds are like parachutes—they only function when open.
Lord Thomas Dewar

Minds, like bodies, will often fall into a pimpled, ill-conditioned state from mere excess of comfort.
Charles Dickens

There is nothing so elastic as the human mind. The more we are obliged to do, the more we are able to accomplish.
Tryon Edwards

A chief event of life is the day in which we have encountered a mind that startled us.
Ralph Waldo Emerson

Nothing is at last sacred but the integrity of your own mind.
Ralph Waldo Emerson

When the Master of the universe has points to carry in his government he impresses his will in the structure of minds.
Ralph Waldo Emerson

We are making stupendous effort to extend the physical and economic life of the many. But of what high consequence is that extension unless the activity of the mind is also extended, unless we strive ever to live better, rather than simply to make a better living?
Dr. John H. Finley

We do not have to visit a madhouse to find disordered minds; our planet is the mental institution of the universe.
Johann Wolfgang von Goethe

A mind too vigorous and active, serves only to consume the body to which it is joined.
Oliver Goldsmith

It is impossible to live without brains, either one's own or borrowed.
Baltasar Gracián

Each man has, each year, his moment of madness, when he ties a rope around his neck, hands the end to his worst enemy, and says "Pull."
John P. Grier

On earth there is nothing great but man; in man there is nothing great but mind.
Sir William Hamilton

A great mind is one that can forget or look beyond itself.
William Hazlitt

The resolved mind hath no cares.
George Herbert

A mind becomes a detriment when it acquires more intelligence than its integrity can handle.
Cullen Hightower

The only way some of us exercise our minds is by jumping to conclusions.
Cullen Hightower

A vacant mind invites dangerous inmates, as a deserted mansion tempts wandering outcasts to enter and take up their abode in its desolate apartments.
George Stillman Hilliard

Just as a particular soil wants some one element to fertilize it, just as the body in some conditions has a kind of famine for one special food, so the mind has its wants, which do not always call for what is best, but which know themselves and

are as peremptory as the salt-sick sailor's call for a lemon or raw potato.
Oliver Wendell Holmes

Insanity is hereditary. You get it from your children.
Lillian Holstein

Riches, honors and pleasure are the sweets which destroy the mind's appetite for heavenly food; poverty, disgrace and pain are the bitters which restore it.
George Horne

Great minds have purposes, others have wishes.
Washington Irving

To be a real philosopher all that is necessary is to hate some one else's type of thinking.
William James

The inlet of a man's mind is what he learns; the outlet is what he accomplishes. If his mind is not fed by a continued supply of new ideas which he puts to work with purpose, and if there is no outlet in action, his mind becomes stagnant. Such a mind is a danger to the individual who owns it and is useless to the community.
Jeremiah W. Jenks

A merchant may, perhaps, be a man of an enlarged mind, but there is nothing in trade connected with an enlarged mind.
Samuel Johnson

A truly strong and sound mind is the mind that can equally embrace great things and small.
Samuel Johnson

There will always be a frontier where there is an open mind and a willing hand.
Charles F. Kettering

Whenever you look at a piece of work and you think the fellow was crazy, then you want to pay some attention to that. One of you is likely to be, and you had better find out which one it is. It makes an awful lot of difference.
Charles F. Kettering

They copied all they could copy,
But they couldn't copy my mind;
And I left them sweatin' and stealin',
A year and a half behind.
Rudyard Kipling

No business, no movement, no activity on the part of man or a group of men can become any greater than the thinking minds and consciousness of the people who are back of the movement.
H. Spencer Lewis

When he was expected to use his mind, he felt like a right-handed person who has to do something with his left.
Georg C. Lichtenberg

Our reliance in this country is on the inquiring, individual human mind. Our strength is founded there; our resilience, our ability to face an ever-changing future and to master it. We are not frozen into the backward-facing impotence of those societies, fixed in the rigidness of an official dogma, to which the future is the mirror of the past. We are free to make the future for ourselves.
Archibald MacLeish

Only in a quiet mind is adequate perception of the world.
Hans Margolius

How can great minds be produced in a country where the test of great minds is agreeing in the opinion of small minds?
John Stuart Mill

The mind is its own place, and in itself can make a heaven of Hell, a hell of Heaven.
John Milton

The worth of the mind consisteth not in going high, but in marching orderly.
Michel de Montaigne

Read every day something no one else is reading. Think every day something no one else is thinking. It is bad for the mind to be always a part of a unanimity.
Christopher Morley

The mind is like the stomach. It is not how much you put into it that counts, but how much it digests.
A.J. Nock

Only fools and dead men don't change their minds. Fools won't. Dead men can't.
John H. Patterson

The mind longs for what it has missed.
Petronius Arbiter

If a man be endowed with a generous mind, this is the best kind of nobility.
Plato

The great business of man is to improve his mind, and govern his manners; all other projects and pursuits, whether in our power to compass or not, are only amusements.
Pliny

The richest soil, if uncultivated, produces the rankest weeds.
Plutarch

Our minds are like our stomachs; they are whetted by the change of their food, and variety supplies both with fresh appetite.
Quintilian

The best minds are not in government. If they were, business would hire them away.
Ronald Reagan

Not the state of the body but the state of the mind and soul is the measure of the wellbeing of each of us.
Winfred Rhoades

The mind grows narrow in proportion as the soul grows corrupt.
Jean-Jacques Rousseau

You cannot fathom your mind. . . . The more you draw from it, the more clear and fruitful it will be.
George A. Sala

Anything that the human mind can conceive can be produced ultimately.
David Sarnoff

The mind, like the body, is subject to be hurt by everything it taketh for a remedy.
George Savile

Great minds are like eagles, and build their nest in some lofty solitude.
Arthur Schopenhauer

A willing mind makes a light foot.
Scottish proverb

A good mind is lord of a kingdom.
Seneca

A golden mind stoops not to shows of dross.
William Shakespeare

It is the mind that makes the body rich.
William Shakespeare

There is no better sign of a brave mind than a hard hand.
William Shakespeare

It is a very fine thing to have an open mind. But it is a fine thing only if you have the ability to make a decision after considering all sides of a question.
James E. Smith

A light and trifling mind never takes in great ideas, and never accomplishes anything great or good.
William Sprague

Quiet minds cannot be perplexed or frightened but go on in fortune or misfortune at their own private pace, like a clock during a thunderstorm.
Robert Louis Stevenson

For God hath not given us the spirit of fear; but of power, and of love, and of a sound mind.
II Timothy 1:7

The mind has transformed the world, and the world is repaying it with interest. It has led man where he had no idea how to go.
Paul Valery

Iron rusts from disuse, stagnant water loses its purity and in cold weather becomes frozen; even so does inaction sap the vigors of the mind.
Leonardo da Vinci

The mind's the standard of the man.
Alan Watts

If we work marble, it will perish; if we work upon brass, time will efface it; if we rear temples, they will crumble into dust; but if we work upon immortal minds and instill into them just principles, we are then engraving upon tablets which no time will efface, but will brighten and brighten to all eternity.
Daniel Webster

Mind is the great lever of all things; human thought is the process by which human ends are answered.
Daniel Webster

The only man who can't change his mind is a man who hasn't got one.
Edward Noyes Wescott

An open mind is all very well in its way, but it ought not to be so open that there is no keeping anything in or out of it.
Alfred North Whitehead

MISFORTUNE

Better be wise by the misfortunes of others than by your own.
Aesop

There is no misfortune, but to bear it nobly is good fortune.
Marcus Aurelius Antoninus

Misfortune makes of certain souls a vast desert through which rings the voice of God.
Honoré de Balzac

The greatest misfortune of all is not to be able to bear misfortune.
Bias

Calamities are of two kinds: misfortune to ourselves and good fortune to others.
Ambrose Bierce

Heaven sends us misfortunes as a moral tonic.
Lady Marguerite Blessington

Most of our misfortunes are more supportable than the comments of our friends upon them.
Charles Caleb Colton

If a great man struggling with misfortunes is a noble object, a little man that despises them is no contemptible one.
William Cowper

Misfortunes always come in by the door that has been left open for them.
Czech proverb

I never did anything worth doing by accident, nor did any of my inventions come by accident; they came by work.
Thomas A. Edison

There is no calamity that right words will not begin to redness.
Ralph Waldo Emerson

On the occasion of every accident that befalls you, remember to turn to yourself and inquire what power you have for turning it to use.
Epictetus

There is in the worst of fortune the best of chances for a happy change.
Euripides

The effect of great and inevitable misfortune is to elevate those souls which it does not deprive of all virtue.
François Guizot

There is an ambush everywhere from the army of accidents; therefore the rider of life runs with loosened reins.
Hafiz

Misfortune does not always wait on vice; nor is success the constant guest of virtue.
William Havard

The rice grain suffers under the blow of the pestle. But admire its whiteness once the order is over. So it is with men and the world we live in. To be a man one must suffer the blows of misfortune.
Ho Chi Minh

A calamity that affects everyone is only half a calamity.
Italian proverb

When any calamity has been suffered, the first thing to be remembered, is, how much has been escaped.
Samuel Johnson

No accidents are so unlucky but that the wise may draw some advantage from them; nor are there any so lucky but that the foolish may turn them to their own prejudice.
Francois de La Rochefoucauld

It costs a man only a little exertion to bring misfortune on himself.
Menander

We feel a kind of bittersweet pricking of malicious delight in contemplating the misfortunes of others.
Michel de Montaigne

If fortune turns against you, even jelly breaks your tooth.
Persian proverb

Some people think that all the world should share their misfortunes, though they do not share in the sufferings of any one else.
A. Poincelot

We can profit only by our own misfortunes and those of others. The former, though they may be the more beneficial, are also the more painful; let us turn, then, to the latter.
Polybius

Calamity is virtue's opportunity.
Seneca

If all our misfortunes were laid in one common heap, whence everyone must take an equal portion, most people would be content to take their own and depart.
Socrates

The wise man sees in the misfortunes of others what he should avoid.
Publilius Syrus

Life is thickly sown with thorns, and I know no other remedy than to pass quickly through them. The longer we dwell on our misfortunes, the greater is their power to harm us.
Voltaire

Show not yourself glad at the misfortune of another, though he were your enemy.
George Washington

From fortune to misfortune is but a step; from misfortune to fortune is a long way.
Yiddish proverb

MISTAKES

More people would learn from their mistakes if they weren't so busy denying that they made them.
Anonymous

If I had to live my life again, I'd make the same mistakes, only sooner.
Tallulah Bankhead

My only solution for the problem of habitual accidents is to stay in bed all day. Even then, there is always the chance that you will fall out.
Robert Benchley

The errors of a wise man make your rule, Rather than the perfections of a fool.
William Blake

An expert is a man who has made all the mistakes that can be made in a very narrow field.
Niels Bohr

It is only an error in judgment to make a mistake, but it shows infirmity of character to adhere to it when discovered.
Christian Bovée

Wise men learn by other men's mistakes, fools by their own.
H.G. Bohn

Three-fourths of the mistakes a man makes are made because he does not

really know the things he thinks he
knows.
James Bryce

Every great mistake has a halfway
moment, a split second when it can be
recalled and perhaps remedied.
Pearl S. Buck

Mistakes are costly and somebody must
pay. The time to correct a mistake is
before it is made. The causes of mistakes
are, first, I didn't know; second, I didn't
think; third, I didn't care.
Henry H. Buckley

A man who has committed a mistake and
doesn't correct it is committing another
mistake.
Confucius

Life is very interesting, if you make
mistakes.
Georges Carpentier

I can pardon everybody's mistakes
except my own.
Marcus Cato

Who has credit enough in this world to
pay for his mistakes?
Edward Dahlberg

He who makes no mistakes never makes
anything.
English proverb

Mistakes occur when a man is overworked or overconfident.
William Feather

Making mistakes is human. Repeating
'em is too.
Malcolm Forbes

None mess up more often than the old—
except the young.
Malcolm Forbes

An honest mistake always favors the
restaurant.
Robert Half

The greatest mistake you can make in life
is to be continually fearing you will make
one.
Elbert Hubbard

I can't even say I made my own mistakes.
Really—one has to ask oneself—what
dignity is there in that?
Kazuo Ishiguro

When I make a mistake, it's a beaut.
Fiorello La Guardia

Mistakes are part of the dues one pays
for a full life.
Sophia Loren

How could I lose to such an idiot?
Aaron Nimzovich

To make no mistakes is not in the
power of man; but from their errors
and mistakes the wise and good learn
wisdom for the future.
Plutarch

The fellow who never makes a mistake
takes his orders from one who does.
Herbert V. Prochnow

He who never made a mistake never
made a discovery.
Samuel Smiles

I don't care what people say about me. I
do care about my mistakes.
Socrates

I love to make a mistake. It is my only
assurance that I cannot reasonably be
expected to assume the responsibility of
omniscience.
Rex Stout

The mistakes are all there waiting to be made.
Savielly Tartakower

None are more liable to mistakes than those who act only on second thoughts.
Marquis de Vauvenargues

The sages do not consider that making no mistakes is a blessing. They believe, rather, that the great virtue of man lies in his ability to correct his mistakes and continually to make a new man of himself.
Wang Yang-Ming

When you make a mistake, don't look back at it long. Take the reason of the thing into your mind, and then look forward. Mistakes are lessons of wisdom. The past cannot be changed. The future is yet in your power.
Hugh White

MODERATION

Moderation is the key of lasting enjoyment.
Hosea Ballou

I believe in moderation in all things, including moderation.
J.F. Carter

Fortify yourself with moderation; for this is an impregnable fortress.
Epictetus

The true boundary of man is moderation. When once we pass that pale, our guardian angel quits his charge of us.
Owen Feltham

In moderating, not in satisfying desires, lies peace.
Reginald Heber

Moderation is commonly firm, and firmness is commonly successful.
Samuel Johnson

Excess on occasion is exhilarating. It prevents moderation from acquiring the deadening effect of a habit.
Somerset Maugham

Let your moderation be known unto all men. The Lord is at hand. Be careful for nothing; but in every thing by prayer and supplication with thanksgiving let your requests be made known unto God.
Philippians 4:5–6

The man who makes everything that leads to happiness depend upon himself, and not upon other men, has adopted the very best plan for living happily. This is the man of moderation, the man of manly character and of wisdom.
Plato

Temperance and labor are the two best physicians of man; labor sharpens the appetite, and temperance prevents from indulging to excess.
Jean-Jacques Rousseau

Power exercised with violence has seldom been of long duration, but temper and moderation generally produce permanence in all things.
Seneca

MONEY

Capital is to the progress of society what gas is to a car.
James Truslow Adams

A man who is furnished with arguments from the mint will convince his antagonist much sooner than one who draws them from reason and philosophy.
Joseph Addison

I'm not in business to make money for the other guy. I'm in business to make money for myself.
Sheldon Adelson

Increased borrowing must be matched by increased ability to repay. Otherwise we aren't expanding the economy, we're merely puffing it up.
Henry C. Alexander

If only God would give me some clear sign! Like making a deposit in my name in a Swiss bank account.
Woody Allen

Money is better than poverty, if only for financial reasons.
Woody Allen

Money doesn't mind if we say it's evil, it goes from strength to strength. It's a fiction, an addiction, and a tacit conspiracy.
Martin Amis

There are more important things in life than a little money, and one of them is a lot of money.
Anonymous

Dress not thy thoughts in too fine a raiment. And be not a man of superfluous words or superfluous deeds.
Marcus Aurelius Antoninus

Money is a guarantee that we may have what we want in the future. Though we need nothing at the moment it insures the possibility of satisfying a new desire when it arises.
Aristotle

No social system will bring us happiness, health and prosperity unless it is inspired by something greater than materialism.
Clement R. Attlee

To acquire money requires valor, to keep money requires prudence, and to spend money well is an art.
Berthold Auerbach

More people should learn to tell their dollars where to go instead of asking them where they went.
Roger Babson

Money is like muck, not good unless spread.
Francis Bacon

It seems to be a law of American life that whatever enriches us anywhere except in the wallet inevitably becomes uneconomic.
Russell Baker

Money, it turned out, was exactly like sex; you thought of nothing else if you didn't have it and thought of other things if you did.
James Baldwin

The nice thing about having people make money is that they don't stick around unless they want to. It is a nice filtering process.
Steve Ballmer

Money is a terrible master but an excellent servant.
P.T. Barnum

Increased wages, higher pensions, more unemployment insurance, all are of no avail if the purchasing power of money falls faster.
Bernard M. Baruch

Money: A dream, a piece of paper on which is imprinted in invisible ink the dream of all the things it will buy, all the trinkets and all the power over others.
David T. Bazelon

Here we are sitting in a shower of gold, with nothing to hold up but a pitchfork.
Jules Bertillon

Let us keep a firm grip upon our money, for without it the whole assembly of virtues are but as blades of grass.
Bhartrihari

Money: A blessing that is of no advantage excepting when we part with it. An evidence of culture and a passport to polite society.
Ambrose Bierce

Carl Icahn is smart and unrelenting, he doesn't care what other people think, and even though he is not always right, I would never bet against him.
Leon Black

The more men, generally speaking, will do for a Dollar when they make it, the more that Dollar will do for them when they spend it.
William J.H. Boetcker

What our country really needs most are those things which money cannot buy.
William J.H. Boetcker

When men are so busy making money that they have no time for anything else, then the day is not far off when they will have no money for anything else.
William J.H. Boetcker

Abstinence from enjoyment is the only source of capital.
Thomas Brassey

To turn $100 into $110 is work. To turn $100 million into $110 million is inevitable.
Edgar Bronfman

Frugality is founded on the principle that all riches have limits.
Edmund Burke

If money isn't loosened up, this could go down.
George W. Bush

Money is the symbol of duty. It is the sacrament of having done for mankind that which mankind wanted.
Samuel Butler

They say that knowledge is power. I used to think so, but I now know that they meant money. Every guinea is a philosopher's stone.
Lord Byron

Money never starts an idea; it is the idea that starts the money.
W.J. Cameron

Put all good eggs in one basket and then watch that basket.
Andrew Carnegie

On his Manhattan real estate holdings:
A total accident. I just needed a place to put all the money I was making.
John Catsimatidis

Never stand begging for that which you have the power to earn.
Miguel de Cervantes

To desire money is much nobler than to desire success. Desiring money may mean desiring to return to your country, or marry the woman you love, or ransom your father from brigands. But desiring success must mean that you take an abstract pleasure in the unbrotherly act of distancing and disgracing other men.
G.K. Chesterton

Anywhere in the world salt is good to eat; anywhere in the world money is good to use.
Chinese proverb

Frugality includes all the other virtues.
Cicero

Nothing so cements and holds together all the parts of a society as faith or credit, which can never be kept up unless men are under some force or necessity of honestly paying what they owe to one another.
Cicero

It is a common observation that any fool can get money; but they are not wise that think so.
Charles Caleb Colton

There is no dignity quite so impressive and no independence quite so important as living within your means.
Calvin Coolidge

Liking money like I like it is nothing less than mysticism. Money is a glory.
Salvador Dalí

One penny on land is better than ten on the sea.
Danish proverb

Before this recession, people were spending their perceived wealth. The values of their homes were up, their investments and their 401(k)s were up. Now, that wealth is gone and they're back to spending their real income.
Pam Danziger

As a general rule, nobody has money who ought to have it.
Benjamin Disraeli

What's money? A man is a success if he gets up in the morning and gets to bed at night and in between does what he wants to do.
Bob Dylan

A feast is made for laughter, and wine maketh merry; but money answereth all things.
Ecclesiastes 10:19

Money is just a method of keeping score now. I certainly don't need more money. No one needs this much money.
Lawrence Ellison

Money, which represents the prose of life, and is hardly spoken of in parlors without apology, is, in its effects and laws, as beautiful as roses.
Ralph Waldo Emerson

Spend, and God will send.
English proverb

'Tis money that begets money.
English proverb

A peculiarity of capital is that it cannot be employed productively without benefiting the community in which it is used.
William Feather

Make money your God, and it will plague you like the devil.
Henry Fielding

Why shouldn't the American people take half my money from me? I took all of it from them.
Edward A. Filene

A man with a surplus can control circumstances, but a man without a surplus is controlled by them, and often he has no opportunity to exercise judgment.
Harvey Firestone

Of all the icy blasts that blow on love, a request for money is the most chilling and havoc-wreaking.
Gustave Flaubert

My problem lies in reconciling my gross habits with my net income.
Errol Flynn

A rich American, intellectually brilliant but without mental or financial scruple, recently died. He was sore, sour, bitter. His sole concern in life was to leave a certain number of millions to his children—his wife didn't rate importantly. He freely admitted to intimates that he didn't care how or where he acquired wealth—he was out to get it by hook or crook. If such a life isn't a miserable failure in the eyes of both God and man, what is?

B.C. Forbes (1937)

He is a wise man who seeks by every legitimate means to make all the money he can honestly, for money can do so many worthwhile things in this world, not merely for one's self but for others. But he is an unmitigated fool who imagines for a moment that it is more important to make the money than to make it honestly. One of the advantages of possessing money is that it facilitates one's independence and mental attitude. The man head over heels in debt is more slave than independent.

B.C. Forbes

How many men I know who are earning dollars aplenty, but who are really earning little of what counts. They are so overwhelmingly engrossed in business that they get nothing from their dollars. The Juggernaut of dollar-making has crushed out of them every capacity for genuine enjoyment, every grace, every unselfish sentiment and instinct.

B.C. Forbes

A lot of money doesn't make anyone more often right. It just makes him harder to correct.

Malcolm Forbes

All work and no play makes jack. With enough jack, Jack needn't be a dull boy.

Malcolm Forbes

Anybody who thinks gold is a substitute for productivity is not a productive thinker.

Malcolm Forbes

Fifteen percent of the bill for the waiter; another 5% of the bill for the captain, in the places where he makes the salad and generally works at the job; one dollar per bottle for the wine steward; and/or a buck for the bartender if he had made several drinks. [And don't think] you can walk out without tipping if you have been dissatisfied. . . .

Malcolm Forbes

Why, just a couple of economic seasons ago, was idle cash considered an indication of bad management or lazy management? Because it meant that management didn't have this money out at work . . . Now look. Presto! A new fashion! Cash is back in! Denigrating liquidity has dropped quicker than hemlines. A management is now saluted if it has some cash, some liquidity, doesn't have to go to the money market at huge interest rates to get the wherewithal to keep going and growing. Along with Ben Franklin, my father and your father would understand and applaud this new economic fashion. . . .

Malcolm Forbes

The cure for materialism is to have enough for everybody and to share. When people are sure of having what they need they cease to think about it.

Henry Ford

The highest use of capital is not to make more money, but to make money do more for the betterment of life.

Henry Ford

Money doesn't change men, it merely unmasks them. If a man is naturally

selfish or arrogant or greedy, the money brings that out, that is all.
Henry Ford

Money is like an arm or leg—use it or lose it.
Henry Ford

Old men are always advising young men to save money. That is bad advice. Don't save every nickel. Invest in yourself. I never saved a dollar until I was forty years old.
Henry Ford

My mother used to sew flour sacks together to make sheets, so cotton sheets were a real treat. I knew I had to marry a rich girl.
Sidney Frank

Beware of little expenses; a small leak will sink a great ship.
Benjamin Franklin

Great spenders are bad lenders.
Benjamin Franklin

He that is of opinion money will do everything may well be suspected of doing everything for money.
Benjamin Franklin

Money is of a prolific generating nature. Money can beget money, and its offspring can beget more.
Benjamin Franklin

Remember, that time is money. . . . Remember, that credit is money . . . Remember that money is of the prolific, generating nature. . . . Remember, that six pounds a year is but a groat a day. . . . Remember this saying, "The good prayer is lord of another man's purse." He that is known to pay punctually and exactly to the time he promises, may at any time, and on any occasion, raise all the money his friends can spare. . . . In short, the

way to wealth, if you desire it, is as plain as the way to market. It depends chiefly on two words, industry and frugality; that is, waste neither time nor money, but make the best use of both.
Benjamin Franklin

The use of money is all the advantage there is in having money.
Benjamin Franklin

God makes, and apparel shapes: but 'tis money that finishes the man.
Thomas Fuller

If anything is evident about people who manage money, it is that the task attracts a very low level of talent, one that is protected in its highly imperfect profession by the mystery that is thought to enfold the subject of economics in general and of money in particular.
John Kenneth Galbraith

I am not rich. I am a poor man with money, which is not the same thing.
Gabriel García Márquez

The most popular labor-saving device is still money.
Phyllis George

Money is like love; it kills slowly and painfully the one who withholds it, and it enlivens the other who turns it upon his fellow man.
Kahlil Gibran

If frugality were established in the state, if our expenses were laid out rather in the necessaries than the superfluities of life, there might be fewer wants, and even fewer pleasures, but infinitely more happiness.
Oliver Goldsmith

Central banks have gotten out of the central banking business and into the central planning business, meaning that

they are devoted to raising up—if they can—economic growth and employment through the dubious means of suppressing interest rates and printing money. The nice thing about gold is that you can't print it.
James Grant

The darkest hour in any man's life is when he sits down to plan how to get money without earning it.
Horace Greeley

A treasure is to be valued for its own sake and not for what it will buy.
Graham Greene

Greek shipowners like to boast, "I bought ships at the bottom of the market, and now they're worth ten times as much." It goes back to the days of Onassis and Niarchos competing with each other over who had the biggest fleet, the biggest yacht and the most famous girlfriend.
Stelios Haji-Ioannou

I pity that man who wants a coat so cheap that the man or woman who produces the cloth shall starve in the process.
Benjamin Harrison

It is often easier to assemble armies than it is to assemble army revenues.
Benjamin Harrison

On the benefits of his being kidnapped:
Very good for the waistline. One of the best reducing programs.
Alfred Heineken

Money is life to us wretched mortals.
Hesiod

Money can be fickle, having a lasting relationship with a few and a brief fling with others, while just flirting with the rest of us.
Cullen Hightower

Money spent on myself may be a millstone about my neck; money spent on others may give me wings like the angels.
Roswell D. Hitchcock

The obsession with gold, actually and politically, occurs among those who regard economics as a branch of morality. Gold is solid, gold is durable, gold is rare, gold is even (in certain very peculiar circumstances) convertible. To believe in thrift, solidity and soundness is to believe in some way in the properties of gold.
Christopher Hitchens

American business needs a lifting purpose greater than the struggle of materialism.
Herbert Hoover

A bank is a place that will lend you money if you can prove that you don't need it.
Bob Hope

I don't want you to put any phony figures in there because I'll rip them down. Because when they [the public] ask me about it, I have to go into a routine. I don't have it. And if my estate's worth over $50 million, I'll kiss your ass. I mean that.
Bob Hope

Germans live with a haunting fear that we might fail. That attitude is a clear disadvantage.
Dietmar Hopp

Get money first; virtue comes after.
Horace

He that hath money in his purse cannot want a head for his shoulders.
James Howell

The safest way to double your money is to fold it over and put it in your pocket.
Kin Hubbard

It's a terribly hard job to spend a billion dollars and get your money's worth.
George Humphrey

Everything you gather is just one that you can lose.
Robert Hunter

Money may be the husk of many things, but not the kernel. It brings you food, but not appetite; medicine, but not health; acquaintances, but not friends; servants, but not faithfulness; days of joy, but not peace or happiness.
Henrik Ibsen

I would rather be a beggar and spend my money like a king, than be a king and spend money like a beggar.
Robert G. Ingersoll

Women prefer men who have something tender about them—especially the legal kind.
Kay Ingram

Getting money is like digging with a needle; spending it is like water soaking into sand.
Japanese proverb

Money and time are the heaviest burdens of life, and the unhappiest of all mortals are those who have more of either than they know how to use.
Samuel Johnson

Sir, no man but a blockhead ever wrote except for money.
Samuel Johnson

There are few ways in which a man can be more innocently employed than in getting money.
Samuel Johnson

The covetous man never has money; the prodigal will have none shortly.
Ben Jonson

There is no subtler, no surer means of overturning the existing basis of society than to debauch the currency. The process engages all the hidden forces of economic law on the side of destruction, and does it in a manner which not one man in a million is able to diagnose. . . .
John Maynard Keynes

There is nothing so disastrous as a rational investment policy in an irrational world.
John Maynard Keynes

All the money in the world is no use to a man or his country if he spends it as fast as he makes it. All he has left is his bills and the reputation for being a fool.
Rudyard Kipling

Under the gold standard America had no major financial panics other than in 1873, 1884, 1890, 1893, 1907, 1930, 1931, 1932, and 1933.
Paul Krugman

Will gold return to its high-street penetration through mass-market jewelers? I doubt it very much. Will it increasingly be center stage at Tiffany and in Bond Street? Absolutely.
David Lamb

It is easy to be generous with other people's money.
Latin proverb

Oh, the poor folks hate the rich folks,
And the rich folks hate the poor folks.
All of my folks hate all of your folks,
It's as American as apple pie.
Tom Lehrer

I got what no millionaires got, I got no money.
Gerald Lieberman

People die, but money never does.
Penelope Lively

Love of money is the disease which makes men most groveling and pitiful.
Cassius Longinus

But for money and the need of it, there would not be half the friendship in the world. It is powerful for good if divinely used. Give it plenty of air and it is sweet as the hawthorn; shut it up and it cankers and breeds worms.
George MacDonald

The love for money is only one among many.
Alfred Marshall

For what is a man profited, if he shall gain the whole world, and lose his own soul?
Matthew 16:26

Money is like a sixth sense—and you can't make use of the other five without it.
Somerset Maugham

I do not prize the word *cheap*. It is not a word of inspiration. It is the badge of poverty, the signal of distress. Cheap merchandise means cheap men and cheap men mean a cheap country.
William McKinley

We cannot gamble with anything so sacred as money.
William McKinley

The chief value of money lies in the fact that one lives in a world in which it is overestimated.
H.L. Mencken

Much work is merely a way to make money; much leisure is merely a way to spend it.
C. Wright Mills

A man's treatment of money is the most decisive test of his character—how he makes it and how he spends it.
James Moffatt

The most substantial people are the most frugal, and make the least show, and live at the least expense.
Francis Moore

He who makes money pleases God.
Muhammad

I'm living so far beyond my income that we may almost be said to be living apart.
H.H. Munro

A credit card is a money tool, not a supplement to money. The failure to make this distinction has supplemented many a poor soul right into bankruptcy.
Paula Nelson

Society can transport money from rich to poor only in a leaky bucket.
Arthur M. Okun

How to make the summer months pass quickly: Borrow money in June, make the note payable in three months, and fall will be here before you know it.
Old Southern saying

After a certain point money is meaningless. It's the game that counts.
Aristotle Onassis

Public money ought to be touched with the most scrupulous conscientiousness of honor. It is not the produce of riches only, but of the hard earnings of labor and poverty. It is drawn even from the bitterness of want and misery. Not a beggar passes, or perishes in the streets, whose mite is not in that mass.
Thomas Paine

The two most beautiful words in the
English language are "Check enclosed."
Dorothy Parker

Frugality is good, if liberality be joined
with it. The first is leaving off superfluous
expenses; the last bestowing them to
the benefit of others that need. The first
without the last begets covetousness;
the last with the first begets prodigality.
Both together make an excellent temper.
Happy the place where that is found.
William Penn

Nothing is cheap which is superfluous,
for what one does not need, is dear at a
penny.
Plutarch

Without counsel purposes are disappointed: but in the multitude of counselors they are established.
Proverbs 15:22

Therefore I love your commandments
above gold, above fine gold.
Psalms 119:127

Money was made for the free-hearted
and generous.
John Ray

I finally know what distinguishes man
from the beasts: financial worries.
Jules Renard

There is a certain Buddhistic calm that
comes from having . . . money in the bank.
Tom Robbins

I believe that the power to make money
is a gift from God.
John D. Rockefeller

Money can't buy happiness, but neither
can poverty.
Leo Rosten

Its not all about the money, its about
transforming something and what you
leave behind.
Stephen Ross

Why, money isn't everything to an
Englishman. There are other considerations when he marries, for instance,
fondness for the girl.
Dowager Duchess of Roxburghe

Money can't buy you happiness, but it
can buy you a yacht big enough to pull up
right alongside it.
David Lee Roth

When money speaks, the truth keeps
silent.
Russian proverb

*On how a $270 million investment
returned him $970 million:* What can I
say? I'm a lucky man.
Haim Saban

Earn enough money so you can afford to
waste time.
Kiyoshi Sagawa

The Lord maketh poor, and maketh rich:
he bringeth low, and lifteth up.
I Samuel 2:7

Finance: the art of passing currency from
hand to hand until it finally disappears.
Robert W. Sarnoff

A cement king's prediction in 1993: In this
business you have to find countries that
need to build an infrastructure. What
we're really excited about is the Far East.
In 20 years all the money will be there
and not in the U.S.
Thomas Schmidheiny

Money is human happiness in the
abstract: he, then, who is no longer
capable of enjoying human happiness in

the concrete devotes himself utterly to money.
Arthur Schopenhauer

Money is like sea-water: The more we drink the thirstier we become; and the same is true of fame.
Arthur Schopenhauer

Credit is like a looking glass, which, when once sullied by a breath, may be wiped clear again, but if once cracked can never be repaired.
Sir Walter Scott

Ask thy purse what thou should spend.
Scottish proverb

With parsimony a little is sufficient; without it nothing is sufficient; but frugality makes a poor man rich.
Seneca

In nature all is managed for the best with perfect frugality and just reserve, profuse to none, but bountiful to all; never employing on one thing more than enough, but with exact economy retrenching the superfluous, and adding force to what is principal in everything.
Lord Shaftesbury

Financiers live in a world of illusion. They count on something which they call the capital of the country, which has no existence.
George Bernard Shaw

It happens a little unluckily that the persons who have the most infinite contempt of money are the same that have the strongest appetite for the pleasures it procures.
William Shenstone

I do what I like, and theres no reason that paper money should change that.
Gil Shwed

If each year slightly less capital is invested in industry, the time will eventually come when the amount of equipment per laborer and, in consequence, the productivity and the wages of labor are less than they otherwise would be.
Sumner H. Slichter

Money and sex are forces too unruly for our reason; they can only be controlled by taboos which we tamper with at our peril.
Logan Pearsall Smith

Money alone is only a mean; it presupposes a man to use it. The rich man can go where he pleases, but perhaps please himself nowhere. He can buy a library or visit the whole world, but perhaps has neither patience to read nor intelligence to see. . . . The purse may be full and the heart empty. He may have gained the world and lost himself; and with all his wealth around him . . . he may live as blank a life as any tattered ditcher.
Robert Louis Stevenson

I like Paris. They don't talk so much of money, but more of sex.
Vera Stravinsky

A wise man should have money in his head, but not in his heart.
Jonathan Swift

No man will take counsel, but every man will take money. Therefore, money is better than counsel.
Jonathan Swift

We are all dependent upon the investment of capital.
William Howard Taft

The philosophy which affects to teach us a contempt of money does not run very deep.
Henry J. Taylor

Why tie to gold? Why not 1982 Bordeaux?
Richard Thaler

It is difficult to begin without borrowing, but perhaps it is the most generous course thus to permit your fellow-men to have an interest in your enterprise.
Henry David Thoreau

But they that will be rich fall into temptation and a snare, and into many foolish and hurtful lusts, which drown men in destruction and perdition.
I Timothy 6:9

His money is twice tainted: 'taint yours and 'taint mine.
Mark Twain

I never write "metropolis" for seven cents because I can get the same price for "city." I never write "policeman" because I can get the same money for "cop."
Mark Twain

The more money an American accumulates, the less interesting he becomes.
Gore Vidal

The contempt of money is no more a virtue than to wash one's hand is one; but one does not willingly shake hands with a man that never washes his.
Horace Walpole

Let us be happy and live within our means, even if we have to borrow money to do it with.
Artemus Ward

Credit has done a thousand times more to enrich mankind than all the gold mines in the world. It has exalted labor, stimulated manufacture and pushed commerce over every sea.
Daniel Webster

If you divorce capital from labor, capital is hoarded, and labor starves.
Daniel Webster

Get all you can, without hurting your soul, your body, or your neighbor. Save all you can, cutting off every needless expense. Give all you can.
John Wesley

What a man does with his wealth depends upon his idea of happiness. Those who draw prizes in life are apt to spend tastelessly, if not viciously; not knowing that it requires as much talent to spend as to make.
Edwin P. Whipple

The great rule is not to talk about money with people who have much more or much less than you.
Katharine Whitehorn

Never get deeply in debt to someone who cried at the end of *Scarface*.
Robert S. Wieder

The way to stop financial joyriding is to arrest the chauffeur, not the automobile.
Woodrow Wilson

Money makes up in a measure all other wants in men.
William Wycherley

With money in your pocket, you are wise and you are handsome and you sing well too.
Yiddish proverb

MORALS

Morality is a private and costly luxury.
Henry Adams

A person may be qualified to do greater good to mankind and become more

beneficial to the world, by morality without faith than by faith without morality.
Joseph Addison

Morality represents for everybody a thoroughly definite and ascertained idea: the idea of human conduct regulated in a certain manner.
Matthew Arnold

Never let your sense of morals prevent you from doing what is right.
Isaac Asimov

The relationship of morality and power is a very subtle one. Because ultimately power without morality is no longer power.
James Baldwin

Morality is character and conduct such as is required by the circle or community in which the man's life happens to be placed. It shows how much good men require of us.
Henry Ward Beecher

Moral: Conforming to a local and mutable standard of right; having the quality of general expediency.
Ambrose Bierce

I like the English. They have the most rigid code of immorality in the world.
Malcolm Bradbury

Morality is the custom of one's country and the current feeling of one's peers.
Samuel Butler

The foundations of morality are like all other foundations: If you dig too much about them the superstructure will come tumbling down.
Samuel Butler

Not on morality, but on cookery, let us build our stronghold: there brandishing our frying-pan, as censer, let us offer sweet incense to the Devil, and live at ease on the fat things he has provided for his elect!
Thomas Carlyle

There can be no high civility without a deep morality.
Ralph Waldo Emerson

If moral thoughtfulness can be erected into a guiding philosophy of business, there is a long day of usefulness ahead for the system.
B.C. Forbes

If you think of standardization as the best that you know today, but which is to be improved tomorrow—you get somewhere.
Henry Ford

What is moral is what you feel good after and what is immoral is what you feel bad after.
Ernest Hemingway

When moral courage feels that it is in the right, there is no personal daring of which it is incapable.
Leigh Hunt

Every act of every man is a moral act, to be tested by moral, and not by economic, criteria.
Robert M. Hutchins

Morality is always the product of terror; its chains and strait-waistcoats are fashioned by those who dare not trust others, because they do not dare to trust themselves, to walk in liberty.
Aldous Huxley

He who steadily observes those moral precepts in which all religions concur will never be questioned at the gates of

heaven as to the dogmas in which they all differ.
Thomas Jefferson

Two things fill the mind with ever new and increasing wonder and awe—the starry heavens above me, and the moral law within me.
Immanuel Kant

With intellectuals, moral thought is often less a tonic that quickens ethical action than a narcotic that deadens it.
Louis Kronenberger

We are a kind of chameleons, taking our hue—the hue of our moral character—from those who are about us.
John Locke

Why, a moral truth is a hollow tooth which must be propped with gold.
Edgar Lee Masters

The foundations of the world will be shaky until the moral props are restored.
Anne O'Hare McCormick

Nothing is politically right which is morally wrong.
Daniel O'Connell

Without civic morality communities perish; without personal morality their survival has no value.
Bertrand Russell

Morality without religion is a tree without roots; a stream without any spring to feed it; a house built on the sand; a pleasant place to live in till the heavens grow dark, and the storm begins to beat.
James B. Shaw

To have a respect for ourselves guides our morals; and to have a deference for others governs our manners.
Laurence Sterne

If thy morals make thee dreary, depend upon it they are wrong.
Robert Louis Stevenson

You must regulate your life by the standards you admire when you are at your best.
John M. Thomas

It is not best when we use our morals on weekdays; it gets them out of repair for Sundays.
Mark Twain

No matter what theory of the origin of government you adopt, if you follow it out to its legitimate conclusions it will bring you face to face with the moral law.
Henry van Dyke

Morality is religion in practice; religion is morality in principle.
Joseph Wardlaw

Morality is simply the attitude we adopt toward people whom we personally dislike.
Oscar Wilde

N

NAMES

Whatever you lend let it be your money, and not your name. Money you may get again, and, if not, you may contrive to do without it; name once lost you cannot get again, and, if you cannot contrive to do without it, you had better never have been born.
Edward Bulwer-Lytton

The inheritance of a distinguished and noble name is a proud inheritance to him who lives worthily of it.
Charles Caleb Colton

I don't remember anybody's name. How do you think the dahling thing started?
Eva Gabor

A man's name is not like a mantle which merely hangs about him, and which one perchance may safely twitch and pull, but a perfectly fitting garment, which, like the skin, has grown over him, at which one cannot rake and scrape without injuring the man himself.
Johann Wolfgang von Goethe

The invisible thing called a Good Name is made up of the breath of numbers that speak well of you.
Lord Halifax

A good name, like good will, is got by many actions and lost by one.
Lord Jeffrey

NATION

There are three things which make a nation great and prosperous—a fertile soil, busy workshops, and easy conveyance for men and commodities.
Francis Bacon

The state is the great fictitious entity by which everyone seeks to live at the expense of everyone else.
Claude Frédéric Bastiat

Caution and conservatism are expected of old age; but when the young men of a nation are possessed of such a spirit, when they are afraid of the noise and strife caused by the applications of the truth, heaven save the land! Its funeral bell has already rung.
Henry Ward Beecher

The modern state no longer has anything but rights; it does not recognize duties any more.
Georges Bernanos

A state without some means of change is without the means of its conservation.
Edmund Burke

A thousand years scarce serve to form a state; an hour may lay it in the dust.
Lord Byron

The whole history of the world is summed up in the fact that, when nations are strong, they are not always just, and when they wish to be just, they are often no longer strong.
Winston Churchill

A nation's character is the sum of its splendid deeds, they constitute one common patrimony, the nation's inheritance. They awe foreign powers, they arouse and animate our own people.
Henry Clay

No nation ever had an army large enough to guarantee it against attack in time of peace or insure it victory in time of war.
Calvin Coolidge

The nation which forgets its defenders will itself be forgotten.
Calvin Coolidge

The greatest asset of any nation is the spirit of its people, and the greatest danger that can menace any nation is the breakdown of that spirit—the will to win and the courage to work.
George B. Cortelyou

Individuals may form communities, but it is institutions alone that can create a nation.
Benjamin Disraeli

Nationalism: An infantile disease. It is the measles of mankind.
Albert Einstein

The state is made for man, not man for the state.
Albert Einstein

Every actual state is corrupt. Good men must not obey the laws too well.
Ralph Waldo Emerson

Nationalism and internationalism! Both must stand together or the human race will be utterly destroyed. We shall never be able to destroy nationalism and we shall never be able to live without internationalism.
Linus R. Fike

A great nation cannot abandon its responsibilities. Responsibilities abandoned today return as more acute crises tomorrow.
Gerald Ford

God grant not only the love of liberty but a thorough knowledge of the rights of man may pervade all the nations of the earth—so that a philosopher may set his foot anywhere on its surface and say, This is my Country.
Benjamin Franklin

We cannot too often tell ourselves that the real wealth of a nation—the only enduring, worthwhile wealth—is in the spiritual, mental and physical health of the citizens, and that in a democracy we are all trustees.
Sir Herbert Gepp

The nationalist has a broad hatred and a narrow love.
André Gide

Altogether, national hatred is something peculiar. You will always find it strongest and most violent where there is the lowest degree of culture.
Johann Wolfgang von Goethe

A nation without dregs and malcontents is orderly, peaceful and pleasant, but perhaps without the seed of things to come.
Eric Hoffer

A nation may be said to consist of its territory, its people and its laws. The territory is the only part which is of certain durability. Laws change, people die, the land remains.
Abraham Lincoln

The worth of a state, in the long run, is the worth of the individuals composing it.
John Stuart Mill

Nationalism: One of the effective ways in which the modern man escapes life's ethical problems.
Reinhold Niebuhr

What makes a nation great is not primarily its great men, but the stature of its innumerable mediocre ones.
Jose Ortega y Gasset

Great nations write their autobiography in three manuscripts—the book of their deeds, the book of their words, and the book of their art.
John Ruskin

Every nation thinks its own madness normal and requisite; more passion and more fancy it calls folly, less it calls imbecility.
George Santayana

Every nation ridicules other nations, and all are right.
Arthur Schopenhauer

For every nation that lives peaceably, there will be many others to grow hard

and push their arrogance to extremes; the gods attend to these things slowly. But they attend to those who put off God and turn to madness.
Sophocles

There will never be a really free and enlightened state until the state comes to recognize the individual as a higher and independent power, from which all its own power and authority are derived, and treats him accordingly.
Henry David Thoreau

Local assemblies of the people constitute the strength of free nations. Municipal institutions are to liberty what primary schools are to science: they bring it within the people's reach, and teach them how to use and enjoy it. A nation may establish a system of free government, but without the spirit of municipal institutions it cannot have the spirit of liberty.
Alexis de Tocqueville

All nations have present, or past, or future reasons for thinking themselves incomparable.
Paul Valery

Nationalism has two fatal charms for its devotees: It presupposes local self-sufficiency, which is a pleasant and desirable condition, and it suggests, very subtly, a certain personal superiority by reason of one's belonging to a place which is definable and familiar, as against a place that is strange, remote.
E.B. White

An individual is as superb as a nation when he has the qualities which make a superb nation.
Walt Whitman

NATURE

A cloudy day, or a little sunshine, have as great an influence on many constitutions as the most real blessings or misfortunes.
Joseph Addison

I am at two with nature.
Woody Allen

Nature has no mercy at all. Nature says, "I'm going to snow. If you have on a bikini and no snowshoes, that's tough. I am going to snow anyway."
Maya Angelou

Farm: What a city man dreams of at 5 p.m., never at 5 a.m.
Anonymous

Nature is a hanging judge.
Anonymous

The guy who wrote "A job well done never needs doing again" never weeded a garden.
Anonymous

Thou hast existed as a part; thou shalt disappear into that which produced thee. This, too, nature wills. Pass then through this little space of time conformably to nature and end thy journey in content, just as the olive falls when it is ripe, thanking the tree on which it grew and blessing the nature that gave it birth.
Marcus Aurelius Antoninus

A tree that affords thee shade, do not order it to be cut down.
Arabian proverb

Ride the tributaries to reach the sea.
Arabian proverb

Nature is a labyrinth in which the very haste you move with will make you lose your way.
Francis Bacon

When ages grow to civility and elegancy, men come to build stately sooner than to garden finely, as if gardening were the greater perfection.
Francis Bacon

Rain! whose soft architectural hands have power to cut stones and chisel to shapes of grandeur the very mountains.
Henry Ward Beecher

The three great elemental sounds in nature are the sound of rain, the sound of wind in a primeval wood, and the sound of outer ocean on a beach.
Henry Beston

Do no dishonor to the earth lest you dishonor the spirit of man.
Henry Beston

To see a World in a Grain of Sand
And a heaven in a Wild Flower,
Hold Infinity in the palm of your hand
And Eternity in an hour.
William Blake

Pray to God for a good harvest, but don't stop hoeing.
Bohemian proverb

If the voice of the brook was not the first song of celebration, it must have been at least an obbligato for that event.
Hal Borland

The fouling of the nest which has been typical of man's activity in the past on a local scale now seems to be extending to the whole system.
Kenneth Boulding

To cultivate a garden is to walk with God.
Christian Bovée

There is something infinitely healing in the repeated refrains of nature—the

assurance that dawn comes after night, and spring after the winter.
Rachel Carson

I love to think of nature as an unlimited broadcasting station, through which God speaks to us every hour, if we will only tune in.
George Washington Carver

For us who live in cities Nature is not natural. Nature is supernatural. Just as monks watched and strove to get a glimpse of heaven, so we watch and strive to get a glimpse of earth. It is as if men had cake and wine every day but were sometimes allowed common bread.
G.K. Chesterton

He who keeps the hills, burns the wood; he who keeps the streams drinks the water.
Chinese proverb

Nature is that lovely lady to whom we owe polio, leprosy, smallpox, syphilis, tuberculosis, cancer.
Stanley Cohen

The only stock I ever invested in always had four legs attached to it.
Conservative farmer

Beware pathetic fallacy. Man's confident assumption that his environment is so sympathetic to his moods as to kick in with complimentary props when he requires them bespeaks the kind of arrogance that invites comeuppance.
Alan Coren

How things look on the outside of us depends on how things are on the inside of us. Stay close to the heart of nature and forget this troubled world. Remember, there is nothing wrong with nature; the trouble is in ourselves.
Parks Cousins

Our world is evolving without consideration, and the result is a loss of biodiversity, energy issues, congestion in cities. But geography, if used correctly, can be used to redesign sustainable and more livable cities.
Jack Dangermond

We talk of our mastery of nature, which sounds very grand; but the fact is we respectfully adapt ourselves, first, to her ways.
Clarence Day

Complete adaptation to environment means death. The essential point in all response is the desire to control environment.
John Dewey

Nature gives to every time and season some beauties of its own; and from morning to night, as from the cradle to the grave, is but a succession of changes so gentle and easy that we can scarcely mark their progress.
Charles Dickens

A pool is, for many of us in the West, a symbol not of affluence but of order, of control over the uncontrollable.
Joan Didion

We are the children of our landscape.
Lawrence Durrell

I don't dig nature at all. I think nature is very unnatural. I think the truly natural things are dreams, which nature can't touch with decay.
Bob Dylan

All the rivers run into the sea; yet the sea is not full; unto the place from whence the rivers come, thither they return again.
Ecclesiastes 1:7

Surely there is something in the unruffled calm of nature that overawes our little anxieties and doubts: the sight of the deep-blue sky, and the clustering stars above, seem to impart a quiet to the mind.
Jonathan Edwards

Farming looks mighty easy when your plow is a pencil, and you're a thousand miles from a corn field.
Dwight D. Eisenhower

All men are poets at heart. They serve nature for bread, but her loveliness overcomes them sometimes.
Ralph Waldo Emerson

The good rain, like a bad preacher, does not know when to leave off.
Ralph Waldo Emerson

Nature is reckless of the individual. When she has points to carry, she carries them.
Ralph Waldo Emerson

Sail! quoth the king; Hold! saith the wind.
English proverb

Deep snow in winter; tall grain in summer.
Estonian proverb

Whatever nature has in store for mankind, unpleasant as it may be, men must accept, for ignorance is never better than knowledge.
Enrico Fermi

I hope a start at getting some oil out of the enormous Alaska field isn't indefinitely mired in a bureaucratic morass as a result of our national concern for the ecology. This concern must not be so misguided, misdirected, misused that it serves to stop economic growth, to bankrupt companies, to stifle new development, new jobs, new horizons. In fighting new pollution and stemming present pollution, exciting, sometimes

costly means and methods exist and others will evolve. But blanket legislative naysaying to expanding power and energy sources is stupid, self-defeating.
Malcolm Forbes (1970)

When a fissure off the California coast started pumping and dumping oil on the nearby towns and beaches, everybody started dumping on Union Oil. Matters weren't helped one iota by a manufactured quotation attributed to Union's president, Fred Hartley, alleging his amazement at the publicity for the loss of a few birds. . . .

Fred Hartley never said what the press reported, as the transcript and the Senate committee members definitely established. But I don't suppose the truth will ever catch up with the more colorful falsehood.
Malcolm Forbes

Will this massive outcry [about pollution] continue long enough to have effective results? Will federal and state laws be enacted with effective enforcement clauses? Will people be concerned long enough to pay the bill through higher prices? Will towns tolerate lost jobs when it proves too costly to clean obsolete plants?. . .

I think so, but it sure won't be as easy as the present outcry and political oratory suggest. The answers to preserving a livable environment are not all simple, and some of the nuts now pushing simplistic cure-alls won't help bring about any lasting solutions.
Malcolm Forbes (1970)

Nature has no principles. She furnishes us with no reason to believe that human life is to be respected. Nature, in her indifference, makes no distinction between good and evil.
Anatole France

Hollywood: the only place you can wake up in the morning and hear the birds coughing in the trees.
Joe Frisco

The winds and waves are always on the side of the ablest navigators.
Edward Gibbon

Is a park any better than a coal mine? What's a mountain got that a slag pile hasn't? What would you rather have in your garden—an almond tree or an oil well?
Jean Giradoux

Nature knows no pause in progress and development, and attaches her curse on all inaction.
Johann Wolfgang von Goethe

Nature goes on her way, and all that to us seems an exception is really according to order.
Johann Wolfgang von Goethe

There is no trifling with nature; it is always true, grave, and severe; it is always in the light, and the faults and errors fall to our share. It defies incompetency, but reveals its secrets to the competent, the truthful, and the pure.
Johann Wolfgang von Goethe

Nature often lets us down when we most need her; let us turn to art.
Baltasar Gracían

He who thinks everything must be in bloom when the strawberries are in bloom doesn't know anything about apples.
Greek proverb

We do not know, in most cases, how far social failure and success are due to heredity, and how far to environment. But environment is the easier of the two to improve.
J.B.S. Haldane

I have come to see the nonsense of trying to describe fine scenery.
Nathaniel Hawthorne

There are only three pleasures in life pure and lasting, and all derived from inanimate things—books, pictures and the face of nature.
William Hazlitt

To the natural philosopher, there is no natural object unimportant or trifling. From the least of Nature's works he may learn the greatest lessons.
Sir John Herschel

A goose flies by a chart which the Royal Geographical Society could not improve.
Oliver Wendell Holmes

Everyone goes to the forest; some go for a walk to be inspired, and others go to cut down the trees.
Vladimir Horowitz

Art may make a suit of clothes, but nature must produce a man.
David Hume

The chessboard is the world; the pieces are the phenomena of the universe; the rules of the game are what we call laws of nature.
Thomas H. Huxley

Different people have different duties assigned them by Nature; Nature has given one the power or the desire to do this, the other that. Each bird must sing with his own throat.
Henrik Ibsen

In nature there are neither rewards nor punishments; there are consequences.
Robert Ingersoll

A man who lives with nature is used to violence and is companionable with death. There is more violence in an English hedgerow than in the meanest streets of a great city.
P.D. James

A man finds in the productions of nature an inexhaustible stock of material on which he can employ himself, without any temptations to envy or malevolence, and has always a certain prospect of discovering new reasons for adoring the sovereign author of the universe.
Samuel Johnson

Rain is good for vegetables, and for the animals who eat those vegetables, and for the animals who eat those animals.
Samuel Johnson

I want to be freed neither from human beings, nor from myself, nor from nature; for all these appear to me the greatest of miracles.
Carl Jung

What is more gentle than a wind is summer?
John Keats

Nature uses as little as possible of anything.
Johannes Kepler

Nature is garrulous to the point of confusion; let the artist be truly taciturn.
Paul Klee

We listen too much to the telephone and too little to nature. The wind is one of my sounds. A lonely sound, perhaps, but soothing.
Andre Kostelanetz

Nature takes no account of even the most reasonable of human excuses.
Joseph Wood Krutch

In the world there is nothing more submissive and weak than water. Yet for attacking that which is hard and strong nothing can surpass it.
Lao-tzu

Nothing that is natural is disgraceful.
Latin proverb

Conservation is a state of harmony between men and land.
Aldo Leopold

And when ye reap the harvest of your land, thou shalt not wholly reap the corners of thy field, neither shalt thou gather the gleanings of thy harvest.
Leviticus 19:9

Into each life some rain must fall, some days must be dark and dreary.
Henry Wadsworth Longfellow

In wilderness I sense the miracle of life, and behind it our scientific accomplishments fade to trivia.
Charles Lindbergh

On seeing Niagara Falls: Fortissimo at last!
Gustav Mahler

Rivers in the United States are so polluted that acid rain makes them cleaner.
Andrew Malcolm

In those vernal seasons of the year when the air is calm and pleasant, it were an injury and sullenness against nature not to go out and see her riches, and partake in her rejoicing with heaven and earth.
John Milton

This grand show is eternal. It is always sunrise somewhere; the dew is never all dried at once; a shower is forever falling; vapor is ever rising. Eternal sunrise, eternal sunset, eternal dawn and gloaming, on sea and continents and islands, each in its turn, as the round earth rolls.
John Muir

We came unto the land whither thou sentest us, and surely it floweth with milk and honey, and this is the fruit of it.
Numbers 13:27

Worship of nature may be ancient, but seeing nature as cuddlesome, hug-a-bear and too cute for words is strictly a modern fashion.
P.J. O'Rourke

There's so much pollution in the air now that if it weren't for our lungs there'd be no place to put it all.
Robert Orben

Nature has perfections, in order to show that she is the image of God; and defects, to show that she is only his image.
Blaise Pascal

Nature imitates herself. A grain thrown into good ground brings forth fruit; a principle thrown into a good mind brings forth fruit. Everything is created and conducted by the same Master—the root, the branch, the fruits—the principles, the consequences.
Blaise Pascal

It were happy if we studied nature more in natural things; and acted according to nature, whose rules are few, plain, and most reasonable.
William Penn

We ought not to treat living creatures like shoes or household belongings, which when worn with use we throw away.
Plutarch

There be three things which are too wonderful for me, yea, four which I know not: The way of an eagle in the air; the way of a serpent upon a rock; the way of a ship in the midst of the sea; and the way of a man with a maid.
Proverbs 30:18–19

The floods have lifted up, O Lord, the floods have lifted up their voice; the floods life up their waves. The Lord on high is mightier than the noise of many waters, yea, than the mighty waves of the sea.
Psalms 93:3–4

The nation that destroys its soil destroys itself.
Franklin D. Roosevelt

In the range of inorganic nature. I doubt if any object can be found more perfectly beautiful than a fresh, deep snowdrift, seen under warm light.
John Ruskin

On why he took his 6-year-old son to see the destruction in Sendai shortly after the quake: I wanted him to see this. I want him to remember what happened to his country. He doesn't show that he was scared, but he's having nightmares.
Tadashi Sato

Nature never quite goes along with us. She is somber at weddings, sunny at funerals, and she frowns on ninety-nine out of a hundred picnics.
Alexander Smith

The best fertilizer is the owner's footprint.
South Carolina saying

The trash and litter of nature disappears into the ground with the passing of each year, but man's litter has more permanence.
John Steinbeck

The long fight to save wild beauty represents democracy at its best. It requires citizens to practice the hardest of virtues: self-restraint.
Edwin Way Teale

Wide flush the fields; the softening air is balm; echo the mountains round; the forest smiles and every heart is joy.
James Thomson

I felt a positive yearning toward one bush this afternoon. There was a match found for me at last. I fell in love with a shrub oak.
Henry David Thoreau

However much you knock at nature's door, she will never answer you in comprehensible words.
Ivan Turgenev

Nature cares nothing for our logic, our human logic; she has her own, which we do not recognize and do not acknowledge until we are crunched under its wheel.
Ivan Turgenev

Nature is full of infinite causes that have never occurred in experience.
Leonardo da Vinci

Animals have these advantages over man: They have no theologians to instruct them, their funerals cost them nothing, and no one starts lawsuits over their wills.
Voltaire

What a man needs in gardening is a cast-iron back, with a hinge in it.
Charles Dudley Warner

They kill good trees to put out bad newspapers.
James Watt

I think I could turn and live with the animals. They are so placid and self-contained. They do not sweat and whine

about their condition. Not one is dissatisfied. Not one is demented with the mania of owning things. Not one is disrespectful or unhappy over the world.
Walt Whitman

The world is too must: with us; late and soon, getting and spending we lay waste our powers. Little we see in nature that is ours.
William Wordsworth

NECESSITY

Make yourself necessary to somebody.
Ralph Waldo Emerson

Where necessity ends, curiosity begins; and no sooner are we supplied with everything that nature can demand than we sit down to contrive artificial appetites.
Samuel Johnson

There is no contending with necessity, and we should be very tender how we censure those that submit to it. 'Tis one thing to be at liberty to do what we will, and another thing to be tied up to do what we must.
Roger L'Estrange

Necessity is the plea for every infringement of human freedom. It is the argument of tyrants; it is the creed of slaves.
William Pitt

Necessity is the constant scourge of the lower classes, ennui of the higher ones.
Arthur Schopenhauer

Necessity is the mother of invention is a silly proverb. Necessity is the mother of futile dodges is much nearer the truth.
Alfred North Whitehead

NEIGHBORS

The love of our neighbor hath its bounds in each man's love of himself.
St. Augustine

It is discouraging to try to be a good neighbor in a bad neighborhood.
William Castle

We make our friends; we make our enemies; but God makes our next-door neighbor.
G.K. Chesterton

A good neighbor—a found treasure.
Chinese proverb

No one is rich enough to do without a neighbor.
Danish proverb

Love your neighbor, yet pull not down your hedge.
English proverb

Good fences make good neighbors.
Robert Frost

We can live without our friends, but not without our neighbors.
Thomas Fuller

It is your interest that is at stake when your neighbor's wall is ablaze.
Horace

Your neighbor is the man who needs you.
Elbert Hubbard

Nothing makes you more tolerant of a neighbor's noisy party than being there.
Franklin P. Jones

How seldom we weigh our neighbor in the same balance with ourselves!
Thomas à Kempis

The good neighbor looks beyond the external accidents and discerns those

inner qualities that make all men human
and, therefore, brothers.
Martin Luther King, Jr.

Someone said of nations—but it might
well have been said of individuals,
too—that they require of their neighbors
something sufficiently akin to be understood, something sufficiently different to
provoke attention, and something sufficiently great to command admiration.
Phoebe Low

All social life, stability, progress, depend
upon each man's confidence in his
neighbor, a reliance upon him to do his
duty.
A. Lawrence Lowell

Live for thy neighbor if thou wouldst live
for thyself.
Seneca

More and more clearly every day, out
of biology, anthropology, sociology,
history, economic analysis, psychological insight, plain human decency and
common sense, the necessary mandate
of survival—that we shall love all our
neighbors as we do ourselves—is being
confirmed and reaffirmed.
Ordway Tead

A little among neighbors is worth more
than riches in a wilderness.
Welsh proverb

We are made for one another, and each is
to be a supply to his neighbor.
Benjamin Whichcote

NEWS

The evil that men do lives on the front
pages of greedy newspapers, but the
good is oft interred apathetically inside.
Brooks Atkinson

Journalism is popular, but it is popular
mainly as fiction. Life is one world, and
life seen in the newspapers another.
G.K. Chesterton

The tabloid newspaper actually means
to the typical American what the Bible
is popularly supposed to have meant to
the typical Pilgrim Father: a very present
help in time of trouble, plus a means of
keeping out of trouble via harmless, since
vicarious, indulgence in the pomps and
vanities of this wicked world.
e.e. cummings

Evil report carries faster than any
applause.
Baltasar Gracián

News is the first rough draft of history.
Philip L. Graham

Were it left to me to decide whether we
should have a government without newspapers, or newspapers without a government, I should not hesitate to prefer the
latter.
Thomas Jefferson

A good newspaper, I suppose, is a nation
talking to itself.
Arthur Miller

A reporter is always concerned with
tomorrow. There's nothing tangible
of yesterday. All I can say I've done is
agitate the air ten or fifteen minutes and
then boom—it's gone.
Edward R. Murrow

I do not like to get the news, because
there has never been an era when so
many things have been going right for so
many of the wrong persons.
Ogden Nash

A newspaper column, like a fish, should be consumed when fresh; otherwise it is not only indigestible but unspeakable.
James Reston

To a philosopher all news, as it is called, is gossip, and those who edit and read it are old women over their tea.
Henry David Thoreau

News is what a chap who doesn't care much about anything wants to read. And it's only news until he's read it. After that it's dead.
Evelyn Waugh

NO

No is always a door-closing word; Yes is a door-opening word.
Thomas Dreier

A gilded No is more satisfactory than a dry Yes.
Baltasar Gracián

The super-salesman neither permits his subconscious mind to broadcast negative thoughts nor give expression to them through words, for the reason that he understands that like attracts like and negative suggestions attract negative action and negative decisions from prospective buyers.
Napoleon Hill

The man who has not learned to say No will be a weak if not a wretched man as long as he lives.
A. Maclaren

So many of us know what we are against, but not what we are for—what we disbelieve, not what we believe. A negative life easily becomes neutral and futile.
Joseph Fort Newton

We should all be very careful when we say no to a suggested improvement or plan made by a subordinate. A no in most cases is final. We are usually more careful when we say yes because we know that our yes decisions will have to stand the test of performance or further approval. As a matter of fact, we should be more careful with our noes for the very reason that they do not have to stand the test of performance or further approval.
A.W. Robertson

It is a great evil, as well as a misfortune, to be unable to utter a prompt and decided No.
Charles Simmons

When we can say no, not only to things that are wrong and sinful, but also to things pleasant, profitable, and good which would hinder and clog our grand duties and our chief work, we shall understand more fully what life is worth, and how to make the most of it.
Charles A. Stoddard

NOBILITY

A noble man compares and estimates himself by an idea which is higher than himself, and a mean man, by one lower than himself.
Henry Ward Beecher

Those who think nobly are noble.
Isaac Bickerstaff

A degenerate nobleman, or one that is proud of his birth, is like a turnip: there is nothing good of him but that which is underground.
Samuel Butler

Nobility of birth does not always insure a corresponding unity of mind; if it did, it would always act as a stimulus to noble

actions; but it sometimes acts as a clog rather than a spur.
Charles Caleb Colton

Every noble activity makes room for itself.
Ralph Waldo Emerson

The essence of true nobility is neglect of self.
James A. Froude

Be noble, and the nobleness that lies in other men, sleeping but never dead, will rise in majesty to meet thine own.
James Russell Lowell

The noble soul has reverence for itself.
Friedrich Wilhelm Nietzsche

We need above all to learn again to believe in the possibility of nobility of spirit in ourselves.
Eugene O'Neill

If a man be endowed with a generous mind, this is the best kind of nobility.
Plato

Do not think it wasted time to submit yourself to any influence that will bring upon you any noble feeling.
John Ruskin

We are all sculptors and painters, and our material is our own flesh and blood and bones. Any nobleness begins at once to refine a man's features, and any meanness or sensuality to imbrute them.
Henry David Thoreau

OBLIGATIONS

Happy the man to whom heaven has given a morsel of bread without laying him under the obligation of thanking any other for it than heaven itself.
Miguel de Cervantes

Small obligations, given habitually, are what preserve the heart and secure comfort.
William Davy

It is well known to all great men, that by conferring an obligation they do not always procure a friend, but are certain of creating many enemies.
Henry Fielding

We are always much better pleased to see those whom we have obliged than those who have obliged us.
François La Rochefoucauld

The more obligations we accept that are self-imposed, the freer we are.
John C. Schroeder

Most men remember obligations, but not often to be grateful; the proud are made sour by the remembrance and the vain silent.
William Simms

To feel oppressed by obligation is only to prove that we are incapable of a proper sentiment of gratitude. To receive favors from the unworthy is to admit that our selfishness is superior to our pride.
William Simms

We cannot always oblige, but we can always speak obligingly.
Voltaire

OBSTACLES

The great pleasure in life is doing what people say you cannot do.
Walter Bagehot

The block of granite which was an obstacle in the path of the weak, becomes a steppingstone in the path of the strong.
Thomas Carlyle

If you find a path with no obstacles, it probably doesn't lead anywhere.
Frank A. Clark

It is a hard rule of life, and I believe a healthy one, that no great plan is ever carried out without meeting and overcoming endless obstacles that come up to try the skill of man's hand, the quality of his courage, and the endurance of his faith.
Donald Wills Douglas

Braving obstacles and hardships is nobler than retreat to tranquility. The butterfly that hovers around the lamp until it dies is more admirable than the mole that lives in the dark tunnel.
Kahlil Gibran

Some minds seem almost to create themselves, springing up under every disadvantage and working their solitary but irresistible way through a thousand obstacles.
Washington Irving

The worst obstructionist in any community is not the man who is opposed to doing anything, but the man who will not do what he can because he cannot do what he would like to do.
J.L. Long

The greater the obstacle the more glory in overcoming it.
Molière

Obstacles are those frightful things you see when you take your eyes off the goal.
Hanna More

OPINIONS

He who is master of all opinions can never be the bigot of any.
William R. Alter

Opinion is the main thing which does good or harm in the world. It is our false opinions of things which ruin us.
Marcus Aurelius Antoninus

So long as there are earnest believers in the world, they will always wish to punish opinions, even if their judgment tells them it is unwise and their conscience that it is wrong.
Walter Bagehot

We should allow others' excellences, to preserve a modest opinion of our own.
Isaac Barrow

Absurdity: A statement or belief manifestly inconsistent with one's own opinion.
Ambrose Bierce

The man who never alters his opinion is like standing water, and breeds reptiles of the mind.
William Blake

One of the mistakes in the conduct of human life is to suppose that other men's opinions are to make us happy.
Richard Burton

He that complies against his will, is of his own opinion still.
Samuel Butler

Popular opinion is the greatest lie in the world.
Thomas Carlyle

No liberal man would impute a charge of unsteadiness to another for having changed his opinion.
Cicero

Opinions, like showers, are generated in high places, but they invariably descend into lower ones, and ultimately flow down to the people, as rain unto the sea.
Charles Caleb Colton

He that never changes his opinions, never corrects his mistakes, and will never be wiser on the morrow than he is today.
Tryon Edwards

A man cannot utter two or three sentences without disclosing to intelligent ears precisely where he stands in life and thought, whether in the kingdom of the senses and the understanding, or in that of ideas and imagination, or in the realm of intuitions and duty.
Ralph Waldo Emerson

Every man should periodically be compelled to listen to opinions which are infuriating to him. To hear nothing but what is pleasing to one is to make a pillow of the mind.
St. John Ervine

The most distinctive mark of a cultured mind is the ability to take another's point of view; to put one's self in another's place, and see life and its problems from a point of view different from one's own. To be willing to test a new idea; to be able to live on the edge of difference in all matters intellectually; to examine without heat the burning question of the day; to have imaginative sympathy, openness and flexibility of mind, steadiness and poise of feeling, cool calmness of judgment, is to have culture.
Arthur H.R. Fairchild

Sometimes only a change of viewpoint is needed to convert a tiresome duty into an interesting opportunity.
Alberta Flanders

The bell of public opinion is today making the Morgan-Rockefeller-Vanderbilt class jump. Nor are the strongest of our corporations immune. The railroads have had to jump pretty lively, and certain gigantic industrial combinations are also being put through their paces.
B.C. Forbes

The free expression of opinion, as experience has taught us, is the safety-valve of passion. The noise of the rushing steam, when it escapes, alarms the timid; but it is the sign that we are safe. The concession of reasonable privilege anticipates the growth of furious appetite.
William Gladstone

In two opposite opinions, if one be perfectly reasonable, the other can't be perfectly right.
Oliver Goldsmith

I do not regret having braved public opinion, when I knew it was wrong and was sure it would be merciless.
Horace Greeley

We are very much what others think of us. The reception our observations meet with gives us courage to proceed, or damps our efforts.
William Hazlitt

The men of the past had convictions, while we moderns have only opinions.
Heinrich Heine

We should be eternally vigilant against attempts to check the expression of opinions that we loathe.
Oliver Wendell Holmes

Honest differences of views and honest debate are not disunity. They are the vital process of policy-making among free men.
Herbert Hoover

I tolerate with the utmost latitude the right of others to differ from me in opinion.
Thomas Jefferson

In every country where man is free to think and to speak, difference of opinion will arise from difference of perception, and the imperfection of reason; but these differences, when permitted, as in this happy country, to purify themselves by free discussion, are but as passing clouds overspreading our land transiently, and leaving our horizon more bright and serene.
Thomas Jefferson

The opinions of men are not the object of civil government, nor under its jurisdiction.
Thomas Jefferson

As for the differences of opinion upon speculative questions, if we wait till they are reconciled, the action of human affairs must be suspended forever. But neither are we to look for perfection in any one man, nor for agreement among many.
Junius

He who has no opinion of his own, but depends upon the opinion and taste of others, is a slave.
Friedrich Gottlieb Klopstock

It is a golden rule that one should never judge men by their opinions, but rather by what their opinions make of them.
Georg C. Lichtenberg

I shall adopt new views as fast as they shall appear to be true views.
Abraham Lincoln

It is the man who does not want to express an opinion whose opinion I want.
Abraham Lincoln

New opinions are always suspected and usually opposed because they are not already common.
John Locke

Reactionaries must be deprived of the right to voice their opinions; only the people have that right.
Mao Tse-tung

Men are never so good or so bad as their opinions.
James Mackintosh

Opinions cannot survive if one has no chance to fight for them.
Thomas Mann

In a discussion the difficulty lies, not in being able to defend your opinion, but to know it.
André Maurois

If all mankind minus one were of one opinion, and only one person were of the contrary opinion, mankind would be no more justified in silencing that one person, than he, if he had the power, would be justified in silencing mankind.
John Stuart Mill

To be absolutely certain about something, one must know everything or nothing about it.
Olin Miller

I look upon the too-good opinion that man has of himself, as the nursing mother of all false opinions, both public and private.
Michel de Montaigne

Today's public opinion, though it may appear as light as air, may become tomorrow's legislation—for better or for worse.
Earl Newsom

Man is a gregarious animal, and much more so in his mind than in his body. He may like to go alone for a walk, but he hates to stand alone in his opinions.
George Santayana

If you want to discover your true opinion of anybody, observe the impression made on you by the first sight of a letter from him.
Arthur Schopenhauer

Opinion is something wherein I go about to give reasons why all the world should think as I think.
John Selden

The circumstances of the world are so variable, that an irrevocable purpose or opinion is almost synonymous with a foolish one.
W.H. Seward

Wind puffs up empty bladders; opinion, fools.
Socrates

Extreme views are never just; something always turns up which disturbs the calculations founded on their data.
Tancred

Public opinion is a weak tyrant compared with our own private opinion.
Henry David Thoreau

It is the difference of opinion that makes horse races.
Mark Twain

What others think of us would be of little moment did it not, when known, so deeply tinge what we think of ourselves.
Paul Valéry

The more opinions you have, the less you see.
Wim Wenders

One can give a really unbiased opinion only about things that do not interest one, which is no doubt the reason an unbiased opinion is always valueless. The man who sees both sides of a question is a man who sees absolutely nothing.
Oscar Wilde

All empty souls tend to extreme opinion. It is only in those who have built up a rich world of memories and habits of thought that extreme opinions affront the sense of probability. Propositions, for instance, which set all the truth upon one side can only enter rich minds to dislocate and strain, if they can enter at all, and sooner or later the mind expels them by instinct.
William Butler Yeats

OPPORTUNITIES

Most of us never recognize opportunity until it goes to work in our competitor's business.
P.L. Andarr

Four things come not back—the spoken word, the sped arrow, the past life, and the neglected opportunity.
Arabian proverb

No one wearies of benefits received.
Marcus Aurelius Antoninus

Opportunities do not come with their values stamped upon them. Every one must be challenged. A day dawns, quite like other days; in it a single hour comes, quite like other hours; but in that day and in that hour, the chance of a lifetime faces us. The face every opportunity of life thoughtfully and ask its meaning

bravely and earnestly, is the only way to meet the supreme opportunities when they come, whether open-faced or disguised.
Maltbie Babcock

A wise man will make more opportunities than he finds.
Francis Bacon

When one door closes another door opens; but we often look so long and so regretfully upon the closed door that we do not see the ones which open for us.
Alexander Graham Bell

There is nothing in the world really beneficial that does not lie within the reach of an informed understanding and a well-protected pursuit.
Edmund Burke

The lure of the distant and the difficult is deceptive. The great opportunity is where you are.
John Burroughs

The sure way to miss success is to miss the opportunity.
Victor Chasles

What helps luck is a habit of watching for opportunities, of having a patient, but restless mind, of sacrificing one's ease or vanity, of uniting a love of detail to foresight, and of passing through hard times bravely and cheerfully.
Charles Victor Cherbuliez

An optimist sees an opportunity in every calamity; a pessimist sees a calamity in every opportunity.
Winston Churchill

If we are to achieve a victorious standard of living today we must look for the opportunity in every difficult instead of being paralyzed at the thought of the difficulty in every opportunity.
Walter E. Cole

Every one has a fair turn to be as great as he pleases.
Jeremy Collier

Small opportunities are often the beginning of great enterprises.
Demosthenes

Next to knowing when to seize an opportunity, the most important thing in life is to know when to forego an advantage.
Benjamin Disraeli

The great secret of success in life is for a man to be ready when his opportunity comes.
Benjamin Disraeli

There is hook in every benefit, that sticks in his jaws that takes that benefit, and draws him whither the benefactor will.
John Donne

Great opportunities come to all, but many do not know they have met them. The only preparation to take advantage of them is simple fidelity to watch what each day brings.
Albert E. Dunning

When blocked or defeated in an enterprise I had much at heart, I always turned immediately to another field of work where progress looked possible, biding my time for a chance to resume the obstructed road.
Charles W. Eliot

It's them as take advantage that get advantage i' this world.
George Eliot

What is opportunity to the man who can't use it? An unfecundated egg,

which the waves of time wash away into nonentity.
George Eliot

No great man ever complains of want of opportunity.
Ralph Waldo Emerson

The prizes go to those who meet emergencies successfully. And the way to meet emergencies is to do each daily task the best we can; to act as though the eye of opportunity were always upon us. In the hundred-yard race the winter doesn't cross the tape line a dozen strides ahead of the field. He wins by inches. So we find it in ordinary business life. The big things that come our way are seldom the result of long thought or careful planning, but rather they are the fruit of seed planted in the daily routine of our work.
William Feather

If you were to visit a certain rural section of Vermont, you would be shown two farms only a few miles apart, and you would be told that a lad raised on one of the farms today occupies the most responsible position in the whole world, the Presidency of the United States. From the other farm, you would be told, there went forth another lad who is today the head of one of the leading railroads in the U.S. . . . Whenever I hear wild denunciations of this country and its institutions I cannot but feel that . . . no other country on earth offers such advantages and opportunities for children born in humble circumstances.
B.C. Forbes

The majority of America's colossal fortunes have been made by entering industries in their early stages and developing leadership in them. . . . Think of what opportunities the present and the future contain in such fields as ship-building and ship-owning, aircraft, electrical development, the oil industry, different branches of the automotive industry, foreign trade, international banking, invention, the chemical industry, moving pictures, color photography, and, one night add, labor leadership.
B.C. Forbes (1921)

I think luck is the sense to recognize an opportunity and the ability to take advantage of it. Every one has bad breaks, but every one also has opportunities. The man who can smile at his breaks and grab his chances gets on.
Samuel Goldwyn

If you want to succeed in the world you must make your own opportunities as you go on. The man who waits for some seventh wave to toss him on dry land will find that the seventh wave is a long time coming.
John B. Gough

If it exists, it's possible.
John P. Grier

We didn't have any plans when we started. We were just opportunistic.
William Hewlett

Most of us don't recognize opportunity until we see it working for a competitor.
Jay Huenfeld

We must dream of an aristocracy of achievement arising out of a democracy of opportunity.
Thomas Jefferson

Genius and great abilities are often wanting; sometimes, only opportunities. Some deserve praise for what they have done; others for what they would have done.
Jean de La Bruyère

To be a great man it is necessary to turn to account all opportunities.
François de La Rochefoucauld

And I say unto you, Ask, and it shall be given you; seek, and ye shall find; knock, and it shall be opened unto you.
Luke 11:9

There is no security on this earth. Only opportunity.
Douglas MacArthur

Injuries should be done all together, so that being, less tasted, they will give less offense. Benefits should be granted little by little, so that they may be better enjoyed.
Niccolò Machiavelli

A pessimist is one who makes difficulties of his opportunities; an optimist is one who makes opportunities of his difficulties.
Reginald B. Mansell

Opportunity has hair in front but is bald behind.
Phaedrus

No man's abilities are so remarkably shining as not to stand in need of a proper opportunity.
Pliny

Opportunity rarely knocks until you are ready. And few people have ever been really ready without receiving opportunity's call.
Channing Pollock

In this world the one thing supremely worth having is the opportunity to do well and worthily a piece of work of vital consequence to the welfare of mankind.
Theodore Roosevelt

More is more.
Mstislav Rostropovich

Opportunity has power over all things.
Sophocles

Opportunity is the best captain of all endeavor.
Sophocles

I've always had the courage to take advantage of opportunities when they come my way.
James Sorenson

It is less important to redistribute wealth than it is to redistribute opportunity.
Arthur H. Vandenberg

America is the land of, and for, uncommon men not only because it affords free choice and opportunity for people to become expert in their chosen occupations, but also because it has mechanisms and incentives for providing the tools of production that the skilled must operate if their skill is to have full fruition in abundant production.
Enders M. Voorhees

The man who works need never be a problem to anyone. Opportunities multiply as they are seized; they die when neglected. Life is a long line of opportunities. Wealth is not in making money, but in making the man while he is making money. Production, not destruction, leads to success.
John Wicker

To every man his chance, to every man, regardless of his birth, his shining golden opportunity. To every man the right to live, to work, to be himself, and to become whatever thing his manhood and his vision can contribute to make him.
Thomas Wolfe

ORDER

The less of routine, the more of life.
Amos Bronson Alcott

Order means light and peace, inward liberty and free command over one's self; order is power.
Henri Frederik Ariel

Nothing is orderly till man takes hold of it. Everything in creation lies around loose.
Henry Ward Beecher

Every great man exhibits the talent of organization or construction, whether it be in a poem, a philosophical system, a policy, or a strategy. And without method there is no organization nor construction.
Edward Bulwer-Lytton

Good order is the foundation of all good things.
Edmund Burke

When liberty destroys order, the hunger for order will destroy liberty.
Will Durant

Have a time and place for everything, and do everything in its time and place, and you will not only accomplish more, but have far more leisure than those who are always hurrying, as if vainly attempting to overtake time that had been lost.
Tryon Edwards

The prizes go to those who meet emergencies successfully. And the way to meet emergencies is to do each daily task the best we can; to act as though the eye of opportunity were always upon us. In the hundred-yard race the winner doesn't cross the tape line a dozen strides ahead of the field. He wins by inches. So we find it in ordinary business life. The big things that come our way are seldom the result of long thought or careful planning, but rather they are the fruit of seed planted in the daily routine of our work.
William Feather

Method will teach you to win time.
Johann Wolfgang von Goethe

We are rational creatures: Our virtue and perfection is to love reason, or rather to love order.
Nicolas Malebranche

Order and simplification are the first steps toward the master of a subject. The actual enemy is the unknown.
Thomas Mann

There is no course of life so weak and sottish as that which is managed by order, method and discipline.
Michel de Montaigne

Almost all men are intelligent. It is method that they lack.
F.W. Nichol

Most of life is routine—dull and grubby, but routine is the momentum that keeps a man going. If you wait for inspiration you'll be standing on the corner after the parade is a mile down the street.
Ben Nicholas

After you've done a thing the same way for two years, look it over carefully. After five years, look at it with suspicion. And after ten years, throw it away and start all over.
Alfred E. Perlman

Sameness is the mother of disgust, variety the cure.
Petrarch

I'm working to improve my methods, and every hour I save is an hour added to my life.
Ayn Rand

Mere lack of success does not discredit a method, for there are many things that determine and perpetuate our sanctified ways of doing things besides their success in reaching their proposed ends.
James Harvey Robinson

Order is the sanity of the mind, the health of the body, the peace of the city, the security of the state. As the beams to a house, as the bones to the microcosm of man, so is order to all things.
Robert Southey

There is no lostness like that which comes to a man when a perfect and certain pattern has dissolved about him.
John Steinbeck

Methods are the masters of masters.
Charles-Maurice de Talleyrand

It is remarkable how easily and insensibly we fall into a particular route, and make a beaten track for ourselves.
Henry David Thoreau

Routine is a ground to stand on, a wall to retreat to; we cannot draw on our boots without bracing ourselves against it.
Henry David Thoreau

The art of progress is to preserve order amid change and to preserve change amid order.
Alfred North Whitehead

That which is to be most desired in America is oneness and not sameness. Sameness is the worst thing that could happen to the people of this country. To make all people the same would lower their quality, but oneness would raise it.
Stephen S. Wise

ORGANIZATION

Large organization is loose organization. Nay, it would be almost as true to say that organization is always disorganization.
G.K. Chesterton

The primary asset of any business is its organization.
William Feather

The young man who addresses himself in stern earnest to organizing his life—his habits, his associations, his reading, his study, his work—stands far more chance of rising to a position affording him opportunity to exercise his organizing abilities than the fellow who dawdles along without chart or compass, without plan or purpose, without self-improvement and self-discipline.
B.C. Forbes

Organization is the art of getting men to respond like thoroughbreds. When you cluck to a thoroughbred, he gives you all of the speed and strength of heart and sinew he has in him. When you cluck to a jackass, he kicks.
C.R. House

We trained hard—but it seemed that every time we were beginning to form into teams, we would be reorganized. I was to learn later in life that we tend to meet any new situation by reorganizing; and what a wonderful method it can be for creating the illusion of progress while producing confusion, inefficiency and demoralization.
Petronius

An architect's arch is a heap of stones until and unless it is organized and grouped around a keystone. The keystone holds the pattern together. So it is with life. Unless there is some keystone conviction by which experience

is organized, the individual remains little more than a bundle of feelings.
Martin H. Scharleman

The secret of all victory lies in the organization of the nonobvious.
Oswald Spengler

P

PASSIONS

Whereas the law is passionless, passion must ever sway the heart of man.
Aristotle

Art is moral passion married to entertainment. Moral passion without entertainment is propaganda, and entertainment without moral passion is television.
Rita Mae Brown

When you have found out the prevailing passion of any man, remember never to trust him where that passion is concerned.
Lord Chesterfield

We are ne'er like angels till our passion dies.
Thomas Dekker

A man in a passion rides a wild horse.
Benjamin Franklin

Passion, joined with power, produceth thunder and ruin.
Thomas Fuller

The passions are the humors of the mind, and the least excess sickens our judgment. If the disease spreads to the mouth, your reputation will be in danger.
Baltasar Gracián

To rule self and subdue our passions is the more praiseworthy because so few know how to do it.
Francesco Guicciardini

Passions unguided are for the most part mere madness.
Thomas Hobbes

Absence diminishes little passions and increases great ones, as wind extinguishes candles and fans a fire.
François de La Rochefoucauld

Three passions, simple but overwhelmingly strong, have governed my life: the longing for love, the search for knowledge, and unbearable pity for the suffering of mankind.
Bertrand Russell

The only difference between a caprice and a lifelong passion is that the caprice lasts a little longer.
Oscar Wilde

PAST

Only one accomplishment is beyond both the power and the mercy of the Gods. They cannot make the past as though it had never been.
Aeschylus

This only is denied even to God: the power to undo the past.
Agathon

Forget the past. No one becomes successful in the past.
Anonymous

Man is a history-making creature who can neither repeat his past nor leave it behind.
W.H. Auden

The true picture of the past flits by. The past can be seized only as an image which flashes up at the instant when it can be recognized and is never seen again.
Walter Benjamin

The past grows gradually around one, like a placenta for dying.
John Berger

Many are always praising the bygone time, for it is natural that the old should extol the days of their youth; the weak, the time of their strength; the sick, the season of their vigor; and the disappointed, the springtide of their hopes.
Caleb Bingham

One may return to the place of his birth, He cannot go back to his youth.
John Burroughs

God cannot alter the past, that is why he is obliged to connive at the existence of historians.
Samuel Butler

We cannot fling ourselves into the blank future; we can only call up images from the past. This being so, the important principle follows, that how many images we have largely depends on how much past we have.
G.K. Chesterton

To be ignorant of what occurred before you were born is to remain always a child.
Cicero

Study the past if you would divine the future.
Confucius

The past is the only dead thing that smells sweet.
Cyril Connolly

We are well advised to keep on nodding terms with the people we used to be, whether we find them attractive company or not. Otherwise they turn up unannounced and surprise us, hammering on the mind's door at 4 a.m. of a dark night and demand to know who deserted them, who betrayed them, who is going to make amends.
Joan Didion

The past always looks better than it was; it's only pleasant because it isn't here.
Finley Peter Dunne

We are not free to use today, or to promise tomorrow, because we are already mortgaged to yesterday.
Ralph Waldo Emerson

It is sadder to find the past again and find it inadequate to the present than it is to have it elude you and remain forever a harmonious conception of memory.
F. Scott Fitzgerald

When I reflect, as I frequently do, upon the felicity I have enjoyed, I sometimes say to myself, that, were the offer made me, I would engage to run again, from beginning to end, the same career of life. All I would ask, should be the privilege of an author, to correct in a second edition, certain errors of the first.
Benjamin Franklin

Nostalgia combines regularly with manifest respectability to give credence to old error as opposed to new truth.
John Kenneth Galbraith

It is delightful to transport one's self into the spirit of the past, to see how a wise man has thought before us, and to what a glorious height we have at last reached. Human life may be regarded as a succession of frontispieces. The way to be satisfied is never to look back.
William Hazlitt

Nothing impresses the mind with a deeper feeling of loneliness than to tread the silent and deserted scene of former flow and pageant.
Washington Irving

Nothing changes more constantly than the past; for the past that influences our lives does not consist of what happened, but of what men believe happened.
Gerald W. Johnston

I don't like nostalgia unless it's mine.
Lou Reed

The past is a bucket of ashes, so live not in your yesterdays, nor just for tomorrow, but in the here and now. Keep moving and forget the postmortems. And remember, no one can get the jump on the future.
Carl Sandburg

It is foolish to try to live on past experience. It is very dangerous, if not a fatal habit, to judge ourselves to be safe because of something that we felt or did twenty years ago.
Charles H. Spurgeon

I said there was but one solitary thing about the past worth remembering and that was the fact that it is past—can't be restored.
Mark Twain

The past is only the present become invisible and mute; its memoried glances and its murmurs are infinitely precious.
Mary Webb

The great achievements of the past were the adventures of the past. Only the adventurous can understand the greatness of the past.
Alfred North Whitehead

PATIENCE

Patience is passion tamed.
Lyman Abbott

The remedy of time is patience.
Arabian proverb

Patience is so like fortitude that she seems either her sister or her daughter.
Aristotle

Patience is the companion of wisdom.
St. Augustine

Prayer of the modern American: Dear God, I pray for patience. And I want it right now!
Oren Arnold

Patience is a minor form of despair, disguised as a virtue.
Ambrose Bierce

There is one form of hope which is never unwise, and which certainly does not diminish with the increase of knowledge. In that form it changes its name, and we call it patience.
Edward Bulwer-Lytton

It is not necessary for all men to be great in action. The greatest and sublimest power is often simple patience.
Horace Bushnell

Impatience never commanded success.
Edwin H. Chapin

Patience, and the mulberry leaf becomes a silk gown.
Chinese proverb

For national leaders it is sometimes easier to fight than to talk. Impatient cries for total victory are usually more popular than the patient tolerance required of a people whose leaders are

seeking peaceful change down the intricate paths of diplomacy.
Harlan Cleveland

Patience is a necessary ingredient of genius.
Benjamin Disraeli

Possess your soul with patience.
John Dryden

In prosperity, caution; in adversity, patience.
Dutch proverb

Successful salesman, authors, executives and workmen of every sort need patience. The great liability of youth is not inexperience but impatience.
William Feather

Whether it's marriage of business, patience is the first rule of success.
William Feather

Having patience with all things, but chiefly have patience with yourself. Do not lose courage in considering your own imperfections, but instantly start remedying them—every day begin the task anew.
St. Francis de Sales

Job was not so miserable in his sufferings as happy in his patience.
Thomas Fuller

Patience is the virtue of an ass that trots beneath his burden, and is quiet.
George Granville

Patience strengthens the spirit, sweetens the temper, stifles anger, extinguishes envy, subdues pride, bridles the tongue.
George Horne

The sharpest sting of adversity it borrows from our own impatience.
George Horne

He that has no patience has nothing at all.
Italian proverb

My brethren, count it all joy when ye fall into divers temptations; Knowing this, that the trying of your faith worketh patience. But let patience have her perfect work, that ye may be perfect and entire, wanting nothing.
James 1:2–4

The mental disease of the present generation is impatience of study, contempt of the great masters of ancient wisdom, and a disposition to rely wholly upon unassisted genius and natural sagacity.
Samuel Johnson

All men command patience, although few be willing to practice it.
Thomas à Kempis

No road is too long to the man who advances deliberately and without undue haste; and no honors are too distant for the man who prepares himself for them with patience.
Jean de La Bruyère

Patience and time do more than strength or passion.
Jean de La Fontaine

He surely is most in need of another's patience, who has none of his own.
Johann Lavater

Endurance is the crowning quality, and patience all the passion of great hearts.
James Russell Lowell

Genius is eternal patience.
Michelangelo

A man must learn to endure that patiently which he cannot avoid conveniently.
Michel de Montaigne

The general order of things that takes care of fleas and moles also takes care of men, if they will have the same patience that fleas and moles have, to leave it to itself.
Michel de Montaigne

He invites a new injury who bears the old patiently.
Fynes Moryson

Patience is bitter, but its fruits are sweet.
Jean-Jacques Rousseau

On the whole, it is patience which makes the final difference between those who succeed or fail in all things. All the greatest people have it in an infinite degree, and among the less, the patient weak ones always conquer the impatient strong.
John Ruskin

Have patience. All things are difficult before they become easy.
Sa'di

Only those who have the patience to do simple things perfectly will acquire the skill to do difficult things easily.
Johann Friedrich von Schiller

How poor are they who have not patience! What wound did ever heal but by degrees.
William Shakespeare

Have patient and the mulberry leaf will become satin.
Spanish proverb

A wise man does not try to hurry history. Many wars have been avoided by patience, and many have been precipitated by reckless haste.
Adlai Stevenson

Patience is the art of hoping.
Luc de Vauvenargues

PATRIOTISM

Patriotism is a lively sense of responsibility. Nationalism is a silly cock crowing on its own dunghill.
Richard Aldington

Patriotism: The first resort of a scoundrel.
Ambrose Bierce

On the House Un-American Activities Committee: They'll nail anyone who ever scratched his ass during the National Anthem.
Humphrey Bogart

Patriotism takes the place of religion in France. In the service of *la patrie*, the doing of one's duty is elevated into the sphere of exalted emotion.
W.C. Brownell

What scoundrels we would be if we did for ourselves what we are ready to do for Italy.
Camillo Benso di Cavour

Patriotism is easy to understand in America. It means looking out for yourself by looking out for your country.
Calvin Coolidge

Patriotic talk is no proof of patriotism. Anyone can wave a flag. The real patriot lives his patriotism in everything he does.
John M. Devine

No matter that patriotism is too often the refuge of scoundrels. Dissent, rebellion, and all-around hell-raising remain the true duty of patriots.
Barbara Ehrenreich

When a whole nation is roaring patriotism at the top of its voice, I am fain to explore the cleanness of its hands and the purity of its heart.
Ralph Waldo Emerson

Patriotism is collective responsibility.
Arnold Glasow

I want to caution that we must not confuse patriotism with blind endorsement of bad policies.
Mark O. Hatfield

Every man who loves his country, or wishes well to the best interests of society, will show himself a decided friend not only of morality and the laws, but of religious institutions, and honorably bear his part in supporting them.
Josiah Hawes

My country gave me schooling, independence of action and opportunity for service. I am indebted to my country beyond any human power to repay.
Herbert Hoover

What is patriotism but the love of the good things we ate in our childhood?
Lin Yutang

No man is worth his salt who is not ready at all times to risk his body, to risk his well-being, to risk his life, in a great cause.
Theodore Roosevelt

Patriotism: Your conviction that this country is superior to all other countries because you were born in it.
George Bernard Shaw

No other factor in history, not even religion, has produced so many wars as has the clash of national egotisms sanctified by the name of patriotism.
Preserved Smith

True patriotism is not manifested in short, frenzied bursts of emotion. It is the tranquil, steady dedication of a lifetime.
Adlai Stevenson

In the beginning of a change, the patriot is a scarce man, and brave, and hated and scorned. When his cause succeeds, the timid join him, for then it costs nothing to be a patriot.
Mark Twain

A real patriot is the fellow who gets a parking ticket and rejoices that the system works.
Bill Vaughan

Guard against the postures of pretended patriotism.
George Washington

You're not supposed to be so blind with patriotism that you can't face reality. Wrong is wrong, no matter who does it or who says it.
Malcolm X

PEACE

Calmness of mind is one of the beautiful jewels of wisdom. It is the result of long and patient effort in self-control. Its presence is an indication of ripened experience and of a more than ordinary knowledge of the laws and operations of thought.
James Allen

A time will come when the science of destruction shall bend before the arts of peace; when the genius which multiplies our powers, which creates new products, which diffuses comfort and happiness among the great mass of the people, shall occupy in the general estimation of mankind that rank which reason and common sense now assign to it.
François Arago

It is more difficult to organize peace than to win a war; but the fruits of victory will be lost if the peace is not well organized.
Aristotle

The lesson which wars and depressions have taught is that if we want peace, prosperity and happiness at home we must help to establish them abroad.
Hugo L. Black

Tranquil pleasures last the longest. We are not fitted to bear long the burdens of great joy.
Christian Bovée

Vast and fearsome as the human scene has become, personal contacts of the right people, in the right places, at the right time, may yet have a potent and valuable part to play in the cause of peace which is in our hearts.
Winston Churchill

The great task of the peace is to work morals into it. The only sort of peace that will be real is one in which everybody takes his share of responsibility. World organizations and conferences will be of no value unless there is improvement in the relation of men to men.
Sir Frederick Eggleston

Peace does not dwell in outward things, but within the soul; we may preserve it in the midst of the bitterest pain, if our will remain firm and submissive. Peace in this life springs from acquiescence, not in an exemption from suffering.
François Fénelon

Universal peace will be realized, not because man will become better, but because a new order of things, a new science, new economic necessities, will impose peace.
Anatole France

You can legislate many conditions—but you cannot legislate harmony into the hearts of men. To attain industrial peace, we need more than by-laws and compulsory rules.
Clarence Francis

Lord, make us instruments of Thy peace. Where there is hatred, let us sow love; where there is injury, pardon; where there is discord, union; where there is doubt, faith; where there is despair, hope; where there is darkness, light; where there is sadness, joy.
St. Francis of Assisi

The thing for which we prepare and which we earnestly expect usually comes upon us. Food is prepared to be eaten; clothing is made to be worn; munitions of war are produced to be used in warfare. Just as truly, preparations made for purposes of peace help to bring about the peaceful condition for which they are prepared.
Francis J. Gable

He is the happiest, be he king or peasant, who finds peace in his home.
Johann Wolfgang von Goethe

Peace among the nations, like happiness for the individual, is not an end, but a by-product that usually comes when you live right.
Edward Howard Griggs

If our hours were all serene, we might probably take almost as little note of them as the dial does of those that are clouded.
William Hazlitt

Peace is such a precious jewel that I would give anything for it but truth.
Matthew Henry

Peace is a nursing mother to the land.
Hesiod

The first and fundamental law of nature is to seek peace and follow it.
Thomas Hobbes

With intelligence and humility and dedication as our ammunition, we can wage the peace throughout the world with a strength beyond armies, destroying nothing except hate and greed and distrust.
Paul G. Hoffman

The pursuit of peace resembles the building of a great cathedral. It is the work of a generation. In concept it requires a master-architect; in execution, the labors of many.
Hubert Humphrey

Nothing gives one person so much advantage over another as to remain cool and unruffled under all circumstances.
Thomas Jefferson

For I know the thoughts that I think toward you, saith the Lord, thoughts of peace, and not of evil, to give you an expected end. Then shall ye call upon me, and ye shall go and pray unto me, and I will hearken unto you.
Jeremiah 29:11–12

We love peace, but not peace at any price. There is a peace more destructive of the manhood of living man, than war is destructive of his body. Chains are worse than bayonets.
Douglas Jerrold

Peace I leave with you, my peace I give unto you: not as the world giveth, give I unto you. Let not your heart be troubled, neither let it be afraid.
John 14:27

These things I have spoken unto you, that in me ye might have peace. In the world ye shall have tribulation: but be of good cheer; I have overcome the world.
John 16:33

Beauty I have learned from the ugly, charity from the unkind and peace from the turmoil of the world.
Frederick Ward Kates

Great tranquility of heart is his who cares for neither praise nor blame.
Thomas à Kempis

I am a man of peace. God knows how I love peace. But I hope I shall never be such a coward as to mistake oppression for peace.
Louis Kossuth

If we have not peace within ourselves, it is in vain to seek it from outward sources.
François de La Rochefoucauld

There is but one bond of peace that is both permanent and enriching: The increasing knowledge of the world in which experiment occurs.
Walter Lippmann

You can't take a crash course in serenity.
Shirley MacLaine

To be at peace with self, to find company and nourishment in self—this would be the test of the free and productive psyche.
Marya Mannes

Only in quiet waters things mirror themselves undistorted. Only in a quiet mind is adequate perception of the world.
Hans Margolius

If you are yourself at peace, then there is at least some peace in the world. Then share your peace with everyone, and everyone will be at peace.
Thomas Merton

Much remains to conquer still; peace hath her victories no less renowned than war.
John Milton

No sacrifice short of the sacrifice of individual liberty, individual self-respect, and individual enterprise is too great a price to pay for permanent peace.
Clark H. Minor

Peace is not merely an absence of war. It is also a state of mind.
Jawaharlal Nehru

Let the world see that this nation can bear prosperity; and that her honest virtue in time of peace is equal to her bravest valor in time of war.
Thomas Paine

There will be no peace so long as God remains unseated at the conference table.
William M. Peck

Five great enemies to peace inhabit with us: viz., avarice, ambition, envy, anger and pride. If those enemies were to be banished, we should infallibly enjoy perpetual peace.
Petrarch

For peace, with justice and honor, is the fairest and most profitable of possessions, but with disgrace and shameful cowardice, it is the most infamous and harmful of all.
Polybius

But the meek shall inherit the earth; and shall delight themselves in the abundance of peace.
Psalms 37:11

If it be possible, as much as lieth in you, live peaceably with all men.
Romans 12:18

Unless man has the wit and the grit to build his civilization on something better than material power, it is surely idle to talk of plans for a stable peace.
Francis B. Sayre

A peace is of the nature of a conquest. For then both parties nobly are subdued, and neither party loses.
William Shakespeare

Peace is not merely a vacuum left by the ending of wars. It is the creation of two eternal principles, justice and freedom.
James T. Shotwell

Peace is not absence of war, it is a virtue, a state of mind, a disposition for benevolence, confidence, justice.
Baruch Spinoza

Go placidly amid the noise and the haste, and remember what peace there may be in silence. As far as possible without surrender be on good terms with all persons. You are a child of the universe no less than the trees and the stars.
Adlai Stevenson

The language of excitement is at best picturesque. You must be calm before you can utter oracles.
Henry David Thoreau

Peace is a militant state, which is not secured by wishful thinking. . . . If we are to be sure of our liberty, we must be ready to fight for it.
Gen. Jonathan Wainwright

Nations have no existence apart from their people. If every person in the world loved peace, every nation would love peace. If all men refused to fight one another, nations could not fight one another.
J. Sherman Wallace

There is no kind of peace which may be purchased on the bargain counter.
Carey Williams

Peace, if it ever exists, will not be based on the fear of war but on the love of peace.
Herman Wouk

If peace is to come, it must be peace within your own mind and heart. If hatred is to die, you must scotch it within yourself. If intelligence is to triumph, you must be intelligent. There is no other pathway, no other salvation.
Henry M. Wriston

PERFECTION

Culture is properly described as the love of perfection; it is a study of perfection.
Matthew Arnold

The humorous man recognizes that absolute purity, absolute justice, absolute logic and perfection are beyond human achievement and that men have been able to live happily for thousands of years in a state of genial frailty.
Brooks Atkinson

Imperfection means perfection hid.
Robert Browning

Aim at perfection in everything, though in most things it is unattainable. However, they who aim at it, and persevere, will come much nearer to it than those whose laziness and despondency make them give it up as unattainable.
Lord Chesterfield

The gem cannot be polished without friction, nor man perfected without trials.
Chinese proverb

To talk about the need for perfection in man is to talk about the need for another species. The essence of man is imperfection. Imperfection and blazing contradictions—between mixed good and evil, altruism and selfishness, co-operativeness and combativeness, optimism and fatalism, affirmation and negation.
Norman Cousins

As natural selection works solely by and for the good of each being, all corporeal and mental endowments will tend to progress toward perfection.
Charles Darwin

To arrive at perfection, a man should have very sincere friends or inveterate enemies; because he would be made sensible of his good or ill conduct, either by the censures of the one or the admonitions of the other.
Diogenes

The feeling of having done a job well is rewarding; the feeling of having done it perfectly is fatal.
Donley Feddersen

If you're looking for perfection, look in the mirror. If you find it there, expect it elsewhere.
Malcolm Forbes

Perfectionism is a dangerous state of mind in an imperfect world. The best way is to forget doubts and set about the task in hand. . . . If you are doing your best, you will not have time to worry about failure.
Robert Hillyer

If you are pleased at finding faults, you are displeased at finding perfections.
Johann Lavater

A great deal of the joy of life consists in doing perfectly, or at least to the best of one's ability, everything which one attempts to do. There is a sense of satisfaction, a pride in surveying such a work,

a work which is rounded, full, exact, complete in all its parts—which the superficial man, who leaves his work in a slovenly, slipshod, half-finished condition can never know. It is this conscientious completeness which turns work into art. The smallest thing, well done, becomes artistic.
William Matthews

Trifles make perfection and perfection is not trifle.
Michelangelo

Perfection does not exist; to understand it is the triumph of human intelligence; to expect to possess it is the most dangerous kind of madness.
Alfred de Musset

A man can do his best only by confidently seeking (and perpetually missing) an unattainable perfection.
Ralph Barton Perry

The closest to perfection a person ever comes is when he fills out a job application form.
Stanley J. Randall

If we pretend to have reached either perfection or satisfaction, we have degraded ourselves and our work. God's work only may express that, but ours may never have that sentence written upon it, "Behold, it was very good."
John Ruskin

Do not lose courage in considering your own imperfections, but instantly set about remedying them.
St. Francis de Sales

Perfection is attained by slow degrees; it requires the hand of time.
Voltaire

PERSEVERANCE

Our delight in any particular study, art or science rises in proportion to the application which we bestow upon it. Thus, what was at first an exercise becomes at length an entertainment.
Joseph Addison

Perseverance is failing 19 times and succeeding the 20th.
Julie Andrews

Everything yields to diligence.
Antiphanes

Diligence is the greatest of teachers.
Arabian proverb

God is with those who patiently persevere.
Arabian proverb

Vigilance is not only the price of liberty, but of success of any sort.
Henry Ward Beecher

Fate gave to man the courage of endurance.
Ludwig van Beethoven

He whipped his horses withal, and put his shoulder to the wheel.
Robert Burton

In commitment, we dash the hopes of a thousand potential selves.
Lord Byron

Diligence is the mother of good fortune, and idleness, its opposite, never brought a man to the goal of any of his best wishes.
Miguel de Cervantes

It is not necessary to hope in order to undertake, nor to succeed in order to persevere.
Charles the Bold

This is no time for ease and comfort. It is the time to dare and endure.
Winston Churchill

Diligence, as it avails in all things, is also of the utmost moment in pleading causes. Diligence is to be particularly cultivated by us; it is to be constantly exerted, it is capable of effecting almost everything.
Cicero

The expectations of life depend upon diligence; the mechanic that would perfect his work must first sharpen his tools.
Confucius

It is the common fate of the indolent to see their rights become a prey to the active. The condition upon which God hath given liberty to man is eternal vigilance.
John P. Curran

I have begun several things many times, and I have often succeeded at last. I will sit down, but the time will come when you will hear me.
Benjamin Disraeli

I have brought myself by long meditation to the conviction that a human being with a settled purpose must accomplish it, and that nothing can resist a will which will stake even existence upon its fulfillment.
Benjamin Disraeli

Vacillating people seldom succeed. They seldom win the solid respect of their fellows. Successful men and women are very careful in reaching decisions and very persistent and determined in action thereafter.
L.G. Elliott

A determination to succeed is the only way to succeed that I know anything about.
William Feather

How you start is important, very important, but in the end it is how you finish that counts. It is easier to be a self-starter than a self-finisher. The victor in the race is not the one who dashes off swiftest but the one who leads at the finish. In the race for success, speed is less important than stamina. The sticker outlasts the sprinter in life's race. In America we breed many hares but not so many tortoises.
B.C. Forbes

When the worms are scarce, what does a hen do? Does she stop scratching? She does not. She scratches all the harder. A lot of businessmen have been showing less sense than a hen since orders became scarce. They have laid off salesmen; they have stopped or reduced their advertising; they have simply resigned themselves to inaction and, of course, to pessimism. If a hen knows enough to scratch all the harder when the worms are scarce, surely businessmen . . . ought to have gumption enough to scratch all the harder for business.
B.C. Forbes

In business, eternal vigilance is the price of liquidity.
Morris Franklin

In the realm of ideas, everything depends on enthusiasm; in the real world, all rests on perseverance.
Johann Wolfgang von Goethe

Whatever necessity lays upon thee, endure; whatever she commands, do.
Johann Wolfgang von Goethe

Mediocrity obtains more with application than superiority without it.
Baltasar Gracián

For me, hard work represents the supreme luxury of life.
Albert M. Greenfield

Persistence is what makes the impossible possible, the possible likely, and the likely definite.
Robert Half

You may be whatever you resolve to be. Determine to be something in the world, and you will be something. I cannot, never accomplished anything: I will try, has wrought wonders.
Joel Hawes

Whoever perseveres will be crowned.
Johann Gottfried von Herder

A determined soul will do more with a rusty monkey wrench than a loafer will accomplish with all the tools in a machine shop.
Rupert Hughes

When we see ourselves in a situation which must be endured and gone through, it is best to make up our minds to it, meet it with firmness, and accommodate everything to it in the best way practicable. This lessens the evil; while fretting and fuming only serves to increase your own torments.
Thomas Jefferson

All the performances of human art, at which we look with praise or wonder, are instances of the resistless force of perseverance.
Samuel Johnson

Few things are impossible to diligence and skill.
Samuel Johnson

Great works are performed not by strength but by perseverance.
Samuel Johnson

Failure is only postponed success as long as courage coaches ambition. The habit of persistence is the habit of victory.
Herbert Kaufman

Keep on going, and the chances are that you will stumble on something, perhaps when you are least expecting it. I never heard of anyone ever stumbling on something sitting down.
Charles F. Kettering

When you want a thing deeply, earnestly and intensely, this feeling of desire reinforces your will and arouses in you the determination to work for the desired object. When you have a distinct purpose in view, your work becomes of absorbing interest. You bend your best powers to it; you give it concentrated attention; you think of little else than the realization of this purpose; your will is stimulated into unusual activity, and as a consequence you do your work with an increasing sense of power.
Grenville Kleiser

Press on. Nothing in the world can take the place of persistence.
Ray A. Kroc

Few things are impracticable in themselves; and it is for want of application, rather than of means, that men fail of success.
François de La Rochefoucauld

Act with a determination not to be turned aside by thoughts of the past and fears of the future.
Robert E. Lee

To live is not to learn, but to apply.
Legouvé

Individual commitment to a group effort—that is what makes a team work, a company work, a society work, a civilization work.
Vince Lombardi

Perseverance and audacity generally win.
Dorothée Luzy

Thankfully, perseverance is a great substitute for talent.
Steve Martin

As long as the day lasts, let's give it all we got.
David O. McKay

Until one is committed, there is hesitancy, the chance to draw back, always ineffectiveness. Concerning all acts of initiative (and creation), there is one elementary truth, the ignorance of which kills countless ideas and splendid plans. That the moment one definitely commits oneself, then providence moves, too. All sorts of things occur to help one that would never otherwise have occurred.
William H. Murray

Genius is perseverance in disguise.
Mike Newlin

He conquers who endures.
Persius

Perserverance is more prevailing than violence; and many things which cannot be overcome when they are together, yield themselves up when taken little by little.
Plutarch

When business is not all that it should be there is a temptation to sit back and say, Well, what's the use! We've done everything possible to stir up a little business and there is nothing doing so what's the use of trying! There is always a way. There was a way in and there is a

way out. And success comes to the man who grits his teeth, squares his jaw, and says, There is a way for me and, by jingo, I'll find it. The stagnator gathers green scum, finally dries up and leaves an unsightly hollow.
Clifford Sloan

By perseverance the snail reached the Ark.
Charles H. Spurgeon

'Tis known by the name of perseverance in a good cause, and obstinacy in a bad one.
Laurence Sterne

There are two ways of attaining an important end—force and perseverance. Force falls to the lot only of the privileged few, but austere and sustained perseverance can be practised by the most insignificant.
Anne Sophie Swetchine

It's dogged as does it.
Anthony Trollope

An ounce of application is worth a ton of abstraction.
Booker T. Washington

To persevere in one's duty, and be silent, is the best answer to calumny.
George Washington

Without perseverance talent is a barren bed.
Welsh proverb

Even in social life, it is persistency which attracts confidence more than talents and accomplishments.
Edwin P. Whipple

It is not necessary to hope in order to act, nor to succeed in order to persevere.
William of Orange

PERSONALITY

A man's nature is best perceived in privateness, for there is no affectation; in passion, for that putteth a man out of his precepts; and in a new case or experiment, for there custom leaveth him.
Francis Bacon

Nobody can be exactly like me. Sometimes even I have trouble doing it.
Tallulah Bankhead

As the sun is best seen at his rising and setting, so men's native dispositions are clearest seen when they are children, and when they are dying.
Robert Boyle

The well-developed, well-patterned individual human being is, in a strictly scientific sense, the highest phenomenon of which we have any knowledge; and the variety of individual personalities is the world's highest richness.
Julian Huxley

An appealing personality is not something grafted on from without. It is not like a coat of paint applied to a building or cosmetics used on the face. It is expressed through the body, the mind, the heart and the spirit. Although some persons seem to have been born with an exceptionally appealing personality, no one has a monopoly on it.
Edith Johnson

He that fancies himself very enlightened, because he sees the deficiencies of others, may be very ignorant, because he has not studied his own.
Edward Lytton-Bulwer

The search for a new personality is futile; what is fruitful is the human interest the old personality can take in new activities.
Cesare Pavese

If I were asked to sum up in a single phrase the main purpose of individual life I would express it as the enlargement of personality. Unless an individual can transcend the limits of class, sex, race, age and creed, his personality remains of necessity to that extent incomplete.
F.W. Pethick-Lawrence

Every person in the world may not become a personage. But every person may become a personality. The happiest people are those who think the most interesting thoughts. Interesting thoughts can live only in cultivated minds. Those who decide to use leisure as a means of mental development, who love good music, good books, good pictures, good plays at the theater, good company, good conversation—what are they? They are the happiest people in the world; and they are not only happy in themselves, they are the cause of happiness in others.
William Lyon Phelps

The globe has been circumnavigated, but no man ever yet has; you may survey a kingdom and note the result in maps, but all the savants in the world could not produce a reliable map of the poorest human personality.
Alexander Smith

No theory of the universe can be satisfactory which does not adequately account for the phenomena of life, especially in that richest form which finds expression in human personality.
B.H. Streeter

Men have yet to learn the value of human personality. The fact that a person is white, or black, or yellow, of one race or another, of this religion or that—these things are not ill-important. It is the human personality that should come first.

John R. Van Sickle

PHILANTHROPY

To give away money is an easy matter, and in any man's power. But to decide to whom to give it, and how large and when, and for what purpose and how, is neither in every man's power—nor an easy matter. Hence it is that such excellence is rare, praiseworthy and noble.

Aristotle

The word "philanthropy" brings up an image of somebody who's had an illustrious career, has retired and is giving to highly established institutions that may or may not have ivy growing up their walls. I personally have felt the need to give philanthropy a reboot.

Laura Arrillaga-Andreessen

Many people, including, I'm proud to say, my three children, give extensively of their own time and talents to help others. Gifts of this kind often prove far more valuable than money. A struggling child, befriended and nurtured by a caring mentor, receives a gift whose value far exceeds what can be bestowed by a check.

Warren Buffett

Mark Zuckerberg will be a hero to many young entrepreneurs 20 years from now. Bill Gates will be a hero to others, and they will look to those [people] like I read books when I was in my teens about Rockefeller or Carnegie.

Warren Buffett

On his Giving Pledge philanthropy: The way I got the message out was to get a copy of *Forbes*, look down that 400 list and start making phone calls! Bill and Melinda [Gates] did the same thing. So keep publishing the list so I can milk it.

Warren Buffett

What gets my goat is not being able to give somebody something you want them to have.

Truman Capote

So let each one give as he purposes in his heart, not grudgingly or of necessity.

II Corinthians 9:7

I tell thee, thou foolish philanthropist, that I grudge the dollar, the dime, the cent I give to such men as do not belong to me and to whom I do not belong.

Ralph Waldo Emerson

Philanthropies and charities have a certain air of quackery.

Ralph Waldo Emerson

When you've got the money, you spend it. When you've spent it all, let someone else get going and spend theirs.

Charles Feeney

On his work vaccinating the world's poor: The magic tool of health intervention is the vaccine, because they can be made very inexpensively. We had to choose what the most impactful thing to give would be—not just money, but our time, energy, voice.

Bill Gates

We say at our dinner table, "Diarrhea is a discussion we can have," and the kids will go, "Ugh!" Diarrhea kills a million and a half kids a year. Sometimes we overdo it, I think, at the dinner table.

Melinda Gates

One can't indefinitely do for somebody what he is reluctant to do for himself.

Christopher Hitchens

Share your blessings in whatever form they come and to whatever level you have been blessed.
Jon Huntsman, Sr.

You just work day and night if the cause in your heart is justified. You just go out and drive yourself to get the money. And you have fun doing it. It's a real rush. The people I particularly dislike are those who say, "I'm going to leave it in my will." What they're really saying is, "If I could live forever, I wouldn't give any of it away."
Jon Huntsman, Sr.

By understanding and harnessing the forces that drive human behavior, you can create a self-sustaining philanthropic effort that reaches millions of people. It begins with an entrepreneurial attitude: Take an idea and execute on that idea.
Naveen Jain

If a free society cannot help the many who are poor, it cannot save the few who are rich.
John F. Kennedy

Philanthropy is commendable but it must not cause the philanthropist to overlook the circumstances of economic injustice which make philanthropy necessary.
Martin Luther King, Jr.

Money is only unused power. The real purpose of wealth, after food, clothing and shelter, is philanthropy.
Leon Levy

There are eight rungs in charity. The highest is when you help a man to help himself.
Maimonides

A large part of altruism, even when it is perfectly honest, is grounded upon the fact that it is uncomfortable to have unhappy people about one.
H.L. Mencken

In the United States, doing good has come to be, like patriotism, a favorite device of persons with something to sell.
H.L. Mencken

Business is about profit, yes, and it is about more than profit. At its best, it is about expanding the possibilities of humanity.
Jon Miller

Our lives are connected by a thousand invisible threads, and along these sympathetic fibers, our actions run as causes and return to us as results.
Herman Melville

Money giving is a very good criterion, in a way, of a person's mental health. Generous people are rarely mentally ill people.
Dr. Karl Menninger

What is the whole point of having rich people wandering around among us? To engage in certain frivolous mischief that the public benefits from enormously.
Peter Norton

Everybody wants to save the earth; nobody wants to help Mom do the dishes.
P.J. O'Rourke

I do not know how wicked American millionaires are, but as I travel about and see the results of their generosity in the form of hospitals, churches, public libraries, universities, parks, recreation grounds, art museums and theatres I wonder what on earth we should do without them.
William Lyon Phelps

He hath dispersed, he hath given to the poor; his righteousness endureth forever; his horn shall be exalted with honor.
Psalms 112:9

A good deal of philanthropy arises in general from mere vanity and love of distinction gilded over to others and to themselves with some show of benevolent sentiment.
Sir Walter Scott

I worry not about my kids but about the third generation; I don't want them to be trust fund babies living an empty, useless life. I want them to have the legacy that you have to give back, make a contribution to worthwhile things so your own existence has some meaning.
Ronald Stanton

The dead carry with them to the grave in their clutched hands only that which they have given away.
DeWitt Wallace

Society can't wait. It's sad there are so many entrepreneurs, business successes and venture capitalists who give no thought to society.
Leslie H. Wexner

Philanthropy [has become] simply the refuge of people who wish to annoy their fellow creatures.
Oscar Wilde

PHILOSOPHY

Every one of us, unconsciously, works out a personal philosophy of life, by which we are guided, inspired, and corrected, as time goes on. It is this philosophy by which we measure out our days, and by which we advertise to all about us the man, or woman, that we are. . . . It takes but a brief time to scent the life philosophy of anyone. It is defined in the conversation, in the look of the eye, and in the general mien of the person. It has no hiding place. It's like the perfume of the flower—unseen, but known almost instantly. It is the possession of the successful, and the happy. And it can be greatly embellished by the absorption of ideas and experiences of the useful of this earth.
George Matthew Adams

Philosopher: A man up in a balloon, with his family and friends holding the ropes which confine him to earth and trying to haul him down.
Louisa May Alcott

Philosophy is a route of many roads leading from nowhere to nothing.
Ambrose Bierce

Philosophy recovers itself when it ceases to be the device for dealing with the problems of philosophers and becomes the method, cultivated by philosophers, for dealing with the problems of men.
John Dewey

All philosophy lies in two words, sustain and abstain.
Epictetus

Philosophy can add to our happiness in no other manner but by diminishing our misery; it should not pretend to increase our present stock, but make us economists of what we are possessed of. Happy were we all born philosophers; all born with a talent of thus dissipating our own cares by spreading them upon all mankind.
Oliver Goldsmith

The creative mind is the playful mind. Philosophy is the play and dance of ideas.
Eric Hoffer

Philosophy should be an energy; it should find its aim and its effect in the amelioration of mankind.
Victor Hugo

Be a philosopher, but amid all your philosophy, be still a man.
David Hume

A philosophy which speaks, even indirectly, only to philosophers is no philosophy at all; and I think the same is true if it speaks only to scientists, or only to jurists, or priests, or any other special class.
Abraham Kaplan

Philosophy triumphs easily over past, and over future evils, but present evils triumph over philosophy.
François de La Rochefoucauld

Philosophy is the art of living.
Plutarch

All work is an act of philosophy.
Ayn Rand

We need fewer philosophies and more philosophers.
Frank Romer

When men comfort themselves with philosophy, 'tis not because they have got two or three sentences, but because they have digested those sentences, and made them their own: philosophy is nothing but discretion.
John Selden

There was never yet a philosopher that could endure the toothache patiently.
William Shakespeare

The discovery of what is true and the practice of that which is good, are the two most important aims of philosophy.
Voltaire

Philosophy may teach us to bear with equanimity the misfortunes of our neighbors.
Oscar Wilde

PLANNING

We can't cross a bridge until we come to it; but I always like to lay down a pontoon ahead of time.
Bernard M. Baruch

The method of the enterprising is to plan with audacity and execute with vigor.
Christian Bovée

Make no little plans, they have no magic to stir men's blood. Make big plans, aim high in hope and work and let your watchword be order and your beacon beauty.
David Burnham

The man who is prepared has his battle half fought.
Miguel de Cervantes

The executive of the future will be rated by his ability to anticipate his problems rather than to meet them as they come.
Howard Coonley

Make your plans as fantastic as you like, because 25 years from now, they will seem mediocre. Make your plans ten times as great as you first planned, and 25 years from now you will wonder why you did not make them 50 times as great.
Henry Curtis

Plan ahead: It wasn't raining when Noah built the ark.
Richard Cushing

We [often] have fine theories, but, somehow, we are not always able to carry them out in this workaday world. A chief executive, for example, can draw

up a perfect organization chart—and then he wonders why it doesn't function smoothly in practice.... If even a Tiffany watch cannot be guaranteed to keep correct time when put to the test of everyday wear and tear, must we not be prepared to make allowance for erring mortals? It is right that executives should draw up perfect plans on paper; but it is all wrong for them to expect their paper plans to work out to perfection in this imperfect world.
B.C. Forbes

By failing to prepare you are preparing to fail.
Benjamin Franklin

Thousands of engineers can design bridges, calculate strains and stresses, and draw up specifications for machines, but the great engineer is the man who can tell whether the bridge or the machine should be built at all, where it should be built, and when.
Eugene G. Grace

You and I must not complain if our plans break down if we have done our part. That probably means that the plans of one who knows more than we do have succeeded.
Edward E. Hale

I try to have no plans the failure of which would greatly annoy me. Half the unhappiness in the world is due to the failure of plans which were never reasonable, and often impossible.
Edgar W. Howe

He who every morning plans the transactions of the day and follows out that plan carries a thread that will guide him through the labyrinth of the most busy life. The orderly arrangement of his time is like a ray of life which darts itself through all his occupations. But where

no plan is laid, where the disposal of time is surrendered merely to the chance of incident, chaos will soon reign.
Victor Hugo

Expect only 5% of an intelligence report to be accurate. The trick of a good commander is to isolate the 5%.
Douglas MacArthur

Most business men generally are so busy coping with immediate and piecemeal matters that there is a lamentable tendency to let the long run or future take care of itself. We often are so busy putting out fires, so to speak, that we find it difficult to do the planning that would prevent those fires from occurring in the first place. As a prominent educator has expressed it, Americans generally spend so much time on things that are urgent that we have none left to spend on those that are important.
Gustav Metzman

The best preparation for tomorrow is to do today's work superbly well.
William Osler

Perfection of planning is a symptom of decay. During a period of exciting discovery or progress, there is no time to plan the perfect headquarters. The time for that comes later, when all the important work has been done.
C. Northcote Parkinson

I thatched my roof when the sun was shining, and now I am not afraid of the storm.
George F. Stivers

An intelligent plan is the first step to success. The man who plans knows where he is going, knows what progress he is making and has a pretty good idea when he will arrive. Planning is the open road to your destination. If you don't

know where you are going, how can you expect to get there?
Basil S. Walsh

The will to win is worthless if you do not have the will to prepare.
Thane Yost

PLEASE

Flattery, if judiciously administered, is always acceptable.
Lady Marguerite Blessington

If you will please people, you must please them in their own way.
Lord Chesterfield

An appeaser is one who feeds a crocodile—hoping it will eat him last.
Winston Churchill

He that can please nobody is not so much to be pitied as he that nobody can please.
Charles Caleb Colton

He who cannot love must learn to flatter.
Johann Wolfgang von Goethe

He who endeavors to please must appear pleased.
Samuel Johnson

We all live in the hope of pleasing somebody; and the pleasure of pleasing ought to be greatest, and always will be greatest, when our endeavors are exerted in consequence of our duty.
Samuel Johnson

We sometimes imagine we hate flattery, but we only hate the way we are flattered.
François de La Rochefoucauld

Pleasant dealing in the ordinary business of life is the oil, the grease, if you please, for the wheels; it facilitates the performance of that business, and lengthens the life of the human machines that do the work of the world.
Walter R. Rutherford

What really flatters a man is that you think him worth flattering.
George Bernard Shaw

Nothing is so great an instance of ill-manner as flattery. If you flatter all the company, you please none; if you flatter only one or two, you affront the rest.
Jonathan Swift

'Tis an old maxim in the schools that flattery is the food of fools. Yet now and then your men of wit will condescend to take a bit.
Jonathan Swift

PLEASURE

Play so you may be serious.
Anacharsis

A fool bolts pleasure, then complains of moral indigestion.
Minna Antrim

It is not abstinence from pleasures that is best, but mastery over them without being worsted.
Aristippus

The great pleasure in life is doing what people say you cannot do.
Walter Bagehot

People seem to enjoy things more when they know a lot of other people have been left out on the pleasure.
Russell Baker

Pleasure only starts once the worm has got into the fruit; to become delightful, happiness must be tainted with poison.
Georges Bataille

Pleasure is in itself a good; nay, even setting aside immunity from pain, the only good.
Jeremy Bentham

Abstainer: A weak person who yields to the temptation of denying himself a pleasure.
Ambrose Bierce

Play is the exultation of the possible.
Martin Buber

Perhaps one has to be very old before one learns how to be amused rather than shocked.
Pearl S. Buck

Pleasure's a sin, and sometimes sin's a pleasure.
Lord Byron

It is not a virtue, but a deceptive copy and imitation of virtue, when we are led to the performance of duty by pleasure as its recompense.
Cicero

Game, noun: Any unserious occupation designed for the relaxation of busy people and the distraction of idle ones. It's used to take people to whom we have nothing to say off our hands, and sometimes even ourselves.
Étienne Bonnot de Condillac

Honor is a public enemy, and conscience a domestic, and he that would secure his pleasure, must pay a tribute to one and go halves with t'other.
William Congreve

Pleasure admitted in undue degree, enslaves the will, nor leaves the judgment free.
William Cowper

If once a man indulges himself in murder, very soon he comes to think very little of robbing, and from robbing he comes next to drinking and Sabbath breaking, and from that to incivility and procrastination.
Thomas De Quincey

We enjoy thoroughly only the pleasure that we give.
Alexandre Dumas

The pleasure of life is according to the man that lives it, and not according to the work or place.
Ralph Waldo Emerson

Pleasure is the first good. It is the beginning of every choice and every aversion. It is the absence of pain in the body and of troubles in the soul.
Epicurus

Business is always interfering with pleasure—but it makes other pleasures possible.
William Feather

We must always skim over pleasures. They are like marshy lands that we must travel nimbly, hardly daring to put down our feet.
Bernard de Fontenelle

Pleasure is the most real good in this life.
Frederick the Great

Choose such pleasures as recreate much and cost little.
Richard Fuller

The best pleasures of this world are not quite true.
Johann Wolfgang von Goethe

We have more days to live through than pleasures. Be slow in enjoyment, quick at work, for men see work ended with pleasure, pleasure ended with regret.
Baltasar Gracián

Who will in time present pleasure refrain, shall in time to come the more pleasure obtain.
John Heywood

Fresh air and innocence are good if you don't take too much of them—but I always remember that most of the achievements and pleasures of life are in bad air.
Oliver Wendell Holmes

I wish for the superfluous, for the useless, for the extravagant, for the too much, for that which is not good for anything.
Victor Hugo

Do not bite at the bait of pleasure till you know there is no hook beneath it.
Thomas Jefferson

The ugliest of trades have their moments of pleasure. If I were a grave digger, or even a hangman, there are some people I could work for with a good deal of enjoyment.
Douglas Jerrold

The great source of pleasure is variety.
Samuel Johnson

The liberty of using harmless pleasure will not be disputed; but it is still to be examined what pleasures are harmless.
Samuel Johnson

Give me books, fruit, French wine and fine weather and a little music out of doors, played by someone I do not know. I admire lolling on a lawn by a water-lilied pond to eat white currants and see goldfish, and go to the fair in the evening if I'm good.
John Keats

I wasted my substance, I know I did, on riotous living, so I did, but there's nothing on record to show I did more than my betters have done.
Rudyard Kipling

Old age is a tyrant, which forbids the pleasures of youth on pain of death.
François de La Rochefoucauld

Love of pleasure is the disease which makes men most despicable.
Cassius Longinus

You can't live on amusement. It is the froth on water—an inch deep and then the mud.
George MacDonald

What we learn with pleasure we never forget.
Louis Mercier

My chief study all my life has been to lighten misfortunes and multiply plea-sures, as far as human nature can.
Mary Wortley Montague

Scratching is one of nature's sweetest gratifications, and the one nearest to hand.
Michel de Montaigne

Ill-luck is, in nine cases out of ten, the result of taking pleasure first and duty second, instead of duty first and pleasure second.
Theodore T. Munger

A life merely of pleasure, or chiefly of pleasure, is always a poor and worthless life.
Theodore W. Parker

Amusement that is excessive and followed only for its own sake, allures and deceives us.
Blaise Pascal

The mind ought sometimes to be amused that it may the better return to thought and to itself.
Phaedrus

Amusement is the happiness of those who cannot think.
Alexander Pope

There is no such thing as pure pleasure; some anxiety always goes with it.
Ovid

I can think of nothing less pleasurable than a life devoted to pleasure.
John D. Rockefeller, Jr.

A man who knows how to mix pleasures with business is never entirely possessed by them; he either quits or resumes them at his will; and in the use he makes of them he rather finds a relaxation than a dangerous charm that might corrupt him.
Charles de Saint-Évremond

Indulge yourself in pleasures only in so far as they are necessary for the preservation of health.
Baruch Spinoza

Pleasure, when it is a man's chief purpose, disappoints itself; and the constant application to it palls the faculty of enjoying it.
Richard Steele

No pleasure lasts long unless there is variety in it.
Publilius Syrus

That man is richest whose pleasures are the cheapest.
Henry David Thoreau

Pleasure has its time; so too, has wisdom. Make love in thy youth, and in old age attend to thy salvation.
Voltaire

A cigarette is the perfect type of a perfect pleasure. It is exquisite, and it leaves one unsatisfied. What more can one want?
Oscar Wilde

Pleasure is Nature's test, her sign of approval. When man is happy, he is in harmony with himself and with his environment.
Oscar Wilde

Pleasure is the only thing to live for. Nothing ages like happiness.
Oscar Wilde

Simple pleasures are the last refuge of the complex.
Oscar Wilde

Excesses accomplish nothing. Disorder immediately defeats itself.
Woodrow Wilson

All the things I really like to do are either illegal, immoral or fattening.
Alexander Woollcott

POETRY

A paranoiac, like a poet, is born, not made.
Luis Buñuel

You don't have to suffer to be a poet. Adolescence is enough suffering for anyone.
John Ciardi

Take a commonplace, clean and polish it, light it so that it produces the same effect of youth and freshness and spontaneity as it did originally, and you have done a poet's job.
Jean Cocteau

You campaign in poetry. You govern in prose.
Mario Cuomo

Poetry is boned with ideas, nerved and blooded with emotions, and held together with the tough, delicate skin of words.
Paul Engle

Poetry is the renewal of words, setting them free, and that's what a poet is doing: loosening the words.
Robert Frost

Writing free verse is like playing tennis with the net down.
Robert Frost

Poetry is not an expression of the party line. It's that time of night, lying in bed, thinking what you really think, making the private world public, that's what the poet does.
Allen Ginsberg

There's no money in poetry, but then there's no poetry in money either.
Robert Graves

Poetry is the shortest way of saying something. It lets us express a dime's worth of ideas, or a quarter's worth of emotion, with a nickel's worth of words.
John P. Grier

You will find poetry nowhere unless you bring some of it with you.
Joseph Joubert

When power leads man to arrogance, poetry reminds him of his limitations. When power narrows the area of man's concern, poetry reminds him of the richness and diversity of his existence. When power corrupts, poetry cleanses.
John F. Kennedy

I can't understand these chaps who go round American universities explaining how they write poems. It's like going round explaining how you sleep with your wife.
Philip Larkin

Perhaps no person can be a poet, or can even enjoy poetry, without a certain unsoundness of the mind.
Thomas B. Macaulay

Publishing a volume of verse is like dropping a rose-petal down the Grand Canyon and waiting for the echo.
Don Marquis

Certainly Kipling has gifts; the fairy godmothers were all tipsy at his christening: What will he do with them?
Somerset Maugham

It is easier to write a mediocre poem than to understand a good one.
Michel de Montaigne

Poetry is adolescence fermented, and thus preserved.
José Ortega y Gasset

In his youth, Wordsworth sympathized with the French Revolution, went to France, wrote good poetry and had a natural daughter. At this period, he was a bad man. Then he became good, abandoned his daughter, adopted correct principles and wrote bad poetry.
Bertrand Russell

Poetry is a sword of lightning, ever unsheathed, which consumes the scabbard that would contain it.
Percy Bysshe Shelley

Meredith is a prose Browning, and so is Browning; he used poetry as a medium for writing in prose.
Oscar Wilde

Poetry has never brought me in enough money to buy shoestrings.
William Wordsworth

POLITENESS

There is no policy like politeness; and a good manner is the best thing in the world either to get a good name, or to supply the want of it.
Edward Bulwer-Lytton

Politeness is an inexpensive way of making friends.
William Feather

New York and surrounding country have been experiencing the worst snowstorms in years. Curiously, they have brought out the best qualities in human nature. Ordinarily, on the streets and in country roads, each man, each driver, is out for himself and delights in scoring over others. But I have noticed, both in the city and in the country, and entirely different spirit since travel became extremely difficult, sometimes impossible. Wagon drivers and truck drivers have shown the greatest readiness to help out others. Politeness not ordinarily witnessed has been the rule rather than the exception. . . .
B.C. Forbes

Politeness is the result of good sense and good nature.
Oliver Goldsmith

Politeness is the chief sign of culture.
Baltasar Gracián

Moving parts in contact require lubrication to avoid excessive wear. Honorifics and formal politeness provide lubrication where people rub together. Often, the very young, the untraveled, the naïve, the unsophisticated deplore these formalities as empty, meaningless, or dishonest, and scorn to use them. No matter how pure their motives, they thereby throw sand into the machinery that does not work too well at best.
Robert A. Heinlein

Politeness is fictitious benevolence.
Samuel Johnson

Tact, the kind of tact you should cultivate, is not a form of deception or make-believe, but a cultivated taste which gives fine perception in seeing and doing what is best under all circumstances. There is nothing which will so readily bring you into favor, or disarm an opponent, as the right use of tact.
Grenville Kleiser

Politeness has been well defined as benevolence in small things.
Thomas B. Macaulay

Be sure, when you think you are being extremely tactful, that you are not in reality running away from something you ought to face.
Frank Medlicott

The spirit of politeness is a desire to bring about by our words and manners, that others may be pleased with us and with themselves.
Montesquieu

Tact is the knack of making a point without making an enemy.
Howard W. Newton

Tact is the interpreter of all riddles, the surmounter of all difficulties, the remover of all obstacles.
William Scargill

A quick and sound judgment, good common sense, kind feeling, and an instinctive perception of character, in these are the elements of what is called tact, which has so much to do with acceptability and success in life.
Charles Simmons

Tact is one of the first mental virtues, the absence of which is often fatal to the best of talents; it supplies the place of many talents.
William Simms

Politeness is good nature regulated by good sense.
Sydney Smith

It's a pity so many of us persist in regarding politeness as being merely a superficial social grace instead of what it really is, namely one of the necessities of life. Quite apart from politeness for its own sake, and as a matter of plain justice, it is invaluable as a sort of cushion or buffer to hold off the jolt that would otherwise disrupt the harmony of things.
Zealandia

Tact is the great ability to see other people as they think you see them.
Carl Zuckmayer

POLITICS

Every politician, when he leaves office, ought to go straight to jail and serve his time.
American folk saying

Go already, my arm's starting to hurt.
Anti-Mubarak placard

Wherever the relevance of speech is at stake, matters become political by definition, for speech is what makes man a political being.
Hannah Arendt

The most radical revolutionary will become a conservative the day after the revolution.
Hannah Arendt

We're not Sunni. We're not Shiite. We just want to be free.
Bahraini protesters

Vote for the man who promises least; he'll be the least disappointing.
Bernard M. Baruch

In Israel, in order to be a realist you must believe in miracles.
David Ben-Gurion

Alliance: In international politics, the union of two thieves who have their hands so deeply into each other's pocket that they cannot separately plunder a third.
Ambrose Bierce

In politics, merit is rewarded by the possessor being raised, like a target, to a position to be fired at.
Christian Bovée

Government is too big and important to be left to the politicians.
Chester Bowles

If you do have to look at polls, you should do it no more than once every few days, to get a general sense of the state of the race. I've seen the work on information overload, which makes people depressed, stressed and freezes their brains. I know that checking the polls constantly is a recipe for self-deception and anxiety.
David Brooks

Nowhere are prejudices more mistaken for truth, passion for reason and invective for documentation than in politics.
John Mason Brown

It is the misfortune of all miscellaneous political combinations, that with the purest motives of their more generous members are ever mixed the most sordid

interests and the fiercest passions of mean confederates.
Edward Bulwer-Lytton

Diplomacy means the art of nearly deceiving all your friends, but not quite deceiving all your enemies.
Kofi Busia

An honest politician is one who when he is bought will stay bought.
Simon Cameron

Every revolutionary ends by becoming either an oppressor or a heretic.
Albert Camus

When [a politician] is in opposition, he is an expert on the means to some end; and when he is in office he is an expert on the obstacles to it. In short, when he is impotent he proves to us that the thing is easy; and when he is omnipotent he proves that it is impossible.
G.K. Chesterton

I have always felt that a politician is to be judged by the animosities he excites among his opponents.
Winston Churchill

A politician thinks of the next election; a statesman of the next generation. A politician looks for the success of his party; a statesman for that of his country. The statesman wishes to steer, while the politician is satisfied to drift.
James Freeman Clarke

It is fortunate that diplomats have long noses since they usually cannot see beyond them.
Paul Claudel

This is quite a game, politics. There are no permanent enemies, and no permanent friends, only permanent interests.
William Clay

On Bill Clinton: I have a simple question: Who's the last President to give you a balanced budget?
Bill Clinton

Real rebels are rarely anything but second rate outside their rebellion; the drain of time and temper is ruinous to any other accomplishment.
James Gould Cozzens

A politician is a man who can be verbose in fewer words than anyone else.
Peter De Vries

To be a liberal one doesn't have to be a wastrel.
Paul H. Douglas

Political controls in the sense that we think of bureaus or departments of government can never operate to produce collaboration between groups in the inner wheels of our industrial organization. It must come from inner compulsions and desires.
William O. Douglas

The political machine triumphs because it is a united minority acting against a divided majority.
Will Durant

When I was first here, we had the advantages of the underdog. Now we have the disadvantages of the overdog.
Abba Eban

I despise all adjectives that try to describe people as liberal or conservative, rightist or leftist, as long as they stay in the useful part of the road.
Dwight D. Eisenhower

I get weary of the European habit of taking our money, resenting any slight hint as to what they should do, and then

assuming, in addition, full right to criticize us as bitterly as they may desire.
Dwight D. Eisenhower

All conservatives are such from personal defects. They have been effiminated by position of nature, born halt and blind, through luxury of their parents, and can only, like invalids, act on the defensive.
Ralph Waldo Emerson

Conservatism stands on man's confessed limitations; reform on his indisputable infinitude; conservatism on circumstance; liberalism on power; one goes to make an adroit member of the social frame; the other to postpone all things to the man himself.
Ralph Waldo Emerson

Men are conservatives when they are least vigorous or when they are most luxurious—they are conservatives after dinner.
Ralph Waldo Emerson

Accuse American businessmen of being responsible for radicalism and they would indignantly deny the accusation. Yet, in one fundamental sense, they are responsible. They are responsible in the sense that they have utterly neglected to take part in the work and the organization which precede the choosing of candidates for political office. Local political organizations all over the land are conducted and controlled, as a rule, by politicians. . . .

Businessmen have shirked such responsibilities, leaving an untrammeled field to others less capable of carrying on the administration of government.
B.C. Forbes

It is not a case of whether we want to wash our hands of Europe or want to help her to regain her feet. The troubles of Europe have been laid on our doorstep, so to speak, and will plague us, if we do nothing to cure them, whether we like it or not.
B.C. Forbes

Let's give the gate to "gating" every crisis, scandal or event that comes along. I'll wager more things have been termed "-gate" than there are gates.
Malcolm Forbes

It's clear that something must be done about the effectively disruptive tactics of anarchistic handfuls [at political rallies]. Handling the occasional heckler is a storied, valuable art in politics; but a militant group of grubs [have] announced their determination to rape the right of candidates to be heard and of citizens to hear. Far, far too often these stinky finkies succeeded. . . .

Free speech is the first requisite of freedom and a viable, functioning democracy. The exercise of it cannot be at the option of those who think the right to dissent includes the right to destroy.
Malcolm Forbes

On retiring from dealmaking: Why does a painter paint? I live, breathe and eat this stuff. I don't do anything else well enough.
Gerald Ford

Memorable recent campaign slogan: He's not a total moron.
Karl Fornes

A liberal is a man too broadminded to take his own side in a quarrel.
Robert Frost

We have the power to do any damn fool thing we want to do, and we seem to do it about every ten minutes.
J. William Fulbright

Politics consists of choosing between the disastrous and the unpalatable.
John Kenneth Galbraith

I have come to the conclusion that politics are too serious a matter to be left to politicians.
Charles de Gaulle

This is a very, very tough neighborhood.
Dan Gillerman, former Israeli ambassador to the UN

In every election in American history both parties have their clichés. The party that has the clichés that ring true wins.
Newt Gingrich

Twist the dial during an election year and you hear someone twisting the truth.
Arnold Glasow

A liberal is a man who is willing to spend somebody else's money.
Carter Glass

I hate all bungling as I do sin, but particularly bungling in politics, which leads to the misery and ruin of many thousands and millions of people.
Johann Wolfgang von Goethe

Politics is an excellent career, unless you get caught.
Robert Half

The end of all political effort must be the well-being of the individual in the life of safety and freedom.
Dag Hammarskjöld

In the end it is worse to suppress dissent than to run the risk of heresy.
Learned Hand

You do not become a "dissident" just because you decide one day to take up this most unusual career. It begins as an attempt to do your work well, and ends with being branded an enemy of society.
Vaclav Havel

Diplomacy is living in state.
Oliver Herford

Haven't we all heard some irritating person saying that if so-and-so is elected, then he/she is absolutely definitely leaving the country? There must be some reason why it is mainly liberals who tend to say this, but the chief thing to note about the promise is that it is usually an empty one.
Christopher Hitchens

In modern Greek history, there is a close relationship between national humiliation and political radicalization.
Christopher Hitchens

The role of dissident is not, and should not be, a claim of membership in a communion of saints. In other words, the more fallible the mammal, the truer the example.
Christopher Hitchens

A heresy can only spring from a system that is in full vigor.
Eric Hoffer

I was probably the only revolutionary ever referred to as "cute."
Abbie Hoffman

Presidents cannot always kick evil-minded persons out of the front door. Such persons are often selected by the electors to represent them.
Herbert Hoover

It is my firm belief that I have a link with the past and a responsibility to the future. I cannot give up. I cannot despair. There's a whole future, generations to come. I have to keep trying.
King Hussein of Jordan

But thus saith the Lord, Even the captives of the mighty shall be taken away, and the prey of the terrible shall be delivered.
Isaiah 49:25

Boxing taught me something that can be used to good advantage in politics—when you see the other fellow getting ready for a punch, hit him first and hit him hard!
Sen. Hiram W. Johnson

The first lady is, and always has been, an unpaid public servant elected by one person, her husband.
Lady Bird Johnson

Of all kinds of credulity, the most obstinate is that of party-spirit; of men, who, being numbered, they know not why, in any party, resign the use of their own eyes and ears, and resolve to believe nothing that does not favor those whom they profess to follow.
Samuel Johnson

A newspaper reported that I spent $30,000 a year buying Paris clothes and that women hate me for it. I couldn't spend that much unless I wore sable underwear.
Jacqueline Kennedy

I am the one person who can truthfully say, I got my job through the *New York Times*.
John F. Kennedy

Politics is a jungle—torn between doing the right thing and staying in office.
John F. Kennedy

Those who make peaceful revolution impossible will make violent revolution inevitable.
John F. Kennedy

I thought they'd get one of us, but Jack, after all he's been through, never worried about it. I thought it would be me.
Robert F. Kennedy

One blames politicians, not for inconsistency but for obstinacy. They are the interpreters, not the masters, of our fate. It is their job, in fact, to register the fact accompli.
John Maynard Keynes

If you feed the people just with revolutionary slogans they will listen today, they will listen tomorrow, they will listen the day after tomorrow, but on the fourth day they will say, "To hell with you."
Nikita Khrushchev

Politicians are the same all over. They promise to build a bridge where there is no river.
Nikita Khrushchev

You can't make war in the Middle East without Egypt and you can't make peace without Syria.
Henry Kissinger

When smashing monuments, save the pedestals—they always come in handy.
Stanislaw Jerzy Lec

What is conservatism? Is it not adherence to the old and tried, against the new and untried?
Abraham Lincoln

The justification of majority rule in politics is not to be found in its ethical superiority.
Walter Lippmann

The politicians were talking themselves red, white and blue in the face.
Clare Boothe Luce

In a chameleon-like change of face, the ruling elite that nurtured the

kleptocracy, the waste of the state, irrationality and impunity have become the torchbearers of austerity, but only in regard to those beneath them. The more impudent among them are even wagging their finger at society.
Stavros Lygeros

Men who use terrorism as a means to power, rule by terror once they are in power.
Helen MacInnes

It is easier to run a revolution than a government.
Ferdinand Marcos

In America you can go on the air and kid the politicians, and the politicians can go on the air and kid the people.
Groucho Marx

Politics is the art of looking for trouble, finding it everywhere, diagnosing it incorrectly and applying the wrong remedies.
Groucho Marx

Rule number one in [election night] cocktail parties: Never make anyone uncomfortable in your home—even morons.
Mary Matalin

The politician will be only too happy to abdicate in favor of his image, because the image will be much more powerful than he could ever be.
Marshall McLuhan

If experience teaches us anything at all, it teaches us this: that a good politician, under democracy, is quite as unthinkable as an honest burglar.
H.L. Mencken

A party of order or stability, and a party of progress or reform, are both necessary elements of a healthy state of political life.
John Stuart Mill

The proper memory for a politician is one that knows what to remember and what to forget.
John Morley

We must not confuse dissent with disloyalty. When the loyal opposition dies, I think the soul of America dies with it.
Edward R. Murrow

There is no longer a way out of our present situation except by forging a road toward our objective, violently and by force, over a sea of blood and under a horizon blazing with fire.
Gamal Abdel Nasser

Politics is the diversion of trivial men who, when they succeed at it, become important in the eyes of more trivial men.
George Jean Nathan

Maybe a nation that consumes as much booze and dope as we do and has our kind of divorce statistics should pipe down about "character issues."
P.J O'Rourke

Is this a joke? It's the last thing I would expect. It mocks us and what we are going through right now. All it will do is infuriate people here.
Chrisoula Panagiotidi

Great political questions stir the deepest nature of one-half the nation, but they pass far above and over the heads of the other half.
Wendell Phillips

Politics is just like show business. You have a hell of an opening, coast for a while, and then have a hell of a close.
Ronald Reagan

Every time we have an election, we get in worse men and the country keeps right on going. Times have proven only one thing and that is you can't ruin this country, even with politics.
Will Rogers

All revolutions devour their own children.
Ernst Rohm

A radical is a man with both feet firmly planted—in the air. A conservative is a man with two perfectly good legs, who, however, has never learned to walk forward. A reactionary is a somnambulist walking backwards. A liberal is a man who uses his legs and hands at the behest of his head.
Franklin D. Roosevelt

The most successful politician is he who says what the people are thinking most often and in the loudest voice.
Theodore Roosevelt

We were eyeball-to-eyeball and the other fellow just blinked.
Dean Rusk

If one man offers you democracy and another offers you a bag of grain, at what stage of starvation do you prefer the grain to the vote?
Bertrand Russell

In America, unlike Europe, there is both a peculiarly immediate sense of hostility and a coarse, on the whole unnuanced, attitude toward Islam.
Edward Said

Revolutions never go backward.
William Henry Seward

He knows nothing and thinks he knows everything. That points clearly to a political career.
George Bernard Shaw

The dictatorship tries to create the myth that it's either them or all hell breaks loose. We fall into that trap by believing there is going to be a civil war after the regime falls.
Nadim Shehadi, Middle East scholar

Even the pyramids might one day disappear, but not the Palestinians longing for their homeland.
Eduard Shevardnadze

The question of questions for the politicians should ever be—What type of social structure am I tending to produce? But this is a question he never entertains.
Herbert Spencer

Politics is perhaps the only profession for which no preparation is thought necessary.
Robert Louis Stevenson

If you allow a political catchword to go on and grow, you will awaken some day to find it standing over you, arbiter of your destiny, against which you are powerless.
William Graham Sumner

There are no personal sympathies in politics.
Margaret Thatcher

Discussion in America means dissent.
James Thurber

We can go into history, or we can go in the garbage of history.
Tarek Tohamy, Egyptian

Revolutions are always verbose.
Leon Trotsky

Political corruption is the toboggan to national disruption.
John A. Ward

To sin by silence, when we should protest, makes cowards of us all.
Ella Wheeler Wilcox

Every man who takes office in Washington either grows or swells, and when I give a man an office, I watch him carefully to see whether he is growing or swelling.
Woodrow Wilson

There is scarcely anything more harmless than political or party malice. It is best to leave it to itself. Opposition and contradiction are the only means of giving it life or duration.
John Witherspoon

POOR

The unfortunate need people who will be kind to them; the prosperous need people to be kind to.
Aristotle

Poverty is an anomaly to rich people. It is very difficult to make out why people who want dinner do not ring the bell.
Walter Bagehot

Anyone who has ever struggled with poverty knows how extremely expensive it is to be poor.
James Baldwin

Come away; poverty's catching.
Aphra Behn

Everything that poverty touches becomes frightful.
Nicolas Boileau

Ignorance and poverty are the best condiments for the great feast of the world, but the inexperienced and poor are never invited to it.
Anthony Burgess

When I give food to the poor, they call me a Saint. When I ask why the poor have no food, they call me a Communist.
Hélder Câmara

One is weary of hearing about the omnipotence of money. I will say rather that, for a genuine man, it is not evil to be poor.
Thomas Carlyle

There's a point of poverty at which the spirit isn't with the body all the time. It finds the body really too unbearable. So it's almost as if you were talking to the soul itself. And a soul's not properly responsible.
Louis-Ferdinand Céline

Thousands upon thousands are yearly brought into a state of real poverty by their great anxiety not to be thought poor.
William Cobbett

In a country well governed, poverty is something to be ashamed of. In a country badly governed, wealth is something to be ashamed of.
Confucius

For the poor shall never cease out of the land; therefore I command thee, saying, Thou shalt open thine hand wide unto thy brother, to thy poor, and to thy needy, in thy land.
Deuteronomy 15:11

To be a poor man is hard, but to be a poor race in a land of dollars is the very bottom of hardships.
W.E.B. Du Bois

One must be poor to know the luxury of giving.
George Eliot

Grant me the treasure of sublime poverty: Permit the distinctive sign of our order to be that it does not possess anything of its own beneath the sun, for the glory of your name, and that it have no other patrimony than begging.
St. Francis of Assisi

Poverty often deprives a man of all spirit and virtue, it is hard for an empty bag to stand upright.
Benjamin Franklin

For every talent that poverty has stimulated it has blighted a hundred.
John W. Gardner

Poverty is uncomfortable; but nine times out of ten the best thing that can happen to a young man is to be tossed overboard and compelled to sink or swim.
James A. Garfield

Only the poor can know all the disadvantages of poverty. Only the rich can know all the disadvantages of wealth.
Cullen Hightower

America has the best-dressed poverty the world has ever known.
Michael Harrington

The poor tread lightest on the earth. The higher our income, the more resources we control and the more havoc we wreak.
Paul Harrison

Of all the advantages which come to any young man, I believe it to be demonstrably true that poverty is the greatest.
Josiah G. Holland

Poverty urges us to do and suffer anything that we may escape from it, and so leads us away from virtue.
Horace

There is hardly an American citizen above the poverty level whose tax conscience is so clear that he isn't scared of being audited.
IRS agent

Woe to them that decree unrighteous decrees, and which write grievousness that they have prescribed. To turn aside the needy from judgment, and to take away the right from the poor of my people, that widows may be their prey, and that they may rob the fatherless!
Isaiah 10:1–2

He who knows how to be poor knows everything.
Jules Michelet

A decent provision for the poor is the true test of civilization.
Samuel Johnson

Poverty is a great enemy to human happiness; it certainly destroys liberty, and it makes some virtues impracticable, and others extremely difficult.
Samuel Johnson

That man is to be accounted poor, of whatever rank he be, and suffers the pains of poverty, whose expenses exceed his resources; and no man is, property speaking, poor, but he.
William Paley

We Athenians hold that it is not poverty that is disgraceful but the failure to struggle against it.
Pericles

Poverty is not dishonorable in itself, but only when it comes from idleness, intemperance, extravagance, and folly.
Plutarch

It is well known that, when two authors meet, they at once start talking about money—like everyone else.
V.S. Pritchett

The profession of letters is, after all, the only one in which one can make no money without being ridiculous.
Jules Renard

Wealth is conspicuous, but poverty hides.
James Reston

Poverty is not disgrace to a man, but it is confoundedly inconvenient.
Sydney Smith

The doctrine of thrift for the poor is dumb and cruel, like advising them to try and lift themselves by their bootstraps.
Norman Thomas

I've never been poor, only broke. Being poor is a frame of mind. Being broke is only a temporary situation.
Mike Todd

We who are liberal and progressive know that the poor are our equals in every sense except that of being equal to us.
Lionel Trilling

In the small town of Hannibal, Missouri, when I was a boy, everybody was poor, but didn't know it; and everybody was comfortable and did know it.
Mark Twain

There is only one class in the community that thinks more abut money than the rich, and that is the poor. The poor can think of nothing else. That is the misery of being poor.
Oscar Wilde

POSSESSIONS

What a man has honestly acquired is absolutely his own, which he may freely give, but cannot be taken from him without his consent.
Samuel Adams

Give thy mind more to what thou has than to what thou hast not.
Marcus Aurelius Antoninus

Why grab possessions like thieves, or divide them like socialists, when you can ignore them like wise men?
Natalie Clifford Barney

There is, of course, a difference between what a man seizes and what he really possesses.
Pearl S. Buck

Thieves respect property. They merely wish the property to become their property that they may more perfectly respect it.
G.K. Chesterton

Our most valuable possessions are those which can be shared without lessening—those which, when shared, multiply. Our least valuable possessions, on the other hand, are those which, when divided, are diminished.
William H. Danforth

Americans are uneasy with their possessions, guilty about power, all of which is difficult for Europeans to perceive because they themselves are so truly

materialistic, so versed in the uses of power.
Joan Didion

Possessions, outward success, publicity, luxury—to me these have always been contemptible. I believe that a simple and unassuming manner of life is best for everyone, best both for the body and the mind.
Albert Einstein

Some men are born to own; can animate all their possessions. Others cannot; their owning is not graceful; seems to be a compromise of their character; they seem to steal their own dividends.
Ralph Waldo Emerson

Mankind, by the perverse depravity of their nature, esteem that which they have most desired as of no value the moment it is possessed, and torment themselves with fruitless wishes for that which is beyond their reach.
François Fénelon

Our life on earth is, and ought to be, material and carnal. But we have not yet learned to manage our materialism and carnalism properly; they are still entangled with our desire for ownership.
E.M. Forster

What I possess I would gladly retain. Change amuses the mind, yet scarcely profits.
Johann Wolfgang von Goethe

Possession hinders enjoyment. It merely gives you the right to keep things for or from others, and thus you gain more enemies than friends.
Baltasar Gracián

Nothing can be so perfect while we possess it as it will seem when remembered.
Oliver Wendell Holmes

Many possessions, if they do not make a man better, are at least expected to make his children happier; and this pathetic hope is behind many exertions.
Wilhelm von Humboldt

Things may come to those who wait, but only the things left by those who hustle.
Abraham Lincoln

Sell that ye have, and give alms; provide yourselves bags which wax not old, a treasure in the heavens that faileth not, where no thief approacheth, nor moth corrupteth.
Luke 12:33

Two things are as big as the man who possesses them—neither bigger nor smaller. One is a minute, the other a dollar.
Channing Pollock

Every increased possession loads us with new weariness.
John Ruskin

Everything comes to us that belongs to us if we create the capacity to receive it.
Rabindranath Tagore

Have a place for everything and keep the thing somewhere else; this is not advice, it is merely custom.
Mark Twain

He who possesses most must be most afraid of loss.
Leonardo da Vinci

That anyone should be able to make it the sole purpose of his life-work, to sink into the grave weighed down with a great material load of money and goods, seems explicable only as the product of a perverse imagination.
Max Weber

POWER

An honest private man often grows cruel and abandoned when converted into an absolute prince. Give a man power of doing what he pleases with impunity, you extinguish his fear, and consequently overturn in him one of the great pillars of morality.
Joseph Addison

The man whose authority is recent is always stern.
Aeschylus

The price of power is responsibility for the public good.
Winthrop W. Aldrich

I have yet to encounter that common myth of weak men, an insurmountable barrier.
James Lane Allen

Where a man does his best with only moderate powers, he will have the advantage over negligent superiority.
Jane Austen

It is a strange desire, to seek power, and to lose liberty; or to seek power over others, and to lose power over a man's self.
Francis Bacon

All human power is a compound of time and patience.
Honoré de Balzac

Power is not revealed by striking hard or often, but by striking true.
Honoré de Balzac

If any man is rich and powerful he comes under the law of God by which the higher branches must take the burnings of the sun, and shade those that are lower; by which the tall trees must protect the weak plants beneath them.
Henry Ward Beecher

I know of nothing sublime which is not some modification of power.
Edmund Burke

Immense power is acquired by assuring yourself in your secret reveries that you were born to control affairs.
Andrew Carnegie

You philosophers are lucky men. You write on paper, which is patient. Unfortunate Empress that I am, I write on the susceptible skins of living beings.
Catherine the Great

Those who seek power for personal ends eventually run afoul of popular opinion.
Chinese proverb

Orators are most vehement when they have the weakest cause, as men get on horseback when they cannot walk.
Cicero

Far from diminishing the appetite for power, suffering exasperates it.
E.M. Cioran

To know the pains of power, we must go to those who have it. To know its pleasures, we must go to those who are seeking it. The pains of power are real, its pleasures imaginary.
Charles Caleb Colton

Law is but a heathen word for power.
Daniel Defoe

Next to the assumption of power is the responsibility of relinquishing it.
Benjamin Disraeli

A great man is one who can have power and not abuse it.
Henry L. Doherty

I have never known there to be groupies around generals. But just like in every other field of endeavor, there is a certain excitement around people that have great power. And generals, like captains of industry and certain kinds of celebrities, wield a certain kind of power.
Jacey Eckhart

Every natural power exhilarates; a true talent delights the possessor first.
Ralph Waldo Emerson

Men, such as they are, very naturally seek money or power; and power because it is as good as money.
Ralph Waldo Emerson

The power which resides in him is new in nature, and none but he knows what that is which he can do, nor does he know until he has tried.
Ralph Waldo Emerson

Authority's for sharing only when the sharer is sure of his (or hers).
Malcolm Forbes

Clout is something some seem to have—until they try exercising it.
Malcolm Forbes

Those carried away by power are soon carried away.
Malcolm Forbes

Power doesn't corrupt people; people corrupt power.
William Gaddis

Power is not happiness. Security and peace are more to be desired than a man at which nations tremble.
William Godwin

Beware of dissipating your powers; strive constantly to concentrate them. Genius thinks it can do whatever it sees others doing, but it is sure to repent of every ill-judged outlay.
Johann Wolfgang von Goethe

In the general course of human nature, a power over a man's subsistence amounts to a power over his will.
Alexander Hamilton

The admiration of power in others is as common to man as the love of it in himself; the one makes him a tyrant, the other a slave.
William Hazlitt

Real power has fullness and variety. It is not narrow like lightning, but broad like light. The man who truly and worthily excels in any one line of endeavor might also, under a change of circumstances, have excelled in some other line. Power is a thing of solidity and wholeness.
Roswell D. Hitchcock

Responsibilities gravitate to the person who can shoulder them; power flows to the man who knows how.
Elbert Hubbard

Every great advance in natural knowledge has involved the absolute rejection of authority.
Thomas Huxley

I have never been able to conceive how any rational being could propose happiness to himself from the exercise of power over others.
Thomas Jefferson

The general story of mankind will evince that lawful and settled authority is very seldom resisted when it is well employed.
Samuel Johnson

The possession of power inevitably spoils the free use of reason.
Immanuel Kant

The power in which we must have faith if we would be well, is the creative and curative power which exists in every living thing.
John Harvey Kellogg

I have two basic convictions: First, more harm has been done by weak persons than by wicked persons; secondly, the problems of the world are caused by the weakness of goodness rather than by the strength of evil. It is evident that we have allowed technology to outstrip social controls. . . . Man must catch up with what he has created.
Harry S. Kennedy

Nothing more impairs authority than a too frequent or indiscreet use of it. If thunder itself was to be continual, it would excite no more terror than the noise of a mill.
Alfred Kingston

Anyone entrusted with power will abuse it if not also animated with the love of truth and virtue, no matter whether he be a prince, or one of the people.
Jean de La Fontaine

Power corrupts, but absolute power is really neat.
Ex-Navy Secretary John Lehman

Nearly all men can stand adversity, but if you want to test a man's character, give him power.
Abraham Lincoln

The great question which, in all ages, has disturbed mankind, and brought on them the greatest part of those mischiefs, which have ruined cities, depopulated countries, and disordered the peace of the world, has been, not whether there be power in the world, not whence it came, but who should have it.
John Locke

The highest proof of virtue is to possess boundless power without abusing it.
Thomas B. Macaulay

He is free who knows how to keep in his own hands the power to decide, at each step, the course of his life, and who lives in a society which does not block the exercise of that power.
Salvador de Madariaga

The only purpose for which power can be rightfully exercised over any member of a civilized community, against his will, is to prevent harm to others. His own good, either physical or moral, is not a sufficient warrant.
John Stuart Mill

The best test of a man is authority.
Montenegran proverb

The culminating point of administration is to know well how much power, great or small, we ought to use in all circumstances.
Montesquieu

The power of the state is measured by the power that men surrender to it.
Felix Morley

Life is an instinct for growth, for survival, for the accumulation of forces, for power.
Friedrich Wilhelm Nietzsche

What is evil?—Whatever springs from weakness.
Friedrich Wilhelm Nietzsche

What is good? Whatever augments the feeling of power, the will to power, power itself, in man.
Friedrich Wilhelm Nietzsche

If thou wouldst conquer thy weakness thou must not gratify it.
William Penn

Unlimited power is worse for the average person than unlimited alcohol; and the resulting intoxication is more damaging for others. Very few have not deteriorated when given absolute dominion. It is worse for the governor than for the governed.
William Lyon Phelps

It has been said that absolute power corrupts absolutely, but many it not be truer to say that to be absolutely powerful a man must first corrupt himself?
Terence Rattigan

How a minority, reaching majority, seizing authority, hates a minority.
Leonard H. Robbins

To be able to endure odium is the first art to be learned by those who aspire to power.
Seneca

The weak and insipid white wine makes at length excellent vinegar.
William Shenstone

Access to secret intelligence is one of the more potent aphrodisiacs of power.
David Stafford

You cannot run away from a weakness. You must sometimes fight it out or perish; and if that be so, why not now, and where you stand?
Robert Louis Stevenson

The cause of all these evils was the desire for power which greed and ambition inspire.
Thucydides

Power, from the standpoint of experience, is merely the relation that exists between the expression of someone's will and the execution of that will by others.
Leo Tolstoy

The prevailin' weakness of most public men is to slop over. G. Washington . . . never slopt over!
Artemus Ward

Nothing in the world is more haughty than a man of moderate capacity when once raised to power.
Baron Wessenburg

Right and truth are greater than any power, and all power is limited by right.
Benjamin Whichcote

We all have weaknesses. But I have figured that others have put up with mine so tolerably that I would be much less than fair not to make a reasonable discount for theirs.
William Allen White

Wherever there is a man who exercises authority, there is a man who resists authority.
Oscar Wilde

As a matter of fact and experience, the more power is divided the more irresponsible it becomes.
Woodrow Wilson

PRAISE

Consider how many do not even know your name, and how many will soon forget it, and how those who now praise you will presently blame you.
Marcus Aurelius Antoninus

The high-minded man is fond of conferring benefits, but it shames him to receive them.
Aristotle

Applause is the echo of a platitude.
Ambrose Bierce

A man's inner nature is revealed by what he praises—a man is self-judged by what he says of others. Thus a man is judged by his standards, by what he considers the best. And you can't find a more crucial test. It reveals the soul.
Hugh Black

Praise is a debt we owe unto the virtue of others, and due unto our own from all whom malice hath not made mutes, or envy struck dumb.
Thomas Browne

To dispense with ceremony is the most delicate mode of conferring a compliment.
Edward Bulwer-Lytton

We all are imbued with the love of praise.
Cicero

There are two modes of establishing our reputation: to be praised by honest men, and to be abused by rogues. It is best, however, to secure the former, because it will invariably be accompanied by the latter.
Charles Caleb Colton

The superior man does not mind being in office; all he minds about is whether he has qualities that entitle him to office. He does not mind failing to get recognition; he is too busy doing the things that entitle him to recognition.
Confucius

Whoever pays you more court than he is accustomed to pay, either intends to deceive you or finds you necessary to him.
John Courtenay

I love criticism just so long as it is unqualified praise.
Noël Coward

He wants worth who dares not praise a foe.
John Dryden

Sweet praise is like perfume. It is fine if you don't swallow it.
Dwight D. Eisenhower

We thirst for approbation, yet cannot forgive the approver.
Ralph Waldo Emerson

Any fact is better established by two or three good testimonies, than by a thousand arguments.
Nathaniel Emmons

Spite of all modesty, a man must own a pleasure in the hearing of his praise.
George Farquhar

That they value not praise will never do anything worthy of praise.
Thomas Fuller

Applause is the only appreciated interruption.
Arnold Glasow

Reprove privately, praise publicly.
Arnold Glasow

The praises of others may be of us in teaching us not what we are, but what we ought to be.
Augustus Hare

There is no verbal vitamin more potent than praise.
Frederick B. Harris

Applause abates diligence.
Samuel Johnson

He who praises everybody praises nobody.
Samuel Johnson

The applause of a single human being is of great consequence.
Samuel Johnson

Praise, like gold diamonds, owes its value to its scarcity.
Samuel Johnson

It would be a kind of ferocity to reject indifferently all sorts of praise. One should be glad to have that which comes from good men who praise in sincerity things that are really praiseworthy.
Jean de La Bruyère

Praise is sometimes a good thing for the diffident and despondent. It teaches them properly to rely on the kindness of others.
Letitia Landon

Consider carefully before you say a hard word to a man, but never let a chance to say a good one go by. Praise judiciously bestowed is money invested.
George Horace Lorimer

Praise is warming and desirable, what the human race lives on like bread. But praise is an earned thing. It has to be deserved like an honorary degree or a hug from a child. A compliment is manna, a free gift.
Phyllis McGinley

He praises the big horse and rides the small one.
Mexican proverb

He who freely magnifies what hath been nobly done, and fears not to declares as freely what might be done better, gives ye the best covenant of his fidelity.
John Milton

I much prefer a compliment, insincere or not, to sincere criticism.
Plautus

Those who are greedy of praise prove that they are poor in merit.
Plutarch

It is not he who searches for praise who finds it.
Antoine de Rivarol

I have yet to find a man, whatever his situation in life, who did not do better work and put forth greater effort under a spirit of approval than he ever would do under a spirit of criticism.
Charles M. Schwab

It is great happiness to be praised of them who are most praiseworthy.
Sir Philip Sidney

Among the smaller duties of life, I hardly know any one more important than that of not praising where praise is not due.
Sydney Smith

Reprove thy friend privately, commend him publicly.
Solon

I know of no manner of speaking so offensive as that of giving praise, and closing with an exception.
Richard Steele

Whenever you commend, add your reasons for doing so; it is this which distinguishes the approbation of a man of sense from the flattery of sycophants and admiration of fools.
Richard Steele

Praise is the daughter of present power.
Jonathan Swift

In modern life nothing produces such an effect as a good platitude. It makes the whole world kind.
Oscar Wilde

Women are never disarmed by compliments. Men always are. That is the difference between the two sexes.
Oscar Wilde

Recognition for a job well done is high on the list of motivating influences for all people; more important in many instances than compensation itself. When someone is promoted, a promotion that everyone could see coming because of an excellent record, the entire department is stimulated. For it is clear, then, that promotions are based on merit. A promotion that seems to come out of the blue, which is always the case when no one knows what the next fellow is doing, causes nothing but resentment and a further weakening of the will to work.
John M. Wilson

The sweetest of all sounds is praise.
Xenophon

PRAYER

The minds of people are so cluttered up with everyday living these days that they don't, or won't, take time out for a little prayer—for mental cleansing, just as they take a bath for physical outer cleansing. Both are necessary.
Jo Ann Carlson

Prayer is a force as real as terrestrial gravity. As a physician, I have seen men, after all other therapy had failed, lifted out of disease and melancholy by the serene effort of prayer. Only in prayer do we achieve that complete and harmonious assembly of body, mind and spirit which gives the frail human reed its unshakable strength.
Alexis Carrel

Prayer, like radium, is a luminous and self-generating form of energy.
Alexis Carrel

The most powerful form of energy one can generate is not mechanical, electronic or even atomic energy, but prayer energy.
Alexis Carrel

The influence of prayer on the human mind and body is as demonstrable as that of secreting glands. Its results can be measured in terms of increased physical buoyancy, greater intellectual vigor, moral stamina, and a deeper understanding of the realities underlying human relationship.
Alexis Carrel

If a pig could pray, it would pray for swill. What do you pray for?
B.C. Forbes

Men have prayed in prison, men have prayed in slums and concentration camps. It's only the middle classes who demand to pray in suitable surroundings.
Graham Greene

Prayer does not change God, but changes him who prays.
Søren Kierkegaard

When we pray "Our Father," I am praying for you, you are praying for me. In fact, if men everywhere would only learn to pray aright, "Our Father," there would be no differences to settle. It would not be long before Communist, imperialist, capitalist and what have you would stop their cold war and start to live at peace with one another.
Albert N. Neibacker, D.D.

We are all weak, finite, simple human beings, standing in the need of prayer. None need it so much as those who think

they are strong, those who know it not but are deluded by self-sufficiency.
Harold Cooke Phillips, D.D.

A generous prayer is never presented in vain; the petition may be refused, but the petitioner is always, I believe, rewarded by some gracious visitation.
Robert Louis Stevenson

We believe that prayer works miracles, and that all prayers are answered. But the greatest miracle is that some of them are actually answered exactly as we ourselves wish them to be.
Glenn Stewart

We should not be discouraged if our prayers go unanswered; if some were, we most certainly would have grave reservations about the sanity of God.
J.K. Stuart

More tears are shed over answered prayers than unanswered ones.
St. Theresa of Ávila

When the gods choose to punish us, they merely answer our prayers.
Oscar Wilde

PREJUDICE

Nothing is harder to topple than a fact that supports a deeply held prejudice denied by its holder.
Russell L. Ackoff

We can get the new world we want, if we want it enough to abandon our prejudices, every day, everywhere. We can build this world if we practise now what we said we were fighting for.
Gwen Bristow

Even in an advanced stage of civilization, there is always a tendency to prefer those parts of literature which favor ancient prejudices, rather than those which oppose them; and in cases where this tendency is very strong, the only effect of great learning will be to supply the materials which may corroborate old errors and confirm old superstitions. In our time such instances are not uncommon; and we frequently meet with men whose erudition ministers to their ignorance, and who, the more they read the less they know.
Henry Thomas Buckle

Our prejudices are our mistresses; reason is at best our wife, very often needed but seldom minded.
Lord Chesterfield

America owes most of its social prejudices to the exaggerated religious opinions of the different sects which were so instrumental in establishing the colonies.
James Fenimore Cooper

Prejudice, which sees what it pleases, cannot see what is plain.
Aubrey deVere

He that is possessed with a prejudice is possessed with a devil.
Tryon Edwards

Too many of us vote for our prejudices instead of our desires.
William Feather

An unprejudiced mind is probably the rarest thing in the world; to nonprejudice I attach the greatest value.
André Gide

He who never leaves his country is full of prejudices.
Carlo Goldoni

Prejudices are the principles of people we dislike.
John P. Grier

Dogs bark at a person whom they do not know.
Heraclitus

A great number of people think they are thinking when they are merely rearranging their prejudices.
William James

The world is as large as the range of one's interests. A narrow-minded man has a narrow outlook. The walls of his world shut out the broader horizon of affairs. Prejudice can maintain walls that no invention can remove.
Joseph Jastrow

Beware prejudices. They are like rats, and men's minds are like traps; prejudices get in easily, but it is doubtful if they ever get out.
Francis Jeffrey

One may no more live in the world without picking up the moral prejudices of the world than one will be able to go to hell without perspiring.
H.L. Mencken

Everyone is a prisoner of his own experiences. No one can eliminate prejudices— just recognize them.
Edward R. Murrow

Prejudice is a mist, which in our journey through the world often dims the brightest and obscures the best of all the good and glorious objects that meet us on our way.
Lord Shaftesbury

We are chameleons, and our partialities and prejudices change places with an easy and blessed facility.
Mark Twain

Prejudice is not held against people because they have evil qualities. Evil qualities are imputed to people because prejudices are held against them.
Marshall Wingfield

PRESENT

Bad times, hard times—this is what people keep saying; but let us live well, and times shall be good. We are the times: Such as we are, such are the times.
St. Augustine

It is difficult to live in the present, ridiculous to live in the future, and impossible to live in the past.
Jim Bishop

Our grand business is not to see what lies dimly in the distance, but to do what lies clearly at hand.
Thomas Carlyle

Men spend their lives in anticipations, in determining to be vastly happy at some period when they have time. But the present time has one advantage over every other—it is our own. Past opportunities are gone, future are not come. We may lay in a stock of pleasures, as we would lay in a stock of wine; but if we defer the tasting of them too long, we shall find that both are soured by age.
Charles Caleb Colton

One of the illusions of life is that the present hour is not the critical, decisive hour. Write it on your heart that every day is the best day of the year.
Ralph Waldo Emerson

This time, like all other times, is a very good one, if we but know what to do with it.
Ralph Waldo Emerson

We cannot overstate our debt to the past, but the moment has the supreme claim.
Ralph Waldo Emerson

Let us think only of spending the present day well. Then when tomorrow shall have come, it will be called today, and then we will think about it.
St. Francis de Sales

Let us . . . quietly accept our times, with the firm conviction that just as much good can be done today as at any time in the past, provided only that we have the will and the way to do it.
Étienne Gilson

The present is burdened too much with the past. We have not time, in our earthly existence, to appreciate what is warm with life, and immediately around us.
Nathaniel Hawthorne

It is common to overlook what is near by keeping the eye fixed on something remote. In the same manner present opportunities are neglected, and attainable good is slighted by minds busied in extensive ranges and intent upon future advantages.
Samuel Johnson

The road recedes as the traveler advances, leaving a continuous present.
Richard Le Gallienne

The dogmas of the quiet past are inadequate to the stormy present. . . . As our case is new, so we must think anew and act anew.
Abraham Lincoln

Who controls the past controls the future; who controls the present controls the past.
George Orwell

Banish the future. Live only for the hour and its allotted work. Think not of the amount to be accomplished, the difficulties to be overcome, or the end to be attained, but set earnestly at the little task at your elbow, letting that be sufficient for the day.
William Osler

Let ancient times delight other folk, I rejoice that I was not born till now.
Ovid

Let any man examine his thoughts, and he will find them ever occupied with the past or the future. We scarcely think at all of the present; or if we do, it is only to borrow the light which it gives for regulating the future. The present is never our object; the past and the present we use as means; the future only is our end. Thus, we never live, we only hope to live.
Blaise Pascal

"Now" is the watchword of the wise.
Charles H. Spurgeon

You must live in the present, launch yourself on every wave, find your eternity in each moment.
Henry David Thoreau

He who governed the world before I was born shall take care of it likewise when I am dead. My part is to improve the present moment.
John Wesley

PRIDE

Pride is a great urge to action; but remember, the pride must be on the part

of the buyer. On the part of the seller, it is vanity.
James R. Adams

Riches are apt to betray a man into arrogance.
Joseph Addison

Conceit is God's gift to little men.
Bruce Barton

A proud man is seldom a grateful man, for he never thinks he gets as much as he deserves.
Henry Ward Beecher

It is pride which plies the world with so much harshness and severity. We are as rigorous to offenses as if we had never offended.
Paxton Blair

Some of the proudest and most arrogant people I have known were morons and paupers, while some of the most wonderful and humble were wealthy.
F. Howard Callahan

If I had only one sermon to preach it would be a sermon against pride.
G.K. Chesterton

The disesteem and contempt of others is inseparable from pride. It is hardly possible to overvalue ourselves but by undervaluing our neighbors.
Lord Clarendon

A great business success was probably never attained by chasing the dollar, but is due to pride in one's work—the pride that makes business an art.
Henry L. Doherty

I've never any pity for conceited people, because I think they carry their comfort about with them.
George Eliot

Every time I see an Erie Railroad engine bearing the name of its faithful driver a thrill goes through me, for I know that the man guiding it has won this rare honor by many years of the most loyal and efficient service. Who will argue that only public men and corporation heads are entitled to have their names emblazoned on the scroll of honor?

All workmen care about is money, you say? Wrong. Workers are made of exactly the same stuff as generals or senators or presidents or governors or industrial leaders. It is just as fitting to honor the worthiest of our wage earners as it is to honor others.
B.C. Forbes

"I don't feel myself that I know it all, but I have enough conceit to be successful." That observation was made by a businessman in his 30s who was making notable headway, although his path bristled with difficulties. Business places no premiums on shrinking violets. Employers prefer men who have self-assurance, forcefulness, go-aheadness, men who know their jobs and know that they know it.
B.C. Forbes

A man given to pride is usually proud of the wrong thing.
Henry Ford

Every man has a right to be conceited until he is successful.
Benjamin Franklin

Conceit is the quicksand of success.
Arnold Glasow

Pride is a deeply rooted ailment of the soul. The penalty is misery; the remedy lies in the sincere, life-long cultivation of humility, which means true

self-evaluation and a proper perspective toward past, present and future.
Robert Gordis

Nothing so obstinately stands in the way of all sorts of progress as pride of opinion; while nothing is so foolish and baseless.
J.G. Holland

When men are most sure and arrogant they are commonly most mistaken, giving views to passion without that proper deliberation which alone can secure them from the grossest absurdities.
David Hume

Conceit causes more conversation than wit.
François de La Rochefoucauld

Every good thought that we have, and every good action that we perform, lays us open to pride, and thus exposes us to the various assaults of vanity and self-satisfaction.
William Law

Pride is a form of selfishness.
David Lawrence

Whenever nature leaves a hole in a person's mind, she generally plasters it over with a thick coat of self-conceit.
Henry Wadsworth Longfellow

Conceit is to nature what paint is to beauty; it is not only needless, but it impairs what it would improve.
Alexander Pope

Conceit may puff a man up, but can never prop him up.
John Ruskin

Pride is at the bottom of all great mistakes.
John Ruskin

Look out how you use proud words; when you let proud words go, it is not easy to call them back.
Carl Sandburg

To knock a thing down, especially if it is cocked at an arrogant angle, is a deep delight to the blood.
George Santayana

Pride may be allowed to this or that degree, else a man cannot keep up his dignity.
John Selden

My pride fell with my fortunes.
William Shakespeare

Pride is a fruitful source of uneasiness. It keeps the mind in disquiet. Humility is the antidote to this evil.
Lydia Sigourney

If a proud man makes me keep my distance, the comfort is that he keeps his at the same time.
Jonathan Swift

He that is proud of riches is a fool. For if he be exalted above his neighbors because he hath more gold, how much inferior is he to a gold mine.
Jeremy Taylor

We can believe almost anything if it be necessary to protect our pride.
Dr. Douglas A. Thom

Undertake not to teach your equal in the art himself professes; it savors arrogancy.
George Washington

Take away the self-conceited, and there will be elbowroom in the world.
Benjamin Whichcote

Remember, when the peacock struts his stuff the shows his backside to half the world.
Herve Wiener

Early in life I had to choose between honest arrogance and hypocritical humility. I chose honest arrogance and have seen no occasion to change.
Frank Lloyd Wright

Conceit and confidence are both of them cheats. The first always imposes on itself; the second frequently deceives others.
Johann Zimmerman

PRINCIPLES

Always vote for a principle, though you vote alone, and you may cherish the sweet reflection that your vote is never lost.
John Quincy Adams

He who floats with the current, who does not guide himself according to higher principles, who has no ideal, no convictions—such a man is a mere article of the world's furniture—a thing moved, instead of a living and moving being—an echo, not a voice.
Henri Frédéric Amiel

Do not consider anything for your interest which makes you break your word, quit your modesty or inclines you to any practice which will not bear the light or look the world in the face.
Marcus Aurelius Antoninus

In any assembly, the simplest way to stop the transacting of business and split the ranks is to appeal to a principle.
Jacques Barzun

Expedients are for an hour, but principles are for the ages. Just because the rains descend, and the winds blow, we cannot afford to build on the shifting sands.
Henry Ward Beecher

Great ideals and principles do not live from generation to generation just because they are right, nor even because they have been carefully legislated. Ideals and principles continue from generation to generation only when they are built into the hearts of the children as they grow up.
George S. Benson

Many people are liberal in principle, reluctant in practice.
John M. Burgess

Our inheritance of well-founded, slowly conceived codes of honor, morals and manners, the passionate convictions which so many hundreds of millions share together of the principles of freedom and justice, are far more precious to us than anything which scientific discoveries could bestow.
Winston Churchill

He who merely knows right principles is not equal to him who loves them.
Confucius

Men of principle are always bold, but those who are bold are not always men of principle.
Confucius

A precedent embalms a principle.
Benjamin Disraeli

We have always found that, if our principles were right, the area over which they were applied did not matter. Size is only a matter of the multiplication table.
Henry Ford

The principles we live by, in business and in social life, are the most important part of happiness. We need to be careful,

upon achieving happiness, not to lose the virtues which have produced it.
Harry Harrison

So act that your principle of action might safely be made a law for the whole world.
Immanuel Kant

Many men do not allow their principles to take root, but pull them up every now and then, as children do the flowers they have planted, to see if they are growing.
Henry Wadsworth Longfellow

Principle—particularly moral principle—can never be a weathervane, spinning around this way and that with the shifting winds of expediency. Moral principle is a compass forever fixed and forever true—and that is as important in business as it is in the classroom.
Edward R. Lyman

In vain do they talk of happiness who never subdued an impulse in obedience to a principle. He who never sacrificed a present to a future good, or a personal to a general one, can speak of happiness only as the blind speak of color.
Horace Mann

One thing I certainly never was made for, and that is to put principles on and off at the dictation of a party, as a lackey changes his livery at his master's command.
Horace Mann

The principles which men profess on any controverted subject are usually a very incomplete exponent of the opinions they really hold.
John Stuart Mill

I love the man that can smile in trouble, that can gather strength from distress, and grow brave by reflection. 'Tis the business of little minds to shrink, but he whose heart is firm, and whose

conscience approves his conduct, will pursue his principles unto death.
Thomas Paine

There is a point, of course, where a man must take the isolated peak and break with all his associates for clear principle; but until that time comes he must work, if he would be of use, with men as they are. As long as the good in them overbalances the evil, let him work with them for the best that can be obtained.
Theodore Roosevelt

Our principles are the springs of our actions; our actions, the springs of our happiness or misery. Too much care, therefore, cannot be taken in forming our principles.
Philip Skelton

It is often easier to fight for a principle than to live up to it.
Adlai Stevenson

Men with intellectual light alone may make advances without moral principle, but without that moral principle which gospel faith produces, permanent progress is impossible.
James B. Walker

PROBLEMS

Nearly all our ills are the result of neglect in some way or other. And this truth may be said to apply to the ills of nations as well. Negligence is at the bottom of all decay. And decay always starts by showing little signs—or warnings. Then is the time to show interest and to be alert. There is nothing quite so easy as to neglect, and nothing quite so difficult as to repair that negligence. Negligence always carries a high price. It costs nothing to avoid it!
George Matthew Adams

A soul exasperated by its ills falls out with everything, with its friends and also with itself.
Joseph Addison

Those who do not complain are never pitied.
Jane Austen

You can overcome anything if you don't bellyache.
Bernard M. Baruch

It is a general error to suppose the loudest complainers for the public to be the most anxious for the welfare.
Edmund Burke

If you think there's a solution, you're a part of the problem.
George Carlin

An unaspiring person always complains. There is no end to his complaints. He bitterly complains even when the blessings of opportunity knock at his very door.
Sri Chinmoy

There are three modes of bearing the ills of life: by indifference, by philosophy, and by religion.
Charles Caleb Colton

Problems always appear big when incompetent men are working on them.
William Feather

It's so much easier to suggest solutions when you don't know too much about the problem.
Malcolm Forbes

When things are bad we take a bit of comfort in the thought that they could always be worse. And when they are, we find hope in the thought that things are so bad they have to get better.
Malcolm Forbes

The reward for being a good problem solver is to be heaped with more and more difficult problems to solve!
Buckminster Fuller

Should one look through a red glass at a white lily, he would seem to see a red lily. But there would be no red lily. So it is with humanity's problems. They consist of false mental pictures.
Miriam D. Garbrick

No one is more definite about the solution than the one who doesn't understand the problem.
Robert Half

All problems become smaller if you don't dodge them but confront them. Touch a thistle timidly, and it pricks you; grasp it boldly, and its spines crumble.
William F. Halsey

There are people who always find a hair in their soup for the simple reason that when they sit down before it, they shake their heads until one falls in.
Friedrich Hebbel

Problems worthy of attack prove their worth by hitting back.
Piet Hein

Every age has its problem, by solving which, humanity is helped forward.
Heinrich Heine

Problems are the price of progress: Don't bring me anything but trouble—good news weakens me.
Charles F. Kettering

Meddling with another man's folly is always thankless work.
Rudyard Kipling

It's not the tragedies that kill us, it's the messes.
Dorothy Parker

Every man has a rainy corner in his life, from which bad weather besets him.
Jean Paul Richter

Suffer the ill and look for the good.
James Sandford

If this nation is going to survive meaningfully, and then perhaps grow decently, it has got to begin to know and accept enormous deprivation.
William Saroyan

We have no more right to put our discordant states of mind into the lives of those around us and rob them of their sunshine and brightness than we have to enter their houses and steal their silverware.
Julia Seton

A great part of this life consists of contemplating what we cannot cure.
Robert Louis Stevenson

We may be pretty certain that persons whom all the world treats ill deserve the treatment they get. The world is a looking glass, and gives back to every man the reflection of his own face.
William Makepeace Thackeray

Conceal thy domestic ills.
Thales

The most important thing to do in solving a problem is to begin.
Frank Tyger

PROCRASTINATION

But is a word that cools many a warm impulse, stifles many a kindly thought, puts a dead stop to many a brotherly deed. No one would ever love his neighbor as himself if he listened to all the buts that could be said.
Edward Bulwer-Lytton

By the street of By-and-By, one arrives at the house of Never.
Miguel de Cervantes

Postponement: the sincerest form of rejection.
Robert Half

There is no pleasure in having nothing to do; the fun is in having lots to do and not doing it.
Mary Little

Putting off a hard thing makes it impossible.
George Horace Lorimer

Procrastination is the art of keeping up with yesterday.
Don Marquis

Do you often start projects that you don't begin?
Suzanne O'Neill

While we are postponing, life speeds by.
Seneca

PRODUCTION

Unless each man produces more than he receives, increases his output, there will be less for him and all the others.
Bernard M. Baruch

Hating hard work can get to be such an obsession that you won't let it pile up.
H.C. Brown

Produce, produce! Were it but the pitifulest, infinitesimal fraction of a product, produce it in God's name. 'Tis the utmost thou hast in thee? Out with it then! Up, up! Whatsoever thy hand findeth to do, do it with thy whole might.
Thomas Carlyle

It is not size that counts in business. Some companies with $500,000 capital

net more profits than other companies with $5,000,000. Size is a handicap unless efficiency goes with it.
Herbert N. Casson

Efficiency is doing things—not wishing you could do them, dreaming about them, or wondering if you can do them.
Frank Crane

There can be no economy where there is no efficiency.
Benjamin Disraeli

Let every employer get this into his mind: Production resulting from long hours worked unwillingly cannot but be less satisfactory than production from shorter hours worked willingly. . . . A willing, cheerful worker, with his heart in his job, will turn out more work and more satisfactory work in 44 hours a week than an unwilling worker, dissatisfied with his conditions, will turn out in 54 hours. It is good business, therefore, for every employer to go as far as he possibly can in reaching a schedule agreeable to his people.
B.C. Forbes

As it is with an individual, so it is with a nation. One must produce to have, or one will become a have-not.
Henry George

The best hope of raising our own standards lies in the progressive expansion of production both here and abroad and making sure that the gains of increased productivity are, in fact, applied to social advance.
Carter Goodrich

The genius of America is production; and a large percentage of our productive enterprises are headed by men who have come up from the worker's bench.
William S. Knudsen

Historically the phenomenal growth of capacity of the American economy has come from a relatively large increase in production per man-hour and a much smaller increase in the size of the labor force; it has taken place in spite of a 25% reduction in working hours over the past 50 years.
Frank D. Newbury

To contrive is nothing! To construct is something! To produce is everything!
Edward Rickenbacker

The efficiency of most workers is beyond the control of the management and depends more than has been supposed upon the willingness of men to do their best.
Sumner H. Slichter

Only in more production and in new production can the American standard of living be increased and the economy be sound.
Alfred P. Sloan, Jr.

PROFIT

What needs to be cultivated among men interested in social relationships whether as owner, manager or employee, producer or consumer, seller or buyer, partner or competitor, is self-control, refraining from unfair advantage, determination to give value as well as to take it; the appreciation that immediate gain is not the principal consideration; that one group can not continue to profit at the expense of another without eventual loss to both; that all classes of men are mutually dependent on the services of each other; that the best service yields the greatest profit.
Preston S. Arkwright

Higher prices are themselves inflation and not merely the result of it. They are accelerated and not stopped by taxation. . . . It isn't high prices that persuade the high cost and marginal producer to make the investment necessary to bring him into production. It is the promise of profit. High prices without profit merely requires more investment to support turnover and inventory.
Bernard M. Baruch

I don't want to do business with those who don't make a profit, because they can't give the best service.
Lee Bristol

If you mean to profit, learn to please.
Winston Churchill

It is a socialist idea that making profits is a vice. I consider the real vice is making losses.
Winston Churchill

Civilization and profits go hand in hand.
Calvin Coolidge

When shallow critics denounce the profit motive inherent in our system of private enterprise, they ignore the fact that it is an economic support of every human right we possess and without it, all rights would disappear.
Dwight D. Eisenhower

Several weeks of summer vacation in the Thirties I spent working at $15 a week in the *Forbes* office. . . . I worked in the mail cage, where envelopes were slit and subscription payments extracted. Dad used to come pounding down the office aisle and pause long enough to ask, How much today? Inevitably the answer was inadequate—except once. That day the controller said excitedly, Mr. Forbes, the ledger shows a slight profit this month! . . . My father turned to him and said, Young man, I don't give a damn what your books show. Do we have any money in the bank?
Malcolm Forbes

When profit is unshared, it's less likely to grow greater.
Malcolm Forbes

The profit system is simply a fair and just reward for effort, and it applies to every executive and every workman.
Ernest Hermann

Where profit is, loss is hidden near by.
Japanese proverb

If thou will receive profit, read with humility, simplicity and faith, and seek not at any time the fame of being learned.
Thomas à Kempis

Nothing contributes so much to the prosperity and happiness of a country as high profits.
David Ricardo

Profit is the ignition system of our economic engine.
Charles Sawyer

No profit grows where is no pleasure taken; in brief, sir, study what you most affect.
William Shakespeare

PROGRESS

Modern invention has banished the spinning wheel, and the same law of progress makes the woman of today a different woman from her grandmother.
Susan B. Anthony

The measure of progress of civilization is the progress of the people.
George Bancroft

Progress: He retired from doing business paperwork at the office to doing health paperwork at home.
Cecil Baxter

We should so live and labor in our time that what came to us as seed may go to the next generation as blossom, and that which came to us as blossom may go to them as fruit. That is what we mean by progress.
Henry Ward Beecher

The grandest of all laws is the law of progressive development. Under it, in the wide sweep of things, men grow wiser as they grow older, and societies better.
Christian Bovée

Progress is the law of life; man is not a man as yet.
Robert Browning

Nothing in progression can rest on its original plan. We might as well think of rocking a grown man in the cradle of an infant.
Edmund Burke

All progress is based upon the universal innate desire on the part of every organism to live beyond its income.
Samuel Butler

The whole story of human and personal progress is an unmitigated tale of denials today—denials of rest, denials of repose and comfort and ease and pleasure—that tomorrow may be richer.
James Carroll

Progress is the mother of problems.
G.K. Chesterton

Little progress can be made by merely attempting to repress what is evil; over

great hope lies is developing what is good.
Calvin Coolidge

Progress in every age results only from the fact that there are some men and women who refuse to believe that what they knew to be right cannot be done.
Russell W. Davenport

Progress is nothing but the victory of laughter over dogma.
Benjamin DeCasseres

The man who will neither play nor do business unless everything is just to his liking and notions, retards rather than contributes to progress.
Henry L. Doherty

Restlessness and discontent are the first necessities of progress.
Thomas A. Edison

Progress in industry depends very largely on the enterprise of deep-thinking men, who are ahead of the times in their ideas.
Sir William Ellis

All our progress is an unfolding, like the vegetable bud. You have first an instinct, then an opinion, then a knowledge, as the plant has root, bud and fruit. Trust the instinct to the end, though you can render no reason.
Ralph Waldo Emerson

Progress is the activity of today and the assurance of tomorrow.
Ralph Waldo Emerson

No man is able to make progress when he is wavering between opposite things.
Epictetus

The way to get ahead is to start now. If you start now, you will know a lot next year that you don't know now and that

you would not have known next year if you had waited.
William Feather

I am suffocated and lost when I have not the bright feeling of progression.
Margaret Fuller

The progress is made by correcting the mistakes resulting from the making of progress.
Claude Gibb

The concept of progress acts as a protective mechanism to shield us from the terrors of the future.
Frank Herbert

All progress and growth is a matter of change, but change must be growth within our social and government concepts if it should not destroy them.
Herbert Hoover

Anything that interferes with individual progress ultimately will retard group progress.
George H. Houston

Progress comes from the intelligent use of experience.
Elbert Hubbard

You can't sit on the lid of progress. If you do, you will be blown to pieces.
Henry Kaiser

Great steps in human progress are made by things that don't work the way philosophy thought they should. If things always worked the way they should, you could write the history of the world from now on. But they don't, and it is those deviations from the normal that make human progress.
Charles F. Kettering

The price of progress is trouble.
Charles F. Kettering

Life does not stand still. Where there is no progress there is disintegration. Today a thousand doors of enterprise are open to you, inviting you to useful work. To live at this time is an inestimable privilege, and a sacred obligation devolves upon you to make right use of your opportunities. Today is the day in which to attempt and achieve something worth while.
Grenville Kleiser

The moving van is a symbol of more than our restlessness, it is the most conclusive evidence possible of our progress.
Louis Kronenberger

The prudent, penniless beginner in the world labors for wages for a while, saves a surplus with which to buy tools or land for himself another while, and at length hires another new beginner to help him. This is the just and generous and prosperous system which opens the way to all, gives hope to all, and consequently energy, and progress, and improvement of conditions to all.
Abraham Lincoln

The history of England is emphatically the history of progress.
Lord Macaulay

The moment a man ceases to progress, to grow higher, wider and deeper, then his life becomes stagnant.
Orison Swett Marden

Progress consists largely of learning to apply laws and truths that have always existed.
John Allan May

All genuine progress results from finding new facts. No law can be passed to make an acre yield three hundred bushels. God has already established the laws. It is

for us to discover them, and to learn the facts by which we can obey them.
Wheeler McMillen

Progress might have been all right once, but it's gone on too long.
Ogden Nash

By a peculiar prerogative, not only each individual is making daily advances in the sciences, and may make advances in morality (which is the science, by way of eminence, of living well and being happy), but all mankind together is making a continual progress in proportion as the universe grows older. So that the whole human race, during the course of so many ages, may be considered as one man who never ceases to live and learn.
Blaise Pascal

If human progress had been merely a matter of leadership we should be in Utopia today.
Thomas B. Reed

Progress is not made by taking pride in our present standards but by critically examining these standards, hypothetically setting higher standards and attempting to achieve them.
Juda L. Rosenstein

The greater part of progress is the desire to progress.
Seneca

All progress is initiated by challenging current conceptions, and executed by supplanting existing institutions.
George Bernard Shaw

Progress in the half-century ahead will continue to be the creation of mind rather than of hand; of stout hearts rather than stern measures.
Norman G. Shidle

The true law of the race is progress and development. Whenever civilization pauses in the march of conquest, it is overthrown by the barbarian.
William Simms

Progress is always the product of fresh thinking, and much of it thinking which to practical men bears the semblance of dreaming.
Robert Gordon Sproul

Complacency is the enemy of progress.
Dave Stutman

Progress is not created by contented people.
Frank Tyger

Progressiveness is looking forward intelligently, looking within critically, and moving on incessantly.
Waldo Pondray Warren

PROPERTY

People who never had enough thrift and forethought to buy and pay for property in the first place seldom have enough to keep property up after they have gained it in some other way.
Thomas Nixon Carver

Property is desirable as the ground work of moral independence, as a means of improving the faculties, and of doing good to others, and as the agent in all that distinguishes the civilized man from the savage.
James Fenimore Cooper

How can you trust people who are poor and own no property? . . . Inequality of property will exist as long as liberty exists.
Alexander Hamilton

Few rich men own their own property. The property owns them.
Robert Ingersoll

There is a desire of property in the sanest and best men, which Nature seems to have implanted as conservative of her works, and which is necessary to encourage and keep alive the arts.
Walter Savage Landor

The strongest bond of human sympathy, outside of the family relation, should be one uniting all working people, of all nations, and tongues, and kindreds. Nor should this lead us to a war upon property, or the owners of property. Property is the fruit of labor; property is desirable; is a positive good in the world. That some should be rich shows that others may become rich and, hence, is just encouragement to industry and enterprise. Let not him who is houseless pull down the house of another, but let him labor diligently and build one for himself, thus, by example, assuring that his own shall be safe from violence when built.
Abraham Lincoln

PROSPERITY

Just to pile up money for my own sake, I just can't view that as good citizenship.
Walter Annenberg

To rejoice in the prosperity of another is to partake of it.
William Austin

If prosperity is regarded as the reward of virtue, it will be regarded as the symptom of virtue.
G.K. Chesterton

In prosperity let us particularly avoid pride, disdain and arrogance.
Cicero

When prosperity comes, do not use all of it.
Confucius

Prosperity cannot be divorced from humanity.
Calvin Coolidge

Prosperity is only an instrument to be used, not a deity to be worshipped.
Calvin Coolidge

Everything in the world may be endured except continuing prosperity.
Johann Wolfgang von Goethe

Few enjoyments are given from the open and liberal hand of nature; but by art, labor and industry we can extract them in great abundance. Hence, the ideas of property become necessary in all civil society.
David Hume

The trick is to make sure you don't die waiting for prosperity to come.
Lee Iacocca

Prosperity is too apt to prevent us from examining our conduct, but adversity leads us to think properly of our state, and so is most beneficial to us.
Samuel Johnson

The prosperity of a people is proportionate to the number of hands and minds usefully employed. To the community, sedition is a fever, corruption is a gangrene, and idleness is an atrophy. Whatever body or society wastes more than it acquires, must gradually decay, and every being that continues to be fed, and eases to labor, takes away something from the public stock.
Samuel Johnson

In adversity assume the countenance of prosperity, and in prosperity moderate the temper and desires.
Livy

Americans have always been able to handle austerity and even adversity. Prosperity is what is doing us in.
James Reston

You cannot create prosperity by law. Sustained thrift, industry, application, intelligence, are the only things that ever do, or ever will, create prosperity. But you can very easily destroy prosperity by law.
Theodore Roosevelt

Few of us can stand prosperity. Another man's, I mean.
Mark Twain

Prosperity is the surest breeder of insolence I know.
Mark Twain

Take care to be an economist in prosperity: there is no fear of your being one in adversity.
Johann Zimmerman

PRUDENCE

One very clear impression I had of all the Beautiful People was their prudence. It may be that they paid for their own airline tickets, but they paid for little else.
James Brady

Prudence is no doubt a valuable quality, but prudence which degenerates into timidity is very seldom the path to safety.
Viscount Cecil

It is a truth but too well known, that rashness attends youth, as prudence does old age.
Cicero

Prudence is the necessary ingredient in all the virtues, without which they degenerate into folly and excess.
Jeremy Collier

It is impossible to live pleasurably without living prudently, and honorably, and justly; or to live prudently, and honorably, and justly, without living pleasurably.
Epicurus

Prudence is a presumption of the future, contracted from the experience of time past.
Thomas Hobbes

Prudence is but experience, which equal time equally bestows on all men, in all things they equally apply themselves unto.
Thomas Hobbes

No other protection is wanting, provided you are under the guidance of prudence.
Juvenal

Who makes quick us of the moment is a genius of prudence.
Johann Lavater

. . . I think there is some virtue in eagerness, whether its object prove true or false. How utterly dull would be a wholly prudent man. . . !
Aldo Leopold

The prudent, penniless beginner in the world labors for wages for a while, saves a surplus with which to buy tools or land for himself another while, and at length hires another new beginner to help him. This is the just, and generous and prosperous system which opens the way to all, gives hope to all, and consequently energy, and progress, and improvement of conditions to all.
Abraham Lincoln

Temper your enjoyments with prudence, lest there be written on your heart that fearful word "satiety."
Francis Quarles

To act coolly, intelligently and prudently in perilous circumstances is the test of a man and also a nation.
Adlai Stevenson

Where destiny blunders, human prudence will not avail.
Publilius Syrus

Often the prudent, far from making their destinies, succumb to them; it is destiny which makes them prudent.
Voltaire

PUBLICITY

The two things that people want more than sex or money are recognition and praise.
Mary Kay Ash

In Hollywood, an equitable divorce settlement means each party getting 50% of publicity.
Lauren Bacall

Live by publicity, you'll probably die by publicity.
Russell Baker

All publicity is good, except an obituary notice.
Brendan Behan

Publicity is the life of this culture, in so far as without publicity capitalism could not survive, and at the same time publicity is its dream.
John Berger

Formerly, a public man needed a private secretary for a barrier between himself and the public. Nowadays he has a press secretary, to keep him properly in the public eye.
Daniel Boorstin

Without publicity there can be no public spirit, and without public spirit every nation must decay.
Benjamin Disraeli

The very minute a thought is threatened with publicity it seems to shrink towards mediocrity.
Oliver Wendell Holmes

Publicity is a great purifier because it sets in action the forces of public opinion, and in this country public opinion controls the courses of the nation.
Charles Evans Hughes

With publicity comes humiliation.
Tama Janowitz

Of course I'm a publicity hound. Aren't all crusaders? How can you accomplish anything unless people know what you're trying to do?
Vivien Kellems

To have news value is to have a tin can tied to one's tail.
T.E. Lawrence

Ninety-eight percent of the adults in this country are decent, hard-working, honest Americans. It's the other lousy 2% that get all the publicity.
Lily Tomlin

PURPOSE

What men want is not talent, it is purpose; in other words, not the power to achieve, but will to labor. I believe that labor judiciously and continuously applied becomes genius.
Edward Bulwer-Lytton

A man's life may stagnate as literally as water may stagnate, and just as motion and direction are the remedy for one, so purpose and activity are the remedy for the other.
John Burroughs

The man without a purpose is like a ship without a rudder—a waif, a nothing, a no man.
Thomas Carlyle

The purpose of life is to believe, to hope, and to strive.
Indira Gandhi

What our deepest self craves is not mere enjoyment, but some supreme purpose that will enlist all our powers and will give unity and direction to our life. We can never know the profoundest joy without a conviction that our life is significant—not a meaningless episode. The loftiest aim of human life is the ethical perfecting of mankind—the transfiguration of humanity.
Henry J. Golding

Find a purpose in life so big it will challenge every capacity to be at your best.
David O. McKay

A purpose is the eternal condition of success.
Theodore T. Munger

Purpose is what gives life a meaning.
C.H. Parkhurst, D.D.

All the world over it is true that a double-minded man is unstable in all his ways, like a wave on the streamlet, tossed hither and thither with every eddy of its tide. A determinate purpose in life and a steady adhesion to it through all disadvantages, are indispensable conditions of success.
William M. Punshon

The goal of life is imminent in each moment, each thought, word, act, and does not have to be sought apart from these. It consists in no specific achievement, but the state of mind in which everything is done, the quality infused into existence. The function of man is not to attain an object, but to fulfill a purpose; not to accomplish but to be accomplished.
S.E. Stanton

Q

QUALITIES

The nobler sort of man emphasizes the good qualities in others, and does not accentuate the bad. The inferior does the reverse. . . . The nobler sort of man pays special attention to nine points. He is anxious to see clearly, to hear distinctly, to be kindly in his looks, respectful in his demeanor, conscientious in his speech, earnest in his affairs. When in doubt, he is careful to inquire; when in anger, he thinks of the consequences; when offered an opportunity for gain, he thinks only of his duty.
Confucius

It is not enough to have great qualities; we must also have the management of them.
François de La Rochefoucauld

I believe that for permanent survival, man must balance science with other qualities of life, qualities of body and spirit as well as those of mind—qualities he cannot develop when he lets mechanics and luxury insulate him too

greatly from the earth to which he was born.
Charles A. Lindbergh

A great man is made up of qualities that meet or make great occasions.
James Russell Lowell

Credit to the fullest the good qualities to be found in others, even though they may far outshine your own.
William M. Peck

A man has generally the good or ill qualities, which he attributes to mankind.
William Shenstone

Any man will usually get from other men just what he is expecting of them. If he is looking for friendship he will likely receive it. If his attitude is that of indifference, it will beget indifference. And if a man is looking for a fight he will in all likelihood be accommodated in that. Men can be stimulated to show off their good qualities to the leader who seems to think they have good qualities.
John Richelsen

To bring the best human qualities to anything like perfection, to fill them with the sweet juices of courtesy and charity, prosperity, or, at all events, a moderate amount of it, is required.
Alexander Smith

Eliminate your negative qualities. Develop your positive ones. You can't win with the check mark in the wrong place.
M. Winette

QUALITY

Quality isn't something that can be argued into an article or promised into it. It must be put there. If it isn't put there,

the finest sales talk in the world won't act as a substitute.
C.G. Campbell

I have never known a concern to make a decided success that did not do good, honest work, and even in these days of fiercest competition, when everything would seem to be a matter of price, there lies still at the root of great business success the very much more important factor of quality. The effect of attention to quality, upon every man in the service, from the president of the concern down to the humblest laborer, cannot be overestimated.
Andrew Carnegie

The surest foundation of a manufacturing concern is quality. After that, and a long way after, comes cost.
Andrew Carnegie

Quality is never an accident; it is always the result of high intention, sincere effort, intelligent direction and skillful execution; it represents the wise choice of many alternatives, the cumulative experience of many masters of craftsmanship. Quality also marks the search for an ideal after necessity has been satisfied and mere usefulness achieved.
Will A. Foster

High people, Sir, are the best: Take a hundred ladies of quality, you'll find them better wives, better mothers, more willing to sacrifice their own pleasures to their children, than a hundred other women.
Samuel Johnson

People forget how fast you did a job—but they remember how well you did it.
Howard W. Newton

The civilization of a country consists in the quality of life that is lived there, and

this quality shows plainest in the things that people choose to talk about when they talk together, and in the way they choose to talk about them.
Albert J. Nock

No matter how small and unimportant what we are doing may seem, if we do it well, it may soon become the step that will lead us to better things.
Channing Pollock

If a thing is old, it is a sign that it was fit to live. Old families, old customs, old styles survive because they are fit to survive. The guarantee of continuity is quality. Submerge the good in a flood of the new, and the good will come back to join the good which the new brings with it. Old-fashioned hospitality, old-fashioned politeness, old-fashioned honor in business had qualities of survival. These will come back.
Edward Rickenbacker

Quality is never an accident; it is always the result of intelligent efforts.
John Ruskin

Professionalism means consistency of quality.
Frank Tyger

QUESTIONS

A prudent question is one-half of wisdom.
Francis Bacon

"Why" and "how" are words so important that they cannot be too often used.
Napoleon Bonaparte

Charm is a way of getting the answer yes without having asked any clear question.
Albert Camus

It's very flattering to ask others about matters they're little qualified to discuss.
Malcolm Forbes

One who never asks either knows everything or nothing.
Malcolm Forbes

The smart ones ask when they don't know. And, sometimes, when they do.
Malcolm Forbes

It's easier to see both sides of a question than the answer.
Arnold Glasow

Both sides of a question do not belong to the poor old question at all, but to the opposing views which bedevil it.
Henry S. Haskins

Some men see things as they are and ask, "Why?" I dream things that never were and ask, "Why not?"
Robert F. Kennedy

I had six honest serving men—they taught me all I knew: Their names were Where and What and When—and Why and How and Who.
Rudyard Kipling

No man really becomes a fool until he stops asking questions.
Charles P. Steinmetz

It is not every question that deserves an answer.
Publilius Syrus

Questions are never indiscreet, answers sometimes are.
Oscar Wilde

The riddle does not exist. If a question can be put at all, then it can also be answered.
Ludwig Wittgenstein

R

READING

The addictive semiconscious vice of b|bloscopy—having to see what the other person is reading, usually on a train, peering over shoulders, bending down to attend simultaneously to a shoelace and a dust jacket, furtively changing seats.
Nigel Andrew

Reading maketh a full man; conference a ready man; and writing an exact man; and, therefore, if a man write little, he had need have a great memory; if he confer little, he had need have a present wit; and if he read little, he had need have much cunning, to seem to know that he doth not.
Francis Bacon

Lists of books we reread and books we can't finish tell more about us than about the relative worth of the books themselves.
Russell Banks

I read for three things; first, to know what the world has done the last twenty-four hours, and is about to do today; second, for the knowledge that I specially want in my work; and third, for what will bring my mind into a proper mood.
Henry Ward Beecher

Many a person has been saved from summer alcoholism, not to mention hypertoxicity, by Dostoyevsky.
Roy Blount, Jr.

It is well to read everything of something, and something of everything.
Henry Brougham

To read without reflecting is like eating without digesting.
Edmund Burke

Happy is he who has laid up in his youth, and held fast in all fortune, a genuine and passionate love for reading.
Rufus Choate

A man may as well expect to grow stronger by always eating as wiser by always reading.
Jeremy Collyer

On receiving an unsolicited manuscript:
Many thanks; I shall lose no time in reading it.
Benjamin Disraeli

Reading provides the only way I know of by which children can see the whole view of how people who are in earnest about it grow slowly but surely into the habit of right conduct.
Annis Duff

In the mountains, there you feel free. I read, much of the night, and go south in the winter.
T.S. Eliot

We sometimes receive letters from businessmen who say they are too busy to read. The man who is too busy to read is never likely to lead. The executive who aspires to success must keep himself well informed. His reading must not be confined to the reports of his own business laid on his desk, or to strictly trade journals, or to newspaper headlines. He must study what is going on throughout his own country and throughout the world. He must not remain blind to financial, industrial, economic trends, evolutions, revolutions.
B.C. Forbes

If you can read and don't, you're dumb.
Malcolm Forbes

Reading makes a full man, meditation a profound man, discourse a clear man.
Benjamin Franklin

Let us read with method, and propose to ourselves an end to what our studies may point. The use of reading is to aid us in thinking.
Edward Gibbon

To teach people to read without teaching them not to believe everything they read is only to prepare them for a new slavery.
Jean Guehenno

Reading, real reading, is a strenuous and pleasurable contact sport.
Maureen Howard

What sense of superiority it gives one to escape reading some book which everyone else is reading.
Alice James

One ought to read just as inclination takes him, for what he reads as a task will do him little good.
Samuel Johnson

The demand that I make of my reader is that he should devote his whole life to reading my works.
James Joyce

I forget the greater part of what I read, but all the same it nourishes my mind.
Georg C. Lichtenberg

Have you ever rightly considered what the mere ability to read means? That it is the key which admits us to the whole world of thought and fancy and imagination? To the company of saint and sage, of the wisest and the wittiest at their wisest and wittiest moment? That it enables us to see with the keenest eyes, hear with the finest ears, and listen to the sweetest voices of all time? More than that, it annihilates time and space for us.
James Russell Lowell

Resolve to edge in a little reading every day, if it is but a single sentence. If you gain fifteen minutes a day, it will make itself felt at the end of the year.
Horace Mann

No entertainment is so cheap as reading, nor any pleasure so lasting.
Mary Montagu

Read every day something no one else is reading. Think something no one else is thinking. It is bad for the mind to be always a part of unanimity.
Christopher Morley

Starting a novel is opening a door on a misty landscape; you can still see very little but you can smell the earth and feel the wind blowing.
Iris Murdoch

Much reading is an oppression of the mind, and extinguishes the natural candle, which is the reason of so many senseless scholars in the world.
William Penn

Feet in the sand, face to the sea, le Carré books piled within reach,

Why not have a martini or three? For it's summer, time for the beach.
Eno Putain

Even the most ardent readers of detective fiction are not much preoccupied with whether a Colt Magnum revolver or a Bowie knife was used to dispatch the victim. The perpetrator's purpose, the "why," is what impels them to read on.
Ruth Rendell

Never write on a subject without first having read yourself full on it; and never

read on a subject till you have thought yourself hungry on it.
Jean Paul Richter

I like to have exciting evenings on holiday, because after you've spent eight hours reading on the beach you don't feel like turning in early with a good book.
Arthur Smith

Reading is to the mind what exercise is to the body.
Richard Steele

One may as well be asleep as to read for anything but to improve his mind and morals, and regulate his conduct.
Laurence Sterne

My education was the liberty I had to read indiscriminately and all the time, with my eyes hanging out.
Dylan Thomas

The man who does not read good books has no advantage over the man who can't read them.
Mark Twain

My family can always tell when I'm well into a novel because the meals get very crummy.
Anne Tyler

We live in an age that reads too much to be wise.
Oscar Wilde

It is well to read up everything within reach about your business; this not only improves your knowledge, your usefulness and your fitness for more responsible work, but it invests your business with more interest, since you understand its functions, its basic principles, its place in the general scheme of things.
Daniel Willard

REALITY

Some people are still unaware that reality contains unparalleled beauties. The fantastic and unexpected, the ever-changing and renewing is nowhere so exemplified as in real life itself!
Berenice Abbott

What the large print giveth, the small print taketh away.
Anonymous

I have lived long enough to be battered by the realities of life and not too long to be downed by them.
John Mason Brown

The wise men of antiquity, when they wished to make the whole world peaceful and happy, first put their own States into proper order. Before putting their States into proper order, they regulated their own families. Before regulating their families, they regulated themselves. Before regulating themselves, they tried to be sincere in their thoughts. Before being sincere in their thoughts, they tried to see things exactly as they really were.
Confucius

Do people love truth? On the contrary, mankind has employed its subtlest ingenuity and intelligence in efforts to evade or conceal it. . . . Do human beings love justice? The sordid travesties in our courts year after year suggest that they love justice only for themselves. Do they love peace? Can anyone seriously ask the question? Do they love freedom? Only for those who share their views. Love of peace, freedom, justice, truth— this is a myth that has been created by the folk mind, and if the artist does not look behind the myth to the reality, he

will indeed wander amid the phantoms which he creates.
Vardis Fisher

There will always be another reality to make fiction of the truth we think we've arrived at.
Christopher Fry

When dreams are more real than reality, you're alive.
Malcolm Forbes

Few men have imagination enough for reality.
Johann Wolfgang von Goethe

What we need most, is not so much to realize the idea as to idealize the real.
Frederick Hedge

The greatest realities are physical and economic, all the subtleties of life come afterward.
Joyce Carol Oates

For the experienced to survive, reality must be considered.
Charles B. Richardson

It is harder to kill a phantom than a reality.
Virginia Woolf

REASON

If we would guide by the light of reason we must let our minds be bold.
Louis D. Brandeis

Men live by intervals of reason under the sovereignty of caprice and passion.
Thomas Browne

Logical behavior often comes dangerously near toppling over into the absurd.
Louise Cristina

He only employs his passion who can make no use of his reason.
Cicero

I am (thank God) constitutionally superior to reason.
William Wilkie Collins

Free inquiry, if restrained within due bounds, and applied to proper subjects, is a most important privilege of the human mind; and if well conducted, is one of the greatest friends to truth. But when reason knows neither its office nor its limits, and when employed on subjects foreign to its jurisdiction, it then becomes a privilege dangerous to be exercised.
Jean D'Aubigne

He that will not reason is a bigot; he that cannot reason is a fool; and he that dares not reason is a slave.
Sir William Drummond

Good sense and good nature are never separated; and good nature is the product of right reason.
John Dryden

The crossroads of trade are the meeting place of ideas, the attrition ground of rival customs and beliefs; diversities beget conflict, comparison, thought; superstitions cancel one another, and reason begins.
Will Durant

We do not act because we know, but we know because we are called upon to act; the practical reason is the root of all reason.
J.G. Fichte

Neither great poverty nor great riches will hear reason.
Henry Fielding

So convenient a thing it is to be a reasonable creature, since it enables one to find or make a reason for everything one has a mind to do.
Benjamin Franklin

They that will not be counselled, cannot be helped. If you do not hear reason she will rap you on the knuckles.
Benjamin Franklin

Let us not dream that reason can ever be popular. Passions, emotions, may be made popular, but reason remains ever the property of the few.
Johann Wolfgang von Goethe

Nothing is more revealing than movement.
Martha Graham

I used to say that, as Solicitor General, I made three arguments of every case: First came the one that I planned—as I thought, logical, coherent, complete. Second was the one actually presented—interrupted, incoherent, disjointed, disappointing. The third was the utterly devastating argument that I thought of after going to bed that night.
Robert H. Jackson

Error of opinion may be tolerated where reason is left free to combat it.
Thomas Jefferson

The life of sense begins by assuming that we can only fitfully live the life of reason.
Louis Kronenberger

Nothing under the sun is ever accidental.
Gotthold Lessing

When I'm getting ready to reason with a man, I spend one-third of my time thinking about myself and what I am going to say—and two-thirds thinking about him and what he is going to say.
Abraham Lincoln

Human beings are the only creatures who are able to behave irrationally in the name of reason.
Ashley Montagu

He who establishes his argument by noise and command, shows that his reason is weak.
Michel de Montaigne

A man always has two reasons for doing anything: A good reason and a real reason.
J.P. Morgan

We are generally better persuaded by the reasons we discover ourselves than by those given to us by others.
Blaise Pascal

He is liable to try to polish off an argument with a phrase rather as in different circles it might be done by throwing a saucepan.
Alan Pryce-Jones

Real life is, to most men, a long second-best, a perpetual compromise between the ideal and the possible; but the world of pure reason knows no compromise, no practical limitations, no barrier to the creative activity.
Bertrand Russell

When a man has not a good reason for doing a thing, he has one good reason for letting it alone.
Thomas Scott

The open mind never acts—when we have done our utmost to arrive at a reasonable conclusion, we still, when we can reason and investigate no more, must close our minds for the moment with a snap, and act dogmatically on our own conclusion. The man who wants to make an entirely reasonable will dies intestate.
George Bernard Shaw

Reason unites us, not only with our contemporaries, but with men who lived two thousand years before us, and with those who will live after us.
Leo Tolstoy

How difficult it is to persuade a man to reason against his interest; though he is convinced that equity is against him.
John Trusler

Reason, too late perhaps, may convince you of the folly of misspending time.
George Washington

I can stand brute force, but brute reason is quite unbearable. It is hitting below the intellect.
Oscar Wilde

RELIGION

If we make religion our business, God will make it our blessedness.
H.G.J. Adam

He was of the faith chiefly in the sense that the church he currently did not attend was Catholic.
Kingsley Amis

A fanatic is the Devil's plaything.
Armenian proverb

Christmas and Easter can be subjects for poetry, but Good Friday, like Auschwitz, cannot. The reality is so horrible, it is not surprising that people should have found it a stumbling block to faith.
W.H. Auden

I have not been able to find a single useful institution which has not been founded either by an intensely religious man or by the son of a praying father or a praying mother. I have made the statement before the chambers of commerce of all the largest cities of the country and have asked them to bring forward a case that is an exception to this rule. Thus far, I have not heard of a single one.
Roger W. Babson

Jews have God's promise and if we Christians have it, too, then it is only as those chosen with them, as guests in their house, that we are new wood grafted onto their tree.
Karl Barth

A man without religion or spiritual vision is like a captain who finds himself in the midst of an uncharted sea, without compass, rudder and steering wheel. He never knows where he is, which way he is going and where he is going to land.
William J.H. Boetcker

True religion is not a mere doctrine, something that can be taught, but is a way of life. A life in community with God. It must be experienced to be appreciated. A life of service. A living by giving and finding one's own happiness by bringing happiness into the lives of others.
William J.H. Boetcker

Religion is excellent stuff for keeping common people quiet.
Napoleon Bonaparte

The Vatican is against surrogate mothers. Good thing they didn't have that rule when Jesus was born.
Elayne Boosler

To die for a religion is easier than to live it absolutely.
Jorge Luis Borges

Jesus was a Jew, yes, but only on his mother's side.
Archie Bunker

One of the hardest lessons we have to learn in this life, and one that many

persons never learn, is to see the divine, the celestial, the pure, in the common, the near at hand—to see that heaven lies about us here in this world.
John Burroughs

It is the test of a good religion whether you can make a joke about it.
G.K. Chesterton

And Jabez called on the God of Israel, saying, Oh that thou wouldest bless me indeed, and enlarge my coast, and that thine hand might be with me, and that thou wouldest keep me from evil.
I Chronicles 4:10

Have respect therefore to the prayer of thy servant, and to his supplication, O Lord my God.
II Chronicles 6:19

If my people, which are called by my name, shall humble themselves, and pray, and seek my face, and turn from their wicked ways; then will I hear from heaven, and will forgive their sin, and will heal their land.
II Chronicles 7:14

The strength of a country is the strength of its religious convictions.
Calvin Coolidge

Under our institutions the only way to perfect the Government is to perfect the individual citizen. It is necessary to reach the mind and soul of the individual. I know of no way that this can be done save through the influence of religion and education. By religion I do not mean fanaticism or bigotry; by education I do not mean the cant of the schools, but a broad and tolerant faith, loving thy neighbor as thyself, and a training and experience that enables the human mind to see into the heart of things.
Calvin Coolidge

If any man defile the temple of God, him shall God destroy; for the temple of God is holy, which temple ye are.
I Corinthians 3:17

What you are is God's gift to you; what you make of it is your gift to God.
Anthony Dalla Villa

The intellectual content of religions has always finally adapted itself to scientific and social conditions after they have become clear. . . . For this reason I do not think that those who are concerned about the future of a religious attitude should trouble themselves about the conflict of science with traditional doctrines.
John Dewey

The most dangerous madmen are those created by religion, and people whose aim is to disrupt society always know how to make good use of them.
Denis Diderot

The secret things belong unto the Lord our God: but those things which are revealed belong unto us and to our children forever, that we may do all the words of this law.
Deuteronomy 29:29

The cosmic religious experience is the strongest and noblest driving force behind scientific research.
Albert Einstein

The most beautiful thing we can experience is the mysterious. It is the source of all true art and science. He to whom the emotion is a stranger, who can no longer pause to wonder and stand wrapped in awe, is as good as dead; his eyes are closed. The insight into the mystery of life, coupled though it be with fear, has also given rise to religion. To know what is impenetrable to us really exists,

manifesting itself as the highest wisdom and the most radiant beauty, which our dull faculties can comprehend only in their most primitive forms—this knowledge, this feeling is at the center of true religiousness.
Albert Einstein

This is what I found out about religion: It gives you courage to make the decisions you must make in a crisis, and then the confidence to leave the result to a higher Power. Only by trust in God can a man carrying responsibility find repose.
Dwight D. Eisenhower

What the church should be telling the worker is that the first demand religion makes on him is that he should be a good workman. If he is a carpenter he should be a competent carpenter. Church by all means on Sundays—but what is the use of church if at the very center of life a man defrauds his neighbor and insults God by poor craftsmanship.
Dwight D. Eisenhower

The dripping blood our only drink,

The bloody flesh our only food:

In spite of which we like to think

That we are sound, substantial flesh and blood

Again, in spite of that, we call this Friday good.
T.S. Eliot

Religion is as effectively destroyed by bigotry as by indifference.
Ralph Waldo Emerson

So when the crisis is upon you, remember that God, like a trainer of wrestlers, has matched you with a tough and stalwart antagonist—that you may prove a victor at the Great Games. Yet without toil or sweat this may not be.
Epictetus

The man without religion is as a ship without a rudder.
B.C. Forbes

The Seder nights tie me with the centuries before me.
Ludwig Franke

What religion needs today is not more flying with God, or leaping with God, or jumping up and down with God, or going into spasms and convulsions and epileptic fits with God. What religion needs today is more walking with God.
Milo H. Gates, D.D.

And Abraham rose up early in the morning, and took bread, and a bottle of water, and gave it unto Hagar, putting it on her shoulder, and the child, and sent her away: and she departed, and wandered in the wilderness of Beer-sheba.
Genesis 21:14

The various modes of worship which prevailed in the Roman world were all considered by the people as equally true, by the philosophers as equally false, and by the magistrate as equally useful.
Edward Gibbon

White people really deal more with God and black people with Jesus.
Nikki Giovanni

If we had not been taught how to interpret the story of the Passion, would we have been able to say from their actions alone whether it was the jealous Judas or the cowardly Peter who loved Christ?
Graham Greene

Why should a country worship another country's tin gods, when it has tin gods of its own?
John P. Grier

Now no chastening for the present seemeth to be joyous, but grievous: nevertheless afterward it yieldeth the peaceable fruit of righteousness unto them which are exercised thereby.
Hebrews 12:11

Jews who long have drifted from the faith of their fathers are stirred in their inmost parts when the old, familiar Passover sounds chance to fall upon their ears.
Heinrich Heine

Religion must be used in furthering great works of justice and reform. It must be used to establish right relations between different groups of men, and thus to make a reality of brotherhood. It must be used to abolish poverty, the breeding ground of all misery and crime, by distributing equally among men the abundance of the soil. And it must be used to get rid of war and to establish enduring peace. Here is the supreme test of the effectiveness of religion.
John Haynes Holmes

England has two books: the Bible and Shakespeare. England made Shakespeare, but the Bible made England.
Victor Hugo

Even them will I bring to my holy mountain, and make them joyful in my house of prayer: their burnt offerings and their sacrifices shall be accepted upon mine altar.
Isaiah 56:7

For my people have committed two evils; they have forsaken me the fountain of living waters, and hewed them out cisterns, broken cisterns, that can hold no water.
Jeremiah 2:13

If thou hast run with the footmen, and they have wearied thee, then how canst thou contend with horses? And if in the land of peace, wherein thou trustedst, they wearied thee, then how wilt thou do in the swelling of Jordan?
Jeremiah 12:5

For God so loved the world, that He gave His only begotten Son, that whoever believes in Him should not perish, but have eternal life.
John 3:16–17

It often happens that I wake at night and begin to think about a serious problem and decide I must tell the Pope about it. Then I wake up completely and remember that I am the Pope.
Pope John XXIII

Do not abandon yourselves to despair. We are the Easter people and hallelujah is our song.
Pope John Paul II

Passover affirms the great truth that liberty is the inalienable right of every human being.
Morris Joseph

Now unto him that is able to keep you from falling, and to present you faultless before the presence of his glory with exceeding joy, to the only wise God our Saviour, be glory and majesty, dominion and power, both now and ever. Amen.
Jude 1:24–25

What church I go to on Sunday, what dogma of the Catholic Church I believe in, is my business; and whatever faith any other American has is his business.
John F. Kennedy

It has long been recognized that an education which does not provide for an intelligent understanding of religion is incomplete.
Raymond C. Knox

It is as difficult to feast with the right motive on the eve of Yom Kippur as it is to fast with the right motive on the day of Yom Kippur.
Israel Salanter Lipkin

The works of nature and the works of revelation display religion to mankind in characters so large and visible that those who are not quite blind may in them see and read the first principles and most necessary parts of it and from thence penetrate into those infinite depths filled with the treasures of wisdom and knowledge.
John Locke

Every valley shall be filled, and every mountain and hill shall be brought low; and the crooked shall be made straight, and the rough ways shall be made smooth.
Luke 3:5

The Puritan hated bear-baiting, not because it gave pain to the bear, but because it gave pleasure to the spectators.
Thomas B. Macaulay

Now as he walked by the sea of Galilee, he saw Simon and Andrew his brother casting a net into the sea: for they were fishers. And Jesus said unto them, Come ye after me, and I will make you to become fishers of men.
Mark 1:16–17

But seek ye first the kingdom of God, and his righteousness; and all these things shall be added unto you.
Matthew 6:33

The objection to Puritans is not that they try to make us think as they do, but that they try to make us do as they think.
H.L. Mencken

He hath shewed thee, O man, what is good; and what doth the Lord require of thee, but to do justly, and to love mercy, and to walk humbly with thy God?
Micah 6:8

Vatican II was a force that seized the mind of the Roman Catholic Church and carried it across centuries from the 13th to the 20th.
Lance Morrow

There is a divinity that shapes our ends—but we can help by listening for Its voice.
Kathleen Norris

Men never do evil so completely and cheerfully as when they do it from a religious conviction.
Blaise Pascal

On Passover eve the son asks his father, and if the son is unintelligent, his father instructs him to ask: Why is this night different from all other nights?
Mishnah, Pesachim 10:4

What then? notwithstanding, everyway, whether in pretence, or in truth, Christ is preached; and I therein do rejoice, yea, and will rejoice.
Philippians 1:18

The integrity of the upright shall guide them: but the perverseness of transgressors shall destroy them.
Proverbs 11:3

Then shalt thou be pleased with the sacrifices of righteousness, with burnt offering and whole burnt offering.
Psalms 51:19

For thou, Lord, art good, and ready to forgive; and plenteous in mercy unto all them that call upon thee.
Psalms 86:5

What the world craves today is a more spiritual and less formal religion. To the man or woman facing death, great conflict, the big problems of human life, the forms of religion are of minor concern, while the spirit of religion is a desperately needed source of inspiration, comfort and strength.
John D. Rockefeller, Jr.

The New Testament never simply says, "Remember Jesus Christ." That is a half-finished sentence. It says, "Remember Jesus Christ is risen from the dead."
Robert Runcie

My mom used to say that Greek Easter was later because then you get stuff cheaper.
Amy Sedaris

Jews know guilt, Catholics know shame.
Rosemary O'Connell Shmavonian

To live, mankind must recover its essential humanness and its innate divinity; men must recover their capacity for humility, sanity and integrity; soldier and civilians must see their hope in some other world than one completely dominated by the physical and chemical sciences.
George F.G. Stanley

Religion is life and lifts you out of yourself. We must believe God is too big to fail.
Samuel H. Sweeney

We have just enough religion to make us hate, but not enough to make us love one another.
Jonathan Swift

Few sinners are saved after the first 20 minutes of a sermon.
Mark Twain

Our business is not only with eternity but with time, to build up on earth the kingdom of God, to enable man to live worthily and not merely to die in hope.
Lord Tweedsmuir

While just government protects all in their religious rites, true religion affords government its surest support.
George Washington

Science has made the world a great neighborhood, but religion must make it a great brotherhood.
Lester A. Welliver

REPUTATION

A man's character is the reliability of himself. His reputation is the opinion others have formed of him. Character is in him; reputation is from other people.
Henry Ward Beecher

I rather like my reputation, actually, that of a spoiled genius from the Welsh gutter, a drunk, a womanizer; it's rather an attractive image.
Richard Burton

To disregard what the world thinks of us is not only arrogant but utterly shameless.
Cicero

You can't build up a reputation on what you are going to do.
Henry Ford

I have visited many countries, and have been in cities without number, yet never did I enter a town which could not produce ten or twelve little great men; all fancying themselves known to the rest

of the world, and complimenting each other upon their extensive reputation.
Oliver Goldsmith

A man's reputation is not in his own keeping. It lies at the mercy of the profligacy of others.
William Hazlitt

What people say behind your back is your standing in the community in which you live.
Edgar Watson Howe

Whatever ignominy or disgrace we have incurred, it is almost always in our power to reestablish our reputation.
François de La Rochefoucauld

We sometimes speak of winning reputation as though that were the final goal. The truth is contrary to this. Reputation is a reward, to be sure, but it is really the beginning, not the end of endeavor. It should not be the signal for a let down, but rather, a reminder that the standards which won recognition can never again be lowered. From him who gives much— much is forever after expected.
Alvan Macauley

It's a fine thing to have a finger pointed at one, and to hear people say, "That's the man."
Persius

Reputations are longer in the making than the losing.
Paul von Ringelheim

It is better to be nobly remembered than nobly born.
John Ruskin

The way to gain a good reputation is to endeavor to be what you desire to appear.
Socrates

A fair reputation is a plant delicate in its nature, and by no means rapid in its growth. It will not shoot up in a night, like the gourd of the prophet, but like that gourd, it may perish in a night.
Jeremy Taylor

Associate yourself with men of good quality if you esteem your own reputation; for 'tis better to be alone than in bad company.
George Washington

RESEARCH

It has recently been discovered that research causes cancer in rats.
Anonymous

Research is what I'm doing when I don't know what I'm doing.
Wernher von Braun

No research is ever quite complete. It is the glory of a good bit of work that it opens the way for something still better, and this repeatedly leads to its own eclipse.
Mervin Gordon

The best insurance policy for the future of an industry is research, which will help it to foresee future lines of development, to solve its immediate problems, and to improve and cheapen its products.
Sir Harold Hartley

Research is an organized method of trying to find out what you are going to do after you cannot do what you are doing now. It may also be said to be the method of keeping a customer reasonably dissatisfied with what he has. That means constant improvement and change so that the customer will be stimulated to desire the new product enough to buy it to replace the one he has.
Charles F. Kettering

Research . . . is nothing but a state of mind—a friendly, welcoming attitude toward change; going out to look for a change instead of waiting for it to come. Research, for practical men, is an effort to do things better. . . . The research state of mind can apply to anything—personal affairs or any kind of business, big or little.
Charles F. Kettering

Research means that you don't know, but are willing to find out.
Charles F. Kettering

Research is the reconnaissance party of industry, roving the unknown territories ahead independently, yet not without purpose, seeing for the first time what all the following world will see a few years hence.
S.M. Kinter

The common facts of today are the products of yesterday's research.
Duncan MacDonald

Research teaches a man to admit he is wrong and to be proud of the fact that he does so, rather than try with all his energy to defend an unsound plan because he is afraid that admission of error is a confession of weakness when rather it is a sign of strength.
Prof. H.E. Stocher

I salute the workers in physical research as the poets of today. It may be that they do not write in verse, but their communications are of such lively interest that they are on the front pages of our newspapers and command space in agricultural periodicals. They appeal to the imagination of us all. They contribute the warming glow of inspiration to industry, and when industry pulls their ideas down from the heavens to the earth and harnesses them for practical service, it,

too, feels that it is an important actor, not only in the makings of things but on the larger stage of human spirit. There may be enough poetry in the whir of our machines so that our machine age will become immortal.
Owen D. Young

RESOLUTION

Irresolution on the schemes of life which offer themselves to our choice, and inconstancy in pursuing them, are the greatest causes of all our unhappiness.
Joseph Addison

Nothing relieves and ventilates the mind like a resolution.
John Burroughs

He that resolves upon any great and good end, has, by that very resolution, scaled the chief barrier to it. He will find such resolution removing difficulties, searching out or making means, giving courage for despondency, and strength for weakness, and like the star to the wise men of old, ever guiding him nearer and nearer to perfection.
Tryon Edwards

Most good resolutions start too late and end too soon.
Arnold Glasow

We can do anything we want to do if we stick to it long enough.
Helen Keller

No one would have crossed the ocean if he could have gotten off the ship in the storm.
Charles F. Kettering

Good resolutions are a pleasant crop to sow. The seed springs up so readily, and the blossoms open so soon with such a brave show, especially at first. But when

the time of flowers has passed, what as to
the fruit?
Lucas Malet

With irresolute finger he knocked at
each one of the doorways of life, and
abided in none.
Owen Meredith

Every human mind is a great slumbering
power until awakened by keen desire and
by definite resolution to do.
Edgar F. Roberts

Be stirring as the time, be fire with fire,
threaten the threatener, and outface
the brow of bragging horror; so shall
inferior eyes, that borrow their behav-
iors from the great, grow great by your
example and put on the dauntless spirit
of resolution.
William Shakespeare

Experience teacheth that resolution is a
sole help in need.
William Shakespeare

See first that the design is wise and just;
that ascertained, pursue it resolutely.
William Shakespeare

Earnest resolution has often seemed
to have about it almost a savor of
omnipotence.
Samuel Smiles

In no direction that we turn do we find
ease or comfort. If we are honest and
if we have the will to win we find only
danger, hard work and iron resolution.
Wendell Willkie

RESPECT

He who has never learned to obey cannot
be a good commander.
Aristotle

Power, money, that's just the road to
respect. After all, money disappears,
friends die, and you die, but your reputation remains.
Thor Bjorgolfsson

Too often a sense of loyalty depends on
admiration, and if we can't admire, it is
difficult to be loyal.
Aimee Buchanan

All true love is founded on esteem.
George Buckingham

Great souls are always loyally submissive, reverent to what is over them: only
small mean souls are otherwise.
Thomas Carlyle

No nobler feeling than this, of admiration for one higher than himself, dwells
in the breast of man. It is to this hour,
and at all hours, the vivifying influence
in man's life.
Thomas Carlyle

In handling men, there are three feelings
that a man must not possess—fear, dislike
and contempt. If he is afraid of men he
cannot handle them. Neither can he
influence them in his favor if he dislikes
or scorns them. He must neither cringe
nor sneer. He must have both self-respect and respect for others.
Herbert N. Casson

Seek respect mainly from thyself, for it
comes first from within.
Steven H. Coogler

Having the courage to live within one's
means is respectability.
Benjamin Disraeli

Human affairs inspire in noble hearts
only two feelings—admiration or pity.
Anatole France

The respect of those you respect is worth more than the applause of the multitude.
Arnold Glasow

A flippant, frivolous man may ridicule others, may controvert them, scorn them; but he who has any respect for himself seems to have renounced the right of thinking meanly of others.
Johann Wolfgang von Goethe

The way to procure insults is to submit to them. A man meets with no more respect than he exacts.
William Hazlitt

He that respects not is not respected.
George Herbert

People who bite the hand that feeds them usually lick the boot that kicks them.
Eric Hoffer

Respect a man, he will do the more.
James Howell

Every man is to be respected as an absolute end in himself; and it is a crime against the dignity that belongs to him as a human being, to use him as a mere means for some external purpose.
Immanuel Kant

Things hard to come by are much esteemed.
Latin proverb

Esteem has more engaging charms than friendship, or even love. It captivates hearts better, and never makes ingrates.
Stanislaus Leszcynski

We are usually mistaken in esteeming men too much; rarely in esteeming them too little.
Stanislaus Leszcynski

He that respects himself is safe from others; he wears a coat of mail that none can pierce.
Henry Wadsworth Longfellow

Whose best and most fruitful gift was the power of admiration, which made it possible for me to learn. Now, as in my youth, I am looking up to the truly great creations of the past, which I see high above my own and which alone deserve the name of greatness.
Thomas Mann

We have so exalted a notion of the human soul that we cannot bear to be despised, or even not to be esteemed by it. Man, in fact, places all his happiness in this esteem.
Blaise Pascal

This is the final test of a gentleman; his respect for those who can be of no possible service to him.
William Lyon Phelps

Only those who respect the personality of others can be of real use to them.
Albert Schweitzer

Admiration is one of the most bewitching, enthusiastic passions of the mind; and every common moralist knows that it arises from novelty and surprise, the inseparable attendants of imposture.
William Warburton

Nobody likes having salt rubbed into their wounds, even if it is the salt of the earth.
Rebecca West

When one has never heard a man's name in the course of one's life, it speaks volumes for him; he must be quite respectable.
Oscar Wilde

RESPONSIBILITY

No individual raindrop ever considers itself responsible for the flood.
Anonymous

Responsibility is the possibility of opportunity culminating in inevitable fulfillment.
Sri Chinmoy

The price of greatness is responsibility.
Winston Churchill

A power above all human responsibility ought to be above all human attainment.
Charles Caleb Colton

Never mind your happiness; do your duty.
Will Durant

Those who enjoy responsibility usually get it; those who merely like exercising authority usually lose it.
Malcolm Forbes

To let oneself be bound by a duty from the moment you see it approaching is part of the integrity that alone justifies responsibility.
Dag Hammarskjöld

Why did the Lord give us so much quickness of movement unless it was to avoid responsibility?
Ogden Nash

We are not put here on earth to play around. There is work to be done. There are responsibilities to be met. Humanity needs the abilities of every man and woman.
Alden Palmer

I believe that every right implies a responsibility; every opportunity, an obligation; every possession, a duty.
John D. Rockefeller

Every right has its responsibilities. Like the right itself, these responsibilities stem from no man-made law, but from the very nature of man and society. The security, progress and welfare of one group is measured finally in the security, progress and welfare of all mankind.
Lewis Schwellenbach

It is easy to dodge our responsibilities, but we cannot dodge the consequences of dodging our responsibilities.
Sir Josiah Stamp

Men who do things without being told draw the most wages.
Edwin H. Stuart

In your area of responsibility, if you do not control events, you are at the mercy of events.
Harland Svare

The real freedom of any individual can always be measured by the amount of responsibility which he must assume for his own welfare and security.
Robert Welch

I feel the responsibility of the occasion. Responsibility is proportionate to opportunity.
Woodrow Wilson

There is a single reason why 99 out of 100 average businessmen never become leaders. That is their unwillingness to pay the price of responsibility. By the price of responsibility I mean hard driving, continual work . . . the courage to make decisions, to stand the gaff . . . the scourging honesty of never fooling yourself about yourself. You travel the road to leadership heavily laden. While the nine-to-five-o'clock worker takes his ease, you are toiling upward through the night. Laboriously you extend your mental frontiers. Any new effort, the psychologists

say, wears a new groove in the brain. And the grooves that lead to the heights are not made between nine and five. They are burned in by midnight oil.
Owen D. Young

REST

We sleep, but the loom of life never stops and the pattern which was weaving when the sun went down is weaving when it comes up tomorrow.
Henry Ward Beecher

Rest and motion, unrelieved and unchecked, are equally destructive.
Benjamin Cardozo

Rest is a fine medicine. Let your stomachs rest, ye dyspeptics; let your brain rest, you wearied and worried men of business; let your limbs rest, ye children of toil!
Thomas Carlyle

Sleep: The golden chain that ties health and our bodies together.
Thomas Dekker

He that can take rest is greater than he that can take cities.
Benjamin Franklin

There is nothing so insupportable to man as to be in entire repose; without passion, occupation, amusement, or application. Then it is that he feels his own nothingness, isolation, insignificance, dependent nature, powerlessness, emptiness. Immediately there issue from his soul ennui, sadness, chagrin, vexation, despair.
Blaise Pascal

Rest is the sweet sauce of labor.
Plutarch

If we could learn how to balance rest against effort, calmness against strain,

quiet against turmoil, we would assure ourselves of joy in living and psychological health for life.
Josephine Rathbone

The best thing we have is sleep, of course, and what is sleep except the putting aside of everything tentative for another interval of final and everlasting truth? Sleep isn't dying, but it is certainly keeping in tough with it.
William Saroyan

Restlessness is the hallmark of existence.
Arthur Schopenhauer

A man who values a good night's rest will not lie down with enmity in his heart, if he can help it.
Laurence Sterne

Rest is valuable only so far as it is a contrast. Pursued as an end, it becomes a most pitiable condition.
David Swing

When one begins to turn in bed it is time to turn out.
Duke of Wellington

RICHES

The quest for riches darkens the sense of right and wrong.
Antiphanes

One cannot both feast and become rich.
Ashanti proverb

Great riches have sold more men than they have bought.
Francis Bacon

Riches are for spending, and spending for honor and good actions; therefore extraordinary expense must be limited by the worth of the occasion.
Francis Bacon

Why grab possessions like thieves, or divide them like socialists, when you can ignore them like wise men?
Natalie Clifford Barney

The prouder a man is, the more he thinks he deserves, and the more he thinks he deserves, the less he really does deserve.
Henry Ward Beecher

He hath riches sufficient, who hath enough to be charitable.
Sir Thomas Browne

The much-maligned "idle rich" have received a bad rap: They have maintained or increased their wealth while many of the "energetic rich"—aggressive real estate operators, corporate acquirers, oil drillers, etc.—have their fortunes disappear.
Warren Buffett

Riches should be admitted into our houses, but not into our hearts; we may take them into our possession, but not into our affections.
Pierre Charron

A man seldom gets rich without ill-got gain; as a horse does not fatten without feeding in the night.
Chinese proverb

Perhaps you will say a man is not young; I answer, he is rich; he is not gentle, handsome, witty, brave, good-humored, but he is rich, rich, rich, rich, rich—that one word contradicts everything you can say against him.
Henry Fielding

Riches have never fascinated me, unless combined with the greatest charm or distinction.
F. Scott Fitzgerald

Americans are like a rich father who wishes he knew how to give his sons the hardships that made him rich.
Robert Frost

The pleasures of the rich are bought with the tears of the poor.
Thomas Fuller

Come with us to the field, or go with our brothers to the sea and cast your net. For the land and the sea shall be bountiful to you even as to us.
Kahlil Gibran

The riches we impart are the only wealth we shall always retain.
Matthew Henry

Riches ennoble a man's circumstances, but not himself.
Immanuel Kant

Let us not envy some men their accumulated riches; their burden would be too heavy for us; we could not sacrifice, as they do, health, quiet, honor and conscience, to obtain them: It is to pay so dear from them that the bargain is a loss.
Jean de La Bruyère

Plenty and indigence depend upon the opinion every one has of them; and riches, like glory of health, have no more beauty or pleasure than their possessor is pleaded to lend them.
Michel de Montaigne

That plenty should produce either covetousness or prodigality is a perversion of providence; and yet the generality of men are the worse for their riches.
William Penn

Riches are a cause of evil, not because, of themselves, they do any evil, but because they goad men on to evil.
Posidonius

If thou art rich, thou'rt poor;

For, like an ass whose back with ingots bows,

Thou bear'st thy heavy riches but a journey,

And death unloads thee.
William Shakespeare

Those who obtain riches by labor, care, and watching, know their value. Those who impart them to sustain and extend knowledge, virtue, and religion, know their use. Those who lose them by accident or fraud know their vanity. And those who experience the difficulties and dangers of preserving them know their perplexities.
Charles Simmons

He that is proud of riches is a fool. For if he be exalted above his neighbors because he hath more gold, how much inferior is he to a gold mine.
Jeremy Taylor

Leisure and solitude are the best effect of riches, because the mother of thought. Both are avoided by most rich men, who seek company and business, which are signs of being weary of themselves.
Sir William Temple

RIGHT

If any man is able to convince me and show me that I do not think or act right, I will gladly change; for I seek the truth, by which no man was ever injured. But he is injured who abides in his error and ignorance.
Marcus Aurelius Antoninus

Never will God suffer the reward to be lost, of those who do right.
Arabian proverb

A man who lives right, and is right, has more power in his silence than other has by his words.
Phillips Brooks

From a worldly point of view there is no mistake so great as that of being always right.
Samuel Butler

Let a man try faithfully, manfully to be right, he will daily grow more and more right. It is at the bottom of the condition on which all men have to cultivate themselves.
Thomas Carlyle

There are two ways, one is right; the other is wrong. If your work is only about right, then it is wrong.
George Washington Carver

The superior man seeks what is right; the inferior one, what is profitable.
Confucius

To see what is right, and not do it, is want of courage, or of principle.
Confucius

Right actions for the future are the best apologies for wrong ones in the past.
Tryon Edwards

The last temptation is the greatest treason: To do the right deed for the wrong reason.
T.S. Eliot

And they shall teach my people the difference between the holy and profane, and cause them to discern between the unclean and the clean.
Ezekiel 44:23

Being right half the time beats being half right all the time.
Malcolm Forbes

To be engaged in opposing wrong affords but a slender guarantee for being right.
William E. Gladstone

It's easier to remember when you are right than when the other person was right.
Robert Half

I am right and therefore shall not give up the contest.
Rutherford B. Hayes

In a family argument, if it turns out you are right, apologize at once!
Robert A. Heinlein

It is not who is right, but what is right, that is of importance.
Thomas H. Huxley

My principle is to do whatever is right, and leave consequences to him who has the disposal of them.
Thomas Jefferson

Nothing can be truly great which is not right.
Samuel Johnson

The more people who believe something, the more apt it is to be wrong. The person who's right often has to stand alone.
Søren Kierkegaard

Narrow minds think nothing right that is above their own capacity.
François de La Rochefoucauld

If both factions, or neither, shall abuse you, you will probably be about right. Beware of being assailed by one and praised by the other.
Abraham Lincoln

Let us have faith that right makes might; and in that faith let us dare to do our duty as we understand it.
Abraham Lincoln

Stand with anybody that stands right and part with him when he goes wrong.
Abraham Lincoln

Aggressive fighting for the right is the greatest sport in the world.
Theodore Roosevelt

At times, although one is perfectly right, one's legs tremble; at other times, although one is completely in the wrong, birds sing in one's soul.
V.V. Rozinov

No man has a right to do as he pleases, except when he pleases to do right.
Charles Simmons

Always do right. This will gratify some people and astonish the rest.
Mark Twain

Every man, at the bottom of his heart, wants to do right. But only he can do right who knows right; only he knows right who thinks right; only he thinks right who believes right. It takes an army of patriotic and order-obeying soldiers to win a war. But only by an army of public-spirited and law-abiding citizens can we hope to win the peace and maintain and remain a great nation.
Tiorio

It is better to be old-fashioned and right than to be up-to-date and wrong.
Tiorio

RIGHTS

So long as any number among us remains indifferent to the ... rights of our fellow-citizens, or becomes emotionally

unbalanced to the point of overriding such rights, they are striking not at our first, but at our last line of defense.
Francis Biddle

Nations begin to dig their own graves when men talk more of human rights and less of human duties.
William J.H. Boetcker

In a democracy, society must recognize that the individual has rights which are guaranteed, and the individual must recognize that he has responsibilities which are not to be evaded.
Harry Woodburn Chase

We need not concern ourselves much about rights of property if we faithfully observe the rights of persons.
Calvin Coolidge

Men are entitled to equal rights—but to equal rights to unequal things.
Charles James Fox

I am the inferior of any man whose rights I trample underfoot.
Horace Greeley

The true civilization is where every man gives to every other every right he claims for himself.
Robert Green Ingersoll

No man has a natural right to commit aggression on the natural rights of another; and this is all from which the laws ought to restrain him.
Thomas Jefferson

We have talked long enough in this country about equal rights. We have talked for 100 years or more. It is time now to write the next chapter, and to write it in the books of law.
Lyndon Baines Johnson

Majorities must recognize that minorities have rights which ought not to be extinguished and they must remember that history can be written as the record of the follies of the majority.
Lindsay Rogers

S

SALESMANSHIP

There is no more fascinating business in this world than that of selling. Without salesmen there would be little progress made. Selling is behind every successful enterprise of whatever character. Even a country has to have its salesmen. Character is the salesman's stock in trade. It is he who must first sell himself. The product itself is secondary. . . . Truthfulness, enthusiasm, and patience are great assets to every salesman. Without them he could not go far. Courage and courtesy are essential equipment. Leave your prospective customer with a smile and he will welcome you on your next visit. Bear in mind to be always a salesMAN!
George Matthew Adam

Once you have sold a customer, make sure he is satisfied with your goods. Stay with him until the goods are used up or worn out. Your product may be of such long life that you will never sell him again, but he will sell you and your product to his friends.
William Feather

Here's a pointer culled from the careers of men who have attained notable success: Don't sit in your office during the hours prospects can be seen. Do your

office work before or after the hours during which possible customers can be reached. This may mean adding an hour or two quite often to your day's work; but in times like this particularly, the securing of a satisfactory amount of business through the expenditure of an extra hour or two a day is not an unreasonable price to pay.
B.C. Forbes

A salesman, like the storage battery in your car, is constantly discharging energy. Unless he is recharged at frequent intervals he soon runs dry. This is one of the greatest responsibilities of sales leadership.
Richard Grant

I think that American salesmanship can be a weapon more powerful than the atomic bomb.
Henry J. Kaiser

Happy salesmen not only multiply their volume of business and their income, they also multiply themselves.
Walter Russell

We are all salesmen every day of our lives. We are selling our ideas, our plans, our enthusiasms to those with whom we come in contact.
Charles M. Schwab

The salesman who thinks that his first duty is selling is absolutely wrong. Selling is only one of the two important things a salesman is supposed to do—and it is not the more important of the two. The salesman's first duty is to make friends for his house.
Ellsworth M. Statler

SATISFACTION

Be satisfied with your business, and learn to love what you were bred to.
Marcus Aurelius Antoninus

Little minds find satisfaction for their feelings, good or bad, in little things.
Honoré de Balzac

Only man clogs his happiness with care, destroying what is, with thoughts of what may be.
John Dryden

Show me a thoroughly satisfied man— and I will show you a failure.
Thomas A. Edison

A man who is always satisfied with himself is seldom satisfied with others.
François de La Rochefoucauld

To be able to look back upon one's past life with satisfaction is to live twice.
Martial

There have been a few moments when I have known complete satisfaction, but only a few. I have rarely been free from the disturbing realization that my playing might have been better.
Ignacy Jan Paderewski

There's no satisfaction in hanging a man who does not object to it.
George Bernard Shaw

We can achieve the utmost in economies by engineering knowledge; we can conquer new fields by research; we can build plants and machines that shall stand among the wonders of the world; but unless we put the right man in the right place—unless we make it possible for our workers and executives alike to enjoy a sense of satisfaction in their jobs, our efforts will have been in vain.
E.R. Stettinius, Jr.

Only madmen and fools are pleased with themselves; no wise man is good enough for his own satisfaction.
Benjamin Whichcote

SCIENCE

Machines are beneficial to the degree that they eliminate the need for labor, harmful to the degree that they eliminate the need for skill.
W.H. Auden

The quick harvest of applied science is the usable process, the medicine, the machine. The shy fruit of pure science is understanding.
Lincoln Barnett

A tool is but the extension of a man's hand and a machine is but a complex tool; and he that invents a machine augments the power of man and the wellbeing of mankind
Henry Ward Beecher

We owe a lot to Thomas Edison—if it wasn't for him, we'd be watching television by candlelight.
Milton Berle

Science increases our power in proportion as it lowers our pride.
Claude Bernard

Observatory: A place where astronomers conjecture away the guesses of their predecessors.
Ambrose Bierce

Science can give mankind a better standard of living, better health and a better mental life, if mankind in turn gives science the sympathy and support so essential to its progress.
Vannevar Bush

The machine can free man or enslave him; it can make of this world something resembling a paradise or a purgatory. Men have it within their power to achieve a security hitherto dreamed of only by the philosophers, or they may go the way of the dinosaurs, actually disappearing from the earth because they fail to develop the social and political intelligence to adjust to the world where their mechanical intelligence has created.
William G. Carleton

That there is an evolution of one sort or another is now common ground among scientists. Whether or not that evolution is directed is another question.
Pierre Teilhard de Chardin

An archeologist is the best husband any woman can have; the older she gets, the more interested he is in her.
Agatha Christie

Daily it is forced home on the mind of the biologist that nothing, not even the wind that blows, is so unstable as the level of the crust of this earth.
Charles Darwin

I look at the natural geological record as a history of the world imperfectly kept and written in a changing dialect; of this history we possess the last volume alone, relating only to two or three countries. Of this volume, only here and there a short chapter has been preserved; and of each page, only here and there a few lines.
Charles Darwin

Science has sometimes been said to be opposed to faith, and inconsistent with it. But all science, in fact, rests on a basis of faith, for it assumes the permanence and uniformity of natural laws—a thing which can never be demonstrated.
Tryon Edwards

The whole of science is nothing more than a refinement of everyday thinking.
Albert Einstein

The most famous self-made man in the world today is our own Edison. Talk with Mr. Edison and he will tell you he owes much if not most of his success to omnivorous reading. *Forbes* is one of his favorite publications. How closely he reads it can be gathered from a letter just received from him in which he asks the editor to forward a long analytical letter to the writer of a series of articles which contained two figures Mr. Edison questions, and he wants to know exactly on what authority or investigation they were based. Both letters were the product of Mr. Edison and were signed by him.
B.C.Forbes

Thomas Edison reads not for entertainment but to increase his store of knowledge. He sucks in information as eagerly as the bee sucks honey from flowers. The whole world, so to speak, pours its wisdom into his mind. He regards it as a criminal waste of time to go through the slow and painful ordeal of ascertaining things for one's self if these same things have already been ascertained and made available by others. In Edison's mind knowledge is power.
B.C. Forbes

Scientists ofttimes have the greatest faith in a higher power. The more they dig into, establish facts and figures, the more they marvel about the mystery of it all.
Malcolm Forbes

What an exciting super-tomorrow it will be! Americans are today making the greatest scientific developments in our history. That is a promise of new levels of employment, industrial activity and human happiness.
Clarence Francis

It is a mistake to believe that science consists in nothing but conclusively proved propositions, and it is unjust to demand that it should. It is a demand made by those who feel a craving for authority in some form to replace the religious catechism by something else, even a scientific one.
Sigmund Freud

In questions of science, the authority of a thousand is not worth that humble reasoning of a single individual.
Galileo Galilei

Science is the knowledge of consequences, and dependence of one fact upon another.
Thomas Hobbes

New discoveries in science . . . will continue to create a thousand new frontiers for those who would still adventure.
Herbert Hoover

We are just in the kindergarten of uncovering things; there is no downcurve in science.
Charles F. Kettering

Science has always promised two things not necessarily related—an increase first in our powers, second in our happiness and wisdom; and we have come to realize that it is the first and less important of the two promises which it has kept most abundantly.
Joseph Wood Krutch

Science itself is humanist in the sense that it doesn't discriminate between human beings, but it is also morally

neutral. It is no better or worse than the ethos with and for which it is being used.
Max Lerner

It is chiefly upon the lay citizen, informed about science but not its practitioner, that the country must depend in determining the use to which science is put, in resolving the many public policy questions that scientific discoveries constantly force upon us.
David E. Lilienthal

While becoming nuclear giants we have remained ethical infants.
Clifford McEntarfer

Science belongs to no one country.
Louis Pasteur

Take interest, I implore you, in those sacred dwellings which are designated by the expressive term, laboratories. Demand that they be multiplied and advanced. These are the temples of the future, temples of well-being and happiness . . . where humanity grows greater, stronger, better.
Louis Pasteur

Science seeks truth and discovers rightness. Religion seeks righteousness and discovers truth. Both have acquired knowledge of creative and destructive ways, and both point the same way of right living.
William G. Patten

I like talking to engineers best. They built bridges, they're very precise, very disciplined, yet I find they have roving minds.
Ralph Richardson

The work of science is to substitute facts for appearances and demonstrations for impressions.
John Ruskin

In art nothing worth doing can be done without genius; in science even a very moderate capacity can contribute to a supreme achievement.
Bertrand Russell

If we are to become the masters of science, not its slaves, we must learn to use its immense power to good purpose. The machine itself has neither mind nor soul nor moral sense. Only man has been endowed with these godlike attributes. Every age has its destined duty. Ours is to nurture an awareness of those divine attributes and a sense of responsibility in giving them expression.
David Sarnoff

The greatest engineering is the engineering of men.
Robert Louis Stevenson

Science has its being in a perpetual mental restlessness.
William Temple

Science moves, but slowly, slowly, creeping on from point to point.
Alfred Tennyson

Civilization requires slaves. Human slavery is wrong, insecure and demoralizing. On mechanical slavery, on the slavery of the machine, the future of the world depends.
Oscar Wilde

Material science now has the clear possibility and promise of the systematic utilization of all the natural resources of the earth for the good of the whole human race. . . . Maintaining and improving the standard of living of all the peoples of the earth through increasing use of mechanical horsepower and the scientific approach is now one of the keys to peace in the world.
Charles E. Wilson

SEASONS

On the influx of shark-watching tourists in recent years to Chatham, Mass.: We wanted to be known as a nice, quiet, laid-back community. We've been having this problem where sharks have been visiting us. It certainly does put you in the limelight.
Mike Ambriscoe

Summer: The time of year that children slam the door they left open all winter.
Anonymous

To sit in the shade on a fine day, and look upon verdure is the most perfect refreshment.
Jane Austen

Ah, summer, what power you have to make us suffer and like it.
Russell Baker

Sweet daughter of a rough and stormy sire, hoar winter's blooming child, delightful spring.
Anna Barbauld

The quality of life, which in the ardour of spring was personal and sexual, becomes social in midsummer.
Henry Beston

Summer ends, and autumn comes, and he who would have it otherwise would have high tide always and a full moon every night.
Hal Borland

Autumn arrives early in the morning, but spring at the close of a winter day.
Elizabeth Bowen

June reared the bunch of flowers you carry from seeds of April's sowing.
Robert Browning

And the spring comes slowly up this way.
Robert Burns

The tendinous part of the mind, so to speak, is more developed in winter; the fleshy, in summer. I should say winter has given the bone and sinew to literature, summer the tissues and blood.
John Burroughs

In the midst of winter, I finally learned that there was in me an invincible summer.
Albert Camus

Spring is sooner recognized by plants than by men.
Chinese proverb

Summer has set in with its usual severity.
Samuel Taylor Coleridge

The summer holidays! The magic words! The mere mention of them used to send shivers of joy rippling over my skin.
Roald Dahl

Summer: The season of inferior sledding.
Eskimo proverb

Alas, that spring should vanish with the rose!
Edward Fitzgerald

Summer, with its dog days, its vacations, its distractions, is over. We have had our holidays, our rest, our recreation. The fall season, with its new opportunities for effort, enterprise and achievement, is upon us. Let us rip off our coats and get down to business. We may have allowed pessimism to grip us during the summer months. We may even have allowed laziness to enter our bones. Now it is up to us to throw off both lassitude and pessimism. The time has come for action, for aggressiveness. . . .
B.C. Forbes

One cannot walk into an April day in a negative way. With spring, each man's plans and hopes result in new efforts, fresh actions.

All of which has a mighty important bearing on the economy. There are those of us who think that the psychology of man, each and together, has more impact on markets, business, services and building and all the fabric of an economy than all the more measurable statistical indices.
Malcolm Forbes

I should like to enjoy this summer flower by flower, as if it were to be the last one for me.
André Gide

Here is the ghost of a summer that lived for us. Here is a promise of summer to be.
William E. Henley

Summer treads on heels of spring.
Horace

Summer afternoon, summer afternoon; to me those have always been the two most beautiful words in the English language.
Henry James

When a poet mentions the spring we know that the zephyrs are about to whisper, that the groves are to recover their verdure, the linnets to warble forth their notes of love, and the flocks and herds to frisk over vales painted with flowers.
Samuel Johnson

Season of mists and mellow fruitfulness.
John Keats

Deep summer is when laziness finds respectability.
Sam Keen

In a summer season when soft was the sun.
William Langland

The course of the seasons is a piece of clockwork, with a cuckoo to call when it is spring.
Georg C. Lichtenberg

If Spring came but once a century instead of once a year or burst forth with the sound of an earthquake and not in silence, what wonder and expectation there would be in all hearts to behold the miraculous change.
Henry Wadsworth Longfellow

Magnificent autumn! He comes not like a pilgrim, clad in russet weeds; not like a hermit, clad in gray; but like a warrior with the stain of blood in his brazen mail.
Henry Wadsworth Longfellow

Oh, the long and dreary winter! Oh, the cold and cruel winter!
Henry Wadsworth Longfellow

What is so rare as a day in June? Then, if ever, come perfect days.
James Russell Lowell

Autumn is the American season. In Europe the leaves turn yellow or brown, and fall. Here they take fire on the trees and hang there flaming. We think this frost-fire is a portent somehow: a promise that the continent has given us. Life, too, we think, is capable of taking fire in this country; of creating beauty never seen.
Archibald MacLeish

There are few things in life more doleful than a child looking at a closed pool on a steamy summer day, and yet that sad scene has become as common as sunburns and mosquito bites as struggling local governments make the painful

choice to shut their pools to save the budget.
Jesse McKinley

In those vernal seasons of the year when the air is calm and pleasant, it were an injury and sullenness against nature not to go out and see her riches, and partake in her rejoicing with heaven and earth.
John Milton

I played as much golf as I could in North Dakota, but summer up there is pretty short. It usually falls on Tuesday.
Mike Morley

On recent beach casualties in Malibu: We had a sea lion that bit a couple of people, [but] the bites were superficial.
Merrill Riley

Summer makes a silence after spring.
Vita Sackville-West

Unusual commencement advice: Ladies and gentlemen of the class of '97: Wear sunscreen. If I could offer you only one tip for the future, sunscreen would be it.
Mary Schmich

The summer night is like a perfection of thought.
Wallace Stevens

In summer, the song sings itself.
William Carlos Williams

It's a sure sign of summer if the chair gets up when you do.
Walter Winchell

SECURITY

We will never have real safety and security for the wage earners unless we provide for safety and security for the wage payers and the wage savers, investors, and then, by all means, protection for both against reckless wasters and wage spenders.
William. J.H. Boetcker

Security is a false god; begin making sacrifices to it and you are lost.
Paul Bowles

Too many people are thinking of security instead of opportunity. They seem more afraid of life than of death.
James F. Byrnes

There is not much collective security in a flock of sheep on the way to the butcher.
Winston Churchill

The habits and language of clandestinity can intoxicate even its own practitioners.
William Colby

The best leaks always take place in the urinal.
John Cole

Curse not the king, no not in thy thought; and curse not the rich in thy bedchamber: for a bird of the air shall carry the voice, and that which hath wings shall tell the matter.
Ecclesiastes 10:20

We believe that our truly urgent need is to make our nation secure, our economy strong and our dollar sound. For every American this matter of the sound dollar is crucial. Without a sound dollar, every American family would face a renewal of inflation, an ever-increasing cost of living, the withering away of savings and life insurance policies.
Dwight D. Eisenhower

Security isn't securities. It's knowing that someone cares whether you are or cease to be.
Malcolm Forbes

The ultimate in futility is owning important jewelry. Insurers often insist on the wearing of paste replicas because necks with real rocks around 'em risk wringing.
Malcolm Forbes

No government can guarantee security. It can only tax production, distribution and service and gradually crush the power to pay taxes. That settles nothing. It only uses up the gains of the past and postpones the developments of the future.
Henry Ford

The farther we get away from the land, the greater our insecurity.
Henry Ford

On Foreign Secretary Robin Cook: If a man cannot keep a measly affair secret, what is he doing in charge of the Intelligence Service?
Frederick Forsyth

He that has eyes to see and ears to hear may convince himself that no mortal can keep a secret. If his lips are silent, he chatters with his fingertips; betrayal oozes out of him at every pore.
Sigmund Freud

Secrecy has become a god in this country, and those people who have secrets travel in a kind of fraternity and they will not speak to anyone else.
William Fulbright

Security is the mother of danger and the grandmother of destruction.
Thomas Fuller

Whoever created the name life insurance had to be the sales genius of all time.
Robert Half

It is when we all play safe that we create a world of utmost insecurity.
Dag Hammarskjöld

Security is mostly a superstition. It does not exist in nature, nor do the children of men as a whole experience it. Avoiding danger is no safer in the long run than outright exposure. The fearful are caught as often as the bold. Faith alone defends.
Helen Keller

What do you think spies are: priests, saints and martyrs? They're a squalid procession of vain fools, traitors, too; yes, pansies, sadists and drunkards, people who play cowboys and Indians to brighten their rotten lives.
John le Carré

He who is firmly seated in authority soon learns to think security, and not progress, the highest lesson of statecraft.
James Russell Lowell

The trouble with worrying so much about your security in the future is that you feel so insecure in the present.
Harlan Miller

Secrecy is as essential to intelligence as vestments and incense to a Mass or darkness to a spiritualist séance and must at all times be maintained, quite irrespective of whether or not it serves any purpose.
Malcolm Muggeridge

The fire at the manufacturing plant was due to friction caused by a large inventory rubbing up against an insurance policy.
Old Southern saying

We know that the wages of secrecy are corruption. We know that in secrecy, error undetected will flourish and subvert.
J. Robert Oppenheimer

The first rule in keeping secrets is nothing on paper: paper can be lost or stolen or simply inherited by the wrong

people; if you really want to keep something secret, don't write it down.
Thomas Powers

It takes a very strong head to keep secrets for years and not go slightly mad. It isn't wise to be advised by anyone slightly mad.
C.P. Snow

Happiness has many roots, but none more important than security.
E.R. Stettinius, Jr.

The desire for safety stands against every great and noble enterprise.
Tacitus

Be secret and exult,
Because of all things known
That is most difficult.
William Butler Yeats

SELF

If somebody tells you you have ears like a donkey, pay no attention. But if two people tell you, buy yourself a saddle.
Sholem Aleichem

He who asks of life nothing but the improvement of his own nature . . . is less liable than anyone else to miss and waste life.
Henri Frédéric Amiel

Man must be arched and buttressed from within, else the temple will crumble to dust.
Marcus Aurelius Antoninus

Never esteem anything as of advantage to thee that shall make thee break thy word or lose thy self-respect.
Marcus Aurelius Antoninus

Every man must scratch his head with his own nails.
Arabian proverb

I count him braver who overcomes his desires than him who conquers his enemies; for the hardest victory is the victory over self.
Aristotle

Whatever task you undertake, do it with all your heart and soul. Always be courteous, never be discouraged. Beware of him who promises something for nothing. Do not blame anybody for your mistakes and failures. Do not look for approval except the consciousness of doing your best.
Bernard M. Baruch

To be ambitious for wealth, and yet always expecting to be poor; to be always doubting your ability to get what you long for, is like trying to reach east by traveling west. There is no philosophy which will help man to succeed when he is always doubting his ability to do so, and thus attracting failure. No matter how hard you work for success if your thought is saturated with the fear of failure, it will kill your efforts, neutralize your endeavors and make success impossible.
Charles Baudouin

A man without self-restraint is like a barrel without hoops, and tumbles to pieces.
Henry Ward Beecher

A man's true estate of power and riches is to be in himself; not in his dwelling or position or external relations, but in his own essential character.
Henry Ward Beecher

No bird soars too high, if he soars on his own wings.
William Blake

If you want to know how rich you really are, find out what would be left of you tomorrow if you should lose every dollar you own tonight.
William J.H. Boetcker

That you may retain your self-respect—it is better to displease the people by doing what you know is right, than to temporarily please them by doing what you know is wrong.
William J.H. Boetcker

He that is master of himself will soon be master of others.
H.G. Bohn

Self-distrust is the cause of most of our failures. In the assurance of strength, there is strength, and they are the weakest, however strong, who have no faith in themselves or their own powers.
Christian Bovée

O wad some Pow'r the giftie gie us
To see oursels as ithers see us!
Robert Burns

The world will always be governed by self-interest: we should not try to stop this: we should try and make the self-interest of cads a little more coincident with that of decent people.
Samuel Butler

Self-laudation abounds among the unpolished, but nothing can stamp a man more sharply as ill-bred.
Charles Buxton

To know oneself, one should assert oneself.
Albert Camus

Let every man mind his own business.
Miguel de Cervantes

There is such a thing as honest pride and self-respect.
Edwin H. Chapin

Our own self-love draws a thick veil between us and our faults.
Lord Chesterfield

Those whom you can make like themselves better will, I promise you, like you very well.
Lord Chesterfield

It is necessary to try to surpass one's self always; this occupation ought to last as long as life.
Queen Christina of Sweden

Every man is the painter and the sculptor of his own life.
St. John Chrysostom

Be yourself. Ape no greatness. Be willing to pass for what you are.
Samuel Coley

People who have nothing to do are quickly tired by their own company.
Jeremy Collier

A man's best friends are his ten fingers.
Robert Collyer

We are all serving a self-sentence in the dungeon of self.
Cyril Connolly

To be nobody-but-yourself—in a world which is doing its best, night and day, to make you everybody but yourself—means to fight the hardest battle which any human being can fight, and never stop fighting.
e.e. cummings

We never understand a thing so well, and make it our own, as when we have discovered it for ourselves.
René Descartes

Self government is no less essential to the development, growth, and happiness of the individual than to the nation.
William H. Douglas

Self-defense is Nature's oldest law.
John Dryden

A person who doubts himself is like a man who would enlist in the ranks of his enemies and bear arms against himself. He makes his failure certain by himself being the first person to be convicted of it.
Alexandre Dumas

One's self-satisfaction is an untaxed kind of property which it is very unpleasant to find depreciated.
George Eliot

There is a great deal of unmapped country within us.
George Eliot

Men who know themselves are no longer fools; they stand on the threshold of the Door of Wisdom.
Havelock Ellis

All are needed by each one. Nothing is fair or good alone.
Ralph Waldo Emerson

Do not spill thy soul in running hither and yon, grieving over the mistakes and the vices of others. The one person whom it is most necessary to reform is yourself.
Ralph Waldo Emerson

No man is free who is not master of himself.
Epictetus

Blow your own horn loud. If you succeed, people will forgive your noise; if you fail, they'll forget it.
William Feather

Invest in yourself—if you have confidence in yourself.
William Feather

It is better to rely on yourself than on your friends.
William Feather

Self-restraint is feeling your oats without sowing them.
Shanon Fife

Each of us is an impregnable fortress that can be laid waste only from within.
Timothy J. Flynn

The man who is bigger than his job keeps cool. He does not lose his head, he refuses to become rattled, to fly off in a temper. The man who would control others must be able to control himself. There is something admirable, something inspiring, something soul-stirring about a man who displays coolness and courage under extremely trying circumstances. A good temper is not only a business asset. It is the secret of health. The longer you live, the more you will learn that a disordered temper breeds a disordered body.
B.C. Forbes

What you have outside you counts less than what you have inside you.
B.C. Forbes

Where you're from only matters in relation to where you are.
Malcolm Forbes

We reproach people for talking about themselves, but it is the subject they treat best.
Anatole France

He that falls in love with himself will have no rivals.
Benjamin Franklin

If you would have a faithful servant and one that you like, serve yourself.
Benjamin Franklin

What is best for people is what they do for themselves.
Benjamin Franklin

A man is little the better for liking himself if nobody else likes him.
Thomas Fuller

There is no dependence that can be sure but a dependence upon one's self.
John Gay

Every man is two men; one is awake in the darkness, the other asleep in the light.
Kahlil Gibran

You give but little when you give of your possessions. It is when you give of yourself that you truly give.
Kahlil Gibran

Let everyone sweep in front of his own door and the whole world will be clean.
Johann Wolfgang von Goethe

The fortunate circumstances of our lives are generally found, at last, to be of our own producing.
Oliver Goldsmith

I am only one, but still I am one; I cannot do everything, but still I can do something; and because I cannot do everything I will not refuse to do the something that I can do.
Edward E. Hale

He is great enough that is his own master.
Joseph Hall

Every person is responsible for all the good within the scope of his abilities, and for no more, and none can tell whose sphere is the largest.
Gail Hamilton

A self-made man may prefer a self-made name.
Learned Hand

No man would, I think, exchange his existence with any other man, however fortunate. We had as lief not be, as not be ourselves.
William Hazlitt

What lies behind us and what lies before us are tiny matters compared with what lies within us.
Oliver Wendell Holmes

The average man plays to the gallery of his own self-esteem.
Elbert Hubbard

Probably the most neglected friend you have is you.
L. Ron Hubbard

A man has to live with himself, and he should see to it that he always has good company.
Charles Evans Hughes

The strongest man in the world is he who stands most alone.
Henrik Ibsen

Everyone gives himself credit for more brains than he has and less money.
Italian proverb

I am of a sect by myself, as far as I know.
Thomas Jefferson

Every man is of importance to himself.
Samuel Johnson

Few men survey themselves with so much severity as not to admit prejudices in their own favor.
Samuel Johnson

Your levelers wish to level down as far as themselves, but they cannot bear leveling up to themselves.
Samuel Johnson

I am only one; but I am still one. I cannot do everything, but still I can do something. I will not refuse to do the something I can do.
Helen Keller

Self-pity is our worst enemy, and if we yield to it, we can never do anything wise in the world.
Helen Keller

Humility is the part of wisdom, and is most becoming in men. But let no one discourage self-reliance; it is, of all the rest, the greatest quality of true manliness.
Louis Kossuth

He who gains a victory over other men is strong; but he who gains a victory over himself is all powerful.
Lao-tzu

He who knows others is clever, but he who knows himself is enlightened.
Lao-tzu

Than self-restraint there is nothing better.
Lao-tzu

A man's mind is the man himself.
Latin proverb

Every man has a property in his own person; this nobody has a right to but himself.
John Locke

Truly, this world can get on without us, if we would but think so.
Henry Wadsworth Longfellow

There is little that can withstand a man who can conquer himself.
King Louis XIV

The greatest service we can perform for others is to help them to help themselves.
Horace Mann

Follow your own path, no matter what people say.
Karl Marx

If you love men and they are unfriendly, look into your love; if you rule men and they are unruly, look into your wisdom; if you are courteous to them and they do not respond, look into your courtesy. If what you do is vain, always seek within.
Mencius

Excess of self-inflation, as self-deflation, is unwise and unworthy of a mature man.
Henry G. Mendelson

He who reigns within himself, and rules passions, desires, and fears, is more than a king.
John Milton

Ofttimes nothing profits more than self-esteem, grounded on just and right well manag'd.
John Milton

The pious and just honoring of ourselves may be thought the fountainhead from whence every laudable and worthy enterprise issues forth.
John Milton

We are all mortals, and each is for himself.
Molière

I care not so much what I am in the opinion of others as what I am in my own; I would be rich of myself and not by borrowing.
Michel de Montaigne

Men throw themselves on foreign assistances to spare their own, which, after all, are the only certain and sufficient ones.
Michel de Montaigne

My library is my kingdom, and here I try to make my rule absolute—shutting off this single nook from wife, daughter and society. Elsewhere I have only a verbal authority, and vague. Unhappy is the man, in my opinion, who has no spot at home where he can be at home to himself—to court himself and hide away.
Michel de Montaigne

The great thing in the world is to know how to be sufficient unto oneself.
Michel de Montaigne

Lack of something to feel important about is almost the greatest tragedy a man may have.
Arthur E. Morgan

What lies behind us and what lies before are tiny matters compared to what lies within us.
William Morrow

Robinson had a servant even better than Friday: His name was Crusoe.
Friedrich Wilhelm Nietzsche

I am I plus my surroundings and if I do not preserve the latter, I do not preserve myself.
José Ortega y Gasset

Do you wish men to speak well of you? Then never speak well of yourself.
Blaise Pascal

We are more easily persuaded, in general, by the reasons we ourselves discover than by those which are given to us by others.
Blaise Pascal

We are only falsehood, duplicity, contradiction; we both conceal and disguise ourselves from ourselves.
Blaise Pascal

The cause of all the blunders committed by man arises from excessive self-love. He who intends to be a great man ought to love neither himself nor his own things, but only what is just, whether it happens to be done by himself or by another.
Plato

One of the very best of all earthly possessions is self-possession.
George D. Prentice

Civilization is the progress of a society towards privacy. The savage's whole existence is public, ruled by the laws of his tribe. Civilization is the process of setting man free from men.
Ayn Rand

We have always known that heedless self-interest was bad morals; we know now that it is bad economics.
Franklin D. Roosevelt

As soon as any man says of the affairs of State, What does it matter to me? that State may be given up for lost.
Jean-Jacques Rousseau

Keep cool and you command everybody.
Louis Léon de Saint-Just

There is but one virtue—the eternal sacrifice of self.
George Sand

Nobody, but nobody, is going to tell me I'm not the most. I am. I was the most when everybody else was struggling bitterly to become a little.
William Saroyan

We forfeit three-fourths of ourselves in order to be like other people.
Arthur Schopenhauer

Teach self-denial and make its practice pleasure, and you can create for the world a destiny more sublime that ever issued from the brain of the wildest dreamer.
Sir Walter Scott

A man is a lion for his own cause.
Scottish proverb

Most powerful is he who has himself in his own power.
Seneca

We can be thankful to a friend for a few acres, or a little money; and yet for the freedom and command of the whole earth, and for the great benefits of our being, our life, health, and reason, we look upon ourselves as under no obligation.
Seneca

It is the hardest thing in the world to be a good thinker without being a good self examiner.
Lord Shaftesbury

It is impossible you should take true root but by the fair weather that you make yourself; it is needful that you frame the season for your own harvest.
William Shakespeare

Self-love is not so vile a sin as self-neglecting.
William Shakespeare

Self-denial is not a virtue, it is only the effect of prudence on rascality.
George Bernard Shaw

Who will adhere to him that abandons himself?
Sir Philip Sidney

Self-approbation, when founded in truth and a good conscience, is a source of some of the purest joys known to man.
Charles Simmons

Know thyself.
Socrates

In vain he seeketh others to suppress who hath not learned himself first to subdue.
Edmund Spenser

The greatest pride, or the greatest despondency, is the greatest ignorance of one's self.
Baruch Spinoza

To be honest, to be kind—to earn a little and spend a little less, to make upon the whole a family happier for his presence, to renounce when that shall be necessary and not be embittered, to keep a few friends, but these without capitulation— above all, on the same grim condition, to keep friends with himself—here is a task for all that a man has of fortitude and delicacy.
Robert Louis Stevenson

He conquers twice who conquers himself in victory.
Publilius Syrus

Self-reverence, self-knowledge, self-control, these three alone lead life to sovereign power.
Alfred, Lord Tennyson

He who lives only to benefit himself confers on the world a benefit when he dies.
Tertullian

The most difficult thing in life is to know yourself.
Thales

It is as hard to see oneself as to look backwards without turning around.
Henry David Thoreau

Not till we are lost, in other words, not till we have lost the world, do we begin to find ourselves, and realize where we are and the infinite extent of our relations.
Henry David Thoreau

In his private heart no man much respects himself.
Mark Twain

We can secure other people's approval if we do right and try hard; but our own is worth a hundred of it, and no way has been found out of securing that.
Mark Twain

We do not deal much in facts when we are contemplating ourselves.
Mark Twain

Self-appraisal will do more for you than self-praise will.
Frank Tyger

When you are alone you are all your own.
Leonardo da Vinci

It is not love we should have painted as blind, but self-love.
Voltaire

Self-love is the instrument of our preservation; It resembles the provision for the reproduction of mankind: It is necessary, it gives us pleasure, and we must conceal it.
Voltaire

I set myself on fire and people come to watch me burn.
John Wesley

I don't like myself, I'm crazy about myself.
Mae West

He that neither knows himself nor thinks he can learn of others is not fit for company.
Benjamin Whichcote

Man is a wonder to himself; he can neither govern nor know himself.
Benjamin Whichcote

When I give, I give myself.
Walt Whitman

Other people are quite dreadful. The only possible society is one's self.
Oscar Wilde

Self-denial is simply a method by which man arrests his progress.
Oscar Wilde

There is luxury in self-reproach. When we blame ourselves, we feel no one else has a right to blame us.
Oscar Wilde

The more you speak of yourself, the more likely you are to lie.
Johann Zimmerman

SELFISHNESS

I have been a selfish being all my life, in practice, though not in principle.
Jane Austen

Be unselfish. That is the first and final commandment for those who would be useful, and happy in their usefulness. If you think of yourself only, you cannot develop because you are choking the source of development, which is spiritual expansion through thought for others.
Charles W. Eliot

Selfishness can be a virtue. Selfishness is essential to survival, and without survival we cannot protect those whom we love more than ourselves.
Duke Ellington

Selfishness ultimately begets only unhappiness. Unselfishness begets happiness.
B.C. Forbes

We are unlikely to cease making gods or inventing ceremonies to please them for as long as we are afraid of death, or of the dark, and for as long as we persist in self-centeredness. That could be a lengthy stretch of time.
Christopher Hitchens

The selfish spirit of commerce knows no country, and feels no passion or principle but that of gain.
Thomas Jefferson

The principle of liberty and equality, if coupled with mere selfishness, will make men only devils, each trying to be independent that he may fight only for his own interest. And here is the need of religion and its power, to bring in the principle of benevolence and love to men.
John Randolph

No man can live happily who regards himself alone, who turns everything to his own advantage. Thou must live for another if thou wishest to live for thyself.
Seneca

Unselfish and noble actions are the most radiant pages in the biography of souls.
David Thomas

A man is called selfish, not for pursuing his own good, but for neglecting his neighbor's.
Richard Whately

Selfishness is not living as one wishes to live. It is asking others to live as one wishes to live.
Oscar Wilde

SERVICE

Service makes men competent.
Lyman Abbott

To give real service you must add something which cannot be bought or measured with money, and that is sincerity and integrity.
Douglas Adams

It is only in the giving of oneself to others that we truly live.
Ethel Percy Andrus

If things are not going well with you, begin your effort at correcting the situation by carefully examining the service you are rendering, and especially the spirit in which you are rendering it.
Roger Babson

The more you learn what to do with yourself, and the more you do for others, the more you will learn to enjoy the abundant life.
William J.H. Boetcker

The work an unknown good man has done is like a vein of water flowing hidden underground, secretly making the ground green.
Thomas Carlyle

Service to a just cause rewards the worker with more real happiness and satisfaction than any other venture of life.
Carrie Chapman Catt

Under our institutions each individual is born to sovereignty. Whatever he may adopt as a means of livelihood, his real business is serving his country. He

cannot hold himself above his fellow men. The greatest place of command is really the place of obedience, and the greatest place of honor is really the place of service.
Calvin Coolidge

The vital force in business life is the honest desire to serve. Business, it is said, is the science of service. He profits most who serves best. At the very bottom of the wish to render service must be honesty of purpose, and, as I go along through life, 1 see more and more that honesty in word, thought, and work means success. It spells a life worth living and in business, clean success.
George Eberhard

Service is what life is all about.
Marian Wright Edelman

Only a life lived for others is a life worthwhile.
Albert Einstein

To devote a portion of one's leisure to doing something for someone else is one of the highest forms of recreation.
Gerald B. Fitzgerald

Which is more worthwhile earning: a large fortune or the esteem and gratitude of the nation? This question is prompted anew by the death of ex-Secretary of the Interior [Franklin K.] Lane. He remained in public service, doing most noble work, until his means became absolutely exhausted, and he died before having had the opportunity to reaccumulate any bank account. . . . He died leaving no estate whatsoever. Is what he did leave more to be desired, more to be coveted, than a fortune reaching into six or seven figures?
B.C. Forbes

Service is the rent that we pay for our room on earth.
Lord Halifax

The life of a man consists not in seeing visions and in dreaming dreams, but in active charity and in willing service.
Henry Wadsworth Longfellow

As soon as public service ceases to be the chief business of the citizens, and they would rather serve with their money than with their persons, the state is not far from its fall.
Jean-Jacques Rousseau

One could of course say that a man's due is to be measured by his services to the community, but I cannot imagine how these services are to be estimated. Compare a baker and an opera singer. You could live without the opera singer, but not without the services of the baker. On this ground you might say that the baker performs a greater service; but no lover of music would agree.
Bertrand Russell

One thing I know; the only ones among you who will be really happy are those who will have sought and found how to serve.
Albert Schweitzer

Have I done anything for society? I have then done more for myself. Let that question and truth be always present to thy mind, and work without cessation.
William Simms

When we act upon the formula of giving service we seem to get what we want and we also get it for the other person, too. In the high art of serving others, workers sustain their morale, management keeps its customers, and the nation prospers. One of the indisputable lessons of life is that we cannot get or keep anything for

ourselves alone unless we also get it for others, too.
J. Richard Sneed

A man should inure himself to voluntary labor, and not give up to indulgence and pleasure, as they beget no good constitution of body nor knowledge of mind.
Socrates

In the New Testament it is taught that willing and voluntary service to others is the highest duty and glory in human life. . . . The men of talent are constantly forced to serve the rest. They make the discoveries and inventions, order the battles, write the books, and produce the works of art. The benefit and enjoyment go to the whole. There are those who joyfully order their own lives so that they may serve the welfare of mankind.
William Graham Sumner

Life is a place of service, and in that service one has to suffer a great deal that is hard to bear, but more often to experience a great deal of joy. But that joy can be real only if people look upon their life as a service, and have a definite object in life outside themselves and their personal happiness.
Leo Tolstoy

The sole meaning of life is to serve humanity.
Leo Tolstoy

The vocation of every man and woman is to serve other people.
Leo Tolstoy

SEX

For birth control I rely on my personality.
Milt Abel

The difference between sex and love is that sex relieves tension and love causes it.
Woody Allen

Sexuality is the lyricism of the masses.
Charles Baudelaire

The highest level of sexual excitement is in a monogamous relationship.
Warren Beatty

Being a sex symbol is a heavy load for one to carry, especially when one is tired, hurt and bewildered.
Clara Bow

No office anywhere on earth is so puritanical, impeccable, elegant, sterile or incorruptible as not to contain the yeast for at least one affair, probably more.
Helen Gurley Brown

Sex after 90 is like trying to shoot pool with a rope. Even putting my cigar in its holder is a thrill.
George Burns

It doesn't matter what you do in the bedroom as long as you don't do it in the street and frighten the horses.
Mrs. Patrick Campbell

I don't believe in vitamin pills. I swear by men, darling, and as many as possible.
Joan Collins

For flavor, instant sex will never supersede the stuff you have to peel and cook.
Quentin Crisp

The act of sex, gratifying as it may be, is God's joke on humanity. It is man's last desperate stand at superintendency.
Bette Davis

Once a woman has forgiven her man, she must not reheat his sins for breakfast.
Marlene Dietrich

Sex. In America an obsession. In other parts of the world a fact.
Marlene Dietrich

It's worrisome that the nation's spymaster who had presided in a military where adultery could result in court-martial could not have found a more clandestine manner of talking naughty to his biographer babe than a Gmail drop box, a semiprivate file-sharing system used by terrorists, teenagers and authors.
Maureen Dowd

It's okay to laugh in the bedroom so long as you don't point.
Will Durst

I'm afraid I'm very much the traditionalist. I went down on one knee and dictated a proposal which my secretary faxed over straight away.
Stephen Fry

My dad told me, "Anything worth having is worth waiting for." I waited until I was 15.
Zsa Zsa Gabor

Why did [God] give us genitals then if he wanted us to think clearly?
Graham Greene

All really great lovers are articulate, and verbal seduction is the surest road to actual seduction.
Marya Mannes

Sex and beauty are inseparable, like life and consciousness.
D.H. Lawrence

Before sleeping together today, people should boil themselves.
Richard Lewis

A promiscuous person is someone who is getting more sex than you are.
Victor Lownes

You mustn't force sex to do the work of love or love to do the work of sex.
Mary McCarthy

Sex is one of nine reasons for reincarnation. The other eight are unimportant.
Henry Miller

Pursuit and seduction are the essence of sexuality. It's part of the sizzle.
Camille Paglia

Dating is a social engagement with the threat of sex at its conclusion.
P.J. O'Rourke

After making love I said to my girl, "Was it good for you, too?" And she said, "I don't think this was good for anybody."
Garry Shandling

On recent events in a New York hotel room: What happened was not just inappropriate, it was more than that, it was a fault; a fault toward my wife, my children, my friends, but also a fault toward the French people who placed in me their hope for change.
Dominique Strauss-Kahn

Sex is like money: only too much is enough.
John Updike

Sex is a conversation carried out by other means. If you get on well out of bed, half the problems of bed are solved.
Peter Ustinov

Love is being stupid together.
Paul Valéry

Sex is. There is nothing more to be done about it. Sex builds no roads, writes

no novels and sex certainly gives no meaning to anything in life but itself.
Gore Vidal

It's worth recalling that Dwight D. Eisenhower's liaison with driver Kay Summersby was not treated as grounds for professional defenestration. Maybe our forbears weren't so morally straightjacketed [sic] as we sometimes imagine. Maybe, too, there was more recognition that an indispensable man could be forgiven personal sins. Mr. Petraeus's record as a strategist and battlefield commander was every bit the equal of Creighton Abrams, Eisenhower or George Patton. What a pity that his service should come to a premature end through the collision of personal error and a zero-tolerance culture.
The Wall Street Journal

Sex is more exciting on the screen and between the pages than between the sheets.
Andy Warhol

A former congressman on his sexting habit: I have made terrible mistakes. I have not been honest with myself, my family, my constituents, my friends and supporters and the media.
Anthony Weiner

When people discussed tonics, pick-me-ups after a severe illness, she kept to herself the prescription of a quick dip in bed with someone you liked but were not in love with. A shock of sexual astonishment which could make you feel astonishingly well and high spirited.
Mary Wesley

Talking from morning to night about sex has helped my skiing, because I talk about movement, about looking good, about taking risks.
Ruth Westheimer

A laugh at sex is a laugh at destiny.
Thornton Wilder

SILENCE

He who is silent is forgotten; he who abstains is taken at his word; he who does not advance falls back; he who stops is overwhelmed, distanced, crushed; he who ceases to grow greater becomes smaller; he who leaves off, gives up; the stationary condition is the beginning of the end.
Henri Frédéric Amiel

Most of us know how to say nothing; few of us know when.
Anonymous

Most men talk too much. Much of my success has been due to keeping my mouth shut.
J. Ogden Armour

Drawing on my fine command of language, I said nothing.
Robert Benchley

Thought works in silence; so does virtue. One might erect statues to silence.
Thomas Carlyle

Silence is the unbearable repartee.
G.K. Chesterton

Silence is a true friend that never betrays.
Confucius

One nice thing about silence is that it can't be repeated.
Gary Cooper

Blessed is the man who, having nothing to say, abstains from giving in words evidence of the fact.
George Eliot

Silence is an answer to a wise man.
Euripides

Saying nothing is sometimes the right thing to say.
Malcolm Forbes

Remember not only to say the right thing in the right place, but far more difficult still, to leave unsaid the wrong thing at the tempting moment.
Benjamin Franklin

Silence makes no mistakes.
French proverb

Quiet persons are welcome everywhere.
Thomas Fuller

Silence is argument carried on by other means.
Che Guevara

All noise is waste. So cultivate quietness in your speech, in your thoughts, in your emotions. Speak habitually low. Wait for attention and then your low words will be charged with dynamite.
Elbert Hubbard

He who thinks much says but little in proportion to his thoughts. He selects that language which will convey his ideas in the most explicit and direct manner.
Washington Irving

Silence is a great peacemaker.
Henry Wadsworth Longfellow

Do not the most moving moments of our lives find us without words?
Marcel Marceau

You have not converted a man because you have silenced him.
John Morley

A sage thing is timely silence, and better than any speech.
Plutarch

A talebearer revealeth secrets: but he that is of a faithful spirit concealeth the matter.
Proverbs 11:13

It is better either to be silent or to say things of more value than silence. Sooner throw a pearl at hazard than an idle or useless word; and do not say a little in many words but a great deal in a few.
Pythagoras

A happy life must be to a great extent a quiet life, for it is only in an atmosphere of quiet that true joy can live.
Bertrand Russell

It is difficult to keep quiet if you have nothing to do.
Arthur Schopenhauer

The silence, often of pure innocence, persuades where speaking fails.
William Shakespeare

Silence is the most perfect expression of scorn.
George Bernard Shaw

Silence is one of the hardest arguments to refute.
Maurice R. Shochatt

The world would be happier if men had the same capacity to be silent that they have to speak.
Baruch Spinoza

Let a fool hold his tongue and he will pass for a sage.
Publilius Syrus

Silence is the universal refuge, the sequel to all dull discourses and all foolish acts, a balm to our every chagrin, as welcome after satiety as after disappointment.
Henry David Thoreau

SIMPLICITY

Refined policy has ever been the parent of confusion, and ever will be so, as long as the world endures. Plain good intention, which is as easily discovered at the first view as fraud is surely detected at last, is of no mean force in the government of mankind. Genuine simplicity of heart is a healing and cementing principle.
Edmund Burke

Everything should be made as simple as possible, but not simpler.
Albert Einstein

Possessions, outward success, publicity, luxury—to me these have always been contemptible. I believe that a simple and unassuming manner of life is best for every one, best both for the body and the mind.
Albert Einstein

Nothing is more simple than greatness; indeed, to be simple is to be great.
Ralph Waldo Emerson

Simplicity of character is the natural result of profound thought.
William Hazlitt

In character, in manners, in style, in all things, the supreme excellence is simplicity.
Henry Wadsworth Longfellow

The silence of the place was like a sleep, so full of rest it seemed.
Henry Wadsworth Longfellow

Whenever two hypotheses cover the facts, use the simpler of the two.
William Ockham

Beauty of style and harmony and grace and good rhythm depend on simplicity.
Plato

There is a certain majesty in simplicity which is far above all the quaintness of wit.
Alexander Pope

SINCERITY

The essential element in personal magnetism is a consuming sincerity—an overwhelming faith in the importance of the work one has to do.
Bruce Barton

Earnestness is the devotion of all the faculties.
Christian Bovée

If life must not be taken too seriously, then so neither must death.
Samuel Butler

The sincere alone can recognize sincerity.
Thomas Carlyle

Even where there is talent, culture, knowledge, if there is not earnestness, it does not go to the root of things.
James Freeman Clarke

There is no substitute for thoroughgoing, ardent and sincere earnestness.
Charles Dickens

Sincerity is no test of truth—no evidence of correctness of conduct. You may take poison sincerely believing it the needed medicine, but will it save your life?
Tryon Edwards

It is not so important to be serious as it is to be serious about the important things.
Robert M. Hutchins

It is an old and true maxim that a drop of honey catches more flies than a gallon of gall. So with men, if you would win

a man to your cause, first convince him that you are his sincere friend.
Abraham Lincoln

Sincerity is impossible unless it pervades the whole being, and the pretense of it saps the very foundation of character.
James Russell Lowell

Sincerity in society is like an iron girder in a house of cards.
Somerset Maugham

The great enemy of clear language is insincerity. When there is a gap between one's real and one's declared aims, one turns, as it were, instinctively to long words and exhausted idioms, like a cuttlefish squirting out ink.
George Orwell

To be practical in life means to take everything seriously and nothing tragically.
Arthur Schnitzler

It is dangerous to be sincere unless you are also stupid.
George Bernard Shaw

We are apt to say that money talks, but it speaks a broken, poverty-stricken language. Hearts talk better, clearer and with wider intelligence.
William Allen White

A little sincerity is a dangerous thing, and a great deal of it is absolutely fatal.
Oscar Wilde

SOCIETY

I can think of few important movements for reform in which success was won by any method other than an energetic minority presenting the indifferent majority with a fait accompli, which was then accepted.
Vera Brittain

Has there ever been a society which has died of dissent? Several have died of conformity in our lifetime.
Jacob Bronowski

If you attack the establishment long enough and hard enough, they will make you a member of it.
Art Buchwald

Society is a partnership in all science; a partnership in all art; a partnership in every virtue and in all perfection. As the ends of such a partnership cannot be obtained in many generations, it becomes a partnership not only between those who are living, but between those who are dead and those who are to be born.
Edmund Burke

A man of a right spirit is not a man of narrow and private views, but is greatly interested and concerned for the good of the community to which he belongs, and particularly of the city or village in which he resides, and for the true welfare of the society of which he is a member.
Jonathan Edwards

In this democracy there are no titles. Yet there is no land on the face of the earth where titles are more freely bestowed— or arrogated. If a man isn't known as Judge or Colonel or Doctor or Professor or General or Governor or Senator or Congressman or Ambassador or Secretary or Captain or Chief, then the chances are that he is described as some kind of a king. We have our Tobacco Kings, our Steel Kings, our Lumber Kings, our Chemical Kings, our Automobile Kings, our Coal Kings, our Traction

Kings, and doubtless we will shortly have our Bootlegger Kings.
B.C. Forbes

Empty heads are fond of long titles.
German proverb

The wise sometimes condescend to accept of titles; but none but a fool would imagine them of any real importance. We ought to depend upon intrinsic merit, and not on the slender helps of a title.
Oliver Goldsmith

The delicate balance between modesty and conceit is popularity.
Robert Half

Popularity disarms envy in well-disposed minds. Those are ever the most ready to do justice to others, who feel that the world has done them justice.
William Hazlitt

I have no doubt that when the power of either capital or labor is extended in such a way as to attack the life of the community, those who seek their private interests at such cost are public enemies and should be dealt with as such.
Oliver Wendell Holmes

He will always be a slave who does not know how to live upon a little.
Horace

A community is like a ship; everyone ought to be prepared to take the helm.
Henrik Ibsen

There are only two classes in society: those who get more than they earn, and those who earn more than they get.
Holbrook Jackson

We are not only gregarious animals, liking to be in sight of our fellows, but we have an innate propensity to get ourselves noticed, and noticed favorably, by our kind.
William James

It is an unfinished society that we offer the world—a society that is forever committed to change, to improvement and to growth, that will never stagnate in the certitude of ideology or the finalities of dogma.
Robert F. Kennedy

One-fifth of the people are against everything all the time.
Robert F. Kennedy

Any society that takes away from those most capable and gives to the least will perish.
Abraham Lincoln

It is not titles that honor men, but men that honor titles.
Niccolò Machiavelli

Whatever makes man a slave takes half his worth away.
Alexander Pope

That which happens to the soil when it ceases to be cultivated, happens to man himself when he foolishly forsakes society for solitude; the brambles grow up in his desert heart.
Antoine de Rivarol

Society is like the air; necessary to breathe, but insufficient to live on.
George Santayana

The community in which each man acts like his neighbor is not yet a civilized community.
Archibald Sayce

There are only two classes in good society in England: the equestrian classes and the neurotic classes.
George Bernard Shaw

As are families, so is society. If well ordered, well instructed, and well governed, they are the springs from which go forth the streams of national greatness and prosperity—of civil order and public happiness.
Frank Thayer

I have three chairs in my house; one for solitude, two for friendship and three for society.
Henry David Thoreau

Once a secret society establishes itself within an open society, there is no end to the hideous mistrust it must cause.
Rebecca West

High society is for those who have stopped working and no longer have anything important to do.
Woodrow Wilson

SOLITUDE

For the self-development of men and women it is absolutely necessary that they should be alone with themselves at least one hour each day—to get the blessings of solitude.
William J.H. Boetcker

It is easy in the world to live after the world's opinion—it is easy in solitude to live after your own; but the great man is he who, in the midst of the world, keeps with perfect sweetness the independence of solitude.
Raplh Waldo Emerson

By all means use sometimes to be alone. Salute thyself; see what they soul doth wear.
George Herbert

Many have no happier moments than those that they pass in solitude, abandoned to their own imagination, which

sometimes puts sceptres in their hands or miters on their heads, shifts the scene of pleasure with endless variety, bids all the forms of beauty sparkle before them, and gluts them with every change of visionary luxury.
Samuel Johnson

Solitude: a sweet absence of looks.
Milan Kundera

The great omission in American life is solitude; not loneliness, for this is an alienation that thrives most in the midst of crowds, but that zone of time and space free from outside pressure which is the incubator of the spirit.
Marya Mannes

The heart beats louder and the soul hears quicker in silence and solitude.
Wendell Phillips

Solitude is not measured by the miles of space that intervene between a man and his fellows.
Henry David Thoreau

SORROW

Resolve to be thyself; and know that he who finds himself, loses his misery.
Matthew Arnold

Regrets are as personal as fingerprints. Discarding what is vain or false, facing the facts that should truly disturb your conscience, is worth whatever time it takes or pain it may cause. It can pay to the future what you owe to the past.
Margaret Banning

If there is a hell upon earth it is to be found in a melancholy man's heart.
Robert Burton

Sorrow was made for man, not for beasts; yet if men encourage melancholy too much, they become no better than beasts.
Miguel de Cervantes

There is no greater sorrow than remembering happy times in the midst of misery.
Dante

Waste no tears over the griefs of yesterday.
Euripides

I haven't a clue about the biology or the psychology involved when a person dissolves into tears, but it is quite fascinating to note what turns them on. There are wives who can cascade over a late husband or a burned dinner, and equally pour tears of joy over a new bonnet or a renovated bathroom. . . .

A while ago I took a ship back from Europe. Amid the tumbling confetti . . . I found myself misty-eyed watching a young lady waving a tearful farewell to her boyfriend on the dock. I couldn't figure out if I was crying at her plight, or in delight that he wasn't coming along with us.
Malcolm Forbes

If we are more affected by the ruin of a palace than by the conflagration of a cottage, our humanity must have formed a very erroneous estimate of the miseries of human life.
Edward Gibbon

Life is made up of sobs, sniffles and smiles, with sniffles predominating.
O. Henry

The miserable are very talkative.
Hindu proverb

There are a good many real miseries in life that one cannot help smiling at, but they are the smiles that make wrinkles and not dimples.
Oliver Wendell Holmes

It is wrong to be sorry without ceasing.
Homer

Sorrow is a kind of rust of the soul, which every new idea contributes in its passage to scour away.
Samuel Johnson

There is no wisdom in useless and hopeless sorrow.
Samuel Johnson

Believe me, every man has his secret sorrows, which the world knows not; and oftentimes we call a man cold, when he is only sad.
Henry Wadsworth Longfellow

The first lesson of life is to burn our own smoke; that is, not to inflict on outsiders our personal sorrows and petty morbidness, not to keep thinking of ourselves as exceptional cases.
James Russell Lowell

Regret is an appalling waste of energy; you can't build on it, it's only good for wallowing in.
Katherine Mansfield

There are times when God asks nothing of his children except silence, patience, and tears.
C.S. Robinson

There's such a charm in melancholy I would not, if I could, be gay.
Samuel Rogers

What's gone and what's past help should be past grief.
William Shakespeare

If all men were to bring their miseries together in one place, most would be

glad to take each his own home again rather than take a portion out of the common stock.
Solon

Nature refuses to sympathize with our sorrow. She seems not to have provided for, but by a thousand contrivances against it. She has bevelled the margins of the eyelids that the tears may not overflow on the cheek.
Henry David Thoreau

Pure and complete sorrow is as impossible as pure and complete joy.
Leo Tolstoy

Half of the secular unrest and dismal, profane sadness of modern society comes from the vain idea that every man is bound to be a critic of life.
Henry van Dyke

'Tis impious in a good man to be sad.
Edward Young

SOUL

The athletic fool, to whom what heaven denied of soul, is well compensated in limbs.
John Armstrong

There seems to be an unalterable contradiction between the human mind and its employments. How can a soul be a merchant? What relation to an immortal being have the price of linseed, the brokerage on hemp? Can an undying creature debit petty expenses and charge for carriage paid? The soul ties its shoes; the mind washes its hands in a basin. All is incongruous.
Walter Bagehot

Every human soul is of infinite value, eternal, free; no human being, therefore, is so placed as not to have within

his reach, in himself and others, objects adequate to infinite endeavor.
Lord Balfour

Our bodies are where we stay; Our souls are what we are.
Cecil Baxter

Even in the meanest sorts of labor, the whole soul of a man is composed into a kind of real harmony the instant he sets himself to work.
Norman Carlisle

No iron chain, or outward force of any kind, could ever compel the soul of man to believe or disbelieve.
Thomas Carlyle

You will do the greatest service to the state if you shall raise, not the roofs of the houses, but the souls of the citizens: for it is better that great souls should dwell in small houses rather than for mean slaves to lurk in great houses.
Epictetus

I believe that man will not merely endure, he will prevail. He is immortal not because he alone among creatures has an inexhaustible voice, but because he has a soul.
William Faulkner

Man is so made that when anything fires his soul impossibilities vanish.
Jean de La Fontaine

Food may be essential as fuel for the body, but good food is fuel for the soul.
Malcolm Forbes

I am fully convinced that the soul is indestructible, and that its activity will continue through eternity. It is like the sun, which, to our eyes, seems to set in night; but it has in reality only gone to diffuse its light elsewhere.
Johann Wolfgang von Goethe

Governments know that the life of the world cannot be saved if the soul of the world is allowed to be lost.
Herbert Hoover

The soul's maladies have their relapses like the body's. What we take for a cure is often just a momentary rally or a new form of the disease.
François de La Rochefoucauld

Years may wrinkle the skin, but to give up interest wrinkles the soul.
Douglas MacArthur

What lies behind us and what lies before us are tiny matters compared to what lies within us.
William Morrow

It is not the eye that sees the beauty of the heaven, nor the ear that hears the sweetness of music or the glad tidings of a prosperous occurrence, but the soul, that perceives all the relishes of intellectual perfection.
Jeremy Taylor

Money is not required to buy one necessity of the soul.
Henry David Thoreau

It seems to me that the soul, when alone with itself and speaking to itself, uses only a small number of words, none of them extraordinary.
Paul Valéry

SPEAKING

The basic rule of human nature is that powerful people speak slowly and subservient people quickly, because if they don't speak fast nobody will listen to them.
Michael Caine

The short words are best, and the old words are the best of all.
Winston Churchill

I love quotations because it is a joy to find thoughts one might have, beautifully expressed with much authority by someone recognizably wiser than oneself.
Marlene Dietrich

Let thy speech be better than silence, or be silent.
Dionysius the Elder

I hate quotations. Tell me what you know.
Ralph Waldo Emerson

What you do speaks so loudly that I cannot hear what you say.
Ralph Waldo Emerson

The opposite of talking isn't listening. The opposite of talking is waiting.
Fran Lebowitz

I wish people who have trouble communicating would just shut up.
Tom Lehrer

There are very few people who don't become more interesting when they stop talking.
Mary Lowry

Get out of here and leave me alone. Last words are for fools who haven't said enough already.
Karl Marx

It is not of so much consequence what you say, as how you say it. Memorable sentences are memorable on account of some single irradiating word.
Alexander Smith

There are three things that ought to be considered before some things are

spoken: the manner, the place and the time.
Robert Southey

It is the first rule of oratory that a man must appear such as he would persuade others to be; and that can be accomplished only by the force of his life.
Jonathan Swift

Nature, which gave us two eyes to see and two ears to hear, has given us but one tongue to speak.
Jonathan Swift

Speech is the mirror of the soul; as a man speaks, so he is.
Publilius Syrus

It usually takes more than three weeks to prepare a good impromptu speech.
Mark Twain

There is much to be said for not saying much.
Frank Tyger

All pleasantry should be short; and it might even be as well were the serious short also.
Voltaire

In a free and republican government, you cannot restrain the voice of the multitude. Every man will speak as he thinks, or, more properly, without thinking, and consequently will judge of effects without attending to their causes.
George Washington

Every man is born with the faculty of reason and the faculty of speech, but why should he be able to speak before he has anything to say?
Benjamin Whichcote

I have always been among those who believed that the greatest freedom of speech was the greatest safety, because if a man is a fool the best thing to do is to encourage him to advertise the fact by speaking.
Woodrow Wilson

SPORTS

No athletes talk to themselves like tennis players. Pitchers, golfers, goalkeepers, they mutter to themselves, but tennis players talk to themselves and answer. Tennis players look like lunatics in a public square.
Andre Agassi

God does not charge time spent fishing against a man's allotted life span.
American Indian proverb

A detailed analysis of his four-putt at the 1986 Masters: I miss the putt. I miss the putt. I miss the putt. I make.
Seve Ballesteros

Curling is weird. You can be the world champion and go out there and lose to four guys in their 60s wearing galoshes.
Don Barcome, Jr.

I now realize that the small hills you see on ski slopes are formed around the bodies of 47-year-olds who tried to learn snowboarding.
Dave Barry

Skiing combines outdoor fun with knocking down trees with your face.
Dave Barry

The boys are so powerful off of the baseline now that they don't have to come to the net to finish points. That's the reason we went to the net. To finish the point.

Nowadays, even the big guys can hit winners four feet behind the baseline.
Boris Becker

Baseball: Almost the only place in life where a sacrifice is really appreciated.
Mark Beltaire

On shopping with Ron Guidry during spring training: He buys his roast beef, I buy my bottle of vodka. We get along real good.
Yogi Berra

Academy: A modern school where football is taught.
Ambrose Bierce

I do not participate in any sport with ambulances at the bottom of the hill.
Erma Bombeck

On Rafael Nadal: Every point he plays is like match point. That's why he's the champion right now.
Björn Borg

On Dwyane Wade turning 30: In NBA years that's like 90.
Chris Bosh

When you hang with a bunch of 300-pound linemen, you tend to find the places that are the greasiest and serve the most food.
Tom Brady

If God had meant Wimbledon to be played in great weather, he would have put it in Acapulco.
British tennis official

On coaching: I gave our guys every opportunity to call me an honest son of a bitch. Hockey players are going to call you a son of a bitch at times anyway, in emotion. But they could call me an honest one because everything was up front.
Herb Brooks

Tough words that presumably helped his U.S. hockey team win the 1980 Olympics: You're playing worse every day, and right now you're playing like the middle of next month.
Herb Brooks

On Charles Barkley's physique: What do I remember about Charles? His gluteus maximus. That's the Number 1 thing. That's the biggest gluteus maximus in the world. I didn't have enough gluteus maximus to defend him.
P.J. Brown

Sport is an international phenomenon, like science or music.
Avery Brundage

There's still room for flair and artistry and playing a game that's going to confuse people. Federer has proven that, time and time and time again. Even with the new string technology, which has been around for ten years.
Darren Cahill

In football the object is for the quarterback, also known as the field general, to be on target with his aerial assault, riddling the defense by hitting his receivers with deadly accuracy in spite of the blitz, even if he has to use the shotgun. With short bullet passes and long bombs, he marches his troops into enemy territory, balancing this aerial assault with a sustained ground attack that punches holes in the forward wall of the enemy's defensive line. In baseball the object is to go home! And to be safe! I hope I'll be safe at home!
George Carlin

On the issue of Virginia Rometty, CEO of IBM (a Masters sponsor), becoming Augusta's first female member: [Chairman] Billy Payne, with his history of inclusion and his role with the

Olympics, should finally take the plunge. This is a good opportunity for him to do it.
Marcia Chambers

The greatest hockey player who ever lived: Bobby Orr, and I love him.
Don Cherry

We have not made cricket and football [soccer] professional because of any astonishing avarice or new vulgarity. We have made them professional because we would have them perfect. We have dedicated men to them as to some god of inhuman excellence. We care more for football than for the fun of playing football.
G.K. Chesterton

Larry Bird just throws the ball in the air and God moves the basket underneath it.
Howie Chizek

Athletes have a certain stubbornness that carries us through and makes us do things that people say we can't do.
Kim Clijsters

I don't intend to die.
Jack Kent Cooke

On gender and the Super Bowl: Women are more measured and intellectual when it comes to betting. There are guys out there who throw down $5,000 on the game without checking the line first. You would almost never see that from a woman.
Terry Cox

On being Duke Snider's neighbor in Brooklyn: He would always tell us to keep out of trouble. We just got used to it. A friend of mine used to walk Pee Wee Reese's daughter to school. They were so unpretentious. Baseball was different then.
Florence Cozzolino

Hyping up the Super Bowl ads has gotten even more ridiculous than hyping up the game. Or maybe we should just start running a four-hour block of commercials with little snippets of football in between.
Ned Crowley

Every player should be accorded the privilege of at least one season with the Chicago Cubs. That's baseball as it should be played—in God's own sunshine.
Alvin Dark

The important thing in these Olympics is less to win than to take part. The important thing in life is not the victory but the contest; the essential thing is not to have won but to have fought well.
Pierre de Coubertin

If you don't break a bone you weren't trying hard enough.
Pip Decker's coach

Football is brutal only from a distance. In the middle of it there's a calm, a tranquility. The players accept pain. There's a sense of order even at the end of a running play with bodies strewn everywhere.
Don Delillo

On McIlroy: We had hoped to compare the young Northern Irishman to the great Masters champions but instead had to reach for the compendium of great golfing train wrecks.
Matt Dickinson

If God had wanted man to play soccer, He wouldn't have given us arms.
Mike Ditka

I never questioned the integrity of an umpire. His eyesight, yes.
Leo Duroche

So you wish to conquer in the Olympic Games? But first mark the conditions and the consequences. You will have to put yourself under discipline; to eat by the rule, to avoid cakes and sweetmeats; to take exercise at the appointed hour whether you like it or not, in cold and heat; to abstain from cold drinks and wine at your will; in a word, to give yourself over to the trainer as to a physician.
Epictetus

No way we thought about the gold medal. We figured the Soviets were gonna be the team and nobody was gonna beat them.
Mike Eruzione

On luring Japanese investors to bankroll the Tampa Bay Lightning: The more we drank, the more it made sense. I said, "Hockey." They thought I said, "Sake."
Phil Esposito

If you can react the same way to winning and losing, that's a big accomplishment. That quality is important because it stays with you the rest of your life, and there's going to be a life after tennis that's a lot longer than your tennis life.
Chris Evert

Federer's thoughts on the tweener: Please don't try this at home. I am a professional.
Roger Federer

If a manager of mine ever said someone was indispensable, I'd fire him.
Charlie Finley

Drivers go further than putters.
Malcolm Forbes

There's just no better way to see a game you really want to see than to watch it on TV from multiple angles, with close-ups and instant replay, too.
Malcolm Forbes

He who spends all his life in sport is like one who hears nothing but fringes and eats nothing but sauces.
Richard Fuller

Skiing is better than sex actually, because for me a good round of sex might be seven minutes. Skiing you can do for seven hours.
Spalding Gray

On Roger Federer's no-look, between-the-legs winner at the U.S. Open: This was definitely a wow moment for tennis players, not just for fans, and the scary part was that it looked like he actually knew where he was hitting it.
Tom Gullikson

On being victimized by Bobby Orr's famous "flying" goal to win the Stanley Cup in 1970: I always tell Bobby he was up in the air for so long that I had time to shower and change before he hit the ice.
Glenn Hall

On Michael Vick's $100 million contract: Everything's going good in his life. Can he continue to avoid the negativity, the dark side off the field? Because now this is where the pressure comes from friends, family members, people out in the street, people that he used to hang out with. They see $100 million.
Rodney Harrison

On today's athletes: I wish I could turn back the clock a little bit so I'd have a chance to cut it up with those guys.
Eric Heiden

Gentlemen, it is better to have died as a small boy than to fumble this football.
John Heisman

Bullfighting is the only art in which the artist is in danger of death and in which

the degree of brilliance in the performance is left to the fighter's honor.
Ernest Hemingway

Father always emphasized being a good sportsman. Lose as if you like it, and win as if you were used to it.
Thomas Hitchcock

On the New England Patriots losing the Super Bowl after going 18–0: We set high expectations, now we go down as 18–1, and that is one big zit. It is one big blemish. We choked.
Ellis Hobbs

I have a lifetime contract. That means I can't be fired during the third quarter if we are ahead and moving the ball.
Lou Holtz

The Lord does not deduct from the hours of man those spent in fishing.
Herbert Hoover

On working for his father: I got fired many, many times.
Jim Irsay (son of Robert Irsay)

On former Colts owner Robert Irsay: He's a devil on earth, that one. He was no good. He was a bad boy. I don't want to talk about him.
Robert Irsay's mother

Football is easy if you're crazy as hell.
Bo Jackson

If every college football team had a linebacker like Dick Butkus, all fullbacks would soon be 3 feet tall and sing soprano. Dick Butkus is a special kind of brute whose particular talent is mashing runners into curious shapes.
Dan Jenkins

It is unbecoming for a cardinal to ski badly.
Pope John Paul II

When the new schedule would come out each year, I'd grab it and circle the Boston games. To me, it was The Two and the other 80.
Magic Johnson

He lied and he cheated and he was rude and he was crude and he was Bob Irsay.
Bert Jones

In Chicago, we had to be to the stadium at 6 o'clock for home games, and traffic was so bad it would take us an hour and 15 or an hour and 30 minutes to drive. So now I'm sitting in a car for almost an hour and a half, and I'm very tense. I'm worried about the traffic. So I started smoking a cigar going to the games in 1993. It became a ritual for every home game.
Michael Jordan

I've missed more than 9,000 shots in my career. I've lost almost 300 games. Twenty-six times I've been trusted to take the gamewinning shot and missed. I've failed over and over and over again in my life. And that is why I succeed.
Michael Jordan

On his blown call that robbed Detroit Tigers pitcher Armando Galarraga of a perfect game: I didn't want my 15 minutes of fame to be this; I'd rather be known for a great call at the World Series. I hope my 15 minutes are over.
Jim Joyce, umpire

Two things only the people anxiously desire, bread and the Circus games.
Juvenal

Tennis and golf are best played, not watched.
Roger Kahn

Football today is far too much a sport for the few who can play it well; the rest of us, and too many of our children, get

our exercise from climbing up the seats in stadiums, or from walking across the room to turn on our television sets.
John F. Kennedy

We are inclined to think that if we watch a football game or a baseball game, we have taken part in it.
John F. Kennedy

Football players, like prostitutes, are in the business of ruining their bodies for the pleasure of strangers.
Merle Kessler

Tennis is a perfect combination of violent action taking place in an atmosphere of total tranquility.
Billie Jean King

Football allows the intellectual part of my brain to evolve, but it allows the emotional part to remain unchanged.
Chuck Klosterman

On accusations that football legend and gourmand Abe Gibron was spying: If we were to send a spy, I would think we would be a little more discreet about it. We had to get Abe two seats in the press box. He took up two spaces. We got him two trays of food, so you could hardly say he was not noticeable.
Chuck Knox

On Vegas football betting: A lot of the movement is dictated by the sharps, the professionals, the wise guys—the sophisticated bettors who go with the bigger amounts. They know the value of point spread, while the average Joe just picks who he thinks is the better team.
Jay Kornegay, bookmaker

Rodeoing is about the only sport you can't fix. You'd have to talk to the bulls and horses, and they wouldn't understand you.
Bill Linderman

When he says "Sit down!" I don't even look for a chair.
Player (about Vince Lombardi)

On Lamar Hunt: When you walked in a room and you saw him and saw he was a part of something, you knew it was something that was branded with integrity and solid and something you could stand behind.
Robert Kraft

I walk into the clubhouse, and it's like walking into the Mayo Clinic. We have four doctors, three therapists and five trainers. Back when I broke in, we had one trainer who carried a bottle of rubbing alcohol and by the seventh inning he had drunk it all.
Tommy Lasorda

Hockey captures the essence of Canadian experience in the New World. In a land so inescapably and inhospitably cold, hockey is the chance of life, and an affirmation that despite the deathly chill of winter we are alive.
Stephen Leacock

I've come to the conclusion that the two most important things in life are good friends and a good bullpen.
Bob Lemon

I told my team that this would be my last ride. And I told them I was just at so much peace in where I am with my decision because of everything that I've done in this league. I've done it, I've done it, man.
Ray Lewis

On abusive Florentine soccer fans (quoted in 1998): They were rude about my mother, the poor woman, who is from Florence. But I do think they could leave my father alone. He died six years ago.
Marcello Lippi

Football is only two things: blocking and tackling.
Vince Lombardi

On football sandals and his improper behavior as a booster in the 1980s: Every college has a bunch of fools that are willing to go out and break the rules. Unfortunately, I was one of them. I got utterly frustrated with S.M.U. and other schools beating us. It not only was wrong morally. It was stupid. That dog's dead.
Dick Lowe, Texas Christian U. alumnus

Conventional wisdom notwithstanding, there is no reason either in football or in poetry why the two should not meet in a man's life if he has the weight and cares about the words.
Archibald MacLeish

The fewer rules a coach has, the fewer rules there are for players to break.
John Madden

On the Yankees: New York City revived around the team. I don't think you can look at the recovery of New York from the 1970s without, on some level, talking about Steinbrenner. Even if you're just talking about the feel of the city, he was part of a creation of a new sense of optimism.
Jonathan Mahle

Duke was a fine man, a terrific hitter and a great friend, even though he was a Dodger.
Willie Mays

I don't have concussion problems. I have got a problem with people giving me traumatic blows to the head, that's what I have got a problem with.
Dean McAmmond

You get thrown off balance out there. And I never recovered. Well, I haven't recovered yet.
Rory McIlroy

I can't remember, even though this is a quarterback-driven league, as many remarkable and compelling stories on the quarterback side as you're seeing this year.
Sean McManus

There is nothing quite so limited as being a limited partner of George Steinbrenner's.
John McMullen

When you're rich you don't write checks.
Randy Moss

Wow, I'm tellin' ya, you quarterbacks—you get all the good-lookin' women.
Brent Musburger

Playing well or playing bad, I have to play aggressive. I must play aggressive.
Rafael Nadal

Till I was 13 I thought my name was "Shut Up."
Joe Namath

On Chris Evert: Before I even met her, she stood for everything I admired in this country: poise, ability, sportsmanship, money, style.
Martina Navratilova

On his collapse at the 1996 Masters: I screwed up. It's all on me. But losing this Masters is not the end of the world. I still have a pretty good life. I'll wake up tomorrow, still breathing, I hope.
Greg Norman

I started out as a football player. I liked to inflict pain. In basketball, it was the same thing.
Shaquille O'Neal

Olympics are probably the most important thing for Russians than any other athletes in the whole world. Since I was a little kid and since everybody was a little kid, their dream was playing in Olympic Games, especially if we have a chance to represent our country in Sochi, it's unbelievable and it's going to be a great thing.
Alex Ovechkin

I like linebackers. I collect 'em. You can't have too many good ones.
Bill Parcells

Some people call me the Kitchen, some call me the Dining Room and some call me the Cafeteria!
William (the Refrigerator) Perry

George [Steinbrenner] is a great guy, unless you have to work for him.
Lou Pinella

How would you like a job where, every time you make a mistake, a big red light goes on and 18,000 people boo?
Jacques Plante

What I always say is, "Look good, feel good, play good."
Ian Poulter

The football season is like pain. You forget how terrible it is until it seizes you again.
Sally Quinn

Hanging out with Derek Jeter sucks because all the women flock to him.
Tim Raines

Everywhere I go, people love me, so I'm just blessed. Do you blame them?
Manny Ramirez

Explaining why he shaved his mustache after the Mets' 2007 season-ending collapse: I tried to cut my throat, but I aimed too high.
Willie Randolph

You will be competing against athletes from many nations. But, most important, you are competing against yourself. All we expect is for you to do your very best, to push yourself just one second faster, one notch higher, one inch further.
Ronald Reagan

Temporary rules, 1940: In competitions, during gunfire or while bombs are falling, players may take cover without penalty for ceasing play.
Richmond (England) Golf Club

On Julius (Dr. J) Erving: There have been some better people off the court—like a few mothers and the Pope. But there was only one Dr. J the player.
Pat Riley

On Augusta's exclusive membership policy: It's a private club, and I don't think they're really concerned about how others perceive them. Their ratings will not rise and fall based on how people view this particular topic. Their ratings will rise and fall if Tiger Woods is at the top of his game, if Tiger and Phil Mickelson and Rory McIlroy or some combination of them happen to be in the mix on the final day of the tournament.
Patrick Rishe

It is at the University of Alabama where the doctrine of the Primacy of the Coach has perhaps its purest expression. There are people living right now whose given names are Bear and Saban, the way ancient Egyptian children were named after kings.
Campbell Robertson

On horse racing: There's ten disappointments to every one joy in the horse business.
Jesse Mack Robinson

Football is a game played with arms, legs and shoulders, but mostly from the neck up.
Knute Rockne

When you're having trouble and topping the ball, it means the ground is moving on you.
Chi Chi Rodriguez

CBS's halftime show during the 2004 Super Bowl was a new low for television.
Mike Rogers

In the NFL you get one first-round draft pick if you're lucky. You couldn't really outwork anybody else. In college I could recruit ten players with first-round talent every year.
Nick Saban

The secret of her success with tennis fans: I attract them because I'm beautiful.
Francesca Schiavone

If you're associated with the Philadelphia media or town, you look for negatives. I don't know if there's something about their upbringing or they have too many hoagies, or too much cream cheese.
Mike Schmidt

When a man wants to murder a tiger he calls it sport; when a tiger wants to murder him, he calls it ferocity.
George Bernard Shaw

I may have become a world champion quicker than most, but people should look at me and realize there are all kinds of ways to get where you want to go. Because we didn't plan it. We just did it.
Mikaela Shiffrin

Excessive golfing dwarfs the intellect. Nor is this to be wondered at when we consider that the more fatuously vacant the mind is, the better for play. It has been observed that absolute idiots play the steadiest.
Sir Walter Simpson

You do that, you go to the box, you know. Two minutes, by yourself, and you feel shame, you know. And then you get free.
Line from the movie *Slap Shot*

While in the city and its suburbs, I fed as if in danger of imminent execution. And I was able to confirm earlier reconnaissance: Vancouver is among the best eating towns in the history of the Winter Games.
Sam Sifton

If you can't beat 'em in the alley, you can't beat 'em on the ice.
Conn Smythe

I am absolutely desperate to win a Super Bowl.
Daniel Snyder

Sectional football games have the glory and the despair of war, and when a Texas team takes the field against a foreign state, it is an army with banners.
John Steinbeck

Winning is the most important thing in my life, after breathing. Breathing first, winning next.
George Steinbrenner

The Super Bowl is Americana at its most kitsch and fun.
Sting

On Nordic ski jumping: It terrifies me. Flying through the air at 100 kilometers per hour just seems silly.
Ryan St. Onge

I don't think I can take seriously any game that takes less than three days to reach its conclusion.
Tom Stoppard

I'm forever gonna miss the start to the finish, the rush of racing downhill.
Picabo Street

Most sorts of diversion in men, children and other animals are an imitation of fighting.
Jonathan Swift

Nobody in the game of football should be called a genius. A genius is somebody like Norman Einstein.
Joe Theismann

A serious football fan is never alone. We are legion, and football is often the only thing we have in common.
Hunter S. Thompson

We must have football. What would this country be without football in October?
Hunter S. Thompson

Mixed doubles strategy: Hit at the girl whenever possible.
Bill Tilden

Ideally, the umpire should have the integrity of a Supreme Court justice, the physical agility of an acrobat, the endurance of Job and the imperturbability of Buddha.
Time **Magazine**

American football is an occasion at which dancing girls, bands, tactical huddles and television commercial breaks are interrupted by short bursts of play.
Times of London

On training properly: I used to have a wild time with three women until 5 a.m., but I am getting older. In the Olympic Village here I will live it up with five women, but only until 3 a.m.
Alberto Tomba

If there is any justice in this world, to be a White Sox fan frees a man from any other form of penance.
Bill Veeck

I think my favorite sport in the Olympics is the one in which you make your way through the snow, you stop, you shoot a gun, and then you continue on. In most of the world it is known as the biathlon, except in New York City, where it is known as winter.
Michael Ventre

I see a lot of 32-, 33-year-olds talking about, "Oh my God, I'm tired today." That really pumps me up. Here you are at 43, trying to do the same, and you don't feel that kind of tiredness or soreness. It just makes you feel so good.
Omar Vizquel

I don't give up easily. I have plans to be around for a while.
Lindsey Vonn

On his wife Lindsey Vonn's skiing style: Her chin used to be in front of her tips every section of the course. It was only one gear—full out—but to have longevity in your career in ski racing, you have to know where to put the pedal to the metal and where to hit the brakes.
Thomas Vonn

I'm not surprised that Junior Seau and others have this evidence of brain damage. Junior just didn't report head injuries. If you did report stuff like that, next thing you know you're on waivers. I think they've basically just scratched the surface of a gigantic iceberg. They turned

a blind eye to this for so long, and now it's an avalanche.
Mark Walczak

On Steinbrenner and the Yankees: If things go right, they're his team. If things go wrong, they're your team.
Bob Watson

I knew there was a certain level that I could get to within the sporting world. But as I continued with my career, not only did I grow, but the sport grew. All of a sudden, all of these doors opened to me. It's been amazing. I guess I was born at the right time.
Shaun White

On snowboarding as an Olympic sport: Since I was 6 years old I've been in the mix and watching this grow and change. I never would have expected it to go this far.
Shaun White

On golfer Rory McIlroy's collapse in the final round of the Masters: McIlroy did not fade out of the contest. He crashed out of it, brakes gone and tires screeching, in a welter of debris.
Richard Williams

We're in a little bit of a boom right now. If those guys continue to develop, we'll have a period of time here, kind of a Camelot of quarterbacking.
Steve Young

On the death of George Steinbrenner: Baseball will miss him. He did a lot of great things and some not so great but it's a sad day for baseball, no doubt about it. He was a winner, and he made the Yankees a winner.
Don Zimmer

Willie, Duke and Mickey. They were great players in one city, one town. Duke never got the credit of being the outfielder that Mays and Mantle were. But Duke was a great outfielder. He was a great player.
Don Zimmer

STATESMAN

A disposition to preserve, and an ability to improve, taken together, would be my standard of a statesman.
Edmund Burke

The great difference between the real statesman and the pretender is, that the one sees into the future, while the other regards only the present; the one lives by the day, and acts on expedience; the other acts on enduring principles and for immortality.
Edmund Burke

The three great ends for a statesman are, security to possessors, facility to acquirers, and liberty and hope to the people.
Samuel Taylor Coleridge

Statesmen stand out because politicians are as alike as peas.
Arnold Glasow

The art of statesmanship is to foresee the inevitable and to expedite its occurrence.
Charles-Maurice de Talleyrand

A statesman is a politician who's been dead ten or 15 years.
Harry S Truman

STOCKS

Beware of barbers, beauticians, waiters— of anyone—bringing gifts of "inside" information or "tips." Don't try to buy at the bottom and sell at the top. This can't be done, except by liars.
Bernard M. Baruch

We've created more assets than there are hands to hold them. And we cannot all de-leverage at the same time.
David Beim

Nothing tells in the long run like a good judgment, and no sound judgment can remain with the man whose mind is disturbed by the mercurial changes of the stock exchange. It places him under an influence akin to intoxication. What is not, he sees, and what he sees, is not.
Andrew Carnegie

It would be heroic to jump in [to the stock market]. It would be unwise. You need to admit that these are unprecedented times.
Linda Duessel

High finance isn't burglary or obtaining money by false pretenses, but rather a judicious selection from the best features of those fine arts.
Finley Peter Dunne

Henry Ford has several times sneered at unproductive stockholders. . . . Well, now. Let's see. Who made Henry Ford's own automobile company possible? The stockholders who originally advanced money to him. Who makes it possible for you and me to be carried to and from business by train or street car? Stockholders. . . . Who made our vast telephone and telegraph service possible? Stockholders. . . . Were stockholders all over the country to withdraw their capital from the enterprises in which they are invested, there would be a panic . . . on a scale never before known.
B.C. Forbes

If I owned any of these Hot New Issues that have doubled, tripled, quintupled or umptupled within days and in some cases hours after they were issued, I most certainly would grab my fabulous windfall, thank my lucky stars and invest the money. It's utter nonsense to think any newly issued stock is really worth two, ten or 20 times the [offering] price. . . . A management so stupid as to sell shares [cheap], and an underwriter so obtuse as not to discern the real value, together would provide reason enough for a sensible man to get rid of his shares.
Malcolm Forbes

SM is an abbreviation of both stock market and sadomasochism—and there are those who think they are one and the same.
Malcolm Forbes

Only Americans have mastered the art of being prosperous though broke.
Kelly Fordyce

There are no new forms of financial fraud; in the last several hundred years, there have only been small variations on a few classic designs.
John Kenneth Galbraith

What made him get out of the market before the 2008 crash (he claims): There were billionaires who could not qualify for The Forbes 400. That was one of many warning signs for me to get out.
David Geffen

Any goodwill generated by successful IPOs in early 2012 has been quickly sucked up by the Facebook debacle.
Sam Hamadeh

It was beautiful and simple, as truly great swindles are.
O. Henry

If you can get an IPO, don't buy it. Only buy IPOs you can't get.
Vahan Janjigian

Wall Street is not a casino. The drinks are free in a casino.
Vahan Janjigian

The market is like a beautiful woman—always fascinating, always mystifying.
Edward Johnson III

People have little idea, by and large, of the investment world. They are convinced they have an advantage.
Daniel Kahneman

It's a startling and eye-opening fact that 70% of widows fire their financial advisors within one year of the death of their spouse. When it comes to satisfaction with a product or service, women rank the financial services industry at the bottom of nearly three dozen categories.
Kathleen Burns Kingsbury

The J.P. Morgan loss is manageable. But it allows us to stand back and ask: "What does this say about the banking system?" It appears the trades themselves were so complex that the risks were not well understood. The bank management didn't understand them. The regulators weren't aware of them. And the bank's risk management system didn't pick them up.
Sallie Krawcheck

On arbitragers: We are like a microbe. While the microbe attacks your body it has a wonderful time living, but it ends up killing your body and dies as a result. The arbitrager is exactly the same. When he sees a market inefficiency, he goes to it and makes it efficient. As a consequence, his profit margin disappears.
William Louis-Dreyfus

Never invest in any idea you can't illustrate with a crayon.
Peter Lynch

On the Facebook IPO flop: It's like someone threw a cherry bomb in the Jell-O bowl. Everyone looks bad.
Jamis MacNiven

In today's regulatory environment, it's virtually impossible to violate rules. It's impossible for a violation to go undetected, certainly not for a considerable period of time.
Bernie Madoff

Securitization is like fertilizer. You can grow tomatoes or blow up buildings.
Simon Mikhailovich

The year 1974 taught me that leverage can decimate even the best company when its access to capital is cut off. It also taught me that most people have short memories. That's why most financial people have five-year careers—one market cycle. All these geniuses who bought stock in the mid-1960s thought they had some divine touch and then it all stopped. It hadn't occurred to them that they looked good because virtually everything was going up. In 1983 Drexel published a paper called "The $55 Billion Misunderstanding." That's how much was lost by people following Nifty Fifty growth stocks. It was a trend, and trends end. People who remembered 1970, 1974 and 1981 made a lot of money in 1989 and 1990 buying good, interest-paying junk bonds when they were selling at 40, 50, 60 cents on the dollar, bonds that now sell at a premium.
Michael Milken (1992)

If you buy a few great companies you can sit on your ass.
Charles Munger

Wall Street is a roach walking around on a dinosaur. It's the symptom, not the disease.
Colin Negrych

Don't gamble! Take all your savings and buy some good stock and hold it till it goes up, then sell it. If it don't go up, don't buy it.
Will Rogers

Finance is the art of passing currency from hand to hand until it finally disappears.
Robert Sarnoff

It is not odd that the only generous person I ever knew, who had money to be generous with, should be a stockbroker?
Percy Bysshe Shelley

Unless the public understands why this happened, until it can identify the villains, you can't recover from it. If you don't have someone to blame, other than some schmucks with fancy bonuses, you won't have a recovery.
Michael Steinhardt

Sometimes your best investments are the ones you don't make.
Donald Trump

A recession is like an unfortunate love affair. It's a lot easier to talk your way in than it is to talk your way out.
Bill Vaughan

The only reason to invest in the market is because you think you know something others don't.
R. Foster Winans

STRENGTH

The quality of strength lined with tenderness is an unbeatable combination, as are intelligence and necessity when unblunted by formal education.
Maya Angelou

Look well into thyself; there is a source of strength which will always spring up if thou wilt always look there.
Marcus Aurelius Antoninus

Men seem neither to understand their riches nor their strength. Of the former they believe greater things than they should; of the latter, less.
Francis Bacon

In the assurance of strength there is strength; and they are the weakest, however strong, who have no faith in themselves or their powers.
Christian Bovée

The world abhors closeness, and all but admires extravagance; yet a slack hand shows weakness, and a tight hand strength.
Sir Thomas Buxton

At times to think of one's outer helplessness is good, but to think always of one's inner strength is infinitely better.
Sri Chinmoy

Live in terms of your strong points. Magnify them. Let your weaknesses shrivel up and die from lack of nourishment.
William Young Elliott

The opinion of the strongest is always the best.
Jean de La Fontaine

The difference between towering and cowering is totally a matter of inner posture.
Malcolm Forbes

Only a strong tree can stand alone.
Arnold Glasow

There is nothing magnanimous in bearing misfortunes with fortitude, when the whole world is looking on. . . . He who,

without friends to encourage or even without hope to alleviate his misfortunes, can behave with tranquility and indifference, is truly great.
Oliver Goldsmith

Give us the fortitude to endure the things which cannot be changed, and the courage to change the things which should be changed, and the wisdom to know one from the other.
Oliver J. Hart

These three things deplete man's strength: fear, travel and sin.
Hebrew proverb

Fortitude: That quality of mind which does not care what happens so long as it does not happen to us.
Elbert Hubbard

Know how sublime a thing it is to suffer and be strong.
Henry Wadsworth Longfellow

That cause is strong which has, not a multitude, but one strong man behind it.
James Russell Lowell

A living being seeks, above all, to discharge its strength. Life is will to power.
Freidrich Wilhelm Nietzsche

Anyone who proposes to do good must not expect people to roll stones out of his way, but must accept his lot calmly if they even roll a few more on it. A strength which becomes clearer and stronger through experiences of such obstacles is the only strength that can conquer them. Resistance is only a waste of strength.
Albert Schweitzer

He who has injured thee was either stronger or weaker than thee. If weaker, spare him; if stronger, spare thyself.
Seneca

Oh! it is excellent to have a giant's strength; but it is tyrannous to use it like a giant.
William Shakespeare

Whatever strengthens and purifies the affections, enlarges the imagination, and adds spirit to sense, is useful.
Percy Bysshe Shelley

Nothing is so strong as gentleness, and nothing is so gentle as real strength.
Ralph Sockman

Whatever increases the strength and authority of your body over your mind, that is sin to you, however, innocent it may be in itself.
Robert Southey

Strength alone knows conflict; weakness is below even defeat, and is born vanquished.
Anne Sophie Swetchine

Although men are accused of not knowing their own weakness, yet perhaps few know their own strength. It is in men as in soils, where sometimes there is a vein of gold which the owner knows not of.
Jonathan Swift

No rock so hard but that a little wave may beat admission in a thousand years.
Alfred, Lord Tennyson

STUDY

Concentration is my motto—first honesty, then industry, then concentration.
Andrew Carnegie

Concentration is the secret of strength in politics, in war, in trade, in short in all management of human affairs.
Ralph Waldo Emerson

Concentrate on your job and you will forget your other troubles.
William Feather

The love of study, a passion which derives fresh vigor from enjoyment, supplies each day and hour with a perpetual source of independent and rational pleasure.
Edward Gibbon

The use of a thing is only a part of its significance. To know anything thoroughly, to have the full command of it in all its appliances, we must study it on its own account, independently of any special application.
Johann Wolfgang von Goethe

I will study and get ready and someday my chance will come.
Abraham Lincoln

If the study to which you apply yourself has a tendency to weaken your affection, and to destroy your taste for those simple pleasures in which no alloy can possibly mix, then that study is certainly unlawful, that is to say, not befitting the human mind.
Mary Shelley

STUPIDITY

Never ascribe to malice what can perfectly well be explained by stupidity.
Anonymous

The two most common elements in the world are hydrogen and stupidity.
Anonymous

Obstinacy and vehemency in opinion are the surest proof of stupidity.
Bernard Barton

There must always be some who are brighter and some who are stupider. The latter make up for it by being better workers.
Bertolt Brecht

The dumbest people I know are those who Know It All.
Malcolm Forbes

There is no stupid work, there are only stupid people.
French proverb

The hardest thing to cope with is not selfishness or vanity or deceitfulness, but sheer stupidity.
Eric Hoffer

Genius may have its limitations, but stupidity is not thus handicapped.
Elbert Hubbard

He that reads and grows no wiser seldom suspects his own deficiency, but complains of hard words and obscure sentences, and asks why books are written which cannot be understood.
Samuel Johnson

Stupidity is an elemental force for which no earthquake is a match.
Karl Kraus

The trouble with the world is that the stupid are cocksure and the intelligent full of doubt.
Bertrand Russell

Tell a man something is bad, and he's not at all sure he wants to give it up. Describe it as stupid, and he knows it's the better part of caution to listen.
David Seabury

The great mistake made by intelligent people is to refuse to believe that the world is as stupid as it is.
Madame de Tencin

Strange as it may seem, no amount of learning can cure stupidity, and formal education positively fortifies it.
Stephen Vizinczey

There is no sin except stupidity.
Oscar Wilde

Whenever a man does a thoroughly stupid thing it is always from the noblest motive.
Oscar Wilde

SUCCESS

The penalty of success is to be bored by the people who used to snub you.
Nancy Astor

There is no such thing as a self-made man. We are made up of thousands of others. Every one who has ever done a kind deed for us, or spoken one word of encouragement to us, has entered into the make-up of our character and of our thoughts, as well as our success.
George Matthew Adams

Tis not in mortals to command success, but we'll do more, Sempronius, we'll deserve it.
Joseph Addison

We mount to heaven mostly on the ruins of our cherished schemes, finding our failures were successes.
Amos Bronson Alcott

Distinction is the consequence, never the object, of a great mind.
Washington Allston

All men seek one goal: success or happiness. The only way to achieve true success is to express yourself completely in service to society. First, have a definite, clear, practical ideal—a goal, an objective. Second, have the necessary means to achieve your ends—wisdom, money, materials and methods. Third, adjust all your means to that end.
Aristotle

For success, attitude is equally as important as ability.
Harry F. Banks

Recipe for success: Be polite, prepare yourself for whatever you are asked to do, keep yourself tidy, be cheerful, don't be envious, be honest with yourself so you will be honest with others, be helpful, interest yourself in your job, don't pity yourself, be quick to praise, be loyal to your friends, avoid prejudices, be independent, interest yourself in politics, and read the newspapers.
Bernard M. Baruch

There is a certain cowardice, a certain weakness, rather, among respectable folk. Only brigands are convinced—of what? That they must succeed. And so they do succeed.
Charles Baudelaire

Success is full of promise till men get it; and then it is a last-year's nest from which the birds have flown.
Henry Ward Beecher

The toughest thing about success is that you've got to keep on being a success. Talent is only a starting point in business. You've got to keep working that talent.
Irving Berlin

Success is the one unpardonable sin against one's fellows.
Ambrose Bierce

Never mind what others do; do better than yourself, beat your own record from day to day, and you are a success.
William J.H. Boetcker

The victory of success is half won when one gains the habit of work.
Sarah K. Bolton

I believe the true road to preeminent success in any line is to make yourself master of that line.
Andrew Carnegie

True success is the only thing that you cannot have unless and until you have offered it to others.
Sri Chinmoy

By different methods different men excel, but where is he who can do all things well?
Charles Churchill

To know a man, observe how he wins his object, rather than how he loses it; for when we fail, our pride supports; when we succeed, it betrays us.
Charles Caleb Colton

The superior man makes the difficulty to be overcome his first interest; success comes only later.
Confucius

And every man that striveth for the mastery is temperate in all things. Now they do it to obtain a corruptible crown; but we an incorruptible
I Corinthians 9:25

You do not succeed because you do not know what you want, or you don't want it intensely enough.
Frank Crane

Being called very, very difficult is the beginning of success. Until you're called very, very difficult you're really nobody at all.
Bette Davis

Real success is not on the stage, but off the stage as a human being, and how you get along with your fellow men.
Sammy Davis, Jr.

Success unshared is total failure.
John Paul DeJoria

Success is counted sweetest by those who ne'er succeed.
Emily Dickinson

I have begun several times many things, and I have often succeeded at last.
Benjamin Disraeli

Success is the child of audacity.
Benjamin Disraeli

Be awful nice to 'em goin' up, because you're gonna meet 'em all comin' down.
Jimmy Durante

The best augury of a man's success in his profession is that he thinks it is the finest in the world.
George Eliot

Success is relative: It is what we can make of the mess we have made of things.
T.S. Eliot

I have had all the disadvantages required for success.
Larry Ellison

I look on that man as happy, who, when there is a question of success, looks into his work for a reply.
Ralph Waldo Emerson

The line between failure and success is so fine that we scarcely know when we pass it—so fine that we often are on the line and do not know it.
Ralph Waldo Emerson

The secret of success in society is a certain heartiness and sympathy. A man who is not happy in company cannot find any word in his memory that will fit the occasion; all his information is a little impertinent. A man who is happy there, finds in every turn of the conversation occasions for the introduction of what he has to say. The favorites of society are able men, and of more spirit than wit, who have no uncomfortable egotism, but who exactly fill the hour and the company, contended and contenting.
Ralph Waldo Emerson

To laugh often and much: To win the respect of intelligent people and the affection of children, to earn the appreciation of honest critics and endure the betrayal of false friends; to appreciate beauty, to find the best in others, to leave the world a bit better whether by a healthy child, a garden patch, or a redeemed social condition; to know even one life has breathed easier because you lived. This is to have succeeded.
Ralph Waldo Emerson

Along with success comes a reputation for wisdom.
Euripides

He that succeeds makes an important thing of the immediate task.
William Feather

Call the roll in your memory of conspicuously successful [business] giants and, if you know anything about their careers, you will be struck by the fact that almost every one of them encountered inordinate difficulties sufficient to crush all but the gamest of spirits. Edison went hungry many times before he became famous.
B.C. Forbes

For my part, I rather distrust men or concerns that rise up with the speed of rockets. Sudden rises are sometimes followed by equally sudden falls. I have most faith in the individual or enterprise that advances step by step. A mushroom can spring up in a day; an oak takes 50 years or more to reach maturity. Mushrooms don't last; oaks do. The real cause for an enormous number of business failures is premature over-expansion, attempting to gallop before learning to creep. Sudden successes often invite sudden reverses.
B.C. Forbes

Madame Curie didn't stumble upon radium by accident. She searched and experimented and sweated and suffered years before she found it. Success rarely is an accident.
B.C. Forbes

Success is finding, or making, that position which enables you to contribute to the world the very greatest services of which you are capable, through the diligent, persevering, resolute cultivation of all the faculties God has endowed you with, and doing it all with cheerfulness, scorning to allow difficulties or defeats to drive you to pessimism or despair. Success consists of being and doing, not simply accumulating. The businessman or business enterprise that aspires to win the highest recognition for success must distinguish himself or itself, not by the magnitude of the profits, but by the value of service performed.
B.C. Forbes

The fittest, not the richest, make the most enviable mark. Pampered sons of plutocrats may shine for a time in society, but not in the world of affairs and of service unless they rip off their coats and get to work early and stay late. To be born with a golden spoon in the mouth is more of a

handicap than a help in attaining worthwhile success in this age.
B.C. Forbes

There is more genuine joy in climbing
the hill of success, even though sweat
may be spent and toes may be stubbed,
than in aimlessly sliding down the path
to failure. If a straight, honorable path
has been chosen, the gaining of the
summit yields lasting satisfaction. The
morass of failure, if reached through
laziness, indifference or other avoidable
fault, yields nothing but ignominy and
sorrow for self and family and friends.
B.C. Forbes

Nothing recedes like success.
Bryan Forbes

Try hard enough.
Malcolm Forbes

In a commencement address: The only
advice I can think of that's of any value
to anybody that is eager to have success—
whatever that means in life—is to do
what turns you on. If you're not doing
something that's got you all, got you all
wrapped up, you just can't do it well.
You're going to lay an egg.
Malcolm Forbes (1988)

You have to come up in the world before
it's worthwhile for those worth less to
put you down.
Malcolm Forbes

If there is any great secret of success in
life, it lies in the ability to put yourself in
the other person's place and to see things
from his point of view—as well as your
own.
Henry Ford

Success has ruin'd many a man.
Benjamin Franklin

It's fine to celebrate success, but it's
more important to heed the lessons of
failure.
Bill Gates

Formula for success: Rise early, work
hard, strike oil.
J. Paul Getty

Success is simple. Do what's right, the
right way, at the right time.
Arnold Glasow

Men are so constituted that every
one undertakes what he sees another
successful in, whether he has aptitude
for it or not.
Johann Wolfgang von Goethe

Success rarely brings satisfaction.
Baltasar Gracián

Take care to make things turn out well.
Some people scruple more over pointing
things in the right direction than over
successfully reaching their goals. The
disgrace of failure outweighs the diligence they showed. A winner is never
asked for explanations.
Baltasar Gracián

The way to secure success is to be more
anxious about obtaining than about
deserving it.
William Hazlitt

Failure can be bought on easy terms;
success must be paid for in advance.
Cullen Hightower

Pray that success will not come any
faster than you are able to endure it.
Elbert Hubbard

The moral flabbiness born of the exclusive worship of the bitch-goddess

SUCCESS. That—with the squalid cash interpretation put on the word success—is our national disease.
William James

It turned out that getting fired from Apple was the best thing that could have ever happened to me. The heaviness of being successful was replaced by the lightness of being a beginner again.
Steve Jobs

This book of the law shall not depart out of thy mouth; but thou shalt meditate therein day and night, that thou mayest observe to do according to all that is written therein: for then thou shalt make thy way prosperous, and then thou shalt have good success.
Joshua 1:8

What separates a winner from a loser at the grandmaster level is the willingness to do the unthinkable. A brilliant strategy is, certainly, a matter of intelligence, but intelligence without audaciousness is not enough. I must have the guts to explode the game, to upend my opponent's thinking and, in so doing, unnerve him.
Garry Kasparov

You sit at the board and suddenly your heart leaps. Your hand trembles to pick up the piece and move it. But what chess teaches you is that you must sit there calmly and think about whether it's really a good idea and whether there are other, better ideas.
Stanley Kubrick

Success didn't spoil me; I've always been insufferable.
Fran Lebowitz

We can't take our eye off the ball, because if we lose it, we'll have a bitch of a time getting it back.
Philip Knight

The talent of success is nothing more than doing what you can do well and doing well whatever you do without thought of fame.
Henry Wadsworth Longfellow

The successful people are the ones who can think up stuff for the rest of the world to keep busy at.
Don Marquis

Only a mediocre person is always at his best.
Somerset Maugham

The common idea that success spoils people by making them vain, egotistic and self-complacent is erroneous; on the contrary, it makes them for the most part, humble, tolerant and kind. Failure makes people cruel and bitter.
Somerset Maugham

The secret of success in life is known only to those who have not succeeded.
Michel de Montaigne

The essence of success is that it is never necessary to think of a new idea. It is far better to wait until somebody else does it, and then to copy him in every detail except his mistakes.
Aubrey Menen

I have always observed that to succeed in the world one should appear like a fool but be wise.
Montesquieu

In most things success depends on knowing how long it takes to succeed.
Montesquieu

When I might have been a college freshman, I had already found oil, had 40 employees, owed $100,000. Being a freshman didn't appeal to me.
Charles Haywood Murphy, Jr.

I'll play some of these really crazy moves that people are not going to be expecting. The way I play is not like most people. The moves are more computeresque. They're not the moves that most humans are going to play.
Hikaru Nakamura

Either attempt it not, or succeed.
Ovid

These three things—work, will, success—fill human existences. Will opens the door to success, both brilliant and happy. Work passes these doors, and at the end of the journey success comes in to crown one's efforts.
Louis Pasteur

Success in business does not depend upon genius. Any young man of ordinary intelligence who is normally sound and not afraid to work should succeed in spite of obstacles and handicaps if he plays the game fairly and keeps everlastingly at it.
J.C. Penney

Success is dangerous. One begins to copy oneself, and to copy oneself is more dangerous than to copy others. It leads to sterility.
Pablo Picasso

What have appeared to be the most striking successes have often, if they are not rightly used, brought the most overwhelming disasters in their train, and conversely the most terrible calamities have, if bravely endured, actually turned out to benefit the sufferers.
Polybius

Rest satisfied with doing well, and leave others to talk of you as they please.
Pythagoras

On the clarity of your ideas depends the scope of your success in any endeavor.
James Robertson

If you want to succeed you should strike out on new paths rather than travel the worn paths of accepted success.
John D. Rockefeller

The most important single ingredient in the formula of success is knowing how to get along with people.
Theodore Roosevelt

The Great don't innovate, they fertilize seeds planted by lackeys, then leave to others the inhaling of the flowers whose roots they've manured.
Ned Rorem

Unless a man has been taught what to do with success after getting it, the achievement of it must inevitably leave him prey to boredom.
Bertrand Russell

In my mind, talent plus knowledge, plus effort account for success.
Gertrude Samuels

Stay true to what you believe and work at it relentlessly. From my first paper route to running a multibillion-dollar company, my success has been driven by working hard.
Richard Schulze

The best place to succeed is where you are with what you have.
Charles M. Schwab

His head was turned by too great success.
Seneca

The conditions of conquest are always easy. We have but to toil awhile, endure awhile, believe always, and never turn back.
Seneca

Success does not consist in never making blunders, but in never making the same one the second time.
Henry Wheeler Shaw

Faith in your own powers and confidence in your individual methods are essential to success.
Roderick Stevens

The higher a monkey climbs, the more you see of its behind.
Gen. Joseph "Vinegar Joe" Stillwell

One only gets to the top rung on the ladder by steadily climbing up one at a time, and suddenly all sorts of powers, all sort of abilities which you thought never belonged to you—suddenly become within your own possibility and you think, Well, I'll have a go, too.
Margaret Thatcher

Men are born to succeed—not to fail.
Henry David Thoreau

Success usually comes to those who are too busy to be looking for it.
Henry David Thoreau

The life which men praise and regard as successful is but one kind. Why should we exaggerate any one kind at the expense of the others?
Henry David Thoreau

People get frightened that success is going to take them out of life. They're no longer going to be on the corner of Bedlam and Squalor; life will only be something you can get through the mail.
Tom Waits

I have learned that success is to be measured not so much by the position that one has reached in life as by the obstacles which he has overcome while trying to succeed.
Booker T. Washington

When a man does all he can, though it succeeds not well, blame not him that did it.
George Washington

Who never climbs as rarely falls.
John Greenleaf Whittier

SUFFERING

Our real blessings often appear to us in the shape of pains, losses and disappointments; but let us have patience, and we soon shall see them in their proper figures.
Joseph Addison

Take heart. Suffering, when it climbs the highest, lasts but a little time.
Aeschylus

Suffering becomes beautiful when anyone bears great calamities with cheerfulness, not through insensibility but through greatness of mind.
Aristotle

The wise man does not expose himself needlessly to danger, since there are few things for which he cares sufficiently; but he is willing, in great crises to give even his life—knowing that under certain conditions it is not worthwhile to live.
Aristotle

The important thing is this: to be able at any moment to sacrifice what we are for what we could become.
Charles Du Bos

To make sacrifices in big things is easy, but to make sacrifices in little things is what we are seldom capable of.
Johann Wolfgang von Goethe

To suffer and to endure is the lot of humanity.
Pope Leo XIII

It is not true that suffering ennobles the character; happiness does that sometimes, but suffering for the most part makes men petty and vindictive.
Somerset Maugham

We must learn to suffer what we cannot evade; our life, like the harmony of the world, is composed of contrary things, and one part is no less necessary than the other.
Michel de Montaigne

Distrust all in whom the impulse to punish is powerful.
Friedrich Wilhelm Nietzsche

Every step forward is made at the cost of mental and physical pain to someone.
Friedrich Wilhelm Nietzsche

What really makes one indignant about suffering isn't the thing itself but the senselessness of it.
Friedrich Wilhelm Nietzsche

It stands to reason that where there's sacrifice, there's someone collecting sacrificial offerings. Where there is service, there is someone being served. The man who speaks to you of sacrifice speaks of slaves and masters. And intends to be master.
Ayn Rand

He jests at scars that never felt a wound.
William Shakespeare

Count no mortal fortunate till he has departed this life free from pain.
Sophocles

SUPERIORITY

I love being superior to myself better than [to] my equals.
Samuel Taylor Coleridge

The superior man is slow in his words and earnest in his conduct.
Confucius

The way of a superior man is threefold: virtuous, he is free from anxieties; wise, he is free from perplexities; bold, he is free from fear.
Confucius

There is no such thing as human superiority.
Dwight D. Eisenhower

Superiority is always detested.
Baltasar Gracián

People who look down on other people don't end up being looked up to.
Robert Half

There was one who thought he was above me, and he was above me until he had that thought.
Elbert Hubbard

The superior man is the providence of the inferior. He is eyes for the blind, strength for the weak, and a shield for the defenseless. He stands erect by bending above the fallen. He rises by lifting others.
Robert Ingersoll

The superior man is he who develops, in harmonious proportions, his moral, intellectual and physical nature.
Douglas William Jerrold

The superiority of some men is merely local. They are great because their associates are little.
Samuel Johnson

I caught sight of a haze upon his face—of that mist which arises invariably from the blissful feeling that one is superior to others.
Georg C. Lichtenberg

STYLE

Of all the things you wear, your expression is the most important.
Anonymous

Style is always in fashion.
Wilma Askinas

Fashions are born and they die too quickly for anyone to learn to love them.
Bettina Ballard

What is exhilarating in bad taste is the aristocratic pleasure of giving offense.
Charles Baudelaire

When in doubt, wear red.
Bill Blass

If alcohol is queen, then tobacco is her consort. It's a fond companion for all occasions, a loyal friend through fair weather and foul. People smoke to celebrate a happy moment, or to hide a bitter regret. Whether you're alone or with friends, it's a joy for all the senses.
Luis Buñuel

A big cigar in a young face requires the best of both.
Malcolm Forbes

A pipe for the hour of work; a cigarette for the hour of conception; a cigar for the hour of vacuity.
George Gissing

You are only as good as the people you dress.
Halston

In matters of style, swim with the current. In matters of principle, stand like a rock.
Thomas Jefferson

Only the minute and the future are interesting in fashion—it exists to be destroyed. If everybody did everything with respect, you'd go nowhere.
Karl Lagerfeld

In my estimation, the only thing that is more to be guarded against than bad taste is good taste.
Russell Lynes

I wish I had invented blue jeans. They have expression, modesty, sex appeal, simplicity, all I hope for in my clothes.
Yves Saint Laurent

Cuban cigars are an acquired taste, like Scotch whisky. If you're not used to them, you'll get a headache, you'll find them much too strong. But to a cigar connoisseur, a longtime smoker, if you have a well-made, well-aged one, there is nothing like a Cuban cigar. Getting them is the ultimate mission; any cigar lover would do anything.
Marvin R. Shanken

To call a fashion wearable is the kiss of death. No new fashion worth its salt is ever wearable.
Eugenia Sheppard

Taste has no system and no proofs.
Susan Sontag

Being a sex symbol has to do with an attitude, not looks. Most men think it's looks; most women know otherwise.
Kathleen Turner

Blue jeans are the most beautiful things since the gondola.
Diana Vreeland

T

TALENT

The English instinctively admire any man who has no talent and is modest about it.
James Agee

To do easily what is difficult for others is the mark of talent.
Henry Frédéric Amiel

It takes little talent to see what lies under one's nose, a good deal to know in what direction to point that organ.
W.H. Auden

Genius is the gold in the mine; talent is the miner that works and brings it out.
Lady Marguerite Blessington

Everyone has talent at 25. The difficulty is to have it at 50.
Edgar Degas

It always seemed to me a sort of clever stupidity only to have one sort of talent— like a carrier pigeon.
George Eliot

No one respects a talent that is concealed.
Erasmus

If a man can make typewriters better than anyone else, let us, in the name of common sense, keep him on the job of making typewriters.
William Feather

Hide not your talents, they for use were made.

What's a sundial in the shade?
Benjamin Franklin

If the power to do hard work is not talent, it is the best possible substitute for it.
James A. Garfield

Don't show off every day, or you'll stop surprising people. There must always be some novelty left over. The person who displays a little more of it each day keeps up expectations, and no one ever discovers the limits of his talent.
Baltasar Gracián

Talent does you no good unless it's recognized by someone else.
Robert Half

There must always be some advantage on one side or the other, and it is better that advantage should be had by talents than by chance.
Samuel Johnson

There are some bad qualities which make great talents.
François de La Rochefoucauld

Talent is that which is in a man's power; genius is that in whose power a man is.
James Russell Lowell

Each man has to seek out his own special aptitude for a higher life in the midst of the humble and inevitable reality of daily existance. Than this, there can be no nobler aim in life.
Maurice Maeterlinck

Hidden talent counts for nothing.
Nero

Shun no toil to make yourself remarkable by some one talent. Yet do not devote yourself to one branch exclusively. Strive to get clear notions about all. Give up no science entirely, for all science is one.
Seneca

If a man has a talent and cannot use it, he has failed. If he has a talent and uses only half of it, he has partly failed. If he has talent and learns somehow to use the whole of it, he has gloriously succeeded, and won a satisfaction and a triumph few men will ever know.
Thomas Wolfe

TALK

When I was born I was so surprised I didn't talk for a year and a half.
Gracie Allen

Conversation: Something that starts the moment you put your foot through the television set.
Anonymous

I think the first prerequisite to civilization is an ability to make polite conversation.
W.H. Auden

The habit of common and continuous speech is a symptom of mental deficiency. It proceeds from not knowing what is going on in other people's minds.
Walter Bagehot

Talk is cheap until you hire a lawyer.
P.T. Barnum

Anybody at all has the right to talk about himself—provided he knows how to be entertaining.
Charles Baudelaire

Civilized people can talk about anything. For them no subject is taboo. . . . In civilized societies there will be no intellectual bogeys at sight of which great grownup babies are expected to hide their eyes.
Clive Bell

Conversation: A fair for the display of the minor mental commodities, each exhibitor being too intent upon the arrangement of his own wares to observe those of his neighbor.
Ambrose Bierce

Two great talkers will not travel far together.
George Borrow

Talkers will refrain from evil speaking when listeners refrain from evil hearing.
Edward Bulwer-Lytton

No mortal has a right to wag his tongue, much less to wag his pen, without saying something.
Thomas Carlyle

Talk that does not end in any kind of action is better suppressed altogether.
Thomas Carlyle

Eloquence is vehement simplicity.
Richard Cecil

A man does not know what he is saying until he knows what he is not saying.
G.K. Chesterton

Who thinks an inch, but talks a yard, needs a kick in the foot.
Chinese proverb

He is an eloquent man who can treat humble subjects with delicacy, lofty things impressively, and moderate things temperately.
Cicero

Never close your lips to those to whom you have opened your heart.
Charles Dickens

Read my lips.
Dirty Harry

When the eyes say one thing and the tongue another, a practiced man relies on the language of the first.
Ralph Waldo Emerson

Those who talk loudly are rarely listened to.
Malcolm Forbes

A man is seldom better than his conversation.
German proverb

Streams of oratory do not always come from mountains of thought.
Charles Grant

The time to stop talking is when the other person nods his head affirmatively but says nothing.
Henry S. Haskins

Conversation: The slowest form of human communication.
Don Herold

We need few words when we have something to say, but all the words in all the dictionaries will not suffice when we have nothing to say.
Eric Hoffer

Writing or printing is like shooting with a rifle; you may hit your reader's mind or miss it. But talking is like playing at a mark with the pipe of an engine; if it is within reach, and you have time enough, you can't help hitting it.
Oliver Wendell Holmes

The most valuable of talents is that of never using two words when one will do.
Thomas Jefferson

If you haven't struck oil in your first three minutes, stop boring!
George Jessel

The happiest conversation is that of which nothing is distinctly remembered, but a general effect of pleasing impression.
Samuel Johnson

How ironical that it is by means of speech that man can degrade himself below the level of dumb creation—for a chatterbox is truly of a lower category than a dumb creature.
Søren Kierkegaard

A gossip is one who talks to you about others; a bore is one who talks to you about himself; and a brilliant conversationalist is one who talks to you about yourself.
Lisa Kirk

A perfect conversation would run much less to brilliant sentences than to unfinished ones.
Louis Kronenberger

The great gift of conversation lies less in displaying it ourselves than in drawing it out of others. He who leaves your company pleased with himself and his own cleverness is perfectly well pleased with you.
Jean de La Bruyère

I attribute the little I know to my not having been ashamed to ask for information, and to my rule of conversing with all descriptions of men on those topics that form their own peculiar professions and pursuits.
John Locke

No pleasure is fully delightful without communications, and no delight absolute except imparted.
Michel de Montaigne

Those who have few affairs to attend to are great talkers. The less men think, the more they talk.
Montesquieu

My great-grandfather used to say to his wife, my great-grandmother, who in turn told her daughter, my grandmother, who repeated it to her daughter, my mother, who used to remind her daughter, my own sister, that to talk well and eloquently was a very great art, but that an equally great one was to know the right moment to stop.
Wolfgang Amadeus Mozart

With a gun stuck in your mouth and the barrel of the gun between your teeth, you can only talk in vowels.
Chuck Palahniuk

We Athenians . . . instead of looking on discussion as a stumbling block in the way of action, think of it as an indispensable preliminary to any wise action at all.
Pericles

And 'tis remarkable that they who talk most are those who have the least to say.
Matthew Prior

They never taste who always drink;
They always talk who never think.
Matthew Prior

You talk, you talk, that's all you know how to do.
Raymond Queneau

It is not what we learn in conversation that enriches us.

It is the elation that comes of swift contact with tingling currents of thought.
Agnes Repplier

Can we talk?
Joan Rivers

What a people talk about means something. What they don't talk about means something.
William Saroyan

I distrust the incommunicable; it is the source of all violence.
Jean-Paul Sartre

The pith of conversation does not consist in exhibiting your own superior knowledge on matters of small importance, but enlarging, improving and correcting information you possess, by the authority of others.
Walter Scott

Wise men say nothing in dangerous times.
John Selden

Conversation should be pleasant without scurrility, witty without affectation, free without indecency, learned without conceitedness, novel without falsehood.
William Shakespeare

Talk is by far the most accessible of pleasures. It costs nothing in money, it is all profit, it completes our education, founds and fosters our friendships, and can be enjoyed at any age and in almost any state of health.
Robert Louis Stevenson

Remember, every time you open your mouth to talk, your mind walks out and parades up and down the words.
Edwin H. Stuart

Conversation is the image of the mind. As the man is, so is his talk.
Publilius Syrus

Brisk talkers are usually slow thinkers. There is, indeed, no wild beast more to be dreaded than a communicative man having nothing to communicate. If you

are civil to the voluble they will abuse your patience; if brusque, your character.
Jonathan Swift

I was gratified to be able to answer promptly, and I did. I said I didn't know.
Mark Twain

People have to talk about something just to keep their voice boxes in working order, so they'll have good voice boxes in case there's ever anything really meaningful to say.
Kurt Vonnegut

Let your discourse with men of business always be short and comprehensive.
George Washington

My skepticism long ago led me to the belief that writers write for themselves and not for their readers, and that art has nothing to do with communication between person and person, but only between different parts of a person's mind.
Rebecca West

Conversation should touch everything but should concentrate itself on nothing.
Oscar Wilde

TAXES

Count the day when, turning on its axis, this earth imposes no additional taxes.
Franklin P. Adams

An income tax form is like a laundry list—either way you lose your shirt.
Fred Allen

Our Founding Fathers objected to taxation without representation. They should see it today with representation.
Anonymous

Governments last as long as the under-taxed can defend them against the overtaxed.
Bernard Berenson

An economy breathes through its tax loopholes.
Barry Bracewell-Milnes

Why does a small tax increase cost you two hundred dollars and a substantial tax cut save you thirty cents?
Peg Bracken

Like mothers, taxes are often misunder-stood but seldom forgotten.
Lord Bramwell

The tax-exempt privilege is a feature always reflected in the market price of [municipal] bonds. The investor pays for it.
Justice Louis D. Brandeis

There is just one thing I can promise you about the outer-space program: Your tax dollar will go further.
Wernher von Braun

Taxing is an easy business. Any projector can contrive new impositions; any bungler can add to the old; but is it alto-gether wise to have no other bounds to your impositions than the patience of those who are to bear them?
Edmund Burke

A citizen can hardly distinguish between a tax and a fine, except that a fine is generally much lighter.
G.K. Chesterton

The imposition of taxes has its limits. There is a maximum which cannot be transcended. Suppose the citizen to be taxed by the general government to the utmost extent of his ability, or a thing as much as it can possibly bear, and the

state imposes a tax at the same time, which authority is to take it?
Henry Clay

The art of taxation consists in so plucking the goose as to obtain the largest possible amount of feathers with the smallest possible amount of hissing.
Jean-Baptiste Colbert

The only thing that hurts more than paying an income tax is not having to pay an income tax.
Thomas R. Dewar

The hardest thing in the world to understand is the income tax.
Albert Einstein

It is easier to start taxes than to stop them. A tax an inch long can easily become a yard long. That has been the history of the income tax. Would not the sales tax be likely to have a similar history [in the U.S.]? . . . Canadian newspapers report that an increase in the sales tax threatens to drive the Mackenzie King administration out of office. Canada began with a sales tax of 2%. . . . Starting this month the tax is 6%. The burden, in other words, has already been increased 200% . . . What the U.S. needs is not new taxes, is not more taxes, but fewer and lower taxes.
B.C. Forbes

Friends and neighbors complain that taxes are indeed very heavy, and if those laid on by the government were the only ones we had to pay, we might the more easily discharge them; but we have many others, and much more grievous to some of us. We are taxed twice as much by our idleness, three times as much by our pride, and four times as much by our folly.
Benjamin Franklin

A taxpaying public that doesn't understand the law is a taxpaying public that can't comply with the law.
Lawrence Gibbs

When making out your income tax, it's better to give than to deceive.
Arnold Glasow

I'm proud to be paying taxes to the U.S. The only thing is—I could be just as proud for half the money.
Arthur Godfrey

We have long had death and taxes as the two standards of inevitability. But there are those who believe that death is the preferable of the two.
Erwin N. Griswold

No taxation without misrepresentation.
Samuel Hoffenstein

The wisdom of man never yet contrived a system of taxation that would operate with perfect equality.
Andrew Jackson

The suppression of unnecessary offices, of useless establishments and expenses, enabled us to discontinue our internal taxes. These, covering our land with officers, and opening our doors to their intrusions, had already begun that process of domiciliary vexation which, once entered, is scarcely to be restrained from reaching, successively, every article of property and produce.
Thomas Jefferson

Taxes grow without rain.
Jewish proverb

In 1790, the nation which had fought a revolution against taxation without representation discovered that some of its citizens weren't much happier about taxation with representation.
Lyndon Baines Johnson

The avoidance of taxes is the only intellectual pursuit that carries any reward.
John Maynard Keynes

Always overpay your income taxes. That way, you'll get a refund.
Meyer Lansky

And it came to pass in those days, that there went out a decree from Caesar Augustus, that all the world should be taxed.
Luke 2:1

If Einstein and the agents of the Internal Revenue Service cannot understand the Tax Code, then the ordinary taxpayers of the U.S. are entitled to a little help.
Warren Magnuson

Unquestionably, there is progress. The average American now pays out almost as much in taxes alone as he formerly got in wages.
H.L. Mencken

Each citizen contributes to the revenues of the State a portion of his property in order that his tenure of the rest may be secure.
Montesquieu

Avoid falsehoods like the plague except in matters of taxation, which do not count, since here you are not lying to take someone else's goods, but to prevent your own from being unjustly seized.
Giovanni Morelli

Where there is an income tax, the just man will pay more and the unjust less on the same income.
Plato

The wages of sin are death, but by the time taxes are taken out, it's just sort of a tired feeling.
Paula Poundstone

Next to being shot at and missed, nothing is really quite as satisfying as an income tax refund.
F.J. Raymond

The taxpayer: Someone who works for the government but doesn't have to take a civil service examination.
Ronald Reagan

The income tax has made more liars out of the American people than golf has. Even when you make a tax form out on the level, you don't know when it's through if you are a crook or a martyr.
Will Rogers

Taxes are paid in the sweat of every man who labors. If those taxes are excessive, they are reflected in idle factories, tax-sold farms and in hordes of hungry people, tramping the streets and seeking jobs in vain.
Franklin D. Roosevelt

The Tax Collector's letters are invariably mimeographed, and all they say is that you still haven't paid him.
William Saroyan

A government which robs Peter to pay Paul can always count on Paul's support.
George Bernard Shaw

What is the difference between a taxidermist and a tax collector? The taxidermist takes only your skin.
Mark Twain

Every country in the world has its hands up to the elbows in the American taxpayer's pocket.
Kenneth Wherry

Income tax returns are the most imaginative fiction being written today.
Herman Wouk

TECHNOLOGY

Electronic aids, particularly domestic computers, will help the inner migration, the opting out of reality. Reality is no longer going to be the stuff out there, but the stuff inside your head. It's going to be commercial and nasty at the same time.
J.G. Ballard

Science and technology multiply around us. To an increasing extent they dictate the languages in which we speak and think. Either we use those languages, or we remain mute.
J.G Ballard

There is nothing more mysterious than a TV set left on in an empty room. It is even stranger than a man talking to himself or a woman standing dreaming at her stove. It is as if another planet is communicating with you.
Jean Baudrillard

The Englishman's telephone box is his castle. Like the London taxi, it can be entered by a gentleman in a top hat. It protects the user's privacy, keeps him warm and is large enough for a small cocktail party.
Mary Blume

Technology is so much fun but we can drown in our technology. The fog of information can drive out knowledge.
Daniel Boorstin

As a means of espionage, writs of assistance and general warrants are but puny instruments of tyranny and oppression when compared with wire-tapping.
Louis D. Brandeis

If the phone doesn't ring, it's me.
Jimmy Buffett

All phone calls are obscene.
Karen Elizabeth Gordon

Man is still the most extraordinary computer of all.
John F. Kennedy

God seems to have left the receiver off the hook.
Arthur Koestler

However far modern science and technics have fallen short of their inherent possibilities, they have taught mankind at least one lesson: Nothing is impossible.
Lewis Mumford

The press, the machine, the railway, the telegraph are premises whose thousand-year conclusion no one has yet dared to draw.
Friedrich Wilhelm Nietzsche

Men are only as good as their technical development allows them to be.
George Orwell

The effectiveness of a telephone conversation is in inverse proportion to the time spent on it.
C. Northcote Parkinson

There are three roads to ruin: women, gambling and technicians. The most pleasant is with women, the quickest

is with gambling, but the surest is with technicians.
Georges Pompidou

When I die I'm going to have a phone in one hand and my phone book in the other.
Nancy Reagan

Once there was an elephant,
Who tried to use the telephant—
No! No! I mean an elephone
Who tried to use the telephone—
Laura Elizabeth Richards

Technology is a queer thing: It brings you great gifts with one hand and it stabs you in the back with the other.
C.P. Snow

The Internet is a telephone system that's gotten uppity.
Clifford Stoll

It is said that one machine can do the work of 50 ordinary men. No machine, however, can do the work of one extraordinary man.
Hsieh Tehyi

Man is only man at the surface. Remove his skin, dissect, and immediately you come to machinery.
Paul Valéry

The greatest discoveries in nanotech have been 20 years away for 20 years.
Ted Waitt

TEMPER

We must interpret a bad temper as the sign of an inferiority complex.
Alfred Adler

Bad temper is its own scourge. Few things are more bitter than to feel bitter.

A man's venom poisons himself more than his victim.
Charles Buxton

Men who have had a great deal of experience learn not to lose their temper.
Charles Victor Cherbuliez

A man who cannot command his temper should not think of being a man of business.
Lord Chesterfield

The difficult part of good temper consists in forbearance, and accommodation to the ill-humor of others.
William Empson

Avoid letting temper block progress— keep cool.
William Feather

Good temper is an estate for life.
William Hazlitt

He who restrains his temper will have all his sins forgiven.
Hebrew proverb

More than half the difficulties of the world would be allayed or removed by the exhibition of good temper.
Sir Arthur Helps

Civility is a charm that attracts the love of all men.
George Horne

A tart temper never mellows with age, and a sharp tongue is the only edged tool that grows keener with constant use.
Washington Irving

Good temper, like a sunny day, sheds a ray of brightness over everything; it is the sweetener of toil and the soother of disquietude!
Washington Irving

He was so generally civil that nobody thanked him for it.
Samuel Johnson

Civility costs nothing and buys everything.
Mary Wortley Montagu

The growth of wisdom may be gauged accurately by the decline of ill temper.
Friedrich Wilhelm Nietzsche

Don't hit at all if it is honorably possible to avoid hitting; but never hit soft.
Theodore Roosevelt

THOUGHT

Man tends to treat all his opinions as principles.
Herbert Agar

Thought means life, since those who do not think do not live in any high or real sense. Thinking makes the man.
Amos Bronson Alcott

Our life is what our thoughts make it. A man will find that as he alters his thoughts toward things and other people, things and other people will alter towards him.
James Allen

The happiness of your life depends upon the quality of your thoughts.
Marcus Aurelius Antoninus

Thinking cannot be clear until it has had expression—we must write, or speak, or act our thoughts, or they will remain in half torpid form. Our feelings must have expression, or they will be as clouds, which, till they descend in rain, will never bring up fruit or flowers. So it is with all the inward feelings; expression gives them development—thought is the blossom; language is the opening bud; action the fruit behind it.
Henry Ward Beecher

Good thoughts and acts will soon improve the health and strength of man, for man was made to think and act according to God's plan; and plan God did that man should live a decent, honest life, enjoying health and happiness, the better with a wife.
Alonzo Newton Benn

There is no less invention in aptly applying a thought found in a book, than in being the first author of the thought.
Robert Boyle

A thought once awakened does not again slumber.
Thomas Carlyle

As soon as true thought has entered our mind, it gives a light which makes us see a crowd of other objects which we have never perceived before.
François de Châteaubriand

Silence and reserve suggest latent power. What some men think has more effect than what others say.
Lord Chesterfield

Mental pleasures never cloy; unlike those of the body, they are increased by reputation, approved by reflection, and strengthened by enjoyment.
Charles Caleb Colton

It is impossible for men engaged in low and groveling pursuits to have noble and generous sentiments. A man's thought must always follow his employment.
Demosthenes

Nurture your mind with great thoughts; to believe in the heroic makes heroes.
Benjamin Disraeli

What we call public opinion is generally public sentiment.
Benjamin Disraeli

It is remarkable to what lengths people will go to avoid thought.
Thomas A. Edison

Few people are capable of expressing with equanimity opinions which differ from the prejudices of their social environment.
Albert Einstein

One couldn't carry on life comfortably without a little blindness to the fact that everything has been said better than we can put it ourselves.
George Eliot

Our thoughts are often worse than we are.
George Eliot

The last change in our point of view gives the whole world a pictorial air.
Ralph Waldo Emerson

What is the hardest task in the world? To think.
Ralph Waldo Emerson

Men are not influenced by things, but by their thoughts about things.
Epictetus

Every definition is dangerous
Erasmus

Second thoughts are ever wiser.
Euripides

Thinkers perish, thoughts don't.
Malcolm Forbes

No one can have a higher opinion of him than I have, and I think he's a dirty little beast.
William S. Gilbert

Have you not learned that not stocks or bonds or stately homes, or products of mill or field are our country? It is the splendid thought that is in our minds.
Benjamin Harrison

Nothing is more unaccountable than the spell that often lurks in a spoken word. A thought may be present to the mind, and two minds conscious of the same thought, but as long as it remains unspoken their familiar talk flows quietly over the hidden idea.
Nathaniel Hawthorne

Thought precedes action as lighting does thunder.
Heinrich Heine

Thus we build in the ice, thus we write on the waves of the sea; the roaring waves pass away, the ice melts, and away goes our palace, like our thoughts.
Johann Gottfried von Herder

What luck for rulers that men do not think.
Adolf Hitler

The world is governed by opinion.
Thomas Hobbes

A man is not idle because he is absorbed in thought. There is a visible labor and there is an invisible labor.
Victor Hugo

Certain thoughts are prayers. There are certain moments when, whatever be the attitude of the body, the soul is on its knees.
Victor Hugo

American public opinion is like an ocean—it cannot be stirred by a teaspoon.
Hubert Humphrey

Single-mindedness is all very well in cows or baboons; in an animal claiming to belong to the same species as Shakespeare, it is simply disgraceful.
Aldous Huxley

Public opinion, a vulgar, impertinent, anonymous tyrant who deliberately makes life unpleasant for anyone who is not content to be the average man.
William Ralph Inge

After the ship has sunk, everyone knows how she might have been saved.
Italian proverb

Compulsory unification of opinion achieves only the unanimity of the graveyard.
Robert Jackson

The glow of one warm thought is to me worth more than money.
Thomas Jefferson

The only means of strengthening one's intellect is to make up one's mind about nothing—to let the mind be a thoroughfare for all thoughts.
John Keats

Nothing is more conducive to peace of mind than not having any opinions at all.
Georg C. Lichtenberg

The thoughts that come often unsought, and, as it were, drop into the mind, are commonly the most valuable of any we have, and therefore should be secured, because they seldom return again.
John Locke

It will be a shock to men when they realize that thoughts that were fast enough for today are not fast enough for tomorrow. But thinking tomorrow's thoughts today is one kind of future life.
Christopher Morley

If I have done the public any service, it is due to patient thought.
Sir Isaac Newton

When we talk in company we lose our unique tone of voice, and this leads us to make statements which in no way correspond to our real thoughts.
Friedrich Wilhelm Nietzsche

There are some things only intellectuals are crazy enough to believe.
George Orwell

There are two distinct classes of what are called thoughts: those that we produce in ourselves by reflection and the act of thinking and those that bolt into the mind of their own accord.
Thomas Paine

All of our dignity consists in thought. Let us endeavor then to think well; this is the principle of morality.
Blaise Pascal

Public opinion is a compound of folly, weakness, prejudice, wrong feeling, right feeling, obstinacy and newspaper paragraphs.
Sir Robert Peel

Always remember to bound thy thoughts to the present occasion.
William Penn

Clear therefore thy head, and rally, and manage thy thoughts rightly, and thou wilt save time, and see and do thy business well; for thy judgment will be distinct, thy mind free, and the faculties strong and regular.
William Penn

Man being made a reasonable, and so a thinking creature, there is nothing more worthy of his being, than the right direction and employment of his thoughts; since upon this depends both his usefulness to the public, and his own present and future benefit in all respects.
William Penn

The intellect is a very nice whirligig toy, but how people take it seriously is more than I can understand.
Ezra Pound

Make yourselves nests of pleasant thoughts. None of us knows what fairy palaces we may build of beautiful thought—proof against all adversity. Bright fancies, satisfied memories, noble histories, faithful sayings, treasure houses of precious and restful thoughts, which care cannot disturb, nor pain make gloomy, nor poverty take away from us.
John Ruskin

The first essential character [of civilization], I should say, is forethought. This, I would say, is what distinguishes men from brutes and adults from children.
Bertrand Russell

Think left and think right and think low and think high. Oh, the thinks you can think up if only you try!
Dr. Seuss

Thoughts are but dreams till their effect be tried.
William Shakespeare

The sound of tireless voices is the price we pay for the right to hear the music of our own opinions.
Adlai Stevenson

They are never alone that are accompanied with noble thoughts.
Sir Philip Sydney

We have only to change the point of view and the greatest action looks mean.
William Makepeace Thackeray

Be a Columbus to whole new continents and worlds within you, opening new channels, not of trade, but of thought.
Henry David Thoreau

Each thought that is welcomed and recorded is a nest egg, by the side of which more will be laid.
Henry David Thoreau

Consciousness is a disease.
Miguel de Unamuno

A man is infinitely more complicated than his thoughts.
Paul Valéry

The second, sober thought of the people is seldom wrong, and always efficient.
Martin Van Buren

Intellectual passion drives out sensuality.
Leonardo da Vinci

His words span rivers and mountains, but his thoughts are still only six inches long.
E.B. White

All thought is immoral. Its very essence is destruction. If you think of anything you kill it. Nothing survives being thought of.
Oscar Wilde

He that will not command his thoughts will soon lose the command of his actions.
Woodrow Wilson

Never stay up on the barren heights of cleverness, but come down into the green valleys of silliness.
Ludwig Wittgenstein

TODAY

Each day of your life, as soon as you open your eyes in the morning, you can square away for a happy and successful day. It's the mood and the purpose of the inception of each day that are the important facts in charting your course for the day. We can always square away for a fresh start, no matter what the past has been. It's today that is the paramount problem always. Yesterday is but history.
George Matthew Adams

No matter what looms ahead, if you can eat today, enjoy the sunlight today, mix good cheer with friends today, enjoy it and bless God for it. Do not look back on happiness—or dream of it in the future. You are only sure of today; do not let yourself be cheated out of it.
Henry Ward Beecher

But what minutes! Count them by sensation, and not by calendars, and each moment is a day.
Benjamin Disraeli

One today is worth two tomorrows; what I am to be, I am now becoming.
Benjamin Franklin

Never regret yesterday. Life is in you today, and you make your tomorrow.
L. Ron Hubbard

Do today's duty, fight today's temptation; do not weaken and distract yourself by looking forward to things you cannot see, and could not understand if you saw them.
Charles Kingsley

I will utter what I believe today, if it should contradict all I said yesterday.
Wendell Phillips

Lay hold of today's task and you will not depend so much upon tomorrow's.
Seneca

The past, the present and the future are really one—they are today.
Harriet Beecher Stowe

Today is the pupil of yesterday.
Publilius Syrus

TOLERANCE

Half the secret of getting along with people is consideration of their views; the other half is tolerance in one's own views.
Daniel Frohman

Tolerance comes with age. I see no fault committed that I myself could not have committed at some time or other.
Johann Wolfgang von Goethe

Intolerance is the Do Not Touch sign on something that cannot bear touching. We do not mind having our hair ruffled, but we will not tolerate any familiarity with the toupée that covers our baldness.
Eric Hoffer

The mind of a bigot is like the pupil of the eye; the more light you pour upon it, the more it will contract.
Oliver Wendell Holmes

What is objectionable, what is dangerous about extremists is not that they are extreme, but that they are intolerant. The evil is not what they say about their cause, but what they say about their opponents.
Robert F. Kennedy

Tolerance is the positive and cordial effort to understand another's beliefs,

practices and habits without necessarily sharing or accepting them.
Joshua L. Liebman

We are in favor of tolerance, but it is a very difficult thing to tolerate the intolerant and impossible to tolerate the intolerable.
George D. Prentice

Nothing is so difficult as to achieve results in this world if one is full of great tolerance and the milk of human kindness.
Corinne Robinson

It is easy to be tolerant when you do not care.
Clement F. Rogers

It is not a merit to tolerate, but rather a crime to be intolerant.
Percy Bysshe Shelley

The resource of bigotry and intolerance, when convicted of error, is always the same; silenced by argument, it endeavors to silence by persecution, in old times by fire and sword, in modern days by the tongue.
Gerald J. Simmons

Toleration has never been the cause of civil war; while, on the contrary, persecution has covered the earth with blood and carnage.
Voltaire

TRAGEDY

Life is a dream for the wise, a game for the fool, a comedy for the rich, a tragedy for the poor.
Sholom Aleichem

It is restful, tragedy, because one knows that there is no more lousy hope left. You know you're caught, caught at last like a rat with all the world on its back. And the only thing left to do is shout.
Jean Anouilh

Only a great mind that is overthrown yields tragedy.
Jacques Barzun

Tragedy is when I cut my finger. Comedy is when you fall into an open sewer and die.
Mel Brooks

Satire is tragedy plus time.
Lenny Bruce

The essence of tragedy is to know the end.
Charles W. Ferguson

In tragedy every moment is eternity; in comedy, eternity is a moment.
Christopher Fry

If you believe, as the Greeks did, that man is at the mercy of the gods, then you write tragedy. The end is inevitable from the beginning.
Lillian Hellman

Tragedy and comedy are simply questions of value; a little misfit in life makes us laugh; a great one is tragedy and cause for expression of grief.
Elbert Hubbard

Tragedy is like strong acid; it dissolves away all but the very gold of truth.
D.H. Lawrence

Farce is tragedy played at a thousand revolutions per minute.
John Mortimer

A tragic situation exists precisely when virtue does not triumph but when it is still felt that man is nobler than the forces which destroy him.
George Orwell

The bad end unhappily, the good unluckily. That is what tragedy means.
Tom Stoppard

When you close your eyes to tragedy, you close your eyes to greatness.
Stephen Vizinczey

TROUBLE

Troubles are usually the brooms and shovels that smooth the road to a good man's fortune; and many a man curses the rain that falls upon his head, and knows not that it brings abundance to drive away hunger.
St. Basil

This is the mark of a really admirable man: steadfastness in the face of trouble.
Ludwig van Beethoven

Many modern (so-called) Reformers are just as dangerous as the physician who makes a wrong diagnosis of a disease. They see the trouble from without and prescribe external remedies, while the cause of the trouble is within and needs internal treatment.
William J.H. Boetcker

There are nettles everywhere, but smooth, green grasses are more common still; the blue of heaven is larger than the cloud.
E.B. Browning

Half the trouble in the world arises from men trying to anticipate their time and season, and the other half from their trying to prolong them.
Arthur Bryant

If you would not have affliction visit you twice, listen at once to what it teaches.
James Burgh

We can outrun the wind and the storm, but we cannot outrun the demon of Hurry.
John Burroughs

The thorns which I have reap'd are of the tree I planted; they have torn me, and I bleed.
Lord Byron

I have had a long, long life full of troubles, but there is one curious fact about them—nine-tenths of them never happened.
Andrew Carnegie

The average man takes life as a trouble. He is in a chronic state of irritation at the whole performance. He does not learn to differentiate between troubles and difficulties, usually, until some real trouble bowls him over. He fusses about pin-pricks until a mule kicks him. Then he learns the difference.
Herbert N. Casson

It is pleasant to recall past troubles.
Cicero

If you see ten troubles coming down the road, you can be sure that nine will run into the ditch before they reach you and you have to battle with only one of them.
Calvin Coolidge

Being oppressed . . . and sorry can be a way of life, just like any other.
John Corry

The cares of today are seldom those of tomorrow; and when we lie down at night we may safely say to most of our troubles, Ye have done your worst, and we shall see you no more.
William Cowper

This world has cares enough to plague us; but he who meditates on others' woe, shall, in that meditation, lose his own.
Richard Cumberland

After great pain, a formal feeling comes
The nerves sit ceremonious, like Tombs.
Emily Dickinson

When I go to bed, I leave my troubles in my clothes.
Dutch proverb

The world is full of cactus, but we don't have to sit on it.
Will Foley

Whenever calamity howlers shake their heads and impress upon you that this, that, and the next dire catastrophe is to befall this nation or the nations of the world—such as, for example, that exhaustion of the world's oil supply will bring all transportation and machinery to a standstill through lack of lubrication, or that exhaustion of the earth's stores of coal will make life unlivable in these cold climates—just smile and reply that the worst troubles of all are those that never happen [and] that you prefer not to cross shaky bridges until you come to them. . . .
B.C. Forbes

A danger foreseen is half avoided.
Thomas Fuller

Most troubles arise from loafing when we should be working or talking when we should be listening.
Arnold Glasow

The world is full of thorns and thistles. It's all in how you grasp them.
Arnold Glasow

The best remedy for disturbances is to let them run their course, for so they quiet down.
Baltasar Gracián

It is doubtful whether the oppressed ever fight for freedom. They fight for pride and power—power to oppress others.
Eric Hoffer

He who would have no trouble in this world must not be born in it.
Italian proverb

Men do not get up and do mischief, without there is someone in the head of it.
Andrew Jackson

A man used to vicissitudes is not easily dejected.
Samuel Johnson

Borrow trouble for yourself, if that's your nature, but don't lend it to your neighbors.
Rudyard Kipling

Just because the river is quiet does not mean the crocodiles have left.
Malay proverb

I love the man that can smile in trouble, that can gather strength from distress, and grow brave by reflection. 'Tis the business of little minds to shrink, but he whose heart is firm, and whose conscience approves his conduct, will pursue his principles unto death.
Thomas Paine

The harder the conflict, the more glorious the triumph. What we obtain too cheap, we esteem too lightly; 'tis dearness only that gives everything its value. I love the man that can smile in trouble, that can gather strength from distress, and grow brave by reflection. 'Tis the business of little minds to shrink; but he whose heart is firm, and whose conscience approves his conduct, will pursue his principles until death.
Thomas Paine

The best education in the world is that got by struggling to get a living.
Wendell Phillips

Our greatest troubles spring from something that is as admirable as it is dangerous . . . our impatience to better the lot of our fellows.
Karl Popper

He who foresees calamities, suffers them twice over.
Beilby Porteus

He that passeth by, and meddleth with strife not belonging to him, is like one that taketh a dog by the ears.
Proverbs 26:17

Though I walk in the midst of trouble, thou wilt revive me: thou shalt stretch forth thine hand against the wrath of mine enemies, and thy right hand shall save me.
Psalms 138:7

It is only necessary to make war with five things: with the maladies of the body, the ignorances of the mind, with the passions of the body, with the seditions of the city, and the discords of families.
Pythagoras

A bright day is easily clouded by a murky road.
Charles B. Rogers

The wise man thinks about his troubles only when there is some purpose in doing so; at other times he thinks about other things.
Bertrand Russell

The process of living is the process of reacting to stress.
Stanley Sarnoff

Danger and delight grow on one stalk.
Scottish proverb

Every stress leaves an indelible scar, and the organism pays for its survival after a stressful situation by becoming a little older.
Hans Selye

No evil is without its compensation. The less money, the less trouble; the less favor, the less envy. Even in those cases which put us out of wits, it is not the loss itself, but the estimate of the loss that troubles us.
Seneca

We are not here to play, to dream, to drift;

We have hard work to do and loads to lift;

Shun not the struggle—face it, 'tis God's gift.
Lord Shaftesbury

May you be a mail carrier and have sore feet.
Spanish gypsy curse

We must do what we can to reduce, not increase, tensions. We must do what we can to present only the facts as we know them, not as we imagine them to be. We must learn to live with crisis in an age which calls for cool heads and accurate appraisals.
Percy C. Spender

He is most free from danger, who, even when safe, is on his guard.
Publilius Syrus

He who shares the afflictions of others will merit to behold the comforting of humanity.
Talmudic saying

If thou has a bundle of thorns in thy lot, there is no need to sit down on it.
Jeremy Taylor

In times of great stress, in times of depression, the public mind loses its balance and becomes the victim of the catchword.
Sir Henry Thornton

Temper is what gets most of us into trouble. Pride is what keeps us there.
Mark Twain

If some great catastrophe is not announced every morning, we feel a certain void. Nothing in the paper today, we sigh.
Paul Valéry

Trouble will come soon enough, and when he does come receive him as pleasantly as possible. Like the tax collector, he is a disagreeable chap to have in one's house, but the more amiably you greet him the sooner he will go away.
Artemus Ward

Let your heart feel for the affliction and distress of every one.
George Washington

Humanity either makes, or breeds, or tolerates all its afflictions, great or small.
H.G. Wells

TRUST

Suspicion is far more apt to be wrong than right; oftener unjust than just. It is no friend to virtue, and always an enemy to happiness.
Hosea Ballou

A man is already of consequence in the world when it is known that we can implicitly rely upon him. Often I have known a man to be preferred in stations of honor and profit because he had this reputation: When he said he knew a thing, he knew it, and when he said he would do a thing, he did it.
Edward Bulwer-Lytton

The man who trusts men will make fewer mistakes than he who distrusts them.
Camillo di Cavour

Suspicion is a thing very few people can entertain without letting the hypothesis turn, in their minds, into fact . . . only scientists can walk around and around a hypothesis without even beginning to confuse it with truth.
David Cort

What has not been examined impartially has not been well examined. Skepticism is therefore the first step toward truth.
Denis Diderot

Man's life would be wretched and confined if it were to miss the candid intimacy developed by mutual trust and esteem.
Edwin Dummer

It is a good maxim to trust a person entirely or not at all.
Henry Fielding

Mistrust carries one such further than trust.
German proverb

The hundred-point man is one who is true to every trust; who keeps his word; who is loyal to the firm that employs him; who does not listen for insults nor look for slights; who carries a civil tongue in his head; who is polite to strangers without being fresh; who is considerate toward servants; who is moderate in his eating and drinking; who is willing to learn; who is cautious and yet courageous.
Elbert Hubbard

The trust that we put in ourselves makes us feel trust in others.
François de La Rochefoucauld

A feeling of distrust is always the last which a great mind acquires.
Jean-Baptiste Racine

I have never accepted a bad check from anyone I did not trust.
Ron Rasmus

I think we may safely trust a good deal more than we do. We may waive just so much care of ourselves as we honestly bestow elsewhere.
Henry David Thoreau

We are always paid for our suspicion by finding what we suspect.
Henry David Thoreau

My father used to say: Never suspect people. It's better to be deceived or mistaken, which is only human, after all, than to be suspicious, which is common.
Stark Young

TRUTH

You get so used to lying that after a while it's hard to remember what the truth is.
Philip Agee

Truth is the secret of eloquence and virtue, the basis of moral authority; it is the highest summit of art and of life.
Henri Frédéric Amiel

If you want to annoy your neighbors, tell the truth about them.
Pietro Aretino

The search for truth is in one way hard and in another way easy, for it is evident that no one can master it fully or miss it wholly. But each adds a little to our knowledge of nature, and from all the facts assembled there arises a certain grandeur.
Aristotle

We must hold fast to the austere but true doctrine as to what really governs politics and saves or destroys states. Having in mind things true, things elevated, things just, things pure, things amiable, things of good report; having these in mind, studying and loving these, is what saves states.
Matthew Arnold

Truth is the daughter of time, not of authority.
Francis Bacon

Power is not revealed by striking hard or often, but by striking true.
Honoré de Balzac

Any man can work when every stroke of his hand brings down the fruit rattling from the tree to the ground; but to labor in season and out of season, under every discouragement, by the power of truth . . . that requires a heroism which is transcendent.
Henry Ward Beecher

Truth is the cry of all, but the game of the few.
George Berkeley

It is not moral to lie, but you don't always have to tell the truth.
Ignas Bernstein

Everything that is possible to be believed is an image of the truth.
William Blake

Truth can never be told so as to be understood and not be believed.
William Blake

Truth never hurts the teller.
Robert Browning

Truth is a gem that is found at a great depth; whilst on the surface of the world all things are weighed by the false scale of custom.
Lord Byron

Can there be a more horrible object in existence than an eloquent man not speaking the truth?
Thomas Carlyle

Truth will rise above falsehood as oil above water.
Miguel de Cervantes

We live in the present, we dream of the future and we learn eternal truths from the past.
Mme. Chiang Kai-shek

Men occasionally stumble over the truth, but most of them pick themselves up and hurry off as if nothing had happened.
Winston Churchill

To all new truths, or renovation of old truths, it must be as in the ark between the destroyed and the about-to-be renovated world. The raven must be sent out before the dove, and ominous controversy must precede peace and the olive wreath.
Samuel Taylor Coleridge

We must not let go manifest truths because we cannot answer all questions about them.
Jeremy Collier

The pursuit of truth shall set you free—even if you never catch up with it.
Clarence Darrow

The love of truth is the stimulus to all noble conversation. This is the root of all the charities. The tree which springs from it may have a thousand branches, but they will all bear a golden and generous fruitage.
Orville Dewey

Frank and explicit: That is the right line to take when you wish to conceal your mind and confuse the minds of others.
Benjamin Disraeli

There is no wisdom like frankness.
Benjamin Disraeli

Truth is never to be expected from authors whose understanding is warped with enthusiasm.
John Dryden

Accuracy is the twin brother of honesty; inaccuracy is a near kin to falsehood.
Tryon Edwards

Keep true, never be ashamed of doing right; decide on what you think is right, and stick to it.
George Eliot

Every violation of truth is not only a sort of suicide in the liar, but is a stab at the health of human society.
Ralph Waldo Emerson

God offers to every mind its choice between truth and repose. Take which you please—you can never have both.
Rlaph Waldo Emerson

Some men's words I remember so well that I must often use them to express my thought. Yes, because I perceive that we have heard the same truth, but they have heard it better.
Ralph Waldo Emerson

The greatest homage we can pay to truth is to use it.
Ralph Waldo Emerson

A man who seeks truth and loves it must be reckoned precious to any human society.
Frederick the Great

The greatest and noblest pleasure which men can have in this world is to discover new truths; and the next is to shake off old prejudices.
Frederick the Great

Truth is the nursing mother of genius. No man can be absolutely true to himself, eschewing cant, compromise, servile imitation, and complaisance without becoming original.
Margaret Fuller

Beware of telling an improbable truth.
Thomas Fuller

An exaggeration is a truth that has lost its temper.
Kahlil Gibran

Truth is a deep kindness that teaches us to be content in our everyday life and share with the people the same happiness.
Kahlil Gibran

Truth must be repeated again and again, because error is constantly being preached round about.
Johann Wolfgang von Goethe

I don't want any yes-men around me. I want everyone to tell me the truth—even though it costs him his job.
Samuel Goldwyn

It is as hard to tell the truth as to hide it.
Baltasar Gracián

The sense of ultimate truth is the intellectual counterpart of the esthetic sense of perfect beauty, or the moral sense of perfect good.
Lord Halifax

Truth is suppressed, not to protect the country from enemy agents but to protect the Government of the day against the people.
Roy Hattersley

No man can, for any considerable time, wear one face to himself, and another to the multitude, without finally getting bewildered as to which is the true one.
Nathaniel Hawthorne

The best test of truth is the power of the thought to get itself accepted in the competition of the market.
Oliver Wendell Holmes

Truth is tough. It will not break, like a bubble, at a touch; nay, you may kick it about all day, like a football, and it will be round and full at evening.
Oliver Wendell Holmes

Truth, when not sought after, rarely comes to light.
Oliver Wendell Holmes

The search for truth is really a lot of good fun.
Vernon Howard

We must be truthful and fair in the ordinary affairs of life before we can be truthful and fair in patriotism and religion.
Edgar Watson Howe

History has its truth; and so has legend hers.
Victor Hugo

Nothing great in science has ever been done by men, whatever their powers, in whom the divine afflatus of the truth-seeker was wanting.
Thomas H. Huxley

There is no alleviation for the sufferings of mankind except veracity of thought

and action, and the resolute facing of the world as it is.
Thomas H. Huxley

The spirit of truth and the spirit of freedom—they are the pillars of society.
Henrik Ibsen

If people are not being told the truth about their problems, the majority not only may, but invariably must, make the wrong judgments.
Ralph Ingersoll

The ultimate test of what a truth means is the conduct it dictates or inspires.
William James

There is no worse lie than a truth misunderstood by those who hear it.
William James

We have to live today by what truth we can get today and be ready tomorrow to call it falsehood.
William James

Any truth is only true up to a certain point. When one oversteps the mark, it becomes a non-truth.
Søren Kierkegaard

Be sure of the foundation of your life. Know why you live as you do. Be ready to give a reason for it. Do not, in such a matter as life, build an opinion or custom on what you guess is true. Make it a matter of certainty and science.
Thomas Starr King

Let your desire for truth transcend all minor considerations. Ignorance is invariably confident. The man of knowledge learns to realize his own needs. Be honest and severe in your self-appraisal. Learn the art of learning, and you are well on the way to achievement. True greatness is reflective, not assertive.
Grenville Kleiser

The real truths are those that can be invented.
Karl Kraus

The exact contrary of what is generally believed is often the truth.
Jean de La Bruyère

The trouble with too many people is they believe the realm of truth always lies within their vision.
Abraham Lincoln

Truth is often eclipsed but never extinguished.
Livy

It is one thing to show a man that he is in error, and another to put him in possession of truth.
John Locke

Let us then be what we are, and speak what we think, and in all things keep ourselves loyal to truth.
Henry Wadsworth Longfellow

Great truths are portions of the soul of man.
James Russell Lowell

Peace if possible, but truth at any rate.
Martin Luther

There is no wisdom save in truth. Truth is everlasting, but our ideas about truth are changeable. Only a little of the first fruits of wisdom, only a few fragments of the boundless heights, breadths and depths of truth, have I been able to gather.
Martin Luther

And in the end, through the long ages of our quest for light, it will be found that truth is still mightier than the sword. For out of the welter of human carnage and human sorrow and human weal the

indestructible thing that will always live is a sound idea.
Douglas MacArthur

Let us labor for that larger comprehension of truth, and that more thorough repudiation of error, which shall make the history of mankind a series of ascending developments.
Horace Mann

You need not tell all the truth, unless to those who have a right to know it all. But let all you tell be truth.
Horace Mann

Not the violent conflict between parts of the truth, but the quiet suppression of half of it, is the formidable evil; there is always hope when people are forced to listen to both sides; it is when they attend to only one that errors harden into prejudices, and truth itself ceases to have the effect of truth, by being exaggerated into falsehood.
John Stuart Mill

Truth is not a crystal one can put in one's pocket, but an infinite fluid into which one falls headlong.
Robert Musil

In the mountains of truth you never climb in vain.
Friedrich Wilhlem Nietzsche

Nobody dies nowadays of fatal truths: there are too many antidotes to them.
Friedrich Wilhelm Nietzsche

We know truth, not only by reason, but also by the heart, and it is from this last that we know first principles; and reason, which has nothing to do with it, tries in vain to combat them. The skeptics who desire truth alone labor in vain.
Blaise Pascal

There are certain times when most people are in a disposition of being informed, and 'tis incredible what a vast good a little truth might do, spoken in such seasons.
Alexander Pope

Tell the truth and shame the Devil.
François Rabelais

When a man tells you that he knows the exact truth about anything you are safe in inferring that he is an inexact man.
Bertrand Russell

Purity of soul cannot be lost without consent.
St. Augustine

It is a great advantage for a system of philosophy to be substantially true.
George Santayana

This above all, to thine own self be true, and it must follow, as the night the day, thou canst not then be false to any man.
William Shakespeare

My way of joking is to tell the truth; it's the funniest joke in the world.
George Bernard Shaw

Weigh not so much what men assert, as what they prove. Truth is simple and naked, and needs not invention to apparel her comeliness.
Sir Philip Sidney

The priceless heritage of the free and independent interchange of thought is not to be kept without ceaseless vigilance. Only by guarding the truth itself can we guard the greatest of all our liberties—the right to proclaim the truth. On that liberty rests the destiny of millions.
Lord Southwood

Fear is not in the habit of speaking truth; when perfect sincerity is expected,

perfect freedom must be allowed; nor has anyone who is apt to be angry when he hears the truth any cause to wonder that he does not hear it.
Tacitus

A cliche is a truth one doesn't believe.
Bernard Taper

It takes two to speak the truth—one to speak and another to hear.
Henry David Thoreau

Study to show thyself approved unto God, a workman that needeth not to be ashamed, rightly dividing the word of truth.
II Timothy 3:15

There is no philosopher in the world so great but he believes a million things on the faith of other people and accepts a great many more truths than he demonstrates.
Alexis de Tocqueville

Most writers regard truth as their most valuable possession, and therefore are most economical in its use.
Mark Twain

When in doubt, tell the truth.
Mark Twain

If a man never contradicts himself, it is because he never says anything.
Miguel de Unamuno

There is no conflict between the Old and the New; the conflict is between the False and the True.
Henry van Dyke

There are truths which are not for all men, nor for all occasions.
Voltaire

Associate yourself with men of good quality, if you esteem your reputation.

Be not apt to relate news, if you know not the truth thereof. Speak no evil of the absent, for it is unjust. Undertake not what you cannot perform, but be careful to keep your promise. There is but one straight course, and that is to seek truth, and pursue it steadily. Nothing but harmony, honesty, industry and frugality are necessary to make us a great and happy nation.
George Washington

At a distance from the theater of action, truth is not always related without embellishment.
George Washington

Truth will ultimately prevail where there are plans taken to bring it to light.
George Washington

Every one wishes to have truth on his side, but it is not every one that sincerely wishes to be on the side of truth.
Richard Whately

It is more important that a proposition be interesting than that it be true.
Alfred North Whitehead

Do I contradict myself? Very well, then, I contradict myself; (I am large. I contain multitudes).
Walt Whitman

A truth ceases to be true when more than one person believes in it.
Oscar Wilde

It is perfectly monstrous the way people go about nowadays saying things against one, behind one's back, that are absolutely and entirely true.
Oscar Wilde

All cruel people describe themselves as paragons of frankness.
Tennessee Williams

TRYING

God lends a helping hand to the man who tries hard.
Aeschylus

Man can have but what he strives for.
Arabian proverb

Experiment is folly when experience shows the way.
Roger Babson

As plants take hold, not for the sake of staying, but only that they may climb higher, so it is with men. By every part of our nature we clasp things above us, one after another, not for the sake of remaining where we take hold, but that we may go higher.
Henry Ward Beecher

Striving for excellence motivates you; striving for perfection is demoralizing.
Harriet Braiker

'Tis not what man does which exalts him, but what man would do!
Robert Browning

All life is an experiment. The more experiments you make the better.
Ralph Waldo Emerson

Venture nothing, and life is less than it should be.
Malcolm Forbes

Until you try, you don't know what you can't do.
Henry James

Nothing will ever be attempted, if all possible objections must first be overcome.
Samuel Johnson

Keep on going and the chances are that you will stumble on something, perhaps when you are least expecting it. I have never heard of anyone stumbling on something sitting down.
Charles F. Kettering

During the first period of a man's life the greatest danger is: not to take the risk. When once the risk has really been taken, then the greatest danger is to risk too much.
Søren Kierkegaard

Without risk, faith is an impossibility.
Søren Kierkegaard

Many a man never fails because he never tries.
Norman MacEwan

To be alive at all involves some risk.
Harold Macmillan

Every noble acquisition is attended with its risks; he who fears to encounter the one must not expect to obtain the other.
Pietro Metastasio

Either do not attempt at all, or go through with it.
Ovid

Contrary to the commonly accepted belief, it is the risk element in our capitalistic system which produces an economy of security. Risk brings out the ingenuity and resourcefulness which insure the success of enough ventures to keep the economy growing and secure.
Robert Rawls

Trying is the touchstone to accomplishment.
Paul von Ringelheim

Whatever course you have chosen for yourself, it will not be a chore but an adventure if you bring to it a sense of the

glory of striving—if your sights are set far above the merely secure and mediocre.
David Sarnoff

The attempt and not the deed confounds us.
William Shakespeare

For want of a block, man will stumble at a straw.
Jonathan Swift

No mistake or failure is as bad as to stop and not try again.
John Wanamaker

TYRANNY

It is far easier to act under conditions of tyranny than to think.
Hannah Arendt

A tyrant is the worst disease, and the cause of all others.
William Blake

No totalitarians, no wars, no fears, famines or perils of any kind can really break a man's spirit until he breaks it himself by surrendering. Tyranny has many dread powers, but not the power to rule the spirit.
Edgar Sheffield Brightman

Many of the greatest tyrants on the records of history have begun their reigns in the fairest manner. But this unnatural power corrupts both the heart and the understanding.
Edmund Burke

Tyrants forego all respect for humanity in proportion as they are sunk beneath it. Taught to believe themselves of a different species, they really become so, lose their participation with their kind,

and in mimicking the god dwindle into the brute.
William Hazlitt

The harshest tyranny is that which acts under the protection of legality and the banner of justice.
Montesquieu

It is time to fear when tyrants seem to kiss.
William Shakespeare

U

UNDERSTANDING

The eye of the understanding is like the eye of the sense; for as you may see great objects through small crannies or holes, so you may see great axioms of nature through small and contemptible instances.
Francis Bacon

Men are admitted into heaven not because they have curbed or governed their passions, but because they have cultivate their understandings.
William Blake

He who calls in the aid of an equal understanding doubles his own; and he who profits of a superior understanding raises his powers to a level with the height of the superior understanding he unites with.
Edward Burke

Martyrs must choose between being forgotten, mocked or made use of. As for being understood, never!
Albert Camus

Be not disturbed at being misunderstood; be disturbed rather at not being understanding.
Chinese proverb

Brethren, be not children in understanding: how-beit in malice be ye children, but in understanding be men.
I Corinthians 14:20

What a delightful thing is the conversation of specialists! One understands absolutely nothing, and it's charming.
Edgar Degas

What better way is there to make men love one another than to make men understand one another. True charity comes only with clarity—just as mercy is but justice that understands. Surely the root of all evil is the inability to see clearly that which is.
Will Durant

There exists a passion for comprehension, just as there exists a passion for music. That passion is rather common in children, but gets lost in most people later on. Without this passion there would be neither mathematics nor natural science.
Albert Einstein

With all thy getting, get understanding, is the banner under which these *Forbes* editorials have appeared since the first issue of the publication. We have no illusions about what great wealth can do and what it cannot do. We believe in the worth-whileness of striving by all worthy means to attain success and to attain wealth. Simply because we are convinced that no amount of money is worth the sacrifice of one's better instincts, of one's self-respect—of one's soul, if you wish—simply because we are convinced that riches not gained legitimately and decently are not worth having. . . .
B.C. Forbes

If you want understanding try giving some.
Malcolm Forbes

When you don't understand, it's sometimes easier to look like you do.
Malcolm Forbes

To understand and to be understood makes our happiness on earth.
German proverb

The great need today in every phase of our social, economical and political life is understanding. It has always been so, but today the need is even greater.
Charles R. Hook

Understanding is more comprehensive than intellect because it intuits truths that cautious intellect can get sight of but never embrace—like a sea-gazer who never plunges in. When we understand, we have left intellect on the shore and don't need it and its crabbed analyses.
David S. Jones

The great art of learning is to understand but little at a time.
John Locke

A man of understanding finds less difficulty in submitting to a wrong-headed fellow, than in attempting to set him right.
François de La Rochefoucauld

There are three kinds of brains: One understands of itself, another can be taught to understand, and the third can neither understand to itself or be taught to understand.
Niccolò Machiavelli

A point of view can be a dangerous luxury when substituted for insight and understanding.
Marshall McLuhan

Thoughts are wonderful things, that they can bring two people, so far apart, into harmony and understanding for even a little while.
Ernest Pyle

If you wish to please people, you must begin by understanding them.
Charles Reade

The ways to knowledge are multitudinous—the way to understanding is devious.
Charles B. Rogers

Our greatest opportunities for advancing productivity and improving living standards are to be found in the field of human relationships. Having achieved a better understanding of each other and their common responsibility to consumers and investors, both management and labor should do all in their power to educate the American public to understanding of the simple economic facts that underlie our industrial and business relationships.
Louis Ruthenburg

Our dignity is not in what we do but what we understand. The whole world is doing things.
George Santayana

No one really understands the grief or joy of another. We always imagine that we are approaching some other, but our lines of travel are actually parallel.
Franz Schubert

It is the great destiny of human science, not to ease man's labors or prolong his life, noble as those ends may be, nor to serve the ends of power, but to enable man to walk upright without fear in a world which he at length will understand and which is his home.
Paul B. Sears

When the heart is won, the understanding is easily convinced.
Charles Simmons

Understanding comes through communication, and through understanding we find the way to peace.
Ralph C. Smedley

I have tried sedulously not to laugh at the acts of man, nor to lament them, nor to detest them, but to understand them.
Baruch Spinoza

I know no evil so great as the abuse of the understanding, and yet there is no one vice more common.
Richard Steele

My intimate contact with those great producing organizations and the men in them has given me great confidence in the machinery and the spirit now available for the building of a proper world. I do not mean that our industrial system is as good as it should be, but if I am looking for intelligent and unselfish understanding of our problems, and a generous approach to their solutions, I shall seek it among the makers and builders with far more confidence than among the talkers, the manipulators and the vote seekers.
Walter Teague

We shall see but little if we require to understand what we see. How few things can a man measure with the tape of his understanding.
Henry David Thoreau

USEFULNESS

Nothing in this world is so good as usefulness, It binds your fellow creatures to you, and you to them; it tends to the improvement of your own characters and gives you a real importance in society, much beyond what any artificial station can bestow.
B.C. Brodie

Everyone knows the usefulness of the useful, but no one knows the usefulness of the useless.
Chuang-tzu

All the good things of the world are no further good to us than as they are of use, and of all we may heap we enjoy only as much as we can use, and no more.
Daniel Defoe

Whatever you have, you must either use or lose.
Henry Ford

A useless life is only an early death.
Johann Wolfgang von Goethe

What praise is implied in the simple epithet "useful"! What reproach in the contrary.
David Hume

A barking dog is more useful than a sleeping lion.
Washington Irving

We must make automatic and habitual, as early as possible, as many useful actions as we can. . . . The more of the details of our daily life we can hand over to the effortless custody of automatism, the more our higher powers of mind will be set free for their own proper work.
William James

Success can corrupt, usefulness can only exalt.
Dimitri Mitroplous

When no new thoughts fill the mind—when no horizons beckon—when life is in the past, not in the future—you are on your way to uselessness.
Dr. Frederick K. Stamm

It is not paradox to say that in our most theoretical moods we may be nearest to our most practical applications.
Alfred North Whitehead

V

VACATIONS

Nothing is more memorable than a smell. One scent can be unexpected, momentary and fleeting, yet conjure up a childhood summer beside a lake in the mountains.
Diane Ackerman

Reached only by boat, seaplane and, with less surety, telephone—this is Fire Island, a pile of sand beneath a pile of people.
Alfred Aronowitz

On fashionable suntans: Skins tanned to the consistency of well-traveled alligator suitcases.
Russell Baker

What an odd thing tourism is. You fly off to a strange land, eagerly abandoning all the comforts of home, and then expend vast quantities of time and money in a largely futile attempt to recapture the

comforts that you wouldn't have lost if you hadn't left home in the first place.
Bill Bryson

A vacation is a sunburn at premium prices.
Hal Chadwicke

There are good books, even great books, that you read happily but with a faint feeling of duty. Then there are the books, often less pedigreed, that you read in a haze of compulsion, as if their pages emitted a drug. Summer is the season for the latter.
Ben Dolnick

On the preferred gender of her awaited third great-grandchild: I don't think I mind. I would very much like it to arrive. I'm going on holiday.
Queen Elizabeth II

Temporary release from work, through vacations, becomes more welcome, more pleasurable, even more necessary, as we grow older.
B.C. Forbes

Vacations for wage earners have proved both popular with workers and profitable for employers. Unfortunately, the majority of large employers have not yet followed the example set by a number of progressive corporations. I don't know of a single company that has abandoned vacations for wage earners after having tried the experiment. But I do know many that are delighted with the fruits they have gathered. Under some of the plans vacations with pay must be earned by good behavior, punctuality, etc. . . . The best results have come where the treatment has been regarded as most liberal.
B.C. Forbes

A tourist is a fellow who drives thousands of miles so he can be photographed standing in front of his car.
Émile Genest

The average vacation is one-tenth playing—nine-tenths paying.
Arnold Glasow

For me, the life of the angler is an almost flawless example of how not to have a good time.
Christopher Hitchens

To travel is to discover that everybody is wrong. The philosophies, the civilizations which seem, at a distance, so superior to those current at home, all prove on a close inspection to be in their own way just as hopelessly imperfect.
Aldous Huxley

A luxury liner is just a bad play surrounded by water.
Clive James

I hate vacations. If you can build buildings, why sit on the beach?
Philip Johnson

"Angling" is the name given to fishing by people who can't fish.
Stephen Leacock

Whenever summer rolls around I begin to realize that I'm a complete and utter book snob. In relation to reading, I have absolutely no guilty pleasures at all. No graphic novels. No murder mysteries. My summer read is really no different from my winter read. I know many bookshops and magazines would have me believe that our summer forays are different, but literature is literature, and unfortunately snobbery is snobbery.
Colum McCann

To go out with the setting sun on an empty beach is to truly embrace your solitude.
Jeanne Moreau

Everybody in 15th century Spain was wrong about where China was and as a result, Columbus discovered Caribbean vacations.
P.J. O'Rourke

The longing to get away from it all never was so great as in our present time of tension and trouble. We want something to lift us out of the mess into which much of life seems to have fallen.
Glenn Stewart

Vacation is that time when you wish you had something to do while doing nothing.
Frank Tyger

A vacation is what you take when you can no longer take what you've been taking.
Earl Wilson

Babies don't need vacations, but I still see them at the beach.
Steven Wright

VALUES

One of the great arts in living is to learn the art of accurately appraising values. Everything that we think, that we earn, that we have given to us, that in any way touches our consciousness, has its own value. These values are apt to change with the mood, with time, or because of circumstances. We cannot safely tie to any material value. The values of all material possessions change continually, sometimes overnight. Nothing of this nature has any permanent set value. The real values are those that stay by you,

give you happiness and enrich you. They are the human values.
George Matthew Adams

He, whose first emotion on the view of an excellent production is to undervalue it, will never have one of his own to show.
John Aiken

Look beneath the surface; let not the several quality of a thing nor its worth escape thee.
Marcus Aurelius Antoninus

Nothing of worth or weight can be achieved with half a mind, with a faint heart and with lame endeavor.
Isaac Barrow

I know it is more agreeable to walk upon carpets than to lie upon dungeon floors; I know it is pleasant to have all the comforts and luxuries of civilization; but he who cares only for these things is worth no more than a butterfly contented and thoughtless upon a morning flower; and who ever thought of rearing a tombstone to a last-summer's butterfly?
Henry Ward Beecher

Everything is worth precisely as much as a belch, the difference being that a belch is more satisfying.
Ingmar Bergman

Men are valued, not for what they are, but for what they seem to be.
Edward Bulwer-Lytton

No literature can outdo real life when it comes to cynicism. You're not going to get a person drunk with a jigger when he's just polished off a barrel.
Anton Chekhov

Cynicism is intellectual treason.
Norman Cousins

Sometimes one pays most for the things one gets for nothing.
Albert Einstein

Try not to become a man of success, but rather a man of value.
Albert Einstein

In the real dark night of the soul it is always three o'clock in the morning.
F. Scott Fitzgerald

One's real worth is never a quantifiable thing.
Malcolm Forbes

Victory is sweetest when you've known defeat.

Ability will never catch up with the demand for it.

You pay for everything, even including speaking your mind (with or without one).

Too many people overvalue what they are not and undervalue what they are.
Malcolm Forbes

There is too much stress today on material things. I try to teach my children not so much the value of cents, but a sense of values.
Morris Franklin

The worthless usually live long.
Baltasar Gracián

The function of values is to give us the illusion of purpose in life.
John P. Grier

A true measure of your worth includes all the benefits others have gained from your success.
Cullen Hightower

A man's worth is what he is divided by what he thinks he is.
Eric Hoffer

Irony differentiates. Cynicism never does.
Paul Horgan

Obsolescence is a factor which says that the new thing I bring you is worth more than the unused value of the old thing.
Charles F. Kettering

Today's value system considers holding on to one's money as important as holding on to one's sanity.
James A. Knight

Every man is valued in this world as he shows by his conduct that he wishes to be valued.
Jean de La Bruyère

Civilization ceases when we no longer respect and no longer put into their correct places the fundamental values, such as work, family and country; such as the individual, honor and religion.
R.P. Lebret

Today we are afraid of simple words like goodness and mercy and kindness. We don't believe in the good old words because we don't believe in the good old values anymore.
Lin Yutang

It is difficult to make a man miserable while he feels he is worthy of himself and claims kindred to the great God who made him.
Abraham Lincoln

Sometimes great life-changing values come to us in brief moments of contact with high-potential personalities.
Walter MacPeek

Minds are cluttered from the age of six with the values of others—values which bear little relation to their own private capacities, needs and desires.
Marya Mannes

Newspapermen, as journalists used to be called, have long been charged with the sin of cynicism, a characterization that many of us encourage to deflect attention from our far more widespread flaw, incorrigible sentimentalism.
Robert Manning

A cynic is a man who, when he smells flowers, looks around for a coffin.
H.L. Mencken

Man's chief purpose . . . is the creation and preservation of values; that is what gives meaning to our civilization, and the participation in this is what gives significance, ultimately, to the individual human life.
Lewis Mumford

There ought to be a club in which preachers and journalists could come together and have the sentimentalism of the one matched with the cynicism of the other. That ought to bring them pretty close to the truth.
Reinhold Niebuhr

A cynic is a person searching for an honest man, with a stolen lantern.
Edgar A. Shoaff

The greatest gains and values are farthest from being appreciated. We easily come to doubt if they exist. We soon forget them. They are the highest reality.
Henry David Thoreau

There is no readier way for a man to bring his own worth into question than by endeavoring to detract from the worth of other men.
John Tillotson

A sentimentalist is a man who sees an absurd value in everything and doesn't know the market price of a single thing.
Oscar Wilde

VANITY

An ostentatious man will rather relate a blunder or an absurdity he has committed, than be debarred from talking of his own dear person.
Joseph Addison

Vanity is a mortgage that must be deducted from the value of a man.
Otto Edward Bismarck

Don't you feel disgusted when you see some fellow strutting along with the air of a peacock? Doesn't the pompous gentleman cause you to laugh—or swear? Isn't vanity the essence of childishness? I have been trying to analyze in my own mind whether more or fewer of our so-called big men are obsessed with pride today than 20 years ago. I believe that more of our leaders are now democratic, approachable, likeable fellows than was the case in the earlier years of this century. . . . The press and the people have abundantly brought it home to the rich that their riches do not entitle them to any special deference or homage. . . .
B.C. Forbes

I have seldom seen much ostentation and much learning met together.
Joseph Hall

Vanity is truly the motive-power that moves humanity, and it is flattery that greases the wheels.
Jerome K. Jerome

Nothing so soothes our vanity as a display of greater vanity in others; it makes us vain, in fact, of our modesty.
Louis Kronenberger

When you are disposed to be vain of your mental acquirements, look up to those who are more accomplished than yourself, that you may be fired with

emulation; but when you feel dissatisfied with your circumstances, look down on those beneath you, that you may learn contentment.
Hannah More

He who denies his own vanity usually has it in so brutal a form that he must shut his eyes in order to avoid despising himself.
Friedrich Wilhelm Nietzsche

One will not go far wrong if one attributes extreme actions to vanity, average ones to habit and petty ones to fear.
Friedrich Wilhelm Nietzsche

There are no grades of vanity, there are only grades of ability in concealing it.
Mark Twain

It is curious how vanity helps the successful man and wrecks the failure.
Oscar Wilde

The surest cure for vanity is loneliness.
Thomas Wolfe

VIOLENCE

Violence is the last refuge of the incompetent.
Isaac Asimov

If you think of all the publicity about the terrible tragedy of Virginia Tech, we have a Virginia Tech in this country every day. It's just spread across 50 states.
Michael Bloomberg

Violence is as American as cherry pie.
H. Rap Brown

When in doubt have a man come through a door with a gun in his hand.
Raymond Chandler

Violence is just when kindness is vain.
Pierre Corneille

Popular culture tells you that schools and parents don't know what's going on, the police are dogs, politicians are all liars and scum, and any crime that's not committed by the Mafia is done by the CIA.
Stanley Crouch

Violent excitement exhausts the mind and leaves it withered and sterile.
François Fénelon

Can you understand why the Congress, most states and most cities refuse to pass legislation requiring the registration and licensing of any and all guns? For the life of me, I can't. We must register our cars and be licensed to drive. In many places we must get licenses for dogs and even bicycles. Being required to register firearms and show the competence and capacity to handle them hardly seems unreasonable, hardly seems an infringement of freedom.

What is it that blocks such legislation? Why do they block it? How are they able to block it?
Malcolm Forbes

Violence ever defeats its own ends. Where you cannot drive you can always persuade. A gentle word, a kind look, a good-natured smile can work wonders and accomplish miracles. There is a secret pride in every human heart that revolts at tyranny. You may order and drive an individual, but you cannot make him respect you.
William Hazlitt

What a vast difference there is between the barbarism that precedes culture and the barbarism that follows it.
Friedrich Hebbel

It is bad enough to persevere in barbarism; it is worse to relapse into it; but worst of all is consciously to seek it out.
Aurel Kolnai

Nothing good ever comes of violence.
Martin Luther

On the murder of New York deli owner Abe Lebewohl: It's almost like wiping out Carnegie Hall. A sandwich to a Jew is just as important as a country to a Gentile.
Jackie Mason

A doctor could make a million dollars if he could figure out a way to bring a boy into the world without a trigger finger.
Arthur Miller

Salvation and justice are not to be found in revolution, but in evolution through concord. Violence has ever achieved only destruction, not construction; the kindling of passions, not their pacification; the accumulation of hate and destruction, not the reconciliation of the contending parties; and it has reduced men and parties to the difficult task of building slowly after sad experience on the ruins of discord.
Pope Pius XII

A criminal is a person with predatory instincts without sufficient capital to form a corporation.
Howard Scott

If you injure your neighbor, better not do it by halves.
George Bernard Shaw

Violence can only be concealed by a lie, and the lie can only be maintained by violence. Any man who has once proclaimed violence as his method is inevitably forced to take the lie as his principle.
Alexander Solzhenitsyn

It's better to be wanted for murder than not to be wanted at all.
Marty Winch

VIRTUE

When we live habitually with the wicked, we become necessarily their victims or their disciples; on the contrary, when we associate with the virtuous we form ourselves in imitation of their virtues, or at least lose, every day, something of our faults.
Agapet

There is virtue in country houses, in gardens and orchards, in fields, streams and groves, in rustic recreations and plain manners, that neither cities nor universities enjoy.
Amos Bronson Alcott

There are some jobs in which it is impossible for a man to be virtuous.
Aristotle

I'm as pure as the driven slush.
Tallulah Bankhead

Only have enough of little virtues and common fidelities, and you need not mourn because you are neither a hero nor a saint.
Henry Ward Beecher

It is a very easy thing to devise good laws; the difficulty is to make them effective. The great mistake is that of looking on all men as virtuous, or thinking that they can be made so by laws; and consequently the greatest art of a politician is to render vices serviceable to the cause of virtue.
Lord Bolingbroke

The virtues which keep this world sweet and the faithfulness which keeps it steadfast are chiefly those of the average

man. The danger of the two-talent man is that he will be content with mediocrity.
W. Russell Bowie

Virtue, as such, naturally procures considerable advantages to the virtuous.
Joseph Butler

For most men, and most circumstances, pleasure—tangible material prosperity in this world—is the safest test of virtue. Progress has ever been through the pleasures rather than through the extreme sharp virtues, and the most virtuous have leaned to excess rather than to asceticism.
Samuel Butler

Ethical living is the indispensable condition of all that is most worthwhile in the world.
Ernest Caldecott

I have always thought it would be easier to redeem a man steeped in vice and crime than a greedy, narrow-minded, pitiless merchant.
Albert Camus

We are all exceptional cases. Each man insists on being innocent, even if it means accusing the whole human race, and heaven.
Albert Camus

Virtue is like health: the harmony of the whole man.
Thomas Carlyle

What is virtue? Reason in practice.
J.J. de Chenier

The door to virtue is heavy and hard to push.
Chinese proverb

The more virtuous any man is, the less easily does he suspect others to be vicious.
Cicero

Virtue and decency are so nearly related that it is difficult to separate them from each other but in our imagination.
Cicero

Virtue is its own reward.
Cicero

Cannot our ethical system be taught upon a non-sectarian basis in all schools, squaring it up with the sciences to the end that our boys and girls, when they emerge, are not ripe fruit for the disbelieving skeptics and the intellectual exhibitionists?
Andrew V. Clements

Nothing more completely baffles one who is full of tricks and duplicity than straightforward and simple integrity in another.
Charles Caleb Colton

Sincerity and truth are the basis of every virtue.
Confucius

A little integrity is better than any career.
Ralph Waldo Emerson

The only reward of virtue is virtue.
Ralph Waldo Emerson

If virtue promises happiness, prosperity and peace, then progress in virtue is progress in each of these; for to whatever point the perfection of anything brings us, progress is always an approach toward it.
Epictetus

The soul that companies with virtue is like an ever-flowing source. It is a pure, clear, and wholesome draught, sweet, rich and generous of its store, that injures not, neither destroys.
Epictetus

When grown people speak of the innocence of children, they don't really know
what they mean. Pressed, they will go
a step further and say, Well, ignorance
then. The child is neither. There is no
crime which a boy of 11 has not envis-
aged long ago. His only innocence is, he
may not yet be old enough to desire the
fruits of it. His ignorance is, he does not
know how to commit it.
William Faulkner

Integrity begins with a person being
willing to be honest with himself.
Cort R. Flint

Compliment others on the virtues they
have; and they're not half as pleased as
being complimented for the ones they
don't have.
Malcolm Forbes

You're fortunate when you can afford to
be virtuous.
Malcolm Forbes

What is called virtue in the common
sense of the word has nothing to do with
this or that man's prosperity, or even
happiness.
James A. Froude

Want of prudence is too frequently the
want of virtue.
Oliver Goldsmith

There can be no final truth in ethics any
more than in physics, until the last man
has had his experience and said his say.
William James

There is a natural aristocracy among
men. The grounds for this are virtue
and talents.
Thomas Jefferson

Integrity without knowledge is weak and
useless, and knowledge without integrity
is dangerous and dreadful.
Samuel Johnson

Let them call it mischief; when it is past
and prospered, it will be virtue.
Ben Jonson

Wisdom is knowing what to do next,
virtue is doing it.
David Starr Jordan

Virtue by calculation is the virtue of vice.
Joseph Joubert

Integrity is praised, and starves.
Juvenal

Courage, energy and patience are the
virtues which appeal to my heart.
Fritz Kreisler

It is easier to enrich ourselves with
a thousand virtues, than to correct
ourselves of a single fault.
Jean de La Bruyère

If vanity does not entirely overthrow the
virtues, at least it makes them all totter.
François de La Rouchefoucauld

What we take for virtue is often nothing
but an assemblage of different actions,
and of different interests, that fortune or
our industry knows how to arrange.
François de La Rochefoucauld

I have three precious things which I hold
fast and prize. The first is gentleness; the
second is frugality; the third is humility,
which keeps me from putting myself
before others. Be gentle and you can be
bold; be frugal and you can be liberal;
avoid putting yourself before others and
you can become a leader among men.
Lao-tzu

What do I owe to my times, to my country, to my neighbors, to my friends? Such are the questions which a virtuous man ought often to ask himself.
Johann Lavater

The morals of men are more governed by their pursuits than by their opinions. A type of virtue is first formed by circumstances, and men afterwards make it the model upon which their theories are framed.
W.E.H. Lecky

Deliberate virtue is never worth much: The virtue of feeling or habit is the thing.
Georg C. Lichtenberg

Virtue is everywhere that which is thought praiseworthy; and nothing else but that which has the allowance of public esteem is called virtue.
John Locke

A man can be as truly a saint in a factory as in a monastery, and there is as much need of him in the one as in the other.
Robert J. McCracken

Most men admire virtue, who follow not her lore.
John Milton

Industry, economy, honesty and kindness form a quartet of virtue that will never be improved upon.
James Oliver

When we are planning for posterity, we ought to remember that virtue is not hereditary.
Thomas Paine

In all things preserve integrity; and the consciousness of thine own uprightness will alleviate the toil of business.
William Paley

The strength of a man's virtue must not be measured by his occasional efforts, but by his ordinary life.
Blaise Pascal

We are apt to love praise, but not to deserve it. But if we would deserve it, we must love virtue more than that.
William Penn

Virtue, though she gets her beginning from nature, yet receives her finishing touches from learning.
Quintilian

If self-knowledge is the road to virtue, so is virtue still more the road to self-knowledge.
Jean Paul Richter

A virtue and a muscle are alike. If either of them is exercised they get weak and flabby.
Richard L. Rooney

Though conditions have grown puzzling in their complexity, though changes have been vast, yet we may remain absolutely sure of one thing; that now as ever in the past, and as it will ever be in the future, there can be no substitute for elemental virtues, for the elemental qualities to which we allude when we speak of a man, not only as a good man, but as emphatically a man. We can build up the standard of individual citizenship and individual well-being, we can raise the national standard and make it what it can and shall be made, only by each of us steadfastly keeping in mind that there can be no substitute for the world-old commonplace qualities of truth, justice, and courage, thrift, industry, common sense and genuine sympathy with the fellow feelings of others.
Theodore Roosevelt

No virtue is safe that is not enthusiastic.
John Seeley

Nature does not bestow virtue; to be good is an art.
Seneca

To be ambitious of true honor, of the true glory and perfection of our natures, is the very principle and incentive of virtue.
Philip Sidney

Integrity is the first step to true greatness. Men love to praise, but are slow to practice it.
Charles Simmons

The shortest and surest way to live with honor in the world is to be in reality what we would appear to be; and if we observe, we shall find that all human virtues increase and strengthen themselves by the practice and experience of them.
Socrates

We live in a war of two antagonistic ethical philosophies, the ethical policy taught in the books and schools, and the success policy.
William Graham Sumner

The wicked are wicked, no doubt, and they go astray and they fall, and they come by their deserts; but who can tell the mischief which the very virtuous do?
William Makepeace Thackeray

Virtue has never been as respectable as money.
Mark Twain

Good company and good discourse are the sinews of virtue.
Izaak Walton

Few men have virtue to withstand the highest bidder.
George Washington

The pure are not fortune's favorites.
Welsh proverb

Virtue has its own reward, but no sale at the box office.
Mae West

One should seek virtue for its own sake and not from hope or fear, or any external motive. It is in virtue that happiness consists, for virtue is the state of mind which tends to make the whole of life harmonious.
Zeno

VOTING

Always vote for a principle, though you vote alone, and you may cherish the sweet reflection that your vote is never lost.
John Quincy Adams

If the people are to be the final tribunal then they must vote for what is right rather than according to their own selfish interests, else we are treading the path of danger.
Henry L. Doherty

Our American heritage is threatened as much by our own indifference as it is by the most unscrupulous office or by the most powerful foreign threat. The future of this republic is in the hands of the American voter.
Dwight D. Eisenhower

A lot of voters always cast their ballot for the candidate who seems to them to be one of the people. That means he must have the same superstitions, the same unbalanced prejudices, and the same lack of understanding of public finances that are characteristic of the majority. A better choice would be a candidate who has a closer understanding and a better education than the majority. Too much

voting is based on affability rather than on ability.
William Feather

People vote their resentment, not their appreciation. The average man does not vote for anything, but against something.
William Bennett Munro

W

WAGES

A fair day's-wage for a fair day's-work: It is as just a demand as governed men ever made of governing. It is the everlasting right of man.
Thomas Carlyle

Always remember that there is a law of compensation which operates just as infallibly as gravitation, and that victory goes at last where it ought to, and that this is just as true of individuals as of nations.
William Feather

Note to salary setters: Pay your people the least possible and you'll get from them the same.
Malcolm Forbes

Of course, it is not the employer who pays wages. He only handles the money. It is the product that pays wages and it is the management that arranges the production so that the product may pay the wages.
Henry Ford

I've noticed two things about men who get big salaries. They are almost invariably men who, in conversation or in conference, are adaptable.

They quickly get the other fellow's view. They are more eager to do this than to express their own ideas. Also, they state their own point of view convincingly.
John Hallock

A day's pay for a day's work is more than adequate when both the work and the pay are appreciated as much as they are expected.
Cullen Hightower

Anybody who has any doubt about the resourcefulness or the ingenuity of a plumber never got a bill from one.
George Meany

One of labor's long-range objectives is to achieve in every basic industry a guaranteed annual wage so that the consumers of this country can have a sustained income month in and month out, because only on that basis can we sustain an economy of full employment and full production and full distribution.
Walter P. Reuther

Even Noah got no salary for the first six months—partly on account of the weather and partly because he was learning navigation.
Mark Twain

WAR

Lesson learned as infantryman in World War II: Stay the hell out of war!
S. Daniel Abraham

Anyone who has looked into the glazed eyes of a soldier dying on the battlefield will think hard before starting a war.
Otto von Bismarck

After the Cuban missile crisis I asked both McGeorge Bundy and Robert Kennedy if they would tell me how much that single evaluated piece of photographic evidence was worth, and they each said it fully justified all that the CIA had cost the country in all its preceding years.
Ray Cline

In peace the sons bury their fathers, but in war the fathers bury their sons.
Croesus

No business in the country today is important except as it contributes toward winning the war.
Allan B. Forbes

The Korean outlook still constitutes an enigma.
B.C. Forbes (1951)

A little while ago I visited Omaha Beach for the second time in my life. In the intervening 26 years, nearly 20,000 tides had come and gone and little remains visible of the greatest military landing in man's history of endless warring. What's to be seen is mostly in a superb museum and a panoramic cemetery. The cemetery memorializes with dignity and grandeur the event and the dead, and moves one deeply.

Before they die less precipitously and/or in lesser purpose, Americans who can should visit World War II's Normandy Beach. Such seeing and remembering helps a man's perspective.
Malcolm Forbes

Bringing Home The Boys has been a top objective of Americans ever since we first sent some of them overseas decades ago. At the close of World War I the phrase flowered, though I'll bet it was used in connection with the Spanish American War. Probably even before

that, when Americans stormed the forts outside Mexico City in 1847. Thank God we're doing so again from Vietnam. But the Return of Americans shouldn't be confined to battle zones. We are neither wanted, nor needed, nor should we be in large numbers in such places as Germany, Korea, Thailand, Okinawa, Japan, the Philippines, Turkey, Spain and so on, ad nauseam.
Malcolm Forbes

It is a damned sight easier to start wars than to end them. This truth has been stated for as long and as often as it has been ignored. High time and thank God, we are at least moving toward de-escalation in Vietnam. The road to extrication will be long, painful, bitter. But it must be trod. We are so bogged down in Vietnam that we cannot respond effectively anywhere else in the world to a military power play except through atomic bombardment.
Malcolm Forbes

Wars almost never end the way starters had in mind.
Malcolm Forbes

There never was a good war or a bad peace.
Benjamin Franklin

To win the war our government must have steel and more steel. It is clear we must prepare ourselves for a long and uninterrupted continuance of hostilities. The foe is strong and desperate.
Elbert H. Gary

Those who in quarrels interpose, must often wipe a bloody nose.
John Gay

There can be no profit in the making or selling of things to be destroyed in war. Men may think that they have such

profit, but in the end the profit will turn out to be a loss.
Alexander Hamilton

The Gulf War was like teenage sex. We got in too soon and out too soon.
Tom Harkin

We become accomplices in evil every time we seek to soothe the unslakable appetites of the crime family that sits in Pyongyang.
Christopher Hitchens

On invading Russia: The beginning of every war is like opening the door into a dark room. One never knows what is hidden in the darkness.
Adolf Hitler

It is the blood of the soldier that makes the general great.
Italian proverb

None but an armed nation can dispense with a standing army.
Thomas Jefferson

Working in a newsroom in Seoul, it certainly does not feel like I'm living in a country that is in a state of war.
Chery Kang

The only war is the war you fought in. Every veteran knows that.
Allan Keller

The most persistent sound which reverberates through man's history is the beating of war drums.
Arthur Koestler

As we head to war with Iraq, President Bush wants to make one thing clear: This war is not about oil, it's about gasoline.
Jay Leno

I know war as few other men now living know it, and nothing to me is more revolting. I have long advocated its complete abolition, as its very destructiveness on both friend and foe has rendered it useless as a method of settling international disputes.
Douglas MacArthur

In war, you win or lose, live or die, and the difference is just an eyelash.
Douglas MacArthur

They died hard, those savage men, like wounded wolves at bay. They were filthy, and they were lousy, and they stunk. And I loved them.
Douglas MacArthur

One ought never to allow a disorder to take place in order to avoid war, for war is not thereby avoided, but only deferred to your disadvantage.
Niccolò Machiavelli

Of all the evils to public liberty, war is perhaps the most to be dreaded, because it comprises and develops every other. War is the patent of armies; from these proceed debts and taxes. And armies, and debts, and taxes, are the known instruments for bringing the many under the dominion of the few. In war, too, the discretionary power of the executive is extended; its influence in dealing out offices, honors, and emoluments is multiplied; and all the means of seducing the minds are added to those of subduing the force of the people! No nation could preserve its freedom in the midst of continual warfare.
James Madison

War is only a cowardly escape from the problems of peace.
Thomas Mann

And when you hear of wars and rumors of wars, do not be alarmed. This must take place, but the end is not yet.
Mark 13:7

The instruments of war can be manufactured . . . human blood cannot be; and the lack of just one pint could mean the life of an American serviceman.
George C. Marshall

Always remember that a soldier's pack is lighter than a slave's chains.
David O. McKay

All of us who grew up before World War II are immigrants in time, immigrants from an earlier world, living in an age essentially different from anything we knew before.
Margaret Mead

War will disappear, like the dinosaur, when changes in world conditions have destroyed its survival value.
Robert A. Millikan

War hath no fury like a noncombatant.
Charles Edward Montague

All eyes, all attention at the federal level, are on al Qaeda and the war on terror. Fact is, al Qaeda wouldn't last a day in parts of Philadelphia. I've got gangsters with .45s that would run them outta town.
Michael Nutter

The world cannot continue to wage war like physical giants and to seek peace like intellectual pygmies.
Basil O'Connor

There remains the possibility of Korean reunification. Between that peaceful scenario and recollections of the horrors of their civil war, Koreans on both sides of the DMZ have little appetite for

full-blown warfare. So relax, and enjoy the next hit from PSY.
Ana Marie Pamintuan

You can no more win a war than you can win an earthquake.
Jeannette Rankin

We understand what kind of regime North Korea is, but we also understand that North Korea is playing games.
Sun Zhe

In the eyes of the people, the general who wins a battle has made no mistakes.
Voltaire

War is partially the result of the greed of men, of imperialistic ambitions, the desire to reach out and possess what others possess. We have seen the hatred of one people for another, notably the persecution of the Jews. Such hatred, however, as well as the cruelty and unkindness that may exist below the veneer of our civilization, are transitory.
Alfred Grant Walton, D.D.

It was necessary for us to discover greater powers of destruction than our enemies. We did. But after every war we have followed through with a new rise in our standard of living by the application of war-taught knowledge for the benefit of the world. It will be the same with the atomic bomb principles.
Thomas J. Watson

As long as war is looked upon as wicked, it will always have its fascination. When it is looked upon as vulgar, it will cease to be popular.
Oscar Wilde

WASTE

An extravagance is anything you buy that is of no earthly use to your wife.
Franklin Pierce Adams

Next to the dog, the wastebasket is man's best friend.
Anonymous

The road of excess leads to the palace of wisdom; for we never know what is enough until we know what is more than enough.
William Blake

What is taken from the fortune, also, may haply be so much lifted from the soul. The greatness of a loss, as the proverb suggests, is determinable, not so much by what we have lost, as by what we have left.
Christian Bovée

The excesses of our youth are drafts upon our old age.
Charles Caleb Colton

The injury of prodigality leads to this, that he that will not economize will have to agonize.
Confucius

From time waste there can be no salvage. It is the easiest of all waste and the hardest to correct because it does not litter the floor.
Henry Ford

The government in business may waste time and money without rendering service. In the end the public pays in taxes. The corporation cannot waste or it will fall. It cannot make unfair rulings or give high-handed, expensive service, for there are not enough people willing to accept inferior service to make a volume of business that will pay dividends.
Henry Ford

Rust wastes more than use.
French proverb

Many people take no care of their money till they come nearly to the end of it, and others do just the same with their time.
Johann Wolfgang von Goethe

Excesses are essentially gestures. It is easy to be extremely cruel, magnanimous, humble or self-sacrificing when we see ourselves as actors in a performance.
Eric Hoffer

Man's chief difference from the brutes lies in the exuberant excess of his subjective propensities. Prune his extravagance, sober him, and you undo him.
William James

By eating what is sufficient man is enabled to work; he is hindered from working and becomes heavy, idle, and stupid if he takes too much. As to bodily distempers occasioned by excess, there is no end of them.
Thomas R. Jones

He who is the cause of another's advancement is thereby the cause of his own ruin.
Niccolò Machiavelli

Losses are comparative, imagination only makes them of any moment.
Blaise Pascal

Spend and be free, but make no waste.
John Ray

No hour is to be considered a waste which teaches one what not to do.
Charles B. Rogers

Why shouldn't things be largely absurd, futile and transitory? They are so; and

we are so, and they and we go very well together.
George Santayana

Wasted time means wasted lives.
R. Shannon

Hundreds would never have known want if they had not at first known waste.
Charles H. Spurgeon

Benjamin Franklin went through life an altered man because he once paid too dearly for a penny whistle. My concern springs usually from a deeper source, to wit, from having bought a whistle when I did not want one.
Robert Louis Stevenson

We are forced to measure each moment partly in and of itself, for if everything is justified solely by the future, life becomes rather futile.
Malcolm R. Sutherland, Jr.

I hold this to be the rule of life, Too much of anything is bad.
Terence

Too much of a good thing can be wonderful.
Mae West

WEALTH

A poor American feels guilty at being poor, but less guilty than an American rentier who has inherited wealth but is doing nothing to increase it; what can the latter do but take to drink and psychoanalysis?
W.H. Auden

There is a growing sentiment in America that regular saving should be ignored—that the government will take care of people and give them security when they get beyond a certain age or become old

and unable to work, but it must be borne in mind that the people who earn and do save, take care of the government! Were it not for the thrifty and the willing workers, the government would be in a bad way.
George Matthew Adams

Another advantage of being rich is that all your faults are called eccentricities.
Anonymous

Save for gold, jewels, works of art, perhaps good agricultural land, and a very few other things, there ain't no such animal as a permanent investment.
Bernard M. Baruch

The true way to gain much, is never to desire to gain too much. He is not rich that possesses much, but he that covets no more; and he is not poor that enjoys little, but he that wants too much.
Francis Beaumont

If any man is rich and powerful he comes under the law of God by which the higher branches must take the burnings of the sun, and shade those that are lower; by which the tall trees must protect the weak plants beneath them.
Henry Ward Beecher

In this world it is not what we take up, but what we give up, that makes us rich.
Henry Ward Beecher

Very few men acquire wealth in such a manner as to receive pleasure from it.
Henry Ward Beecher

I can walk. It's just that I'm so rich I don't need to.
Alan Bennett

The ascending spiral of greatness in America has risen because industry has produced wealth, which in turn has supported educational institutions,

which in turn have supplied leadership to industry in order that with each succeeding generation it might produce more wealth.
Wallace F. Bennett

The best condition in life is not to be so rich as to be envied nor so poor as to be damned.
Josh Billings

If the majority of people of a country, no matter how great its natural resources, organize and conspire to get more out and put less in, to do less and get more, how long will, how long can it last?
William J.H. Boetcker

The more you learn what to do with yourself, and the more you do for others, the more you will learn to enjoy the abundant life.
William J.H. Boetcker

Getting fired can produce a particularly bountiful payday for a CEO. He can "earn" more in that single day, while cleaning out his desk, than an American worker earns in a lifetime of cleaning toilets. Today, in the executive suite, the all-too-prevalent rule is nothing succeeds like failure.
Warren Buffett

If we command our wealth, we shall be rich and free; if our wealth commands us, we are poor indeed.
Edmund Burke

For anything worth having one must pay the price; and the price is always work, patience, love, self-sacrifice—no paper currency, no promises to pay, but the goal of real service.
John Burroughs

The wealth of man is the number of things which he loves and blesses, which he is loved and blessed by.
Thomas Carlyle

At the end, the acquisition of wealth is ignoble in the extreme. I assume that you save and long for wealth only as a means of enabling you the better to do some good in your day and generation.
Andrew Carnegie

Surplus wealth is a sacred trust which its possessor is bound to administer in his lifetime for the good of the community.
Andrew Carnegie

The gratification of wealth is not found in mere possession or in lavish expenditure, but in its wise application.
Miguel de Cervantes

I knew once a very covetous, sordid fellow who used to say, Take care of the pence, for the pounds will take care of themselves.
Lord Chesterfield

It is difficult to set bounds to the price unless you first set bounds to the wish.
Cicero

There is enough for all. The earth is a generous mother; she will provide in plentiful abundance food for all her children if they will but cultivate her soil in justice and in peace.
Bourke Cockran

That which we acquire with the most difficulty we retain the longest; as those who have earned a fortune are usually more careful of it than those who have inherited one.
Charles Caleb Colton

Money is power. Every good man and woman ought to strive for power, to do

good with it when obtained. I say, get rich, get rich!
Russell Herman Conwell

To acquire wealth is difficult, to preserve it more difficult, but to spend it wisely most difficult of all.
Edward Day

But thou shalt remember the Lord thy God: for it is he that giveth thee power to get wealth, that he may establish his covenant which he sware unto thy fathers, as it is this day.
Deuteronomy 8:18

The secret point of money and power in America is neither the things that money can buy nor power for power's sake but absolute personal freedom, mobility, privacy.
Joan Didion

A billion dollars here, a billion dollars there, and pretty soon you're talking about real money.
Everett Dirksen

All heiresses are beautiful.
John Dryden

Each man also to whom God hath given riches and wealth, and hath given him power to eat thereof, and to take his portion, and to rejoice in his labor; this is the gift of God. For he shall not much remember the days of his life; because God answereth him in the joy of his heart.
Ecclesiastes 5:19–20

If rich men would remember that shrouds have no pockets, they would, while living, share their wealth with their children, and give for the good of others, and so know the highest pleasure wealth can give.
Tryon Edwards

It requires a great deal of boldness and a great deal of caution to make a great fortune, and when you have got it, it requires ten times as much wit to keep it.
Ralph Waldo Emerson

Wealth brings with it its own checks and balances. The basis of political economy is noninterference. The only safe rule is found in the self-adjusting meter of demand and supply. Open the doors of opportunity to talent and virtue and they will do themselves justice, and property will not be in bad hands. In a free and just commonwealth, property rushes from the idle and imbecile to the industrious, brave and persevering.
Ralph Waldo Emerson

Bare-faced covetousness was the moving spirit of civilization from the first dawn to the present day; wealth, and again wealth, and for the third time wealth; wealth, not of society, but of the puny individual, was its only and final aim.
Friedrich Engels

Poor men seek meat for their stomachs, rich men stomachs for their meat.
English proverb

Lampis the shipowner, on being asked how he acquired his great wealth, replied, My great wealth was acquired with no difficulty, but my small wealth, my first gains, with much labor.
Epictetus

When the anger of the gods is incurred, wealth or power only bring more devastating punishment.
Euripides

Let me tell you about the very rich. They are different from you and me. They possess and enjoy early, and it does something to them, makes them soft where we are trustful, in a way that,

unless you were born rich, it is very difficult to understand.
F. Scott Fitzgerald

A nation's economic salvation does not
lie in the amount of money its rich inhabitants can squander recklessly. A nation's
economic salvation lies in the amount
of money its inhabitants can save and
invest after providing themselves with
all the necessaries and all the reasonable
comforts of life.
B.C. Forbes

A young financial writer once brought
ridicule upon himself by stating that
a certain company had nothing to
commend it except excellent earnings.
Well, there are companies whose earnings are excellent but whose stocks I
would never recommend. In selecting
investments, I attach prime importance
to the men behind them. I'd rather buy
brains and character than earnings.
Earnings can be good one year and poor
the next. But if you put your money
into securities run by men combining
conspicuous brains and unimpeachable
character, the likelihood is that the financial results will prove satisfactory.
B.C. Forbes

Are your desires purely selfish? Do your
tastes run to a grand home, automobiles,
fine clothes, an abundance of amusements, and so forth? If so, look around
you at people who have such things in
superabundance. Are they any happier,
do you think, than you are? Are they any
better morally? Are they any stronger
physically? Are they better liked by their
friends than you are by your friends? . . .
Carnegie said, Millionaires rarely smile.
This is substantially true.
B.C. Forbes

If the United States is to produce a
nation of investors—as we must if we are
to gain financial world-leadership—it is
imperative that boards of directors be so
constituted as to adequately represent
the interests and inspire the complete
confidence of investors of moderate
substance.
B.C. Forbes

Remember, diamonds are only lumps of
coal that stuck to their jobs.
B.C. Forbes

In all the thrashing about that results
from our dwindling gold reserves, it's
about time that this country and other
countries get some perspective on the
situation.

The day this country is out of the stuff,
that day gold becomes what it's worth
as a metal and no longer will have much
significance as a monetary measurement.

It isn't the gold we have that makes this
nation rich. It's what we make, our know
how, our productivity. So long as this
country produces more and better, the
world will continue to want what we
make.
Malcolm Forbes

Investor: One who bought stocks that
went up.
Malcolm Forbes

Wherever desirable superfluities are
imported, industry is excited, and
thereby plenty is produced. Were only
necessaries permitted to be purchased,
men would work no more than was
necessary for that purpose.
Benjamin Franklin

He is not fit for riches who is afraid to
use them.
Thomas Fuller

Let me gain by you, and no matter
whether you love me or not.
Thomas Fuller

Wealth is a means to an end, not the end itself. As a synonym for health and happiness, it has had a fair trial and failed dismally.
John Galsworthy

I am indeed rich, since my income is superior to my expense, and my expense is equal to my wishes.
Edward Gibbon

Hereditary wealth is in reality a premium paid to idleness.
William Godwin

One is led astray alike by sympathy and coldness, by praise and by blame.
Johann Wolfgang von Goethe

His greatest riches—ignorance of wealth.
Oliver Goldsmith

Ill fares the land
To hastening ills a prey
When wealth accumulates
But men decay.
Oliver Goldsmith

The jests of the rich are ever successful.
Oliver Goldsmith

Rich people should consider that they are only trustees for what they possess, and should show their wealth to be more in doing good than merely in having it.
Joseph Hall

Sometimes the best gain is to lose.
George Herbert

I wish I were either rich enough or poor enough to do a lot of things that are impossible in my present comfortable circumstances.
Don Herold

Take away play, fancies and luxuries and you will turn man into a dull, sluggish creature, barely energetic enough to obtain a bare subsistence.
Eric Hoffer

Wealth is a great thing to have and a great thing to share.
Harold Honickman

High descent and meritorious deeds, unless united to wealth, are as useless as seaweed.
Horace

When I caution you against becoming a miser, I do not therefore advise you to become a prodigal or a spendthrift.
Horace

He is rich who owes nothing.
Hungarian proverb

Every gain made by individuals or societies is almost instantly taken for granted. The luminous ceiling toward which we raise our longing eyes becomes, when we have climbed to the next floor, a stretch of disregarded lino-leum beneath our feet.
Aldous Huxley

No man is any the worse off because another acquires wealth by trade, or by the exercise of a profession; on the contrary, he cannot have acquired his wealth except by benefiting others to the extent of what they considered to be its value.
Thomas H. Huxley

In America 18% of people are below the poverty level. Tell me how you can justify this, given our great country and the fact that top management are being paid what they're paid.
Carl Icahn

Speculation is the romance of trade, and casts contempt upon all its sober realities. It renders the stock-jobber a

magician, and the exchange a region of enchantment.
Washington Irving

Go to now, ye rich men, weep and howl for your miseries that shall come upon you. Your riches are corrupted, and your garments are motheaten.
James 5:1–2

In the practical as in the theoretic life, the man whose acquisitions stick is the man who is always achieving and advancing, whilst his neighbors, spending most of their time in relearning what they once knew but have forgotten, simply hold their own.
William James

Nothing is more fallacious than wealth. Today it is for thee, tomorrow it is against thee. It arms the eyes of the envious everywhere. It is a hostile comrade, a domestic enemy.
St. John Chrysostom

Bounty always receives part of its value from the manner in which it is bestowed.
Samuel Johnson

A man who both spends and saves money is the happiest man, because he has both enjoyments.
Samuel Johnson

Few enterprises of great labor or hazard would be undertaken if we had not the power of magnifying the advantages we expect from them.
Samuel Johnson

It is better to live rich than to die rich.
Samuel Johnson

We do not commonly find men of superior sense amongst those of the highest fortune.
Juvenal

A speculator is one who runs risks of which he is aware, and an investor is one who runs risks of which he is unaware.
John Maynard Keynes

Savings represent much more than mere money value. They are the proof that the saver is worth something in himself. Any fool can waste; any fool can muddle; but it takes something more of a man to save and the more he saves the more of a man he makes of himself. Waste and extravagance unsettle a man's mind for every crisis; thrift, which means some form of self-restraint, steadies it.
Rudyard Kipling

Misers are neither relations, nor friends, nor citizens, nor Christians, nor perhaps even human beings.
Jean de La Bruyère

We all covet wealth, but not its perils.
Jean de La Bruyère

Never say you know a man until you have divided an inheritance with him.
Johann Lavater

One's strongest asset is simultaneously his point of strongest vulnerability.
Harry Levinson

If the wealth of this country were distributed, 90 per cent. would be destroyed by the act of distribution. The resulting starvation and anarchy would destroy the rest in less than thirty days.
James F. Lincoln

I've been more bossed by my fortune than it has been bossed by me.
John P. Lippett

Never buy at the bottom, and always sell too soon.
Jesse L. Livermore

Wealth may be an excellent thing, for it means power, leisure and liberty.
James Russell Lowell

Wealth is the smallest thing on earth, the least gift that God has bestowed on mankind.
Martin Luther

Luxury makes a man so soft that it is hard to please him, and easy to trouble him; so that his pleasures at last become his burden. Luxury is a nice master, hard to be pleased.
Sir G. Mackenzie

When a man tells you he got rich through hard work, ask him: Whose?
Don Marquis

For whosoever hath, to him shall be given, and he shall have more abundance; but whosoever hath not, from him shall be taken away even that he hath.
Matthew 13:12

God must love the rich or he wouldn't divide so much among so few of them.
H.L. Mencken

The most valuable of human possessions, next to a superior and disdainful air, is the reputation of being well-to-do. Nothing else so neatly eases one's way through life, especially in democratic countries.
H.L. Mencken

A man's true wealth is the good he does in this world.
Muhammad

Although wealth may not bring happiness, the immediate prospect of it provides a wonderfully close imitation.
Patrick O'Brian

Why is it no one ever sent me yet
One perfect limousine, do you suppose?

Ah no, it's always just my luck to get
One perfect rose.
Dorothy Parker

Those who condemn wealth are those who have none and see no chance of getting it.
William Penn Patrick

Every luxury must be paid for, and everything is a luxury, starting with being in the world.
Cesare Pavese

Luxury is the first, second and third cause of the ruin of republics. It is the vampire which soothes us into a fatal slumber while it sucks the life-blood of our veins.
Payson

There is no sound basis upon which it may be assumed that all poor men are godly and all rich men are evil, no more than it could be assumed that all rich men are good and all poor men are bad.
Norman Vincent Peale, D.D.

Get place and wealth, if possible with grace; if not, by any means get wealth and place.
Alexander Pope

To whom can riches give repute, or trust, content, or pleasure, but the good and the just?
Alexander Pope

He that oppresseth the poor to increase his riches, and he that giveth to the rich, shall surely come to want.
Proverbs 22:16

Be not thou afraid when one is made rich, when the glory of his house is increased; for when he dieth he shall carry nothing away: his glory shall not descend after him.
Psalms 49:16–17

Well, yes, you could say we have independent means.
John D. Rockefeller III

Probably the greatest harm done by vast wealth is the harm that we of moderate means do to ourselves when we let the vices of envy and hatred enter deep into our own natures.
Theodore Roosevelt

It takes a great deal of boldness mixed with a vast deal of caution to acquire a great fortune; but then it takes ten times as much wit to keep it after you have got it as it took you to make it.
Baron Rothschild

A fool and her money are soon courted.
Helen Rowland

Why is one man richer than another? Because he is more industrious, more persevering and more sagacious.
John Ruskin

Look at a gown of gold, and you will at least get a sleeve of it.
Walter Scott

A great fortune is a great slavery.
Seneca

A miser grows rich by seeming poor; an extravagant man grows poor by seeming rich.
William Shakespeare

Abundance consists not alone in material possession, but in an uncovetous spirit.
Charles M. Sheldon

Wealth is a dangerous inheritance, unless the inheritor is trained to active benevolence.
Charles Simmons

You can never be too rich or too thin.
Wallis Simpson

The real price of everything is the toil and trouble of acquiring it.
Adam Smith

Whatever a person saves from his revenue he adds to his capital, and either employs it himself in maintaining an additional number of productive hands, or enables some person to do so . . . for a share of profits. As the capital of an individual can be increased only by what he saves . . . so the capital of a society can be increased only in the same manner.
Adam Smith

Solvency is entirely a matter of temperament and not of income.
Logan Pearsall Smith

If a rich man is proud of his wealth, he should not be praised until it is known how he employs it.
Socrates

Luxury, today, is solitude and silence.
Paul-Henri Spaak

We shall have better business when everyone realizes that while it pays to invest money in their industries and develop natural resources, it pays still higher dividends to improve mankind and develop human resources.
H.E. Steiner

Just as war is waged with the blood of others, fortunes are made with other people's money.
André Suarès

There is no gain so certain as that which arises from sparing what you have.
Publilius Syrus

There must be a reason why some people can afford to live well. They must have worked for it. I only feel angry when I

see waste. When I see people throwing away things we could use.
Mother Teresa

A man is rich in proportion to the number of things which he can afford to let alone.
Henry David Thoreau

Most of the luxuries, and many of the so-called comforts of life are not only indispensible, but positive hindrances to the elevation of mankind.
Henry David Thoreau

Superfluous wealth can buy superfluities only.
Henry David Thoreau

What is most important for democracy is not that great fortunes should not exist, but that great fortunes should not remain in the same hands. In that way they do not form a class.
Alexis de Tocqueville

I think that the reason why we Americans seem to be so addicted to trying to get rich suddenly is merely because the opportunity to make promising efforts in that direction has offered itself to us with a frequency out of all proportion to the European experience.
Mark Twain

There are two times in a man's life when he should not speculate: when he can't afford it, and when he can.
Mark Twain

Enough is often too much in our material world, but seldom enough in our material world.
Robert L. Upshur

He who wishes to be rich in a day will be hanged in a year.
Leonardo da Vinci

He had so much money that he could afford to look poor.
Edgar Wallace

Make all you can, save all you can, give all you can.
John Wesley

No man is rich enough to buy back his past.
Oscar Wilde

I am grateful for the blessings of wealth, but it hasn't changed who I am. My feet are still on the ground; I'm just wearing better shoes.
Oprah Winfrey

If a man successful in business expends a part of his income in things of no real use, while the poor employed by him pass through difficulties in getting the necessaries of life, this requires his serious attention.
John Woolman

Rich man down and poor man up—they are still not even.
Yiddish proverb

I have about concluded that wealth is a state of mind, and that anyone can acquire a wealthy state of mind by thinking rich thoughts.
Edward Young

Much learning shows how little mortals know; much wealth, how little worldlings enjoy.
Edward Young

If I could, I wouldn't even be on [The Forbes 400].
Mark Zuckerberg

WEATHER

What dreadful hot weather we have! It keeps me in a continual state of inelegance.
Jane Austen

What men call gallantry, and gods adultery, Is much more common where the climate's sultry.
Lord Byron

For the man sound in body and serene in mind there is no such thing as bad weather; every sky has its beauty, and storms which whip the blood do but make it pulse more vigorously.
George Gissing

Weather in towns is like a skylark in a counting-house—out of place and in the way.
Jerome K. Jerome

Climate has much to do with cheerfulness, but nourishing food, a good digestion, and good health much more.
Alexander Rhodes

Sunshine is delicious, rain is refreshing, wind braces up, snow is exhilarating; there is no such thing as bad weather, only different kinds of good weather.
John Ruskin

Weather is a literary specialty, and no untrained hand can turn out a good article on it.
Mark Twain

Beautiful snow! It can do nothing wrong.
John Whittaker Watson

A hard, dull bitterness of cold.
John Greenleaf Whittier

Whenever people talk to me about the weather, I always feel certain that they mean something else.
Oscar Wilde

WILL

For purposes of action nothing is more useful than narrowness of thought combined with energy of will.
Henri Frédéric Amiel

Great souls have wills; feeble ones have only wishes.
Chinese proverb

There is no power in man greater to effect anything than a will determined to exert its utmost force.
Richard Cumberland

Let not thy will roar when thy power can but whisper.
Thomas Fuller

If we will it, it is no dream.
Theodor Herzl

People do not lack strength; they lack will.
Victor Hugo

We have more power than will; and it is only to exculpate ourselves that we often say that things are impracticable.
François de La Rochefoucauld

Will is character in action.
William McDougall

Nothing is impossible to the man who can will.
Comte de Mirabeau

We cannot be held to what is beyond our strength and means; for at times the accomplishment and execution may not be in our power, and indeed there is nothing really in our own power except the will: on this are necessarily based and founded all the principles that regulate the duty of man.
Michel de Montaigne

Lack of will power has caused more failure than lack of intelligence or ability.
Flower A. Newhouse

Will opens the door to success, both brilliant and happy.
Louis Pasteur

Work usually follows will.
Louis Pasteur

Every man stamps his value on himself. The price we challenge for ourselves is given us by others. Man is made great or little by his own will.
Johann Friedrich von Schiller

The will is the strong blind man who carries on his shoulders the lame man who can see.
Arthur Schopenhauer

To will and not to do when there is opportunity, is in reality not to will; and to love what is good and not to do it, when it is possible, is in reality not to love it.
Emanuel Swedenborg

In the moral world there is nothing impossible if we can bring a thorough will to do it. Man can do everything with himself, but he must not attempt to do too much with others.
Wilhelm von Humboldt

WINNING

There are hundreds who can stand failure to one who can stand success; the good loser is far more common than the good winner.
Franklin Pierce Adams

Anybody can win unless there happens to be a second entry.
George Ade

Victories that are easy are cheap. Those only are worth having which come as the result of hard work.
Henry Ward Beecher

Be it jewel or toy, not the prize gives the joy, but the striving to win the prize.
Edward Bulwer-Lytton

Know ye not that they which run in a race run all, but that one receiveth the prize? So run, that ye may obtain.
I Corinthians 9:24

A winner must first know what losing's like.
Malcolm Forbes

After the fact, our hearts always go out to the fallen Goliaths. Yet we invariably root for their Davids. Until they're winners.
Malcolm Forbes

If you've had a good time playing the game, you're a winner even if you lose.
Malcolm Forbes

The game is the thing. The wins and losses are not the thing. One loses every time one wins, for he then has no game.
L. Ron Hubbard

The man who wins may have been counted out several times, but he didn't hear the referee.
H.E. Jansen

Spurts don't count. The final score makes no mention of a splendid start if the finish proves that you were an also-ran.
Herbert Kaufman

You can't expect to win unless you know why you lose.
Benjamin Lipson

Winning isn't everything, but wanting to win is.
Vince Lombardi

The first thing any man has to know is how to handle himself. Training counts. You can't win any game unless you are ready to win.
Connie Mack

Nothing is ever gained by winning an argument and losing a customer.
C.F. Norton

There may be as much nobility in being last as in being first, because the two positions are equally necessary in the world, one to complement the other.
José Ortega y Gasset

Ten Commandments for Victory

1. Obey orders always, honestly, cheerfully and conscientiously!

2. Do your duty on time all the time!

3. Practice self-control and self-denial always!

4. Be considerate of others; be willing to give before you take!

5. Be neat and clean in person as well as in speech!

6. Don't find fault, lest you find time for little else!

7. Whatever you do, do it just a little bit better than anyone else!

8. Resolve to win, always on the alert for Victory!

9. Be true to yourself, your comrades, your God and your country!

10. Be faithful and dependable, ever mindful of your sacred privilege in serving America!
Manfred Pakas

When it comes to winning, you need the skill and the will.
Frank Tyger

WISDOM

We cannot advance without new experiments in living, but no wise man tries every day what he has proved wrong the day before.
James Truslow Adams

Wisdom consists in rising superior both to madness and to common sense, and is lending oneself to the universal illusion without becoming its dupe.
Henri Frédéric Amiel

Wisdom is divided into two parts: (a) having a great deal to say, and (b) not saying it.
Anonymous

Keep the gold and keep the silver, but give us wisdom.
Arabian proverb

Wise men, though all laws were abolished, would lead the same life.
Aristophanes

A prudent question is one-half of wisdom.
Francis Bacon

Nothing doth more hurt in a state than that cunning men pass for wise.
Francis Bacon

The price of wisdom is eternal thought.
Frank Birch

He who is virtuous is wise; and he who is wise is good; and he who is good is happy.
Boethius

True wisdom lies in gathering the precious things out of each day as it goes by.
E.S. Bouton

Mixing one's wines may be a mistake, but old and new wisdom mix admirably.
Bertolt Brecht

As a solid rock is not shaken by a strong gale, so wise persons remain unaffected by praise or censure.
Buddha

There is a courageous wisdom; there is also a false reptile prudence, the result, not of caution, but of fear.
Edmund Burke

A man doesn't begin to attain wisdom until he recognizes he is no longer indispensable.
Richard E. Byrd

Great men are the commissioned guides of mankind, who rule their fellows because they are wiser.
Thomas Carlyle

True wisdom comes from the overcoming of suffering and sin. All true wisdom is therefore touched with sadness.
Whittaker Chambers

Be wiser than other people if you can; but do not tell them so.
Lord Chesterfield

Wise people may say what they will, but one passion is never cured by another.
Lord Chesterfield

It is better to speak wisdom foolishly, like the saints, rather than to speak folly wisely, like the dons.
G.K. Chesterton

A single conversation across the table with a wise man is worth a month's study of books.
Chinese proverb

The chief aim of wisdom is to enable one to bear with the stupidity of the ignorant.
Winston Churchill

He that sympathizes in all the happiness of others, perhaps himself enjoys the safest happiness; and he that is warned by the folly of others has perhaps attained the soundest wisdom.
Charles Caleb Colton

Any fool can carry on, but only the wise man knows how to shorten sail.
Joseph Conrad

Knowledge comes, but wisdom lingers. It may not be difficult to store up in the mind a vast quantity of facts within a comparatively short time, but the ability to form judgments requires the severe discipline of hard work and the tempering heat of experience and maturity.
Calvin Coolidge

Knowledge is proud that he has learned so much; wisdom is humble that he knows no more.
William Cowper

The height of human wisdom is to bring our tempers down to our circumstances, and to make a calm within, under the weight of the greatest storm without.
Daniel Defoe

When we know how to read our own hearts, we acquire wisdom of the hearts of others.
Denis Diderot

The wisdom of the wise and the experience of ages may be preserved by quotation.
Benjamin Disraeli

All wisdom may be reduced to two words—wait and hope.
Alexandre Dumas

Science gives us knowledge, but only philosophy can give us wisdom.
Will Durant

For wisdom is a defence, and money is a defence: but the excellency of knowledge is, that wisdom giveth life to them that have it.
Ecclesiastes 7:12

The words of wise men are heard in quiet more than the cry of him that ruleth among fools. Wisdom is better than weapons of war; but one sinner destroyeth much good.
Ecclesiastes 9:17–18

Wisdom is like electricity. There is no permanently wise man, but men capable of wisdom, who, being put into certain company, or other favorable conditions, become wise for a while, as glasses being rubbed acquire electric power for a while.
Ralph Waldo Emerson

Wisdom will never let us stand with any man on an unfriendly footing. We refuse sympathy and intimacy with people, as if we waited for some better sympathy or intimacy to come. But whence and when: Tomorrow will be like today. Life wastes itself while we are preparing to live.
Ralph Waldo Emerson

The two powers which in my opinion constitute a wise man are those of bearing and forbearing.
Epictetus

Wisdom is knowing when to speak your mind and when to mind your speech.
Evangel

Stoicism is the wisdom of madness and cynicism the madness of wisdom.
Bergen Evans

Speakers have been showering us with pearls of wisdom for centuries, and if all of their valuable advice were laid end to end, it would still be just as good as new. Very little of it has ever been used.
Benjamin F. Fairless

He who hesitates is sometimes wise.
Malcolm Forbes

Once in a while there's wisdom in recognizing that the Boss is.
Malcolm Forbes

It is human nature to think wisely and act foolishly.
Anatole France

When you assemble a number of men to have the advantage of their joint wisdom, you inevitably assemble with those men all their prejudices, their passions, their errors of opinion, their local interests and their selfish views.
Benjamin Franklin

Wisdom in a poor man is a diamond set in lead.
Thomas Fuller

Wisdom, itself, is often an abstraction associated not with fact or reality, but with the man who asserts it and the manner of its assertion.
John Kenneth Galbraith

The man who questions opinion is wise; the man who quarrels with facts is a fool.
Frank A. Garbutt

Wisdom ceases to be wisdom when it becomes too proud to weep, too grave to laugh, and too self-ful to seek other than itself.
Kahlil Gibran

To comprehend a man's life, it is necessary to know not merely what he does, but also what he purposely leaves undone. There is a limit to the work that can be got out of a human body or a human brain, and he is a wise man who wastes no energy on pursuits for which he is not fitted; and he is still wiser who, from among the things that he can do well, chooses and resolutely follows the best.
William E. Gladstone

All truly wise thoughts have been thought already thousands of times; but to make them truly ours, we must think them over again honestly till they take firm root in our personal experience.
Friedrich Wolfgang von Goethe

The mind is found most acute and most uneasy in the morning. Uneasiness is, indeed, a species of sagacity—a passive sagacity. Fools are never uneasy.
Friedrich Wolfgang von Goethe

Wisdom makes but a slow defense against trouble, though at last a sure one.
Oliver Goldsmith

Knowledge without wisdom is double folly.
Baltasar Gracián

The sage has one advantage: He is immortal. If this is not his century, many others will be.
Baltasar Gracián

The intellect of the wise is like glass: It admits the light of heaven and reflects it.
Augustus Hare

The wise know the value of riches, but the rich do not know the pleasures of wisdom.
Hebrew proverb

Ninety percent of all human wisdom is the ability to mind your own business.
Robert A. Heinlein

Where wisdom is called for, force is of little use.
Herodotus

Knowledge can be communicated, but not wisdom. One can find it, live it, be fortified by it, do wonders through it, but one cannot communicate and teach it.
Herman Hesse

Such is the nature of men that howsoever they may acknowledge many others to be more witty, or more eloquent, or more learned, yet they will hardly believe there may be many so wise as themselves.
Thomas Hobbes

It is the folly of the world, constantly, which confounds its wisdom.
Oliver Wendell Holmes

It is the province of knowledge to speak, and it is the privilege of wisdom to listen.
Oliver Wendell Holmes

How prone to doubt, how cautious are the wise!
Homer

Those unacquainted with the world take pleasure in intimacy with great men; those who are wiser fear the consequences.
Horace

True wisdom is to know what is best worth knowing, and to do what is best worth doing.
Edward Porter Humphrey

Wisdom denotes the pursuing of the best ends by the best means.
Frances Hutcheson

Nature will not forgive those who fail to fulfill the law of their being. The law of human beings is wisdom and goodness, not unlimited acquisition.
Robert M. Hutchins

He is great who can do what he wishes; he is wise who wishes to do what he can.
August Iffland

The wisdom of the wise is an uncommon degree of common sense.
William Ralph Inge

The art of being wise is the art of knowing what to overlook.
William James

Knowledge without wisdom is a load of books on the back of an ass.
Japanese proverb

The wise men are ashamed, they are dismayed and taken: lo, they have rejected the word of the Lord; and what wisdom is in them?
Jeremiah 8:9

Thus saith the Lord, Let not the wise man glory in his wisdom.
Jeremiah 9:23

Whence then cometh wisdom? and where is the place of understanding? Seeing it is hid from the eyes of all living, and kept close from the fowls of the air.
Job 23:20–21

Very few men are wise by their own counsel, or learned by their own teaching; for he that was only taught by himself had a fool as his master.
Ben Jonson

Maxims are to the intellect what laws are to actions: They do not enlighten, but guide and direct, and though themselves blind, are protecting.
Joseph Joubert

It is a maxim received in life that, in general, we can determine more wisely for others than for ourselves. The reason of it is so clear in argument that it hardly wants the confirming of experience.
Junius

The constancy of sages is nothing but the art of locking up their agitation in their hearts.
François de La Rochefoucauld

Wisdom is to the mind what health is to the body.
François de La Rochefoucauld

The first point of wisdom is to discern that which is false; the second to know that which is true.
Lactantius

Make wisdom your provision for the journey from youth to old age, for it is a more certain support than all other possessions.
Diogenes Laertius

I do not think much of a man who is not wiser today than he was yesterday.
Abraham Lincoln

Be wise; soar not too high to fall, but stoop to rise.
Philip Massinger

If 40 million people say a foolish thing it does not become a wise one, but the wise man is foolish to give them the lie.
Somerset Maugham

To know that which before us lies in daily life is the prime wisdom.
John Milton

What is strength without a double share of wisdom? Strength's not made to rule, but to subserve, where wisdom bears command.
John Milton

A wise man sees as much as he ought, not as much as he can.
Michel de Montaigne

Wisdom comes not from experience but from meditating on experience and assimilating it.
Joy Elmer Morgan

Knowledge comes by taking things apart: analysis. But wisdom comes by putting things together.
John A. Morrison

The growth of wisdom may be gauged accurately by the decline of ill temper.
Friedrich Wilhelm Nietzsche

He who is taught to live upon little owes more to his father's wisdom than he who has a great deal left him does to his father's care.
William Penn

The wise man will want to be ever with him who is better than himself.
Plato

The wisest have the most authority.
Plato

Every man, however wise, needs the advice of some sagacious friend in the affairs of life.
Plautus

He is happy in his wisdom who has learned at another's expense.
Plautus

Wisdom thoroughly learned, will never be forgotten.
Pythagoras

Be wisely worldly, but not worldly wise.
Francis Quarles

Nine-tenths of wisdom consists in being wise in time.
Theodore Roosevelt

The difference between a wise guy and a wise man is plenty!
Galen Star Ross

Good people are good because they've come to wisdom through failure.
William Saroyan

Fools are aye fond o' flittin' and wise men o' sittin'.
Scottish proverb

Precepts or maxims are of great weight; and a few useful ones at hand do more toward a happy life than whole volumes that we know not where to find.
Seneca

Wisdom does not show itself so much in precept as in life—in firmness of mind and a mastery of appetite. It teaches us to do as well as to talk; and to make our words and actions all of a color.
Seneca

Wisely and slow; they stumble that run fast.
William Shakespeare

Wisdom makes but a slow defense against trouble, though at last a sure one.
Oliver Smith

Much wisdom often goes with fewer words.
Sophocles

Wisdom outweighs any wealth.
Sophocles

The wise man must remember that while he is a descendant of the past, he is a parent of the future.
Herbert Spencer

It is sometimes wise to forget who we are.
Publilius Syrus

The stupid neither forgive nor forget; the naive forgive and forget; the wise forgive but do not forget.
Thomas Szasz

Immortal gods! How much does one man excel another! What a difference there is between a wise man and a fool.
Terence

A man never reaches that dizzy height of wisdom that he can no longer be led by the nose.
Mark Twain

He is a hard man who is only just, and a sad one who is only wise.
Voltaire

Wisdom is oftimes nearer when we stoop than when we soar.
William Wordsworth

WIT

New Year's resolution: To refrain from saying witty, unkind things, unless they are really witty and irreparably damaging.
James Agate

Wit has truth in it; wisecracking is simply calisthenics with words. Dorothy Parker Wit is a treacherous dart. It is perhaps the only weapon with which it is possible to stab oneself in one's own back.
Goeffrey Bocca

Better the fragrant herb of wit and a little cream of affability than all the pretty cups in the world.
Van Wyck Brooks

Repartee is what you wish you'd said.
Heywood Broun

If you have wit, use it to please and not to hurt: you may shine like the sun in the temperate zones without scorching.
Lord Chesterfield

Wit is the salt of conversation, not the food.
William Hazlitt

Impropriety is the soul of wit.
Somerset Maugham

Wit has a deadly aim and it is possible to prick a large pretense with a small pin.
Marya Mannes

Brevity is the soul of lingerie.
Dorothy Parker

As empty vessels make the loudest sound, so they that have the least wit are the greatest blabbers.
Plato

He that would pun would pick a pocket.
Alexander Pope

WOMEN

We don't want so much to see a female Einstein become an assistant professor. We want a woman schlemiel to get promoted as quickly as a male schlemiel.
Bella Abzug

You can never trust a woman; she may be true to you.
Douglas Ainslie

There's a special place in hell for women who don't help other women.
Madeleine Albright

The average woman would rather have beauty than brains because the average man can see better than he can think.
Anonymous

A youthful figure is what you get when you ask a woman her age.
Anonymous

When a woman is very, very bad, she is awful, but when a man is correspondingly good, he is weird.
Minna Antrim

Women bear rule over king and beggar alike.
Apocrypha: Patriarchs, Judah 15:5

The first time Adam had a chance, he laid the blame on women.
Nancy Astor

A woman, especially if she have the misfortune of knowing anything, should conceal it as well as she can.
Jane Austen

In my ballets, woman is first. Men are consorts. God made men to sing the praises of women. They are not equal to men: they are better.
George Balanchine

The man who enters his wife's dressing room is either a philosopher or a fool.
Honoré de Balzac

It is the good girls who keep the diaries; the bad girls never have the time.
Tallulah Bankhead

The trouble with life is that there are so many beautiful women—and so little time.
John Barrymore

The way to fight a woman is with your hat. Grab it and run.
John Barrymore

Behind almost every woman you ever heard of stands a man who let her down.
Naomi Bliven

Intimacies between women often go backwards, beginning in revelations and ending up in small talk without loss of esteem.
Elizabeth Bowen

Most beautiful but dumb girls think they are smart and get away with it because other people, on the whole, aren't much smarter.
Louise Brooks

I never liked the looks of the life that was programmed for me—ordinary, hillbilly and poor—and I repudiated it from the time I was 7 years old.
Helen Gurley Brown

Some guy said to me, "Don't you think you're too old to sing rock 'n' roll?' I said, "You'd better check with Mick Jagger."
Cher

The trouble with some women is that they get all excited about nothing—and then marry him.
Cher

Being a woman is a terribly difficult trade, since it consists principally of dealing with men.
Joseph Conrad

The average man is more interested in a woman who is interested in him than he is in a woman with beautiful legs.
Marlene Dietrich

Men like women who write. Even though they don't say so. A writer is a foreign country.
Marguerite Duras

I know I have the body of a weak and feeble woman, but I have the heart and stomach of a king, and of a king of England, too.
Queen Elizabeth I

Man is not the enemy here, but the fellow victim. The real enemy is women's denigration of themselves.
Betty Friedan

Contrary to popular belief, English women do not wear tweed nightgowns.
Hermione Gingold

There is only one proper way to wear a beautiful dress: to forget you are wearing it.
Mme. de Girardin

A faithful woman looks to the spring, a good book, perfume, earthquakes, and divine revelation for the experience others find in a lover. They deceive their husbands, so to speak, with the entire world, men excepted.
Jean Giraudoux

Most men who rail against women are railing at one woman only.
Remy de Gourmont

The hardest years in a woman's life are those between 10 and 70.
Helen Hayes (at 83)

Margaret Thatcher has shown that there is power and dignity to be won by defying the status quo and the majority rather than by adapting to them. If the British left, which she froze into immobility like Medusa, could bring itself to learn from this, then we might not have to look upon her like again.
Christopher Hitchens

A man is in general better pleased when he has a good dinner upon his table, than when his wife talks Greek.
Samuel Johnson

The media's enthusiasm for Marissa Mayer as the mascot for women in tech ignores the truth: She is just one woman. She is one hell of a smart and accomplished woman, but she's not a superhero.
Anneke Jong

If you care so much about Marissa Mayer that you question her choices, then stop gossiping and mobilize to change things for all women. Her choice to take a huge job when she's pregnant isn't going to hurt you, or your daughters, or women in general.
Amy Keyishian

The colonel's lady and Judy O'Grady are sisters under their skins.
Rudyard Kipling

A woman's guess is much more accurate than a man's certainty.
Rudyard Kipling

All one's life as a young woman one is on show, a focus of attention, people notice you. You set yourself up to being noticed and admired. And then, not expecting it, you become middle-aged and anonymous.
Doris Lessing

On her rapidly growing wealth (she's ranked No. 8 on Forbes' *list of top-earning female athletes):* I still like to use my husband's credit card because I want to save my money.
Li Na

I always say that a girl never really looks as well as she does on board a steamship, or even a yacht.
Anita Loos

But if God had wanted us to think with our wombs, why did he give us a brain?
Clare Boothe Luce

You don't know a woman until you've met her in court.
Norman Mailer

Our bodies are shaped to bear children, and our lives are a working out of the processes of creation. All our ambitions and intelligence are beside that great elemental point.
Phyllis McGinley

I don't mind living in a man's world as long as I can be a woman in it.
Marilyn Monroe

People in the U.S. used to think that if girls were good at sports their sexuality would be affected. Being feminine meant being a cheerleader, not an athlete. The image of women is changing now. You don't have to be pretty for people to come and see you play.
Martina Navratilova

Women are the untapped market. More than China and more than India, it's women around the world who are this great force to be tapped.
Alyse Nelson

Woman was God's second mistake.
Friedrich Wilhelm Nietzsche

Thoughts on what it's like being a woman: How the hell should I know?
Suzy O'Neill

If women didn't exist, all the money in the world would have no meaning.
Aristotle Onassis

When the candles are out, all women are fair.
Plutarch

On Thailand's first female prime minister, Yingluck Shinawatra: There will be no honeymoon for Yingluck. She has to hit the ground running. There are all kinds of questions and bumpy challenges confronting her.
Thitinan Pongsudhirak

I remember it vividly. I was watching *Bridesmaids.* Twenty minutes in, I suddenly got an incredible rush because I suddenly realized I had been starving and didn't even know it. What I was watching was so unnecessarily rare— women on screen, in a smart, hysterical, poignant film.
Gina Prince-Bythewood

The charms of a passing woman are usually in direct relation to the speed of her passing.
Marcel Proust

She openeth her mouth with wisdom; and in her tongue is the law of kindness.
Proverbs 31:26

I never expected to see the day when girls would get sunburned in the places they now do.
Will Rogers

On Ellen DeGeneres' show replacing Oprah Winfrey's: I don't see how DeGeneres can possibly live up to Oprah's numbers. It's like replacing David Ortiz with a rookie from Pawtucket.
Steve Safran

In the future, there will be no female leaders. There will just be leaders.
Sheryl Sandberg

Any woman who has a great deal to offer the world is in trouble.
Hazel Scott

No man is a match for a woman, except with a poker and a hobnailed pair of boots—and not always even then.
George Bernard Shaw

Think what cowards men would be if they had to bear children. Women are altogether a superior species.
George Bernard Shaw

Like a talented politician, Helen Gurley Brown had a vision of how American society would and could change. In her 32 years as editor in chief of *Cosmopolitan* magazine, she fostered, amplified and embodied in her own life the ideal of a liberated woman who compounds her impact by partnering with an equally liberated man.
Gail Sheehy

If Hollywood could wrap its collective brain around the fact that women want to see and talk about movies just as much as men do, then more jobs for women in film would follow.
Melissa Silverstein

No one has ever asked an actor, "You're playing a strong-minded man. . . ." We assume that men are strong-minded or have opinions. But a strong-minded woman is a different animal.
Meryl Streep

The cocks may crow, but it's the hen that lays the egg.
Margaret Thatcher

On what she thought in 1969: No woman in my time will be Prime Minister or Chancellor or Foreign Secretary—not the top jobs.
Margaret Thatcher

I'm 65 and I guess that puts me in the geriatrics. But if there were 15 months in the year, I'd only be 48. That's the trouble with us. We number everything.

Take women, for example. I think they deserve to have more than 12 years between the ages of 28 and 40.
James Thurber

Every man has a secret ambition: To outsmart horses, fish and women.
Mark Twain

My advice to girls: first, don't smoke—to excess; second, don't drink—to excess; third, don't marry—to excess.
Mark Twain

On Angela Merkel remaining on vacation during Europe's economic crisis: There is no debate raging about Germany's creditworthiness or the risks associated with its budget. Therefore Merkel is sending precisely the right signals, namely of dependability and consistency.
Unnamed German official

One should never trust a woman who tells one her real age. A woman who would tell that would tell anything.
Oscar Wilde

I have bursts of being a lady, but it doesn't last long.
Shelley Winters

For most of history, Anonymous was a woman.
Virginia Woolf

WORDS

We have too many high-sounding words, and too few actions that correspond with them.
Abigail Adams

Ideas in the mind are the transcript of the world, words are the transcript of ideas; and writing and printing are the transcript of words.
Joseph Addison

Propaganda is a soft weapon: Hold it in your hands too long and it will move like a snake and strike the other way.
Jean Anouilh

Words once printed assume a life of their own.
Wilma Askinas

When you have spoken the word, it reigns over you. When it is unspoken you reign over it.
Arabian proverb

The word virus has established itself so firmly as an accepted part of the human organism that it can now sneer at gangster viruses like smallpox and turn them in to the Pasteur Institute.
William S. Burroughs

Words fascinate me. For me, browsing in a dictionary is like being turned loose in a bank.
Eddie Cantor

Speak English, said the Eaglet. I don't know the meaning of half these long words, and what's more, I don't believe you do either.
Lewis Carroll

A quote is a personal possession and you have no right to change it.
Ray Cave

Short words are best and the old words when short are best of all.
Winston Churchill

For one word a man is often deemed to be wise, and for one word he is often deemed to be foolish. We should be careful indeed what we say.
Confucius

There is never enough time to say our last word—the last word of our love, of our desire, faith, remorse, submission, revolt.
Joseph Conrad

Propaganda is the art of persuading others of what you don't believe yourself.
Abba Eban

Although words exist for the most part for the transmission of ideas, there are some which produce such violent disturbance in our feelings that the role they play in the transmission of ideas is lost in the background.
Albert Einstein

Because his wife is of such a delicate nature, a man avoids using certain words all through his married life, and then one day he picks up a bestseller she is reading and finds five of the words in the first chapter.
William Feather

You can stroke people with words.
F. Scott Fitzgerald

The power of words is immense. A well-chosen word has often sufficed to stop a flying army, to change defeat into victory, and to save an empire.
Émile de Girardin

Nothing is more unaccountable than the spell that often lurks in a spoken word. A thought may be present to the mind, and two minds conscious of the same thought, but as long as it remains unspoken their familiar talk flows quietly over the hidden idea.
Nathaniel Hawthorne

Sticks and stones can break your bones, but words can make your blood boil.
Cullen Hightower

When I feel inclined to read poetry I take down my dictionary. The poetry of words is quite as beautiful as that of sentences. The author may arrange the gems

effectively, but their shape and lustre have been given by the attrition of ages.
Oliver Wendell Holmes, Sr.

Language rarely lies. It can reveal the insincerity of a writer's claims simply through a grating adjective or an inflated phrase. We come upon a frenzy of words and suspect it hides a paucity of feeling.
Irving Howe

Propaganda, to be effective, must be believed. To be believed, it must be credible. To be credible, it must be true.
Hubert Humphrey

Anybody can become pope; the proof of this is that I have become one.
Pope John XXIII

Words, like eyeglasses, blur everything that they do not make more clear.
Joseph Joubert

Words are the most powerful drug used by mankind.
Rudyard Kipling

The closer the look one takes at a word, the greater distance from which it looks back.
Karl Kraus

At the beginning there was the Word—at the end just the Cliché.
Stanislaw Jerzy Lec

A man who has humility will have acquired in the last reaches of his beliefs the saving doubt of his own certainty.
Walter Lippmann

We should have a great many fewer disputes in the world if words were taken for what they are, the signs of our ideas only, and not for things themselves.
John Locke

But I say unto you, That every idle word that men shall speak, they shall give account thereof in the day of judgement.
Matthew 12:36

The world is satisfied with words, few care to dive beneath the surface.
Blaise Pascal

If a civil word or two will render a man happy, he must be a wretch indeed who will not tell them to him.
William Penn

A word fitly spoken is like apples of gold in pictures of silver.
Proverbs 25:11

Let the words of my mouth, and the meditation of my heart, be acceptable in thy sight, O Lord, my strength and my redeemer.
Psalms 19:14

Why is propaganda so much more successful when it stirs up hatred than when it tries to stir up friendly feeling?
Bertrand Russell

Words are loaded pistols.
Jean-Paul Sartre

A word too much always defeats its purpose.
Arthur Schopenhauer

Such as thy words are, such will thine affections be esteemed; and such as thine affections, will be thy deeds; and such as thy deeds will be thy life.
Socrates

A powerful agent is the right word. Whenever we come upon one of those intensely right words in a book or a

newspaper the resulting effect is physical as well as spiritual, and electrically prompt.
Mark Twain

He'd be a much nicer fellow if he had a good swear now and then.
John Tyndall

No one working in the English language now comes close to my exuberance, my passion, my fidelity to words.
Jeanette Winterson

One great use of words is to hide our thoughts.
Voltaire

A wise man hears one word and understands two.
Yiddish proverb

WORK

Without rest, a man cannot work; without work, the rest does not give you any benefit.
Abkhazian proverb

People do not get tired out from working where work is intelligently handled. Work, if it is interesting, is a stimulant. It's worry and a lack of interest in what one does that tire and discourage. Every one of us should have our pet interests— as many as we can handle efficiently and happily. Our interests should never be allowed to lag or get cold so that all enthusiasm is spent. Each day can be one of triumph if you keep up to your interests—feeding them as they feed you!
George Matthew Adams

Most of the trades, professions, and ways of living among mankind, take

their original either from the love of the pleasure, or the fear of want. The former, when it becomes too violent, degenerates into luxury, and the latter into avarice.
Joseph Addison

Work only tires a woman, but it ruins a man.
African Proverb

A work of real merit finds favor at last.
Amos Bronson Alcott

Doing nothing is the hardest work of all.
Anonymous

If you feel that you are indispensable, put your finger in a glass of water, withdraw it, and note the hole you have left.
Anonymous

Tell your boss what you think of him, and the truth will set you free.
Anonymous

I don't want to work. I want to smoke.
Apollinaire

He works and blows the coals, and has plenty of other irons in the fire.
Aristophanes

They are happy men whose natures sort with their vocations.
Francis Bacon

It is necessary to work, if not from inclination, at least from despair. Everything considered, work is less boring than amusing oneself.
Charles Baudelaire

If we would have anything of benefit, we must earn it, and earning it becomes shrewd, inventive, ingenious, active, enterprising.
Henry Ward Beecher

No fine work can be done without concentration and self-sacrifice and toil and doubt.
Max Beerbohm

Anyone can do any amount of work, provided it isn't the work he is supposed to be doing at that moment.
Robert Benchley

Less shirk means less irk in work!
Alonzo Newton Benn

Men are more important than tools. If you don't believe so, put a good tool into the hands of a poor workman.
John J. Bernet

No man can make good during working hours who does the wrong thing outside of working hours.
William J.H. Boetcker

You can employ men and hire hands to work for you, but you will have to win their hearts to have them work with you.
William J.H. Boetcker

The true wealth of a state consists in the number of its inhabitants, in their toil and industry.
Napoleon Bonaparte

The noblest workers of this world bequeath us nothing so great as the image of themselves. Their task, be it ever so glorious, is historical and transient, but the majesty of their spirit is essential and eternal.
George Brown

If your work is work to you and you don't see beyond that work and see the pleasure in work and the pleasure in service, look out; you are in danger of standing in your present station for a long, long time.
Milan R. Bump

Employment, which Galen calls nature's physician, is so essential to human happiness that indolence is justly considered as the mother of misery.
Robert Burton

Work with some men is as besetting a sin as idleness with others.
Samuel Butler

I never work hard when I am working; I only work hard when I am not working.
Irving Caesar

It is an article of faith in my creed to pick the man who does not take himself seriously, but does take his work seriously.
Michael C. Cahill

Blessed is he who has found his work; let him ask no other blessedness.
Thomas Carlyle

Work is a grand cure for all the maladies and miseries that ever beset mankind—honest work, which you intend getting done.
Thomas Carlyle

Set me a task in which I can put something of my very self, and it is a task no longer; it is joy; it is art.
Bliss Carman

It marks a big step in a man's development when he comes to realize that other men can be called in to help him do a better job than he can do alone.
Andrew Carnegie

I hold that a man had better be dead than alive when his work is done.
Alice Cary

It is an undoubted truth that the less one has to do the less time one finds to do it in. One yawns, one procrastinates, one can do it when one will, and, therefore, one seldom does it at all; whereas those

who have a great deal of business must (to use a vulgar expression) buckle to it; and then they always find time enough to do it in.
Lord Chesterfield

Let every man practice the art that he knows best.
Cicero

A windmill is eternally at work to accomplish one end, although it shifts with every variation of the weathercock, and assumes ten different positions in a day.
Charles Caleb Colton

All one's work might have been better done; but this is a sort of reflection a worker must put aside courageously if he doesn't mean every one of his conceptions to remain forever a private vision, an evanescent reverie.
Joseph Conrad

A man is a worker. If he is not that he is nothing.
Joseph Conrad

All growth depends upon activity. There is no development physically or intellectually without effort, and effort means work. Work is not a curse; it is the prerogative of intelligence, the only means to manhood, and the measure of civilization.
Calvin Coolidge

The man who builds a factory builds a temple; the man who works there worships there; and to each is due not scorn and blame but reverence and praise.
Calvin Coolidge

No matter how much work a man can do, no matter how engaging his personality may be, he will not advance far in business if he cannot work through others.
John Craig

It's the men behind who make the man ahead.
Merle Crowell

The more help a man has in his garden, the less it belongs to him.
William H. Davies

We would rather have one man or woman working with us than three merely working for us.
J. Dabney Day

Nothing is really work unless you would rather be doing something else.
Chub De Wolfe

The workers are the saviors of society, the redeemers of the race.
Eugene V. Debs

Thoughts on cubicles: I'm genetically not wired to be an employee.
Bharat Desai

My idea of the real aristocrat is the master workman, no matter what his line of work may be.
Henry L. Doherty

When you find a man who knows his job and is willing to take responsibility, keep out of his way and don't bother him with unnecessary supervision. What you may think is cooperation is nothing but interference.
Thomas Dreier

Work is hard if you're paid to do it, and it's pleasure if you pay to be allowed to do it.
Finley Peter Dunne

Whatsoever thy hand findeth to do, do it with thy might; for there is no work, nor device, nor knowledge, nor wisdom, in the grave, whither thou goest.
Ecclesiastes 9:10

If I were to suggest a general rule for happiness, I would say, Work a little harder; work a little longer; work!
Frederick H. Ecker

I am wondering what would have happened to me if some fluent talker had converted me to the theory of the eight-hour day and convinced me that it was not fair to my fellow workers to put forth my best efforts in my work. I am glad that the eight-hour day had not been invented when I was a young man. If my life had been made up of eight-hour days I do not believe I could have accomplished a great deal. This country would not amount to as much as it does if the young men of fifty years ago had been afraid that they might earn more than they were paid for.
Thomas A. Edison

Happiest is a man who has his vocation as a hobby.
Murray Edwards

How do I work? I grope.
Albert Einstein

Many times a day I realize how my own outer and inner life is built upon the labors of my fellow men, both living and dead, and how earnestly I must exert myself in return as much as I have received.
Albert Einstein

A man is relieved and gay when he has put his heart into his work and done his best; what he has said or done otherwise shall give him no peace.
Ralph Waldo Emerson

The shoemaker makes a good shoe because he makes nothing else.
Ralph Waldo Emerson

The sum of wisdom is that time is never lost that is devoted to work.
Ralph Waldo Emerson

Elbow grease is the best polish.
English proverb

Let him that stole steal no more: but rather let him labor, working with his hands the thing which is good, that he may have to give to him that needeth.
Ephesians 4:28

One of the saddest things is that the only thing a man can do for eight hours a day, day after day, is work. You can't eat eight hours a day nor drink for eight hours a day nor make love for eight hours.
William Faulkner

It's not the increasing competition; it's going back to real work that most of us complain about.
William Feather

The right man can make a good job out of any job.
William Feather

Here below is not the land of happiness; it is only the land of toil; and every joy which comes to us is only to strengthen us for some greater labor that is to succeed.
Immanuel Fichte

Conditions never get so bad in this country but that a man who works can get business.
Lawrence P. Fisher

Failures are few among people who have found a work they like enough to do it well. You invest money in your work; invest love in it too. Like your work. Like the materials and the tools with which you work. Like the people with whom

you work. Like the place where you work. It pays well.
Clarence E. Flynn

Genius is often a short way of spelling hard work. Poverty, obscurity, struggle and ambition formed the foundation for many careers of transcendent achievement. Few marks are made in the world's history by eight-hour-day men.... Sir Joshua Reynolds had but one maxim for success: Work, work, work. Is not rigid and continuous training necessary for the making of strong athletes? Hard work is not fatal to real success. *Vouloir c'est pouvoir*.
B.C. Forbes

Has your work become very easy? Do you find you can do it with little effort? Has it ceased to impose any strain or fatigue upon you? Do you no longer feel loss of vitality after a long spell of it? Can you now do it as easy as water rolls off a duck's back? If so, look out! Do some stock-taking. Examine your output.... Work done with little effort is likely to yield little result. Every job can be done excellently or indifferently. Excellence necessitates effort—hard, sustained, concentrated effort.
B.C. Forbes

J.P. Morgan, then past 70, was asked by the son of an eminent father why he [Morgan] didn't retire. When did your father retire? asked Mr. Morgan, without looking up from his desk. In 1902. When did he die? Oh, at the end of 1904. Huh! snapped Mr. Morgan, If he had kept on working he would have been alive still. Work is God's best medicine. It is God's medicine for man.
B.C. Forbes

Ugliness, squalor are breeding grounds for revolution. Beauty is conducive to tranquillity, happiness. Beautifying of

homes and places of worship began with the dawn of civilization. Beautifying of workplaces is only in its infancy. Yet, since men normally spend more than half of their waking hours at work, surely it is important that adequate attention be devoted to elevating their working environment, whether office or factory, foundry or machine shop, mine or warehouse. Beautiful surroundings subtly encourage beautiful living. Drab surroundings, bad air, bad light, evoke bad reactions.
B.C. Forbes

When the snow and the ice were inches deep at home I was able to journey southwards where there was no snow and plenty of sunshine. How I revelled in my leisure during the first few days.... Gradually, however, my zest for play subsided. Even golf began to savor of monotony and work. By the end of two weeks I was eager to return to the daily grind. I found, too, that men and women who had nothing to do ... were a rather dissatisfied, peevish lot. Work, even too much work, is preferable to too much play. Play can become harder work than work.
B.C. Forbes

Whimpering never kept a leaking vessel from foundering. Vigorously manning the pumps has. Get busy with your head and hands, not your chin.
B.C. Forbes

In these striking times there's an understandable tendency on the part of those struck to deplore with vehemence the ready availability of unemployment insurance for workers not working. In fact, only a fraction of those collecting unemployment compensation are strikers. And only a small percentage of those collecting unemployment compensation are unwilling to work. In these times of wide and widening

unemployment—reaching near to 5 million at the moment—it shouldn't take much thought to make one glad unemployment insurance is as substantial and of as long duration as it is.
Malcolm Forbes (1971)

If you have a job without any aggravations, you don't have a job.
Malcolm Forbes

The hardest work of all: Doing nothing.
Malcolm Forbes

When anyone has enough money not to work, it's usually because he does.
Malcolm Forbes

When the joy of the job's gone, when it's no fun trying anymore, quit before you're fired.
Malcolm Forbes

When those with ability at their job get to thinking they can't be done without, they're already on their way out.
Malcolm Forbes

Working at what you enjoy is far more important than what you're working at.
Malcolm Forbes

Life is work, and everything you do is so much more experience. Sometimes you work for wages, sometimes not, but what does anybody make but a living? And whatever you have you must either use or lose.
Henry Ford

Nobody can think straight who does not work. Idleness warps the mind. Thinking without constructive action becomes a disease.
Henry Ford

The object of living is work, experience, happiness. There is joy in work. All that money can do is buy us some one else's

work in exchange for our own. There is no happiness except in the realization that we have accomplished something.
Henry Ford

There are two ways of making yourself stand out from the crowd. One is by having a job so big you can go home before the bell rings if you want to. The other is by finding so much to do that you must stay after the others have gone. The one who enjoys the former once took advantage of the latter.
Henry Ford

There are two things needed in these days; first for rich men to find out how poor men live; and second, for poor men to know how rich men work.
John Foster

I early found that when I worked for myself alone, myself alone worked for me; but when I worked for others also, others worked also for me.
Benjamin Franklin

The six laws of work are:

1. A man must drive his energy, not be driven by it.

2. A man must be master of his hours and days, not their servant.

3. The way to push things through to a finish effectively must be learned.

4. A man must earnestly want.

5. Never permit failure to become a habit.

6. Learn to adust yourself to the conditions you have to endure, but make a point of trying to alter or correct conditions so that they are most favorable to you.
William Frederick

It's all very well in practice, but it will never work in theory.
French management saying

Work has a greater effect than any other technique of living in the direction of binding the individual more closely to reality; in his work, at least, he is securely attached to a part of reality, the human community.
Sigmund Freud

Your work is really important. Even the smallest job has such a definite place it might be likened to a piece in a jigsaw puzzle; the puzzle would not be complete without it.
Francis J. Gable

But let every man prove his own work, and then shall he have rejoicing in himself alone, and not in another.
Galatians 6:4

No ethic is as ethical as the work ethic.
John Kenneth Galbraith

Unemployment is rarely considered desirable except by those who have not experienced it.
John Kenneth Galbraith

Employment is nature's physician, and is essential to human happiness.
Galen

My grandfather once told me that there are two kinds of people: those who do the work and those who take the credit. He told me to try to be in the first group; there was much less competition there.
Indira Gandhi

You work that you may keep pace with the earth and the soul of the earth. For to be idle is to become a stranger unto the seasons, and to step out of life's procession, that marches in majesty and proud submission towards the infinite.
Kahlil Gibran

Man must work. That is certain as the sun. But he may work grudgingly or he many work gratefully; he may work as a man, or he may work as a machine. There is no work so rude, that he may not exalt it; no work so impassive, that he may not breathe a soul into it; no work so dull that he may not enliven it.
Henry Giles

There is no work so rude that man may not exalt it; no work so impassive that he may not breathe a soul into it; no work so dull that he may not enliven it.
Henry Giles

On U.S. border policies for it workers: Why restrict the best and the brightest people from coming into your country?
James Goodnight

When work is a pleasure, life is a joy. When work is duty, life is slavery.
Maxim Gorky

Quit while you're ahead. All the best gamblers do.
Baltasar Gracián

Work is the price that is paid for reputation.
Baltasar Gracián

Work is uninspiring, unappreciated and underpaid—unless you're out of it.
Robert Half

A man is never astonished that he doesn't know what another does, but he is surprised at the gross ignorance of the other in not knowing he does.
Thomas C. Haliburton

Work is a great blessing; after evil came into the world, it was given as an antidote, not as a punishing.
Arthur S. Hardy

Have you ever noticed that it is generally the same people who talk about the need for incentive to make a man

work successfully, who resent the idea of incentive to make a man think successfully?
Sydney Harris

He who does nothing renders himself incapable of doing any thing; but while we are executing any work, we are preparing and qualifying ourselves to undertake another.
William Hazlitt

The only time some people work like a horse is when the boss rides them.
Gabriel Heatter

A man at work at his trade is the equal of the most learned doctor.
Hebrew proverb

One's lifework, I have learned, grows with the working and the living. Do it as if your life depended on it, and the first thing you know, you'll have made a life out of it.
Theresa Helburn

He that labors and thrives spins gold.
George Herbert

Work is the greatest thing in the world, so we should always save some of it for tomorrow.
Don Herold

They must hunger in frost that will not work in heat.
John Heywood

Do not waste a minute—not a second—in trying to demonstrate to others the merits of your performance. If your work does not vindicate itself, you cannot vindicate it.
Thomas W. Higginson

In our nation there are two classes of nobility: the law-abiding workers and the law-abiding employers who sustain each other.
Cullen Hightower

Incentives are spurs that goad a man to do what he doesn't particularly like, to get something he does particularly want. They are rewards he voluntarily strives for.
Paul G. Hoffman

It is by work that man carves his way to that measure of power which will fit him for his destiny.
Josiah G. Holland

A day's impact is better than a month of dead pull.
Oliver Wendell Holmes

Light is the task where many share the toil.
Homer

We work to become, not to acquire.
Elbert Hubbard

The person who studiously avoids work usually works far harder than the man who pleasantly confronts it and does it. Men who cannot work are not happy men.
L. Ron Hubbard

I believe in work, hard work and long hours of work. Men do not break down from overwork, but from worry and dissipation.
Charles Evans Hughes

Like every man of sense and good feeling, I abominate work.
Aldous Huxley

If you want to leave your footprints on the sands of time, be sure you're wearing work shoes.
Italian proverb

Nothing is so fatiguing as the eternal hanging on of an uncompleted task.
William James

Occupation was one of the pleasures of paradise, and we cannot be happy without it.
Anna Jameson

Never fear the want of business. A man who qualifies himself well for his calling, never fails of employment.
Thomas Jefferson

I like work, it fascinates me. I can sit and look at it for hours. I love to keep it by me: the idea of getting rid of it nearly breaks my heart.
Jerome K. Jerome

The man who works for the gold in the job rather than for the money in the pay envelope, is the fellow who gets on.
Joseph French Johnson

Amateurs hope; professionals work.
Garson Kanin

People who decide they came to earth to work, who make work their personal philosophy, are kept very busy.
Constantine Karamanlis

My share of the work of the world may be limited, but the fact that it is work makes it precious. Darwin could work only half an hour at a time; but in many diligent half-hours he laid anew the foundations of philosophy. Green, the historian, tells us that the world is moved not only by the mighty shoves of the heroes, but also by the aggregate of the tiny pushes of each honest worker.
Helen Keller

There has never been any 30-hour week for men who had anything to do.
Charles F. Kettering

Being forced to work, and forced to do your best, will breed in you temperance and self-control, diligence and strength of will, cheerfulness and content, and a hundred virtues which the idle never know.
Charles Kingsley

Too much work and too much energy kill a man just as effectively as too much assorted vice or too much drink.
Rudyard Kipling

More men have died from overwork than the importance of the word justifies.
Rudyard Kipling

There is honor in labor. Work is the medicine of the soul. It is more: it is your very life, without which you would amount to little.
Grenville Kleiser

I plan to work until they carry me out.
John Kluge

For the last third of life there remains only work. It alone is always stimulating, rejuvenating, exciting and satisfying.
Käthe Kollwitz

If you are poor, work. If you are burdened with seemingly unfair responsibilities, work. If you are happy, work. Idleness gives room for doubts and fears. If disappointments come, keep right on working. If sorrow overwhelms you and loved ones seem not true, work. If health is threatened, work. When faith falters and reason fails, just work. When dreams are shattered and hope seems dead, work. Work as if your life were in peril. It really is. No matter what ails you, work. Work faithfully—work with faith. Work is the greatest remedy available for both mental and physical afflictions.
Korsaren

There are only two ways of getting on in this world; by one's own industry or by the weakness of others.
Jean de La Bruyère

The only way to eliminate unemployment is to eliminate unemployment benefits.
Philip Larkin

To industry nothing is impossible.
Latin proverb

In the democratic way of life it is not the best things in life are free, but rather the best things in life are worth working for!
Ruth M. Leverton

If ever this free people, if this government itself is ever utterly demoralized, it will come from this human wiggle and struggle for office—that is, a way to live without work.
Abraham Lincoln

If you intend to go to work, there is no better place than right where you are; if you do not intend to go to work, you cannot get along anywhere. Squirming and crawling about from place to place can do no good.
Abraham Lincoln

A people, secure in their jobs, taking pride in their work, and sure of just recognition, will help our society grow to new heights. If all industry should adopt an incentive system, the standard of living of all peoples would be quadrupled; friction between labor and management would disappear, and the satisfaction of all workers would be greatly enhanced.
James F. Lincoln

My main hobby is working. I love what I do.
Carl Lindner

No man is born into the world whose work is not born with him. There is always work, and tools to work with, for those who will, and blessed are the horny hands of toil. The busy world shoves angrily aside the man who stands with arms akimbo until occasion tells him what to do; and he who waits to have his task marked out shall die and leave his errand unfulfilled.
James Russell Lowell

In the final analysis, there is no other solution to a man's problems but the day's honest work, the day's honest decisions, the day's generous utterance, and the day's good deed.
Clare Booth Luce

The highest genius is willingness and ability to do hard work. Any other conception of genius makes it a doubtful, if not a dangerous, possession.
Robert S. MacArthur

Work is a dull thing; you cannot get away from that. The only agreeable existence is one of idleness, and that is not, unfortunately, always compatible with continuing to exist at all.
Rose Macaulay

Find something you love to do and you'll never have to work a day in your life.
Harvey Mackay

We thoroughly enjoy the work of a man only if the enjoyment of his work can be applied with respect and love for the man.
Hans Margolius

He worked like hell in the country so he could live in the city, where he worked like hell so he could live in the country.
Don Marquis

Work is the true elixir of life. The busiest man is the happiest man. Excellence in

any art or profession is attained only by hard and persistent work. Never believe that you are perfect. When a man imagines, even after years of striving, that he has attained perfection, his decline begins.
Sir Theodore Martin

The big mistake people make is thinking it's a party, when it's really a business affair. One should go with the recognition that the bosses and the human resources people are watching them.
John McKee

The only liberty an inferior man really cherishes is the liberty to quit work, stretch out in the sun, and scratch himself.
H.L. Mencken

There comes a point in any organization where too much supervision means that supervisors spend too much time writing memorandums to one another, making needless telephone calls to one another, and the like, with no more productive work being accomplished in the aggregate, and possibly even less. We must strike the correct balance between too much supervision, and too little supervision.
Gustav Metzman

The bad workmen who form the majority of the operatives in many branches of industry are decidedly of the opinion that bad workmen ought to receive the same wages as good.
John Stuart Mill

Let us go forth and resolutely dare with sweat of brow to toil our little day.
John Milton

The more I work, the more I want to work.
Joan Miró

Elbow grease; the kind that won't soil a shirt.
Garry Moore

Give me love and work—these two only.
William Morris

Though a little one, the master-word (work) looms large in meaning. It is the open sesame to every mortal, the great equalizer in the world, the true philosopher's stone which transmutes all the base metal of humanity into goal.
William Osler

I never knew a man escape failures, in either mind or body, who worked seven days in a week.
Sir Robert Peel

But make not more business necessary than is so; and rather lessen than augment work for thyself.
William Penn

Nor yet be overeager in pursuit of any thing; for the mercurial too often happen to leave judgment behind them, and sometimes make work for repentance.
William Penn

. . . Human society is not a machine, and it must not be made such, even in the economic field. . . . Access to employment [shall not be] made to depend on registration in certain parties or in organization which deal with the distribution of employment. . . . It is necessary that humanity turn its gaze toward the action of God . . . to aid and redeem mankind from all its ills.
Pope Pius XII

We must infer that all things are produced more plentifully and easily and

of a better quality when one man does one thing which is natural to him and does it at the right time, and leaves other things.
Plato

There is a singing ecstasy in good work.
Channing Pollock

What I still ask for daily—for life as long as I have work to do, and work as long as I have life.
Reynolds Price

I see no virtues where I smell no sweat.
Francis Quarles

Whatever you do, if you do it hard enough you'll enjoy it. The important thing is to work and work hard.
David Rockefeller

When work goes out of style we may expect to see civilization totter and fall.
John D. Rockefeller

Extend pity to no man because he has to work. If he is worth his salt, he will work. I envy the man who has work worth doing and does it well. There never has been devised, and there never will be devised, any law which will enable a man to succeed save by the exercise of those qualities which have always been the prerequisites of success, the qualities of hard work, of keen intelligence, of unflinching will.
Theodore Roosevelt

Far and away the best prize that life offers is the chance to work hard at work worth doing.
Theodore Roosevelt

The world is moved not only by the mighty shoves of the heroes, but also by the aggregate of the tiny pushes of each honest worker.
Frank C. Ross

In order that people may be happy in their work, these three things are needed: They must be fit for it. They must not do too much of it. And they must have a sense of success in it.
John Ruskin

The highest reward for a person's toil is not what he gets for it, but what he becomes by it.
John Ruskin

There is rough work to be done, and rough men must do it; there is gentle work to be done, and gentlemen must do it.
John Ruskin

Work is of two kinds: first, altering the position of matter at or near the earth's surface relatively to other such matter; second, telling other people to do so. The first kind is unpleasant and ill paid; the second is pleasant and highly paid.
Bertrand Russell

The Lord recompense thy work, and a full reward be given thee of the Lord God of Israel, under whose wings thou art come to trust.
Ruth 4:12

We are not here to play, to dream, to drift;

We have hard work to do and loads to lift;

Shun not the struggle—face it, 'tis God's gift.
Lord Shaftesbury

The terrible newly imported American doctrine that everyone ought to do something.
Osbert Sitwell

I am suggesting to you the simple idea that people work harder and smarter if they find their work satisfying and know that it is appreciated.
Robert F. Six

Those who have the most to do, and are willing to work, will find the most time.
Samuel Smiles

The one who doesn't pull his weight is not asked to pull, while the one who does, pulls for two.
Alexander Solzhenitsyn

Without labor nothing prospers.
Sophocles

The true craftsman has a light in his eye that money can't buy.
Hal Stebbins

If a man love the labor of any trade, apart from any question of success or fame, the gods have called him.
Robert Louis Stevenson

There is no boon in nature. All the blessings we enjoy are the fruits of labor, toil, self-denial, and study.
W.G. Sumner

The only method by which people can be supported is out of the effort of those who are earning their own way. We must not create a deterrent to hard work.
Robert A. Taft

The day is short, and the work is great, and the laborers are sluggish and the reward is much, and the Master of the house is urgent.
Rabbi Tarfon

Whatsoever we beg of God, let us also work for it.
Jeremy Taylor

We beseech you, brethren, that ye increase more and more; And that ye study to be quiet, and to do your own business, and to work with your own hands.
I Thessalonians 4:10–11

Know them which labor among you . . . esteem them very highly in love for their work's sake.
I Thessalonians 5:12

For even when we were with you, this we commanded you, that if any would not work, neither should he eat.
II Thessalonians 3:10

Good for the body is the work of the body, good for the soul is the work of the soul, and good for either the work of the other.
Henry David Thoreau

Next to us is not the workman whom we have hired, with whom we love so well to talk, but the workman whose work we are.
Henry David Thoreau

Among a democratic people, where there is no hereditary wealth, every man works to earn a living, or is born of parents who have worked. The notion of labor is therefore presented to the mind, on every side, as the necessary, natural, and honest condition.
Alexis de Tocqueville

I do not like work even when someone else does it.
Mark Twain

Let us be grateful to Adam our bene-factor. He cut us out of the blessing of idleness and won for us the curse of labor.
Mark Twain

The law of work does seem utterly unfair—but there it is, and nothing can change it; the higher the pay in enjoy-ment the worker gets out of it, the higher shall be his pay in money also.
Mark Twain

When you like your work, every day is a holiday.
Frank Tyger

It is easier to do a job right than to explain why you didn't.
Martin Van Buren

God sells us all things at the price of labor.
Leonardo da Vinci

Work is often the father of pleasure.
Voltaire

Work spares us from three great evils: boredom, vice and need.
Voltaire

My destiny is solitude, and my life is work.
Richard Wagner

Accepting government aid is like taking drugs—pleasant at first, habit-forming later, damning at last.
William W. Ward

Employment gives health, sobriety, and morals. Constant employment and well-paid labor produce, in a country like ours, general prosperity, content and cheerfulness.
Daniel Webster

Even the strongest personality will regress and eventually may disintegrate if there is no incentive (other than threat of punishment) for the work he does. When there is no feeling of accomplishment, children fail to develop properly and old people rapidly decline.
Joseph Whitney

The man who works need never be a problem to anyone. Opportunities multiply as they are seized; they die when neglected. Life is a long line of opportunities. Wealth is not in making money, but in making the man while he is making money. Production, not destruction, leads to success.
John Wicker

Work is the curse of the drinking classes.
Oscar Wilde

Work is the refuge of people who have nothing better to do.
Oscar Wilde

It is better to lay your life upon the altar of worthy endeavor than to luxuriate and perish as a weed.
Albert L. Williams

Work only a half a day. It makes no difference which half—the first 12 hours or the last 12 hours.
Kemmons Wilson

Never try to work a man who will work you to death trying to work him.
Robert Lewis Wilson

No task, rightly done, is truly private. It is part of the world's work.
Woodrow Wilson

Because I helped to wind the clock, I come to hear it strike.
William Butler Yeats

WORLD

Had I been present at the Creation, I would have given some useful hints for the better ordering of the Universe.
Alphonso the Learned

I hear noise but see no grinding.
Arabian proverb

Remember, you can't drain the ocean with a teaspoon.
Ignas Bernstein

The earth is, like our own skin, fated to carry the scars of ancient wounds.
Fernand Braudel

Our sun is one of 100 billion stars in our galaxy. Our galaxy is one of the billions of galaxies populating the universe. It would be the height of presumption to think that we are the only living things within that enormous immensity.
Werner von Braun

The biggest problem in the world could have been solved when it was small.
Witter Bynner

The world is a thing that a man must learn to despise, and even to neglect, before he can learn to reverence it, and work in it and for it.
Thomas Carlyle

This world, after all our science and sciences, is still a miracle, wonderful, inscrutable, magical and more, to whoso-ever will think of it.
Thomas Carlyle

The task for us now, if we are to survive, is to build the earth.
Teilhard de Chardin

The real trouble with this world of ours is not that it is an unreasonable one. The trouble is that it is nearly reasonable, but not quite.
G.K. Chesterton

Every blade of grass has its spot on earth whence it draws its life, its strength; and so is man rooted to the land from which he draws his faith together with his life.
Joseph Conrad

Most people are quiet in the world, and live in it tentatively, as if it were not their own.
E.L. Doctorow

The world has forgotten, in its concern with Left and Right, that there is an Above and Below.
Galen Drake

The World is a great mirror. It reflects back to you what you are. If you are loving, if you are friendly, if you are helpful, the World will prove loving and friendly and helpful to you. The World is what you are.
Thomas Dreier

The free world has need that its foreign policies should fairly measure the realities of the world in which we live. There are certain principles to which we hold: the sanctity of treaties, good faith between nations, the interdependence of peoples from which no country, however powerful, can altogether escape.
Anthony Eden

Here is the world, sound as a nut, perfect, not the smallest piece of chaos left, never a stitch nor an end, nor a mark of haste, or botching, or a second thought; but the theory of the world is a thing of shreds and patches.
Ralph Waldo Emerson

God has made no one absolute. The rich depend on the poor, as well as the poor on the rich. The world is but a magnificent building; all the stones are gradually cemented together. No one subsists by himself.
Owen Feltham

I am satisfied with, and stand firm as a rock on the belief that all that happens in God's world is for the best, but what is merely germ, what blossom and what fruit I do not know.
Johann Fichte

The world is a book and he who stays at home reads only one page.
M.K. Frelinghuysen

The world is so filled with interesting things to do that the longest human life could not exhaust more than a small fraction of them.
Frank Gaines

You can't shut out the world without shutting yourself in.
Arnold Glasow

I do not have to make over the universe; I have only to do my job, great or small, and to look often at the trees and the hills and the sky, and be friendly with all men.
David Grayson

To him who looks upon the world rationally, the world in its turn presents a rational aspect. The relation is mutual.
Georg Wilhelm Hegel

Maybe this world is another planet's hell.
Aldous Huxley

This may not be the best of all possible worlds, but to say that it is the worst is mere petulant nonsense.
Thomas H. Huxley

Admiration for ourselves and our institutions is too often measured by our contempt and dislike for foreigners.
William Ralph Inge

Man will never be entirely willing to give up this world for the next nor the next world for this.
William Ralph Inge

All the people like us are We,
And everyone else is They.
And They live over the sea,
While We live over the way.
But—would you believe it?—

They look upon We
As only a sort of They.
Rudyard Kipling

Half the world wants to be like Thoreau worrying about the noise of traffic on the way up to Boston; the other half use up their lives being part of that noise. I like the second half.
Franz Kline

Sometimes, when one person is missing, the whole world seems depopulated.
Alphonse de Lamartine

When the world is destroyed, it will be destroyed not by its madmen but by the sanity of its experts and the superior ignorance of its bureaucrats.
John le Carré

Not for himself, but for the world he lives.
Lucan

The more noise a man or a motor makes the less power there is available.
W.R. McGeary

It is ridiculous ever to forget that you and your business are each implanted in the society of the moment. . . . We cannot ignore the world of our time. We had better understand it.
J. Irwin Miller

The universe is full of magical things, patiently waiting for our wits to grow sharper.
Eden Philpotts

Noise is manufactured in the city, just as goods are manufactured. The city is the place where noise is kept in stock, completely detached from the object from which it came.
Max Picard

It is with narrow-souled people as with narrow-necked bottles; the less they

have in it, the more noise they make in pouring it out.
Alexander Pope

O Lord, how manifold are thy works! in wisdom hast thou made them all: the earth is full of thy riches.
Psalms 104:24

When you look at the world in a narrow way, how narrow it seems! When you look at it in a mean way, how mean it is! When you look at it selfishly, how selfish it is! But when you look at it in a broad, generous, friendly spirit, what wonderful people you find in it.
Horace Rutledge

The universe, as far as we can observe it, is a wonderful and immense engine. . . . If we dramatize its life and conceive its spirit, we are filled with wonder, terror and amusement, so magnificent is the spirit.
George Santayana

The whole world and every human being in it is everybody's business.
William Saroyan

The world as it is has been humanly made and must be humanly remade.
Minot Simons

This is a good world. We need not approve of all the items in it, nor of all the individuals in it; but the world itself— which is more than its parts or individuals; which has a soul, a spirit, a fundamental relation to each of us deeper than all other relations—is a friendly world.
Jan Christiaan Smuts

Once you kick the world, and the world and you will live together at a reasonably good understanding.
Jonathan Swift

The world is a looking glass and gives back to every man the reflection of his own face. Frown at it and it will in turn look sourly upon you; laugh at it and with it and it is a jolly kind companion.
William Makepeace Thackeray

If the world is cold, make it your business to build fires.
Horace Traubel

A federation of all humanity, together with a sufficient measure of social justice to ensure health, education and a rough equality of opportunity, would mean such a release and increase of human energy as to open a new phase in human history.
H.G. Wells

WORRY

There's many a pessimist who got that way by financing an optimist.
Anonymous

Worry is rust upon the blade.
Henry Ward Beecher

Worry is evidence of an ill-controlled brain; it is merely a stupid waste of time in unpleasantness. If men and women practiced mental calisthenics as they do physical calisthenics, they would purge their brains of this foolishness.
Arnold Bennett

There are people who are always anticipating trouble, and in this way they manage to enjoy many sorrows that never really happen to them.
Josh Billings

Anxiety is the poison of human life, the parent of many sins and of more miseries. In a world where everything is doubtful, and where we may be disappointed, and be blessed in

disappointment, why this restless stir and commotion of mind? Can it alter the cause, or unravel the mystery of human events?
Paxton Blair

The man of regular life and rational mind never despairs.
Charlotte Brontë

Better be despised for too-anxious apprehensions, than ruined by too-confident security.
Edmund Burke

A friend of mine tells me that a Beethoven symphony can solve for him a problem of conduct. I've no doubt that it does so simply by giving him a sense of the tragedy and the greatness of human destiny, which makes his personal anxieties seem small, which throws them into a new proportion.
Joyce Cary

Sing away sorrow, cast away care.
Miguel de Cervantes

Do not lie in a ditch and say, God help me; use the lawful tools He hath lent thee.
George Chapman

Nobody should ever look anxious except those who have no anxiety.
Benjamin Disraeli

As a cure for worrying, work is better than whiskey.
Thomas A. Edison

What we call despair is often the painful eagerness of unfed hope.
George Eliot

When one seeks assurance, there's none from those who respond, Now, don't you worry about a thing. If you weren't worried, you wouldn't have asked. If you are concerned, it's nice to know that those you query are, too. I'll take a worrier any day over a platitudinous reassurer.
Malcolm Forbes

Do not anticipate trouble, or worry about what may never happen. Keep in the sunlight.
Benjamin Franklin

Industry pays debts, despair increases them.
Benjamin Franklin

You'll break the worry habit the day you decide you can meet and master the worst that can happen to you.
Arnold Glasow

Worry compounds the futility of being trapped on a dead-end street. Thinking opens new avenues.
Cullen Hightower

Worry is interest paid on trouble before it becomes due.
William Ralph Inge

We care what happens to people only in proportion as we know what people are.
Henry James

Pessimism leads to weakness; optimism to power.
William James

There is little peace or comfort in life if we are always anxious as to future events. He that worries himself with the dread of possible contingences will never be at rest.
Samuel Johnson

Life is too short for mean anxieties.
Charles Kingsley

It is certainly wrong to despair; and if despair is wrong hope is right.
John Lubbock

The mere apprehension of a coming evil has put many into a situation of the utmost danger.
Lucan

A pessimist is one who makes difficulties of his opportunities; an optimist is one who makes opportunities of his difficulties.
Reginald B. Mansell

Worry affects the circulation, the heart, the glands, the whole nervous system, and profoundly affects the health. I have never known a man who died from overwork, but many who died from doubt.
Charles W. Mayo

To stabilize society, pachinkos contribute much. They really soothe people's anxiety.
Kenkichi Nakajima

Anxiety is love's greatest killer. It makes one feel as you might when a drowning man holds on to you. You want to save him, but you know he will strangle you in his panic.
Anaïs Nin

Agitation prevents rebellion, keeps the peace, and secures progress. Every step she gains is gained forever. Muskets are the weapons of animals. Agitation is the atmosphere of the brains.
Wendell Phillips

A pound of worry won't pay an ounce of debt.
John Ray

Worry is a thin stream of fear trickling through the mind. If encouraged, it cuts a channel into which all other thoughts are drained.
Arthur Somers Roche

A job becomes work only when you worry about it.
Josephine Schaefer

The mind that is anxious about the future is miserable.
Seneca

Care's an enemy of life.
William Shakespeare

A pessimist is a man who thinks everybody as nasty as himself, and hates them for it.
George Bernard Shaw

Our cares are the mothers not only of our charities and virtues, but of our best joys, and most cheering and enduring pleasures.
William Simms

In being realistic we do not always have to be pessimistic. Christ never blinked his eyes at bad things. But he never became so obsessed with human evil that he lost faith in man.
Ralph W. Sockman

Worry, whatever its source, weakens, takes away courage, and shortens life.
John Lancaster Spalding

There is no sadder sight than a young pessimist.
Mark Twain

Despair not only aggravates our misery but our weakness.
Luc de Vauvenargues

Peace of mind: The contentment of the man who is too busy to worry by day, and too sleepy to worry at night.
Woodrow Wilson

WRITING

Walter Scott has no business to write novels, especially good ones. He has fame and profit enough as a poet, and should not be taking the bread out of other people's mouths.
Jane Austen

A curious thing about written literature: It is about four thousand years old, but we have no way of knowing whether four thousand years constitutes senility or the maiden blush of youth.
John Barth

By its very looseness, by its way of evoking rather than defining, suggesting rather than saying, English is a magnificent vehicle for emotional poetry.
Max Beerbohm

A writer is in the broadest sense a spokesman of his community. Through him that community comes to know its heart. Without such knowledge, how long can it survive?
Saul Bellow

Propaganda is to a democracy what violence is to a dictatorship.
William Blum

Writers seldom choose as friends those self-contained characters who are never in trouble, never unhappy or ill, never make mistakes, and always count their change when it is handed to them.
Catherine Drinker Bowen

It is by sitting down to write every morning that one becomes a writer. Those who do not do this remain amateurs.
Gerald Brenan

Hemingway was a prisoner of his style. No one can talk like the characters in Hemingway except the characters in Hemingway. His style in the wildest sense finally killed him.
William S. Burroughs

One of the pleasures of reading old letters is the knowledge that they need no answer.
Lord Byron

Those who write clearly have readers; those who write obscurely have commentators.
Albert Camus

There is a great discovery still to be made in literature—that of paying literary men by the quantity they do not write.
Thomas Carlyle

Next to doing things that deserve to be written, nothing gets a man more credit, or gives him more pleasure than to write things that deserve to be read.
Lord Chesterfield

The most durable thing in writing is style, and style is the most valuable investment a writer can make with his time.
Raymond Chandler

Would you convey my compliments to the purist who reads your proofs and tell him or her that I write in a sort of broken-down patois which is something like the way a Swiss waiter talks, and that when I split an infinitive, God damn it, I split it so it will stay split.
Raymond Chandler

I can't write without a reader. It's precisely like a kiss—you can't do it alone.
John Cheever

Everyone seems to assume that the unscrupulous parts of journalism will be the frivolous or jocular parts. This is against all ethical experience. Jokes are generally honest. Complete solemnity is

almost always dishonest. The writer of the snippet merely refers to a frivolous and fugitive fact in a frivolous and fugitive way. The writer of the leading article has to write about a fact he has known for 20 minutes as though he has studied it for 20 years.
G.K. Chesterton

The best time for planning a book is while you're doing the dishes.
Agatha Christie

As in political, so in literary action, a man wins friends for himself mostly by the passion of his prejudices.
Joseph Conrad

Propaganda is that branch of the art of lying which consists in nearly deceiving your friends without quite deceiving your enemies.
F.M. Cornford

In America only the successful writer is important, in France all writers are important, in England no writer is important, in Australia you have to explain what a writer is.
Geoffrey Cotterell

I can't read ten pages of Steinbeck without throwing up.
James Gould Cozzens

Words are made for a certain exactness of thought, as tears are for a certain degree of pain. What is least distinct cannot be named; what is clearest is unutterable.
René Daumal

An editor should tell the author his writing is better than it is. Not a lot better, a little better.
T.S. Eliot

I am seldom interested in what he [Ezra Pound] is saying, but only in the way he says it.
T.S. Eliot

Some editors are failed writers, but so are most writers.
T.S. Eliot

Someone said: The dead writers are remote from us because we know so much more than they did. Precisely, and they are what we know.
T.S. Eliot

Mr. Faulkner, of course, is interested in making your mind rather than your flesh creep.
Clifton Fadiman

Great editors do not discover nor produce great authors; great authors create and produce great publishers.
John Farrar

Henry James was one of the nicest old ladies I ever met.
William Faulkner

If a writer has to rob his mother, he will not hesitate; the "Ode on a Grecian Urn" is worth any number of old ladies.
William Faulkner

You should approach Joyce's *Ulysses* as the illiterate Baptist preacher approaches the Old Testament: with faith.
William Faulkner

One major problem is his [John Dewey's] writing style, which has the monotonous consistency of peanut butter.
Joseph Featherstone

The ideal view for daily writing, hour on hour, is the blank brick wall of a

cold-storage warehouse. Failing this, a stretch of sky will do, cloudless if possible.
Edna Ferber

The real literary editors have mostly been fired. Those that remain are all "bottom line" editors; everything depends on the money.
Lawrence Ferlinghetti

May the founder of *Forbes* make a confession? The motive underlying the creation of *Forbes* was the furthering of better understanding between employers and employees, between the strong and the weak, between the high and the low, between the rich and the poor, between the haves and the have-nots. It was foreseen years ago that, unless those who ruled were understandingly interpreted to those ruled, unless those who ruled could be induced to treat more humanely those whom they rule . . . this country would be in danger of suffering political and social upheavals. . . .
B.C. Forbes

It ticks me no end when people get ticked off at those of us who comment audibly and in print on events and problems. That's what we're paid for. Why clutter up your mind with a bunch of facts that might inhibit the solve-ability of us who must express an opinion? After all, all the world cries out for a solution to its problems, and we supply them right and left. Come to think of it, it's we who should be giving our deplorers and detractors the blast; because 99% of the time they don't do as we say.
Malcolm Forbes

Personal & Confidential.
Letters so marked should be. When the contents are only printed matter, though, the minifrauder succeeds in sowing ill will & ire.
Malcolm Forbes

Putting pen to paper lights more fire than matches ever will.
Malcolm Forbes

Real writers—that is, capital W Writers—rarely make much money. Their biggest reward is the occasional reader's response. Commentators-in-print voicing big fat opinions—you might call us small w writers—get considerably more feedback than Writers. The letters I personally find most flattering are not the very rare ones that speak well of my editorials, but the occasional reader who wants to know who writes them. I always happily assume the letter-writer is implying that the editorials are so good that I couldn't have written them myself.
Malcolm Forbes

All the fun's in how you say a thing.
Robert Frost

The ear is the only true writer and the only true reader.
Robert Frost

It's a damn good story. If you have any comments, write them on the back of a check.
Erle Stanley Gardner

Our writers are full of clichés just as old barns are full of bats. Anything that you suspect of being a cliché obviously is one and had better be removed.
Wolcott Gibbs

I suppose I am a born novelist, for the things I imagine are more vital and vivid to me than the things I remember.
Ellen Glasgow

There is no need for propaganda to be rich in intellectual content.
Paul Joseph Goebbels

Nothing you write, if you hope to be any good, will ever come out as you had first hoped.
Lillian Hellman

All modern American literature comes from one book by Mark Twain called *Huckleberry Finn*.
Ernest Hemingway

Poor Faulkner. Does he really think big emotions come from big words? He thinks I don't know the ten-dollar words. I know them all right. But there are older and simpler and better words, and those are the ones I use.
Ernest Hemingway

Writing and travel broaden your ass if not your mind.
Ernest Hemingway

I have Graham Greene's telephone number, but I wouldn't dream of using it. I don't seek out writers because we all want to be alone.
Patricia Highsmith

As soon as by one's own propaganda even a glimpse of right on the other side is admitted, the cause for doubting one's own right is laid.
Adolf Hitler

Nothing comes easily. My work smells of sweat.
Eric Hoffer

No poems can live long or please that are written by water-drinkers.
Horace

This method answers the purpose for which it was devised; it saves lazy editors from working and stupid editors from thinking.
A.E. Housman

Editor: a person employed by a newspaper, whose business it is to separate the wheat from the chaff, and to see that the chaff is printed.
Elbert Hubbard

It takes a great deal of history to produce a little literature.
Henry James

Editing Hemingway was like wrestling with a god.
Tom Jenks

In all pointed sentences, some degree of accuracy must be sacrificed to conciseness.
Samuel Johnson

The only end of writing is to enable readers better to enjoy life or better to endure it.
Samuel Johnson

Your manuscript is both good and original, but the part that is good is not original, and the part that is original is not good.
Samuel Johnson

What is an editor but a cross between a fall guy and a father figure?
Arthur Koestler

One must never judge the writer by the man; but one may fairly judge the man by the writer.
Louis Kronenberger

Some things can only be said in fiction, but that doesn't mean they aren't true.
Aaron Latham

She was a copy editor, possessed of the rare capacity to sit all day in a small cubicle, like a monk in a cell, and read with an almost penitential rigor.
David Leavitt

He is as good as his word and his word is no good.
Seumas MacManus

Looking back, I imagine I was always writing. Twaddle it was too. But far better write twaddle or anything, anything, than nothing at all.
Katherine Mansfield

If you want to get rich from writing, write the sort of thing that's read by persons who move their lips when they're reading to themselves.
Don Marquis

A good style should show no sign of effort. What is written should seem a happy accident.
Somerset Maugham

There are three rules for writing a novel. Unfortunately, no one knows what they are.
Somerset Maugham

In literature as in love, we are astonished at what is chosen by others.
André Maurois

Most clear writing is a sign that there is no exploration going on. Clear prose indicates the absence of thought.
Marshall McLuhan

The successor to politics will be propaganda. Propaganda, not in the sense of a message or ideology, but as the impact of the whole technology of the times.
Marshall McLuhan

An author is a fool who, not content with having bored those who have lived with him, insists on boring future generations.
Montesquieu

I'm the kind of writer that people think other people are reading.
V.S. Naipaul

To write well consists of continuously making small erosions, wearing away grammar in its established form, current norms of language. It is an act of permanent rebellion and subversion against social environs.
José Ortega y Gasset

Asking a working writer what he thinks about critics is like asking a lamppost what it feels about dogs.
John Osborne

He's a writer for the ages—for the ages 4 to 8.
Dorothy Parker

All those writers who write about their childhood! If I wrote about mine you wouldn't sit in the same room with me.
Dorothy Parker

If, at the close of business each evening, I myself can understand what I've written, I feel the day hasn't been totally wasted.
S.J. Perelman

Among our literary scenes, Saddest this sight to me, The graves of little magazines That died to make verse free.
Keith Preston

Editing is the same as quarreling with writers—same thing exactly.
Harold Ross

I write fiction and I'm told it's autobiography, I write autobiography and I'm told it's fiction, so since I'm so dim and

they're so smart, let them decide what it is or it isn't.
Philip Roth

To me, writing is a horseback ride into heaven and hell and back. I am grateful if I can crawl back alive.
Thomas Sanchez

I became a writer because during several of the most important years of my life, writing seemed to me to be the most unreal, unattractive, and unecessary idea ever imposed upon the human race.
William Saroyan

Most novelists, knowing that ongoing work is fed by ongoing life, prize their telephones, their correspondence, and their daily rubbing up against family and friends.
Carol Shields

Virginia Woolf, I enjoyed talking to her, but thought nothing of her writing. I considered her "a beautiful little knitter."
Edith Sitwell

As a novelist, I tell stories, and people give me money. Then financial planners tell me stories, and I give them money.
Martin Cruz Smith

I'm told that when Auden died, they found his *Oxford English Dictionary* all but clawed to pieces. That is the way a poet and his dictionary should come out.
Francis Steegmuller

One man was so mad at me that he ended his letter: "Beware. You will never get out of this world alive."
John Steinbeck

Writing, when properly managed, is but a different name for conversation.
Laurence Sterne

Man does not live by words alone, despite the fact that he sometimes has to eat them.
Adlai Stevenson

With 60 staring me in the face, I have developed inflammation of the sentence structure and a definite hardening of the paragraphs.
James Thurber

Adam was the only man who, when he said a good thing, knew that nobody had said it before him.
Mark Twain

I was sorry to hear my name mentioned as one of the great authors, because they have a sad habit of dying off. Chaucer is dead, so is Milton, so is Shakespeare, and I am not feeling very well myself.
Mark Twain

My own luck has been curious all my literary life; I could never tell a lie that anyone would doubt, nor a truth that anyone would believe.
Mark Twain

Whenever the literary German dives into a sentence, that in the last you are going to see of him until he emerges on the other side of his Atlantic with his verb in his mouth.
Mark Twain

Style is knowing who you are, what you want to say, and not giving a damn.
Gore Vidal

Mark Twain was so good with crowds that he became, in competition with singers and dancers and actors and acrobats, one of the most popular performers of his time. It is so unusual, and so psychologically unlikely, too, for a great writer to be a great performer, too. . . .
Kurt Vonnegut

I am persuaded that foolish writers and foolish readers are created for each other; and that fortune provides readers as she does mates for ugly women.
Horace Walpole

Anyone could write a novel given six weeks, pen, paper and no telephone or wife.
Evelyn Waugh

To see him [Stephen Spender] fumbling with our rich and delicate language is to experience all the horror of seeing a Sèvres vase in the hands of a chimpanzee.
Evelyn Waugh

Editing is the most companionable form of education.
Edward Weeks

Journalism justifies its own existence by the great Darwinian principle of the survival of the vulgarist.
Oscar Wilde

On women's magazines: Page one is a diet, page two is a chocolate cake. It's a no-win situation.
Kim Williams

The way Bernard Shaw believes in himself is very refreshing in these atheistic days when so many believe in no God at all.
Israel Zangwill

WRONG

A wrong-doer is often a man that has left something undone, not always he that has done something.
Marcus Aurelius Antoninus

The surest method against scandal is to live it down in well-doing.
Hermann Boerhaave

Those who cause divisions, in order to injure other people; are in fact preparing pitfalls for their own ruin.
Chinese proverb

It is better to do the wrong thing that to do nothing.
Winston Churchill

Faults of the head are punished in this world: those of the heart in another; but as most of our vices are compound, so is their punishment.
Charles Caleb Colton

I have never been hurt by anything I didn't say.
Calvin Coolidge

Never put a man in the wrong. He will hold it against you forever.
Will Durant

A man in the wrong may more easily be convinced than one half right.
Ralph Waldo Emerson

His heart was as great as the world, but there was no room in it to hold the memory of a wrong.
Ralph Waldo Emerson

Hoarding one's hurts hurts only the hoarder.
Malcolm Forbes

Sin lies in hurting other people unnecessarily. All other sins are invented nonsense.
Robert A. Heinlein

It is better to suffer wrong than to do it, and happier to be sometimes cheated than not to trust.
Samuel Johnson

When our vices quit us we flatter ourselves with the belief that it is we who quit them.
François de La Rochefoucauld

Never do a wrong thing to make a friend or to keep one.
Robert E. Lee

It has ever been my experience that folks who have no vices have very few virtues.
Abraham Lincoln

The worst-tempered people I've ever met were people who know they were wrong.
Wilson Mizner

Believe nothing against another but on good authority; and never report what may hurt another, unless it be a greater hurt to some other to conceal it.
William Penn

A man should never be ashamed to own he has been in the wrong, which is but saying in other words, that he is wiser today than he was yesterday.
Alexander Pope

What once were vices are now manners.
Seneca

He who injured you was either stronger or weaker. If he was weaker, spare him; if he was stronger, spare yourself.
Seneca

To persist in doing wrong extenuates not the wrong, but makes it much more heavy.
William Shakespeare

The best remedy for an injury is to forget it.
Publilius Syrus

He who commits a wrong will himself inevitably see the writing on the wall, though the world may not count him guilty.
Martin Tupper

It's often wrong to do the thing you have a right to do.
Frank Tyger

The individual who cultivates grievances, and who is perpetually exacting explanations of his assumed wrongs, can only be ignored, and left to the education of time and of development. . . . One does not argue or contend with the foul miasma that settles over stagnant water; one leaves it and climbs to a higher region, where the air is pure and the sunshine fair.
Lillian Whiting

XYZ

YOUTH

In case you're worried about what's going to become of the younger generation, it's going to grow up and start worrying about the younger generation.
Roger Allen

The young are permanently in a state resembling intoxication; for youth is sweet and they are growing.
Aristotle

You can be young without money but you can't be old without it.
Aristotle

Youth loves honor and victory more than money.
Aristotle

Youth has the resilience to absorb disaster and weave it into the pattern of its life, no mater how anguishing the thorn that penetrates its flesh.
Sholem Asch

Young men are fitter to invent than to judge; fitter for execution than for counsel; and fitter for new projects than for settled business.
Francis Bacon

The old repeat themselves and the young have nothing to say. The boredom is mutual.
Jacques Bainville

Americans began by loving youth, and now, out of adult self-pity, they worship it.
Jacques Barzun

[Coward] has become a fat old turtle with slits for eyes, no upper teeth, the lower lip bulging outwards, hunched bent, the lot. How sad. He was once the very spirit of youth.
Cecil Beaton

If you want to capture your youth, cut off his allowance.
Al Bernstein

Affection is certain deformity. By forming themselves on fantastic models, the young begin with being ridiculous and often end in being vicious.
Hugh Blair

Youth is young life plus curiosity minus understanding.
Anthony Brooks

The youth of today and the youth of tomorrow will be accorded an almost unequaled opportunity for great accomplishment and for human service.
Dr. Nicholas Murray Butler

My supply of Scotch caution never has been small; but I was apparently something of a daredevil now and then to the manufacturing fathers of Pittsburgh. They were old and I was young, which made all the difference.
Andrew Carnegie

Young men are apt to think themselves wise enough, as drunken men are apt to think themselves sober enough.
Lord Chesterfield

Youth is always too serious, and just now it is too serious about frivolity.
G.K. Chesterton

Elderly people and those in authority cannot always be relied upon to take enlightened and comprehending views of what they call the indiscretions of youth.
Winston Churchill

The joy of the young is to disobey but the trouble is, there are no longer any orders.
Jean Cocteau

Youth is a period of missed opportunities.
Cyril Connolly

I remember my youth and the feeling that will never come back any more—the feeling that I could last forever, outlast the sea, the earth, and all men.
Joseph Conrad

A boy who isn't handicapped is handicapped.
E.L. Cord

The young always have the same problem—how to rebel and conform at the same time. They have now solved this by defying their parents and copying one another.
Quentin Crisp

If I had the opportunity to say a fine word to all the young people of America, it would be this: Don't think too much about yourselves. Try to cultivate the habit of thinking of others; this will reward you. Nourish your minds by good reading, constant reading. Discover what your lifework is, work in which you can do most good, in which you can be happiest. Be unafraid in all things when you know you are in the right.
Charles W. Eliot

Tell me how a young man spends his evenings and I will tell you how far he is likely to go in the world. The popular notion is that a youth's progress depends upon how he acts during his working hours. It doesn't. It depends far more upon how he utilizes his leisure. . . . If he spends it in harmless idleness, he is likely to be kept on the payroll, but that will be about all. If he diligently utilizes his own time . . . to fit himself for more responsible duties, then the greater responsibilities—and greater rewards—are almost certain to come to him.
B.C. Forbes

This is a youth-oriented society, and the joke is on them because youth is a disease from which we all recover.
Dorothy Fuldheim

The intolerance of young people appeals to me. It's a good sign when a youngster is temperamentally in revolt against the world in general.
Roger Martin du Gard

I leave everything to the young men. You've got to give youthful men authority and responsibility if you're going to build up an organization. Otherwise you'll always be the boss yourself and you won't leave anything behind you.
A.P. Giannini (age 70)

You're immature if you can't accept reality or responsibility.
Arnold Glasow

Girls we love for what they are; young men for what they promise to be.
Johann Wolfgang von Goethe

The destiny of any nation, at any given time, depends on the opinions of its young men under five-and-twenty.
Johann Wolfgang von Goethe

You are only young once, but you can be immature forever.
John P. Grier

When a man is young he is so wild he is insufferable. When he is old he plays the saint and becomes insufferable again.
Nikolai Gogol

Immaturity can last a lifetime.
Robert Half

Young man: Be honest; train yourself for useful work; love God.
Milton S. Hershey

I would not waste the springtime of my youth in idle dalliance; I would plant rich seeds to blossom in my manhood, and bear fruit when I am old.
Richard Hillhouse

A compilation of what outstanding people said or wrote at the age of 20 would make a collection of asinine pronouncements.
Eric Hoffer

If a society is to preserve stability and a degree of continuity, it must know how to keep its adolescents from imposing their tastes, attitudes, values and fantasies on everyday life.
Eric Hoffer

It is the malady of our age that the young are so busy teaching us that they have no time left to learn.
Eric Hoffer

Youth is a frightening age . . . so many problems; so little wisdom to solve them.
Walter Hoving

People have this obsession. They want you to be like you were in 1969. They want you to because otherwise their youth goes with you. It's very selfish but it's understandable.
Mick Jagger

Develop in youth the devotion to home interests and home affairs, to community interests and community affairs that led the founding fathers to establish a nation of communities upon this continent, dedicated to a decent, free life of equal opportunity under God, and consecrated to the principle that the State exists as an instrument for serving the individual, not for enslaving him. So instructed, American youth can be trusted.
Joseph P. Kennedy

The surest way to corrupt a young man is to teach him to esteem more highly those who think alike than those who think differently.
Friedrich Wilhelm Nietzsche

Youth doesn't reason, it acts. The old man reasons and would like to make others act in his place.
Francis Picabia

The real lost souls don't wear their hair long and play guitars. They have crew cuts, trained minds, sign on for research in biological warfare and don't give their parents a moment's worry.
J.B. Priestley

Youth cannot know how age thinks and feels. But old men are guilty if they forget what it was to be young.
J.K. Rowling

To the young I should offer two maxims: Don't accept superficial solutions of difficult problems. It is better to do a little good than much harm. I should not offer anything more specific; every young person should decide on his or her own credo.
Bertrand Russell

In youth we run into difficulties. In old age difficulties run into us.
Beverly Sills

There is nothing that you can have when you are old that can replace being young and having nothing.
Mary Wallace Smith

The closest you can get to your youth is to start repeatin' your follies.
Reg Smythe in Andy Capp

All sorts of allowances are made for the illusions of youth; and none, or almost none, for the disenchantments of age.
Robert Louis Stevenson

The best rules to form a young man are: to talk a little, to hear much, to reflect alone upon what has passed in company, to distrust one's own opinions, and value others' that deserve it.
Sir William Temple

Youth is a time when we find the books we give up but do not get over.
Lionel Trilling

Life would be infinitely happier if we could only be born at the age of 80 and gradually approach 18.
Mark Twain

Not everyone grows to be old, but everyone has been younger than he is now.
Evelyn Waugh

There is no trade or employment but the young man following it may become a hero.
Walt Whitman

Youth is a circumstance you can't do anything about. The trick is to grow up without getting old.
Frank Lloyd Wright

ZEAL

The greatest dangers to liberty lurk in insidious encroachment by men of zeal, well meaning but without understanding.
Louis D. Brandeis

Zeal without knowledge is like fire without a grate to contain it; like a sword without a hilt to wield it by; like a high-bred horse without a bridle to guide him. It speaks without thinking, acts without planning, seeks to accomplish a good end without the adoption of becoming means.
Julius Bate

Experience shows that success is due less to ability than to zeal. The winner is he who gives himself to his work body and soul.
Charles Buxton

A fanatic is one who can't change his mind and won't change the subject.
Winston Churchill

The fanatic is incorruptible: If he kills for an idea, he can just as well get himself killed for one; in either case, tyrant or martyr, he is a monster.
E.M. Cioran

Zeal is fit only for wise men, but is found mostly in fools.
Thomas Fuller

Zeal without knowledge is fire without light.
Thomas Fuller

Political extremism involves two prime ingredients: an excessively simple diagnosis of the world's ills and a conviction that there are identifiable villains back of it all.
John W. Gardner

I do not love a man who is zealous for nothing.
Oliver Goldsmith

Defoe says that there were a hundred thousand country fellows in his time ready to fight to the death against popery, without knowing whether popery was a man or a horse.
William Hazlitt

At least two-thirds of our miseries spring from human stupidity, human malice and those great motivators and justifiers of malice and stupidity: idealism, dogmatism and proselytizing zeal on behalf of religious or political ideas.
Aldous Huxley

In the fevered state of our country, no good can ever result from any attempt to set one of these fiery zealots to rights, either in fact or in principle. They are determined as to the facts they will believe and the opinions on which they will act.
Thomas Jefferson

Zeal is very blind, or badly regulated, when it encroaches upon the rights of others.
Pasquier Quesnel

Fanaticism consists in redoubling your efforts when you have forgotten your aim.
George Santayana

Zeal for the public good is the characteristic of a man of honor and a gentleman, and must take the place of pleasures, profits, and all other private gratifications. Whoever wants this motive, is an open enemy, or an inglorious neuter to mankind, in proportion to the misapplied advantages with which nature and fortune have blessed him.
Richard Steele

Nothing spoils human nature more than false zeal. The good nature of a heathen is more God-like than the furious zeal of a Christian.
Benjamin Whichcote

An infallible method of making fanatics is to persuade before you instruct.
Voltaire

SOURCES

2,548 Best Things Anybody Ever Said
A Man Without a Country, by Kurt Vonnegut
AARP
Adage.com
Airman's Odyssey, by Antoine de Saint-Exupéry
Associated Press
Bartleby.com
Bartlett's *Familiar Quotations*
BBC
Business Insider
Columbia Dictionary of Quotations
Cubanmissilecrisis.org (Harvard Kennedy
    School, Belfer Center)
Dailybeast.com
Detroit Free Press
Diary of Anaïs Nin, Volume 1
Dictionary of Proverbs
Eating the Dinosaur, by Chuck Klosterman
Education: Free and Compulsory, by Murray
    Rothbard
Encyclopedia of Religious Quotations
ESPN
Football and Philosophy: Going Deep, by Michael
    Austin
Football Physics: The Science of the Game, by
    Timothy Gay
Forbes
Forbes.com
Foxsports.com
Goodreads.com
Grubstreet.com
Hey Rube, by Hunter S. Thompson
Ideas for Our Time
Intelligent Investor
International Thesaurus of Quotations
Jesting Pilate
Language and Cultural Descriptions, by Charles
    O. Frake
The Last Word on Making Money, by Rolf B. White
The Literary Spy
Mercurynews.com
Military.com
New International Dictionary Of Quotations

New York Magazine
The New York Times
Newyorker.com
Nytimes.com
On Photography, by Susan Sontag
Oxford Dictionary of Humorous Quotations
*Persistence of the Classical: Essays on
    Architecture,* by Frank Salmon
Peter's Quotations
Philippine Star
Pimco.com
Pops, by Terry Teachout
Quotable Chesterton
Quotable Hitchens: From Alcohol to Zionism
Reuters
Royal Wisdom, by Kate Petrella
*Sad and Luminous Days: Cuba's Struggle with the
    Superpowers After the Missile Crisis,* by James
    G. Blight and Phillip Brenner
SBS-CNBC
Simpson's Contemporary Quotations
Sports Illustrated
Sports Justice: The Law & The Business of Sports,
    by Roger I. Abrams
Suzanne O'Neill
Tallulah: My Autobiography, by Tallulah
    Bankhead
Thehill.com
Treasury of Jewish Quotations
Unabridged Devil's Dictionary, by Ambrose Bierce
University of Notre Dame Institute for
    Educational Initiatives
USA Today
Vulture.com.
The Washington Post
Washingtonpost.com.
Wild Mountain Thyme, by Rosamunde Pilcher
The Wit & Wisdom of Winston Churchill, by James
    C. Hume and Richard M. Nixon
WSJ.com
Yale Book of Quotations.
Zero History, by William Gibson

INDEX